G000136217

# *Before They Were Heroes at King's Mountain*

**Other titles by Randell Jones**

*In the Footsteps of Daniel Boone,* 2005, John F. Blair, Publisher
Willie Parker Peace History Book Award, 2006
North Carolina Society of Historians

*On the Trail of Daniel Boone,* companion DVD,
Daniel Boone Footsteps, publisher
Paul Green Multimedia Award, 2006
North Carolina Society of Historians

*In the Footsteps of Davy Crockett,* 2006, John F. Blair, Publisher

*Scoundrels, Rogues, and Heroes of the Old North State*
by Dr. H.G. Jones, co-editors: Randell and Caitlin Jones
2004, The History Press, Charleston, SC

All available through Daniel Boone Footsteps
www.danielboonefootsteps.com
1959 N. Peace Haven Rd., #105
Winston-Salem, NC 27106
DBooneFootsteps@gmail.com

BEFORE THEY WERE HEROES AT KING'S MOUNTAIN

# Before
# They Were Heroes
# at King's Mountain

by Randell Jones

To Edna Cooper,

Nov. 11, 2011

**Daniel Boone Footsteps**
Winston-Salem, North Carolina

Copyright 2011 Randell Jones
All Rights Reserved

Daniel Boone Footsteps
*www.danielboonefootsteps.com*
*DBooneFootsteps@gmail.com*

*For Dad*
*and all the heroes*
*aboard the* Sangamon
*May 4, 1945*

BEFORE THEY WERE HEROES AT KING'S MOUNTAIN

"A numerous and unexpected enemy
came from the mountains.
As they had good horses,
their movements were rapid."

– Lord Charles Cornwallis

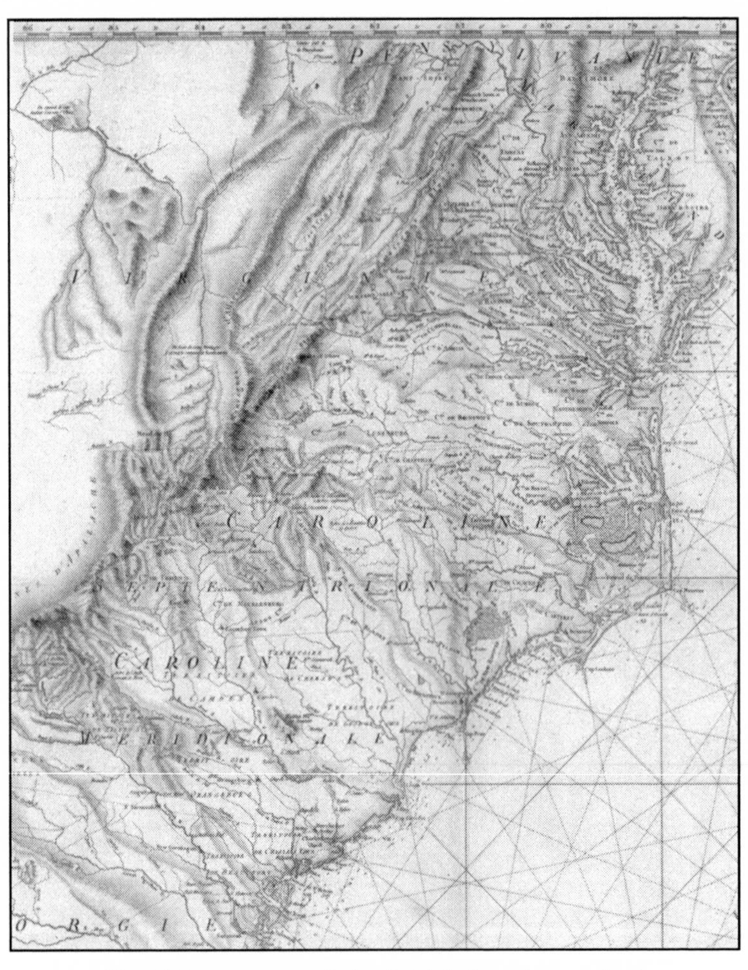

**Detail from a map of the British American colonies by French cartographer, Antoine de Sartine, 1778**

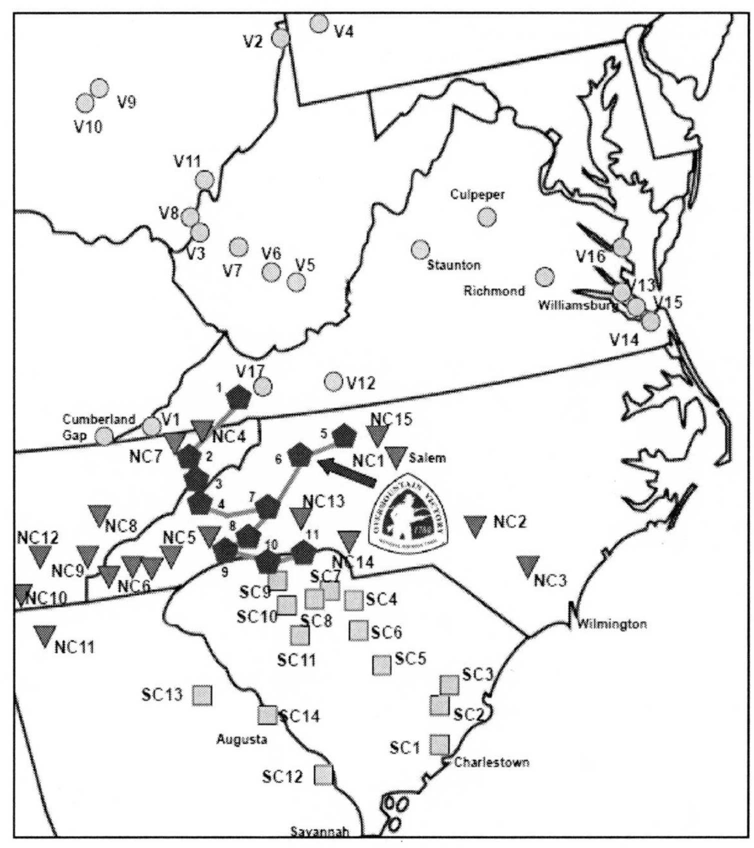


**This map shows the locations of key sites for events from 1774 to 1780. Many additional nearby sites are mentioned in the accounts. This map shows current state outlines of the Southern region to help orient readers to the places mentioned in the accounts.**

Numbered sites for the Overmountain Victory National Historic Trail are:

1 - Abingdon Muster Grounds
2 - Sycamore Shoals
3 - Yellow Mountain Gap
4 - Gillespie Gap
5 - Surry Mustering Grounds
6 - Tory Oak and The Round About
7 - Quaker Meadows
8 - Gilbert Town
9 - Green River ford (Alexander's)
10 - The Cowpens
11 - Little King's Mountian

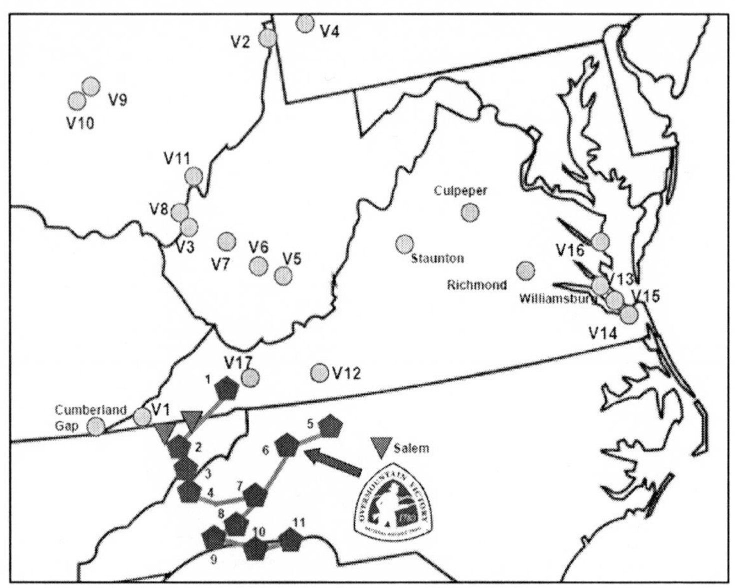


**Sites in Virginia, West Virginia, Pennsylvania, and Ohio**

V1 – Martin's Station, Wilderness Road State Park
V2 – Yellow Creek Massacre
V3 – George Washington's Land Grant
V4 – Fort Dunmore (site of Fort Pitt)
V5 – Camp Union (today's Lewisburg, WV)
V6 – Grandview State Park
V7 – Kanawha River at Elk River (today's Charleston, WV)
V8 – Battle of Point Pleasant (Tu-Endie-Wei State Park)
V9 – Camp Charlotte
V10 – Logan Elm State Memorial
V11 – Fort Gower
V12 – Lead Mines
V13 – Williamsburg
V14 – Battle of Great Bridge
V15 – Bombardment of Norfolk
V16 – Gwynn's Island
V17 – Aspenvale

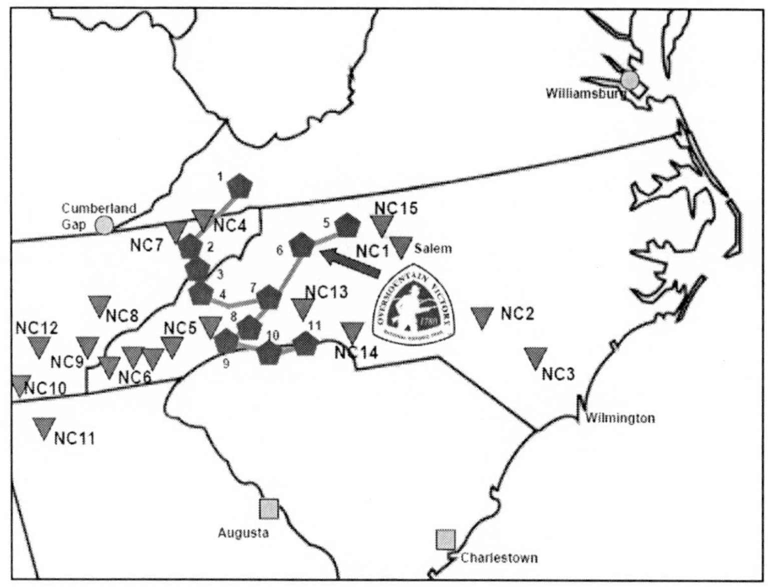


**Sites in North Carolina and Tennessee**

NC1 – Salem
NC2 – Cross Creek (Fayetteville)
NC3 – Moores Creek National Battlefield
NC4 – Overmountain Region (Holston, Watauga, and Nolichucky river valleys)
NC5 – Fort Davidson (Old Fort)
NC6 – Middle Towns of Cherokee (Rutherford's Campaign)
NC7 – Long Island of the Holston (Kingsport)
NC8 – Warrior's Path, French Broad River
NC9 – Towns of the Overhill Cherokee
NC10 – Chickamauga Creek (Chattanooga)
NC11 – Chickamauga refuge
NC12 – Sale Creek
NC13 – Battle of Ramsour's Mill
NC14 – Battle of Charlotte
NC15 – Bethabara and Bethania

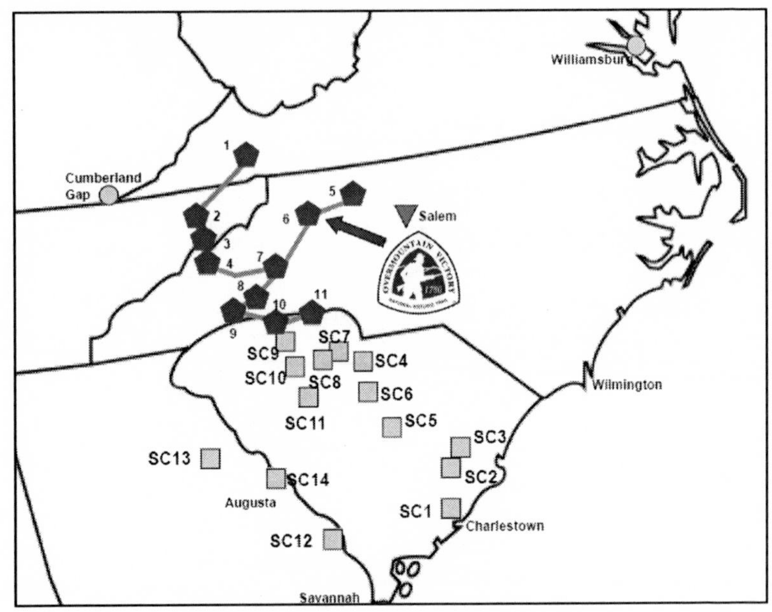


**Sites in South Carolina and Georgia**

SC1 – Charlestown
SC2 – Biggin's Bridge (Monck's Corner)
SC3 – Lenud's Ferry
SC4 – Waxhaws (Buford's Massacre)
SC5 – High Hills of Santee (Thomas Sumter's home)
SC6 –Camden
SC7 – Rocky Mount
SC8 – Hanging Rock
SC9 – Thicketty Fort
SC10 –Musgrove's Mill
SC11 – Ninety Six
SC12 – Battle of Briar Creek
SC13 – Battle of Kettle Creek
SC14 – Siege of Augusta

# Preface

The book you are holding is the **full edition** of *Before They Were Heroes at King's Mountain.*

## Three Regional Editions

Three regional editions are also available. These regional editions feature selected chapters from the full edition that may appeal primarily to readers with an interest in a smaller geographic area. Of course, each of the three regional editions is priced less than the full text, helping provide a range of opportunities for readers to access this exciting story of America's Revolutionary War heritage in the South. A "trail guide" edition for the Overmountain Victory National Historic Trail is also available.

All editions include the story of the campaign, fighting, and aftermath connected to the Battle of Kings Mountain. That portion of the story leads readers along the Overmountain Victory National Historic Trail (www.NPS.gov/ovvi) and ends at Kings Mountain National Military Park (www.NPS.gov/kimo).

The Virginia regional edition features the story of Lord Dunmore's War against the Shawnee, the story of Virginia's defeat of its royal governor at the Battle of Great Bridge and his eventual departure from the rebel colony under a barrage of cannon fire from General

Andrew Lewis and then-Captain William Campbell. As well, it recounts Campbell's relentless campaigns against the Tory opposition including his excursions into North Carolina to the Moravian towns.

The North Carolina regional edition features the chapters that tell the story of Royal Governor Josiah Martin giving birth to the notion of a Southern Strategy, the Battle at Moore's Creek Bridge, and the events in the backcountry which led up to that conflict between Whig and Loyalist factions. It recounts the efforts of the Cherokees to prevent further encroachments on their lands in the Overmountain region, Griffith Rutherford's expedition against the Cherokees in 1776, William Christian's invasion of the Overhill Cherokee homeland, and the Chickamauga Campaign of 1779 led by Evan Shelby. It recounts as well the Battle of Ramsour's Mill, a battle between Loyalist and Whig militia that foreshadowed the Battle of King's Mountain. It recounts the campaigns of Benjamin Cleaveland, the "Terror of the Tories," throughout the Yadkin and New River valleys as well as into Virginia. It also shares the story of the Patriot withdrawal from King's Mountain with prisoners and the unexpected descent of these needy captives and their Whig guards on the Moravian community of Bethabara. Included, too, is the story of Cornwallis's actions in and around Charlotte Town, events concurrent with the campaign and battle at King's Mountain.

The South Carolina regional edition features the chapters that tell the story of the British Southern Campaign that began the day after Christmas in 1779. Sir Henry Clinton reveled in the surrender of Charlestown. British Legion forces spread out across South Carolina and Georgia's Savannah River corridor. Cornwallis's march northward saw the rout of the Continental Army's Southern Department at the Battle of Camden but also the rise of the backcountry militia whose resistance preceded the Battle of King's Mountain. Battles at Rocky Mount, Hanging Rock, Fishing Creek, Williamson's Plantation, Thicketty Fort, Musgrove's Mill, and other skirmishes were an important part of preparing for the conflict with Major Patrick Ferguson. The Siege of Augusta by partisan Elijah Clarke and his retreat in the face of reinforcements is an often ignored part of the whole story.

A companion DVD is also available. It takes the viewer on a tour of the sites spread across a half-dozen states—from the Ohio River to Charleston, South Carolina and from Williamsburg, Virginia to Cumberland Gap. Visit www.danielboonefootsteps.com for more information.

**A word about "Kings" and "King's"**

Over time, authors have referred to both "Kings Mountain" and "King's Mountain." I use both in this book, but not randomly. The National Park Service and Lyman C. Draper have used "Kings," and when referring to the National Military Park or the event, "the Battle of Kings Mountain," I have used that form. I found enough usage of "King's" in historical documents, that I chose to retain the apostrophe in this current treatment. Therefore, I refer to "the battle at King's Mountain" and use "King's" in other instances as well. Both are correct. I have tried to be consistent in my usage, but in any case, I do not think the matter interferes with the story. Similarly, I have chosen to use "Cleaveland" rather than "Cleveland." Both spellings can be supported, but I find the former at least piques the reader's interest.

I have pursued writing this book in earnest since 2007. Since 1994, I have had a deep and abiding interest in the story of the Overmountain Men of 1780 and the Battle at Kings Mountain. I have researched and read a great deal, but I have not read everything, I suspect. I will continue, I am sure, to meet people who know something I do not know or who have a different perspective on a point that I might make. I welcome all comments.

Much has been written about the American Revolution in the South. It is a great story and others have pursued it and continue to pursue it enthusiastically. I have written this book for those who want to know a little more. I have added what I think is an interesting amount of detail without delving into such depths as to extinguish the interest of the reader. I invite your comments to help me discern if I have achieved that intended balance.

My first book, *In the Footsteps of Daniel Boone*, received in 2006 the Willie Parker Peace History Book Award from the North Carolina Society of Historians. In the five years since its release, I have been gratified by the response and appreciation so many readers of all ages have expressed to me. It seems that book struck a good balance between sharing historical detail and moving the story along. As I had hoped, it provided enough of a story to get its readers interested in learning more. I trust this current book does the same.

What more could an author hope to achieve than to provide the impetus, if not the source, for someone's new discovery? I hope you find this book fulfills my part of that exchange. I am pleased that you have chosen to read this story and to learn more about the American Revolution in the South. Let us explore that story together.

R. J.

# Foreword

The late, popular historian Stephen Ambrose wrote that for him the study of history was like telling a series of stories. I wholeheartedly agree; and, I have found that when one reads history, one often finds himself connecting one story with another, sometimes unexpectedly, and discovering in the process the profound effects some events have on future ones.

*Before They Were Heroes at King's Mountain* is a detailed account of American history and patriotism revealed through a series of stories woven together tightly in their telling. All of the stories are connected with the people and the places associated with one important and improbable event—the Patriot victory at the Battle of Kings Mountain. That victory in October 1780 did have a profound effect on bringing about, at Yorktown just twelve months and twelve days later, an end to the then seven-years-long American Revolution. As many have heard me say previously when I have spoken on this subject, if there had been no victory at Kings Mountain, there would have been no victory by General Daniel Morgan at Cowpens. If there had been no Cowpens, there would have been no Battle of Guilford Courthouse. (Without these losses, Cornwallis would have been at full strength, General Greene would have been powerless to stop him, and Cornwallis's invasion of North Carolina would have been largely successful.) And, if there had been no Battle of Guilford Courthouse, there would have been no Yorktown and no surrendering of the British troops under Lord Cornwallis. So, the victory at Kings Mountain initiated a chain of events that ended with America's freedom. Thomas Jefferson said the same two hundred years ago, calling that Patriot victory at Kings Mountain "the joyful annunciation of that turn of the tide of success which terminated the Revolutionary War, with the seal of our independence."

Randell Jones has written other stories of great frontiersmen in the history of our country, including the award-winning *In the Footsteps of Daniel Boone* and *In the Footsteps of Davy Crockett.* He is eminently qualified to tell the story of the Battle of Kings Mountain. He has spent a decade immersed in its history. Along the way, he has served as president of the Overmountain Victory Trail Association, the organization of men and women who have worked tirelessly for years to keep alive the memory of what happened there on that mountain top in 1780, and why that victory meant so much in bringing an end to the conflict. During his term, he wrote "Footsteps for Freedom," the story of the campaign and battle explained at a $4^{th}$ grade-student level. He wrote the $25^{th}$ anniversary history of the Trail's 1980 founding and created the curricula-based education program for the Overmountain Victory National Historic Trail offered free-of-charge to teachers by the National Park Service. More recently he penned the account of the campaign and battle for LearnNC (*www.LearnNC.org*), the online educational resource supported by Universtiy of North Carolina at Chapel Hill. And, since 2007, he has lectured around the state as a member of the Road Scholars Speakers' Bureau of the North Carolina Humanities Council. Randell knows the history of the struggle itself, he knows the history of the Trail, and he tells a good story.

I have a deep, personal interest in the story and the Trail as well. I grew up in my home town of Lenoir, North Carolina hearing stories of this battle. I knew some of the descendants of the heroes who fought in this battle. Fort Defiance, located in my home county of Caldwell, was the home of one of the heroes of the Battle of Kings Mountain, William Lenoir, who was a Captain at that time, and later rose to become the General of Militia for Western North Carolina.

But, my interest in the story and the Trail runs deeper still. In 1975, a remarkable group of dedicated men and women came to me as a Member of Congress and asked me to become involved in seeking federal recognition of the route that was used by these early Patriots as they came out of the mountains to pursue the threatening British forces. This group also asked that we make every effort to preserve the route so that future generations of Americans could not only use the trail but embrace a piece of history and see what hardships their ancestors had to surmount to win the victory that secured their Liberty.

The work we did together over the following five years culminated in the passage of federal legislation that I had sponsored. The bill was signed into law by President Jimmy Carter in August 1980, thus making the Overmountain Victory Trail a part of the National Historic Trails System. This Act provided for marking the Trail and took the initial steps to preserve the Trail for all time. Ever since the Overmountain Victory National Historic Trail was founded, significant steps have been taken to preserve the route. Moreover, the Overmountain Victory Trail Association is still alive and well, one of several dozen Trail partners supporting and collaborating with the National Park Service. The OVTA continues to tell the story of the Campaign and Battle of Kings Mountain all year-round, and especial-

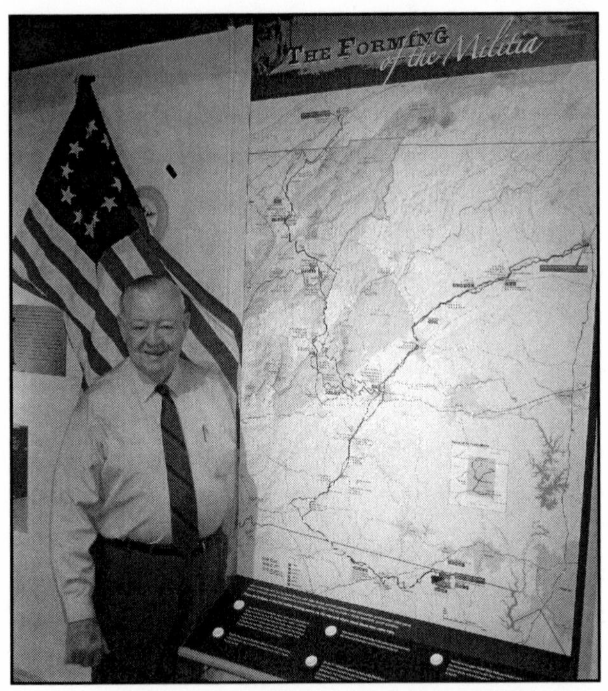


**Senator James T. Broyhill introduced federal legislation in 1977 to create the Overmountain Victory National Historic Trail.**

ly during the annual reenactment of the heroic march each September and October.

This book tells the story of the battle, but more importantly it emphasizes the stories of these early American Patriots and the surprising connections they had to each other and to previous events that affected their preparedness for and participation in the campaign to what became the Battle of Kings Mountain. This book also guides today's visitors along the Overmountain Victory National Historic Trail, revealing how these Patriots got to the site of the battle and sharing the stories that unfolded at those sites along the way. Unique in its perspective and coverage, it guides the reader through the exciting experiences of these brave men during the six years before they mustered at Sycamore Shoals in pursuit of Patrick Ferguson—six years during which the reputation of the backwoodsman and the overmountain Patriots grew in notoriety, legend, and respect.

Randell Jones has made a most worthwhile contribution to the telling of American history. If you love America and if you like a good story, this book is for you. I am proud to recommend this book to all who have an interest in the early history of our country, and trust that it will do much to keep alive the story of the victory at the Battle of Kings Mountain in the war that won for us all our Freedoms as Americans.

Jim Broyhill

Senator James T. Broyhill of North Carolina
Former Member of Congress, 1963-1987

# Overmountain Victory Trail Association

We keep **The Story** alive!

The story of the Overmountain Men and their campaign to the Battle of Kings Mountain is a story of the American Spirit. Faced with a threat to invade their Overmountain homelands, men and women of pioneer stock and frontier spunk rallied to the cause. They left their homes already at peril to renegade Cherokees and crossed over the mountains to answer the threat of Major Patrick Ferguson and the advancing British Legion.

The Overmountain Men along with other Patriots from the Piedmont sections of North Carolina, South Carolina and Georgia took the initiative to meet the threat head on. During two weeks, they pursued Patrick Ferguson's army of Loyalists, catching them atop Little Kings Mountain on October 7, 1780. In a monumental battle, this band of experienced militiamen—but still only citizen farmers, hunters, shopkeepers, and tradesmen—defeated Patrick Ferguson and forced the retreat of Lord Cornwallis and the most powerful army in the world.

Nearly two centuries later, in 1975, a group of private citizens began efforts to see the campaign route to the Battle of Kings Mountain designated as a National Historic Trail. With the partnership and efforts of U.S. Senator James T. Broyhill of North Carolina, this was accomplished in 1980. The Overmountain Victory National Historic Trail became the first such trail east of the Mississippi River and is today one of an elite number of historic trails in the country. During their early efforts to achieve this coveted designation, these citizens organized the Overmountain Victory Trail Association, chartered in 1977.

Since its inception, the OVTA has been keeping alive the story of the Campaign to the Battle of Kings Mountain. The OVTA has retraced the daily steps of the heroes on this campaign every year since 1975. This annual event continues to grow. Our band of commemorative marchers and reenactors moves down the Trail, encamping in the same locations on the same dates of the calendar as the Patriot militia did in 1780. During the march each year, OVTA educates the public. In the past two years alone, OVTA has told The Story to over 21,000 people during this annual commemorative march along the Trail corridor. Most are students learning firsthand that history teaches important values essential to what it means to be an American. They learn about how people lived two centuries ago and why some of them made the choices they did, choices that still benefit all Americans today.

We invite you to join in our effort. Join the Overmountain Victory Trail Association and help us keep the story alive. Visit us online at *www.OVTA.org* and become a member today.

Sincerely,

Alan Bowen
President, Overmountain Victory Trail Association, Inc.
www.OVTA.org

# Contents

# Introduction

*"[The victory at Kings Mountain] was the joyful annunciation*
*of that turn of the tide of success*
*which terminated the Revolutionary War,*
*with the seal of our independence."*
– Thomas Jefferson
(Letter to John Campbell, Nov. 10, 1822 from Monticello)

Those who know the story of the Battle of Kings Mountain share in a collective incredulity that every American — or at least those who profess to care about its history and heritage — are not well acquainted with the remarkable account of that event. The American War for Independence was not going well for the rebel Whigs, that faction of the American colonial citizens who wanted independence from Great Britain. After five years of fighting to a stalemate in the New England and mid-Atlantic states (or rebellious colonies, as some were inclined to regard them), the British once again attempted their Southern strategy. The surrender of Charlestown in May 1780 led to the advance of General Lord Cornwallis through South Carolina and to the disastrous defeat of the Continental Army's Southern Department at the Battle of Camden in August. Marching on toward Charlotte Town, Cornwallis looked unstoppable until the commander of his western flank, Major Patrick Ferguson, a Scotsman, imprudently threatened to invade and destroy the Overmountain regions of North Carolina and Virginia. In a response characteristic of their nature, a band of frontier militiamen — descendants of Scots-Irish, Welsh, German, and French Huguenot ancestry, among others — and without a single Continental soldier or officer among them, amassed a fighting force of 2,000 men to pursue and defeat the threatening invaders. Their unexpected victory atop Little King's Mountain on October 7 stunned the British Legion and halted Cornwallis's advance for three months. The victory quelled the enthusiasm of Southern Loyalists and renewed the spirit of the Patriot cause, leading to a succeeding string of victories that ended with Cornwallis's surrender at Yorktown just twelve months and twelve days after the Battle of Kings Mountain. The victory at King's Mountain was, in modern slang, a game-changer.

The story of the battle is commemorated and interpreted today by the National Park Service at Kings Mountain National Military Park. The story of the muster and the march — the campaign of the militiaman that created that confrontation — is commemorated and interpreted by the National Park Service along the 330 miles of the Overmountain Victory National Historic Trail. The OVNH Trail, created in 1980 by federal legislation, became the first national historic trail east of the Mississippi River and took its place alongside the Lewis & Clark Trail and the Oregon Trail as a significant resource for recounting and memorializing an essential part of America's history and heritage. Scores of organizations and thousands of individuals are partners with the OVNH Trail in supporting its charge to continually tell the story of the heroes of King's Mountain.

But, there is more to the story than is usually told. This book pursues that broader, deeper telling. After the battle, many of the men who survived made indelible marks on the history of America. Having fought at the Battle of Kings Mountain was a point of pride and a mark of distinction. Much has been written about these men afterward and their roles in shaping and championing a new America: Isaac Shelby, John Sevier, William Campbell, Benjamin Cleaveland, Joseph Winston, William Lenoir, William Hill, Edward Lacey. The names of the battle's valiant dead redound in history: Williams, Chronicle, Bowen, Edmiston, Sevier, and others. Other men who were not at the battle also played roles in events leading up to the conflict: Charles McDowell, Elijah Clarke, Joseph Williams, William Christian, Joseph Martin, and Thomas Sumter. All these names are etched into America's story.

But, who were these men who mustered in 1780 to confront a threatened British invasion of their homeland? How were they qualified by skill and experience and temperament to undertake such a daunting task? What roles had they played in the movement of the frontier and, in particular, in the fighting for independence that had already occurred? The answers lie, in part, in exploring their actions and activities during the six years prior to that fateful battle.

It is not surprising to find these men fighting against Shawnees and Cherokees, developing the skills that garnered them the fearsome appellation, "the yelling boys." But their skills in Indian fighting and their marksmanship with the Pennsylvania (or Kentucky) longrifle had also gained them a reputation among the ranks of the British army. Lord Dunmore's War in 1774 and the campaigns against the Cherokees in 1776 and 1779 developed their capacity for campaigning through mountainous terrain and fighting tree-to-tree in fierce, hand-to-hand battles. The Battle of Great Bridge in 1775 helped develop the reputation of the "shirtmen" for their expert marksmanship. The Loyalist support in the Southern colonies was tested at Moore's Creek

Bridge and later at Ramsour's Mill. The royal governors of Virginia, North Carolina, and South Carolina escaped their colonies aboard British ships, but lingered off the coast creating trouble and attempting to reinsert themselves into power. British Indian agents on the frontier, acting against official policy, conspired to incite the Cherokees and Creeks to attack the rebel colonists who were spilling over their promised boundary line, the Proclamation Line of 1763. The Cherokees were to be part of a pan-Indian attack reaching south from Fort Detroit and forcing the trespassers back across the Alleghenies, where "the Father, King George III" wanted his colonial subjects to stay. During the revolution, the Upcountry militiaman of South Carolina harassed the advancing British Legion in partisan, guerilla warfare. They set the stage for the conflict in the Carolina Piedmont that would destroy one-third of Cornwallis's army. All these and other skirmishes, battles, and campaigns during the six years before the fall of 1780 prepared these backcountry frontiersmen for the challenges they would face on the way to and at King's Mountain.

Not everyone in America was a Patriot, of course, and that was the situation in the backcountry as well. Bands of Tory militia rode throughout the Carolina Piedmont and the Virginia mountains harassing rebel families. Bands of outlaws — opportunists posing as Tories — also roamed the countryside robbing and plundering frontier families on both sides. William Campbell and Benjamin Cleaveland, in particular, were active in suppressing the activities of Tories and outlaws. Consequently, with threats from Cherokees, Tories, and the British army, the Patriots on the frontiers were more than a little busy just trying to put in a crop, raise a few cattle, hunt for some pelts, and survive in a challenging and sometimes unforgiving natural environment.

The story of these backcountry and Overmountain settlers during the

American Revolution is rich with remarkable and interesting accounts; and one, little-known account, provides a surprising twist in this current telling of the adventures of the Overmountain Men of 1780 and their pursuit of Patrick Ferguson. Three men, each famous in his own right in the history of this frontier, fought in three separate theaters of the American Revolution, yet they each played a role in bringing about the victory at the Battle of Kings Mountain. And although their stories are most often recounted separately, they were, in fact, friends growing up together in the backcountry of Virginia, sharing in the frolicking, gambling, and signature vices of a misspent youth. The separate lives of "Three Friends on the Frontier" each affected the history of America. Their escapades together provide interesting insights into the experiences that helped develop them as frontiersmen and as leaders of men to become venerable icons of the American Revolution in the South.

Leaders such as these and others who rose to occasion, as well as countless backcountry Patriots and Overmountain frontiersmen, forged this country's freedom with their courage, their resolve, and their selfless acts for a noble cause. They deserve our respect and the courtesy and obligation of remembering their sacrifices. All these men were heroes, and their stories are worth telling.

This is their story — before they were heroes at King's Mountain.

# Three Friends on the Frontier

They were rascals. Before they were heroes, three young men, who would later become icons of the Southern Campaign of the American Revolution, were together in their youth reckless, shiftless, carefree lads. For a time on the Virginia frontier in the mid-1700s, these three friends enjoyed times of untroubled, high-spirited living—frolicking, drinking, gambling and paying little heed to making their way in the world. Ben, Tom, and Joe shared the common bond of youthful irresponsibility during their adolescence and early adulthood. Their devil-may-care lives at the time belied the commitment and resolve each would later exhibit to bring about the hard-fought independence of the United States of America.

The celebrated contributions of these three Patriots in support of the cause of Liberty occurred in different theaters of conflict; and, history usually recounts their stories disconnected from each other. However, their heroic efforts and influences did converge in a most unsuspected way. During the summer and fall of 1780, each, in his own way, helped bring about the Battle of Kings Mountain. Thanks to each, that Patriot victory at the hands of militiamen from the back-country turned the direction of the Revolutionary War. Though they were scamps in their youth together, Ben, Tom, and Joe grew in character and action to become the noted partisans: Colonel Benjamin Cleaveland, General Thomas Sumter, and General Joseph Martin.

Their youthful escapades aside, the reputations of these patriots remain indelible in American history. Their connections to one another and to the Battle of Kings Mountain are important links to the broader story of America's beginnings as an independent nation.

**Spirited Young Lads**

Full of themselves and the passions of youth, in the early 1750s, the three friends joined the local militia in Orange County, then the backcountry of settled Virginia. They served together under Colonel Zachariah Burnley at a time when the world was changing around them.[1] In the mid-1750s, the dominance of Great Britain on the frontier of America was called into question. Lt. Colonel George Washington surrendered Fort Necessity in 1754 and marched away, yielding for the moment the upper Ohio Valley to French control. The British attempted a formidable response, but a small party of French militiamen and their northern Indian allies ambushed the British column and defeated what was generally regarded as the best fighting force in the world. British Major General Edward Braddock and his entourage of British Regulars and Provincial Guard were routed in a massacre along the Monongahela River on July 9, 1755. It is remembered today as Braddock's Defeat.

After this shocking insult to the British army, the three young Virginians joined the colonial troops for a time and served during the French and Indian War.[2] Joseph Martin, born in 1740, and Thomas Sumter, six years Martin's senior, served together under Col. William Bird. They joined in General John Forbes's 1758 campaign that captured Fort Duquesne, the French fort Braddock had failed to conquer. That captured, strategic stronghold was renamed Fort Pitt. By the end of the conflict, Sumter, the oldest of the three, earned his stripes as a sergeant at age 24. The particulars of service during the war of the third lad, Benjamin Cleaveland, born in 1738, are lost to history but may have included service under Colonel James "Mad Jimmie" Moore.[3]

During the years following the French and Indian War, life drew the three young men in different directions, yet they also shared similar and important molding experiences. Each was a frontiersman, making his way on the edge of a growing America in a time of revolutionary change. The three friends all served separately as leaders of the back-country militia. They faced down Cherokee and Shawnee resistance to expanding white settlement. They all mined their frontier experiences and honed their skills to become men of ability during the two decades before the American Revolution.

**Bad Blood Between Allies**

The challenges faced by Martin, Sumter, and Cleaveland were rooted in the Colonial period and the betrayal of respect between allies. During the French and Indian War, the Cherokees served as allies of the British. The "Real People" fought alongside the red-coated British Regulars and the uniformed Provincial Guard of the colonies in their fight against the French army and militia and their Indian allies from the north. But, eventually the Cherokees fell from alliance with the British colonists.

Despite making numerous promises, British military leaders mistreated and undersupplied the Cherokees during the first years of the war. In 1758, Cherokee warriors supported Forbes's campaign against Fort Duquesne, but suffered some unstated offense from the British. Cherokee chief Attakullakulla (called Little Carpenter) and nine warriors departed the campaign, but were overtaken at Forbes's instructions and disarmed. The Cherokee braves continued on, bound for home. Before the chief reached his village, another party of Cherokees also departed the campaign unescorted. These allied warriors had not been compensated properly, and during their trip homeward, they felt obliged to take as payment goods and property from any whites they happened upon. They viewed all English as members of the same tribe, each responsible for a common debt. One group of Virginia militiamen, suffering the loss of their horses to the disgruntled Cherokee warriors, felt differently about the matter. They organized themselves and rode down the Cherokees, killing and scalping a dozen or more as horse thieves.[4] When the survivors reached the Cherokee Nation with the story of these murders at the hands of the English, the young Cherokee warriors were outraged. Taking up arms, they set upon white settlements all along the frontier in the Carolinas and Virginia determined to exact revenge in small and swift attacks. In February 1760, a party of Cherokees killed 50 settlers in the Long Canes of South Carolina as the settlers were attempting to make their way to safety in Augusta.[5] In the same month, another party attacked the British garrison at Fort Dobbs on the North Carolina frontier. The Provincial Guard at the fort repelled the attackers, but the Cherokees massacred settlers living nearby. In the face of this uprising, called the Cherokee War, over half of the white settlers retreated from the North Carolina piedmont frontier. Notable among them, Daniel Boone removed his wife Rebecca and their two sons, James and Israel, from the Forks of the Yadkin to a safe community. His family remained in Culpeper County, Virginia for the duration of the conflict, while he returned to the North Carolina mountains for hunting and perhaps service during the war. (See *In the Footsteps of Daniel Boone.*)

Over the next two years, British units under the successive commands of Colonel Archibald Montgomery and Colonel James Grant along with South Carolina militiamen and volunteers eventually subdued the

Cherokees. In two separate campaigns, the 77th Regiment of Foot and the Highlanders marched into the Cherokee Nation, destroying villages and crops. They attacked the Lower Towns and the Middle Towns. In the second campaign, the British killed 60 to 80 Cherokees, taking another 40 as prisoners, mostly women and children. The soldiers did not intend to fight the Cherokees as much as force them into the mountains to die of starvation and exposure. Among those officers marauding through the Cherokees' Lower and Middle Towns and learning the skills of fighting in the backcountry were Andrew Williamson, Andrew Pickens, Francis Marion, William Moultrie, Henry Laurens, and Isaac Huger. All these men would play important roles later during the Southern Campaign of the American Revolution.[6]

Despairing of the destruction of his homeland, Cherokee leader Attakullakulla helped negotiate a peace in both Charlestown, South Carolina and at Fort Robinson, recently built on the Long Island of the Holston River (in today's Kingsport, Tennessee). Speaking for Chief Kanagatucko (called Standing Turkey), Attakullakulla told the Royal governor and the military officers at the two separate treaties that the Cherokee chiefs were sorry they had started a war. When he signed a peace treaty on November 19, 1761 at Fort Robinson, then under the command of Colonel Adam Stephen, Kanagatucko asked that one of the Virginia soldiers carry the treaty to the Overhill Towns to demonstrate the good intentions of the British. Sensing the personal danger this arrangement would create for any courier should the British violate the treaty, Stephen was reluctant to order any of his men to go. Not willing to see the peace pact undone, Lieutenant Henry Timberlake volunteered for the mission. Demonstrating no less courage in the face of such danger, Sergeant Thomas Sumter volunteered to go with him.

**Thomas Sumter**

Though the Cherokees warned Timberlake and Sumter that travel by water would expose them to the hostilities of French-allied northern Indians along the way, the small party departed by canoe on November 28. They expected to arrive in the Overhill Towns by descending the Holston and Cherokee rivers in six days.[7] Joined by an interpreter, John McCormack, the party took with them in a large canoe supplies for ten days and goods enough to trade for horses for their return trip. To outfit this expedition, Sumter borrowed £60 from Alexander McDonald.

Not far below the Long Island, the men ran aground in shallow water. Timberlake recorded, "Sumter the serjeant leaped out, and dragged us near a hundred yards over the shoals until we found deep water again."[8] Suffering the effects of the summer's drought, the river's shallow water plagued the men for the next 19 days as winter quickly approached. They spent much of each day dragging the canoe and supplies. Timberlake recalled, ". . . the weather was so extremely cold, that the ice hung to our cloaths . . ."[9]

With provisions running low, one of the party went ashore to hunt, but one of their two guns broke in firing. From the canoe, Sumter attempted to steady himself for a shot at a bear, but succeeded only in knocking the remaining good rifle overboard, losing it in a deep pool. Their circumstances were dire. "Our provisions were consumed to an ounce of meat and but very little flour," Timberlake wrote, "our guns lost and spoiled, ourselves in the heart of woods, at a season when neither fruit nor roots were to be found, many days journey from any habitation and frequented only by the northern Indians from whom we had more reason to expect scalping than succor."[10] Remarkably, the men succeeded in some unreliable, makeshift manner to repair the broken rifle sufficiently—and with much good luck—to kill a bear. They would not starve, it seemed.

Proceeding down river, they encountered an "amazing quantity of buffaloes, bears, deer, beavers, geese, swans, ducks, turkeys and other game,"[11] Timberlake recounted. They stopped to explore a cave high on a bluff along the river. For lack of light they could not venture far in; and, upon their quick return to the river, they discovered their canoe drifting away. Sumter scampered down the near-vertical face of the bluff, jumped into the river without even removing his coat and swam after the canoe. He caught it a quarter-mile downstream. With Sumter's clothes soaked and frozen stiff, the men built a fire in the cave to dry him out. The three did not sleep much at all that night because of the continual wailing of wild beasts trapped farther back in the cave by the men's campfire at its mouth. When they did depart after two nights, they discovered a substantial waterfall not far below the spot where Sumter had stopped the canoe. Had he not recovered it when he did, they would certainly have lost all their trade goods, their gear, and the renewed supply of meat.

During the next few days, the explorers negotiated their way downriver past massive, stair-stepped waterfalls and broke a path through long expanses of bank-to-bank ice. At the end of that ordeal, a Cherokee hunting party intercepted the adventurers. Taking some pity on the hapless travelers, this band of Cherokees led the expedition downriver and then upstream against the current along a wide tributary to the Overhill Towns. During the following two months, Timberlake and Sumter lived among the Cherokees visiting Tommotley, Chote, Settico, Chilhowee, and other villages along the river. Timberlake kept a detailed diary and sketched a map of the Cherokee towns throughout the region. He named the river for the town of Tanasi and recorded it on his map the way he heard it, "Tennessee." During this time of exploration, Sumter and Timberlake continued developing their skills with the Cherokee language.

On March 10, 1762, Timberlake, Sumter, and the interpreter departed Tommotley and headed back to Fort Robinson, escorted by Chief Ostenaco (also called Judd's Friend or Judge[12]) and some one hundred Cherokee braves and village chieftains. Concluding his visit at the fort, Ostenaco asked if they might go to Williamsburg where he hoped to see the governor. Accommodating the request, Sumter and Timberlake escorted a party of Cherokee chiefs to the Virginia capital where the governor entertained the visiting Cherokee for several weeks. At a departure dinner held at the College of William and Mary, Ostenaco saw a portrait of King George III,[13] and he expressed a desire to meet "the King my father." Initially reluctant to arrange the trip, Lieutenant Governor Francis Fauquier eventually chose to send Ostenaco and two other chiefs, Cunne Shote (called Stalking Turkey) and Wooe (alsoWoyi, called Pidgeon), to London.[14] Timberlake and Sumter accompanied the chiefs along with a new interpreter. Thomas Jefferson, then a student at the college, later recalled hearing Ostenaco bid his people farewell the night before the departure: "The moon was in full splendour, and to her he seemed to address himself in his prayers for his own safety on the voyage and that of his people during his absence. His sounding voice, distinct articulation, animated action, and the solemn silence of his people at their several fires, filled me with awe and veneration, although I did not understand a word he uttered."[15]

On June 16, the Cherokee chiefs and their colonial escorts arrived at Plymouth, England and later London to great curiosity. London soci-

**Cherokee Chief Ostenaco, joined by Cunne Shote and Wooe and escorted by Henry Timberlake and Thomas Sumter, traveled to London to meet with King George III in 1762. The Museum of the Cherokee Indian in Cherokee, NC presents this tableau as part of its "Emissaries of Peace" exhibit, interpreting the 1762 Cherokee and British delegations.**

ety and aristocracy so grandly received the chiefs that Timberlake and Sumter purchased scarlet coats for their uniforms and passed themselves off as British officers. After weeks of various receptions, tours, and portrait sessions, the chiefs enjoyed an audience with King George III, then just 24 years of age and in his second year on the throne. Because the skilled interpreter had died on the voyage over, Sumter and Timberlake stepped in and served as best they could at translating the exchange between his Majesty and the three Cherokees.[16] The parties each offered gifts and pledges of loyalty and friendship. Departing Great Britain, the Cherokees sailed to Charlestown with Sumter escorting them; Timberlake remained behind. The travelers arrived October 28. At the chief's insistence, Sumter rode with them through the South Carolina countryside and stayed for a while longer in the Overhill Towns. During the ride,

**Thomas Sumter opened a store in South Carolina in 1767 after escaping from a jail in Virginia. A badly weathered historical marker along SC Hwy 6 in northwest Berkeley County commemorates his "country store." (See Notes for marker text.)**

Sumter admired the landscape they passed. During his second stay, he earned the Cherokees' deeper friendship. In the spring, Sumter departed the Cherokee villages and returned to Virginia by way of Charlestown, again delighting in the South Carolina backcountry on his journey.

Arriving home in Virginia among friends and family in early 1763, Thomas Sumter was welcomed warmly. He recounted his exploits and experiences of the recent several years to an eager audience of neighbors. Alexander McDonald was glad to see him as well, but for another reason. Sumter had not repaid the £60 he had borrowed for the expedition into the Cherokee Nation more than a year before. For that reason, McDonald swore out a warrant. After the court convened in November, Thomas Sumter was thrown into jail for debt and held in a gaol in Staunton. Good fortune and a good friend, however, soon rescued the adventurer. Joseph Martin was returning home from his service in the military when he arrived in Staunton. Learning of

Sumter's plight, Martin went to visit his old childhood friend. After gaining permission to spend the night at the gaol so he could talk to his friend, Martin departed in the morning, having left Sumter a tomahawk and 10 guineas (pounds sterling). By use of one or both, Sumter escaped the jail the next day and headed south. Arriving safely in South Carolina, the fugitive wrote to Joseph Martin three weeks later from Long Cane Creek, declaring " . . . I am for Ever your Honest Friend."[17]

Shortly thereafter, Thomas Sumter ventured to the land he had spied in passing through South Carolina. He established a store not far off the Santee River, where roads converged, connecting the coastal region with the Upcountry. He prospered quickly and invested his profits in more land. In the summer of 1767, Sumter married; and, he married well. Taking as his wife the widow Mary Jameson, Sumter gained a sizeable plantation at the Great Savannah at Nelson's Ferry across the Santee River.[18] As a prominent member of the community, Sumter and his associates were friends of the government and supporters of the King and Parliament. But, when the revolution came and after hearing the arguments for independence from Great Britain offered by young firebrands in the community, Sumter soon changed his Loyalist attitude and became an ardent supporter of Liberty. [19]

**Joseph Martin**

In his youth, Joseph Martin was regarded as "large, rude, and ungovernable."[20] His unwillingness to attend to his education caused his father to hire him out as an apprentice carpenter. He rebelled against the instruction, ran away, and joined the provincial guard at Fort Pitt with his friends. Returning home after his service, Martin came into a small inheritance from his father who had died in 1760. Though married in 1762, Martin refused to reform his wild ways. He never drank to excess, nor was he given to swearing profanely, but he enjoyed gambling, perhaps too much. Soon enough Martin found his inheritance gone and himself in debt.

Martin was adventurous and resourceful enough, however, to work his way out of financial trouble. He became a long hunter and may well have ventured into southwest Virginia in the early 1760s with Elijah Wallen. (It is said Wallen was the first to have applied the name "Cumberland" from the river, named by Dr. Thomas Walker in 1748, to the prominent pass then known as Cave Gap.) But aside from the hard work of the long hunt, Martin also fancied to find easy ways he might make his living without much toil. Joining him in the effort to shirk such enterprising industry as drudgery was his childhood friend, Benjamin Cleaveland, another notably idle and married roustabout who also favored riotous living.

Cleaveland and Martin were good hunters and certainly much preferred to go on long hunts than to work on their family farms. Martin's "restless spirit could not be patient at the plow," his son later recounted.[21] The pair ranged far and wide through south central Virginia collecting hides, pelts, and furs from the headwaters of the Staunton (Roanoke), Pigg, and Dan rivers. They had a good market for the skins they harvested. By such efforts over several years and by some good success in his continued gambling, Martin worked himself out of debt. He also earned a deserved reputation as a more-than-competent backwoodsman.

In 1767 while still looking for easy ways to make a living, Cleaveland and Martin attempted to plant a crop of wheat on Cleaveland's land along the Pigg River. The young men were rather lazy about tending the crop, however, and did not properly fence it to protect it from wild animals. At harvest time, as was the custom—and certainly their preference—they invited some friends to help with cutting what wheat there was. To ease the anticipated drudgery on the eve of beginning work, Cleaveland and Martin offered the gathering adequate liquor and the inspirations of a fiddler. The group enjoyed a spirited evening of revelry but never did get around to harvesting any grain. The crop and the enterprise were lost.[22]

Two years later, Martin took up a challenge offered by Dr. Thomas Walker to settle land Walker claimed in the Powell River valley (today's Lee County, Virginia). Walker offered two teams of adventurers—Martin's party and the Kirtleys—the challenge to venture west and put in a crop of corn in the prize region. The first group there would win claims on extensive tracts of fertile land. Martin's group stood to gain 21,000 acres of their choosing.

Following a four-day trip from home to Staunton, Martin's group arrived at the New River on March 14, 1769. There at Captain English's fort, they provisioned their party with seed corn and ammunition. When they reached the Holston River, they learned that Captain [Angus?] Rucker[23] and the Kirtleys had days before hired a pilot to take them by the quickest route to the Powell River valley. Martin's party was already behind, they realized. They hired their own pilot and hurried into the fray with an advance party; the remaining party would follow. After three days, the advance team was lost, and spent another three days wandering around looking for a path. They crossed mountains, creeks, laurel, and canebrakes.[24] The land was rugged. The men were hungry and the horses exhausted. They rested another two days, when Martin, exploring some five miles from the camp, came upon the Hunter's Track. He hurried back to camp with the good news. The men departed the next morning on the 24$^{th}$ with

**In 1769, Joseph Martin and his men built a fortified station along Beargrass Creek on the far western Virginia frontier, but it was soon destroyed by Cherokee or Shawnee raiders. Wilderness Road State Park in Lee County, Virginia interprets Martin's Station and hosts juried reenactments.**

renewed hope and no small portion of anger. "With much difficulty," Martin wrote, "I prevented my companions from discharging our pilot with heavy blows." The advance party arrived at the Powell Valley two days later and the remainder of the men arrived on April 1.[25] In short order they began to secure their sustenance from the forest, consuming in six weeks "23 deer—15 bears—2 buffaloes and a great number of turkeys." On the 15th, the Kirtleys arrived, but discovering they had been beat to the site, they turned homeward without looking elsewhere for claims.

Martin was delighted with the land. He described it as possessing "Vast quantities of black Walnut and wild cherries . . .Very good Springs—Bold creeks, big enough for Mills."[26] Word of this rich land had already attracted others. He wrote, "April 24th came several gentlemen from Culpeper, with negroes to Settle. Likewise several gentleman from Bedford, 3 gentlemen from Maryland, to get land to settle 100 families." And while Joseph Martin and his men were busily constructing Martin's Station along Beargrass Creek, Daniel Boone and his party of five other hunters were surprised to happen upon any white settlement that far into the wilderness. Boone had left his home on the Upper Yadkin River on May 1 upon the hope that John Finley did indeed know how to find a passage through the Cumberland Mountains, one that would take them into the abundant hunting lands of Ken-te-ke. (See *In the Footsteps of Daniel Boone.*)

Martin's men erected the frontier station and put in a crop of corn. They too ventured into Ken-te-ke to hunt. A party of Indians—probably Cherokee or Shawnee—befriended the party of hunters long enough to gain their trust. After a time and on a signal, the Indians seized all the inattentive hunters' rifles. The captors sent the men back east through the gap. When the would-be hunters reached the station, they discovered it had been broken up. Despairing of the Indian menace for the time being, Martin and his men abandoned the station and returned home. Martin spent the next three years working as an overseer on a relative's plantation. He saved his earnings and purchased his own tract for farming in Pittsylvania County (later Henry County), Virginia. He moved there in 1773.

**Benjamin Cleaveland**

The seriousness of enterprise that would later mark the life of Benjamin Cleaveland continued to escape the young man who was idly enjoying an undirected life. About 1764 and after serving in some manner during the French and Indian War, he married Mary Graves of Orange County, Virginia. Her father was well-to-do and so there was little pressure for Cleaveland to embark in earnest on his own endeavor. He continued to enjoy horse-racing and gambling. Without apology, he engaged with his circle of rowdy friends, including Joseph Martin, in the frolicking that was customary on the frontier.

Except for the impending (or possibly recent) birth of Cleaveland's third child in 1769, Cleaveland would likely have gone with Joseph Martin on his expedition to the Powell River valley. Or it may be that Cleaveland's father-in-law was too insistent on separating the young man from his frolicking friends. In either case, Benjamin Cleaveland and family departed for the backcountry of North Carolina when that third child was but an infant.

Near 1770, the young Cleaveland family, along with his father-in-law, Mr. Graves, settled in the foothills of the Blue Ridge Mountains along Roaring River, a tributary of the Yadkin River. With labor provided by the workers enslaved by Mr. Graves, a Cleaveland farmstead began raising crops and livestock. Meanwhile, Benjamin Cleaveland continued to hunt. At some point, he scouted far enough to the southeast to find a site where he erected a new home for his family. It lay in a horseshoe bend of the Yadkin River, about three miles downstream from the mouth of Roaring River. There he built his home which he named "The Round About." During 1770, Surry County was formed from Rowan County and Benjamin Cleaveland became one of its prominent leaders, serving as a justice of the court.

After completing his initial two-year long hunt into Ken-te-ke, Daniel Boone returned home to the Upper Yadkin Valley in the spring of 1771 not too far from the home of Benjamin Cleaveland. Boone's brother, Squire, Jr., had returned during the interim on several occasions with deer hides and peltry to sell. He also brought with him stories of the success of their hunts and he told of the herds of buffalo and the forests abundantly rife with deer, elk, otter and beaver. With these stories circulating in the communities of the Yadkin River valley and perhaps after hearing them directly from Daniel Boone himself, Cleaveland decided a hunting expedition would be his next adventure.

In the summer of 1772, Cleaveland, in the company of Jesse Walton, Jesse Bond, Edward Rice, and William Hightower, made his way into Ken-te-ke.[27] The route to Cumberland Gap was known to adventurous hunters. In the Powell Valley, he no doubt passed by the settlement his good friend Joseph Martin had built three years earlier and then shortly abandoned in the face of Indian attacks. After crossing through the Gap, Cleaveland's party was itself set upon by a band of Cherokees. The braves threatened the hunters and then took all their possessions including not only the hides and pelts they had collected, but their horses, guns, powder, and shot. The irate Cherokees also took the trespassers' hats and shoes as well. They warned the explorers never to come back to their hunting grounds and then gave the men an old shotgun and enough powder and shot for just two loads. Cleaveland's party retreated toward North Carolina taking care to save their powder for a sure kill. They did shoot one small deer, but missed the intended mark with the other shot. With luck, they

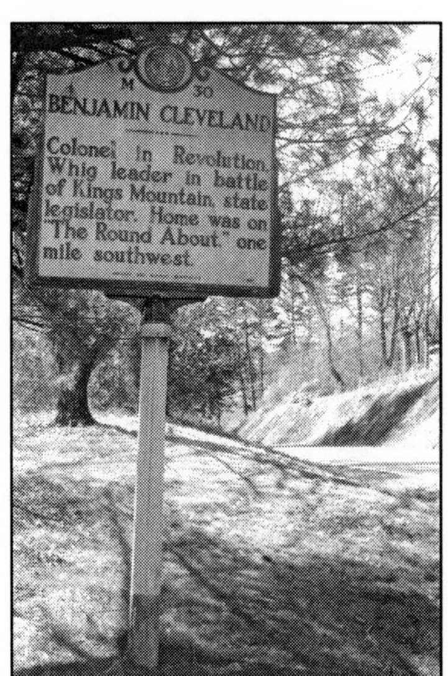


**After living on Roaring River for a few years, Benjamin Cleaveland moved his family to a site in a bend of the Yadkin River. He named the home he built there "The Round About." A marker along NC Hwy 268 near Ronda commemorates his home.**

caught a wild goose suffering with a broken wing. This provided the only other food they had. Nearing starvation, Cleaveland killed his faithful hunting dog to feed himself and his friends. In later years and speaking kindly of this four-legged hunting companion, Cleaveland said it was the "sweetest animal food" he had ever eaten. Supplementing this meager fare with only wild berries and nuts, Cleaveland and his party eventually arrived home, but they were severely undernourished. They had nearly starved to death.

After regaining his strength over the following few months, Cleaveland declared he would recover the horses that had been stolen from him. Hightower, at least, was among the band of hand-picked men who accompanied Cleaveland into Cherokee territory. They arrived first at Nikwasi (Neequasee),[28] the village of the Cherokee chief Yona Equa (called Big Bear).[29] He told Cleaveland that the horses were in the Cherokee towns farther west and that the warriors who had them would likely kill Cleaveland and his party when they arrived. As a compliment, Yona Equa added, "If you were to be killed, I should claim that honor, as one big warrior ought only be slain by another."[30] Cleaveland was indeed uncommonly big and strong, weighing well over 300 pounds even in the prime of life. He boasted that his muscular power was limited only by the strength of his bones.[31] He was a good-natured man, but at times, he could be hot tempered; most definitely he was determined. To help Cleaveland in recovering his stolen property, Yona Equa sent Cherokee escorts along with the hunters.

Cleaveland's party and escorts ventured deeper into the Cherokee Nation and soon without much trouble had reclaimed all the horses except his. When the party rode into the last village, the Cherokee brave who had Cleaveland's horse raised his tomahawk in a threat.

Cleaveland cocked his rifle and pointed it toward the man. One of the escorts threw himself against the brave knocking him to the ground to keep him from being shot. The indignant Cherokee, however, had already thrown his tomahawk. It reached its mark, but only cut away part of Cleaveland's hunting shirt.

Cleaveland mounted his recovered horse and was riding away when the angry brave shot Cleaveland's horse. The injury was not serious and Cleaveland rode on. The party of hunters returned to Yona Equa who, perhaps, was impressed that all the horses had actually been recovered. He increased the number of escorts to see the men safely out of the Cherokee Nation. On their return home, Cleaveland's party rode through the Tugaloo area giving Cleaveland his first look at the picturesque and bountiful land where he would later live.

**A New Time Coming**

In the mid-1770s, tensions between the American colonies and the British Ministers continued to mount as Great Britain sought ways to pay off the heavy debt of having fought the Seven Years' War. Revolution was in the air. The backcountry regions of North Carolina and Virginia, however, were not as preoccupied with revolutionary talk as were the eastern counties, although neighbors and relations were soon to choose sides, just as they would in the backcountry of South Carolina and Georgia. Events soon to unfold would once again test the mettle of the three childhood friends from Virginia's Orange County. This would not be a time for childishness. This was a time for heroes.

# Lord Dunmore's War

**Massacre at Yellow Creek**

On the Ohio River at Yellow Creek, two villages — so different and yet so similar — sat on opposite banks in the spring of 1774. The creek flowed in where the "the beautiful river"[1] first turned due south some fifty miles below where Fort Pitt had stood at the confluence of the Allegheny and Monongahela rivers. Along the west bank of the Ohio River, Tachnechdorus lived with members of his family; he was known to whites as Chief John Logan. He was a leader among the Mingos, a tribe of peoples chased westward from their Iroquois homelands.[2]

On the east side of the river was the white settlement of Baker's Bottom and in it the grog shop of Joshua Baker. That tavern was frequented by trappers, traders, long hunters, and surveyors, those passing through the border area venturing downriver and exploring the wilderness area of Fincastle County, Virginia, most of which became today's Kentucky. The tavern's visitors also included Mingos, Shawnee, Delaware and members of other tribes as well. They enjoyed on occasion, if not the hospitality and welcome of the white patrons, at least the intoxicating beverages served there.

On the morning of April 30, four Mingo men and three woman, one with an infant, crossed the Ohio River in a canoe. The young Mingo mother was the sister of Chief Logan and the wife of a white trader, John Gibson. She had been to the Baker home previously where Joshua's wife provided her with cow's milk for the baby. On the evening before that day's visit, she had come over greatly distressed. After much prodding, she confided in Mrs. Baker that some of the Mingo intended to kill some settlers at Baker's Bottom the next day. The Mingo braves were upset and angry, she said, about recent murderous attacks by Captain Michael Cresap on small parties of Indians elsewhere along the river. The young Mingo men wanted revenge. The warriors intended to restore balance in their world by killing only enough whites to offset the loss to their tribe. Mrs. Baker alerted her husband to the threat. A neighbor, Daniel Greathouse, mustered a party of twenty-one armed men including two others from his family. Four of them hid in readiness in an adjacent room in the tavern, conspiring to thwart any attack that might come. The others hid in the brush along the river, watching for any sign of hostility.

The unarmed Mingos, who had arrived with John Gibson's wife and infant, were loitering around the tavern where they drank through the morning. After some time, they became quite inebriated. In an initially playful act, one donned from a wall peg the coat and hat of a tavern patron, possibly John Sappington or Baker's brother-in-law. The Mingo, Logan's brother, began to parade around in a mocking fashion decrying the arrogance of the whites who were coming down the river. "I'm a white man," the tipsy Mingo said, standing in a mocking way with his arms akimbo. "White man, son of a bitch," he blurted out defiantly, the alcohol or the anger loosening his tongue. Irritated at the spectacle, Sappington demanded the fellow remove the coat and hat. Instead, the reveler headed for the door. Sappington, perhaps having had more than a few drinks himself and acting beyond sober reason, grabbed his rifle. He shot Logan's brother. When they heard the single shot, the men hiding in the next room poured into the tavern. They began shooting the other Indians including the young mother. In her last breath, Logan's sister begged mercy for her infant. Seeing that the first victim, Logan's brother, was still alive, Edward King pounced on him and finished the job with his hunting knife. The Massacre at Yellow Creek had begun.[3]

Unknown to the men hiding inside the tavern, two canoes had pushed off from the Mingo camp to cross the river with seven Indians "all naked, painted and armed completely for war" Sappington later recalled. As the Mingos approached the east bank, they were fired upon by the white men secluded in the brush. The whites shot both warriors in the first canoe; the victims fell into the river as the second canoe turned away. Two more canoes with 18 warriors "painted and armed as the first" tried to land down stream. Each party fired at the other. One Mingo was killed before the others paddled away, retreating down the Ohio River. [4]

Another account of this incident said the white men got some of the Indians drunk and then challenged the armed non-drinkers to a shooting contest. When the Indians had discharged their weapons, the white men killed them all.[5] Most accounts suggest that upon hearing the gunfire from across the river, some of the peaceable Mingos from Logan's camp grabbed their firearms and launched canoes, eager to reach their family and friends. They were recalled as would-be rescuers and not aggressors. Regardless of the actual circumstances and events, the incident was a horrible tragedy precipitated by the lethal combination of fear, arrogance, misunderstandings, and alcohol. Its consequences and the pervasive distrust between cultures it signified spread quickly across the border region.

In all, Daniel Greathouse and the men at Baker's Bottom killed thirteen Mingos; some said eleven. The infant was spared and given to the family of Major William Crawford for a while. Word of the massacre spread like hatred across both sides of the river. Chief Logan, who was away at the time of the killing, was inconsolable. Among the dead, at least, were his sister, a brother, and his mother.

A grieving Logan took two dozen warriors into western Pennsylvania and exacted revenge against settlers he found there. Throughout the summer of 1774, Logan's band of renegades attacked and massacred settlers in the Ohio valley. By some accounts, Logan personally scalped or took prisoner 30 white settlers, traders, trappers, and any others he could find. He took 13 scalps, it was claimed, one for each of his family and tribe killed at Baker's Bottom.

Keigh-tugh-qua (called Cornstalk), chief of the Shawnee, had hoped to persuade Logan not to attack. Cornstalk had promised to protect the fur traders in the area, and he knew they were innocent of this crime. No one, however, was able to stop Logan's rampage. And, although Cornstalk for a time "continue[d] to hold by that Chain of Friendship which ha[d] been put into their hands," by the English settlers, he at last joined Logan in the uprising.[6] He had a change of heart when he saw how the whites behaved; they treated all Indians as their enemy. The attitude and desires of these whites was expressed succinctly in a message, ironically, from Pennsylvania's Governor Penn to Chief Cornstalk. Speaking ill of the Virginians, whom he saw as illegally challenging his own claim to western lands in his colony, Penn warned: "Consider, brethren, that the people of Virginia are like the leaves upon the trees, very numerous, and you but few, and … they will at last wear you out and destroy you."[7] Each of these peoples sought to make the Ohio Valley its home. Unfortunately, the vast breadth of misunderstanding and mistrust that separated these cultures was as wide as the river that for the moment just barely kept them apart.

### The Cream of the Country

The issue at the core of the tension between whites and Indians was land. The Mingo and the Shawnee were not the centuries-old native peoples of the border area, however. Only for the last 50 years or so had the Ohio Valley been the domain of these resident tribes. They had moved to the valley in the first third of the 1700's after the Iroquois chased some groups west and the Cherokee chased others north from their respective homelands. The Delaware also had moved from eastern Pennsylvania where growing white settlements continued to take their lands.

In the mid-18th century, the Shawnee lived in villages to the north of the Ohio River. They regarded the lands south of it as a hunting pre-

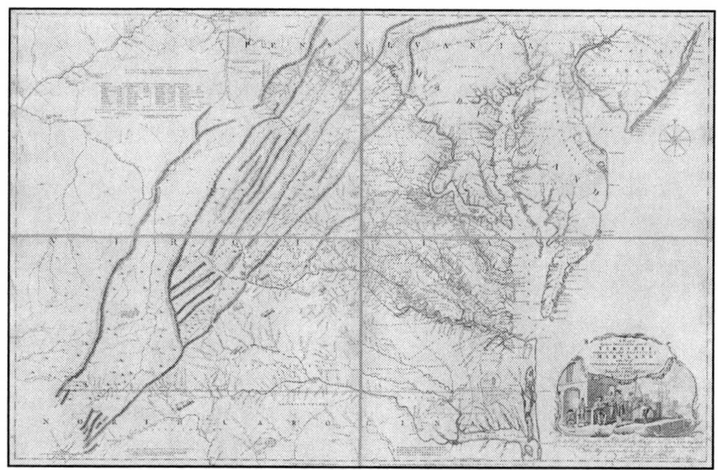

**The western frontier of Virginia, reaching into the Ohio River valley, was little explored and rich with opportunity. This 1751 map by Frye and Jefferson reveals the times' poor knowledge of the west.**

serve, a place for seeking balance with nature and a place from which to take the deerskins they needed to trade with the British for guns and goods they could not make. In the Ohio River valley, the Shawnee had been peaceful under French control because the French treated them as allies. The several tribes of the valley had a testy relationship with the English, however, because after the Seven Years War (known in the Americas as the French and Indian War, 1754-1763), victorious Great Britain treated the Indians as a conquered people. Such haughtiness was immediately resented. North and west of these Ohio Valley tribes were the Great Lakes tribes: the Wyandotte, Ottawa, and Miami. All had joined with the Mingo, Delaware and Shawnee in the pan-regional uprising of 1763 known as Pontiac's Rebellion. After that short-lived assault on the frontier, most whites were wary of all Indians regardless of their tribe.

After the Treaty of Fort Stanwix in 1768 with the Iroquois and since the Treaty of Lochabar (a.k.a. Hard Labor) in 1770 with the Cherokee, more white settlers had been pouring into the upper Ohio Valley and onto lands west of the Appalachians. These treaties had abandoned the Proclamation Line of 1763 on the crest of the Blue Ridge and Allegheny mountains by which the King of Great Britain, "the Great

**George Washington acquired extensive tracts of land in the Ohio River valley in December 1773. A mounted 1932 plaque and historic marker along the Kanawha River commemorate a grant to him for 7,276 acres issued by Lord Dunmore, Governor of Virginia. (See Notes for text on plaque.)**

White Father," had promised to control the westward movement of English colonists. These new treaties created another boundary farther west by which the royal governor of Virginia could secure lands to compensate the soldiers who had fought for the British Crown during the Seven Years' War, known in the colonies as the French and Indian War. The new line was to run north and south connecting the mouth of the Great Kanawha on the Ohio River to Long Island on the Holston River.

The only tribes not included in these two important treaty negotiations were the tribes actually living on and depending upon the land: the Shawnees, the Delawares, and the Mingos. After the treaties, these native inhabitants watched anxiously as numerous parties of surveyors passed down the Ohio River in a rush to mark off and claim the rich tracts of land where these peoples then lived and hunted. Among the surveyors, George Washington had arrived in 1770 with Captain William Crawford, Surveyor of the Soldier Lands, to mark off part of the 200,000 acres which had been promised the soldiers.[8] Washington called the land at the confluence of the Kanawha and Ohio rivers "a most pleasant point."[9] Returning two years later with a party of 30 men, Washington and Crawford marked off over 50,000 acres around the Great Kanawha River. Andrew Lewis received the first tract of nearly 10,000 acres including what became known as Point Pleasant. George Washington claimed over 10,000 acres along the Kanawha River beginning about a mile up from the mouth. Washington later called these tracts "the cream of the Country in which they are."[10]

**Fort Dunmore and Fort Fincastle**

In October 1772, British General Thomas Gage, commander in chief of the North American forces, ordered Fort Pitt abandoned and destroyed. He claimed to need those troops elsewhere in the American

**Dr. John Connolly rebuilt Fort Pitt in 1774 as Fort Dunmore after General Thomas Gage ordered the fort abandoned. The blockhouse built at Fort Pitt in 1764 stands among other remnants of the British fort today at the confluence of the Allegheny and Monongahela rivers in Pittsburgh, PA.**

colonies. Fifteen months later the royal governor of Virginia, Lord Dunmore, ordered the fort rebuilt under the command of Dr. John Connolly. He did so to protect the interests of Virginia in the Ohio Valley. Connolly gave the name Fort Dunmore to the new stockade erected at the site of the abandoned Fort Pitt.

From his post at the head of the Ohio River in April 1774, Connolly created undue alarm. He issued an incendiary and ill-advised circular declaring that a state of war existed between the settlers and the Indians. As a result, many settlers abandoned the Upper Ohio Valley and moved east of the Monongahela River. Some accounts reported that more than a thousand settlers crossed the river in one day. At the same time, those who remained in the valley became belligerent toward all Indians, whether Shawnee, Delaware, Iroquois, Mingo or any other people. Acting with popular support — though he initially counseled against such rash actions — Virginia's Captain Michael Cresap led attacks on small groups of Indians during the spring.[11] His raids and ambushes enraged the area tribes, setting in motion retaliatory assaults. Attack after attack, each side justified its actions, claiming only to be exacting revenge for the most recent outrage perpetrated by the other. Such were the tensions in the spring of 1774 that led to the Massacre at Yellow Creek.

With such distrust and misunderstanding existing between the Virginians and the Shawnee, the frontier could not help but be drawn into hostilities. Rightfully frightened at the prospects of another potentially vicious, frontier Indian war, white settlers living beyond the mountains petitioned their royal governors for help. The two colonies responded differently.

Pennsylvania's assembly refused to get involved; it provided no militia, although it did hire 100 rangers to patrol the area. Virginia's response was more substantial and perhaps politically calculated. John Murray, 4th Earl of Dunmore, Viscount Fincastle and Royal Governor of Virginia, was among those who saw the opportunity to promote the colony's claim to the Ohio River valley including all lands west of the Allegheny crest. Pennsylvania was surprised and even went so far later as to accuse Virginia of fomenting the frontier conflict just so they could move in an armed force and lay claim to Pennsylvania's western territory.

Under orders from Virginia's governor, Dr. John Connolly, Royal Captain Commandant of West Augusta, sent Major William Crawford[12] downriver from Fort Pitt in July 1774 to build a fort at Zane's Station. He named it Fort Fincastle in honor of one of the titles held by Lord Dunmore.[13] Major Angus McDonald, commander of Virginia's northern militia, gathered 400 militiamen at the fort. Those men may have helped strengthen the fortification; some accounts credit them with building it. Regardless of its role in the fort's construction, this army of angry militiamen was not satisfied with taking a defensive posture at the fort. They persuaded McDonald to lead them into the Ohio Valley. Among those involved were Michael Cresap and the later famous general, Daniel Morgan. The militiamen skirmished with a few parties of Shawnee lying in ambush and then destroyed 70 acres of corn in the field and five abandoned Shawnee villages, all evacuated in the face of the advancing militia troops.[14] Cornstalk was not afraid to fight, however; he was busily conferring with other tribes, amassing a force sufficient to strike with effect.

**I Thought I Must Kill Too**

Word of the Indian trouble in the Ohio Valley greatly concerned settlers in other areas, especially those not too far away in the other frontiers of Virginia, west of the Blue Ridge Mountains. Stories of burnings, captures, massacres, and plunderings abounded. With reports that Indians were seen within 30 miles of the courthouse in Botetourt County, frontier settlers moved into the forts of Fincastle County in the Clinch and Holston river valleys.

On July 21, a war club and note were left at the remote cabin of the Roberts family on Reedy Creek of the North Fork of the Holston River (today's Sullivan County in northeast Tennessee.) Inside the cabin were the murdered and scalped bodies of John Roberts, his wife, and all their young children except ten-year-old Jaime, who was taken away. Though it was left hundreds of miles from Yellow Creek, the message was from Logan. It read:

> "To Captain Cresap: What did you kill my people on Yellow Creek for. The white People killed my kin at Coneestoga *(sic)* a great while ago, & I thought nothing of that. But you killed my kin again on Yellow Creek, and took my cousin prisoner. Then I thought I must kill too; and I have been to war three times since but the Indians is not Angry only myself."[15]

With the increasing threat of an uprising, Colonel William Preston, County Lieutenant of Fincastle County militia, feared for the lives of surveyors who were already working far west along the Ohio River. He called for two volunteers to venture into Fincastle County (today's Kentucky) to warn the men of the impending Indian attacks. Captain William Russell of Castle's-wood sent "two of the best Hands I could think of": Daniel Boone and Michael Stoner (also Holsteiner).[16] These experienced woodsmen traveled into the Kentucky wilderness to make certain that the surveyors did not get caught unawares. They ventured as far as the Falls of Ohio (today's Louisville) covering 800 miles in 60 days.[17] Fortunately, all the surveyors escaped, some floating down the Ohio and Mississippi rivers to the Gulf of Mexico.

**Virginia's Royal Governor**

John Murray, Lord Dunmore was the most-reluctant governor of Virginia. He had protested to excess his reassignment from the governorship of New York to the southern province. He had only been New York's governor since September 1770; and. he held Virginia in low regard. He decried how "tiresome" it would be to live in "that country, where there is little or

**John Murray, Lord Dunmore was a proud Scotsman with family connections, which helped him secure a post as a colonial governor. He strongly protested his transfer from New York to Virginia. A full-size copy of the Joshua Reynolds painting of Lord Dunmore is on display at the Hampton History Museum in Hampton, VA.**

no society."[18] Besides, he had been busily collecting substantial personal fees for granting land in New York and acquiring for himself, in an unscrupulous manner, an estate of 51,000 acres along Lake Champlain. When he was eventually confronted with the inevitability of his reassignment, he got drunk, assaulted some of his quests, and declared, "Damn Virginia! — Did I ever seek it?"[19]

The new governor finally arrived in Williamsburg on horseback in September 1771. He was neither inspiring nor gracious. Comparing their new governor with the beloved Lord Botetourt, who had died in office the year before, some Virginians regarded Dunmore in the same spirit he regarded them. "In stature he was low," one wrote, "and though muscular and healthful he bore on his head hoary symptoms of probably a greater age than he had reached. To external accomplishments he pretended not, and his manners and sentiments did not surpass substantial barbarism … not palliated by a particle of native genius nor regulated by one ingredient of religion. His propensities were coarse and depraved."[20]

Among the events early in his administration which best acquainted the citizenry of Virginia with their new governor, Dunmore presided in a court case. It was a salacious and much-too-public affair pitting a "pretty young," not-yet-21 Kitty Eustace against her bride-groom of a day, the also young Dr. James Blair. The suit regarded the consequences of a marriage not consummated to either's satisfaction on the wedding night. Stretching the bounds of equity and propriety and further piquing the public's interest in the matter, the plaintiff, Kitty Eustace, had been (by credible accounts) the mistress of the judge, John Murray, Lord Dunmore, during his time in New York. The court proceedings were made even more colorful by the attorneys involved. Kitty Eustace Blair was represented by political opposites Attorney

General John Randolph and Patrick Henry. The defendant was represented by Edmund Pendleton, George Wythe, Virginia's first law professor at the College of William and Mary, and Wythe's star student, Thomas Jefferson. Although the wedding day and fateful evening were in May 1771, Lord Dunmore did not render his decision on the court case for a year-and-a-half, in November 1773, after the defendant had actually died much too young. Within days of the ruling, Kitty Blair announced an auction on January 1 for her one-half interest in the Blair estate. Thinking that with this case he had somehow recovered his reputation and repaired "the happiness of his government," Dunmore soon found that he had done the opposite. He had given ample evidence to the rising Whig faction in the colony that, beyond being a simple adulterer, he intended to rule Virginia as a despot and without regard to interests other than his own.[21]

What Dunmore needed to boost his popularity in the colony was a celebrated victory over a perceived threat to the interests and safety of the colonists. In the summer of 1774, he put himself at the head of just such a campaign.

### All the Men You Think Willing & Able

Faced with an Indian uprising — even one it created for itself, Virginia prepared to quiet the frontier by force. On July 24, 1774, Lord Dunmore called for the mustering of two divisions of fighting men from Virginia's western lands including the Shenandoah Valley. Dunmore might have preferred to use militia from the eastern provinces as well, but Virginia's assembly, the House of Burgesses, and its eastern citizenry were uncooperative and, at the moment, unempowered. Within Virginia and the other American colonies, a rising tension drifting toward animosity was building between the colonists and the British Parliament. Indeed, the Boston Tea Party had occurred on December 16, 1773 and Parliament had retaliated by shutting down the harbor until the East India Company was compensated for the destroyed shipment of tea. More specifically, Lord Dunmore had dissolved the assembly on May 26 to discipline it for having proclaimed June 1 as a day of fasting and prayer in support of the citizens of Boston. Dunmore saw the House's action as an affront to Crown authorities.

The Virginia citizens and representatives in the east were reluctant to turn their attention and resources to a frontier that did not concern them as much as did the issues of protesting the heavy-handed British ministers. Some saw the conflict on the frontier as a mess of the frontiersmen's own making. Those of that opinion were just as happy to let the frontiersmen take care of the matter themselves. Members of the dissolved House of Burgesses were meeting as the "Association" and planning a convention in Richmond on August 1 to discuss their political situation. Some spoke about the "expert riflemen" of the interior counties and how they might do in combat against British soldiers. Some talked of holding their planned rebel assembly, the August 1 convention, in one of the western towns — Winchester, Frederick, or Lancaster — to have these riflemen at hand for defense.[22]

From his perspective, Dunmore knew that a decisive victory over an Indian uprising, especially if he were in personal command, would make him immensely popular across the colony and help diffuse some of the talk of rebellion.[23] And, indeed, some leaders of the Association (also called the "convention") were not upset by Dunmore's plans to march to the frontier; they would benefit personally. Patrick Henry and George Washington had engaged a surveyor jointly that very summer to explore the region and to secure for them "provisional warrants" on land should London later remove restrictions.[24] Land speculators as well as individual frontier families had an interest in seeing the Shawnee menace subdued. Consequently, for their fighting prowess and for their as-yet unspoiled support of the royal governor, the militiamen of the western counties were Dunmore's best resource from which to gather a fighting force.

Dunmore knew something of these westering folk. He shared his thoughts about them with Lord Dartmouth: "They [backwoodsmen of Pennsylvania and Virginia] acquire no attachment to Place; but wandering about Seems engrafted in their nature; and it is a weakness incident to it, that they Should forever imagine the Lands further off, as Still better than those upon which they are already settled."[25]

Five weeks would be required to recruit, enlist, provision, and muster the troops for the two divisions. According to the plan, the separate armies were to rendezvous along the Ohio River and prepare an attack into the Ohio Valley. Dunmore added in his call for mustering militia that "a Fort at the Conflux of the Great Kanhaway [Kanawha] and the Ohio would answer several good purposes."[26] Perhaps not the least of these was helping secure the governor's personal interests in land speculation for the vast country he soon hoped to secure from the Shawnee — land from which he, no doubt, hoped to profit in opening it to the likes of those who "imagine lands further off as still better."

As part of the preparations for mustering the western militia, Joseph Martin was commissioned a captain of the Pittsylvania militia on August 24 with a specific task. Martin took command of Captain Abraham Penn's company stationed at Culbertson's Bottom, a six-mile meadow along the New River as it cut through mountainous terrain. Several well-used Indian trails converged at the ford there.

Acknowledging Martin's efforts at patrolling the area while others mustered elsewhere for the campaign against the Shawnee, Colonel William Preston wrote to Martin: "I know you have made several long fatiguing scouts with your men, for which I am much obliged to you. The pass is important and I am fully satisfied you will do all you can to guard it."[27] This would not be the last time Martin was called upon to hold a position on the edge of the frontier and to keep the peace in a time of war.

Leaving Williamsburg, in mid-July — in advance of the planned illegal August 1 convention of Burgesses, Lord Dunmore intended to command the first of the two groups, men mustered from Frederick and Dunmore (later Shenandoah) counties. He gathered about 1,200 men (other accounts report up to 1,700 men) who pushed out from Winchester and passed through Fort Cumberland, Maryland. They proceeded north along the Youghiogheny River to Fort Dunmore, following the route Major General Edward Braddock had taken nineteen years earlier in his ill-fated campaign to capture Fort Duquesne.

The second division called for by Lord Dunmore was put under the command of Colonel Andrew Lewis with orders to meet Dunmore at the mouth of the Great Kanawha River on October 2. Dunmore had ordered Lewis to "raise all the Men you think willing & Able & go down immediately to the mouth of the great Kanhaway & there build a Fort."[28] The men came from Augusta and Botetourt counties, which at the time included all the settlements in the Shenandoah Valley between today's Rockingham and Roanoke counties. Added to this southern group were men from Fincastle County, which then included the area west and southwest of Big Lick (i.e., today's Roanoke). Two independent militia groups arrived as well, one from Bedford County, riding under Major Thomas Buford. The other was from

Culpeper County, under the command of Colonel John Fields.[29]

### Andrew Lewis at Camp Union

The men originally mustered at Camp Union (today's Lewisburg, West Virginia). Camp Union stood near Lewis Spring where Andrew Lewis had established himself on the Virginia frontier in 1751. Lewis had served under George Washington in 1754 in the Colonial troops when Washington surrendered at Fort Necessity. It is believed he also marched the following year with Major General Edward Braddock and was at the Battle of the Monongahela on July 9, 1755, also called Braddock's Defeat. Lewis, as a member of the House of Burgesses, was privy to the discussions among his peers pitting immediate concerns about excessive British ministries against threats of an Indian war erupting on the distant frontier. For some, such as Andrew Lewis, Indian wars were not distant actions to be discussed at leisure. They were immediate, real, and fearsome experiences.

In 1763 during Pontiac's Rebellion, Cornstalk had led a war party of Shawnee to attack two nearby settlements at the Big Levels of the Savannah. Cornstalk had gained the trust of the settlers at Muddy Creek and then massacred them. The next day he repeated the betrayal at the Clendenin Settlement, killing 50 settlers; he took many women and children as prisoners. He had completely annihilated the early settlement of the Greenbrier valley. This treachery by Cornstalk was not forgotten by the Virginians, at least not by those who ventured beyond the populated safety of the tidewater towns.

Lewis had the heart of a frontiersman and he knew well how to recruit the men he needed. He promised "to reward every Vollunteer in a handsome manner, over and above his Pay; as the plunder of the Count[r]y will be valuable."[30] About 1,100 men from the frontier of

**Andrew Lewis mustered his militiamen at Camp Union adjacent to Lewis Spring. Plaques and a spring house over Lewis Spring commemorate the 1774 muster in today's Lewisburg, WV. (See Notes for text of plaque.)**

Virginia mustered at Camp Union. These were hunters and trappers, farmers and woodsmen, all tested and hardened by the experience of making a life on the edge of the wilderness. Daniel Boone planned to muster as well, no doubt anticipating a reunion with his old friends, the Greens, the Fields, and the Slaughters from Culpeper County. He departed Russell's Fort at Castle's-wood on August 13, riding northeast with a company of men from the Clinch River valley where he commanded militia at several forts. While en route, however, he received orders from Colonel William Preston to return to his post.[31] The Indian uprising was expected at several points along the frontier. Boone and his men, it was believed, would be needed in that quarter as well.

Although Daniel Boone was recalled, militiamen did arrive at Camp Union from the southern parts of Virginia, from Fincastle County. Among those from the Holston River valley was Captain Evan Shelby with a company of 50 men including his son, Lieutenant Isaac Shelby. Among the militia were also men from the Watauga area including James Robertson and Valentine Sevier (the son, not the immigrant. His brother, John Sevier, was not involved in this campaign.) From Fincastle County were men riding under Captain William Russell of

Castle's-wood including William Bowen. Rees Bowen rode under Captain David Smith.[32] The Bowen brothers served as scouts. (It was Russell's son Henry, age 16, who had been murdered by Shawnee, Cherokee, and Delaware warriors near Kane's Gap along with James Boone, Daniel's first-born child and also 16, on October 9, 1773 as the Russells and Boones first attempted to settle their families in Kentucky. See *In the Footsteps of Daniel Boone*.)

The Virginia militia companies arrived at Camp Union as travel conditions and distances from their home areas dictated. Meanwhile, Colonel Lewis prepared for a departure in early September. Colonel William Christian and his Fincastle men, including Lt. William Edmiston (Edmundson)[33] from the Holston River valley, arrived on September 6 on the eve of departure. That late arrival garnered for Christian and his men, including Captain William Campbell, the inglorious duty of conveying the expedition's baggage and supplies at the rear of the column. Christian's Fincastle troops remained at Camp Union for two weeks collecting provisions and gathering more recruits from those still arriving.[34]

The mustering of such a large army on the frontier had not gone unnoticed. Two days before the march began, one of the officers, Colonel William Fleming, wrote to his wife: "[T]here are some Indian Spies attending us, and now and then firing on a stragling *(sic)* person they can have an advantage over."[35]

**Such As May Be Depended On**

On September 6, the advance party led by Colonel Charles Lewis, brother to Colonel Andrew Lewis, departed Camp Union led by scout Captain Mathew Arbuckle. They drove a herd of beeves and brought along 400 packhorses loaded with flour, salt, and tools. They were to

**Andrew Lewis led his frontier militiamen across the trackless mountians of today's West Virginia. Grandview State Park near Beckley offers an overlook of the beautiful and rugged terrain.**

head for the Elk River where they would build enough canoes to transport all the supplies down the Kanawha River to the Ohio. On the 10th, Colonel John Fields joined this advance party en route with 30 men from Culpeper County. Two days later, Colonel Andrew Lewis's main expedition pushed westward into the mountain wilderness of Virginia. His party also drove a herd of beeves and led a train of packhorses.

Before crossing Gauley Mountain, some of the advance party were menaced by small groups of Indians, probably Shawnee. The entire expedition was tracked daily, in fact, by Indian scouts. The demanding terrain offered as much of a challenge as the harassing Shawnee. Colonel William Fleming, recording in his journal on the 19th the experience of crossing the Gauley Mountain, wrote, "we Met with sudden & frequent Showers of Rain as is usual near these Mountains. It is pritty difficult to Cross being about a mile & half in Ascent & as much in descent."[36]

Colonel Andrew Lewis's men reached the New River on the 21st and proceeded downstream following the narrow gorges and covered about 10 miles a day. On the 23rd, they reached the Elk River where the New River joins to become the Great Kanawha. (Today, this is Charleston, West Virginia.) Rejoining Colonel Charles Lewis's party there after a march they calculated at 108 miles, all the men spent a week building canoes to carry their supplies down the river.[37] By the end of the week, the tedium of camp life tempted these young men to overindulge at liberty in the spirits sold by the suttlers accompanying the march. Because so many militiamen had gotten too drunk, Lewis ordered no further sales of alcohol.[38] During the same week, Colonel Andrew Lewis had sent several scouts downriver to await the arrival of Lord Dunmore. One of the men returned in a few days to report several Indian parties nearby and campfires along the banks of the Kanawha only 15 miles from the Ohio River.

On the 30th, employing their canoes, all the men crossed the Elk River and marched down to its mouth on the Kanawha River. On October 2, they pushed north, following along the Great Kanawha River. Colonel William

**After reaching the Elk River, Lewis's men spent a week building canoes to cross the tributary. They continued down the Great Kanawha River. Charleston, West Virginia sits at the confluence of the Elk and Kanawha rivers.**

Fleming, commanding seven companies of 50 men each from Botetourt County, wrote in his diary, "We marched this day [October 5] about twelve miles through several defiles, & over three or four muddy runs with verry high & steep banks, in many Places the hills came so cloase to the river that the two Columns were oblidged to march in One path."[39]

After marching northward from Camp Union for a month or so through the rugged mountain terrain, the advance units and the main body arrived on October 6 at the mouth of the Great Kanawha River. They made camp on the point between the two rivers where they joined, a *tu-endie-wei*, as the Wyandotte called it, a "mingling of waters." Lewis's army of a thousand or so (Fleming says 800) camped at Point Pleasant, "most of them Woodsmen well armed & such as may be depended on," Fleming wrote. He continued his letter to Colonel Adam Stephen on October 8, then at the mouth of the Hockhocking River: ""Our rear of 200 & odd men [Christians' corps] are within 60 miles of us."[40]

While Lewis's division advanced across the mountainous terrain, Lord Dunmore and his northern division of militiamen stopped at Fort Dunmore for a month. There the governor negotiated a treaty with the Delaware and the Six Nations of Iroquois. At the fort, he enlisted the help of scouts, men who knew well the Ohio River valley. Expecting to treat with a gathering of Shawnee chiefs farther down river, Lord Dunmore proceeded with 700 men in a flotilla of some one hundred canoes, keel boats and pirogues passing by Fort Fincastle on September 13. The other 500 men mustered with Dunmore, those under the command of Major William Crawford, moved overland driving cattle with them. On September 30, some of Dunmore's men arrived at the mouth of the Hockhocking River where they were to meet the Shawnee chiefs. While the militiamen waited, they began work on a stockade. Dunmore named it Fort Gower perhaps to honor his brother-in-law, Earl Gower, one of his chief advocates at court.[41] When Dunmore arrived a few days later, no chiefs had yet arrived. Learning from scouts that the Shawnee chiefs and their warriors had gone to intercept the other division, the one advancing from the south, Dunmore realized he had been tricked. He sent a messenger to advise the other division of a change in plans. The second division was to cross the Ohio River and move north toward the villages of the Shawnee on the Plains of Pickaway. Dunmore would move from the east to catch the warriors in a classic pincer movement.

A few more days passed at Point Pleasant and Dunmore did not appear, though his instructions for Lewis had been left in a hollow tree by two messengers, reportedly the later famous Simon Kenton[42] and the later infamous Simon Girty. Lewis sent his own messengers up the Ohio River to find Dunmore, but on October 8 a messenger from Dunmore did arrive with the new orders. Lewis was to cross the Ohio River and to march up the Scioto River where he would meet Dunmore on the Pickaway Plains. In compliance, Lewis ordered his men to prepare for a morning departure. Unknown to Colonel Andrew Lewis or to any of the men in the camp, however, a war party was preparing a surprise attack. That night Delaware, Mingo, Shawnee, Ottawa, Wyandotte, and Taway (Tawas) warriors numbering between 700 and 1,000, by various accounts, crossed the Ohio River in 70 rafts a few miles above the mouth of the Great Kanawha River.

### Be Strong, Fight and Be Strong

The long march and the days in camp along the Ohio River awaiting Dunmore's arrival had depleted some of Colonel Lewis's supplies. Because Colonel Christian had not yet arrived with the expedition's baggage, parties of hunters were sent out each day to hunt for game to help feed the men. Before dawn on the morning of October 10, the day the army was intending to cross the river, two hunting parties went out early. Evan Shelby had asked Valentine Sevier and James Robison (or Robertson)[43] of his Holston boys to "perch a turkey" to strengthen his ailing son, James Shelby. A second party, James Mooney and Joseph Hughey (some accounts say Hickman), were hunting three miles upstream when they stumbled upon the Shawnee war party preparing for attack. The two hunters bolted for the camp. Hughey was shot by a scout for the Shawnee, Tavenor Ross, a white renegade.[44] The other, Mooney, ran for his life hallooing as he went to alert the camp. He stumbled into the encampment breathless, warning of "a body of Indians covering four acres of ground." Isaac Shelby wrote in a letter a few days later that Valentine Sevier and James Robison returned immediately as well and confirmed the report of the first party of hunters.[45] Colonel Andrew Lewis immediately dispatched his younger brother, Colonel Charles Lewis, and Colonel William Fleming to intercept the oncoming attackers, believing this was just another small group such as had been menacing them throughout their campaign. Andrew Lewis ordered each colonel out with 150 men.

The hurriedly mustered militiamen proceeded north from the camp in two columns in the direction from which Mooney had come. Colonel Charles Lewis with captains Dickerson, Harrison, and Skidmore was on the left. Colonel William Fleming with captains Evan Shelby, William Russell, and Thomas Buford was on the right. "They marched pretty briskly," Fleming wrote, "about 150 or 200 yards apart up the river about half a mile when a Sudden the Enemy lurking behind Bushes & Trees gave the Augusta Line a heavy fire which was briskly followed by a second & third & returned again by our men with much bravery & Courage. This attack was attended with the death of some of our bravest officers & men also with the deaths of a great number of the Enemy. Nor were the Enemy less tardy in their attack on the left Column; for immediately after the fire upon the right line succeeded a heavy one on the left & a return from us with spirit & resolution."[46]

Colonel Charles Lewis was hit early in the battle but did not reveal his condition as he continued to urge on his men. When his stamina flagged and two men carried him from the field, he passed William Bowen, who heard Lewis implore, "Push on boys and never mind me!"[47] Fleming too was soon shot, in the arm and chest; he was led from the field. The colonial forces fell back a little, perhaps 150 or 200 yards, yielding some ground in the confusion to find cover from the ferocious fire of the Shawnee, "attended," Fleming wrote, "with dismal Yells & Screams from the Enemy."[48] The militiamen were soon joined, however, by advancing reinforcements under Colonel John Fields. The woodsmen dug in for a fire fight.

The Shawnee and their allies were fierce warriors. They fought hard, with tenacity. They attacked under the leadership of their chiefs: Cornstalk, his son, Elinipisco, Blue Jacket, Black Hoof, Red Eagle, Captain Dickson, Scoppathus, and Chiyawee. The line of warriors extended from the Ohio River on the west to the Great Kanawha on the south. As the warriors advanced they concentrated the colonial forces which then became targets more susceptible to being struck by any shot fired. The two rivers behind them afforded no escape. Lewis's men would have been trapped and slaughtered at Point Pleasant if they did not prevail in pushing the line outward. Along the front lines, the militiamen could hear Cornstalk and the other chiefs urging on his warriors, "Lye low," "Shoot well," and "Be strong! Fight and be strong!"[49] But, these backwoods militiamen were hunters and expert riflemen. They knew well how to make every shot count.

The fighting had started at first light and continued well into the afternoon. The sides were evenly matched in numbers. During the course of the day, the lines moved only slightly in both directions with each side taking some ground and giving up other. As the militiamen pressed forward, however, the Shawnee were forced to thin their ranks so they could stretch their line from river to river. This afforded some advantage to the militiamen as fighting sometimes erupted in close, hand-to-hand combat. "[The] Enemy being much Suppirour in Number, Disputed the ground," recalled one captain, "after Runung up to the Very Muzels of our Gunes where the[y] as often fell Victims to there Rage."[50]

On that front line and in the heat of the battle, William Bowen fought for his life. He was in a dry streambed loading his rifle when he spied an Indian taking aim, supposedly right at him. When the fellow fired, the shot went high or he had someone else in mind. "As soon as the Indian fired," Draper recorded in his interview notes, "he discovered Bowen and dashed toward him [with] tomahawk, and Bowen with his went to meet his foe. [The] Indian, painted & greased, swank *(sic)* the first blow, but so near that the Indian's hand struck Bowen and the hatchet flew from his hand. When Bowen aimed a tomahawk blow at this foe's head, he missed its aim and struck [the Indian] on his collarbone and cut him open. [Bowen] finished him with his butcher knife, the blood spirting *(sic)* all over him."[51]

About mid-day, Colonel Charles Lewis died of his wounds; and, shortly after arriving with his reinforcements, Colonel John Fields was killed. Captain Evan Shelby took immediate command of the men along that line. Isaac Shelby wrote later, "... the Action continued

Extreemly Hott[. T]he Close underwood, many steep bancks & Loggs greatly favoured their retreat, and the Bravest of their men made the use of themselves, whilst others were throwing their dead into the Ohio, and Carrying of[f] their wounded …"[52]

Late in the afternoon, Evan Shelby conferred with some of the other captains and decided to attempt a tactical maneuver. Captain Shelby, along with captains Arbuckle, Matthews, and Stuart led some men (presumed to include his son Lieutenant Isaac Shelby) along Crooked Creek using the stream bank to shield their movement. They intended to advance up that ravine to gain a position on high ground behind the Shawnee. They were spotted before reaching the advantageous position, but the effort may have worked in their favor, nevertheless. The Shawnee may have mistook these men for the reinforcements that Cornstalk knew from his own scouting parties were coming up behind with Colonel Christian. Expecting a turn in the tide of the battle if reinforcements had arrived, Cornstalk exhorted his braves to retreat. They withdrew skillfully, returning fire intermittently, never allowing the militiamen to gain an advantage that would precipitate a

**The Battle of Point Pleasant was a day-long conflict on October 10, 1774 and the single battle of Lord Dunmore's War. The Battle Monument stands at the center of Tu-Endie-Wei State Park in Point Pleasant, WV, overlooking the Ohio and Kanawha rivers.**

rout. Isaac Shelby wrote: "They had not the satisfaction of scalping any of our men save One or two straglers whom they Killed before the ingagement[. M]any of their dead they scalped rather than we should have them but our troops scalped upwards of Twenty of those who were first killed; Its Beyond a Doubt their Loss in Number farr Exceeds ours, which is Considirable."[53] He continued, "[I]ts realy Impossible for me to Express or you to Concieve Acclamations that we were under, sometimes, the Hidious Cries of the Enemy and the groans of our wound[ed] men lying around was Enough to shuder the stoutest hart."[54] In a familial tone in his closing remarks made in a letter from the camp to his uncle, Isaac Shelby referred briefly to the welfare of his father: "five men that Came in Dadys [daddy's] Company were killed."[55]

As evening came on, Cornstalk and his band of Shawnee-allied warriors re-crossed the Ohio River, yielding the battlefield at Point Pleasant to the colonial militiamen from the frontiers of Virginia. Colonel Andrew Lewis's men had suffered substantial casualties: 75 dead and some 140 or more wounded by some accounts. (Others say 54 and 87.[56]) This was a quarter of their troops. Among the dead was James Mooney — the frontier woodsman who first alerted the camp. Five years earlier, in May 1769, Mooney had joined with Daniel Boone in his first expedition through the Cumberland Gap into Ken-te-ke. These men at Point Pleasant were fighting to secure continued safe access to those same rich wilderness lands for themselves and their families. The Shawnee were fighting to preserve the same hunting lands for their own people, to sustain their culture, and to protect their own threatened way of life.

The Virginia militiamen counted only 35 dead Shawnee, but suspected many more had been carried off, buried, or thrown into the river

**Metal figures of Chief Cornstalk and Col. Andrew Lewis stand in front of an elaborate and detailed battle mural painted on the Ohio River-side of the floodwall protecting the City of Point Pleasant.**

to prevent them from being scalped, a desecration performed by many frontiersmen, they believed.[57] Their concern was justified. Fleming wrote two days after the battle: "This day the scalps of [the] enemy were collected & found to be 17[. T]hey were dressed & hung on a pole near the river Bank ..." The militiamen had scalped "principal warriors amongst the Shawnese camp," Fleming added. One account suggested that 230 warriors were killed or wounded and that the entire band of warriors had been about 430. Others suggested twice that many Indians.[58] Not all warriors were alike, of course. As with the death of some militia leaders, the consequences of some Indian deaths were felt more profoundly. One of the Indian dead was Puckeshinwa, the father of the later famous and militant Shawnee chief, Tecumseh, then age six.

The frontier militiamen from the Shenandoah Valley had held their ground and won a victory in what to that time had been the fiercest fighting ever encountered between whites and Indians. They had fought from tree to tree and rock to rock, fighting on occasion hand-to-hand with knives, tomahawks, and clubs. These were not trained, uniformed soldiers fighting in regimental fashion. These were citizen soldiers, roused to a cause and mustering to the call in their hunting shirts and trousers made of homespun linen. They knew how to handle a rifle in the woods and these backwoods "shirt men," as they were called, had acquitted themselves expertly in battle. As midnight arrived, so did Colonel William Christian with what would have been most helpful reinforcements just a few hours earlier. He also brought the expedition's baggage and additional supplies. Arriving too late to share in either the challenge of the fight or the glory of the victory, Captain William Campbell and Lieutenant William Edmiston were among the fresh troops. Over the next week, they helped care for the wounded, raise a stockade, and provision the troops.[59] Though absent from the battle, these late arrivals had endured the same laborious march through difficult mountainous terrain. Being men of action, they were, no doubt, eager to pursue Cornstalk and to put an end to the Indian threat.

### Not a Drop of My Blood

Colonel Andrew Lewis sent a messenger to inform Lord Dunmore that his men had won the battle at Point Pleasant. Dunmore had heard the gunfire from upriver and had waited anxiously for a report on the outcome. Upon hearing the good news, Dunmore broke camp and continued his march toward the Pickaway Plains. After a few days of marching, another messenger met Dunmore on October 16; this one came from Cornstalk. The messenger was Matthew Eliot, another white renegade living and fighting with the Indians. Eliot brought word that the Shawnee chief knew that he was trapped between advancing armies and he wanted to sue for peace. Dunmore preferred to settle the matter without any additional bloodshed, so he erected a camp about eight miles east of Cornstalk's village. To honor his queen,

**Lord Dunmore called for a treaty at a makeshift camp he named Camp Charlotte. The event is commemorated by a marker and monument south of Circleville, OH in Pickaway County.**

he called the encampment Camp Charlotte, though he may have later told his wife, also named Charlotte, a different account. He wrote the name in red chalk on a sapling in the middle of the enclosure.

After tending to the care of his men for a week, Colonel Andrew Lewis crossed the Ohio River on October 17. Leaving his wounded at camp, Lewis advanced with his remaining militiamen toward the villages at Chillicossee Town, the Shawnee capital on the Scioto River. Meanwhile, Dunmore was at Camp Charlotte planning to negotiate with Cornstalk. Lewis's men, however, were in no mood for negotiations. They wanted to punish Cornstalk and his warriors for the death and damage inflicted on 200 of their friends, neighbors, and fellow men-in-arms. Dunmore immediately sent a message to Lewis to stop his advance toward Cornstalk's village. One account says that Dunmore had to ride to Lewis's camp himself to order Lewis's men to stand down while he pursued peace negotiations. More likely, Lewis's scout had taken the wrong path in an effort to find a site suitable for the men to encamp in compliance with Dunmore's orders. As it was, Lewis's army was advancing, perhaps inadvertently, toward Cornstalk's village rather than toward Camp Charlotte. Confronted by Dunmore, Colonel Lewis and his men obeyed the orders, though many of the Virginia militiamen were angry with Dunmore for interfering with their plans for revenge against the Shawnee warriors. To protect the governor from the wrath of these humorless frontiersmen, extra guards were placed around Dunmore's tent.

As the Shawnee chiefs gathered at Camp Charlotte, Lord Dunmore realized that Chief Logan was not among them. He asked John Gibson, Logan's son-in-law and the husband of the young Mingo mother murdered at Yellow Creek, to see if Logan would come treat with him and the others. Logan refused to come to the treaty, but he shared with Gibson a message for Dunmore. When Gibson returned to Camp Charlotte, he went immediately into a tent and wrote down the message as best he could recall it. He then read the "speech" to the officers gathered. The powerful words became known as Logan's Lament:

> "I appeal to any white man to say if ever he entered Logan's cabin hungry and he gave him not meat; if ever he came cold and naked and he clothed him not. During the course of the last long and bloody war, Logan remained idle in his cabin, an advocate of peace. Such was my love for the whites that my countrymen pointed at me as they passed and said, "Logan is the friend of white men." I had even thought to have lived with you, but for the injuries of one man, Colonel Cresap[60] the last spring in cold blood and unprovoked, murdered all the relatives of Logan, not even sparing my women and children. There runs not a drop of my blood in the veins of any living creature. This called on me for revenge. I have sought

**In 1774, Chief John Logan refused to attend Dunmore's treaty, but offered his sentiments beneath a large elm tree, since died. Several monuments grace Logan Elm State Memorial on OH Hwy 361 one mile east of US Hwy 23 in Pickaway County, OH, near Circleville.**

> it, I have killed many. I have fully glutted my vengeance. For my country I rejoice at the beams of peace. But do not harbor a thought that mine is the joy of fear. Logan never felt fear. He will not turn on his heel to save his life. Who is there to mourn for Logan? Not one." [61]

Without Logan's participation, Lord Dunmore nevertheless negotiated the Treaty of Camp Charlotte. It forced the Shawnee to relinquish their claim to lands south of the Ohio River, even for hunting. The Shawnee were to return hostages, replace stolen horses from their own stock, and permit boats to pass along the river unmolested.[62] Though many historians have declared that the treaty also succeeded in reducing the Indian threat on the frontier for the first two years of the American Revolution — a conflict that had not yet erupted, Indian troubles abounded in small skirmishes all along the western frontier during the ensuing years. Although the military leaders of the Continental Army may have felt comfortable ignoring any Indian threat during 1775 and 1776, those who lived on the frontier were rightfully ever vigilant for threats from the west as well as from the east.

Lord Dunmore's War was finished with the single victory of the colonial militia at the Battle of Point Pleasant and with the Treaty of Camp Charlotte. The royal governor of Virginia returned to Williamsburg to great acclaim. He arrived in Williamsburg on December 4 where he received public praise and congratulatory addresses issued by the city of Williamsburg, the College of William and Mary, and the governor's council. Though he had fired no shots nor lost any men in battle from his division, Lord Dunmore was the hero of the day.

Meanwhile, the backcountry militiamen from the Shenandoah Valley (running from Frederick to Botetourt counties) and from the Holston River valley, those from Fincastle, Bedford and Culpeper counties — the men who had engaged in the fighting — returned to their respective homes. Lord Dunmore had dismissed them at Camp Charlotte and Fort Gower, providing them no supplies for their return trips. These were frontiersmen, however, and as was their capability, they lived off the land during their return home. As they made their way back, they considered their experience and their lessons from combat. They returned to pursuing their lives on the frontier as farmers and hunters, as trappers and traders. They had won a victory, but they nevertheless readied themselves, as always, for the next battle with whatever enemy should come.

**Now Is Our Time**

To help secure the future peace, the Virginia colonial militia established a garrison at Point Pleasant. They built Fort Blair at the confluence of the Great Kanawha and Ohio rivers. It was a palisade fort

Fort Blair and later nearby Fort Randolph were built to secure Virginia's land claims in the Ohio River valley. Isaac Shelby garrisoned there before departing to survey his land claims in Ken-te-ke during 1775 and 1776. A monument on the lawn of a residential community in Point Pleasant commemorates Fort Randolph.

about 80 yards long with blockhouses in two corners. Lieutenant Isaac Shelby, then approaching his 24th birthday in December remained at Fort Blair for the next nine months until the troops there were disbanded. By June 1775, Lord Dunmore had decided it imprudent to have these armed men gathered together when they might be influenced to join the rebellious Whigs and turn against his authority as royal governor.[63] It was not long, however, before Virginia's rebel government ordered Fort Randolph built a short distance upstream from the site of Fort Blair. Captain Mathew Arbuckle commanded the garrison there, protecting the interests of Virginia.

After leaving Fort Blair in the summer of 1775, Isaac Shelby began working for Richard Henderson, the North Carolina justice and land speculator. Henderson had leased a massive tract of land — 20 million acres known as the Transylvania Purchase — from the Cherokee in March of that year at a treaty at Sycamore Shoals on the Watauga River. Also working for Henderson, Daniel Boone had marked a trail through the Cumberland Gap during March and April for others to follow later. After arriving deep in Fincastle County at a site on the banks of the Kentucky River, Boone's party had begun building a settlement the others named Fort Boonesborough.

During the remainder of 1775 and most of 1776, Isaac Shelby explored the Fincastle terrain that became Kentucky County on December 31, 1776. He surveyed his land to further improve his claim; the requirements were very strict. Claimants had to put in a successful crop of corn during 1775. Moreover, the opportunity was given only to those who were "industriously inclined to become an inhabitant and promote the felicity of the whole community." Although Shelby was farther west in Fincastle County, during 1775 Joseph Martin, stationed in the Powell Valley, was responsible for recording land claims as entry taker.[64] On July 20th, Richard Henderson wrote to Martin encouraging him and his men as they withstood attacks to their settlement from Shawnee and Cherokee war parties. "Your spirited conduct gives me great pleasure," Henderson wrote. "Keep your men in heart if possible, now is our time, the Indians must not drive us." To avoid aggravating the Indians further, Henderson warned Martin not to permit any settlement farther down the valley "yet below Cumberland Gap." A year later in the summer of 1776, however, Martin and his men would abandon their station in Powell Valley in the face of a growing Indian uprising.[65]

### At the Expense of Our Lives

Captain William Campbell, then 29, and his men, including his second in command, Lt. William Edmiston, returned to the Holston River valley not having seen action against the Indians at Point Pleasant. Along the way home, they were, nonetheless, part of history.

As some of Dunmore's soldiers and militiamen reached the Ohio River at the mouth of the Hockhocking River, they stopped at Fort

Gower. They may have expanded the fort and reinforced it for future use. While there, they learned that the First Continental Congress, formed in September 1774 to coordinate the collective response of the thirteen colonies, was encouraging colonists to boycott British goods in retaliation for recent British acts, which oppressed the American colonists. Parliament, under the direction of Prime Minister Lord North, 2nd Earl of Guilford, had passed the Coercive Acts — called by the colonists the Intolerable Acts — in response to the Boston Tea Party, a protest of Parliamentary control of colonial commerce. Through the Intolerable Acts, Parliament closed the port of Boston to all trade except food and firewood until the East India Company was compensated for its losses, the tea tossed overboard. The acts also imposed appointed officials, rather than elected ones, on Massachusetts colonists. All the colonies were concerned about an overbearing and heavy-handed Parliament.

Four of the Intolerable Acts affected mostly people along the eastern seaboard and principally Massachusetts. The Quebec Act, however, struck at the heart of the westering colonists' ideals. The act extended the jurisdiction of Quebec to the Ohio River valley, tolerated Roman Catholicism in place of Protestant preferences, and provided for administration of Quebec by an appointed council rather than a body

**After the Treaty of Charlotte, some of the militiamen expressed their collective, supportive sentiments to the First Continental Congress by fashioning the Fort Gower Resolutions. Fort Gower and the resolutions are commemorated in Hockport, OH, where the Hock(hock)ing River flows into the Ohio River.**

of elected representatives. This act affected the western colonial lands. If enforced, the act would prevent these frontiersmen from occupying the lands on which many were already living and from seeking other tracts farther west. They had just fought the Shawnee at Point Pleasant to make these lands safe for settlement and then faced the prospect of being denied by the British Parliament the full use of their land. On November 5, the gathering of officers heard one of their own offer a proposal to assure the country of their readiness to defend it. His remarks suggested that he may well have heard expressions of both pride and concern about the "expert riflemen" of the interior counties. He said:

> Gentlemen: … We have lived about three months in the woods without any intelligence from Boston, or from the Delegates at Philadelphia. It is possible, from the groundless reports of designing men, that our countrymen may be jealous of the use such a body would make of arms in their hands at this critical juncture. That we are a respectable body is certain, when it is considered that we can live weeks without bread or salt; that we can sleep in the open air without any covering but that of the canopy of Heaven; and that our men can march and shoot with any in the known world. Blessed with these talents, let us solemnly engage to one another, and our country in particular, that we will use them to no purpose but for the honour and advantage of America in general, and of Virginia in particular. It behooves us then, for the satisfaction of our country, that we should give them our real sentiment, by way of resolves, at this very alarming crisis."[66]

Thus encouraged, the officers of the militiamen at Fort Gower, with Campbell and Edmiston assumed among them, declared to the First Continental Congress their support for the boycott. They decreed:

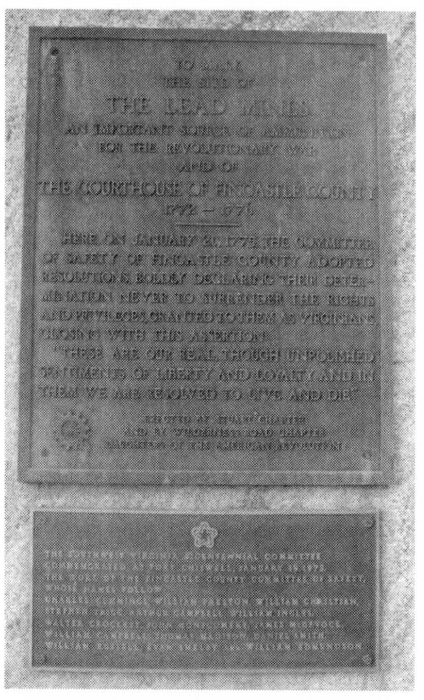



**William Campbell and other leaders signed the Fincastle Resolution in support of the Continental Congress. Two plaques in Austinville, VA commemorate the former county seat, Lead Mines, and the signing. The monument is on Austinville Rd. one-half mile west of the VA Hwy 636 bridge over New River.**

"[A]s the love of Liberty, and attachment to the real interests and just rights of America outweigh every other consideration, we resolve that we will exert every power within us for the defence *(sic)* of American Liberty." Their political statement became known as the Fort Gower Resolutions.[67] The name given to this declaration of their defense of Liberty could not have pleased Lord Dunmore. His brother-in-law, Earl Gower, was a hard-line supporter of Lord North in addressing the insolence of the American colonists.[68]

Upon returning to the Holston River valley, Campbell and Edmiston were parties just a few weeks later to another, similar declaration made January 20, 1775. The thirteen elected representatives of Fincastle County gathered at Lead Mines, the seat of county government, where they pledged their own support to the First Continental Congress. The Fincastle Resolution offered patriotic support for resistance to the oppressions of the British government. It declared "if no pacific measures shall be proposed or adopted by Great Britain, and our enemies attempt to dragoon us out of those inestimable privileges which we are entitled to as subjects, and reduce us to slavery, we declare that we are deliberately and resolutely determined never to surrender them to any power upon earth but at the expense of our lives. These are our real, though unpolished, sentiments of liberty and loyalty, and in them we are resolved to live and die." Joining with a rising chorus of other leaders across Virginia, William Campbell and William Edmiston were publicly committed to retaining the freedoms they believed were the entitlements of British citizens living in the colonies. The Fincastle Resolutions, though decrying any interest in "shaking off our duty and allegiance to our lawful Sovereign," continued, we "cannot think of submitting our liberty or property to the power of a venal British Parliament, or to the will of a corrupt Ministry." The Fincastle Resolution was the earliest such declaration of the willingness of some colonists to expend their lives in the pursuit of Liberty.

Campbell and Edmiston were in good company in this declaration. They were joined in its signing by William Campbell's cousin (and brother-in-law) Colonel Arthur Campbell and by colonels William Preston and William Christian as well as by Evan Shelby, and Thomas Madison, all leaders of Fincastle County. Colonel Christian and Captain Madison shared another connection as well. Each was married to a sister of Whig firebrand Patrick Henry. Christian was married to Anne and Madison to the youngest sister, Susanna. Another of these signers of the Fincastle Resolutions would soon join them in this matrimonial distinction — Captain William Campbell.

# Great Bridge and Norfolk

## (The Rise of the "Shirtmen")

### Give Me Liberty

After the Battle of Point Pleasant in October 1774, Lord Dunmore returned to Williamsburg in December. Following an absence of several months, he resumed his more prosaic duties as royal governor of Virginia, but he did so amidst great public admiration. At the confluence of the Kanawha and Ohio rivers, the frontier militiamen under Colonel Andrew Lewis had decisively defeated Cornstalk and his Shawnee warriors. Over the following days, Dunmore had negotiated a treaty to secure at least a temporary peace on the western frontier. He had made it safe for Virginians to settle on the formerly contested

**Lord Dunmore held a ball at the Governor's Palace after his triumphant treaty with Chief Cornstalk. The Governor's Palace burned in 1781. The palace at Colonial Williamsburg was reconstructed in 1934 on the original foundation.**

lands of the Shawnee, lands that had been promised to men for their service during the French and Indian War. For the next several weeks following his return, Dunmore enjoyed great popularity throughout the colony. On January 19, 1775, he hosted a ball at the Governor's Palace to celebrate two occasions: the Queen's birthday and the christening of his new daughter, Virginia. Amidst such gaiety and public adulation, Lord Dunmore probably could not have imagined the changes that would soon transform his fame of the moment into everlasting infamy.

As the spring of 1775 approached, the growing discontent among American colonists aroused by the Intolerable Acts was giving way to talk of revolution. When the House of Burgesses had called for a day of prayer in support of Boston the year before, Lord Dunmore dissolved the House in May 1774. After gathering initially at the Raleigh Tavern in Williamsburg to discuss their plight, the members convened defiantly that August in Richmond, away from the governor, to talk of how all the colonies could unite in opposition to Parliament's egregious actions. The First Continental Congress, including representatives from 12 of the colonies and convened in Philadelphia at the time of the Battle of Point Pleasant, had called for a boycott of British goods. As the boycott began and other collective actions took effect, Virginia's own revolutionary convention received encouragements from several counties. Colonel William Christian brought forward the Fincastle Resolution as evidence of his region's "real, though unpolished sentiments," their earnest pledge to fight to the death for Liberty.

Fincastle would provide more than words, however, eventually supplying over 1,000 riflemen in the cause of Liberty. These frontiersmen of the western counties were regarded as "the most formidable light infantry in the world," said convention member Richard Henry Lee. It was a testament to what they had just demonstrated, traversing the rugged Appalachian Mountains to fight a monumental battle. Further praising the skills and courage of the Virginians from the west, Lee declared that with the riflemen "every shot is fatal," adding that none "wishes a distance less than 200 yards on a larger object than an Orange."[1]

On March 23, 1775, Patrick Henry addressed the second Virginia convention at St John's Church in Richmond. Some of the men present sincerely hoped to mend the colonial rift with Parliament and to retain their rights at Englishmen. Henry countered that desire, championing a new, radical view: "We indulge the fond hope of peace and reconciliation …in vain." He then declared his revolutionary ambitions for Virginia: "Gentlemen may cry peace, peace, but there is no peace. … What is it that [these] gentlemen wish? Is life so dear, or peace so sweet, as to be purchased at the price of chains and slavery? Forbid it,

**Patrick Henry delivered an impassioned speech at St. John's Church on E. Broad St. in Richmond, VA. The middle section of the modern building was the historic gathering place of the renegade Burgesses who heard Henry declare, "Give me liberty or give me death." The site offers interpretive tours and a visitor center.**

Almighty God! I know not what course others may take, but as for me—give me liberty or give me death."[2] After some impassioned debate and shouts of "Treason!" the convention then passed, though narrowly so, a resolution for "raising a body of armed men in all the counties." [3] These would be volunteers, both mounted and infantry. Henry chaired the committee to implement the plan for establishing regiments of regular soldiers and militia. Serving with him were Thomas Jefferson, Andrew Lewis, George Washington, William Christian, Adam Stephen, and Richard Henry Lee.[4]

**Outcast**

The actions of the second convention to form armed units across the colony aroused concern for Virginia's colonial governor. Dunmore concluded it prudent for him to take possession of the gunpowder stored in the magazine at Williamsburg. (The same concerns by General Thomas Gage, then military royal governor of Massachusetts, initiated similar actions simultaneously in that colony, giving rise to a mustering of Patriots that later became celebrated by Henry Wadsworth Longfellow as "The Midnight Ride of Paul Revere.") Dunmore gave the keys to the walled, octagonal munitions depot to Lieutenant Henry Colins, commander of the *HMS Magdalen*, an armed schooner anchored in the James River. Under Colins's command, a party of royal marines came ashore at night. Before dawn on Friday, April 21, they entered Williamsburg and began loading half-barrels of gunpowder into the governor's wagon. The raid was discovered in progress after 15 kegs had been loaded. The town was alerted with shouts of alarm and with the beating of drums. Local independent militiamen turned out, but the governor succeeded in taking possession of the gunpowder nonetheless.

Word of the governor's theft from the magazine spread rapidly across

**Dunmore's seizing of the colony's gunpowder in 1775 mirrored similar and uncoordinated events in Massachusetts. Both incidents led to revolution. The octagonal powder magazine at Colonial Williamsburg was restored in 1934 after partial collapse and a fire in the late 1800s.**

Virginia. Citizens were outraged. Some of the newly organized militia units began to muster and move toward Williamsburg. Units from the Virginia piedmont, from Orange, Culpeper, and Albemarle counties included troops who had fought on Dunmore's behalf at Point Pleasant just six months earlier. At the suggestion of George Washington, militia from Fredericksburg, numbering 600, stood ready for a call to action. Closer to Williamsburg and moving immediately, Patrick Henry led the militia from his home county, Hanover. As the separate groups of armed men converged on the capital, disturbing news came from afar. On April 28, the first word arrived in Virginia of the fighting that had taken place in Massachusetts on the 19$^{th}$. The anxious Virginians learned that British soldiers and colonial subjects of the King had shot and killed one another on the village greens and along the roads in Lexington and Concord more than a week earlier. Upon that news, life in Virginia changed forever.

With the militia groups gathering outside Williamsburg, Lord Dunmore made his own preparations. He brought cannons to the Palace, trained them on the town, and threatened to destroy Williamsburg if any hostile Virginians should enter the capital. As an additional precaution, should he fail to dissuade the gathering of armed citizens, he removed his wife and family to the safety of the *HMS Fowey* at Yorktown. Dunmore then sent an urgent message to the British command in Boston seeking reinforcements.

Over the next few days a standoff ensued with Patrick Henry waiting outside the city some dozen miles away at Doncastle's ordinary in New Kent County. He commanded an army of militia, variously reported between 150 and 500 men. Fortunately, diplomacy prevailed during the interim. An intermediary succeeded in securing from Lord Dunmore the payment of £330 for the stolen gunpowder. Upon receiving proof of payment for the powder, Patrick Henry disbanded his militia; the potential for immediate hostilities diminished. For the immediate future, the revolution in Virginia would not become the open shooting conflict Massachusetts had suffered. Shortly thereafter Lord Dunmore derided Patrick Henry in a public proclamation intending to reestablish himself as the sole, recognized leader of Virginia. Nothing Dunmore could have done at this point, however, could have helped recover for the colonial governor the rapport and good graces he had only recently enjoyed with many of the citizens of Virginia. More strongly than ever, those with inclinations toward revolution despised the British government and its colonial ministers. Feeling thus threatened, on June 8 Lord Dunmore left Williamsburg and joined his family aboard the *HMS Fowey*.[5] He was no longer able to govern properly his colony; however, Dunmore was not finished making trouble for Virginia and for himself.

**A Capital Mistake**

Deciding that a volunteer militia was not adequate protection for the colony, in July and August, Virginia's third convention formed two regiments of regular troops and five companies for protecting the western borders against Indians.[6] They also formed 16 militia districts and called upon each to raise a battalion of men. The largest battalion was formed in Culpeper District where 14 companies were mustered in Culpeper, Orange, and Fauquier counties. One rifle company from Culpeper became part of a Virginia regiment.[7]

In September 1775, the Committee of Safety, acting as the Convention, made Patrick Henry the commander-in-chief of the provisional army and gave him command of the First Virginia Regiment. Colonel William Woodford commanded the Second Virginia Regiment. Henry's fiery rhetoric easily enabled him to rally men to fight for the freedom he had professed in his famous speech. He was less successful in persuading some of his fellow Burgesses and Assemblymen that a break with Great Britain was best for Virginia.

Patrick Henry's political rivals — those conservatives who sought to appease the King and an arrogant, obstinate Parliament rather than to confront the Crown — thwarted his military career. They conspired to send out troops under Colonel Woodford when they were needed, leaving Henry and his regiment idle in camp. Moreover, Henry was perhaps much better suited to serve the Patriot cause in other than military ways. After later considering Henry's military appointment and frustrated service, George Washington said, "I think my countrymen made a capital mistake when they took Henry out of the senate to place him in the field."[8]

**Painted Like Indians**

As the militiamen of the Virginia backcountry began to muster, one traveler encountered a band of such men, giving an extensive account of his mid-summer meeting for the *Virginia Gazette.*

"Notwithstanding the urgency of my business, I have been

detained three days in this place by an occurrence truly agreeable. I have had the happiness of seeing Captain Michael Cressap *(sic)*, marching at the head of a formidable company, of upwards of 130 men, from the mountains and back woods. Painted like Indians, armed with tomahawks and rifles, dressing in hunting shirts and mockasons, and though some of them had travelled near 800 miles from the banks of the Ohio, they seemed to walk light and easy, and not with less spirit than in the first hour of their march. Health and vigour, after what they had undergone, declared them to be intimate with hardship, and familiar with danger; joy and satisfaction were visible in the crowd that met them. Had lord North been present, and assured that the brave leader could raise thousands of such like to defend his country, what think you? Would not the hatchet and the block have intruded upon his mind? I had an opportunity of attending the captain during his stay in town, and watched the behaviour of his men, and the manner in which they treated him; for it seems that all those who go out to war under him, do not only pay the most willing obedience to him as their commander, but in every instance of distress look up to him as a friend or a father. A great part of his time was spent in listening to and relieving their wants, with kindness and spirit, and on every occasion condescended to please without losing his dignity.

"Yesterday the company were supplied with a small quantity of powder from the magazine, which wanted airing, and was not in good order for rifles; in the evening, however, they were drawn out, to shew [show] the gentlemen of the town their dexterity in shooting; a clapboard with a mark the size of a dollar, was put up; they began to fire off hand, and the bystanders were surprised, few shot being made that were not close to on in the paper; when they had shot for a time in this way, some lay on their backs, some on their breast or side, others ran 20 or 30 steps and firing, appeared to be equally certain of their mark. With this performance the company were more than satisfied, when a young man took up the board in his hand, not by the end but the side, and holding it up, his brother walked to the distance and very coolly show in the white; laying down his rifle, he took the board, and holding it as it was held before, the second brother shot as the former had done. By this exercise I was more astonished than pleased. But will you believe me when I tell you that one of the men took the board, and placing it between his legs, stood with his back to the tree, while another drove the center. What would a regular army, of considerable strength in the forest of America do with 1000 of these men, who want nothing to preserve their health and courage, but water from the spring, with a little parched corn, and what they can easily procure in hunting; and who, wrapped in their blankets in the damp of night, would chuse [choose] the shade of a tree for their covering, and the earth for their bed?" [9]

**All Fine Fellows and Well-armed**

In September, Henry ordered the Culpeper battalion to Williamsburg. Taking several weeks to muster and march the 150 miles, their arrival was noted in the *Virginia Gazette* of October 20: "The Culpeper Minute Men, all fine fellows, and well-armed (near one half of them with rifles) are now within a few hours march of the city."[10]

The men arriving at Williamsburg since June as volunteers had no uniforms and most brought their own firearms, some described as sim-

**Patriot militiamen rendezvoused in Williamsburg and bivuoacked behind the Wren Building at the College of William & Mary during 1775 and 1776. The field is known today as the Sunken Garden.**

ple "fowling pieces." The men from the frontier were distinctively different. Philip Slaughter wrote in his diary that the minute men from the Culpeper District wore "hunting shirts made of strong, brown linen dyed the color of the leaves of the trees and on the breast of each hunting shirt was worked in large white letters the words 'Liberty or Death.'" They carried tomahawks and scalping knives in belts around their shoulders and "all that could procure for love or money buck's tails wore them in their hats." This company of riflemen mustered beneath a flag displaying a coiled rattlesnake emblazoned with "Don't Tread on Me." To the sides of the snake were the words "Liberty or Death" and across the top "The Culpeper Minute Men." These experienced frontiersmen from the Culpeper regiment cut a fearsome image to the inhabitants of the tidewater town. Slaughter continued: "Many people hearing we were from the backwoods … and seeing our dress, were as much afraid of us for a few days as if we had been Indians; but finding that we were orderly and attentive to guarding the city, they treated us with great respect. We took great pride in demeaning ourselves as patriots and gentlemen."[11]

In September 1775, William Campbell, living in Fincastle County, raised the first company from southwest Virginia, the Holston River valley area of Fincastle County, in support of what was called "the common cause." They arrived in Williamsburg where they were put in the First Virginia, under the command of Patrick Henry. Three months later, William Campbell, already a captain in the militia, was commissioned as captain in the new Virginia regiment of Continentals.[12]

The men from all regions of Virginia assembling in Williamsburg changed the appearance of the town. A city of tents rose up in the field behind the College of William and Mary. Others camped in the gardens behind the Royal Palace. With the rains, the troops of men soon turned both bivouacs into vast expanses of mud. To relieve the tedium of camp, the men took to the taverns at night. In the morning, the apothecaries did a brisk business selling remedies for hangovers.[13]

**A Proper Sense of Their Duty**

Lord Dunmore was an outcast from Williamsburg, but the governor reasoned he could find a base of support in Norfolk from which to recapture control of the colony. Indeed, the Whigs considered Norfolk to be a "nest of Tories." Dunmore was now operating from ships in the Elizabeth River and from his land-based refuge at Gosport Shipyard in Plymouth.[14] Along with a number of tenders, he had a fleet of three ships: *Fowey*, *Liverpool*, and *Otter*. But not only the winds of change were against the royal governor, the storms of the Atlantic came ashore that fall and wreaked havoc. On September 7, 1775, the *Virginia Gazette* (Pinkney) reported:

> "The late heavy wind and rain have been productive of great mischief to the mills, corn, etc. etc. in and about this neighborhood. There is hardly a possibility of getting any grain ground for the use of the inhabitants of this city. Large trees are in many places blown up by the roots, and the corn laid level with the ground; the fodder in general is almost entirely

> lost. We are informed that the devastation at Norfolk is inexpressible. Four or five and twenty sail of vessels are run on shore there, many of which are irrecoverably gone. The *Mercury* ship of war is also aground, and it is thought will remain so for some time. One of the tenders, that was in the same predicament, is burnt by some of the people of Hampton, who, we are told have taken six of her men prisoners, among whom is the gunner. Master Squires, the magnanimous commander of this mighty vessel, nearly escaped. He was obliged to take shelter under the trees that agreeable night, and in the morning went in disguise to some negro's cabbin *(sic)*, from whom he borrowed a canoe, by which means he got off."[15]

Apparently incensed at this characterization of him in the paper as a cowardly skulker and for other remarks he considered abusive, Captain Matthew Squires took ashore a raiding party on September 30 to capture John Holt, editor of the *Norfolk Gazette* and an outspoken Whig supporter. Holt escaped out a rear window, but Squires confiscated the printing press and took it out to his ship.[16]

On Thursday morning, October 26, Captain Squires, aboard a schooner, attacked Hampton near Old Point Comfort, across the mouth of the James River from Norfolk. Hampton, a port town, included about 100 buildings and about 2,700 inhabitants, half of them enslaved.[17] Squires fired incendiary shot into the town from the schooner and from five other boats with him. A company of local militia fended off a landing party while others sent to Williamsburg for help. Two companies of Continentals under Colonel William Woodford and a company of Culpeper Minute Men under Captain Abraham Buford rode hard all night through a driving rain, covering

**Captain Squires attacked the thriving port of Hampton, the first British attack in Virginia. The Hampton History Museum interprets this battle and the proud history of this Chesapeake Bay port town from 1608.**

36 miles in 12 hours.[18] Arriving at dawn and taking positions along the waterfront behind trees, houses, rocks, and fences, the backwoods marksmen fired at the ships, taking particular aim at the gunners. Buford's Culpeper Minute Men joined in picking off all the gunners who dared show themselves. Facing such a deadly display of expert riflery, Dunmore's fleet soon ceased its bombardment of Hampton.[19] Squires retreated, sailing away in disgust.[20]

This attack at Hampton was the first such assault on Virginia's citizens by British troops.[21] Six months after Lexington and Concord, the shooting war in Virginia began. "The Battle of Hampton placed Virginia in a perfect state of frenzy," Thomas Jefferson said.[22]

Earlier, at the height of tensions in early May, Dunmore had threatened to emancipate all the enslaved who would rally to his cause and the King. The House of Burgesses had called it a diabolical scheme, "to offer Freedom to our Slaves, and turn them against their Masters."[23] On November 7, Dunmore made good on that earlier proposal from aboard the *HMS William*.[24] Publishing the statement a week later, Lord Dunmore raised the British flag over the ship. He declared martial law and offered freedom to all the enslaved who would come to fight for the Crown. The offer, infamous in the minds of the planter class among the Patriots, became known as Dunmore's Proclamation:

> "… I do in Virtue of the Power and Authority to ME given, by His MAJESTY, determine to execute Martial Law, and cause the same to be executed throughout this Colony: and to [the end that] the Peace and good Order may the sooner be restored, … do hereby further declare all indented [indentured] Servants, Negroes, or others, (appertaining to Rebels,) free that are able and willing to bear Arms, they joining His MAJESTY'S Troops as soon as may be, for the more speedily reducing this Colony to a proper Sense of their Duty, to His MAJESTY'S Crown and Dignity."[25]

As word of the offer spread throughout the area, reports soon followed of enslaved blacks stealing themselves away to join with Dunmore. "Numbers of Negroes and Cowardly Scoundrels flock to his Standard" wrote one member of the Committee of Safety.[26] Mostly able-bodied men came, but some women were captured among the parties attempting to flee their enslavers.[27]

Having declared martial law, Dunmore authorized raids against Virginia planters who supported the rebellious colonists, destroying their property and seizing their enslaved blacks. He raised an army of volunteers, Loyalist militiamen, and British Regulars.[28] He put hundreds of ex-enslaved to work fortifying Norfolk with entrenchments on which he placed numerous cannons. One resident wrote to a friend in England: "Lord Dunmore sails up and down the river and where he finds a defenceless (*sic*) place, he lands, plunders the plantation and carries off the negroes."[29] But Dunmore made good use of the skilled runaways who responded to his proclamation. Many piloted small craft as Dunmore harassed plantations along the Chesapeake Bay.

Indeed, Joseph Harris piloted the *Otter* under recommendation to Captain Squires. "I think him too useful to His Majesty's service to take away," wrote a naval officer, "his being well acquainted with many creeks in the Eastern Shore at York, James River and Nansemond …"[30] Other blacks who fled to Dunmore's protection were used for other tasks on land. They foraged among the plantations, driving livestock toward the coast and pilfering food stocks to feed Dunmore's growing entourage.[31] As the royal governor of a rebellious crown colony, Lord Dunmore was both determined and desperate to regain control of Virginia.

## Hogpen

Responding to Lord Dunmore's threats and punitive actions, the Committee of Safety took action. They sent Colonel William Woodford with the Second Virginia Regiment — the heroes of Hampton — to remove Dunmore from Norfolk. The committee, dominated by Patrick Henry's political enemies, chose to overlook him and the First Virginia Regiment, which he commanded.

Lacking any naval support to cross the river at Jamestown where Dunmore's ships awaited in early November, Woodford's men marched up the James River to Sandy Point. After crossing there, they returned south of the river in a wide arc to avoid the Nansemond and Elizabeth rivers. Woodford marched an army of 700. Learning on November 20 of a planned attack on provisions stored at Suffolk, Woodford sent ahead 215 men on a forced march under Lt. Colonel Charles Scott to thwart the raid. The rest hurried on behind.[32] These vigilant and responsive Patriots did save the supplies from pilferage.

The Tories in Norfolk realized that the Patriots would be attacking from the south. Responding to pleas from the Loyalists in Norfolk to stop any invasion, on the night of November 13, Dunmore marched to the Great Bridge. He was accompanied by a party of Loyalists and two companies of the 14th Regiment of Foot. The regiments, under the command of Captain Samuel Leslie and Captain Charles Fordyce, had just arrived from St. Augustine to support Dunmore. The Great Road crossed the South Branch of the Elizabeth River about 12 miles south of Norfolk. This was the road past the Dismal Swamp used by planters and farmers from North Carolina's Albemarle Sound region to trade through Norfolk. The farmers and landowners there brought to the port by this route cattle, wheat, corn, shingles, and naval stores — tar, pitch, and turpentine — the principal products of North Carolina's northeastern counties at the time. The road, often muddy, was made passable with a corduroy of timbers. It was rough and passage was difficult, but the road was the main route for commerce; the bridge was a key element. Dunmore chose his position north of the crossing. It was a high spot in the marshlands, an island. He ordered

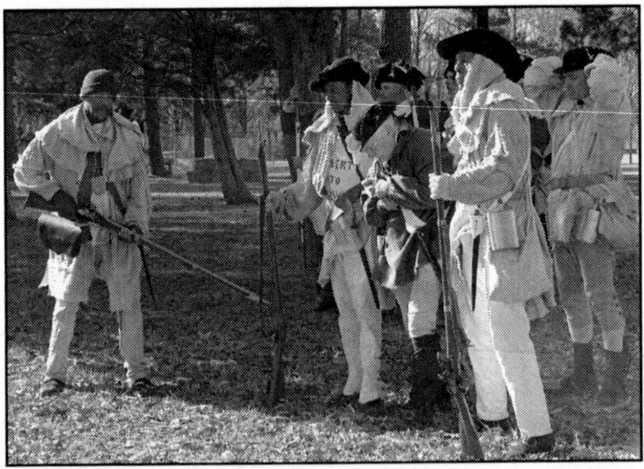

**Fighting under the promise of freedom offered by Dunmore, the formerly enslaved painted "Liberty to Slaves" on their shirts. Reenactors at the annual event for the Great Bridge Battlefield and Waterways History Foundation portray members of Dunmore's Royal Ethiopians capturing Colonel Joseph Hutchins, Patriot commander at Kemp's Landing.**

the erection of a fortification there, intending to control access to Norfolk at the bridge. The formerly enslaved blacks who had rallied to Dunmore provided most of the labor. They threw up the rude fort, making it from planks removed from the bridge, rotting logs, and mounds of earth. They called it Fort Murray, after Dunmore, but there may not have been much honor in that naming. The patriots called it "hogpen."[33] To open the range of fire by which he could protect and control the narrow causeway at the crossing, Dunmore burned several homes and buildings south of the bridge and brought up two field cannons to fortify the position further.

**Lord Dunmore's Ethiopian Regiment**

Learning of a gathering of Patriot militiamen from Princess Anne County nearby, Dunmore struck out for Kemp's Landing about November 14 where his 350 men (some say 150) intercepted the Patriot band of 170 volunteers and militia. With one volley, the Loyalists sent the Patriots in retreat, some dashing into the swamps for cover. Some of the wounded drowned there. Dunmore marched on to the landing, parading in his victory, before returning to Fort Murray. Encouraged by the success of this victory, Dunmore ordered, on November 14, the publication of the proclamation he had issued the week before from on board his ship.[34] He also wrote to General Sir William Howe in Boston apprising him of his circumstances and displaying a certain self-assuredness. He wrote in part, "I must inform you that with our little corps, I think we have done wonders. … And I make no doubt we shall be able to maintain our ground here. … Here we are with only a small part of a regiment contending against the extensive colony of Virginia."[35]

Dunmore made different use of his ex-enslaved in this encounter at Kemp's Landing, arming them with muskets and using them as soldiers. He formed them into Lord Dunmore's Ethiopian Regiment, sometimes called the Royal Ethiopians. The formerly enslaved men proved themselves worthy in the skirmish, capturing one of the two commanding Patriot colonels.[36] Indeed, by the end of November, two weeks after publishing the proclamation, the British had 300 ex-enslaved blacks outfitted for military service. They wore simple frocks with "Liberty to Slaves" painted across the breast. Woodford reported that "all the blacks who are sent to the fort at the great Bridge are supplied with muskets, Cartridges &c[,] strictly ordered to use them defensively and offensively." Runaways intercepted by the Patriots before the battle reported the garrison at Fort Murray had 30 whites and 90 blacks. Even after reinforcements arrived, bringing the total to some 600 soldiers, almost half were Negroes.[37] By early December, Dunmore was arming ex-enslaved blacks "as fast as they came in,"[38] reported at six or eight a day.[39]

**Regulars, Minute-men, Militia, and Volunteers**

Hearing of the defeat of Patriot militia at Kemp's Landing, Woodford hurried a detachment toward Great Bridge. The Culpeper Minute Men were under the command of Lt. Colonel Charles Scott and Major Thomas Marshall. In the company of the major were his black, enslaved manservant and the major's 19-year-old son John, a lieutenant. Though most of the officers wore blue or green frocks with blue, wool leggings, John Marshall, a bit of a dandy, wore "a purple or pale blue hunting shirt and trousers of the same material fringed with white."[40] (John Marshall later became the longest-serving Chief Justice of the United States, serving from 1801 to 1835.) They reached the Great Bridge on November 28, as other Patriot units made their way to the site. Woodford continued forward at a pace that enabled him to gather some provisions. He arrived at Great Bridge on December 2 with the remainder of his Second Virginia regiment.

**The Patriot forces included militiamen from the settled eastern counties and frontier riflemen such as the Culpeper Minute Men from the western counties. Volunteer reenactors load their weapons during the annual reenactment of the Battle of Great Bridge.**

Woodford gathered to his ranks additional forces, including militiamen from Princess Anne and Norfolk counties. He already had the frontier riflemen from western counties including Augusta and Fauquier counties and five companies of militia from Culpeper County under the command of Colonel Edward Stevens. Woodford was pleased also to have 250 men arrive from North Carolina under a Colonel Vail. These were men from Currituck and Pasquotank counties, communities which traded through the port at Norfolk. As reported in the *Virginia Gazette* of December 13, 1775, Woodford said of the North Carolinians, "They were composed of regulars, minutemen, militia, and volunteers and have brought with them 6 cannon." He continued with some concern, however, "I have received no certain account of Colonel [Robert] Howe, where he is, what number of forces he commands, how armed and provided, or when or where he intends to join us." Howe commanded the Second North Carolina Continentals, a regiment just formed on September 1. The offer of assistance from North Carolina made to Virginia's Committee of Safety was most welcomed.

### Exposed to Every Hardship

Arriving south of the bridge on December 2, Woodford's men

**British troops including Captain Fordyce's grenadiers marched confidently toward the Patriot's barricades. Portraying British regulars, reenactors attack at the Battle of Great Bridge.**

stopped when they saw the governor's makeshift fortification. To protect themselves, they erected a 150-foot-long breastworks south of Fort Murray and almost within musket range. The Patriots shaped the seven-foot high redoubt with loopholes for firing from protected positions to provide for catching any advancing enemy in a crossfire; however, neither army advanced. For several days, the two sides exchanged intermittent fire throughout the day from dawn to dusk. On the 7th of December, Colonel Woodford wrote to Patrick Henry, "The enemy are strongly fortified on the other side of the bridge, and a great number of the negroes and Tories with them; my prisoners disagree as to the numbers. We are situated here in the mud and mire, exposed to every hardship that can be conceived, but the want of provisions, of which our stock is but small, the men suffering for shoes; and if ever soldiers deserved a second blanket in any service, they do in this; our stock of ammunition [is] much reduced." Sleeping and walking on the cold, damp ground was wearing on the rebel militiamen. Neither could they find supplies from the community. Colonel Charles Scott wrote that the local residents, "nine-tenths Tories, … are the poorest, miserable wretches, I ever saw." The land was so spare of supplies, he said, that he did not think "there is as much provision within 10 miles round as would serve us one day."

Lord Dunmore and his collection of British Regulars, Loyalist Volunteers, Royal Ethiopians, and others were suffering through the same cool and damp weather. Dunmore's patience gave out first. He had received erroneous information about the number of riflemen entrenched with the patriots. Woodford wrote, "a servant of Major Marshall … deserted [and] informed Lord Dunmore that no more than 300 shirtmen were here. That imprudent man [Dunmore] caught at the bait, and dispatched Captain Leslie with all the regulars …" The informant was playing out a ruse concocted by Woodford, Marshall, and the Whigs. It worked as well as they had hoped.

**A Vast Effusion of Blood**

Despite the advice of his experienced commanders, Lord Dunmore ordered an attack on the Whig breastwork. Holding the Whig militia in low esteem, he imagined that an assault by sixty fearsome grenadiers would easily send the backwoods militiamen scurrying. During the night of December 8, about 200 more British and Loyalist soldiers, the remainder of the 14th Regiment of Foot under the command of Captain Leslie, were brought into Fort Murray from Norfolk. This addition raised Dunmore's fighting force to about 670 men. Hoping, perhaps, to portray the patriot riflemen as barbarians and to instill some ruthlessness into his own troops, Dunmore told his men his opinion of the frontier militiamen who had fought on his behalf a year earlier. Should his Loyalist forces be captured by the "shirt men," he warned them, the captives would likely be scalped because the western riflemen were "the most hardy warlike people in America … in frequent war with their neighbors the Indians." Dunmore's attempt at instilling courage may not have worked as he intended.

At dawn on the 9th, Dunmore's commanders commenced their attack, sending the infantry forward. They replaced some planks on the bridge and rolled cannons into place so they could blast the Whig position from a spot obscured by a bend in the road. Some of the Virginia Patriots serving as sentries in forward positions began to fire at the soldiers coming out of the fort. Most got off three shots before retiring to the breastworks. William "Billy" Flora, a local merchant and a freeman of color, held fast to this position firing eight shots before following the others to the safety of the barricade. While still under heavy musket fire, he pulled in the plank that allowed access over the barricade and into the Patriot's fortified position.[41]

The grenadiers, under the command of Captain Charles Fordyce, marched across the narrow bridge, six abreast and in parade formation, heading for the Patriots' barricade. Woodford wrote, "… none marched up but his majesty's soldiers, who behaved like Englishmen." Behind them 300 volunteers and Royal Ethiopians waited to rush into the Patriot position after the grenadiers had opened it. The advancing British formations alternated their fire by platoons taking only 15 seconds to reload. They cast a continual hail of bullets toward the Whig position, which was manned at the time by only some of the riflemen, perhaps 25 to 30, under the command of a Lieutenant Travis. The patriots at the front hunkered down and waited as more of Woodford's men, surprised by the shots of the early morning attack, ran to take their positions behind the breastworks. Still, those who were in camp more than a few hundred yards back from the barricade, may not have been able to get into position to engage fully in the brief fight.

The British troops advanced unperturbed, not realizing that the

**The British forces retreated when a dozen grenadiers were killed and another 19 wounded in the deadly volley of rifle fire from the Patriot barricade. Reenactors of the Battle of Great Bridge play out the desperate scene that ended with a decisive Patriot victory.**

Patriots were under orders to hold their fire until the enemy was within fifty yards. Neither did they know that more riflemen than they had suspected were bracing for the fight. Having received no fire, Captain Fordyce at fifteen paces from the breastwork took his hat in his hand and waved with a shout to his men, "The day is ours." With the British in range, about 80 Whig militiamen rose up and opened fire with the deadly aim of experienced hunters. Twelve grenadiers fell dead and 19 more were wounded in the immediate volley. Fordyce fell onto the breastworks, his body riddled with 14 holes.

Although Woodford determined a counter charge to be too risky and inconsistent with his orders, Colonel Stevens did lead a hundred of the Culpeper Minute Men in a sweep forward so they could snipe at the artillerymen on the bridge. With casualties falling all around, Dunmore's artillery captain ordered his cannons hurriedly rolled back to Fort Murray.

The fighting had lasted less than half–an-hour. The carnage was substantial among Dunmore's forces with 102 killed and wounded by Woodford's count. Dunmore's records reported fewer casualties — 17 dead and 49 wounded — though he only counted the regular troops. Woodford wrote that from the "blood on the bridge and in the fort, from the accounts of the sentries, who saw many bodies carried out of the fort to be interred, and other circumstances, I conceive their loss to be much greater … and the victory complete." Apparently many volunteers and freed enslaved paid a high price for their loyalty to Dunmore. Captain Richard Meade reported a "vast effusion of blood, so dreadful that it beggars description, a scene, when the dead and wounded were bro't off, was too much; I then saw the horrors of war in perfection, worse than can be imagin'd; 10 and 12 bullets thro' many; limbs broke in 2 or 3 places; brains turning out. Good God, what a sight!" Woodford's men suffered a single casualty — a slight injury to a militiaman's thumb. The marksmanship, bravery, and stealth of the backwoods militiamen had made the difference in the battle. Patriots with rifles, men schooled and tested in fighting Indian wars, had carried the day.

### Friends to the Shirt Men

Rather than attack Fort Murray, Woodford secured a truce so that the dead and wounded could be tended. The Patriots left their breastworks to find and treat many of the wounded Loyalists. As Woodford's men approached them, some of the victims pleaded not to be murdered, apparently recalling the warning from Dunmore that they might be scalped. [42] Recognizing the humane treatment given his men by the Patriots, Captain Leslie stepped out from Fort Murray and bowed in appreciation. The respectful Patriots even buried Captain Fordyce with full military honors.[43]

That night, under the cover of darkness, Dunmore's men spiked the

**The Battle of Great Bridge is commemorated in Chesapeake, Virginia on the Southern Branch of Elizabeth River adjacent to a modern draw bridge.**

cannons to render them useless and retreated in wagons to Norfolk, taking some wounded with them and sending others by water. Once in Norfolk, Dunmore despaired of defending the town. He spiked his twenty cannons[44] there and boarded ships. Meanwhile, a party of the Culpeper Minute Men patrolled the general area at Great Bridge seeking information and capturing Tories. As the Whigs assessed their next move, they were joined by additional troops who had hoped to arrive in advance of the conflict. Colonel Robert Howe arrived with the Second North Carolina Regiment well after the conflict at Great Bridge, but in time to participate in the next confrontation with Dunmore. (Benjamin Cleaveland had been appointed an Ensign in the Second North Carolina on September 1. He declined, preferring instead to serve in his home militia.) Arriving from Henry's First Virginia Regiment were Captain William Campbell and Captain John Gibson, leading two companies of Fincastle County riflemen.[45]

Over the next few days, other troops joined Woodford as well, including militiamen from Amelia, Nansemonde, and South Hampton counties. Woodford reported shortly to the president of the Convention in Williamsburg, Edmund Pendleton, that his troops, combined with the new arrivals, numbered 1,275 men and had control of Norfolk. The defeat, which became known as the Battle of Great Bridge, soon discouraged Loyalists all along the Virginia coast and made it more difficult to muster volunteers in the region to fight for the King. One of the Culpeper Minute Men, Corporal William Wallace, sensed a change in the interest of the Loyalists to fight. He put it bluntly: "All the damn Tories down this way are glad to get a buck's tail to put in their hats now that they may pass for Friends to the Shirt men."

The victory at Great Bridge emboldened the Patriots. A band of backwoods frontiersmen and untrained militia and volunteers had defeated professional soldiers supported by cannons, and they had done so decisively. The Patriot force had proven the value of riflemen who could shoot with accuracy, and in particular had put the British on notice that the "shirt men" from the backcountry were a formidable force not to be taken lightly or disrespected. The reputation of the backwoods Patriots as fearless fighters continued to spread across the colonies among both those who championed them as a potent fighting force and those who dreaded the next encounter with them.

**Knocked About Their Ears**

Dunmore was stung by the defeat at Great Bridge. A year earlier, after the victory at Point Pleasant, he had been the toast of the town; but, after the recent defeat at the hands of what he thought was an undisciplined band of rabble, his reputation was greatly sullied. "His Lordship has much to answer for," wrote one of his officers, "besides sacrificing a handful of brave men, he has ruined every Friend of Government in this Colony & done the Cause much Disservice."

Another soldier called the battle, "an absurd, ridiculous and unnecessary attack, an extravagant folly." The royal governor, having lost control of his colony, was also losing the faith of his supporters.

Dunmore and his followers resorted to living aboard ships in the Elizabeth River; they were a "floating town."[46] Norfolk was under the control of a Patriot force. During December the two sides exchanged rifle and musket fire between ship and shore. Dunmore also sent landing parties ashore to secure water and provisions for those at anchor in the Elizabeth River. He had previously threatened to cannonade Williamsburg and now his plans for such shocking retribution included Norfolk, occupied as it was by Whig recruits and militia. A midshipman aboard the *Otter* wrote in a letter:

> "… Off Norfolk, December 14 … The rebels having now nothing to obstruct their passage, arrived and took possession of Norfolk, and in the evening saluted us with a volley of small arms; on which, the next morning, was sent on shore to their commander, to inform him, that if another shot was fired at the OTTER, they must expect the town to be knocked about their ears …"

Three weeks after retreating from the debacle at Great Bridge, Dunmore ordered the bombarding of Norfolk. It was New Year's Day, 1776. The *Otter*, the *Fowey*, and the *Liverpool* provided a continual barrage from late afternoon well into the night. Over 800 buildings, nearly two-thirds of Norfolk, were destroyed by cannonball and fire. Captain Matthew Squires, Commander of the *HMS Otter*, wrote in his journal:

> "… Jan 1776, Mon. 1; Elisabeth River … Am receiving 3 Hhds [hogsheads] of water by the long boat mostly little wind & fair. At 4 p.m. began a brisk fire from the squadron on the

town and continued till 11 during which time the boats landed & set fire to the different wharfs, had two men wounded by rebel musketry. The rebels set fire to many parts of the back of the town …"

Dunmore received some naval reinforcement in early February with the arrival of Captain Andrew Hammond and the *HMS Roebuck* with its 44 guns. With this support, Dunmore took and held a position on land at Tucker's Mill Point on the Elizabeth River. From there, he continued to menace planters along the Chesapeake Bay, though some of the raids were no more than "chicken stealing expeditions."[47] Skirmishes ensued between Patriot patrols and occasional landing parties, but overall, the Patriots were able to keep Dunmore at bay. In early February, the Patriots set fire to the unburned sections of Norfolk. The town was completely destroyed. The sole building that remained standing in Norfolk was St. Paul's Episcopal Church, though it did incur some damage. It lost its roof and windows. A cannon ball from Dunmore's January 1 barrage struck a wall and left a cavity in the brick. Generations later, a cannon ball was cemented into the cavity as a reminder of the wartime destruction of the largest Atlantic port between New York and Charlestown.

**Lord Dunmore's cannonade destroyed Norfolk on New Year's Day, 1776. A cannonball cemented into a cavity in a surviving wall of St. Paul's Church serves as a reminder of the city's destruction even before independence was declared.**

# All His Majesty's Faithful Subjects

## North Carolina Backcountry

At the middle of the 18th century, a pervasive hunger for affordable, frontier land drove second and third generation settlers and swarms of new immigrants out of the Lancaster Valley of Pennsylvania. They moved south through the Shenandoah Valley of Virginia and into the relatively uninhabited Piedmont of North Carolina. One of the early arrivals, in 1752, was the family of Squire and Sarah Boone, including son Daniel, age 18. Transplanting themselves from a Quaker community in the Oley Valley west of Philadelphia, they settled in the backcountry region known as the Forks of the Yadkin.

In that same year, Moravian Bishop Spangenberg recorded his observations about settlers coming to the area. He wrote from his perspective at the Wachau tract (later Wachovia). The Unitas Fratrum had just purchased some 98,000 acres just east of the big bend in the Yadkin River. On this land, the German-speaking Moravians established Bethabara the next year and Salem in 1766. Spangenberg remarked, "toward the west and near the mountains, many families are moving in from Virginia, Maryland, Pennsylvania, Jersey, and even New England; in this year alone more than four hundred families have come with horse and wagon and cattle. Among them are sturdy farmers and skilled men …"[1]

A dozen years later, royal governor William Tryon gave a similar description of the North Carolina backcountry, although one tinged perhaps with a bit of British class consciousness. He wrote, "The poorer Settlers coming from the Northward Colonies set themselves down in the back Counties where the land is the best but who have not more than a sufficiency to erect a Log House for their families and procure a few Tools to get a little Corn in the ground …"[2]

**Benjamin Cleaveland**

By 1770, enough of these "sturdy farmers and skilled men" had come to northwest North Carolina, "where the land is the best," to warrant establishing Surry County, carved from Rowan County.[3] One of the new county's prominent citizens at its formation, and a recent arrival himself, was Benjamin Cleaveland. Having some success at his plantation, The Round About, Cleaveland became influential in the business of the backcountry. In November 1774, he served as a justice in the county court, and within the following three months he became chairman of the Surry Court. The court system was the seat of real power for the counties; it was an appropriate place for men of means, influence, and ambition. The justices oversaw all criminal and civil trials, handled land titles, deeds, wills, and bills of sale. They levied taxes and constructed public buildings and roads. The chairman oversaw it all. But, Cleaveland was not a full-time politician; he was primarily a farmer and planter. Despite being chairman of the Surry County court and dealing with such a host of responsibilities, he knew his priorities. In February 1775, Cleaveland was granted leave from his duties so he could build on his 10,000-acre estate a grist mill on Roaring River and a bridge over Elkin Creek.[4]

Benjamin Cleaveland was an uncommonly large man, weighing over 350 pounds. He claimed that his muscular power was limited only by the strength of his bones.[5] His imposing presence enabled him to dominate others in his interactions, if he wanted, but he could also be good-natured on occasion. When the situation called for resolve and perseverance, he could be focused and serious. He could also be reckless and seemingly hot-tempered at random. He had a voice like a bull, one writer assessed, and when the issue at hand did not call for a fight, he could and did roar down the opposition.[6] In all, Benjamin Cleaveland was not someone to be tested or trifled with, as many who disagreed with him soon discovered.

**Surry County**

On May 17, 1775, word first arrived in the backcountry of the April 19 calamity in Massachusetts — soldiers and citizens shooting each other at Lexington and Concord. The news came through Salem, the Moravian village of artisans and commerce. Salem was a gateway to the backcountry, and the clearinghouse for information coming to the Upper Yadkin River valley.

In response to the growing political conflict and on appeal from both the Second Continental Congress and North Carolina's Provincial Congress at Hillsborough, the community leaders formed a Committee of Safety for Surry County.[7] They gave it all the responsibilities of the courts and elected Benjamin Cleaveland chairman on August 25.[8] The committee also took control of the militia. On August 26, moving to secure the shot and powder in control of the Tories, the committee resolved "that Benjamin Cleaveland, Jesse Walton, and Benjamin Herndon wait on Mr. Charles Gordon to secure all the Ammunition they shall find in his possession."[9] In short order, Cleaveland was essentially in charge of the civil and militia apparatus of the county. By these actions, the committee ensured that "Liberty Men" would be sent to represent the county in North Carolina's provisional government.

Making their views as Patriots known, the Surry County Committee of Safety issued in its first meeting a series of resolutions protesting British actions, prominently listing among them: "laying taxes on us without our consent and against our protestations." Presenting themselves as defiant but not yet rebellious, the committee headed the list of resolutions with "Liberty or Death — God save the king." They sent the document to the royal governor in New Bern. Benjamin Cleaveland signed it as chairman. William Lenoir signed as clerk.[10]

Not everyone in Surry County, or in the backcountry, was a Whig and a rebel, however. About an equal number were Loyalists. Others declared themselves neutral, as perhaps they had to be to survive in a community were peoples' political loyalties could get them killed. One of the prominent Loyalists of Surry County was Morgan Bryan, the grandfather of Rebecca Bryan, who had married Daniel Boone in 1756 in Rowan (later Surry, then Davie) County. Supporting the King and protecting their rights as Englishmen, the Bryans raised partisan bands of Tories. Many fought under Joseph Bryan, Rebecca's father. Many others fought under the infamous Samuel Bryan, Joseph's brother. Other leaders among the "non-associators" in Surry County also organized local bands of Loyalist militia. In the backcountry, as elsewhere in the Carolinas, the American Revolution was a civil war waged among neighbors and among family members who harbored deeply divisive and passionately held differences of opinion. Also gathering, however, were bands of marauding raiders, horse thieves, and robbers, men of no conscience who preyed on the citizens living in communities of confused jurisdictions. The Surry County militia, Patriots, did not differentiate in how it dealt with either group.

In the fall of 1775, as each rebel province was forming its own standing army, Benjamin Cleaveland was offered the rank of Ensign in the Second Regiment of North Carolina, under the command of Colonel Robert Howe. Cleaveland declined the appointment by the Provincial Congress at Hillsborough, declaring that he preferred to serve as a captain with the Surry County Militia.[11] His first opportunity to serve his rebellious colony under arms was not long in coming.

**Immovably Attached to His Majesty**

In the winter of 1775-76, North Carolina's royal governor Josiah Martin continued his efforts to regain control of his rebellious colony. He was gratified to receive on January 3 a letter from Lord Dartmouth, the British secretary of state for the American colonies.[12] Martin learned that the British ministry liked the idea he had proposed for a strategy to end the rebellion, at least in the southern colonies. It was a plan he had well considered for some time.

During the prior spring, 1775, Governor Martin had witnessed a general unrest across the colonies prompted by Parliament's laying on of taxes judged unfair by the Americans. In support of his King, he had tried to stymie North Carolina's assemblymen from sending delegates to the First Continental Congress. In defiance of the governor, the representatives called their own Provincial Congress and elected delegates anyway. When fighting erupted in Massachusetts in April and nearly the same in Virginia, Josiah Martin decided it was unsafe for him to continue residing in New Bern. He abandoned the governor's palace[13] on May 31. (Lord Dunmore, Martin's counterpart in Virginia, retreated from his palace a week later.) By June 2, Martin had made Fort Johnston on the Lower Cape Fear River his new colonial headquarters. Within a few days, however, Martin had fled a second time to the *HMS Cruizer*, a sloop-of-war anchored in the Cape Fear River.

From aboard ship, he had watched a mob of angry Whig militiamen burn the fort.

Dartmouth's letter, dated November 7, 1775, and reaching Martin two months later, responded to one sent by Martin in early summer. To help reestablish British control in all the southern colonies, Martin had devised a plan while he sat at anchor aboard the *Cruzier*. In his June 30 letter, the optimistic and inventive Martin had suggested his plan to British officials in London.[14] While each of the other royal governors of rebellious colonies was clamoring to be sent troops and ships, Martin asked only for arms and money. He boasted that he could easily raise a large army of men loyal to the Crown. These men mustering to the King's Standard in North Carolina, he claimed, could then "reduce to order and obedience every Colony to the Southward of Pennsylvania." [15] Martin added, "I could collect immediately among the immigrants from the Highlands of Scotland who are settled here and immovably attached to His Majesty and his government, that I am assured by the best authority I may compute at 3,000 men."[16] Martin continued, claiming that two-thirds of the fighting men in the colony, some 30,000 in total, would rally to such a call and fight for the King. "I beg leave …" he proposed, "to raise a Battalion of a Thousand Highlanders here."

William Legge, 2nd Earl of Dartmouth, was intrigued by Martin's intentions to help his situation using a local and loyal populace. Dartmouth embraced the plan in his letter of November 7 and decided to assure its success by sending aid that was not requested: troops and ships. However, Lord Dartmouth soon resigned his office, deciding that he could not wage war against English colonists. His successor, Lord George Germain, taking office on November 10, also embraced the plan after some further consideration. He sent his own letter dated December 23 to Martin elaborating on the plans outlined by Dartmouth.

Receiving Dartmouth's November letter on January 3, 1776, and being unaware of Dartmouth's resignation, Martin learned that a detachment of 2,000 British Regulars was sailing from Boston to Brunswick Town along the Lower Cape Fear River. The troops were under the command of Sir Henry Clinton. Seven regiments of British regulars would arrive from Ireland aboard 54 ships commanded by Admiral Sir Peter Parker. The troops were under the command of Lord Charles, the Earl Cornwallis. Governor Martin's task, according to Dartmouth's plan, was to muster the Loyalists and have them join the arriving British army at Brunswick Town. Knowing from Dartmouth's letter that Cornwallis's troops were departing Cork, Ireland on December 1, Martin estimated their arrival in early February. Time was short, he reasoned; he would need to work quickly to raise his Loyalist army.

Brunswick Town residents visiting Martin's ship clamored for him to take action and enthusiastically assured him that a Loyalist army of 2,000 to 3,000 men could be raised most certainly. Martin expected two primary groups to rally: ex-regulators who had renewed their allegiance after Royal Governor William Tryon had defeated them in 1771, and the Highland Scots living in Cumberland County in the Cape Fear River valley near Cross Creek. Martin sent a messenger to explain the plans to the Highlander chieftains. The untrustworthy courier instead revealed the plans to the Whig rebels. Martin then sent a Scotsman, Alexander McLean, to rally support among the Highlanders. Learning from the local clan chieftains that they could perhaps produce 3,000 men but that no more than 1,000 would be armed, the perhaps overly enthusiastic but committed McLean reported to Martin a potential of 6,000 men, all well equipped.[17]

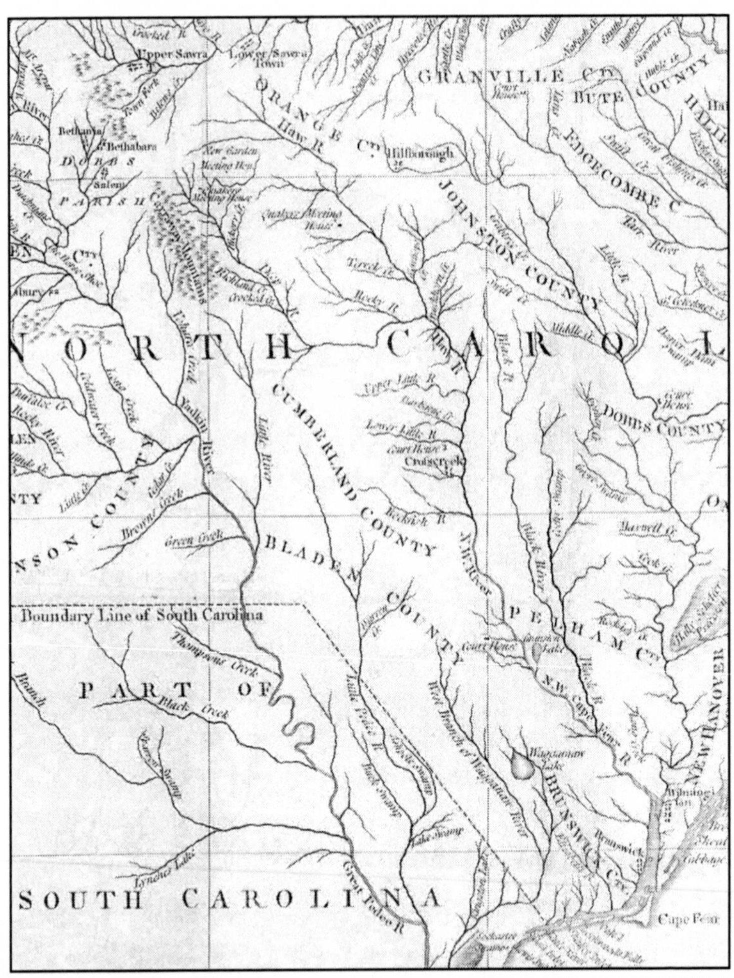


**Loyalists from the backcountry mustered at Cross Creek (center). Most of the Loyalists were Highland Scots who marched toward Brunswick Town (lower right) to meet the landing of a British army. Patriot militia also rode from the Yadkin River valley (upper left corner) but arrived after the battle.**
**["A New and Accurate Map of North Carolina in North America," London, 1779]**

Encouraged by such reports, Martin issued a proclamation on January 10 by which he did "hereby exhort, require and command ... all His Majesty's faithful subjects" to rally against a "most daring, horrid and unnatural Rebellion ... by the base and insidious artifice of certain traitorous, wicked and designing men." Making outlaws of his enemies, Martin continued, declaring "all such Rebels as will not join the Royal banner, Rebels and Traitors, their lives and properties to be forfeited."[18] Martin was confident in the prospects of a Loyalist muster. He reasoned that even if only a fraction of the willing Loyalists he was convinced inhabited the colony did rally, their numbers would still guarantee a citizen militia of the size needed to support the British landing at Brunswick Town.

The British ministers had already identified the Highlanders as a potential source of support; and, the Patriots had already moved to woo them over to the rebel side. To help in assuring the Highlanders' allegiance to the King during the summer, General Thomas Gage had sent two advisors to train these Loyalist recruits. The two Scotsmen, Lt. Colonel Donald MacDonald and Captain Donald McLeod, were selected for the task, in part, because they spoke Gaelic. Moreover, MacDonald was a veteran soldier, having fought under Bonnie Prince Charlie at the Battle of Culloden.[19] The pair, it was believed, would be able to entice many of the Scotsmen living in the backcountry of Cumberland County to rally for the Crown.

The two agents had arrived in the rebellious colony through New Bern attired not in their military uniforms, but in civilian clothes. The local Whig authorities, aware that two such advisors were on their way, had been initially suspicious of the pair; but, after interviewing the two new arrivals, the New Bern Committee of Safety released them. The Committee members bid them farewell and warned them to watch out for and to be wary of any such Tory recruiters.[20] Martin was pleased to learn of the pair's success in fooling the Committee. He promoted MacDonald to brigadier general and McLeod to lieutenant colonel in the militia.[21] These two would lead the recruits to Brunswick Town.

### The Gathering

Commissioned by Governor Martin, Alexander McLean called for a mustering of Loyalists in Cross Creek for February 5. The Highlanders then pledged only 700 and lobbied for a delay in beginning the march until after the British troops arrived. The militant ex-Regulators boasted they would gather 5,000 men and argued for an immediate march.[22]

Elsewhere Donald McLeod was to rally 500 men for marching to Cross Creek. The men who mustered disliked being led by a foreigner. He induced their allegiance for a time by producing a hogshead of rum "which most of them visited industriously." But upon hearing that a large party of Whigs was headed their way, the 500 men dispersed immediately.[23] At Cross Creek, neighbors reported the expected Loyalists "were Sculking *(sic)* & hiding themselves through Swamps & such concealed places."[24] The commitment and bravery of some who mustered was less than ideal. MacDonald fared a little better, bringing 300 men he had recruited for the Royal Highland Emigrant Regiment.[25] Another 500 Highlanders gathered at Cross Hill, enticed by the promise of 200 acres and the exemption of quitrents and taxes for 20 years.

Not surprising on the frontier, rumors traveled more quickly than accurate news. Soon the citizens of the backcountry were hearing various reports including that Governor Martin had landed with 700 Highlanders and with another 700 locals was marching toward

**Loyalist militiamen mustered in Cross Creek, today's Fayetteville. Liberty Point, at Person St. and Bow St., is home to several markers and monuments of the community's early history.**

Salisbury.[26] Loyalists in the western counties were encouraged by this exciting, though false, report and many responded to the call to muster at Cross Creek. The Moravians in Salem witnessed the response. They recorded on February 6 that "various small companies passed toward Cross Creek; it is said that the King's Standard will be raised today sixty miles from here."[27] The Moravians continued: "Feb. 7. Early this morning Giery Wright [a Surry County Loyalist] and some twenty men marched through, but had neither money nor provisions."[28]

These backcountry Loyalists soon returned through Salem, however. The muster at Cross Creek on February 5 had disappointed those who went. Expecting to find the governor and British troops, they found "only one Scotch officer there to command them." Many of the 500 or 600 who had gathered dispersed and returned home. Having declared their loyalty to the King by the act of mustering to the King's banner, these returning Loyalists were treated harshly by the local Liberty Men.[29, 30]

Another circulating rumor, true or not, caused additional concern. Benjamin Cleaveland had heard that the Highlander merchants in Cross Creek where demanding an oath of allegiance to the King before citizens could trade their produce and pelts for sugar, salt, gun powder, iron, and other essential goods. This irked him greatly, and Cleaveland pledged to "dislodge those Scotch scoundrels at Cross Creek."[31] But, first, he preferred to deal with the Loyalists rising from within his own community.

**All Is Alarm and Confusion**

Tradition of questionable authenticity says that Benjamin Cleaveland assembled the men under his command by blowing a large ox horn from atop Rendezvous Mountain in the Upper Yadkin River valley. If he did so on this occasion, as captain he gathered his mounted riflemen and joined with the Surry County Militia under the command of Colonel Martin Armstrong. They were six-hundred strong.

Detachments of these Whig militiamen rode throughout the county and dispersed the Loyalists who were attempting to gather in response to the muster at Cross Creek. Cleaveland and his Whig militiamen persecuted those who sided with the king or even those who wanted to remain neutral. These victims' only failing was not pledging by test oath to join with the "Liberty Men." The Whigs drove many people from their homes, forcing them to hide and live in the woods. The victims became known as "outlyers" and they suffered the brutality of nature. In late January, the Moravians recorded "Very unfriendly weather, with glaze ice and rain, so that one could hardly go out of the house."[32] In the first week of February, they noted that under the burden of such conditions, "ten men from up on the Atkin [Yadkin], [were] fleeing from the hard treatment which is being given to the Non-Associators there" and "last night another party from the Atkin passed on their way to Cross Creek." On February 8, the Moravians recorded in Salem: "From Bethabara we heard that they had been frightened by men wearing buck-tails in the hat, presumably they were from Capt. Waldham's [Walton's] Company, which has been roughly treating people on the Atkin. … [Others] reported that many farms there had been completely abandoned by their owners."[33] "All is alarm and confusion," the Moravians wrote.[34]

Benjamin Cleaveland and the Liberty Men continued to terrorize their neighbors throughout Surry County. They drove many who had desired to remain neutral to seek safety and protection among the Loyalists. (Immediately and over the next few years, the actions of Cleaveland and the Liberty Men likely created more, not fewer, of what they were trying to control — Loyalists and Tories.[35]) Cleaveland and the Surry County militia did capture some of the armed Loyalists. Three prominent Tories, brothers Gideon and Giery Wright and James Glen, were captured around the 15th of February and taken as prisoners to the blacksmith shop in Salem. Cleaveland had the smithy shackle the three men together.[36]

**The Moravian merchants in Salem were compelled to trade with both Loyalist and Whig militia forces. "T. Bagge, Merchant" is open for business today at Old Salem Museums and Gardens in Winston-Salem, NC in the same store on Salem Square which served the Surry County Militia in 1776.**

The Moravians, desiring to remain neutral, easily found themselves in trouble amidst the two opposing factions. In the second week of February, they sent nine wagons to Cross Creek to pick up loads of salt so badly needed in the backcountry. Discovering the Moravian teamsters on the road heading toward Cross Creek with empty wagons, the Whigs accused them of mustering with the Loyalists. After defending themselves successfully against those claims, the drivers loaded their wagons with salt and headed home. Along the road, they were accosted by bands of Loyalist militiamen who were heading to Cross Creek, on the assumption the wagoners were carrying the salt to the aid of the rebels. The Loyalists threatened to spill the salt on the ground and ruin it rather than see it go to "the Boston party,"[37] as they termed the Whigs. After holding the wagoners for 24 hours, the Loyalists released them, but cursed them in their departure as they continued toward Salem.[38] But the Moravians' troubles were not over. The Committee of Safety for the Salisbury District pursued the rumors of their giving "aid and comfort" to the Loyalists. Colonel Martin Armstrong and Captain Jesse Walton investigated the Moravians, calling them to answer to the accusations. Satisfied with their response, Colonel Armstrong issued a certificate on February 15 giving them "a right to Protection both of their Persons and Properties."[39]

**We Could Not Object**

In mid-February, the Patriot militia of Surry County mustered at Salem in preparation for its march against the Loyalists and Tories gathering at Cross Creek. Though six or seven companies mustered at Bethabara, totaling some 1,000 men, only a portion moved on to Salem, including "a Company of Cavalry, and several wagons."[40] "They camped over night beyond the bridge," the Moravians recorded, "their officers were Col. Armstrong, Captains Cleaveland,

Hamelin, Walton and Henry Schmid; they numbered about two hundred; and they behaved well."[41] Cleaveland and the Whig militia took from the stores and workshops what he needed "and had them charged." "We could not object," the Moravians recorded, "though payment is doubtful."[42] The Moravian merchants had little choice. The peaceable community was maintaining a delicate balance. They wanted to support the community in which they lived, even a rebellious one, but they did not want to offend the British Crown as the Unitas Fratrum had many missions in other British colonies around the world. They professed loyalty, they supported their neighbors, and they sought to appease both sides.[43] Not pressing further the issue of Moravian sentiments toward the Whigs, Colonel Armstrong provisioned from Salem 2,000 pounds of meat and enough cornmeal to feed 2,000 men for eight days. Perhaps prudently withholding a display of their collective relief, the Moravians at Salem simply recorded, "Feb. 23. In the afternoon the troops marched away."[44]

**King George and Broadswords**

At Cross Creek on February 12, the expected mustering of several thousand Loyalists was greatly disappointing. They numbered only several hundred with only 130 ex-Regulators, not the five thousand so boldly promised. Few, if any, Loyalists from the backcountry gathered.

Colonel Thomas Rutherford issued another call to arms on the 13th blaming in his manifesto the "idle and false reports spread by wicked and ignorant men" which aroused in the Loyalists "unjust apprehensions of danger." He went on to "command, enjoin, beseech and require all His Majesty's faithful subjects within the County of Cumberland" to muster on the 16th at Cross Creek. "Otherwise," he continued, "they must expect to fall under the melancholy consequences of a declared rebellion and expose themselves to the just resentment of an injured, though gracious Sovereign."[45] (Clearly demonstrating how the political tensions of the day divided the country and even families, Thomas Rutherford was a brother to General Griffith Rutherford, commander of the Patriot militia in the Western [Salisbury] District.)

By February 15, General Donald MacDonald combined his gathering troops from all parts of the region into a command of 1,400 men. Only 520 were armed. He sent a party of light cavalry scrounging for weapons. They returned with another 130 firearms gathered from residents of the countryside.[46] MacDonald confiscated gunpowder stored for the Whigs in Cumberland County and purchased more locally. Hurriedly gathering the supplies he needed, MacDonald prepared for the Loyalist march to Brunswick Town.

### A Curious Sense of Duty

The troops who mustered at Cross Creek were mostly Highland Scots. Many had arrived in North Carolina after the brutal defeat of the Scottish clans at the Battle of Culloden Moor in April 1746. Many Highland Scots had championed Bonnie Prince Charlie, the "Young Pretender," in his attempt to regain the English throne; but, after their ignominious defeat, they lost their claim to the lands on which they lived. These Scots became homeless people, but as subjects of the king hundreds upon hundreds immigrated to Wilmington and then moved up the Cape Fear River where they established a community at Cross Creek. Having been displaced from their homeland by the King of Great Britain, their allegiance to the Crown made for a curious sense of duty. One who came was Flora MacDonald, the woman who had helped the fugitive Bonnie Prince Charlie escape his pursuers while he dressed as her Irish maid, "Betty Burke." She hid the prince throughout the summer of 1746. After others helped spirit the prince to safety in France, Flora MacDonald was captured and thrown into the Tower of London for providing this aid. After her release, she moved to North Carolina with her husband and was living for a time at Cross Creek. Though defeated by the British, these Highland Scots, men of their word, had taken an oath of allegiance to the King. When the muster at Cross Creek was called in 1776, many responded without delay; but, those were mostly the more recent arrivals. Having arrived since 1770, they were enticed by the promise to receive tracts of land confiscated from the soon-to-be defeated rebels and the suspension of property taxes for twenty years. Many long-established Scots families were reluctant to muster. They feared confiscation of their lands by the Patriots.

These mustering Loyalists were farmers, not fighters. The men were not a militia unit nor an army of experienced soldiers. They had not trained together nor fought together, and they were ill equipped and poorly supplied. MacDonald's task was to deliver this band of recruits to the coast where they could be trained and equipped and join in with the British Regulars who were expected. Little if any *esprit de corps* existed, except perhaps among the clans of Highland Scots. Some brought along their broadswords and others their bagpipes. Flora MacDonald, their revered heroine, was there at Cross Creek to wish them well and to send them on their campaign to the coast. Little did they know how soon their courage and resolve would be tested.

### The March to Brunswick Town

The Provincial Congress ordered its military units to intercept the Loyalists marching toward Brunswick Town. Colonel James Moore was the commander of the First North Carolina Regiment of Continentals. During the French and Indian War he was known among his soldiers as "Mad Jimmie" for the bravery he exhibited in battle. Whether or not Cleaveland served under Moore during that war is unknown, but Captain Cleaveland greatly admired the colonel and held him in high esteem as a military leader.[47]

Commanding about 2,000 men including his Continentals and militia from New Hanover County, Moore approached Rockfish Creek at its confluence with the Cape Fear River, a few miles south of Cross Creek. Under him was Colonel Alexander Lillington commanding militia from the Wilmington district. Other Whig militiamen were marching westward from New Bern under Colonel Richard Caswell and eastward from Surry and Guilford counties. (Richard Caswell had represented North Carolina at the First Continental Congress in Philadelphia in 1774, one of 56 delegates from 12 colonies. He was both powerful and influential in Whig circles.)

With orders issued on February 18, Loyalist General MacDonald began his cross-country march to join with the expected landing of British soldiers. News of Whig militias approaching Cross Creek encouraged him to start. Just seven miles below Cross Creek along the Cape Fear River, the Loyalists came face to face across Rockfish Creek with James Moore and his 1,100 Whig militiamen. MacDonald knew he outnumbered the Patriots, so he first demanded they surrender

**Colonel James Moore first confronted the Loyalists across Rockfish Creek only seven miles from Cross Creek. Marker is on NC Hwy 87, 1.6 miles south of I-95.**

immediately. As he expected, he got an equal demand for surrender in return. MacDonald gathered his men into formation and with great show challenged his own men on their willingness to fight for the King's cause. Twenty men laid down their arms and retreated into the woods to the jeers of their former comrades. (Two companies from Anson County with similar sentiments had marched away the night before.) The remaining Loyalists gave themselves a hearty cheer of huzzas in full view of the Patriots.[48] MacDonald then started marching his Loyalist troops back toward Cross Creek, making a show of his troop movement. Just before arriving back at Cross Creek and well out of view of the Patriots, MacDonald's men ferried across the Cape Fear River in boats, which they destroyed once across.[49] They continued toward the coast by another route toward Negro Head Point, gaining an advantage on Moore's troops who did not discover until the following morning that the enemy had escaped. Upon the discovery, Moore ordered Colonel Richard Caswell, marching from New Bern, to position his men at Corbett's Ferry on the Black River. Should he fail to intercept them there, Moore ordered, Caswell was to block the bridge at Widow Moore's Creek. Meanwhile, Moore marched hurriedly down the Cape Fear River attempting to cut off MacDonald's advance at Elizabeth Town and planning to attack the rear of MacDonald's advance if the opportunity arose. Moore sent troops north as well to occupy Cross Creek to cut off that escape route. He also sent 150 men under Colonel Alexander Lillington to reinforce Caswell's position at Moore's Creek.[50]

MacDonald's men pressed on southeastward, moving away from the Cape Fear River. He moved slowly, crossing swampy lands and sending scouts ahead to prevent being ambushed by the Whigs. The Loyalists' wagons, loaded with the supplies such an army would need, required that the bridges they crossed along the way be reinforced.[51]

After three days of this exhausting campaign, MacDonald's forces arrived at Corbett's Ferry on the Black River. As they approached, they captured a party of Whig scouts and learned from them that Caswell's army of about 850 militiamen from Craven County were waiting in the woods across the river. MacDonald again succeeded in avoiding the Whigs with a second ruse. He left a few men at the ferry to make a great deal of noise while he marched the bulk of his men upstream where they built a bridge and crossed the river on February 26. Once across, MacDonald's men overtook a supply train headed for Caswell. They captured 22 men, 21 bullocks, and 2 wagons of cornmeal. Meanwhile, Caswell, suspecting from the noise in the woods that MacDonald was preparing for a crossing at Corbett's Ferry, had told his men to dig in and to prepare for a fight when the Loyalists crossed. When Caswell discovered that the bagpipes, an occasional shot fired, the general commotion, and the sound of drums had fooled him, he ordered his men to march hurriedly toward Moore's Creek Bridge hoping to arrive there ahead of MacDonald. As Caswell proceeded on his mission, Colonel Moore floated his men 60 miles downstream from Elizabeth Town to Dollison's Landing from where he planned to march overland to Moore's Creek.[52]

When Caswell did arrive at Widow Moore's Creek, he found Colonel Alexander Lillington and his 150 Wilmington militiamen on the east side of the bridge preparing earthworks. They had arrived the day before, on the 25$^{th}$. Caswell had his 850 men pitch their tents and make camp on the west side of the bridge, but this was a trick.

When MacDonald arrived within six miles of the bridge, his scouts reported that Caswell had beaten them there. Under the pretext of calling for surrender, MacDonald sent a messenger forward to the Whig encampment. The real purpose was to spy on the conditions of the Whigs' preparations for making a stand.[53]

The forced march by the Loyalists had taken its toll on the 80-year-old MacDonald. He had fallen ill, but received the information from his returning spy. He learned that Caswell's men were encamped on the near side of the bridge and had their backs to the creek. MacDonald called his officers together; they discussed their options. The young officers all expressed an eagerness to attack Caswell's position at dawn the next day. MacDonald was less aggressive in his thinking, but he deferred to his younger officers. Noting his illness, he gave command of the expedition to Lieutenant Colonel Donald McLeod.

During the night, the Highlanders prepared for the attack, although they were at a significant disadvantage. Because half of the men were without firearms,[54] the officers decided that some of the men would go into battle swinging their traditional broadswords. These 75 hand-picked swordsmen were to serve under Captain John Campbell as shock troops. Their mission was to strike fear among the defenders. At an hour past midnight on the morning of February 27, the Loyalists began their march toward the bridge at Widow Moore's Creek.

**Old Mother Covington and Her Daughter**

Passing clouds obscured the light of the moon and the Loyalists became lost in the dark swamp during their six-mile approach to the bridge. They stumbled around in the muck for much of the time until they caught a glimpse of the campfires from Caswell's encampment. The Loyalists formed three columns and advanced quietly and quickly toward the camp well before dawn. They were expecting to catch the Whigs in their tents, but Caswell had provided the decoy this time.[55]

**"Old Mother Covington" (left) and "her daughter" fired swan shot from Colonel Lillington's earthworks into the Loyalist militiamen crossing the impaired bridge. Firing demonstrations are offered at Moores Creek National Battlefield.**

After dark, Caswell had moved his men to the east side of the bridge, leaving the encampment in place and the campfires burning. Caswell's men joined Lillington's forces in the earthworks. The Whigs prepared to defend the bridge employing two pieces of artillery known to the men as "Old Mother Covington and her daughter." The former was a two-and-a-half pound cannon mounted on a galloper carriage. The latter was a half-pound swivel gun for mounting on a tree stump. Both fired swan shot, canvas bags filled with 20 or so pieces of lead. Upon firing, the pellets scattered into a wide and deadly pattern.

The advancing Loyalists entered the camp and quickly discovered that the Whig tents were empty. Sensing a trick, McLeod and his men retreated into the woods; they waited for daylight. The element of surprise had been lost. The Loyalists peered into the darkness looking for the bridge. Likewise, the Whigs from their entrenched positions on the opposite side of the creek carefully watched for the Highlanders. Each side stared into the predawn of February 27.

The Loyalists considered the options for retreating, but McLeod was recklessly ambitious, some concluded later. He moved among his men, who were waiting in the woods, attempting to rally them for the coming attack and informing them to attack when he gave the signal. When McLeod heard some random shots fired before dawn, he accelerated his plans and gave the anticipated signal. His columns advanced into the predawn darkness with the roll of drums and the squeal of bagpipes. They shouted "King George and broadswords" as they moved forward looking for the bridge in the dark.[56]

Caswell and Lillington had prepared the crossing to thwart the Loyalists' advance. The bridge across Moore's Creek was of simple construction and included planks attached to two large logs, running across the stream as stringers. The Whig troops had removed some of the planks and covered the two logs with soap and tallow.[57] Below the bridge was the deep, dark, near motionless water of Widow Moore's Creek about 50 feet wide and fluctuating between five and eight feet deep depending on the tides. The Whigs held their fire as two columns of Loyalists attempted to advance across the crippled bridge. McLeod thrust the tip of his sword into the log to help himself across and then pointed it into the air with another cry of "King George and broadswords!"

When the two logs of the bridge were full of Loyalists, the Whigs opened fire with their muskets and two blasts from "Mother Covington and her Daughter." The first volley cleared the bridge. Dozens of the advancing Loyalists were hit and died instantly; others fell wounded from the bridge into the water and drowned. McLeod was knocked to the ground but he rallied enough to offer one more battle cry before being cut down in a hail of musket fire just a few feet from the Whig entrenchments. John Campbell as well was slain.[58] The Whigs continued to fire and some Loyalists returned the fire from

**Highland Scots made up most of the Loyalist army commanded by General Donald MacDonald. Loyalist reenactors cross a modern bridge spanning Widow Moore's Creek at the site of the battle at Moores Creek National Battlefield.**

behind trees and other cover. Within three minutes, some said, the fighting was over. Highlanders, both privates and officers alike, began running into the woods toward their pervious night's camp. Some of the deserters removed horses from their wagon's harnesses and rode hurriedly away. Others stumbled blindly into the woods and the swamp running as fast as they could, frequently tripping over tree roots and sprawling face-first into the cold, wet mire. The Whigs jumped from behind their entrenchments, restored the bridge, and gave chase. In a short time, Colonel James Moore arrived at the scene of the battle with his troops and organized a full pursuit of the retreating Loyalists.

Some of the Loyalists got away and returned on their own to their homes, but the pursuing Whigs captured many of them, including the ill General MacDonald, whose retreating Highlanders abandoned him. He was lying alone in his tent when the Whigs arrived. The Whigs took MacDonald as a prisoner first to New Bern and then placed him in the jail at Halifax. The other captured Loyalist militia officers were also taken as prisoners to Halifax. Most of the captured privates, some 850 in all, were colonial farmers, Americans all, just as were their Whig captors. The Whigs paroled these captured, rank-and-file militiamen and allowed them to return home after taking an oath not to take up arms ever again against the Patriot cause.[59]

The victors captured the supplies left behind by the retreating Tories. This included 1,500 rifles, 350 shot bags, 150 swords and Scottish dirks, two chests of medical supplies and 13 wagons with horses. Inside a stable in Cross Creek, the Whigs discovered a box of "johannes and guineas" valued at £15,000, money intended to fund the formation of a Loyalist army.[60] ("Johannes" and "jacks" were slang terms for a coin of £5. A guinea was worth one pound and one shilling, that is, 21 shillings.)

## Still Overflowing with Zeal

The conflict at Moore's Creek Bridge was the first battle of the American Revolution fought in North Carolina. It was a civil conflict, one fought between residents of the colony because of their differing political views and allegiances. Suffering only two casualties, only one of which later died, the Patriots killed 30 Loyalists and wounded 40 in the devastating assault. Many others may have drowned beneath the bridge. This overwhelming Whig victory immediately dampened the broad-based Loyalist spirit in North Carolina. Although pockets of Tories would continue in opposition to the Patriots all across the state, after July 4$^{th}$, the newly independent state would be free from the threat of an invading British army for the following four years.

After the victory, the confidence of the Patriots soared. On April 12, 1776, North Carolina's Fourth Provincial Congress, meeting in

**Americans fought Americans at Moores Creek. This monument at Moores Creek National Battlefield commemorates and honors the American Loyalists killed. It was erected in 1909 by the Moore's Creek Monumental Association to honor captains McCleod and Campbell and "about fifty Highland Scots ... They were heroes who did their duty as they saw it ..."**

Halifax, passed a resolution (later known as the Halifax Resolves) becoming the first of the 13 colonies to authorize its delegates to the Second Continental Congress in Philadelphia to vote for independence from Great Britain. Among the 83 delegates voting unanimously for the resolution were Griffith Rutherford of Rowan County, and Joseph Winston and Joseph Williams, both from Surry County.[61]

Sir Henry Clinton did not arrive at Cape Fear until March 14. The first of his flotilla carrying 2,000 soldiers arrived only two days earlier. Clinton learned from Governor Martin that the body of Loyalists expected to meet him had been dispersed two weeks before. Adding insult to injury, Martin received on March 18 the letter of December 23 from Lord Germain advising him of the change in plans. Clinton stayed aboard ship off the coast, considering his next move. During this time, he received onboard the Superintendent of Indian Affairs for the Southern Department, John Stuart, who had traveled from St.

Augustine to meet with him. They discussed the possible roles of Britain's Cherokee allies in helping end the rebellion. On May 7, Lord Cornwallis and the troops from Ireland finally arrived. High winds and heavy seas had delayed them two months.[62]

As Clinton had sailed past the Chesapeake Bay on his way to Cape Fear, he conferred with Lord Dunmore aboard ship, and learned about Dunmore's plight and the events in Virginia. Yet, even after the debacle at Moore's Creek Bridge, Clinton believed that the Loyalists in the southern colonies were "still overflowing with zeal." Nevertheless, because the Loyalists were in the backcountry, he believed they would be of little value until the British established control of a port to which the Loyalists could rally. Consequently, Clinton considered Charlestown as a reasonable next target. He learned that the fortifications on Sullivan's Island, a point regarded as "the key to Charles Town harbor," were unfinished and inadequate. Thus encouraged, Sir Henry Clinton and Admiral Sir Peter Parker sailed their expedition away from Cape Fear on May 31. Josiah Martin, the displaced governor of North Carolina, joined them onboard.[63] The royal governor of South Carolina, who had fled his colony for England in September, joined the expedition as well. They sailed aboard Admiral Parker's flagship, the *HMS Bristol.*

Josiah Martin's grand scheme of recovering the southern colonies using men still loyal to the king had disintegrated in its initial showing. No small part of the bungling was due to the change in British secretaries-of-state in the midst of planning the invasion. The delay in the arrival of the British troops was instrumental as well to the Loyalists' defeat. To their credit, the Continental troops and militia under Moore, Caswell, and Lillington had pursued, entrapped, routed, and captured the unprepared army of Scottish Loyalists. Discounting the significance of any of these factors, however, the London press treated the entire affair as inconsequential and as only a minor check of the rise of Loyalist support in the southern American colonies.

### A Good Deal of Plundering

General Griffith Rutherford had mustered militia of the Salisbury District, including the Surry County Militia, and was marching toward Cross Creek apparently to confront his Loyalist brother on the battlefield. Fortunate for the family perhaps, the general arrived after the conflict.[64] Though some of the Surry County militiamen, those serving under Major Joseph Winston, had arrived in time to participate in the immediate pursuit of the vanquished Tories, those riding under Captain Benjamin Cleaveland did not arrive at Cross Creek until the day after the rout at Moore's Creek. Lieutenant William Lenoir, mustering under Captain Jesse Walton, took ill along the road and was unable to travel. Walton discharged him, and he made his way back to Surry County as best he could, missing the campaign against the Loyalists.

Cleaveland's men quickly joined the campaign to capture the several parties of Tories, who were attempting to return to their homes in the west. At one point, Colonel Moore ordered Cleaveland to escort the prisoners to Hillsborough, but that order was changed. Instead, Cleaveland and his men rode throughout the countryside rounding up Tories. Thus for a time, Captain Cleaveland did serve under "Mad Jimmie," the commander he so much admired. Captain Jesse Walton and his company of Surry County militiamen conveyed the prisoners to Hillsborough.[65]

Some of the ex-Regulators, those who left Cross Creek when they first heard that Captain Cleaveland and the Surry Militia were on their way,

**Patriot casualties were few at the battle at Moore's Creek. Private John Grady was the only Patriot killed, the first North Carolina martyr to freedom. The Grady Monument commemorates all the Patriots who fought.**

did not return to their homes immediately. They and other disgruntled Tories took to marauding across the countryside, harassing and plundering Whigs in the area. As recalled years later by Colonel Ransom Sutherland, a Patriot, some of these renegades "betook themselves to the woods, like outlaws, and continued to commit depredations on lives and properties." Sutherland recalled that Benjamin Cleaveland "scoured the country and picked up several of these outlaws and hung some of them to trees in woods." In tracking down Loyalists and Tories, Cleaveland dispensed his brand of justice for which he would later become infamous. Indeed, after a Captain Jackson had burned Sutherland's house only a few days after the fight at Moore's Creek, Cleaveland captured the rascal and hanged him within a half-mile of the Sutherland homestead. "I don't recollect," added Sutherland, "after Cleaveland had done with them, to have heard much more of those wretches during the war."[66]

The Whig militiamen were no saints themselves, however, and they extracted their own spoils from those whom they thought had wronged them. At Cross Creek, Cleaveland and the other Whig militia leaders decided that each of the men — if the fellow could pay for its transport home — should have a bushel of salt from the stores of the Loyalist merchants in town. "There must have been a good deal of plundering also," the Moravians recorded, "for as the Militia passed through Salem on their return … it was noticed that many of the men wore Scottish clothes."[67]

**A New Threat from an Old Enemy**

As Benjamin Cleaveland and the Surry County Militia returned home to the Yadkin River valley, they soon learned of a new threat to their safety and freedom. The Moravians in Salem recorded their own account on May 18:

> "People were here from many places. Among them were Mr. [Richard] Henderson and Col. [Joseph ?] Williams, coming from Transylvania [Boonesborough]. They brought a report, sworn to by a Indian trader, who had heard it among the Cherokee, that the Southern Indians were going into the war against the neighboring Colonies; that Stuart, Superintendent of Indian Affairs, his Deputy, and other white men, were among them, to help their king, and that they had received much ammunition from Mobile. Mr. Henderson will shortly take a company of soldiers to Transylvania or Powel[l']s Valley [Martin's Station], to defend that settlement against an attack of the enemy."[68]

The war had come to the frontier.

# Gwynn's Island to Aspenvale

## A Resignation and a Wedding

In 1775, the Second Continental Congress had called for each of the rebel provinces to organize standing units for service under the Continental Army. After six months, six of Virginia's nine proposed regiments had been taken. However, Patrick Henry did not receive a commission as brigadier general, as he desired. That post went to Andrew Lewis instead. Henry had been slighted by his political enemies in the Virginia Convention and overlooked for military assignments. Colonel Woodford and the Second Virginia Regiment had garnered all the battlefield glory. Indeed, Woodford had been insubordinate to Henry during the campaign at Great Bridge, communicating directly to Edmund Pendleton and the Committee of Safety.[1] In late February 1776, Henry succumbed to the petty politics of his opponents, relinquishing his role as commander-in-chief.. He resigned his command of the First Virginia Regiment.[2] Patrick Henry would find ways other than the field of battle to contribute to the Common Cause.

Greatly disappointed at Henry's resignation, the men of the First Regiment threatened to leave in protest. They were accustomed to serving under natural leaders, that is, leaders they elected. Ninety officers, including some of Woodford's men, wrote in support of Henry, noting his eloquence as an orator and the spirit of revolution he instilled in them. They encouraged him to disregard how "the envious undermine an established reputation." If not their command, Henry still enjoyed the support of his countrymen.[3]

To his credit, Patrick Henry persuaded the soldiers to stay and to serve under the new commander, Colonel William Christian, as they would have served under him. Captain William Campbell was one of the men affected by the transfer of command, but he benefited in two ways from this turn of events. First, he soon came under the leadership of Brigadier General Andrew Lewis, the hero of the Battle of Point Pleasant. Lewis could teach him much about military command. Second, because he had remained in Williamsburg for some time, he came under the enchantments of Elizabeth Henry, sister to Patrick Henry. In the meantime, William Campbell got a chance to serve Virginia in battle, helping rid the independent commonwealth of its last royal governor.

**That Ever I Should Come to This**

From the beginning of 1776, Norfolk was in ruins. Lord Dunmore had bombarded the city on New Year's Day. British troops and Patriots had finished the job, each setting fires to burn sections of the town figuring any remaining buildings would provide shelter and supplies for its enemy. By the end of February, the city was gone. Meanwhile, Dunmore had taken refuge across the Elizabeth River on a point of land he could defend and from which he continued menacing Patriot planters along the James River and Chesapeake Bay.

On May 20, 1776, Major General Charles Lee, first Commander of the Southern Department of the Continental Army, skirmished from shore with Dunmore's fleet at Tucker's Mill Point, forcing the ex-governor to leave. About June 1,[4] Dunmore pulled up anchor in the

Elizabeth River and sailed away with about 90 ships and boats under 103 sails.[5] He was a man without a home, a governor with no province to govern. Dunmore sailed north along the west shore of Chesapeake Bay to Gwynn's Island, at the mouth of the Piankatank River adjacent to the mouth of the Rappahannock River, where he landed with some 500 crew, soldiers, and ex-slaves. He set up a small, rude fortification there, from which he continued harassing Patriot planters along the Chesapeake Bay.

Later in June, annoyed by the persistent plundering committed by Dunmore, the Committee of Safety asked Brigadier General Andrew Lewis and the Seventh Virginia Regiment to remove the former governor from Gwynn's Island.[6] Lewis's force, which included Colonel Adam Stephen and Captain William Campbell, advanced toward the island with an army of several companies and artillery. Approaching

**From Crickett Hill, Brig. General Andrew Lewis bombarded Lord Dunmore's ships and Loyalist camp on Gwynn's Island. In forcing Dunmore to flee the island, the Patriots drove the last royal governor from the Virginia province.**

the island on July 8, the Patriots took a position at Cricket Hill overlooking the island. Imprudently, Dunmore had left some of his fleet exposed. On the 9th, Lewis fired his cannons at the camp with such ferocity that cannon balls crossed each other in the air.[7] Dunmore's camp included fewer fighting men than it might have. Captain James Barron of the Virginia Navy captured on the Chesapeake a transport with 218 uniformed Highlanders bound to reinforce Dunmore. Lewis fired at the ships as well. "The men of war were hulled several times, and received considerable damage," the *Virginia Gazette* later reported, "particularly the *Dunmore* and *Otter*, which [at] last was obliged to be towed away in the greatest hurry."[8] The ex-governor was wounded in the barrage when a nine-pound ball smashed into his ship's cabin. A sizeable shard of splintered wood struck him in the leg. One possibly spurious account related that as his dinner china crashed all around him, he bemoaned, "Good God, that ever I should come to this!"[9]

Dunmore's camp began to evacuate the island. He had recently been reinforced with 150 Tories from Maryland who brought over cattle as provisions. The refugees had to escape aboard what ships they could move out of range of Lewis's cannons. Many loaded at Cherry Point on the north shore of the island.

### The Shirtmen are Coming

Lewis had no boats to cross over to the island on the 9th, but overnight, he gathered canoes, rafts, and row-galleys to move his men. He took his cannons across as floating batteries. When some 250 Patriots were seen crossing to the island on the morning of July 10, panic struck Dunmore's camp. The Loyalist had faced before, or had heard stories about, the fighters then pouring onto the island. The Tory militia first sent up the alarm, running through the camp shouting, "The shirtmen are coming! The shirtman are coming!"[10] All the camp ran toward Dunmore's ships and boats seeking to escape. Under some 80 sails, much of Dunmore's fleet of war ships and civilian boats pushed away from Gwynn's Island before the Patriots actually landed, leaving behind what, and whom, they could not load in time.

When the Patriots reached Gwynn's Island, Lewis's men were shocked at what they found: many sick and dying, victims of small pox and "jail fever." The people were suffering from living so crowded for so long aboard dirty ships, which had become "floating lazarettos."[11] As evidence of the Tories' flight taken "with precipitation and confusion,"[12] they found half-covered graves and unburied Negroes. Indeed, the ex-enslaved had suffered greatly from disease, mostly small pox. Dunmore had written to Lord Germain in the spring of 1776 noting that "a fever crept in amongst them [the ex-enslaved], which carried

**Andrew Lewis is one of six Virginia leaders featured on the George Washington equestrian monument on Capitol Square in Richmond. It was completed in 1869.**

off a great many very fine fellows."[13] The Patriots also found newly erected baking ovens and incomplete windmills, indicating Dunmore's hope for a longer stay. Lewis's men captured the cattle left behind and confiscated the provisions that had been abandoned.

Escaping entrapment on Gwynn's Island, Dunmore continued to raid and plunder plantations along the Chesapeake Bay. Reportedly, he was intending to sail up the Potomac River, attack Mount Vernon and capture Martha Washington as a hostage. Difficult weather interfered with Dunmore's execution of the scheme. Repelled by cannon fire from all other attempts to find a landing spot,[14] Dunmore sailed down the Chesapeake Bay to St. George's Island where he repaired and watered his ships during the last weeks of July.[15] During this time, he was forced to disperse, run aground, burn, or dismantle 63 of the vessels in his floating town.[16] Learning that Sir Henry Clinton was returning to New York after being repulsed at Charlestown, Lord Dunmore despaired of ever reclaiming his colony. He set sail for New York as well with seven ships, passing through the capes of Chesapeake Bay on August 6.[17] The remaining ships headed for St. Augustine and Bermuda. Aboard them all were some 300 surviving ex-enslaved and Royal Ethiopians, with the healthiest ones going north with Dunmore, some for additional military duty.[18]

Some accounts lingered, however, of a more nefarious ending to Dunmore's time in Virginia. Instead of New York, he sailed south to the Caribbean, some said, carrying aboard those who had remained loyal to him, including about a thousand former enslaved who had accepted his promise of emancipation. According to 19$^{th}$ century historian Benson J. Lossing, upon arriving at a Caribbean port, Lord Dunmore, the last Royal Governor of Virginia, sold the emancipated enslaved back into slavery and then sailed away to join his family in

England.[19] Such accounts were most likely Patriot propaganda intended to besmirch further the name of Lord Dunmore, a man whose reputation had already fallen precipitously from his return just 20 months earlier in victory over the Shawnee of the Ohio Valley. His was an ignoble ending to a once celebrated career.

**A New Virginia**

Just six weeks before his departure from the capes, Lord Dunmore had already been replaced as governor of Virginia. On June 29, 1776, Patrick Henry was elected the first governor of an independent Virginia. Henry and the radicals had overcome the political influence of the conservatives and Edmund Pendleton.[20] Henry's election was helped to some degree by the rising popularity across the colonies for full revolution. In January, Thomas Paine had published *Common Sense*, a pamphlet which spread quite quickly an enthusiasm for the belief that "a government of our own is our natural right."[21] With the eloquence of Henry and his power to persuade, Paine penned, "Ye that dare oppose, not only the tyranny, but the tyrant, stand forth. Freedom hath been haunted round the globe. … Europe regards her like a stranger, and England hath given her warning to depart. O! receive the fugitive, and prepare in time an asylum for mankind."[22]

The personal slight which Henry had suffered in his military career, was rectified in his election as governor. Virginia was independent and shed of its last royal governor. For the next five years, it would also be free of any British incursions.

Captain William Campbell, after returning from Gwynn's Island, continued to court Elizabeth Henry. He married her on April 2, 1776 with plans to take her back to his Holston River valley home, Aspenvale at the end of his commission. During the summer, he learned that

Cherokees were stirring up trouble, attacking settlements in the Watauga and Holston river valleys. He desired to return west to Fincastle County as soon as possible to help protect his mother and sisters, who lived along the Middle Fork of the Holston River. Campbell was unable to resign his position in the regiment, however, and he remained in its service until the end of the year. When he did return to Aspenvale with his bride in January 1777, he arrived to find his home in newly formed Washington County. He continued his service as a justice in the new county and accepted an appointment as Lieutenant Colonel of the militia. He served under Colonel Evan Shelby. The energies of the militia in southwest Virginia turned to face two threats: roaming bands of plundering Tories and the potential unleashing of violent Indian attacks.

# Cherokee Resistance

## A New Menace Rising

During the winter of 1776, North Carolina Patriots had dealt successfully with a Loyalist uprising in the East linked to an invasion of British soldiers. Soon after, they sensed a new imminent danger building on their western regions, one that threatened South Carolina, Georgia, and Virginia, as well. Reports of small raiding parties of Cherokees indiscriminately attacking outlying settlements began arriving more frequently at established communities a safe distance from the frontier. The Moravians at Bethania recorded on May 1 that seventeen settlers in the Holston River valley had been massacred by Indians who had "horribly mutilated them, scalping the entire head, and hacking the body into many pieces."[1] Urgent stories recounted the killing of men in Virginia's Powell Valley, land just east of the Cumberland Gap, the new overland gateway to the bluegrass meadows of "Ken-te-ke." Closer to home, the wife of a man named McFalls, living at either North Cove or Turkey Cove on the North Fork of the Catawba River in Rowan (later Burke) County, was attacked by a raiding party. "The Indians in ambush shot her down and stabbed her we suppose with a scalping knife and took off her scalp down to both ears."[2] She recovered but was "disowned and deserted by her unfeeling husband," a Tory, "because her beauty had been marred."[3] By midsummer, General Griffith Rutherford, militia commander of North Carolina's Western (Salisbury) District reported: "37 I am informed was killed … on the Cuttaba [Catawba] River, I am also informed that Col° McDowel 10 men more & 120 women and Children is Beshaged [besieged], in sume kind of a fort, & the Indins Round them …"[4] In the face of such news, the North Carolina Council of Safety realized it had yet another serious problem to address.

## The Bloody Ground, Dark and Difficult

A year earlier, in March 1775, North Carolina judge and land speculator Richard Henderson had negotiated a treaty with willing Cherokee to lease 20 million acres between the Cumberland River and the Ohio River. (This included today's north central Tennessee and about two-thirds of what is Kentucky.) This lease, of questionable legality, was called the Transylvania Purchase. At the Sycamore Shoals treaty site on the Watauga River, the older Cherokee chiefs, including Oconostota, agreed to trade the land in exchange for currency and wagonloads of goods valued together at 10,000 British pounds. Two days later, on March 19, Charles Robertson, representing the Watauga Association, made another land purchase, the Watauga Purchase, along the Holston and New rivers from Chief Oconostota and the Cherokees.

The Cherokees were accompanied by a number of white traders, who lived in their towns. Among them was Nathaniel Gist.[5] Henderson negotiated for the "Great Grant" and a "Path Deed," the latter being a swath of land enabling white settlers to pass unmolested through Cherokee land to the Cumberland Gap. The joke was on Henderson, however, because the Cherokees did not really control this land; it was the traditional hunting grounds of the Shawnee. While the treaty participants continued to celebrate with a feast following the negotiations, Daniel Boone and 30 axe-men set off on March 17 to mark a path through the Cumberland Gap for Henderson and others to follow shortly into the Kentucky countryside.[6] Known as Boone's Trace, the

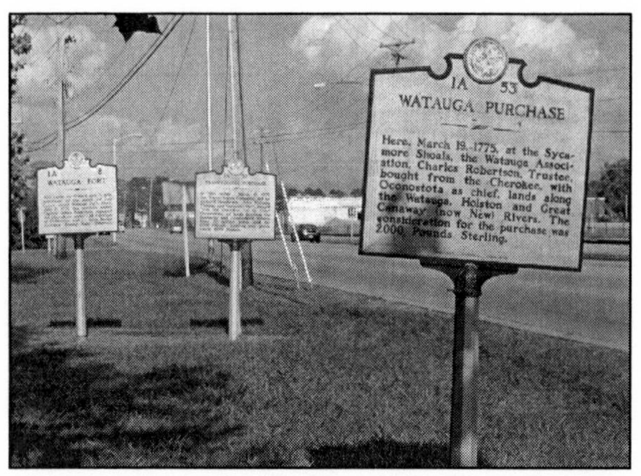


**White settlers convened with Cherokees at Sycamore Shoals in Mach 1775 to purchase tracts of land. Three historical markers at Sycamore Shoals State Historic Area commemorate Fort Watauga, the Watauga Purchase, and the Transylvania Purchase.**

route eventually became part of the Wilderness Road. (See *In the Footsteps of Daniel Boone.*)

Not all the Cherokee leaders present agreed to the Treaty of Sycamore Shoals and the Watauga Purchase. Tsi'yu-gunsini (Dragging Canoe)[7], the young, firebrand Cherokee leader and son of Cherokee civil (or peace) chief Attakullakulla (Little Carpenter), vehemently protested the transactions. Dragging Canoe called the Cumberland "the bloody Ground." Refusing to sign the treaty, he told Henderson the region would be "dark, and difficult to settle."[8] With a following of other young warriors, all disgruntled in the face of a growing menace to their homeland, Dragging Canoe left Sycamore Shoals, vowing to fight those white settlers who continued to trespass on Cherokee lands.

The problem of encroachment on Indian lands was not new, but it had recently begun in earnest on the western side of the mountains, and indeed gave rise to Dunmore's War. At the end of the French and Indian War, the British had set the crest of the Allegheny and Blue Ridge Mountains as the boundary between the two peoples, whites and Indians. King George III proclaimed on October 7, 1763, that no settlers should cross into lands that did not drain to the Atlantic Ocean.[9] Each year, however, Indians of the interior tribes discovered more and more white settlers violating this geographical boundary. They saw whites as moving illegally onto lands King George III had promised to reserve for his allied Indian subjects. It was a promise the King was failing to keep.

**British Indian Agents**

As pre-revolutionary turmoil in the American colonies continued in the early 1770s, the British ministers sought to control the enmity between the Indians and the white settlers, especially those to the west of the Appalachians. Since 1762, John Stuart had been advisor to the Cherokees serving as the Superintendent of Indian Affairs for the Southern Department. After word of the fighting at Lexington and Concord, Massachusetts reached Charlestown, South Carolina in May 1775, revolutionaries circulated rumors that Stuart had ordered the Cherokees and Catawbas to attack the frontier and that 32 families had been slaughtered as a result. The claims were false and unfounded and a misinterpretation of his attempts to assure his superiors of the loyalty and dependability of the Indian tribes, should they be needed. Nevertheless, the rumors were popular and widely believed. Learning that a group of Whigs was planning to capture him, Stuart fled Charlestown for Savannah and then later escaped to St. Augustine, a Loyalist enclave in the British colony of East Florida.[10]

In January 1776, as the city of Norfolk was in flames hundreds of miles away, five dozen Cherokees made the long journey to St.

**Chota was a principal village of the Overhill Cherokees. A series of pedestals representing each of the seven Cherokee clans comprise a monument on a peninsula marking the site of the historic town, now submerged beneath Tellico Lake on the Little Tennessee River in Monroe County, Tennessee.**

Augustine to meet Stuart.[11] Revolutionaries, they told him, had intercepted the powder usually brought by the traders. The chiefs implored Stuart to provide the usual supply of powder and ammunition they needed to hunt game for food, continue their normal trade in buckskins for British goods, and to protect themselves against enemy tribes, Creeks mostly. After the meeting, Superintendent Stuart appointed his younger brother, Henry, as deputy agent and sent him to Pensacola with the powder and lead. From there, Henry Stuart proceeded to Mobile, West Florida, where he met with Dragging Canoe and tried to explain "the cause of the present quarrel and disorders in the Colonies."[12] Afterward, Henry Stuart departed Mobile on or about March 1, 1776 with 30 packhorses loaded with ammunition.[13] He made his way carefully past the Creek nation and through Chickasaw country to the Tennessee River where Dragging Canoe and 80 Cherokees awaited him. From there, and in the company of Nathaniel Gist, the party completed Stuart's 55-day journey to the Overhill

Cherokee village of Toqua on the Little Tennessee River. Along the way, the party of Cherokee met a few boats of white settlers heading down the Tennessee River from the Holston River valley to Natchez on the Mississippi River. The emigrants told the Indians that settlers on the frontier were talking of moving down the Holston River as far as the French Broad River.[14] This alarmed the Cherokees and by the time they reached their villages, they were generally enraged about the growing threat of continued white encroachment.[15]

On April 24, the Cherokees greeted Henry Stuart and his supplies with great ceremony in the Overhill village where another deputy agent, Alexander Cameron, had been resident for a time. The arrival of so much powder and lead in the Cherokee towns was not such a welcome sight to the Overmountain communities who were already suspicious of British alliances with any Indian tribes and especially the Cherokees.[16]

While the Cherokee caravan made its way to the Overhill towns, John Stuart made his way from St. Augustine to the Cape Fear River in North Carolina. There he met with Sir Henry Clinton, who had arrived in March following the too-early mustering of a Loyalist army and its disastrous defeat at Moore's Creek Bridge weeks before he arrived. In support of Clinton's stated plans to attack Georgia and South Carolina from the coast with the fleet of Admiral Sir Peter Parker, Stuart and Clinton discussed the possible use of the Cherokees in some concerted manner to support a British invasion with regular troops or Loyalist forces. Stuart carried with him plans for just such a use of Cherokees and Creeks fighting under white leaders. Thomas Brown, a Georgia Loyalist with vengeance on his mind, had crafted this design. Rebel Whigs in Augusta had recently tarred and feathered Brown, subjecting him to ridicule for his allegiance to the Crown.

However, regardless of Brown's motivations and regardless of precedent or any personal inclinations Clinton or Stuart may have had, the two devised no plans to use Cherokee warriors on the western front. Nevertheless, the pervasive fear and anticipation of just such British-sponsored Indian attacks dominated the thoughts of those who lived on the Georgia and Carolina frontiers.[17]

### Georgia Backcountry

The population of Georgia's backcountry had grown quickly since Royal Governor James Wright had accepted the cession of Indian land in two treaties, in 1763 and 1773. The Second Treaty of Augusta opened about one million acres above the Little River as part of a deal to pay off the trade debts of the Cherokees. The governor wanted many small landowners to populate the area and thus provide a buffer between Savannah at the settled coast and the Indians and Spanish to the west. He had hoped for "the Middling Sort of People, such as have Families and a few Negroes."[18] Unfortunately, those who came, he regarded as "Crackers … a set of Vagabonds often as bad or worse than the Indians themselves."[19]

**In 1763 and 1773, Georgia's governor met with Cherokees and other tribes at the site of Fort Augusta on the Savannah River to negotiate the cession of lands for white settlement. The fort was adjacent to St. Paul's Church (estbl. 1750) at Reynolds St. and 6th St. diagonal to the Augusta Museum of History in Augusta, Georgia. (See notes for partial text of marker.)**

Among the immigrants, both "middling" and otherwise, were many Scots-Irish. They had come down the Great Wagon Road a decade or a generation earlier and settled in the backcountry of Virginia and the Carolinas. After the War of the Regulation in North Carolina in the early 1770s, some of these chastised Regulators had moved over the mountains into the Watauga and Nolichucky river valleys. Some, such as Elijah Clarke, had moved into the Upcountry of South Carolina. When the lands in Georgia opened up for settlement, he and thousands of others with a pioneer spirit migrated across the Savannah River. They provided a buffer, of course, but they also created a problem as many encroached on Indian lands not ceded, and many were outright Indian haters. As occurred with the contact between settlers and Cherokees in the Overmountain region, trouble brewed in the Georgia backcountry.[20]

Royal Governor Wright wanted to maintain trade with the Indians, as deer skins were important to the merchant class in Savannah. But, the inhabitants of the backcountry thought the Indian trade "tended to bring those savages down into the settlements, and they seldom return without either committing murder or robbery or and generally both upon the white people."[21] Also, the settlers resented the Indian traders putting guns and ammunition into the hands of the people these backcountry settlers feared most. From the other side, the Creeks felt betrayed by the ceding of land for Cherokee debts. Unavoidably, Indian wars erupted in the backcountry in the winter of 1773-74.[22]

The governor stopped the Indian trade for a while, initially appeasing the backcountry settlers but displeasing the Indians. When Georgia Whigs rallied in August 1774 in opposition to Parliament's Coercive (Intolerable) Acts, the backcountry settlers signed petitions declaring that the Whigs did not speak for all Georgians. The backcountry settlers depended on British troops and forts for protection against the Indians. Elijah Clarke was among those opposed to the Whig rebel position. Soon, however, Governor Wright restarted the trade. By the end of 1774, Clarke and many of his fellow backcountry colleagues, including Benjamin Few and John Twiggs, switched their allegiances. They became supporters of the Whigs.

In the spring of 1775, news of the fighting in Lexington and Concord, Massachusetts reached Georgia along with false rumors that a British agent (i.e. John Stuart) was inciting the Indians to attack American colonists on the frontier. The Whigs took action. Some "liberty boys" in Savannah broke into the powder magazine and threatened the officials there. Those in the backcountry struck out against those who did not rally in support of the Whigs and their Continental Association. For those who actually tried to organize an opposition movement, worse was in store. Thomas Brown learned this firsthand — or foot first, as it were.

### Thomas Brown

Thomas Brown was the type of immigrant the governor had most wanted to attract. He was an Englishman with a pedigree, and he had become a prominent planter in the backcountry. Brown owned 5,000 acres and had brought in about 150 indentured servants since 1774. He supported the Crown and organized an association of Loyalists. In light of his open opposition to the Whigs, a mob of "liberty boys" went to his home, clubbed him down, shaved his head (if not scalped him) and then tarred and feathered him. They forced him to stand on burning logs (he lost two toes in the incident) and then hauled him through the streets of Augusta in a cart, subjecting him to ridicule. He became known by his antagonists as "Burntfoot" Brown. After such treatment, Brown attempted to rally Loyalist support in South Carolina around Ninety Six, but he was threatened further. He escaped his Patriot pursuers and fled to East Florida.[23]

Meanwhile, British General Thomas Gage, the military royal governor of Massachusetts, did, in fact, instruct John Stuart to use the Indians on the frontier in support of Loyalists who were taking up arms against the rebel Whigs.[24] Learning of this new policy, Thomas Brown, then in East Florida, sought to use it to his advantage. He devised a plan and persuaded the royal governor of East Florida, Patrick Tonyn, to support him. Brown wanted to coordinate an Indian attack on Augusta with a landing of British troops. This would secure an inland port for British shipping and dishearten the backcountry Whigs, the very people who had tortured and ridiculed him. Brown personally delivered a train of fifty packhorses laden with ammunition to the Creeks. He wanted them to attack the frontiers in concert with Sir Henry Clinton's planned attack at Charlestown. Brown's overtures to the Indians cost him the support of some backcountry Loyalists, however. As Tonyn expressed in a letter to Sir Henry Clinton, "the Americans are a thousand times more in dread of the Savages than of any European troops."[25]

General Charles Lee, the first commander of the Southern Department of the Continental Army made plans to defend the southern colonies against a British attack on two fronts. In July 1776, he told Virginia and the Carolinas to send their militia against the Indians on the frontiers. Whatever intentions Lee may have had for how this was done, the sentiments of those facing the continual threat of Indian attacks were clear. William Henry Drayton expressed his expectations clearly in giving his orders to the South Carolina militia officers: "And now a word to the wise. It is expected you make smooth work as you go — that is you cut up every Indian cornfield and burn every Indian town and every Indian taken shall be the slave and the property of the taker and that the nation be extirpated and the lands become the property of the public."[26]

Despite the bellicose calls of the backcountry Georgians "to exterminate and rout those savages out of their nation," few could be rallied to the cause. The Georgians would let the Carolinians and the Virginians do the job. Thomas Brown, however, was more committed to his cause. Knowing that the destruction of the Cherokees and the failure of the Creeks to fight ruined his plans, he retreated to East Florida again. He gathered former Indian traders, "daring fellows" with "the love of plunder," to form the East Florida Rangers.[27] During the next two years, Patriot forces, including Elijah Clarke, pursued Brown's Rangers in the Florida swamps, but unsuccessfully. Soon enough, however, Brown would return to Georgia.

**Young Blades**

In the face of this increasingly feared Indian menace from the west, a call came to send men to help repel the doubtless coming British invasion of Charlestown. While visiting his father, Colonel John Walker, east of the mountains, Felix Walker learned of a need for fighting men.[28] (Felix Walker was then a clerk of the Watauga Association in the Overmountain settlements. His father lived along Cane Creek in Tryon County, later Rutherford County, about five miles northeast of where Gilbert Town was soon to be established.[29]) Walker returned to the Watauga area and recruited a platoon of "young blades"[30] to serve under Colonel Isaac Huger in the defense of Charlestown. They arrived in May, 1776. Among them, historians believe, was Robert Sevier.[31] These skilled hunters initially were stationed on James Island among 500 others as a second line of defense. Known as expert marksmen, these Overmountain hunters were most certainly among the men sent to the rifle pits to defend the incomplete, palmetto-log fortifications on Sullivan Island. Their prowess in helping prevent the landing of Sir Henry Clinton's troops on June 28, 1776, was recounted in the words of one of the riflemen, Morgan Brown. "Our rifles were in prime order, well provided and well charged," he wrote, "every man took deliberate aim at his object, and it really appeared that every ball took fatal effect. … The fire taught the enemy to lie closer behind their banks of oyster shells."[32]

After the British fleet under Clinton and Parker retreated from Charlestown, the platoon of Wataugans remained to help rebuild the fortifications, which were then given the name Fort Moultrie. They worked for a time until they learned of looming Indian troubles back home. The young men resigned their service and immediately returned home to the Watauga River valley settlements.

**Stuart's Letter**

On May 2, 1776, at Chote (Chota), the principal Overhill village, the chiefs met with Henry Stuart. They insisted he write a "talk" to the settlers along the Watauga and Nolichucky rivers. Although during the previous five years British agents and the governor of North Carolina had ordered these stubborn transmontane settlers to vacate the land, they remained. Once again, the Cherokees earnestly sought the help of their British allies in removing these white trespassers.[33]

The agents were convinced of the Cherokees' allegiance to the King in the face of a growing colonial rebellion and even despite the efforts of the rebel governments to persuade the Cherokees to their side. John Stuart wrote: "The Cherokees under the trying circumstances of hunger and nakedness stand firm in their attachment to his Majesty and reject all the temptation thrown in their view."[34] The agents were also convinced of the Cherokees' readiness to support in battle against the rebels any incursion made by Loyalist or British troops. Stuart wrote to his brother, the superintendent: "The young men I know will be ready at the first word[;] but to employ them before Something Effectual can be done may be attended with bad Consequences." Cameron added his thoughts: "I would not willingly have the Indians to Committ *(sic)* any Hostilities before some of the King's Troops were Actually in Arms in N° Carolina[,] S° Carolina or Georgia."[35] With Indian allegiances assured, the principal challenge for Stuart and Cameron was restraining the Cherokees from attacking the settlements along the Watauga and Nolichucky rivers. Stuart warned the Cherokees against any attacks, as "that would doubtless involve their Nation in Ruin."[36]

The Cherokees' "talk" declared as untrue the settlers' claims that the Cherokees had traded them land. The chiefs decried the fraud. They demanded that all "Virginians" (a term they used for all encroaching white settlers) should move to "lands within the white man's bounds."[37] Henry Stuart wrote out the letter, the "talk," and sent it to the Watauga River settlement by way of Isaac Thomas. Thomas was one of the white traders who lived among the Cherokees; he was a large man — a near-giant.[38] Thomas delivered the letter on May 11 to the home of William Bean, from where it was shared with others.[39]

In response to Stuart's letter, Colonel John Carter, writing on May 13 for the Wataugans, declared they had indeed negotiated honestly with "our brothers, the Cherokees" for the land where they lived. Carter said they would willingly give up those claims when "legally called upon" to do so, he wrote, but in any case would need more time to vacate the area than the 20 days presented in Stuart's letter.[40] These settlers were simply stalling, however, and did not intend to give up the lands they regarded as theirs. (These settlers had arrived after 1769 and by 1772 organized themselves as the Watauga Association, a self-governing body independent of any other government, the first such to form with a written compact west of the Alleghenies.[41]) Isaac Thomas carried the Wataugans' response to the Cherokee chiefs. He also took with him separate, more conciliatory responses from settlers on the Nolichucky River. That second letter assured Stuart of their allegiance to the Crown. The Nolichucky River settlers simply asked where they might relocate "untill things should take a turn in the settlements."[42]

Carrying a letter dated May 23 from Cameron and Stuart, Thomas and another trader, John Bryan, returned to the Watauga River settlement. The Cherokees responded from Toqua, granting an additional 20 days for removal but with unwavering determination to reclaim their lands.

The Overmountain leaders sent forward a copy of Stuart's letter to the Committee of Safety of Fincastle County; they may have altered it somewhat to their purposes in requesting aid. (At the time, without an extension of a line marking the North Carolina-Virginia border, some Overmountain settlers believed they were in Virginia.) The Committee's response to the Overmountain settlers was unexpected. The Committee suggested that those settlers over the line move back across the boundary. Moreover, the Committee provided 500 lbs. of powder for each of the frontier Virginia counties with a thousand pounds of lead, but only to those non-trespassing settlers east of the line. Some saw the Overmountain settlers as creating a threat to others on the frontier. William Christian apparently believed that the British agents were indeed encouraging the Cherokees to attack the frontiers. He offered to the Committee his advice for the settlers: "By all means every person over the line ought to move instantly, if they did, perhaps the Indians would not be Wrought upon by our enemies to cross the line for some time, if the people do not move, ruin must overtake them…"[43]

On the night of May 18, 1776, another letter arrived mysteriously in the Watauga River settlement at the home of Charles Robertson. It purported to come from Henry Stuart also. In it, "Stuart" acknowledged the settlers' "great apprehensions of the Indians doing mischief immediately" and offered the Overmountain settlers a remedy. The letter offered protection against the Indians to any of the Overmountain settlers who would sign a paper stating their allegiance to the Crown. The letter continued that "his Majesty will immediately land an army in West Florida, march them through the Creek to the Chickasaw Nation, where five hundred warriors from each nation are to join them, and then come by Chota, who have promised their assistance, and then to take possession of the frontiers of North-Carolina and Virginia …"[44]

The Wataugans read the letter as a clear threat to invade their Overmountain community with a combined force of British soldiers and their Indian allies. The letter, however, may have been a foolhardy attempt by some scheming Loyalist to frighten the settlers into joining the Loyalist side. As the British feared, and had so pointedly discussed between royal ministers and agents, any attack on the settlements by the Indians would likely drive many uncommitted settlers over to the rebel Whig side, thus losing their numbers as reliable Loyalists to support any subsequent British invasion. (Indeed, Stuart later denied that he had written such a letter. Historians believe that Jesse Benton may have been the skillful forger.[45])

**Facing a Cherokee uprising, Overmountain settlers fortified their settlements for protection. An interpreted replica of Fort Watauga stands at Sycamore Shoals State Historic Area in Elizabethton, Tennessee. A museum interprets frontier life, skills, and technology.**

Leaders of the Overmountain settlers sent copies of the second "Stuart" letter to Colonel William Preston and to the Committee of Safety. If the ruse of the Loyalists had failed, the Wataugans used it to their advantage. Even if they believed the letter to be a forgery, they knew that if they used it to associate the threatened Indian attacks with the actions of devious British agents, they would receive support from the revolutionaries in Virginia. The letter was circulated widely into North Carolina and South Carolina where it enflamed anti-British sentiments.[46] Henry Stuart denounced the second letter as a forgery accusing "Villains" of wanting "to involve the Settlements of Virginia and North Carolina in an unjust War with the Indians" just so they could retain the lands they had taken from the Cherokees by fraud, he said.[47]

Sentiments began to favor the Overmountain settlements. William Cocke responded to the Committee reminding its members of the service these Overmountain settlers had provided Virginia previously. He wrote, "… in Every war we have been ready and Ever furnished our Quota of men & have been as ready to Open Our purses …"[48] Moreover, intentional or not, passing along the suspect letter and suggesting the imminent threat of a British-inspired Indian attack got the Wataugans the support they wanted.[49] During the course of the summer, the Wataugans petitioned separately the rebel governments of Virginia and North Carolina for protection.

The Overmountain settlers raised a company of 100 rangers to patrol the area between the settlements and the Cherokee towns. To provision themselves, they purchased ammunition from Virginia.[50] The settlers began building forts: Fort Lee on Limestone Creek of the Nolichucky River and Fort Caswell (Carter's Fort, Fort Watauga) at Sycamore Shoals on the Watauga River. They also fortified outlying homesteads and stations to varying degrees: Eaton's Fort (five miles east of today's Kingsport Tennessee), Shelby's Fort (in today's Bristol, Tennessee), and Womack's Fort, (two miles northeast of today's Bluff City, Tennessee). The Overmountain settlers prepared in earnest for the anticipated attack.

### Better To Die Like Warriors

The Cherokees were growing evermore anxious as they awaited a response from the Wataugans but heard nothing. At the time of this posturing and extended exchange of letters between Watauga River settlers and the Cherokees, a party of 14 Indian warriors and chiefs representing some northern tribes, including Iroquois, Ottawa, Nanticoke (Nancutas), Shawnee, and Delaware, arrived at the Cherokees' Overhill capital of Chote. They were seeking an alliance with the Cherokee for a coordinated, pan-Indian attack against all white settlers encroaching beyond the Allegheny and Appalachian divide. Among them, some believe, was Cornstalk, the Shawnee chief who had attacked Virginia militiamen at Point Pleasant a year-and-a-half earlier. These emissaries spoke of the treachery of the white settlers, the Virginians, and the continuing incursion of these trespassers onto Indian lands all along the frontier. The speaker believed to be Cornstalk was reported as having said, "When a fort appears, you may depend upon it that there will soon be a town and settlement of white men. It is plain that the white people intend to extirpate the Indians. It is better for the red men to die like warriors than to diminish away by inches."[51]

Though it was untrue, the visitors from the North told the Cherokee that rebels had tarred and feathered the British superintendent of Indian affairs for the northern colonies, Guy Johnson.[52] They spoke of the British forces attacking from the sea and proposed that if all Indians attacked from the west, the white settlers would be "as nothing." The chief believed to be Cornstalk declared that any tribes that did not join in the alliance would be a common enemy and that after the tribal alliance had defeated the whites, the victors would turn upon the tribes who did not fight with them.

The northern emissaries continued beseeching Cherokee participation by sharing that the French had outfitted them with supplies, arms, and ammunition in support of their uprising against British interests. Painted black to indicate readiness for war, the northern chiefs offered to Dragging Canoe a decorated, vermillion war belt, nine feet long. The Cherokee chiefs among those gathered who were eager for battle received it one by one and took up the war dance and chant. Dragging Canoe was among those who readily accepted the alliance; some other, older chiefs hesitated or outright refused.[53]

Although not all the Cherokee chiefs accepted the challenge, enough did. Henry Stuart wrote, "After this day, every young Fellow's face in the Overhills Towns appeared Blackened, and nothing was now talked of but War. The people of Tellico and the Island were busily employed in preparing Spears, Clubs, and scalping Knives."[54]

At last, Isaac Thomas returned to the Cherokees with a "talk" from the Fincastle Committee of Safety. Again, the Virginia leaders surprised and disappointed. The tone of this letter was not what the Cherokees were expecting. Henry Stuart wrote that the letter "so exasperated the Indians that we had little hopes after this of being able to restrain them."[55] It warned the Cherokees against allowing themselves to be influenced by the British agents and instructed them that complaints should be taken to the government of Virginia at Williamsburg. Among other such condescending statements, the letter demanded that those Cherokees responsible for recently murdering whites on the path to Kentucky must be punished. A refusal on this point, the letter said, would bring on "the destruction and perhaps the utter extirpation of the Cherokee Nation."[56] Aware of the building of forts and the raising of militia, some Cherokees concluded that an army of whites was forming to invade their towns. In the face of eminent war, Henry Stuart departed for Pensacola and Alexander Cameron later left for the Lower Towns in South Carolina. Nathaniel Gist, employed by British agent Cameron, remained in the Cherokee villages. Despite what the Wataugans had convinced others to believe about a British-Cherokee alliance against them, it is more likely that the urging of the northern Indian tribes and the threats of the Virginia Committee of Safety actually provoked the Cherokee to attack the Overmountain settlements.[57]

**Overmountain Loyalists**

Not all the settlers in the Overmountain communities were Whig rebels; some remained fiercely loyal to the Crown and many more were yet undecided as to which side they might take if called upon to fight for one or the other. Many Overmountain Loyalists lived along the Nolichucky River. Ostensibly to save the lives of Loyalists, Nathaniel Gist agreed to approach the forts there with a handful of other white traders before the planned attack. By design, the Loyalists in the area were to gather and march away with Gist, carrying white cloths in their hands to distinguish them from the others. They would then join the war party of Cherokee. (Gist later claimed convincingly that this was his way of escaping to Virginia.[58]) Getting wind of the plan, Captain James Robertson with Patriot militiamen from Watauga and Captain John Shelby (brother to Major Evan Shelby) with Patriot militiamen from the Holston River valley rode into the Nolichucky River valley and rounded up 70 Loyalists.[59] The Patriots forced the captives to take an oath of allegiance or at least promise to remain neutral in the fight. Not all honored that oath and many were looking for the first opportunity to strike back at the Patriot rebels. [60]

## The Raven, Old Abram, and Dragging Canoe

Incensed at the audacity of the white trespassers, the Cherokees mounted a three-pronged attack against the Overmountain settlements. And, although Henry Stuart left the Cherokee Nation, for a time Alexander Cameron must have agreed to help the Cherokees organize. Old Abram of Chilhowee would lead an attack against the Watauga and Nolichucky River valley settlements, The Raven would attack Carter's Valley, and Dragging Canoe would attack settlements along the Holston River. The surprise of the plan was spoiled, however. In advance of the attacks, Nancy Ward (Nanye-hi), Beloved Woman (Ghighua) of the Cherokee and a cousin to Dragging Canoe, sent word of the planned assault to warn the white settlers. Four white traders, Isaac Thomas, Jarret Williams, William Falling (Faulin), and Isaac Williams (or possibly John Bryan)[61], took the warning by four separate routes to assure that at least one of them got through. At least two of these men were among the traders Nathaniel Gist had hoped to use in rallying Loyalists from the Nolichucky River settlements to join in the Indian cause. Either their sentiments lay with the Patriots or they could not take up arms with the Cherokees against their own. Gist, however, remained under grave suspicions of being a Tory.

Having left the Cherokee Nation on July 8th, Jarret Williams shortly thereafter reported to the settlements what he had observed. He estimated the number of Cherokee warriors at 600. "They propose to take away negroes, horses, and to kill all kinds of cattle, sheep, &c. [etc.], for which purpose they are well stocked with bows and arrows; also to destroy all corn, burn houses, &c.," he attested. Williams also confirmed that Cameron had interrogated a prisoner brought in by the Cherokees. He added that Cameron had instructed Gist to approach the Overmountain forts before attacking and to ask those loyal to the King to leave the settlements and to join with the Indians in fighting. Williams concluded his deposition noting that "a number of the Cherokee of the Lower towns were gone to fall on the frontiers of South-Carolina and Georgia."[62] Alexander Cameron led them.

On the 11$^{th}$, after learning of Williams's account as corroborated by others, John Sevier sent a letter from Fort Lee to alert the leaders of Fincastle County. The four traders, he wrote, "have this moment come in by making their escape from the Indians and say six hundred Indians and whites were to start for this fort, and intend to drive the country up to New River before they return."[63] Anticipating the worst, Sevier and others then set about preparing the already alarmed Overmountain settlements to face the imminent attack.

Simultaneously and hundreds of miles east, North Carolina's political leaders were coming to their own conclusions about the Indian threat. Being so distant from the field of action, they were taking their own actions based on what information they had received. Convinced of a British and Cherokee alliance — true or not — Thomas Jones of the North Carolina Council of Safety wrote in July of "the cruel Indian war brought about by the wicked and diabolical superintendent Cameron who resides in the Overhill Cherokee towns." Attributing at the time almost 200 deaths of men, women and children to British-urged Indian attacks, he added, "I hope a tory will never after this open his mouth in favor of the British government, which, of all governments on earth, I believe at this time is the most tyrannical and bloody."[64]

**The Unacas Are Running**

In July 1776, Cherokee warriors advanced northward with a party numbering between 600 and 700. The Raven ravaged the thinly settled Carter Valley. His warriors burned farmsteads, crops, and livestock and completely cleared the valley of settlers, killing those who did not escape. Another marauding force advanced well into Virginia. "They divided themselves into small detachments," wrote Ramsey, "and carried fire and devastation and massacre into every settlement, from the remotest cabin on Clinch, to the Seven Mile Ford, in Virginia." As they neared Wolf Hills (later Abingdon), they fired upon the Reverend Charles Cummings and four others going into their fields. Three were killed or wounded, but Cummings and his slave fought back until help arrived from nearby Black's Fort. Thereafter, Rev. Cummings and the men of his congregation arrived at church well-armed and sat with their rifles in their hands.[65]

Mustered in Williamsburg, Captain William Campbell learned of the

**The Battle of Island Flats was the first shooting battle in the summer of 1776 between Dragging Canoe's Cherokee warriors and the Overmountain settlers. Two highway historic markers on Memorial Blvd. in Kingsport, Tennessee commemorate this battle.**

attacks at Seven Mile Ford, near his home. He sought to relinquish his commission in the Continental Army so he could return home immediately to defend his home community and siblings through service in the militia. His commanders denied his request.

Dragging Canoe and his 170 to 200 warriors headed for Long Island. The settlers in the Holston Valley had retreated to Eaton's (Heaton's) Station, which they hurriedly fortified with the construction of a rough stockade. About 170 fighting men, five companies comprised mostly of Virginians, gathered there with their families. Under the general command of Captain James Thompson, the companies were led by captains James Shelby, William Buchanan, John Campbell, Thomas Madison[66], and William Cocke. Fearing for the welfare of the settlers who had not sought the safety of the fort, the captains moved out on August 20 to meet the oncoming enemy, reported by scouts to number 300 to 400 warriors. "We marched in two divisions," the captains later reported, "with flankers on each side and scouts before." Late in the afternoon, the scouts spotted about 20 warriors and fired on them. The Cherokees retreated and the militiamen chased them for a short distance. Robert Campbell, brother of Colonel Arthur Campbell, was so far ahead of his companions in pursuit that he was mistaken for a Cherokee and nearly shot. "We took ten bundles and a good deal of plunder," the captains later wrote, "and had good reason to think some of them were wounded."[67]

Having seen the Indians retreat, the captains chose to return to the fort, concluding that a larger party of Indians might be nearby. Moreover, evening was coming. William Cocke was most earnest in his pleas for a return to the fort and was so far ahead of the others in heading that way, that claims of "cowardice" haunted his reputation thereafter. As the militiamen made their way back toward the fort, those in the rear soon raced forward reporting that a large party of warriors was indeed gaining on them. Robert Campbell first alerted the captains, who gave the order for the men to fall into fighting positions amongst the trees. They did this immediately, though with some understandable confusion. Some accounts say the senior officer Captain James Thompson formed the left line and ordered the right line to form. Lieutenant Robert Davis did so, stretching his line to a small rise from which four lookouts could see the oncoming

**In the summer of 1776, Cherokee warriors attacked the settlers encroaching on Cherokee lands. Chiefs led attacks into the Holston, Nolichucky, and Watauga river valleys.**
**(Cherokee reenactors at Fort Dobbs SHS, NC 2009 portraying 1760.)**

Cherokees. In a moment's time, Dragging Canoe and his horde of warriors attacked the militiamen in the woods. Ramsey wrote: "The Indians fought, at first, with great fury; the foremost hallooing, ['T]he Unacas are running, come on and scalp them.[']"[68]

"Our men sustained the attack with great bravery and intrepidity," the captains later reported. "The Indians endeavored to surround us, but were prevented by the uncommon fortitude and vigilance of Captain James Shelby, who took possession of an eminence that prevented their design. Our line of battle extended about a quarter of a mile."[69] Others credit Robert Campbell with preventing the Cherokee from flanking the militiamen. Probably each (and others as well) played important roles in defending the militia's position in the open. Ramsey wrote: "The greater part of the officers and not a few of the privates, gave heroic examples to cause the men to advance and give battle; of the latter, Robert Edmiston [Edmondson] and John Morrison gave conspicuous exertions. They advanced some paces towards the enemy and began the battle by shooting down the foremost of them. The battle then became general."[70] In one instance, a Cherokee warrior charged Robert Campbell and fired his rifle but missed the Virginian. The Indian stopped and stood tall folding his arms across his chest in stately defiance as Campbell fired with greater accuracy, killing the warrior at close range.[71]

At times, the fighting was hand-to-hand. Alexander Moore, in Shelby's company, shot a retreating warrior, wounding him in the knee. The Cherokee dropped into a sinkhole to tie up his wound. Moore pursued him there. The brave drew his knife. Moore grabbed the blade, cutting his hand. The two men clinched into a grappling match, with the warrior trying to stab and slash his white opponent. Moore, as strong and equally sized, threw his opponent to the ground and knocked the knife from the Indian's hand. The two wrestled on the ground, each trying to reach the weapon. Moore kicked the knife away repeatedly. The desperate fight continued until one of Moore's companions came upon them and shot the warrior. Although accounts differ, the companion was likely Charles Young, the younger brother of Robert Young.[72]

The captains stopped counting enemy dead at 13. (Ramsey says 26 Cherokee died on the battlefield with "upwards of forty" dying after those wounded succumbed.[73]) "There were streams of blood every way, and it was generally thought there was never so much execution done in so short a time on the frontiers," the captains wrote. Indeed, Dragging Canoe was wounded in the brief encounter, which lasted perhaps ten minutes. A shot to his leg may have broken a bone. Among the militia at the open-woods skirmish, which became known as the Battle of Island Flats, the captains reported no deaths and "only four men greatly wounded." They closed their report, "The rest of the troops are in high spirits and eager for another engagement."[74]

**Leap the Wall Or Die**

As Old Abram's war party advanced along the foot of the mountains toward Fort Caswell, his warriors fanned out in small raiding parties, killing and capturing isolated settlers. One such party captured Lydia Bean, the wife of William Bean, as she made her way from her home along Boone's Creek to Fort Caswell. At their station camp on the Nolichucky River, the Cherokees interrogated her to discover the strength of the settlers and the number of forts. Through a translator, a fellow captive, she led Old Abram to believe the forts were well armed and adequately manned to resist his attack. The Cherokees took Lydia Bean to their Overhill town where she was condemned to death and placed on the mound for burning. Nancy Ward immediately pardoned her. The fortunate Mrs. Bean lived among the Cherokees for a time teaching their women how to make butter and cheese. Other such captured settlers suffered worse.[75]

The other chiefs regarded Old Abram well as a strategist but thought him less effective in the field. When he attacked the settlers in the Nolichucky and Watauga river valley settlements, most of the community had already gathered at Fort Caswell, named to honor an independent North Carolina's first governor, Richard Caswell, and also called Fort Watauga. Colonel John Carter commanded the fort with the aid of Captain James Robertson and Lieutenant John Sevier. Sevier had been defending Fort Lee on the Nolichucky River, but brought his 15 remaining men and their families with him to defend Fort Caswell. A good portion of the residents of the Nolichucky River valley — regarded as a nest of Loyalists by some — had already departed. Writing two decades later, one observer described the situation at the time: "The inhabitants immediately took alarm, and instead of flocking to the frontier barrier in strong and open ground and thereby securing their country, those of the Nolachucky *(sic)* hastily fled. Carrying off their livestock and provisions ..."[76] Nevertheless,

**Fort Watauga stood on a rise out of the floodplain adjacent to Sycamore Shoals. A monument on G Street at Monument Place in Elizabethton, Tennessee commemorates the historic location of Fort Watauga near Sycamore Shoals State Historic Area.**

the combined militia forces at Fort Caswell numbered 75 fighting men (others say 40) with 150 settlers inside.[77]

Early in the morning of July 21, some women and girls went out from Fort Caswell to tend to the cows. While some distance from safety, they were surprised by Cherokees, who had sneaked close to the fort during the night. The women rushed back toward the fort, running for their lives; the Cherokees killed one and captured others. One lone female figure made exceptional haste for the fort. She was Catherine Sherrill, a young woman who had arrived at the fort with her parents just the day before. Cherokee warriors were in hot pursuit and cut off her angle toward the front gate. Determined to get inside the fort, she ran for the wall and leaped up. "The bullets and arrows came like hail," she recalled many decades later. "It was now leap the wall or die," she declared of the moment, "for I would not live a captive." A man in the fort reached over the wall as far as he could and grabbed her hand. By some calamity, he lost his footing and his grasp. She fell to the ground. Determined to save herself, she leaped again. Another man extended his hand as he leaned over the wall (and some say while others inside were holding onto his legs and britches) and grabbed her hand as she leaped up to grab his arm. John Sevier pulled Catherine over the stockade wall and into the safety of the fort. She recounted finding herself "by the side of one in uniform." Thus did John Sevier and Catherine "Bonnie Kate" Sherrill first meet.[78] (Another account, perhaps more in tune with the independent spirit of Catherine Sherrill, says, "equal to the emergency, she threw her bonnet over the pickets [of the wall], and then clambered over herself, and, as she jumped within, was caught in the arms of John Sevier.[79])

Rifle fire from within Fort Caswell was heavy and accurate as the Overmountain marksmen took careful aim. Evidenced by the amount of blood left on the ground, the Cherokees had suffered greatly in their attempted assault. The Cherokees withdrew a safe distance and laid siege to the fort, expecting to starve out those inside. One day, about 25 warriors attempted to start a fire against the stockade wall at a point where the men could not shoot at them. Tradition recounts that James Robertson's sister, Ann, thwarted their attempt by pouring a kettle of boiling wash water onto the Cherokees. Although she was wounded in the exchange, she kept up her scalding attack until the warriors scattered.

Other settlers were not as fortunate as Ann. Cherokees discovered James Cooper outside the fort along the river. They shot him with arrows and bullets as he attempted to swim to safety but thrashed about in shallow water. In response to his screams for help, Lieutenant Sevier sought to mount a rescue party immediately. Captain Robertson, fearing a ruse to get some of the men into an ambush, kept Sevier inside the fort. The warriors killed Cooper and scalped him. A young boy, Samuel Moore, had gone out with Cooper to get "boards to cover a hut" in the fort. Warriors captured him and later took him to the Cherokee towns. After some time, they tied young Samuel to a stake and burned the poor lad to death.[80]

After two weeks, Old Abram abandoned the siege of Fort Caswell. The Cherokees retreated from their attack against the Overmountain settlements. For the moment, these defiant settlers — some rebel, others perhaps Loyalist — had survived this Indian uprising, many believing, whether true or not, that it was encouraged by British agents.

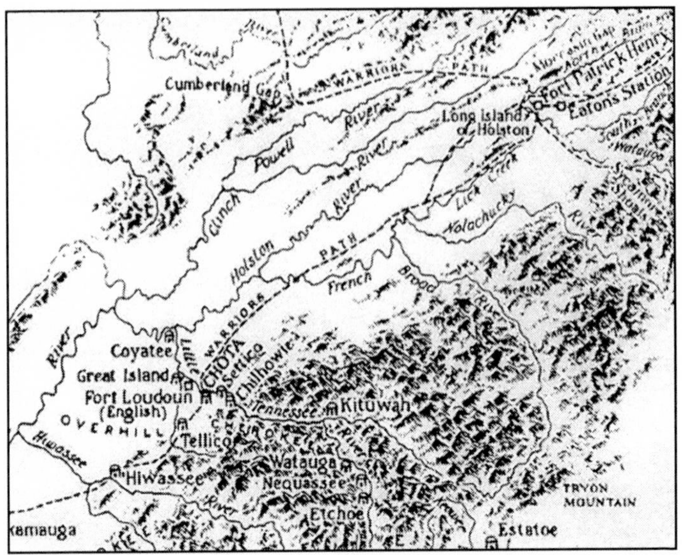


**In 1776, the Overmountain settlements of the encroaching whites, both Patriots and Loyalists, were at the north end of the Warrior's Path leading from the Overhill Cherokee Towns on the Little Tennesse and Hiwassee rivers.**

**[Detail from Coulter and Swanton, *Indian Tribes of North America*, (Washington: USGPO, 1952), p. 76]**

**The story of the Aniyunwiya, the Real People, is presented at the Museum of the Cherokee Indian in Cherokee, NC. It is located on the tribal lands of the Eastern Band of the Cherokee.**

# "A Finel Destruction of the Cherroce Nation"

## The Most Vigorous Measures

As British Indian agents Henry Stuart and Alexander Cameron had feared, the attacks by Dragging Canoe and the Overhill Cherokees on illegal settlements west of the mountains garnered a response that punished the entire Cherokee nation. While Dragging Canoe had been planning his assaults, the Patriots had already decided how to deal with what they regarded as the rising Indian threat. The North Carolina Council of Safety ordered General Griffith Rutherford to assemble militia in readiness to protect the frontier against retaliation by the Cherokees. To some, the Cherokee War of 1759-61 was not long over, and many wanted a long-term solution to the continuing risk of Indian attacks. Rutherford deemed the Council's both limited and limiting instructions as insufficient; he wrote back to the Council on July 5. With reference to Virginia and South Carolina and revealing the extent of his formal education, Rutherford wrote that "if the Frunters, of Each of them Provances will joyn me (with your approbetion & Derection) I have no Doubt of a Finel Destruction of the Cherroce Nation."[1] Two days later, the South Carolina Council of Safety, as if reading Rutherford's mind, suggested to both North Carolina and Virginia a collective campaign against the Cherokees with its Colonel Andrew Williamson advancing against the Lower Towns with 1,100 militiamen. Virginia's troops under Colonel William

Christian would advance against the Overhill Towns. Rutherford was to attack the Middle and Valley Towns. In response to Rutherford's letter, the president of the North Carolina Council of Safety agreed, noting that the backwoods militiamen Rutherford commanded were "as Chosen Rifle-men as any on this Continent … hearty and Determined in the present cause."[2]

The interest in moving immediately against the Cherokee towns may have been encouraged by the fact that 200 volunteer militiamen from Georgia, riding under Colonel Samuel Jack, were already attacking villages in the Lower Valley along the Tugaloo River. They met little resistance as they destroyed several towns and burned the crops. The Cherokees there had escaped in advance of the attack to more remote Cherokee towns. Unfortunately for the Cherokees, those refugees ran to the regions targeted for attack by the forces from South Carolina, North Carolina, and Virginia.

The instructions given to Rutherford by the Council of Safety called for him to take "the most vigorous measures … to put an end to this cruel unjust & wicked Indian war."[3] He was given great latitude in how he was to accomplish this, but he was expected to "act in such a manner as to you in your good sense & judgment may seem best so as effectually to put a stop to the future depredations of those merciless Savages."[4]

Newly elected Virginia Governor Patrick Henry agreed to send 900 militiamen under Colonel William Christian, and he asked that North Carolina supplement that number by adding 300 troops from its ranks. He and others believed that successful attacks in the Lower and Middle Towns would drive the Cherokees into the Overhill Towns where more militiamen would be needed to defeat them. In response,

General Rutherford begrudgingly assigned 300 militiamen from Surry County to ride with the Virginians.[5] The Surry County Militia mustered under Lieutenant Colonel Joseph Williams and Major Joseph Winston.

## Joseph Winston

Joseph Winston was a good choice for a leader. He was experienced in Indian campaigns, having joined at age 17 a punitive expedition against some renegades in 1763. The September campaign was at least coincident with Pontiac's Rebellion if not actually in response to that uprising. Winston rode among a company of 60 rangers from his home in Louisa County, Virginia. The rangers were drawn into an ambuscade on the western frontier near Fort Dinwiddie (about 45 miles west of today's Staunton). Shots from cover along both sides of the trail took their toll. The attackers shot Winston's horse from beneath him and he suffered two wounds himself — in the torso and the thigh. Bleeding and unable to flee, he hid nearby until the Indians (likely Shawnees) gave up their pursuit of survivors. A fellow ranger came back for Winston. Putting the wounded youth on his back, the soldier carried Winston for three days. The two rangers lived solely on wild berries until they reached a frontier cabin

**Joseph Winston is celebrated for his service to North Carolina during and after the American Revolution. A statue and his grave are on the grounds of Guilford Courthouse National Military Park in Greensboro, NC.**

where Winston was taken in and nursed back to health.[6]

Besides his experience pursuing Indians, Winston also understood firsthand the colonists' appetite for western lands. Winston had come to North Carolina only five years prior to Rutherford's current muster of militia, after failing to secure a grant of 10,000 acres for which he petitioned. He was a first cousin to Patrick Henry, the governor who saw westward expansion as the future of Virginia and a means for his own personal wealth as well. As lads growing up, the two boys had often played together as children.[7] Winston was judicious and intelligent as well. He had represented Surry County at the Third Provincial Congress in Hillsborough in 1775. His skills in negotiations and diplomacy would later come into additional play on the frontier, most directly in treating with the Cherokees.

**Desolation**

Though the commanders from each of the three rebel provinces had talked about coordinating their campaigns against the Cherokees, each eventually set out on his own schedule. South Carolina units marched forth in July toward the Cherokee Lower Towns with 1,100 militiamen from South Carolina and Georgia led by about 20 Catawba scouts. Knowing that Dragging Canoe and Alexander Cameron were nearby, Williamson sent ahead a detachment of 300 men. Two hours past midnight on the morning of August 1, Williamson's men stumbled into the camp of the Cherokees and Loyalists. The South Carolinians panicked, but in the cover of the darkness they were able to escape annihilation by the superior enemy forces four times their size. When Captain Andrew Pickens arrived with reinforcements, his men poured in such heavy fire from an adjacent ridge that the Cherokees retreated.[8] Williamson's men advanced into the Cherokee lands, but not without fierce resistance. On August 12, Pickens received everlasting noto-

**Andrew Pickens's men fought valiantly against five times their number of Cherokees at the "Ring Fight" near the site of Tamassee, one of the towns destroyed by the South Carolina militiamen. The Tamassee Town marker is in Oconee County, SC, on Cheohee Valley Road at Tamassee Knob Road.**

riety and later a promotion for his strategic defense and courage shown in the face of an attack by five times his numbers at the skirmish known thereafter as the Ring Fight.[9] By August 14, he reported having spread "Desolation … over all the lower towns." He was credited with (some would say guilty of) attacking and burning Esseneca, Oconee, Tugaloo, Estatoe, Senaca, Tomassee, and Keowee, though some of those towns may have been attacked by Colonel Jack's Georgia militiamen.

Williamson discharged his militiamen to resupply themselves, calling for them to muster at the end of the month at Fort Rutledge, an installation they hurriedly erected over the ruins of Esseneca. When the South Carolina militia marched out on September 13 on its second expedition, the men were joined by Lt. Colonel Thomas Sumter and his command of 300 state riflemen, South Carolina 6th Regiment, who had marched there from Charlestown.[10] The reinforced and resupplied South Carolinians marched northward expecting to rendezvous with General Rutherford's North Carolina force at Nuquassee (Nikwasi).[11]

### Rutherford's Campaign

General Griffith Rutherford departed Salisbury on July 19. From his post there he commanded the militia for western North Carolina, one of the rebel province's six military districts. Though the Continental Congress in Philadelphia had adopted the Declaration of Independence two weeks earlier, word of North Carolina's new status as one of thirteen "Free and Independent States" did not reach the province until July 22. Word arrived first at Halifax and then spread westward at the speed of commerce and express riders. Most likely, Rutherford and his men were oblivious to the new status of their homeland during their campaign against the Cherokees.

Rutherford proceeded west from Salisbury through the Catawba River valley and followed the Island Ford Road. He passed a few miles south of Quaker Meadows and made his way to Davidson's Fort at the base of the Blue Ridge Mountains near where Mill Creek flows into the Catawba River and on Davidson family land. The fort was built by militia in 1776, or perhaps the year before, for the protection of settlers against attacks by Cherokees.[12] Rutherford waited there for militia forces to arrive from throughout the western backcountry of North Carolina. A regiment of militiamen arrived from Rowan County under Joseph McDowell.[13] While Rutherford waited, he selected "a picked force" to ride with him over the Appalachians to menace a party of some 500 Cherokees, who were foraging along the Nolichucky River.[14]

Militiamen responding to the call from Surry County rode under the

**General Griffith Rutherford mustered his militiamen at Davidson's Fort, built at the head of the Catawba River on land of the Davidson family in 1776, not 20 years before the American Revolution as the plaque claims. (The war bonnet headress as shown is also inappropriate for Cherokees.) The fort's presence provided the name for the modern town of Old Fort in McDowell County, NC. The distinctive arrowhead monument is on US Hwy 70 at S. Catawba Ave.**

command of Colonel Martin Armstrong with Benjamin Cleveland serving as captain and William Lenoir as lieutenant.[15] Lenoir kept a detailed diary of the expedition. The Surry County Militia mustered its men in mid-August at Mulberry Fields downstream from the confluence of the Reddies River and the Yadkin River. (Today's Smoot Park in North Wilkesboro sits on land that was once the Mulberry Fields.) There they awaited supplies to arrive from Salem.

The Moravian community of Salem was the center of commerce for the Upper Yadkin River valley and the craftsmen and artisans there were capable of supplying the much-needed fresh meat, flour, salt, corn, and gunpowder for Armstrong's militia although the community had only about 75 adults. Throughout the early Revolution, the peaceable Moravians remained neutral in the conflict between Patriots and Loyalists. As a consequence, their allegiance was often suspected by some, however their actions spoke volumes. When Armstrong asked for a loan to purchase a herd of beeves, Moravian merchant Traugott Bagge provided the sizable sum of £146.[16] On August 6, a printed copy of the American Declaration of Independence was posted at the Salem Tavern. Moreover, the Moravian merchants accepted a depreciating currency as payment for their supplies. By doing so, they willingly lost a little value on every transaction. Still, the neutrality of any person was a concern to the partisan Whigs.

With supplies provided, the Surry County militiamen left the Mulberry Fields on August 17 and proceeded up the Yadkin River on their campaign to join Rutherford.[17] After reaching the head of the Yadkin River, they descended into the Catawba River basin, crossing John's River at McKenny's Ford, passing Quaker Meadows, and crossing the Catawba River at Greenlee's Ford. [18] They camped near Cathey's Fort and then united with Rutherford's force at Davidson's Fort.[19]

By Lenoir's account, Rutherford apparently lived as his men did. "I believe the Genl. himself was without a tent. A few officers and men had something like a wagon cover stretched to shelter them from the rain. … At that time if a gentleman could procure a hunting shirt made of good tow linen and dyed black, with a motto across the breast in large white letters, 'Liberty or Death,' and a pair of stout breeches and leggings of the

**Surry County militiamen, including Benjamin Cleaveland and William Lenoir, camped near Cathey's Fort on their way to rendezvous with General Rutherford. A marker on US Hwy 64 at Brittian Church, seven miles north of Rutherfordton, NC notes the event, although it incorrectly reports the actual date, 1776.**

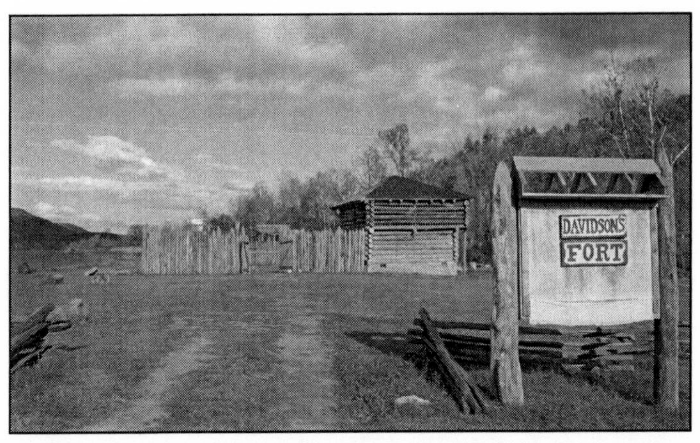


**General Griffith Rutherford mustered his men and gathered provisions in fall 1776 for an expedition against the Cherokees. Visible along I-40, Davidson's Fort Historic Park interprets colonial life on the North Carolina frontier during the American Revolution at its replica fortifcation in Old Fort, McDowell County, NC.**

same texture, and a buck's tail on his wool hat for a cockade, he was fine enough for anything, and in fact, our good Genl's hunting shirt was inferior, it was a dingy colored, ordinary looking one."[20]

Rutherford assembled some 2,500 North Carolina militiamen at Davidson's Fort, at the head of the Catawba River. He had 1,917 privates and 80 light-horsemen. In addition to those, he counted his officers and those who handled the packhorses, which carried the provisions. The supply train for Rutherford's expedition, carrying 40-days of provisions, included 1,400 packhorses and 350 drivers, all overseen by 35 packhorse masters. To help provide for protection at home, Rutherford chose some four hundred men to remain with their captains to protect the frontier. He sent 130 for Tryon County, 175 for Rowan County, and 100 for Surry County.[21]

With forces mustered, General Rutherford's expedition departed

Davidson's Fort on September 1. They headed into a wilderness with no roads and few trails. "We had no government to provide for us," Lenoir wrote later. "We drove some beeves but had no way of carrying any bread stuff, except a few pack horses, along a very bad old Indian path through the mountains, in which horses frequently got mired."[22] The expedition immediately ascended the headwaters of the Catawba River valley and proceeded toward Swannanoa Gap, where they crossed onto the Blue Ridge Plateau and into westward flowing waters. The ascent was difficult and tempers grew short. Lenoir recorded, "Capt. Cleavd. & Capt. [Michael?] Henderson Quarreled."[23] The army of volunteers followed the Swannanoa River for nine miles and on September 3 crossed the French Broad River. Following Hominy Creek upstream, they covered nine miles total that day. Progress was slow. They proceeded generally westward and forded the Pigeon River (near present day Canton) and marched southwesterly to Richland Creek (near present day Waynesville). William Lenoir wrote in his diary that the expedition "marcht in a very Rough way…"[24] Along Richland Creek on September 6, the expedition encountered their first Cherokees. A militiaman spotted five Indians and pursued them with some colleagues, but the militiamen did not overtake the Cherokees. The pursuers "found 1 gun," Lenoir wrote at the time.[25]

**On September 7, 1776, a party of Cherokees ambushed Colonel Francis Lock near Rocky Face Knob. The site is near where US Hwy 23/74 crosses the Blue Ridge Parkway on the Haywood-Jackson county line at Balsam Gap.**

The expedition continued along Richland Creek until they reached Scott Creek, which flowed into the Tuckaseegee River. The men were becoming more eager to encounter the Cherokees. At Scott Creek, the Reverend James Hall, the expedition's chaplain, spied someone running through the woods. It was a black man enslaved by John Scott, a white trader with the Cherokees. Hall mistook the enslaved man for a Cherokee and shot him.

Intending to surprise the Cherokees, Rutherford ordered a thousand men to advance under the command of Colonel Francis Lock. He undertook a forced march across the Tuckaseegee River and down Savannah Creek. Lock hoped to catch the Cherokees living along the Little Tennessee River unaware of his arrival. When Lock's detachment reached the Cowee Mountains on September 7, they were ambushed near Rocky Face Knob[26] by a small party of about 20 Cherokees. Suffering one militiaman wounded, Lock's men pursued the Cherokees but did not overtake them though they covered 20 miles that day. Speaking proudly of the character of the militiamen in this skirmish, the president of the North Carolina Council of Safety later wrote to Virginia's Governor Patrick Henry. He said, "It is but justice to our Troops to observe that when they were fired on, and expected the enemy on every Side, the only contention among them was, who Should be foremost to share the danger and the promised Fight."[27]

On the following day, Sunday, September 8, Lock's party reached the Watauga village where Watauga Creek flows into the Little Tennessee River (at the Porters Bend Dam, three miles north of today's Franklin). [Watauga Creek in southwest North Carolina should not be confused with the Watauga River in today's northeast Tennessee.] Watauga Town was deserted, and Lock remained there to await the arrival of Rutherford's remaining force on September 9. That was the day Rutherford had expected to rendezvous with Colonel Williamson's force advancing from South Carolina, but Williamson had not yet arrived.

On the 10th, Rutherford sent 600 of his men to look for Williamson's army of militiamen. The rest of the North Carolina force moved south, advancing along the Little Tennessee River and searching out Cherokee towns. They found Echoe and Nikwasi (also Nuquassee) within seven miles of Watauga. The militiamen destroyed the corn fields and burned the storehouses holding food supplies. A detachment of about 300 militiamen advanced farther upstream along the Cullasaja River to Sugartown. The men entered the town, which appeared deserted. After they were in the village, the Cherokees opened fire from their secluded positions in brush along the river and within the cover of the forest. The militiamen took shelter in the village inside the Cherokees' cabins, where they were pinned down for three hours. When militia reinforcements arrived after hearing the distant gunfire, the Cherokees retreated without suffering any casualties, but they had killed 18 militiamen and wounded 22 others. Rutherford's men, however, did capture one Cherokee, who upon peril of his life, agreed to lead them to a secluded village where women and children and a herd of cattle were supposedly kept. Rutherford's men advanced up the Cullasaja River with some difficulty. The route was described in one account: "This was 7 miles distant from Nequasee *(sic)* in a narrow valley on the Sugartown [today's Cullasaja] river and surrounded at all points by mountains and was very difficult to approach from the fact that the mountains jutted in abruptly upon the river, in many places scarcely leaving room for a foot path."[28] When the militiamen arrived, they found only a few elderly men and women in the village. Others were seen atop a ridge hundreds of feet above the town look-

**Rutherford's militiamen invaded the abandoned Cherokee town, Cowee, on September 11 and then camped there before burning it. The site is along NC Hwy 28 about eight miles north of Franklin.**

ing down at the men who had just invaded the village. Seeing that the Cherokee men had retreated from the village, the militiamen destroyed the town and what few cattle they found.

Excepting the men who had been sent to look for Colonel Williamson, Rutherford's entire command proceeded down the Little Tennessee River to Cowee, the chief town of the Middle Cherokee. Naturalist William Bartram had visited the village only a few months before and gave this account of the substantial settlement:

> *"I arrived at Cowe about noon. This settlement is esteemed the capital town: it is situated on the bases of the hills on both sides of the river, near to its bank, and here terminates the great vale of Cowe … [where there are] Indian plantations of Corn, which was well cultivated, kept clean of weeds, and well advanced, being near eighteen inches in height … The town of Cowe consists of about one hundred dwellings … the council or town-house is a large rotunda, capable of accommodating several hundred people: it stands at the top of an ancient artificial mount of earth."* [29]

**Rutherford's militiamen occupied Nikwasi, where Reverend Hall violated Cherokee spiritual practices, giving a Christian sermon from atop the Cherokees' sacred mound. The mound, historic marker, and interpretive wayside exhibit are along East Main Street in Franklin, NC.**

Rutherford's men camped at Cowee on Wednesday, September 11. On Thursday, Rutherford sent a small party seven miles downstream along the Little Tennessee River to Allejoy. William Lenoir recorded an account of the encounter: "[We] saw some Indians [and] killed & sculpt 1 Indian Squaw [and] was Fired at by a few Indians who killed Nichl. Peck of Rowan County 2nd Batalion." [30]

Rutherford's men left Cowee after destroying it, and moved back upstream to Nikwasi on the 14th. On Sunday, the 15th, the Reverend Hall violated the Cherokees further, delivering a Christian sermon to the militiamen from atop the sacred Cherokee mound. Afterwards, Rutherford and his militia officers conferred on a plan of action. About half of the troops would go with Rutherford to search out and destroy Cherokees in the Valley region. The remainder would stay at Nikwasi to await the arrival of Colonel Williamson.

On Monday, September 16, Rutherford departed Nikwasi heading west toward the Nantahala Mountains. The terrain was unfamiliar and Rutherford's expedition lost its way. They followed the main branch of the Cartoogechaye River instead of taking the tributary that led to

Wayah Gap. Rutherford thus crossed the ridge, most probably, at Wallace Gap, a place that was not usual. This was fortunate, for the Cherokees had set an ambuscade at Wayah Gap[31], where they expected Rutherford to cross. Thus by dint of luck or fate, Rutherford escaped a certain bruising encounter with the Cherokees. (Willie Jones, president of the North Carolina Council of Safety described it differently to Virginia Governor Patrick Henry, saying "to their great Mortification, [they were] disappointed of an Encounter with about 500 Indians.")[32] Whether lucky or embarrassed, Rutherford pressed on, passing into the Valley Towns by a route farther south than he had intended. By noon on Wednesday, the 17th, the expedition arrived at Nowee, in the headwaters of the Nantahala River. One diary recounts the hardships the men endured during this invasion: the men "marched one mile from Nowee and encamped on the side of a steep mountain, without any fire." Noting the apparent grumbling among the troops, Lenoir scratched through one part of his entry for this day: "men fit to Muternize [mutiny]."[33] On the 18th and proceeding to the southwest, they crossed what Lenoir described as "two very steep Mountains" and they camped at the head of Hiwassee Creek, probably at Shooting Creek. Noting that Colonel Williamson's scouts had finally caught up to Rutherford's expedition, Lenoir added, "Major [Andrew] Pickins *(sic)* Brought Tidings."[34] On the 19th, Rutherford followed Shooting Creek and the Hiwassee River to Quanassee (near today's Hayesville).

Over the next six days, according to Lenoir, Rutherford's men plundered and burned several Valley towns along the Hiwassee River including Hiwassee and Chowa. The militiamen killed several Cherokees and took others as prisoners. They captured horses and cattle and set fire to fields and stores of corn. "We destroyed all their buildings and crops and stocks of every kind that we could find,"

Lenoir later wrote, "and left them in such a state of starvation that they were not able to wage war against us."[35] Rutherford's army of North Carolina militiamen widely menaced the Cherokee villages throughout the Valley area.

On the 18th, the same day Captain Pickens had discovered Rutherford, Colonel Williamson's main body of South Carolina troops reached Nikwasi and set out to find Rutherford in the Valley. When they crossed the Nantahalas at Wayah gap (or possibly arrived at Indian Grave Gap)[36], the place Rutherford had avoided, the South Carolina troops fell into an ambush. From the mountain slopes surrounding the pass, they called the "Black Hole," six hundred Cherokee fired into the South Carolinians below. Arthur Fairie recounted in his journal the fight on Thursday, September 19: "[W]e had gone about 6 miles from camp [at Nikwasi] on the road, we marched into a valley or rather a hollow, named Black Hole, surrounded by mountains on all sides … [T]he Indians … fired on our guard, and all our regiment was soon

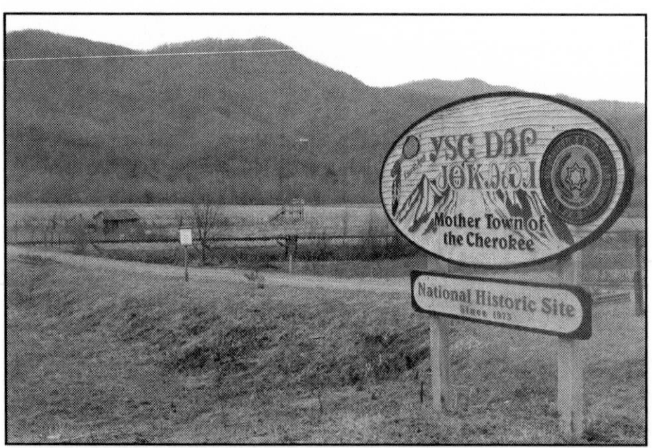


**Kituwah, the Mother Town of the Cherokees, was among those towns destroyed by Rutherford's militiamen. The remnants of the mound is a National Historic Site in the Tuckasegee River valley along US Hwy 19 about 3 miles northeast of Bryson City, NC.**

engaged, & the firing of the Indians was incessant. We continued our fight about one hour, desperate. … Capt. Ross, 41 who was in the front, was shot at and slightly wounded; the Indians thought to have his scalp and made to him and his head being down and bloody the Indians struck him with the gun in his hand, until the force of the strokes broke the butt piece; but the Captain recovering, seized the fellow and overcame him getting his scalp."[37]

In the heated, two hour skirmish, Thomas Sumter placed his riflemen on the mountainside so they could prevent the enemy from circling around behind. Through their perseverance, skill, and courage the South Carolinians prevailed over the Cherokees, who finally gave way as they ran out of ammunition. Williamson's men recovered the gap.[38] Fairie continued his account: "We had to camp here all night on account of burying our dead, & on attending the sick or wounded. A most dreadful sight to behold — our fellow creatures massacred by the heathens, for there were three of our men scalped, and one sadly speared and tomahawked. … [On the 20th, we] continued our march to the Valleys. We started & marched along the greatest of Narrows, where immense numbers of Indian camps. Our road continued up a vast mountain, or rather between two mountains [Wayah Gap?], which led us to the most wildersomest *(sic)* part of the world, allowed by us. … [T]hrough mercy we got safe to the top, allowing it little inferior to the mountain of Ararat."[39]

"The Indians killed 13 or 14 whites," Lenoir wrote later, "who were buried in the swamps and a pole cause-way made, over which we marched as we returned from Hiwassee to the Middle Towns." The militiamen, with 32 wounded among them, pushed on toward the Valley Towns, where they arrived at Hiwassee on the 26th. The South Carolinians were greeted by the North Carolinians with a spirited and hearty salute, Lenoir recorded, "with 13 Swivel Guns." Because Rutherford's men had already destroyed the Valley towns, the two armies briefly considered pushing on through the mountains into the Overhill area, but they decided against it. Williamson departed on the 27th heading for home. Rutherford left Hiwassee on the same day taking for this return the route Williamson had followed through Wayah Gap. Having learned of the ambush there, the North Carolina militiamen were eagerly looking for Cherokees to fight.

Rutherford's army proceeded north and east from Hiwassee. On the 29th, they passed through Wayah Gap where Lenoir recorded sighting evidence of the battle the South Carolinians had fought with the Cherokees: "On Sunday 29th we marched by whare *(sic)* the South army fought the Battle[. S]aw Dead Indians lying and where the [South Carolina troops] buried their dead in a Branch …"[40]

Completing their return march to Nikwasi on the 29th with a march of 15 miles, they rejoined their brigade there and discovered that two men had died during the interim. Having left Davidson's Fort four weeks prior, Rutherford's men were eager to get home; they departed Nikwasi intending to return as quickly as possible. The different companies marched day and night attempting to outdo each other and thus arrived at Davidson's Fort in six days. The hurried march was costly. Lenoir later recalled, "… [while] crossing the Blue Ridge at Swannanoa Gap on rainy day[,] some of our horses were killed by slipping from the path down a steep precipice."[41] The militiamen suffered only a few dozen casualties in actual fighting, but the expedition took its toll on the men in other ways. "The great exposure, hardship, fatigue and privation of this campaign," Lenoir concluded in his later account, "caused a great number of men to die after they returned home. I had a severe trip myself," he added, "but by a divine mercy, aided by a strong constitution, I survived."[42]

In his journal, Lenoir recounted the specific experience of the Surry County Militia returning north on their way to the Yadkin River valley. "On Friday [October] 4th we … Campt. just below Cathey's fort and Colo. Armstrong treated with 6 gals Brandy. On Saty. 5 Capt. Cleavland *(sic)* & Capt. [Jacob] Ferree had very smart quarrel. Capt. Cleaveland & I Treated the men with 2 gallons Brandy & at Cryder's fort he Treated with 7 or 8 Galns. Cyder. … I got home Monday nt. 7 Oct. 1776."[43]

One official report recounted that Rutherford's expedition "destroyed the greater part of the Valley Towns, killed twelve & took nine Indians, and ma[d]e prisoners [of] Seven White Men, from whom he got four Negroes, a considerable Quantity of Stock & Deer leather, about 100 w[eight] of gunpowder & 2000 of Lead …"[44] Beyond the tangible plunder, the campaign against the Middle and Valley towns devastated the Cherokees. With winter coming, these native residents of the mountain vales were left with no food stores and no crops to harvest. Their villages had been destroyed and they had no shelter.[45] The North Carolina Council of Safety gave their assessment of the expedition in a letter sent to the Virginia governor knowing that Colonel William Christian was soon to be marching toward the Overhill towns:

> "[Our source] Supposes that Many of the Indians lay concealed in the Mountains, that some had gone to the Overhills; but that the greater part had fled South Westward, to Coosawatee River, bordering on the Upper Creeks. Should Your Army meet with any Signal Success against the Overhills, or should they only destroy their Towns & Corn,

> we flatter ourselves that the Southern States will suffer no further Damage this Season from the Savages, as it will employ their whole time to provide Sustenance & Shelter for their Squaws & Children."[46]

### The Expedition Against the Overhills

Following the Indian attacks against the settlers of the Holston River valley, the Provincial Council of Virginia instructed Colonel William Christian to attack the Cherokee in the Overhill region. Referring to his mustering of troops, they declared, "... if these forces shall be judged sufficient for the purpose of severely chastising that cruel and perfidious nation, ... you are to do [so] ... in a manner most likely to put a stop to future insults and ravages and that may redound most to the honor of American arms."[47]

Governor Patrick Henry was confident in assigning to Colonel Christian the task of punishing the Overhill Cherokees; he knew the man well. William Christian had served as a lieutenant colonel under Colonel Henry when he commanded the First Virginia Regiment. Christian had studied law under Henry and had married one of Henry's sisters, Anne. Moreover, when Patrick Henry resigned his command, Christian succeeded to the command of the First Virginia, which was placed under Brigadier General Andrew Lewis. Christian and Lewis along with Captain William Campbell rode together and engaged ex-royal governor Lord Dunmore at Gwynn's Island to drive him completely from Virginia soil on July 9, 1776. Later that month, Christian resigned his commission in the regular Continental army to serve as a colonel on the frontier in the Virginia militia.

Most certainly, Colonel Christian was up to the challenge of attacking the Overhill Cherokees, and he had adjusted his thinking. In advance

**Lt. Colonel William Russell and Captain Joseph Martin built Fort Patrick Henry on the Holston River. The likely site of that fort (now occupied by Eastman Chemical Co. in Kingsport) was commemorated by a marker along TN Hwy 93 at the Holston River. (See Notes for marker text.)**

of Rutherford's campaign, Christian wrote him on August 18 saying, "I was doubtful that the way from North Carolina to the Valley Towns was so Mountainous and rugged that [the attack] could not be well done that way. But good men can surmount all difficulties, and the Plan [attacking from three provinces] is undoubtedly an excellent one."[48] Christian was expecting to raise an army of men of at least the same spirit and capability as Rutherford had fielded. As he planned his campaign, no doubt, he was thinking about the specific instructions he had received from his brother-in-law. Governor Patrick Henry asked that Christian insist upon the Cherokees "giving up to justice all persons amongst them who had been concerned in bringing on the present war, particularly Stewart [Stuart], Cameron and Gist."[49]

Christian called for a mustering of militia from the frontier of Virginia. He assembled 1,750 men including the 300 North Carolina militiamen from Surry County under the command of Lieutenant Colonel Joseph Williams, First Major Joseph Winston, and Second Major Jesse Walton.[50] They were to gather on September 20 at the Long Island of the Holston, believed, as it was at the time, to be in Virginia. Among the militiamen arriving early were a company of 50 men raised in Pittsylvania County by Joseph Martin. The men elected him their captain.[51]

Lieutenant Colonel William Russell also arrived at Long Island ahead of many. While he was awaiting the arrival of other militia, he used the intervening six weeks to build a fort. His men and Martin's 50 constructed a stockade 300 feet by 300 feet on the north bank of the Holston River opposite the Long Island and near its eastern end. Three sides were enclosed and the steep riverbank provided protection on the fourth side. The structure included bastions in each corner and a storehouse in the middle with quarters for a commander. Russell named it Fort Patrick Henry in honor of the Whig governor of Virginia. (Fort Patrick Henry was not built at the site of Fort Robinson, as some writers have suggested.)

Though many of the men who mustered may have experienced hostile encounters with Indians, Colonel William Russell had suffered a recent and especially grievous loss. Russell's teenage son, Henry, had been murdered in a wilderness camp along with Daniel Boone's eldest son, James, in October 1773. The two youths, both in their 16th years, and their party had been attacked in the Powell Valley near the Great Warrior Path by Shawnee, Cherokee, and Delaware warriors. (See *In the Footsteps of Daniel Boone.*)

As Colonel Christian proceeded down the Holston River valley to the muster site, he found along the way, as many as 3,000 of the region's settlers "forting up" and seeking protection. They had abandoned their farms and homesteads in fear of continued Indian attacks. Christian noted that many were suffering from the ill effects of close confinement together with so many others. Their supplies were running low. He provided what flour he could spare to some of those in

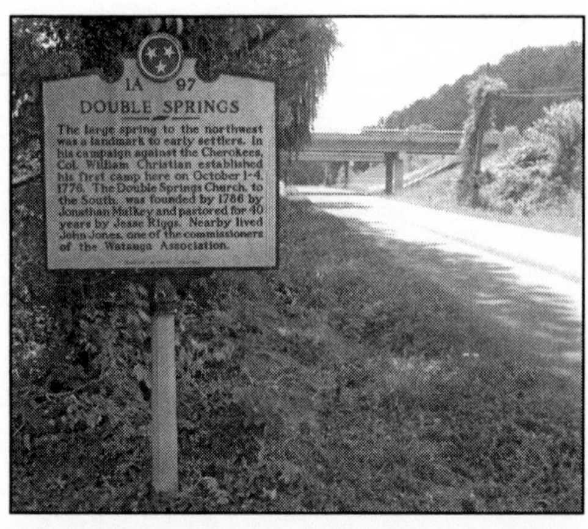


**Colonel William Christian's expedition camped at Double Springs after leaving Fort Patrick Henry. The springs and marker are on Double Springs Road near mile 54.2 on I-81 (seen in background of photo; no exit).**

great need, mostly the wives and widowed mothers of the men who responded to his muster call.

Colonel Christian departed Fort Patrick Henry on or about October 1. Most of the men were on foot and they marched up Horse Creek about six miles the first day ending at Double Springs, a couple of miles east of the base of Chimney Rock Mountain. At this camp, the campaign was joined by others, from the Watauga Settlement under the command of James Robertson and from the Nolichucky River valley under John Sevier. Sevier's reputation as an Indian fighter had earned him the nickname, "Nolichucky Jack." Sevier's men arrived on horseback and provided the campaign its one company of light horse cavalry. Some of the companies mustering at Long Island, those under the command of James Thompson, Daniel Smith, and Gilbert Christian, joined with those from the Watauga Settlement to form a battalion under Major Evan Shelby. Shelby was second in command.

From Double Springs, Colonel Christian sent a report to Governor Henry outlining his plans. He wrote that he was departing with supplies for 30 days and heading toward a crossing of the French Broad River. There he anticipated meeting at the ford a host of Cherokees ready to engage in a fierce fight. He added in his report that he expected to return in five or six weeks.

Christian's expedition pushed south from Double Springs, out of the Holston River watershed, and into the Nolichucky River basin. With his army of 1,800 men, Christian followed an Indian path along Lick Creek. They moved more slowly than they would have liked. Proceeding with such a large army, they had to clear a road sufficient for passage of the supply wagons. In addition, the soft and wet ground along the creek hampered their progress. A mile-long swamp along Lick Creek near its confluence with the Nolichucky River delayed part of the expedition. On the day of that passage, it was near midnight before the packhorses and the herd of beef cattle made their way through that boggy place.

Perhaps becoming somewhat anxious at the slow progress and anticipating a confrontation at the French Broad River, Christian sent ahead 16 men under Valentine Sevier, Jr. to scout the crossing. Probably before they returned with any report, a white trader from the Cherokee towns arrived at Christian's camp under a flag of truce with a message. He explained that 700 to 800 Cherokees were camped on the south side of the crossing. (Another account says the trader reported 3,000 Indians at the crossing.) The trader declared that the Cherokees would most certainly attack Christian's men if they ventured beyond the French Broad River.

The Cherokees, however, were not in such firm agreement on a course of action. The Raven, the Cherokee war chief, championed the idea of appeasing rather than fighting Colonel Christian; the other, older chiefs supported him. Dragging Canoe, manifestly defiant, could not agree to such a move. Encouraged by Alexander Cameron, the deputy British Indian agent, Dragging Canoe suggested the Overhills abandon their towns on the Little Tennessee River and retreat for a firm stand at Hiwassee. Despite his call for armed resistance, the elders carried the argument. They sent forward another white trader from their town to negotiate with Colonel Christian. This messenger was better known to the colonel — Nathaniel Gist.

Meanwhile, Christian received word from his scouts. They told him of evidence spied at the bend in the Nolichucky River (near today's Lowland along the Cocke-Hamblen county line) that large parties of Cherokees had recently encamped there. Christian would not be intimidated, however. He sent the Indian's courier back to the Cherokees with a message that he and his army intended not only to cross the French Broad River but to venture beyond the Little Tennessee as well. On the morning of the next day, Christian's expedition ventured into unfamiliar territory, but he benefitted from following the lead of Isaac Thomas, a trader who knew the area. The men watched out carefully for any ambush along the way as Thomas led them along the Great War Path following Long Creek to its head and then down Dumplin Creek to its confluence with the French Broad River. Near there, the war path shifted a couple of miles east and upstream toward the well-known crossing at Buckingham's Island (Big Island).

Expecting to confront the Cherokees on the south bank of the French Broad River, Christian designed a bit of a ruse to confound the Cherokees. He ordered his men to pitch their tents and to build fires at the north side of the crossing at Buckingham's Island. A couple of hours after sunset, he marched 1,100 of his men some four miles downstream from Buckingham Island to another ford. Sevier's men had discovered this new crossing in their scouting efforts. The plan was to cross the river and in a flanking maneuver before dawn to get behind the Cherokees, who were believed in place on the south bank of the French Broad River.

The river current was swift and the ford not so shallow. The men, including militiaman Robert Campbell, crossed in parties four abreast to brace themselves against the current. At times the water reached above their chests, but they were able to cross while keeping their rifles and powder dry. The night was extremely cold and the men were thoroughly soaked in the crossing, but they could not build fires for fear of revealing their presence to the Cherokees they hoped to surprise. Christian's detachment passed a miserable, restless night on the south bank of the French Broad River. As Lyman Draper recounted militiaman Robert Campbell's experience, they "renew[ed] their march at the dawn of day, with shivering limbs, literally encased in ice."[52]

By first light, Colonel Christian had maneuvered his men behind where he suspected the Cherokees had positioned themselves to attack his force crossing the French Broad River. Meanwhile, another division of 600 men crossed the river at the ford at Buckingham's Island. Captain Joseph Martin led his company of men across first, including two who were ill but who insisted on crossing. Martin stripped to his shirt, put one man across his back, and forded the river. He went back to get the other man and carried him across as well.[53] To the surprise of all after crossing, Christian found no Cherokees waiting to attack.

As the men spent the remainder of that day drying out the equipment, their supplies, and themselves, Nathaniel Gist approached Colonel Christian in camp. Gist brought a message from the Cherokee towns. Gist was a Virginian known to many of the men. Some called him Captain Gist. His father was Christopher Gist, a renowned guide who was the chief scout for Major General Edward Braddock when he was defeated at the Monongahela River on his campaign to capture Fort Duquesne in July 1755. Nathaniel Gist had been on that campaign as well, a lieutenant to his father. The year before, in the winter of 1754-55, the elder Gist had twice saved the life of Major George Washington as well. The Gists, father and son, were friends of Daniel Boone from their time in the Upper Yadkin Valley; Nathaniel Gist and Daniel Boone hunted together in the Blue Ridge Mountains as early as 1760. In 1776, however, Nathaniel Gist was a trader with the Cherokees; he had spent many years living with and among them. By some accounts, in a relationship with the Cherokee woman, Wuh-teh

**Colonel William Christian followed a well-known Indian path through the Tennessee River valley and along Boyd's Creek after fording the French Broad River. This Indian War Trail marker on Boyd's Creek is on US Hwy 441 two miles east of TN Hwy 35 in Sevier County, TN.**

(Wut-teh), of the Paint Clan, Gist fathered a son (born in the early 1770s) who grew up under only his mother's care. The son, though himself illiterate, in a remarkable feat of intellect later created the Cherokee syllabary, the only written American Indian language. The son of Nathaniel Gist (the likely father) and Wuh-teh was the famous Cherokee silversmith, Sequoyah (Sikwayi).[54]

At the camp, Gist told Christian that The Raven had prevailed among the chiefs in arguing for not fighting against Christian's superior numbers. He reported that the Cherokees had camped only four miles south of the river, but had then fallen back to their towns on the Little Tennessee River so they could move their families and supplies to safety. Gist asked Christian to spare the chief village of Chota, though he added that Alexander Cameron had urged the Cherokees to burn their own towns and supplies and to retreat into the villages along the Hiwassee River. Gist added that Cherokees from the Hiwassee villages

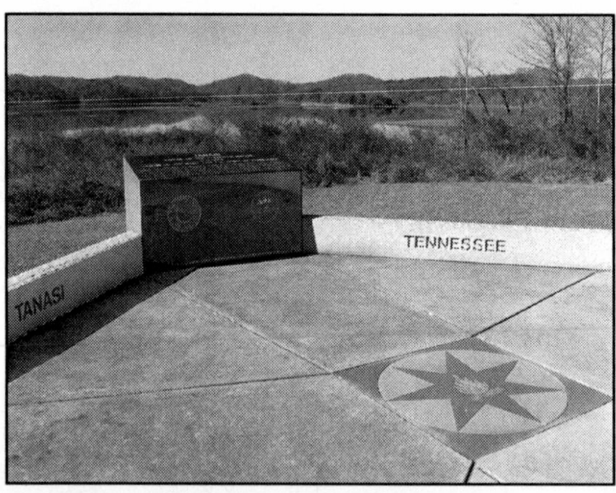


**Christian's expedition marched into the Cherokee towns along the Tanasi River, phonetically spelled by Lt. Henry Timberlake in 1762 as "Tennessee." The town,Tanasi, now submerged beneath Lake Tellico, 300 yards west of this monument, was home in the 1720s to the first elected "Emperor of the Cherokee Nation."**

had already swarmed into the Little Tennessee River towns upon the attacks there by General Rutherford and Colonel Williamson.

Colonel Christian considered what Gist revealed to him. He also considered that his men had mixed feelings about this white trader who lived among the Cherokees. Many wanted to kill him then and there as a friend of the Cherokees, whom they considered hostile; but, some argued in Gist's favor. Those who got to know him over the following days soon found that he had won them over. Gist was popular in Christian's camp. Christian wrote of this matter to Governor Henry, "I believe he is sorry for what he has done. I did intend to put him in irons but the manner of his coming, I believe, will prevent me." Christian noted in conclusion that he was uncertain if Gist wanted to return to the Cherokees. (Gist, in fact, abandoned his wife and child, returned to Virginia, and served during the American Revolution under General George Washington.) Aside from how he intended to deal with Gist, Christian finished his report saying, "I believe I shall push for the island towns and those that bred the war and have thoughts of sparing Chota."[55]

On the next day, Christian's expedition pushed southwest moving upstream along Boyd's Creek. The creek was named for one of two white traders who had been ambushed and killed there the year before. The Cherokee perpetrators threw the bodies into the creek. Many settlers later said this single hostile act was the first of the many that followed and caused the fighting between the Cherokees and the settlers in 1776. Reaching the headwaters of Boyd Creek, Christian crossed the divide and continued down Ellejoy (also Ellijay) Creek to Little River (near today's Maryville, Tennessee) and then south by southwest to the Little Tennessee River where several Cherokee towns sat along the banks.

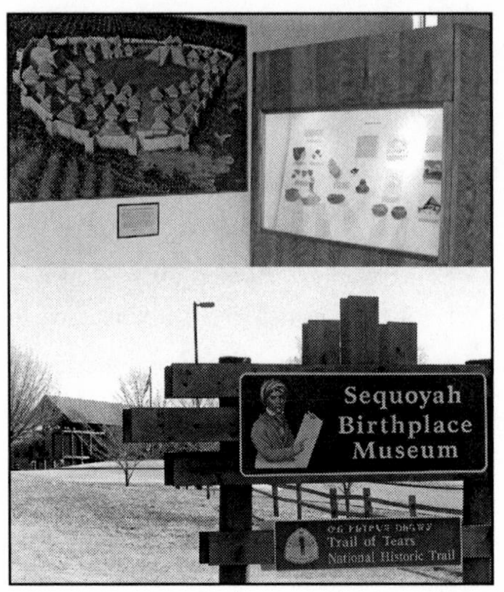


**The Town of Toqua and life in other 18th-century Cherokee villages along the Little Tennessee River are interpreted at the Sequoyah Birthplace Museum on TN Hwy 360 near Vonore in Monroe County, TN.**

Christian probably knew something of what to expect of the Overhill towns. In 1762, Lieutenant Henry Timberlake and Sergeant Thomas Sumter had lived among the Cherokees for three months with Timberlake preparing detailed maps of the Overhill's towns along the Little Tennessee River. As the militiamen entered the river valley following the route Timberlake had labeled on his map "Road to Virginia," they encountered no resistance from the bands of Cherokee warriors rumored to be gathered there. Christian's men arrived first at Toqua Town and then descended downstream to Tommotely where they pitched camp on October 18th. The next day, they moved through Tuskegee to The Great Island Town, Mialoquo (or Amayelegway), where Colonel Christian set up his command post. He discovered there great stores of corn and potatoes left behind by hurriedly departing Cherokees. Many escaping Overhill residents took to canoes and paddled downstream abandoning their livestock as well. The invading militiamen found hogs, horses, cattle, and fowl around the town along with what Colonel Christian later described as 40-50 thousand bushels of corn and 10-15 thousand bushels of potatoes. Other

Cherokees had taken flight overland heading toward Hiwassee (Ayouwasi) or possibly to towns on the lower Hiwassee River.

Colonel Christian sent messengers requesting the Cherokee chiefs to come meet with him. Anticipating that most would come to treat, Christian wrote to Governor Henry explaining his motives and decrying the unnecessary distressing of innocents:

> *"Tomorrow I expect The Raven, Oconostota, The Carpenter* [Attakullakulla] *and many others of the chiefs; and I suppose in three days I can open a treaty or begin to destroy the towns and pursue the Indians towards the Creeks. I know, sir, that I could kill and take hundreds of them and starve hundreds by destroying their corn, but it would be mostly the women and children, as the men could retreat faster than I can follow. And I am convinced that Virginia State would be better pleased to hear that I showed pity to the distressed and spared the suppliants rather than that I should commit one act of barbarity in destroying a whole nation of enemies."*[56]

Christian was not disappointed in his expectation of the Cherokee leaders. The several chiefs arrived ready to negotiate a peace; however, they were unable to deliver the one thing Christian demanded: their turning over to him Dragging Canoe and Alexander Cameron. Each had left the area, the chiefs declared. Dragging Canoe had gathered to the south with Creek allies along Chickamauga Creek. Cameron headed for a union with the Alabama.[57] Moreover, some of the chiefs were guilty of prior offenses against white settlers, it was claimed, and Christian's men demanded justice. The militiamen burned the towns of the accused chiefs, destroying all the provisions that were stored there as well. They burned five towns all together, but they deemed two as essential to destroy. One was the town where the Cherokees had held Lydia, wife of William Bean, after her capture during the attack on Fort Caswell (Watauga Fort) at Sycamore Shoals. The other was the town of Dragging Canoe, where the young, white captive, Samuel Moore, had been killed. In Dragging Canoe's house, the militiamen found seven scalps on display. Outside was the stake around which the warriors had danced while flames consumed young Samuel.

Colonel Christian destroyed the towns as part of the terms for the initial truce. In addition, Christian demanded the release of captured whites and the return of enslaved Negroes and horses taken from the settlers. He also required the chiefs to come to Long Island the following year to negotiate a formal, more binding agreement and to set new boundaries that secured for white settlers the lands on which they lived.

The militiamen left the site of the Overhill towns to return home, but not everyone was pleased with the kinder treatment Christian had afforded the Cherokees. In particular, Colonel Joseph Williams of the Surry County Militia wrote on November 6 to the North Carolina Provincial Congress saying that the expedition had only "burn[ed] five of their towns and patched up a kind of peace."[58] Perhaps disappointed at not exacting greater retribution against the Cherokees, these North Carolina militiamen were among the first to leave for home.

**Captain Moore's Campaign**

After Rutherford's men had returned in early October from their campaign into the Middle and Valley Cherokee Towns, the general thought it strategically advisable to send a small party of militiamen back into the area to harass the Cherokees further. They would as well probably support the efforts of Colonel William Christian, who, Rutherford had learned by this time, was beginning his separate campaign against the Overhill towns. Rutherford ordered Captain William Moore and his light-horsemen and Captain Joseph Hardin with his North Carolina Colonial Light Horse from Tryon County to ride into the area Rutherford had just raided.[59] Mustering their men on October 19, the two companies started back into the Cherokee Nation on October 29 to search and destroy what they might find, anything Rutherford's expedition might have missed.

Finding between the Swannanoa and French Broad rivers evidence of the presence of a small party of Cherokees, the men eagerly pursued the unsuspecting hunters. "After the Moon arose we sent out a Detachment of 13 men," Moore wrote, " … then they Discovered upon the frost, that One Indian had gone Along the Road; they pursued Very Briskly about five miles further and came up with said Indian, Killed and Scalped him."[60]

Moore's men rode onward, learning of the nearby "Town of Too Cowee" (Stecoee[61] or Stekoeh[62]). Realizing their numbers at 97 were too few to surround the scattered village, the two companies rode headlong into the center of the town attempting to catch the inhabitants by surprise. All the Cherokees had fled, however, except two, who were seen trying to escape by jumping into the river. "We pursued to the Bank," Moore recounted later, "& as they were Rising the Bank on the Other Side, we fired upon them and Shot one of them Down & the Other Getting out of reach of our shot, & Making to the Mountain. Some of our men Crossed the river on foot, & pursued, & some went to the ford & crossed on horse, & headed him, Killed & Scalped him with the other."[63]

Moore noted the town had 25 houses, some newly constructed and "one Curious Town house framed & Ready for Covering." Perhaps Cherokee refugees had come to this town seeking a safe haven after

Rutherford's invasion. Noting by the stores they left behind that the Cherokees had abandoned the town hurriedly and only recently, "We took what Corn we stood in need of," Moore recounted, "and what Triffling Plunder was to be got, and then set fire To the Town."[64]

The militiamen continued to seek out Cherokee villages, wherever they might find them. "We marched over a Large Mountain," Moore wrote, "& came upon a Very Beautiful river which we had no Knowledge of."[65] Following signs of Indian camps, the raiders advanced, expecting to discover another Cherokee town. They came upon "two Squaws and a lad" at a creek. Moore's men rode them down in their attempted escape to their camp. The militiamen took all three as prisoners. The three captives led the whites to their camp. Moore's men "found abundance of plunder, of Horses and other Goods ..." Some of the horses had been stolen, it was recognized; the militiamen recovered them and later returned them to "the poor Inhabitants of the frontier."[66]

"That night we lay upon a prodigious Mountain," recalled Moore, "where we had a Severe Shock of an Earthquake, which surprised our men very much."[67] The Cherokee Nation, no doubt, put a different interpretation at that time on the presentment of a rumbling mountain and the shaking earth in the heart of their nation. Ruthless whites had invaded their ancient homelands. The Cherokees might well have believed their world was coming to an end.

The next day the militiamen marched to the Pidgeon River, "Where we Vandued off [auctioned] all Our Plunder." The men and the officers argued about selling the prisoners as slaves. "[T]he Greater part Swore Bloodily that if they were not sold for Slaves upon the spot, they would Kill & Scalp them Immediately," Moore wrote. The officers relented to the violent temper of the men. The Cherokees sold into slavery and all the plunder garnered £1,100 and put the men in the mood for more raiding.[68]

Captains Moore and Hardin completed their expedition by November 17, when Moore reported its outcome to General Rutherford. He noted in closing that he, Colonel [Joseph or Charles?] McDowell and a Captain Davidson would soon interrogate one of the captured, enslaved Cherokee women, promising to advise the general on anything they could learn about the condition of the Cherokees. Moore also added a final statement giving some insight into the difficulty he and Captain Hardin must have encountered in sharing the command. He wrote, "… where there is separate Companys United into one Body, without a head Commander of the whole, I shall never Embark in such an Expedition Hereafter; for where every Officer is a Commander there is no command."[69] (Captain Hardin was a member of the Committee of Safety for Tryon County and served in the North Carolina Provincial Congress at Hillsborough in 1775 and at Halifax in 1776. A monument at his Tennessee cemetery reads "*stern and fearless in discharge of duty.*")[70]

**Avery's Treaty**

The attack of the Cherokees against the Overmountain settlements in the summer of 1776 resulted in a double loss for the Overhill tribes. Not only had the Cherokees failed to prevent further encroachment on their lands by white settlers, who willingly ignored British treaties, but the subsequent invading army of frontier militiamen had viewed up close the lands occupied by the Cherokees. The men who had invaded the Cherokee homeland found the landscape quite promising; they were eager to displace the Cherokees further west and to move into the beautiful and fertile Tennessee River valley west of the

Appalachian Mountains. What they had not taken from the Cherokees with powder, shot, and scalping knives, they prepared to take with pen and paper and with promises they could not keep.

During the months before convening the planned peace treaty, some of the militiamen who mustered for the campaign remained in the area to patrol it. Joseph Martin's men had mustered for six-month's service. Captain Martin and his company garrisoned for the winter and spring of 1777 at the fort at Rye Cove on the Clinch River. Their presence there greatly relieved the concerns of the nearby inhabitants. In April, Martin's company moved to Fort Lee on the Nolichucky River.

As Colonel William Christian had demanded of the Cherokee chiefs at The Great Island Town, they met the following year to negotiate a

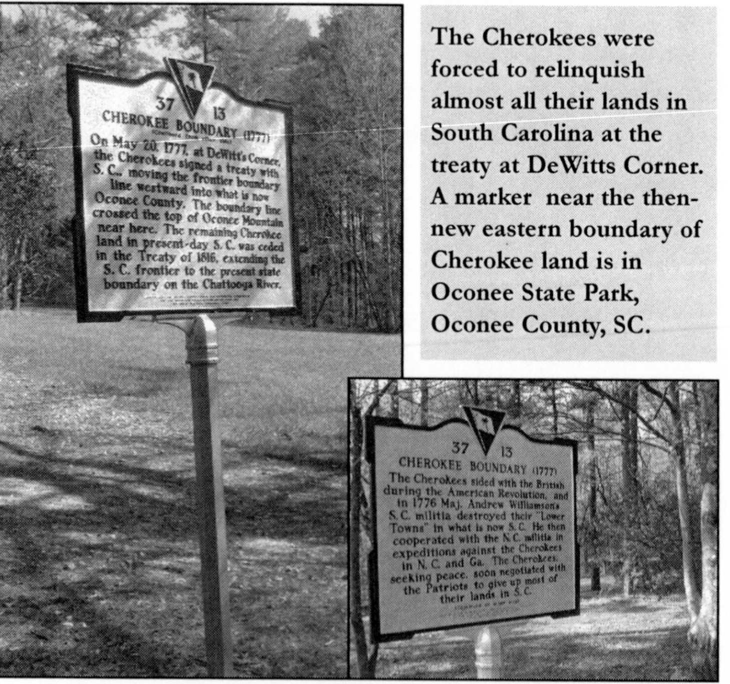


**The Cherokees were forced to relinquish almost all their lands in South Carolina at the treaty at DeWitts Corner. A marker near the then-new eastern boundary of Cherokee land is in Oconee State Park, Oconee County, SC.**

more detailed treaty. On May 20, 1777, South Carolina treated with the Cherokees of the Lower Towns at DeWitts Corner and secured a surrender of all Cherokee lands in that state except for a narrow strip along its western boundary. In July, representatives from Virginia and North Carolina met with the Overhill chiefs at Fort Patrick Henry adjacent to the Long Island of the Holston. In those negotiations and among other considerations, those states secured in the Treaty of the Long Island of the Holston a surrender of all Cherokee lands east of the Blue Ridge Mountains as well as a corridor through the mountains to the Cumberland Gap.

In advance of the summer treaty, Governor Richard Caswell of North Carolina sent two militia companies to the Overmountain area to help protect the settlers who were still being harassed by Dragging Canoe's Chickamauga radicals. Captain Benjamin Cleaveland's company was stationed at Fort Caswell (Carter's Fort or Watauga Fort) at Sycamore Shoals, where he commanded the garrison. Second Major Jesse Walton's company was sent along the Nolichucky River to command Fort Williams, named for Colonel Joseph Williams of Surry County.[71] During this service, Walton became enamored of the "western waters"; he purchased land for a plantation along the Nolichucky River. He later became good friends with John Sevier, visiting at Sevier's home, Mount Pleasant.[72] Just a year and some months later, in January 1779, Jesse Walton introduced a bill at the Assembly in Halifax to authorize the establishing of a new town in Washington County, the first town in North Carolina's trans-Appalachian region. He named it Jonesborough in honor of Willie Jones, prominent promoter of western expansion. The surveyor who laid out the lots for sale was John Gilleland. The first name on the list of purchasers was Robert Sevier.[73]

At the time of the treaty, Cleaveland's company moved to Long Island to patrol and provide protection. Joining in the effort from Virginia was Captain Joseph Martin and the remainder of his company still serving. With his arrival at the site of the treaty, Martin reunited with his good friend Benjamin Cleaveland, his fellow mischief-maker and roustabout from their carefree days together a decade before in Orange County, Virginia.

The different principals began to arrive for the treaty. Nathaniel Gist, promoted to colonel in the Continental Army since Christian's campaign and serving under General George Washington, arrived on June 28 from Chota, escorting a party of Cherokee chiefs. He also brought spurious intelligence claiming that 4,000 British troops had landed at Pensacola and were planning with the Creeks for an attack against Georgia. On June 30, Colonel Christian arrived with Chief Oconostota from Williamsburg. He, along with forty-some other Cherokees, had traveled there to meet with Governor Patrick Henry. Arriving shortly after the party from Williamsburg had arrived, the commissioners for North Carolina reached the fort. The four men appointed on June 12 by Governor Richard Caswell in New Bern to negotiate on behalf of the state were Waightstill Avery, William Sharpe, Robert Lanier, and Major Joseph Winston.[74]

Joseph Winston had served under Colonel Christian in the fall campaign against the Overhills and also as a representative from Surry County at the provincial congresses in Hillsborough in 1775 and in Halifax in 1776. William Sharpe served as an aide to General Rutherford in his expedition against the Cherokees and as a representative at the provincial congresses at New Bern, Hillsborough, and Halifax. Robert Lanier, a brother-in-law to Joseph Winston, represented Surry County in the General Assembly and served as a justice of the peace. He lived at the Shallow Ford on the Yadkin River where he operated a store. Waightstill Avery was a Princeton-educated attorney who helped draft the state constitution at Halifax in November 1776. He had been a delegate to the Hillsborough provincial congress and served as a representative in the General Assembly. Avery had encountered the Cherokees personally once before. In 1776, when the Cherokees came raiding into Burke County, they came down Roaring Creek to the Toe River and crossed into the North Cove settlement. Avery was riding up Roaring Creek when, "hearing the war-hoop behind, [he] spurred his horse and galloped across from the head of the creek to the Watauga settlement on Doe River." He was likely following a route well known as Bright's Trace, a path familiar to those hardy few who crossed the mountains from time to time for business and trade. At the treaty, he learned that the Cherokee warriors had followed him a great distance and had stopped their pursuit only because they thought he was leading them into an ambush.[75] Avery's influence on the treaty at Long Island was so substantial that afterwards it was often called Avery's Treaty.

**Commissioners from Virginia and North Carolina treated with Cherokee chiefs at Long Island of the Holston a year after attacking their villages in the Middle and Overhill Towns. This historic marker on TN Hwy 81 stands on Long Island in Kingsport.**

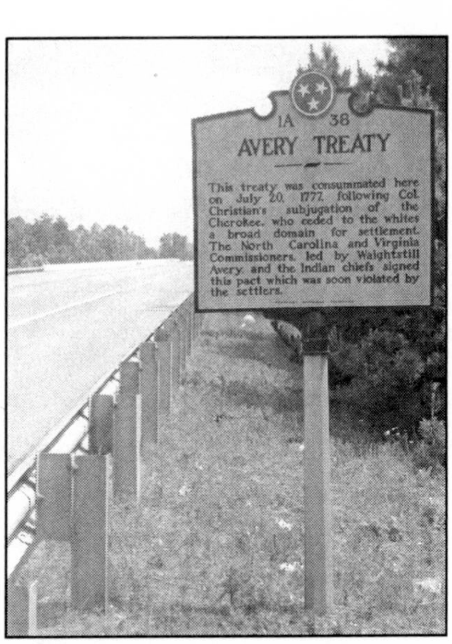

Provisions for all those attending the treaty, including 400 Cherokees, were arranged by captains Isaac Shelby and Thomas Madison. Just that year Virginia's governor, Patrick Henry, had appointed Shelby as commissary for the western garrisons.[76] As Draper wrote, "It was only by his [Shelby's] most indefatigable exertions that the large amount of provisions required [for the garrisons], could be obtained." During the following year, Shelby continued his service as commissary, supplying General Lachlan McIntosh and his Continental Army forces in their failed campaign out of Fort Pitt against Fort Detroit and the British-allied Indians north of the Ohio River.[77]

Shortly after the treaty of peace began, a diplomatic tragedy disrupted it. Not all the local residents were enthralled at the gathering of Cherokees at Long Island, where about 400 had convened to observe and participate in the treaty. On July 2, someone killed one of the Cherokees at "the Great Island," shooting the Cherokee from afar while the Indian sat on the riverbank mending his moccasins. In response, the commissioners posted a notice on the fort's gate offering a reward. It read: "Six Hundred Dollar Reward – Whereas some wicked and evil minded person unknown on the second Instant did in a secret and cowardly manner, feloniously kill and murder a Cherokee Indian, called the Big Bullet, while the said Indian was attending a Treaty of Peace, and by the Law of Nations was entitled to all the protections of a foreign Embassador *(sic)*." Much later, by one account, it was learned that Robert Young, a militiaman serving later under Captain Valentine Sevier, had shot Big Bullet.[78]

During the treaty, the settlers convened at Fort Patrick Henry for a celebration of the first anniversary of Independence Day. The official account of events on July 4 reported, "… the garrison were paraded and fired two rounds, each in six platoons and for the 13th one general volley. The Great Guns were also fired." Captain Benjamin Cleaveland's Surry County Militia were among the celebrants.[79] The commissioners' minutes also noted, "The young warriors then closed the entertainment with a dance." Of this incident, historian Samuel Cole Williams declared, "The redmen … then joined in a celebration of the freedom of the American people from British rule. No counterpart can be found in American history."[80]

By July 11, serious concern about so large a gathering of Cherokees had begun to stir in nearby settlements. Learning of plans among the inhabitants in the Watauga and Nolichucky river valley settlements to harm the Cherokees in some way, Joseph Winston and Waightstill Avery rode out to those communities to help quell the rising alarm. They returned to the fort on July 13 and resumed the treaty on the following day.

**With over 400 Cherokees at the treaty, some settlers became uncomfortable with a large gathering of a people they regarded as a threat. The only recorded hostility was toward the Cherokees, not from them.** **(Cherokee reenactors at Fort Dobbs SHS, NC, 2009)**

Joining the North Carolina commissioners were three men representing Virginia: Colonel William Christian, Colonel William Preston and Major Evan Shelby. (Shelby was absent through much of the negotiation, at home ill; he did not sign the treaty.[81]) During the treaty, Joseph Martin commanded the Virginia troops at Long Island. Afterwards, on November 3, Governor Henry appointed him to serve at Long Island as the Indian agent and superintendent to the Cherokees on behalf of Virginia.[82] Martin served in that capacity for many years and, as was the custom to bind the two nations, in 1778 he took a Cherokee wife. She was Betsy Ward, the daughter of Nancy Ward, the Beloved Woman of the Cherokee. Elizabeth was 21 and Martin was about age 38. Martin already had a wife in Pittsylvania County, Virginia. Each wife knew of the other, and his first wife, Sarah Lucas, was reportedly understanding of the circumstances and graciously welcomed Betsy into her home on occasion. (After Sarah's early death, Martin later married Susannah Graves, the mother of many of his children. Other accounts include speculation about Martin's possible marriage to two other Cherokee women, the Emory sisters, after Betsy moved to South Carolina to care for her aging mother, Nancy Ward.)

The Cherokees attending the Treaty of Long Island included Oconostota and The Raven from Chota, Attakullakulla and Old Tassel (Corntassel) from Toqua (also Toquse). Pot Clay and Abram came from Chilhowee; Mankiller came from Hiwassee (also Highwasaw). Many other chiefs represented their towns as well, but Dragging Canoe did not attend. He did however return a "talk" in response to one offered him from Colonel Gist. As shared by Gist, but recorded by the commissioners, it proclaimed in part: "I have heard your talk and hold them fast as long as I live, for they have opened my Eyes and made me see clear, that Cameron and Stewart [Stuart] have been telling me lies, when we had any talks with the Virginians he was

**The Cherokee chiefs attending the peace treaty were leaders of their respective villages. They agreed to the treaty terms in the hope of stopping the slaughter of their tribes and clans, and satisfying the settlers' desire for more land.**
**(Reenactor at Fort Dobbs SHS, 2006)**

always mad with us, and told us that all that the Virginians wanted was to get our land and kill us …" It is not surprising, perhaps, that the commissioners recorded in their accounts to be read by state officials a statement of contrition completely out of character with Dragging Canoe's sentiments. Dragging Canoe's anger could not likely be so easily assuaged. Moreover, the prevailing belief among the rebel Whigs persisted that Stuart and Cameron, acting as British Indian agents fulfilling British policy, had incited the Cherokees to attack the Overmountain settlements. More likely, Cameron was a renegade agent, acting independently in inciting Dragging Canoe against the Whig rebel settlers.

After a week of talks, the parties signed the final articles of the treaty on July 20, 1777. The Cherokees relinquished their claims to extensive tracts of land east of the Appalachians and land west in the Watauga, Holston, and Nolichucky river valleys. In a closing address, the commissioners from Virginia and North Carolina declared "… we have been here several days delivering good talks to each other. We have brightened the chain of friendship that had contracted some rust; and the beloved man of Chote and our Governors have taken fast hold of it. We have washed the blood out of the path from Chote to this place. … We have established a boundary between the Overhill country and the two Countries of Virginia & North Carolina. A boundary so strong that it cannot be broken down, and so high that our Enemies cannot get over it."

Before signing, Old Tassel offered, "We will not dispose of this Island [Long Island of the Holston] but we reserve it to hold our Great Talks on. Even the grass is for our creatures and the wood to kindle our beloved fire with. People may settle around it, but not on it." He also shared his apprehensions saying, "… ever since I signed a paper for Col. Henderson [the Transylvania Purchase, 1775], I am afraid of signing papers. He told me many lies and deceived us."

Hoping to preserve the right spirit for the treaty, Waightstill Avery spoke in conclusion: "We have now Kindled the beloved fire, smoked the pipe of Peace and joined the hand of friendship which is much augmented by our Brothers of Virginia. We have now made a firm and as we hope a lasting peace that will tend to the prosperity and happiness of both Nations."

While Avery and the other commissioners were making peace, four dozen Wataugans marched off with Captain William Bailey Smith to reinforce the settlers in Kentucky at Fort Boonesborough. That settlement had been under attack through the summer of 1777. Some of the militiamen who went had fought at Point Pleasant. The woodsman skills of the Overmountian men were soon enough tested in Virginia's Kentucky County. (See *In the Footsteps of Daniel Boone.*)

As was the practice of the day, each party in a treaty often provided

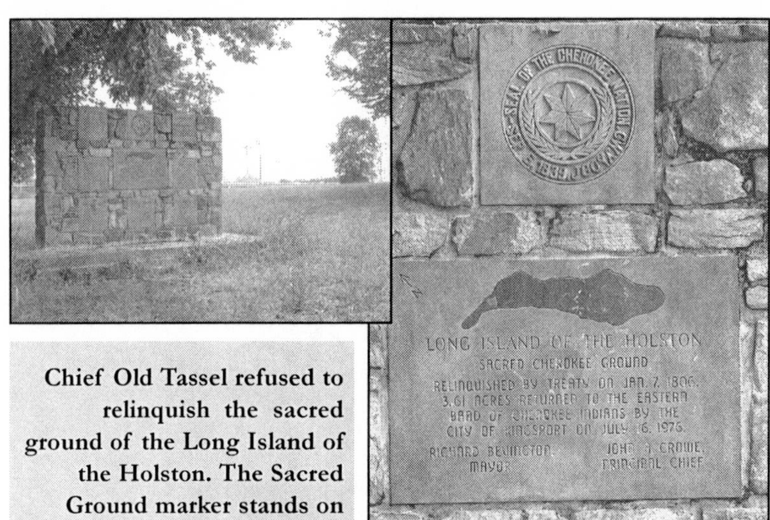


**Chief Old Tassel refused to relinquish the sacred ground of the Long Island of the Holston. The Sacred Ground marker stands on the north end of the island on land returned to the Cherokees in 1976.**

"hostages" for the other to hold in good faith that the provisions of the treaty would be upheld. North Carolina accepted five Cherokees, who volunteered for passage to Rowan County to see three of their captured friends being held. The commissioners issued a letter for their safe passage, first to Quaker Meadows and the home of Colonel Charles McDowell and then on to the home of Commissioner William Sharpe. At the request of Old Tassel for an agent to live with them, Captain James Robertson was appointed to live at Chote as agent on behalf of North Carolina. At the conclusion of the Treaty of the Long Island of the Holston, the Overhill Cherokees received an escort from Fort Patrick Henry part of the way back to their villages on the Little Tennessee River. While the Overhills made their return trip south, Colonel Nathaniel Gist led seventeen Cherokee warriors north to join General George Washington as scouts.[83] These Cherokee scouts were led by Wooe, The Pidgeon, one of the Cherokees who had gone to London in 1761 with Henry Timberlake and Thomas Sumter to meet "the King, my father."[84]

**Attakullakulla (called Little Carpenter) was the Peace Chief (civil leader) of the Cherokees during the invasion of their homelands by white colonial settlers. His son, Tsi'yu-gunsini (called Dragging Canoe), led a renegade faction, called Chickamaugas, in resisting the taking of Cherokee lands. First-person historic interpreter Ron Rambo portrays Attakullakulla throughout the country, shown here at Fort Dobbs State Historic Site, Statesville, NC, 2010.**

# The Chickamauga Campaign

**Renegades and Trespassers**

Replacing a temporary agent, James Robertson served as the Indian liaison in Chota following the Treaty of Long Island of the Holston. In October 1777, he reported in a letter destined for the North Carolina General Assembly that the Overhill Cherokee seemed to be living agreeably with the terms of the latest treaty. He noted, however, that the opportunity for "a lasting peace with them at Chuckemogo [Chickamauga]" did not exist. He added that British sympathizers were stirring up the Chickamauga against the white settlers, all assumed to be Patriots, and that Alexander Cameron was soon expected to arrive. "Cameron may have me taken prisoner," Robertson added, "and any white people he knows to be friends to the American cause." In light of that threat, the white traders left the Cherokee towns.[1]

Indeed, Dragging Canoe and his renegade Cherokee had retreated south to villages along Chickamauga Creek. (It runs from the mountains of today's Walker County, Georgia, into the eastern part of Chattanooga, Tennessee, joining the Tennessee River three miles downstream of Chickamauga Dam. Some believe one village was at the site of an ancient Creek village, Chukko-mah-ko, "meaning dwelling place of the chief."[2]) From these numerous villages, they initiated attacks and raids against outlying settlers beginning soon after the initial truce was called. It was during this time and under one such raid that David Crockett and his wife (name unknown), grandparents to the later-famous frontiersman and Tennessee Congressman, were killed at their homestead near today's Rogersville, Tennessee. John Crockett, later the father of the famous Congressman, was away from the home at the time patrolling the area against just such attacks; but, two of his brothers, Joseph and James, were at home. Joseph suffered a broken arm from a musket ball fired by the Cherokee. James, deaf and mute since birth, was captured by the Cherokee and held for nearly 18 years before his freedom was purchased. (See *In the Footsteps of Davy Crockett.*)

During the months following the Treaty of Long Island of the Holston with the Overhill Cherokee, the character of the Overmountain settlements began to change. A land office was opened in the newly created Washington County, North Carolina, and new residents began arriving in the area. Many came from Virginia, continuing south through the Shenandoah Valley and west from the James River. Others simply moved down the Upper Holston Valley of southwest Virginia, leap-frogging those who had arrived just before them. The land available for settlement was beautiful, fertile, and affordable. Many of those who came were poor but they were seeking opportunity and willing to work hard to build their future in the land so recently conceded by the Cherokees. As were many of those already in the Overmountain region, the new arrivals were second- and third-generation immigrant families of German and Scots-Irish heritage; but, settlers of English, Irish, and French Huguenot stock were among the residents, too. The vast majority were yeomen farmers arriving without wealth or slaves. As in any community, some benefited from having more education than others, but a working knowledge of the forest and the skills of a frontier settler served most well enough.[3]

Some of the new settlers pushed southward beyond the Watauga and Nolichucky river valleys and appeared to be trespassing on lands beyond the 1777 treaty line. Although the numbers were small and the incursions slight in fact (by some accounts, not reaching below today's Greeneville, Tennessee, by 1778), the reports were exaggerated. The North Carolina governor acknowledged having received from the Overhill Cherokees complaints of such trespassing and requests for his intervention. The North Carolina governor also received pleas from Virginia's governor, who was concerned that such incursions might spark renewed hostilities on the western frontier.

Concern for the continued encroachment of white settlers on western lands was not limited to the Cherokee. During the second half of 1777, Lieutenant Governor Henry Hamilton of the British Province of Quebec was making plans to support a pan-Indian attack against the encroaching white settlers in Pennsylvania and Virginia. From Fort Detroit, he served as the Superintendent of Indian Affairs. His plan was to ally with the Indians of the Northwest and support them with British advisors and with warriors of the Cherokees and Chickasaws. Together they would attack white settlers who had crossed the mountains. He did not need to kill the settlers to achieve his goal. As part of the overall British strategy against the Patriots, his intention was "destroying the crops and habitations of all advanced settlers and driving them back upon their brethren of the Atlantic States, whom they would greatly distress by an additional consumption of goods and provisions."[4] He enlisted the help of John Stuart, Superintendent of the Indians for the Southern Department. Stuart revealed his preparedness in a letter to British General William Howe: "The Cherokee [meaning the Chickamauga] were perfectly well affected, and notwithstanding the severe chastisement they lately received, are ready to act when called upon. … They will be immediately followed home by Mr. Cameron who will hold them prepared for any service which may be required of them. I have lately received assurances from those who live near and pretend to be in friendship with the rebels [meaning Tories and Loyalists] that they wish for an opportunity of acting which they will embrace whenever it offers."[5]

**Outrageous Murder and Revenge**

In Pensacola, Alexander Cameron had organized a troop of mounted rangers called the Loyal Refugees (also East Florida Rangers). These were Loyalist traders who had left the frontier in the face of the rebel aggression. By March 1778, he stood ready with these white troops to lead war parties of Chickamauga, Creeks, and Chickasaws in support of Hamilton's plan. Meanwhile, Cameron continued to menace the Southern frontiers.[6] Lt. Governor Hamilton, however, was not successful in enlisting the support of all Indian nations. In particular, Cornstalk, the Shawnee chief punished by Colonel Andrew Lewis at Point Pleasant in 1774, professed his and his tribe's neutrality. Other Shawnee chiefs, including Blue Jacket, however, joined in the uprising. Seeing his fellow chiefs persuaded to attack the whites, Cornstalk changed his mind. To retain his honor in that circumstance, Cornstalk felt compelled to advise the soldiers of his decision. Cornstalk and his two advisors approached Fort Randolph at Point Pleasant in October 1777, under a flag of truce. They were not graciously received; the fort's commander, Captain Mathew Arbuckle, detained Cornstalk in a guarded room. Soon, Cornstalk's son, Elinipsico, also a veteran of the Point Pleasant battle, came to the fort seeking his father. Arbuckle detained the son with the others.

On November 8, word reached the fort that a party of Shawnee had killed and scalped a soldier, Ensign Robert Gilmore, while he was across the river — without permission — and hunting deer. Outraged at the sight of the soldier's bloodied and scalped corpse as others brought it back across the river, a mob of soldiers formed with Gilmore's captain, a relative, at their head. "Let us kill the Indians in the fort!" they shouted. Mathew Arbuckle, the fort's commander, tried to stop them, insisting that the Indians he was holding were innocent of the soldier's murder. Incensed with anger, the soldiers cocked their rifles and threatened to kill Arbuckle if tried to stop them. The soldiers rushed to the fort and slaughtered the defenseless Cornstalk, his son Elinipsico, Red Hawk and Old Yie (some accounts say Patella). Accounts of the killing differ. Most say Cornstalk stood quietly in the doorway, resigned to his fate, as the mob rushed toward the stoic Shawnee. The soldiers probably fired a fusillade into the room where the captives were held, killing Cornstalk and two others instantly. One account says the fourth captive was hacked to death with knives and perhaps tomahawks as he attempted to climb into the chimney for refuge. Cornstalk had been prescient about his death, it seemed. He

**Chief Cornstalk and his son were among those Shawnee leaders massacred by irate soldiers while the chiefs were held prisoners at Fort Randolph. A monument at Tu-Endie-Wei State Park in Point Pleasant, West Virginia, overlooks the Ohio River and marks the spot of Cornstalk's burial.**

had met with the fort's officers that day in council and offered his honest sentiments. "When I was a young man and went to war," he said, "I thought that might be the last time and I would return no more. Now I am here among you; you may kill me if you please; I can die but once; and it is all one to me, now or another time."[7]

After hearing of the treacherous murder of their leaders, the Shawnee were similarly outraged. With more resolve than ever, they sought to support the British-planned attacks against the frontier settlers encroaching on Indian lands.

Reporting to his superiors the preparedness of his plan, in December 1777, Hamilton wrote that "belts have gone from the Cherokee [meaning the Chickamauga] and Chickasaws to the Shawnees and Delawares, requesting them to forget former quarrels and unite against western settlers; and that parties of the Cherokees [Chickamaugas] and Chickasaws were being assembled at the mouth of the Tennessee."

General movements by allied Indians against white settlers began early in 1778. On February 8, in the Kentucky settlements, a party of Shawnee captured Daniel Boone along with 27 other men at the Lower Blue Licks where the party had been out for a month making salt. They were taken to Chillicothe (today's Oldtown, Ohio), the village of Shawnee Chief Blackfish. As a prisoner, Boone walked to Fort Detroit where he was interrogated by Lieutenant Governor Henry Hamilton before returning to live as the adopted son of Blackfish, but still a prisoner, for over four months. He escaped the village in mid-June, covering on foot 160 miles in four days, to warn the settlers at Booneborough of an impending attack. The famous nine-day siege of the fort began in early September with Chief Blackfish and 400

Shawnee warriors supported by British advisors. (See *In the Footsteps of Daniel Boone.*)

**Illinois Country**

As Indian aggression against western settlers was increasing, the young Virginia militia leader, George Rogers Clark, understood that the safety of Kentucky depended on securing control of the Illinois country. This region was protected by British soldiers at Fort Detroit, Fort Sackville, and at the outposts of Kaskaskia and Cahokia on the Mississippi River.[8] Early in 1778, Virginia Governor Patrick Henry took initiative with a military campaign in the West against British interests. He conferred with Colonel George Rogers Clark and sent him on a mission to invade the Illinois country and to capture the cannons at the British outpost, Kaskaskia. Governor Henry wanted these cannon moved to a fort planned at the mouth of the Ohio River to protect Virginia's claim to the vast Ohio River valley. Indeed, Governor Henry's interest in the far west territory included his potential for personal gain. In a business venture, he stood in place of his father-in-law, John Shelton, regarding vague grants issued in 1749 for lands reaching along the Ohio River to the Mississippi River.

Colonel Clark wanted seven companies of 50 men each for his expedition to Kaskaskia. Most of the recruits were mustered from Kentucky County, formed in December 1776 from Fincastle County; however, Clark expected that some of the desired number of recruits would be raised from the Holston and Watauga region. Indeed, Captain William Bailey Smith had been successful in recruiting men from that region in the prior summer to go to the aid and reinforcement against Indian attacks on the new settlements in Kentucky. In 1778, he repeated his recruiting success, raising perhaps 100 men who marched off to Kentucky. Because of the secrecy around Clark's mission, the recruits were never told about their true destination, Kaskaskia. However, due to long delays in getting the Holston and Watauga men marching toward Kentucky, when they did arrive, Clark's men had already departed taking two extra companies from the area. Though about twenty men from the Holston and Watauga rivers region did join up with Clark's force for the expedition, the others remained in Kentucky to help defend the settlements there.

William Bailey Smith was no stranger to the Kentucky region and he knew the Wataugans well. He moved to North Carolina from Virginia. He was present and signed the Treaty of Sycamore Shoals securing the Transylvania Purchase in the spring of 1775. He accompanied Richard Henderson into Kentucky a few days behind Daniel Boone's advance party. The following summer, 1776, Smith was one of the men who helped rescue the Boone and Callaway girls who were kidnapped from Fort Boonesborough on July 14. After returning to North Carolina to recruit militiamen for service in the West, he later played a key role in the 1778 Siege of Fort Boonesborough laid by the British-allied Shawnee under Blackfish. (See *In the Footsteps of Daniel Boone.*)

**The Rogues at Chuckemogo**

As Colonel George Rogers Clark was advancing Virginia's interests in the Illinois country, Joseph Martin, Virginia's agent to the Overhill Cherokee, was reporting a growing menace among the renegade Chickamaugas. Martin had traveled to Williamsburg to deliver his report directly to Governor Patrick Henry. He warned that the Chickamaugas were planning an all-out attack on the white settlements in spring 1779. He reported the Chickamaugas had traveled to Pensacola with 300 pack horses to receive war supplies from British agents there. He added with emphasis, however, that the chiefs of the Overhills wanted to see the Chickamaugas disciplined. This was related by Governor Henry to North Carolina's Governor Richard Caswell in a letter saying "[Martin] observed that the leading men of the Overhill are much exasperated at the conduct of the seceders who perpetually embroiled their public councils and, by repeated violence, instigated by British emissaries, tried to involve the nation at large in the suspicion of hostility and consequent war …" Martin went on to say that despite efforts of the chiefs, some Cherokees from the old towns had joined the Chickamaugas. "Those of the men who may be slain will fall unlamented by their country," Henry interpreted to Caswell of the Overhill chiefs' regard for the renegades and those joining their ranks. James Robertson similarly reported on the attitude of the Overhill chiefs that the Overmountain settlers would be justified in "warring against the rogues at Chuckemogo."

In January 1779, Governor Patrick Henry ordered an attack on the Chickamauga towns. He asked Colonel Evan Shelby to organize 300 men to "totally destroy that and every settlement near it which the offending Indians occupy." Henry wrote to Governor Caswell and asked that he provide an additional 200 men. The North Carolina general assembly assented on January 21 and asked that the men be "furnished from the militia of Washington County, formed by voluntary enlistments if they can be so procured." Major Charles Robertson, then representing Washington County in the senate, took command as lieutenant colonel, reporting to Colonel Shelby. Though the men who volunteered were eager to engage the Chickamaugas, the general assembly asked specifically that women and children of the enemy be treated kindly. They also insisted that the Cherokee chiefs who were living in agreement with the treaty, be told of the raid in advance.

April 1 was the agreed date for mustering the Virginia and North Carolina militiamen.[9] Though they may have gathered first at Long

Island, they did meet at the home of James Robertson, the Indian agent, at Big Creek on the Holston River. (The exact location is unknown, but the creek merges with the Holston River just east of today's Rogersville in Hawkins County, Tennessee. Moreover, James Robertson was not involved in this mustering. He departed that spring on his expedition to establish Nashborough on the Cumberland River, i.e., today's Nashville, Tennessee.) The captains under Colonel Evan Shelby were James Shelby, Aaron Lewis, and Gilbert Christian. Robertson's captains were believed to be William Bean, Thomas Vincent, George Russell, and Robert Sevier. (Because the North Carolinians were volunteers, no muster role was made.) Continuing his service as Commissary to the western garrisons, Captain Isaac Shelby provided the supplies for his father's expedition. He was also elected to represent Washington County in the Virginia legislature. [10] All of Colonel Evan Shelby's sons went on this expedition against the Chickamaugas.

The effort against the Chickamauga was actually more than it first appeared. The campaign was to serve two purposes and only the first served the interests of the Overmountain settlers. The second was in support of Governor Henry's grander scheme for controlling the West. The combined force was, of course, to eradicate the threat of Dragging Canoe and his renegade Chickamaugas. After completing that task, the "twelve-months men" under command of Virginia's Captain John Montgomery were to continue down the Tennessee River to reinforce Colonel George Rogers Clark in the Illinois country.[11] They would welcome any other volunteers who would join them after defeating the Chickamaugas.

The expedition was planned so the men would arrive by water. Gov. Henry's orders to Montgomery said, "You will cause the proper vessels for transporting the troops down the Cherokee [Tennessee] River to be built and ready. Let no time be lost in doing that. Captain Isaac Shelby, it is desired, may prepare the boats. But if he can't do it you must get some other person …"

Though Virginia supplied funds for the construction of the boats, it provided no money for supplying the troops. As Commissary, Captain Isaac Shelby provisioned the expedition under his own good credit. Some of the larger boats, it is believed, were built at Long Island of the Holston, but the others were built at Big Creek. After the men arrived, even more boats were constructed, some from tall poplar trees, which they felled and shaped with axes and other hand tools into long canoes and pirogues.

The flotilla launched on April 10 and the men proceeded down the Holston River to the Tennessee River. (Today's Tennessee River above the Little Tennessee River was then called the Holston River.) Upon reaching that confluence, Colonel Shelby sent the pilot, John Hutson (Hudson), up the river to Chota with a letter advising Indian agent Joseph Martin, who was there at the time, to evacuate to the Long Island. Unfortunately, Hutson drowned in a mishap while completing the mission.

Colonel Evan Shelby continued his course downriver. His pace of advance was aided greatly by the increased currents resulting from spring rains. After but a few days, in mid-April, they reached (South) Chickamauga Creek. Turning upstream just before dawn, they captured an Indian who was asleep near his fish-traps. Shelby forced him to guide the invading militiamen to the main village. Shelby's 350 men and Montgomery's 150 waded with stealth through a flooded cane brake to reach the village, which stretched along the river about one

**The renegade Cherokees, calling themselves Chickamaugas, moved south along the Tennessee River to sites from where they continued to attack settlers, whom they saw as trespassers. A statue of a Cherokee fisherman, located at the Tennessee State Aquarium in Chattanooga, gazes toward the Tennessee River and Ross's Landing.**

mile. Many of the warriors were away. In May, Cameron had been ordered "to assemble a large party of Cherokee to attack the frontiers of Georgia or South Carolina, and join the King's troops there." Cameron's band of Chickamaugas was in Georgia, possibly in the Creek Nation, when the Overmountain men attacked.[12] The unexpected invasion by a water route stunned the some 500 Chickamauga villagers, who offered no resistance. The Chickamaugas abandoned the towns and escaped into the mountains.

The militiamen burned the town as a smaller party chased some of the Chickamaugas who had crossed the river. The pursuing militiamen found a camp along Laurel Creek and scattered the Indians who were there. Other parties of militiamen discovered and burned other outlying towns, including the village of Little Owl. All together, the invaders destroyed 11 towns. They also confiscated 150 horses and 100 cattle. They took, most probably at today's Ross's Landing, a large cache of deerskins and pelts, much of which was owned by one of the traders John McDonald. (McDonald was the grandfather of the later

Cherokee Chief, John Ross, who reluctantly presided over the forced removal of the Cherokees in 1838.) All these items were sold among the militiamen in an auction held on the return trip at a place whose name commemorates the event, Sale Creek. The confiscated animals and goods were valued at 25,000 British pounds. Shelby noted in his report that "20,000 bushels of corn" also had been captured. These were provisions, it was assumed, for the expedition the Chickamaugas were planning to rendezvous with British Lt. Governor Hamilton at the mouth of the Tennessee River.

Having completed its objective of destroying the Chickamauga towns, the militia force divided. Captain John Montgomery continued down the Tennessee River with his men to support Colonel George Rogers Clark in holding the Illinois country. Volunteering to join Montgomery on his expedition down the Tennessee River were Captain James Shelby and about 16 men from his company of Overmountain Men. Unknown to them at the time, Colonel Clark was

**Crawfish Springs in Chickamauga (Walker County), Georgia is in the headwaters of Chickamauga Creek. Chief Crayfish lived here. It may have been a refuge for Chickamaugas escaping Shelby's 1779 attack. The springs and park are on GA Hwy 341 in the heart of Chickamauga, across from the Gordon Lee Mansion.**

**Evan Shelby and his returning militiamen auctioned off the spoils of their raid on the villages of the Chickamaugas. The site of the auction is in the town named for the event, Sale Creek, Tennessee, on US Hwy 27 in Hamilton County between Soddy-Daisy and Dayton.**

having some success against the British in the Illinois country. He had captured Kaskasia and Cahokia. In late February, Clark had captured Fort Sackville at Vincennes and had taken Lt. Governor Henry Hamilton prisoner. With the capture of Hamilton, Alexander Cameron abandoned the plans for a pan-Indian attack along the trans-Appalachian frontier. [13]

**Whetted Appetites**

Colonel Evan Shelby's band of Overmountain men turned toward home. They crossed the Tennessee River to the west side and sank the boats to prevent their use by the Chickamauga. The men started the trek homeward with many delighted to be riding on horseback for the return trip. In fact, the best steed was held out for Colonel Shelby. The receipt for the six-year-old black horse secured at the Sale Creek auction was dated April 27 suggesting the date near the men's departure for home.

The returning militiamen proceeded up the Tennessee River valley northeastward to Post Oak Springs near today's Rockwood, Tennessee. They crossed the Emory and Clinch rivers near there and later crossed the Holston (today's Tennessee) River above the confluence of the French Broad River. By following this route, many of these men of the Holston, Watauga, and Nolichucky river valleys first viewed the vast expanses of rich and fertile land of the Tennessee Valley. Their experience of this new country, especially as viewed in the spring, whetted their appetites for moving farther west from their current homesteads.

With the suppression of the Chickamaugas, at least for the time being, the Overmountain settlers had made the valleys of the Holston River inviting to more settlers. Jesse Walton had moved to the Nolichucky River valley in 1777 where he became friends with John Sevier. In 1778, Walton served on the Washington County commission to locate a courthouse and jail. In 1779, representing Washington County in the North Carolina Assembly, he introduced a bill to form Jonesborough, the first town of white settlers west of the Appalachians. It was founded in May 1779 and named for Willie Jones, a prominent advocate of North Carolina's westward expansion.

**Isaac Shelby**

Following the Chickamauga Campaign and after his election to serve in the Virginia legislature, Isaac Shelby was promoted to major. In that capacity he commanded the escort of guards to protect the party commissioned by Governor Thomas Jefferson to extend westward the boundary line between North Carolina and Virginia. As it passed through the Holston River valley, Shelby and many other Virginians discovered they actually lived in North Carolina. In November 1779, Governor Richard Caswell appointed Shelby as colonel and magistrate for the new Sullivan County. He assumed those duties in February 1780; but, by summer, Shelby was back in Virginia's Kentucky County continuing work on the surveys and land claims he had begun five years earlier while in service to Richard Henderson and the Transylvania Company. [14]

Returning home to the Overmountain settlements in the summer of 1779, the victorious frontiersmen were scarcely aware of the fighting east of the Appalachians. There the Whig rebels of the newly declared independent states pitted their poorly provisioned Continental Army against British Regulars in battles fought mostly north of the Potomac River. The frontier settlers' attention had been for years, and certainly most recently, focused on defending their incursion into the lands of the Shawnees and Cherokees. But, within a year of their return from their raid on the Chickamaugas, the stage was set to engage these westering folk in defending America's own future from another southern invasion. Joining them from Kentucky in this effort was Isaac Shelby, who returned in July 1780 resolved to remain in service to his country until the union of states should secure independence for them all. [15]

**Isaac Shelby returned to Sapling Grove from surveying in Kentucky determined to help the Patriot cause. Markers in Bristol, TN on Shelby Street near 7th Street commemorate the Evan Shelby and Isaac Shelby homes. The mansion in the center of the photo sits at the site of Shelby's Fort at Anderson Steet and 7th Street.**

# Charlestown

The British Southern Strategy hatched in 1775 by North Carolina's Royal Governor Josiah Martin had failed miserably even before the Patriots had declared their independence. Martin and the royal governors of South Carolina and Virginia had each been forced to flee onto British ships to escape their respective rebelling colonies. Indeed, Lord Dunmore had used his ships to attack his own people, Virginian colonists, firing on Norfolk on New Year's Day, 1776. In June of that year, the Second South Carolina regiment under Colonel William Moultrie[1] successfully repelled British attempts to capture Charlestown. Sergeant William Jasper's heroic effort under fire to

**Sergeant William Jasper helped rally Colonel Moultrie's South Carolina Continental troops in stopping the British attack on Charlestown in 1776. Many monuments, including those to William Moultrie and the defenders of 1776, grace the seven-acre White Point Park in Charleston, SC, where the Ashely and Cooper rivers meet at Charleston Harbor.**

*Charlestown*

recover and fly the downed flag rallied the troops at the incomplete, palmetto-log fort on Sullivan's Island defending the harbor's entrance. Cannon fire from the rebel fort, later named for Moultrie, hit the British flagship, *HMS Bristol*, and wounded South Carolina's exiled royal governor with splintered wood. He would die from the injuries over two years later in September 1778, still another two years ahead of events yet to unfold in South Carolina's Upcountry that would provide the irony: The last royal governor of South Carolina bore the name William Campbell.

After the ouster of these royal colonial administrators, no armed British troops set foot in Virginia or North Carolina during the ensuing four years. South Carolina enjoyed a reprieve only a little shorter. During that period, the American Revolution primarily involved engagements much farther north at Boston, New York, Trenton, Philadelphia, Saratoga, and Monmouth. Moreover, after the Patriot victory at Saratoga and with France having entered the war in late 1777 on the side of the Patriots, Great Britain found itself fighting a much broader war. The British ministers were compelled to send troops to the Caribbean, to Canada, and to Florida. With fewer regular troops available for service in the rebellious American colonies, the British commander-in-chief and his advisers were hesitant to launch an all-out attack on the coast of the southern colonies. Nevertheless, for political purposes, the ministers in London needed a smart victory and soon. They looked again to their southernmost opportunities.

**Georgia – Savannah and Augusta**

Tory militia Colonel Thomas Brown's plan for an attack on the frontiers to coincide with a British invasion at the coast had finally garnered the attention and approval of the British colonial authorities. Although he was trapped in East Florida during the preceding months, avoiding capture by bands of Patriot militia, his ideas had been championed by East Florida Royal Governor Patrick Tonyn and in New York by Moses Kirkland, a South Carolina Loyalist of the South Carolina Upcountry. So it was that in late 1778, the British again tried their Southern Strategy.

After arriving aboard ships at Tybee Island, Georgia, on December 23, 1778, a month later than intended, British Lt. Colonel Archibald Campbell advanced toward Savannah. His army included three thousand 71st Highlanders, Hessians, and Loyalist battalions from New York under lieutenant colonels George Turnbull and John Cruger. Patriot Major General Robert Howe arrayed his force of largely untested Continentals and militia a half-mile south of Savannah preparing to confront the British. He was outnumbered four to one. An enslaved man, Quomino Dolly, made the Patriot's prospects for success even more daunting. Perhaps hoping to earn his freedom, Dolly told the British of a path through the swamps, by which about 600 British cavalry and infantry outflanked Howe's force. When the shooting began, some of the Patriots never fired a shot but fled immediately into the city and then out the north side. Howe's men were completely routed, with fewer than half completing the retreat along the Savannah River to Purrysburg. Howe's force suffered 83 dead, 11 wounded, and more than 450 captured. Howe lost the city, also numerous cannons, 94 barrels of gunpowder, and a Spanish ship with 22 guns. Equating his victory at Savannah with a subjugation of the entire rebellious Georgia colony, Archibald Campbell reportedly declared that he would be "the first British officer to [rend] a star and a stripe from the flag of Congress."[2] In any case, the battle cost Howe his stars. On January 3, he relinquished command of the Patriot forces to General Benjamin Lincoln, who had been marching toward Savannah with reinforcements from Charlestown.[3]

Savannah was not the real objective for the British leader, however. Campbell waited at Savannah only long enough for General Augustine Prevost to arrive from St. Augustine, British East Florida. With him came Lt. Colonel Thomas Brown and his East Florida Rangers, whom Campbell disapprovingly called "a mere Rabble of undisciplined free-booters."[4] Brown led them all upriver to Augusta, the real prize in Georgia, he believed. From this point on the river, the British could control navigation in the lower Savannah River; and, through the network of trading paths and roads that crossed at Augusta, they could control the interior countryside and all commerce with the Indians.

In a few weeks, the British force was both gratified and cautioned by the welcome they received from the Loyalists rallying to the British Standard in the backcountry. More than a thousand men took the oath of allegiance; moreover, Tory Colonel James Boyd was riding toward Augusta with a body of some 700 Loyalist militiamen. Although this was positive for the British, this was not the army of 6,000 men Campbell had been expecting to come join the British liberators. Of more immediate concern, Campbell also learned that Patriot forces were moving in his direction.

Patriot General Benjamin Lincoln had ordered Major General John Ashe to advance to a position across the river from Augusta to reinforce Brigadier General Andrew Williamson in an effort to stop the British advance. Williamson was camped there with about 800 South Carolinians. (Among Williamson's officers was Colonel James Williams.) Ashe brought 1,600 men, mostly North Carolina militia from the eastern part of the state. [John Ashe was the Speaker of the Colonial Assembly (1762-65) and led the mob in Wilmington that pursued Royal Governor Josiah Martin in 1775, causing him to seek safety aboard the *HMS Cruizer* in the Cape Fear River. Ashe personally set the fire that consumed Fort Johnston.] In the face of these arriving Patriot reinforcements, British Lt. Colonel Campbell retreated from Augusta on February 14, moving south along the Savannah River. The Loyalists in Augusta, who had declared their allegiance to the Crown so publically, felt betrayed at Campbell's departure.

**Kettle Creek**

Colonel Boyd and his 700 Loyalists were riding toward Augusta from South Carolina's Upcountry, plundering Patriot homesteads as they went. Patriot Colonel Andrew Pickens pursued him with his smaller force of about 340 South Carolina and Georgia militia, among them Lt. Colonel Elijah Clarke and his 60 Georgians. As Boyd was planning to unite with another force at Little River (Georgia) before proceeding to Augusta, Pickens knew he had to overtake and outmaneuver Boyd beforehand. On February 14, Boyd's men came upon a Whig homestead from which they stole some cattle, incurring the ire of the woman of the farm. (Her Whig husband was riding with Colonel Clarke at the time.) Continuing on to a creek, they stopped to slaughter the beeves and prepare their first hot meal in some time. Almost all the men were crowded into a small space between a steep hill and the then-flooding creek. A few lookouts climbed toward the top of a hill and then hunkered down, probably below the ridge, to escape the cold, brisk wind.

When Pickens, searching for Boyd, happened upon the irate settler, he learned about the theft of her cattle and the direction the Loyalists had taken. Pickens pursued them to the camp along the creek. Pickens and his men, numbering only about half Boyd's force, formed three columns and approached the camp, getting close before they were seen. When the pickets spied them and fired on Pickens's men, Boyd

**Colonel Andrew Pickens and Lt. Colonel Elijah Clarke led Patriot militiamen to victory against South Carolina Tories at Kettle Creek in Wilkes County, Georgia. A marker and two monuments (not in picture) along with a cemetery of Revolutionary War veterans is on War Hill about seven miles southwest of Washington, Georgia.**

immediately climbed up the hill with a hundred men to form a line. That initial resistance failed when Boyd's men were outflanked, receiving fire from two sides. Boyd was mortally wounded in that early exchange, hit with three shots. Some of his men retreated, reaching the creek and fleeing across it, many without their horses. They tossed aside their pots and pans, henceforth giving the creek its name, Kettle Creek. Many other Tories were captured before they could cross.

As the escaping Loyalists reached the other side of the creek, Major William Spurgin began to rally the smaller band of Tories. When Clarke saw this, he charged across the river with only 20 or so of his men following initially. His horse was shot from under him, but he remounted on another and continued his charge. Pickens and the others soon followed Clarke's lead. The Patriot militia poured onto the far bank. The entire battle lasted more than two hours, ending when

Spurgin led his men away. Seventy Loyalists were killed and 150 were captured. Only about 270 Loyalists eventually arrived at Lt. Colonel Campbell's lines along the Savannah River. The Patriots fared better suffering only nine killed and 21 wounded. In their recent skirmishes including Kettle Creek, these Patriots had captured a good deal of baggage, as well, and about 600 horses.[5]

The Patriots took the prisoners to Augusta and then marched them to Ninety Six, occupied by the Patriots. A third of the Loyalist prisoners were treated not as prisoners of war, but were tried for treason and crimes. Twenty were sentenced to be hanged on April 17. Eventually five were hanged, which along with such hangings in Salisbury about that time set in motion series after series of summary and brutal retaliatory actions by Whigs and Tories against one another. The "uncivil war" of the backcountry worsened.

**Briar Creek**

During the two weeks following his departure from Augusta, Lt. Colonel Campbell continued to retreat down the Savannah River on the Georgia side. General John Ashe continued to pursue him although his troops were quite exhausted, having walked from Kingston ("Kinston" after 1784), North Carolina and subsisting on limited rations. Ashe's troops crossed the Savannah River, marched south, and on February 26 arrived at Briar (Brier) Creek. They set about rebuilding a bridge and cutting a road toward Mathew's Bluff on the river about five miles to the east, where General Griffith Rutherford's North Carolina militiamen encamped.

During the interim, Colonel Archibald Campbell had turned over command to Lt. Colonel James Mark Prevost, the younger brother of General Augustine Prevost. With Campbell's suggestions, the younger

Prevost planned a trap for General Ashe. He marched forward with 71st Highlanders, light infantry, Grenadiers, some of the militia survivors from Kettle Creek, and Brown's East Florida Rangers (also King's Carolina Rangers). They made a 50-mile arc to the west to get behind General Ashe's encampment as a smaller force made a diversionary movement in front of Ashe. When Prevost presented his force on March 3 to the Patriot's rear, the Patriot militia was slow to react. They did not have adequate supplies and equipment, lacking cartridge boxes and the proper size shot to fit the variety of muskets in use. They also lacked the training and discipline they needed to stand against the experienced British force. Movements by the inexperienced militiamen opened the center of the Patriot line. Prevost's men advanced with a bayonet charge and quickly overran the Patriots, some of whom retreated into the swamps. During the battle, Highlanders slaughtered many of the militiamen in retaliation for a recent butchering of one of their own. Colonel Ashe tried to rally his scattering militia troops, but they fled at such a pace that his efforts on horseback to get in front of them appeared to some as if he were leading the retreat. One group of Patriots fought valiantly, however. Colonel Samuel Elbert's Second Georgia Battalion fought fiercely enough that Prevost called in reinforcements. These Georgia Patriots did not yield, fighting until every man was killed or captured. Their sacrifice mattered not; the victorious British looted the camp.

The Patriots lost 150 to 200 men killed, about 40 wounded, about 170 captured and another 100 missing, many presumed drowned as they tried to cross the 80-foot-wide creek. Some men were burned to death when the British set fire to the brush along the creek in which the wounded and retreating Patriots were holed up. Others died of exposure in the swamps. The brief battle of only a few minutes was disastrous for the Patriots, and the loss negated the recent victory at Kettle

Creek.[6]

Helping some Patriot survivors escape across the river were the militia units of General Griffith Rutherford, who had been only four miles away. Among them was Benjamin Cleaveland, the new colonel of militia for the recently formed Wilkes County, North Carolina. Upon his return home after the devastating battle, he began his service in the state senate.[7] John Ashe had taken leave from his post as treasurer in the same state government to command the militia. Despite his service to the state on many fronts, he could not escape the blame for the debacle at Briar Creek. Ashe's legacy of public service was tainted by a later censure for his "lack of vigilance." Regardless of the cause and responsibility, this rout of Patriot militia along the Savannah River completely turned the momentum in Georgia away from the Patriots and stopped their hope of rebuffing the British advance along the Savannah River into the Georgia and Carolina backcountry.

**A New Vision**

Under his scheme, Thomas Brown had been expecting the Cherokees and Creeks to rally to Augusta in support of the British troop movements. They came, but not in time. When Indian superintendent John Stuart died, conveniently for Brown, in March 1779, Brown ensured his control over those relationships. The Southern Department of Indian Affairs was divided. Brown took control of the eastern division with the Cherokees and Creeks. Alexander Cameron, who had the historic relationship with those tribes, was given the western division to collaborate with the Chickasaws, Choctaws, and others. The letters of commission issued by Lord Germain emphatically declared their objectives: "The King's Service now requires that the procuring, sending out of leading Parties of the Indians to cooperate with His

Majesty's Forces, or otherwise to annoy the Enemy, shou'd be the principal Object of your Attention."[8]

A year before, in May 1778, General Sir Henry Clinton had replaced General Sir William Howe as commander-in-chief of North American British forces. In planning his actions to subdue the rebel colonies, Clinton noted the capture of Savannah in December (1778) and the failure of the Patriots to mount any effective resistance in Georgia during the spring of 1779. Clinton began to plan a more substantial invasion of the southern colonies but had to consider the presence of the French fleet, then supporting the rebel Patriots. The wisdom of that plan was supported the following October, no doubt, by the failure of the Patriots to recapture Savannah. Indeed, the occupying British force at Savannah had withstood the efforts of French Admiral Count d'Estaing and Major General Benjamin Lincoln to retake the city by laying siege to it. . After a disastrous, final battle on October 9, 1779, and in the face of the nearing hurricane season, d'Estaing abandoned the cause. The French fleet sailed to the West Indies, thus leaving the southern coast of the rebel colonies open to attack by any fleet of British ships.

In part to help discourage another possible attempt by Patriots to retake Savannah and to initiate another attempt at executing a Southern Strategy, on the day after Christmas, 1779, Lt. General Sir Henry Clinton sailed from New York with a British force of 8,700 troops.[9] Clinton was a careful planner and a cautious commander. He was painfully aware of the defeat of "Gentleman Johnny" Burgoyne at Saratoga and the embarrassment that had caused the British ministers.[10] He did not want to repeat that disaster. Indeed, it was that Patriot victory in New York which had convinced France's Louis XVI to enter the war with troops. It was also that battle — with Burgoyne's decisive retreat beginning on October 7, 1777 — which gave rise to the reputations of Patriot generals Horatio Gates and Benjamin Lincoln. Both men subsequently rose in their responsibilities.

**Charlestown by Sea**

Clinton had planned to sail for Charlestown on December 19 with a fleet of 90 transport ships carrying 8,700 troops and supplies. They were to be accompanied by five ships of the line, four frigates, two sloops, and two ships with 44 guns and 50 guns respectively. Severe winter weather delayed his departure, and ice damaged a half-dozen of the hundred ships moored in New York harbor. Clinton had previously delayed his departure awaiting word of the whereabouts of the French navy, reportedly in the Caribbean Sea, but on the morning of December 26, 1779, the fleet at last set sail under the command of Admiral Marriot Arbuthnot.

The British expected to lay siege to Charlestown, so they carried equipment and supplies appropriate for that strategy. They carried British infantry, artillerymen, cavalry of the British Legion, and a squadron of the 17$^{th}$ light dragoons. Some of the troops were Hessian (including jaegers and grenadiers), some were British, and some were Loyalist troops from the American colonies called the British Legion.

The British fleet encountered trouble almost immediately. A winter storm confronted the ships at sea on their second day out. Subsequent storms further thwarted their progress and blew some of the ships to England and some to the Bahamas. By one account, on almost half of their days at sea, severe gales and storms tossed about the fleet. The weather slowed their progress terribly. What was usually a ten-day voyage from New York to Savannah stretched into five weeks. The soldiers were exhausted from lack of sleep aboard the rolling, creaking ships and were additionally distressed at the loss of their rum supply. The overloading of ships with extra men taken aboard from the foundered ships overtaxed onboard supplies of food and water. Rats took an additional toll on the rations. Moreover, the British suffered the loss of cargo including a large part of their ordnance and ammunition when one ship sank. The weather-battered ships tossed about the cargo of horses. The crew and soldiers forced the injured animals overboard. When rations ran low, the officers ordered other valuable hoof stock jettisoned into the sea. The expedition completed its voyage with virtually no horses — none for the mounted soldiers and scarcely any for hauling supply wagons or artillery after the expedition should land.

At the end of January 1780, Clinton and Arbuthnot arrived at the mouth of the Savannah River, dividing the rebel colonies of Georgia and South Carolina. Clinton took personal command of the planned assault, intending to isolate Charlestown with attacks from both land and sea. Clinton put ashore 2,500 troops under Brigadier General James Paterson (also Patterson). They were to march along the Savannah River toward Augusta and to patrol the area to prevent Patriot forces from making their way to the relief of Savannah.[11]

From the fleet's rendezvous off Tybee Island, Clinton sailed north toward Charlestown where on February 11 and 12 he brought his remaining troops ashore at North Edisto River and Simmons (Seabrook) Island. With great difficulty, the British units made their way through the marshes of Johns Island and James Island.

Major General Benjamin Lincoln, commander of the Continental Army's Southern Department, had learned in the fall of 1779 about possible British plans to sail an army south. He had requested rein-

**Charlestown had been a walled city with strong defenses since 1704 after its founding on this site in 1680. A powder magazine, built in 1713, was used for a brief time during the American Revolution to store gunpowder for the Patriots. The Old Powder Magazine on Cumberland Street interprets some of Charleston's earliest history as a Lord Proprietors' Colony.**

forcements from General George Washington. Depleting his own strength around New York by a sixth, Washington ordered 800 North Carolina soldiers and 2,500 Virginians to march to Charlestown. Leaving in November and suffering much hardship in such a long expedition on foot, these men arrived in Charlestown in March and early April, well after Clinton had landed his men on James Island. Among the Patriots coming south were 125 cavalry riding under Lt. Colonel William Washington. Needing still more manpower to defend the city, Lincoln had asked North Carolina's Governor Richard Caswell and Virginia's Governor Thomas Jefferson to send more men, especially militia. The day before Clinton disembarked onto James Island, General Alexander Lillington, a hero of the Battle of Moore's Creek Bridge, arrived in Charlestown with 1,200 North Carolina militiamen.[12] Lincoln also wished to raise more men locally for the defense of the city. Lincoln was further frustrated in raising local troops, as few South Carolinians rallied to his call. Many feared leaving their property and family as Tory neighbors were aggressively raiding area farms and the newly-landed British Legion was commandeer-

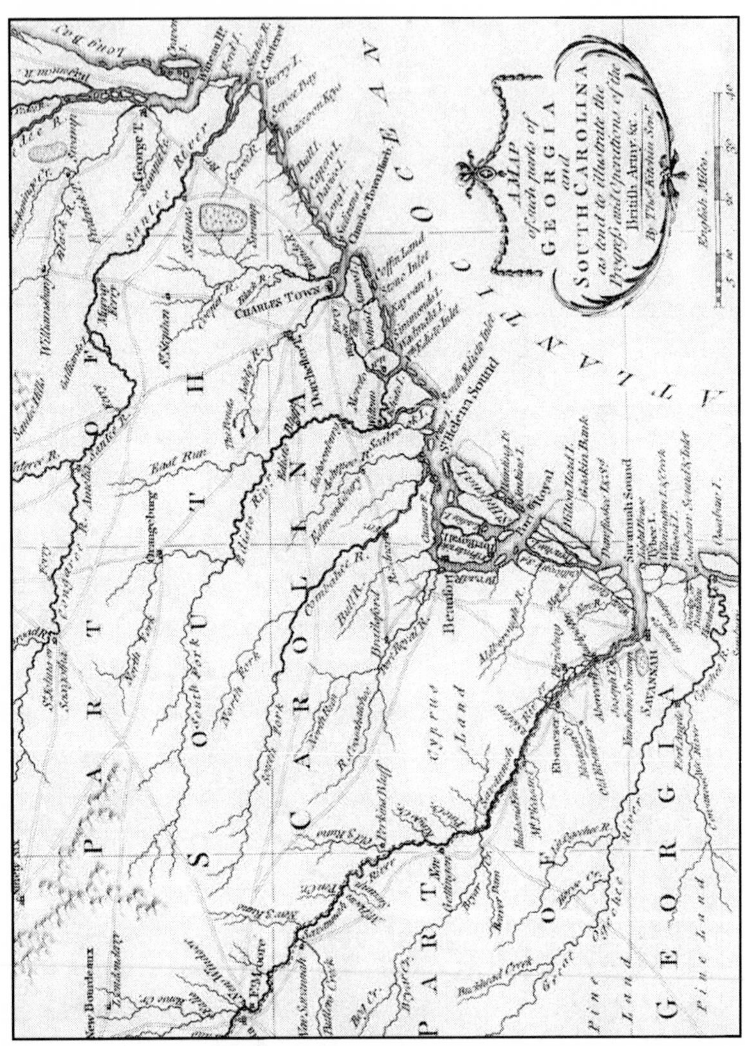


**The Lowcountry of South Carolina and the backcountry of Georgia were the scenes of much activity in 1780 leading up to and following the Siege of Charlestown.**
**["A map of such parts of Georgia and South Carolina as tend to illustrate the Progress and Operations of the British Army, &c," by Thomas Kitchin, Sr., for London Mag., May 1780]**

ing supplies and livestock at will. British foraging parties concluded that any farm that was abandoned was the property of a rebel. Reports of smallpox in Charlestown also kept many fearful South Carolinians away from the city.[13] To fill his need for armed men, Lincoln even considered arming the enslaved with muskets. This was strongly opposed by the legislators who feared a slave revolt. The slave insurrection of 1739, the Stono Rebellion, still haunted the white planter class of South Carolina, which forty years after that revolt was outnumbered several fold by enslaved blacks. Whites were wary of putting muskets into the hands of the enslaved.

As Sir Henry Clinton's effective force of 6,700 advanced north and east across James Island, they confiscated and destroyed property from Lowcountry farms. They took the enslaved, horses, cattle, oxen, corn, and straw. They took from the farms anything they could use to feed or support the British invasion; and, on occasion, over-zealous soldiers terrorized area residents, even those claiming to be friends of the government.

**Advancing to Charlestown**

In early March after landing his troops, Clinton made plans for a siege of Charlestown. Because Clinton needed all his men for the planned blockade, he ordered General Paterson to march his men toward the port city. Clinton especially needed mounted troops to carry messages between James Island lying to the southwest of the city and the siege works planned for the neck north of Charlestown between the Cooper and Ashley rivers. Clinton would also rely on the mounted infantry and cavalry to scout the countryside around the city, especially to the north and east. These dragoons would help prevent the advance of any Patriot reinforcements attempting to relieve Charlestown.

Paterson was several days' march from the city. After its debarkation off Tybee Island on February 1, Paterson's army, including the 71st Regiment, had advanced north along the Savannah River. It included the New York Volunteers under Lt. Colonel George Turnbull; the Royal North Carolina Volunteers; the South Carolina Royalists under Lt. Colonel Alexander Innes; and the American Volunteers under Major Patrick Ferguson. Under Paterson, they had marched north some 25 or 30 miles along the Savannah River. They encountered only one party of rebels in the first week, noted Lieutenant Anthony Allaire in his daily journal: "A foraging party of the Dragoons Fell in with some Rebel Light Horse."[14] Indicative of the care Allaire took in recording accounts of the expedition, he noted that the army suffered some "disagreeable, rainy weather" and had, perhaps, a rather rude introduction to the local Southern flora. "Several men taken suddenly ill with pain and swelling of the extremities," Allaire wrote, "occasioned by a weed that poisons where it touches the naked skin, when the dew is on it."[15]

On March 10 and 11, Paterson's army crossed the Savannah River with some difficulty, the river being "four to ten feet deep," Allaire noted, over usually dry and passable ground. They swam the horses over where "the current sets down very rapid." Once across, the army proceeded with difficulty, passing through swamps and low, marshy ground. On the east side of the river, they first met up with rebels and faced some resistance from the South Carolina Patriot militia. On March 13, Ferguson rode ahead with some of his men to secure the crossings at Bee Creek and the bridges at Coosawhatchie and Tully Finney. A detachment spotted and pursued the rebel militia but did not overtake them. Ferguson proceeded six miles beyond the Tully Finney bridge, where he discovered the abandoned camp of the Patriot militia at McPherson's plantation. Ferguson encamped there the night of March 14. Major Charles Cochrane of Tarleton's British Legion was pursuing another rebel party through the area with his Dismounted Legion infantry unit. Spotting Ferguson's campfires that night and mistaking them for the rebel encampment, Cochrane ordered his men to charge the camp with bayonets. A hot skirmish ensued between the two British units before the two leaders almost simultaneously recognized each other's voices calling out commands. They quickly stopped the fighting, but not before damage was done. Three men were killed and several wounded. Ferguson suffered a bayonet run through his left arm — his remaining good arm. Ferguson had previously lost the permanent use of his right arm when he suffered a musket ball to the arm at the Battle of the Brandywine in 1777. During that earlier period of recovery, he worked diligently to master the use of his saber in his left hand.[16] After suffering this second wound, Ferguson received the sympathy and admiration of his men as the stalwart major rode for a time with the bridle reins in his teeth.[17]

The men remained at McPherson's plantation a few days, resting and recovering in the bounty of their plunder. Allaire wrote of his ride through camp that the men were "living on the fat of the land, the soldiers every side of us roasting turkeys, fowls, pigs, etc., every night in great plenty."[18] Despite their brief respite from battle, these men were needed in Charlestown to begin the siege. Paterson pushed them on, moving eastward.

On March 18 at the crossing of Saltketcher River, resisting Patriot militia formed makeshift breastworks across the road and fired upon the advancing Loyalist units as they first arrived across the river. Paterson sent a raiding party to cross downstream. His loyalist light infantry circled behind the rebel militia and attacked the Patriots from behind with bayonets, killing one officer and 16 privates, and taking five prisoners. After the militia scattered, Paterson continued his march. Allaire described the chore of marching through the Lowcountry: "This day's march was very tedious — a disagreeable, rainy, cold day, and through a swamp where the water was from two to three feet deep."[19] These invaders found South Carolina much less than welcoming.

Lt. Colonel Banastre Tarleton and his British Legion joined with Paterson's army on March 21. Since their landing at the Savannah River, Tarlton had been at Port Royal gathering what horses they could find in the area to remount his dragoons. Tarleton did not think the mounts he found there equal to those he had lost at sea.

As Paterson's British Legion continued marching toward Charlestown, it collected from farms across the countryside a large number of enslaved blacks, cattle, and horses. In particular, Major Ferguson's detachment raided rebel properties along the way. Allaire wrote: "This day Col. Ferguson got the rear guard in order to do his King and country justice, by protecting friends, and widows, and destroying Rebel property, ... collect[ing] live stock for the use of the army, ... [and] by destroying furniture, breaking windows, etc., taking all their horned cattle, horse, mules, sheep, fowls, etc., and their negroes to drive them."[20] Indeed, so many enslaved Africans and African-Americans escaped to the British side that they created a problem in their need for food, clothing, and shelter. General Clinton made use of them, however, putting some to work in the camps and many to work building fortifications. Because the British had not yet secured enough horses and oxen to move the artillery and supplies, he worked some of the refugee enslaved like draught animals, using them to haul overland the monstrously heavy cannons, howitzers, and mortars.[21]

On March 25 and 26, Paterson's army crossed the Stono River with some difficulty over their makeshift bridge. They advanced to make camp near the plantation of South Carolina's rebel governor John Rutledge. As Paterson's army approached, they were confronted by 300 Continental light horse, who retreated from the Legion's dragoons after a brief skirmish. At last, Paterson's army arrived on the west side of the Ashley River where Clinton was assembling his army and preparing to lay siege to Charlestown. Paterson's men camped at Lining's plantation, nearly opposite the city. They remained there while the bulk of Clinton's army crossed over Ashley River on March 29 and 30 at Ashley Ferry and marched southward onto the neck. On April 2, five hundred men began digging trenches and constructing redoubts as parts of the siegeworks. Over the next week, the Patriots and the British forces exchanged cannonades and gunfire as the invaders worked in earnest to sap trenches and parallels closer and closer to the Patriot defenses of Charlestown.[22]

### Monck's Corner

Clinton knew his success in laying siege to the city depended on his ability to seal off the countryside from any relief effort. Indeed, five hundred Patriots under General Isaac Huger were then posted up the Cooper River some 35 miles northeast of Charlestown at Monck's Corner. Their task was to patrol the area and to keep the road and bridge open for relief and, if necessary, for retreat. Their service had immediate effect in Charlestown. On April 8, much to the surprise and consternation of the British invaders and to the visible delight of the besieged, 750 Virginians arrived on board eleven schooners and sloops, sailing down the Cooper River and past the British siegeworks. These men had marched 500 miles in four weeks to reinforce the Continentals at Charlestown. They were under the command of Brigadier General William Woodford, the hero of the Battle of Great Bridge. Pealing bells and shouted huzzas greeted the Virginians as they made their way into the city soon to be encircled.[23]

Two days later, on April 10, Clinton formally called on the Patriot commander, Benjamin Lincoln, to surrender his garrison and the city. Clinton wrote in part: "An alternative is offered at this hour to the inhabitants, of saving their lives and property contained in the town, or of abiding by the fatal consequences of a cannonade and storm." He disclaimed any responsibility for the inevitable "resentment of an exasperated soldiery" should the Patriots decline.[24] Lincoln refused, declaring to Clinton his "Duty and Inclination" to defend the city to "the last extremity." To emphasize his point, Lincoln commenced a cannonade upon the British troops. It continued well into the night.

In his effort to guard Biggin's Bridge at Monck's Corner, General Huger commanded 400 mounted soldiers and 100 poorly equipped North Carolina militia who had just arrived. Some of the latter troops had no ammunition; others among them had arrived without even firearms. Huger placed the useless militia out of the way at nearby Biggin's Church.

Displeased with Lincoln's refusal of his summons to surrender, Clinton chose to thwart the Continental's mission to keep the back-country routes open at Monck's Corner. He issued orders for Colonel Tarleton to menace General Huger in concert with Lt. Colonel James Webster and Major Patrick Ferguson. Ferguson's men were then camped on the opposite side of Charlestown. To participate in this raid, they had a great distance to cover quickly.

In the early evening on April 12, Ferguson began marching from Lining's Plantation west of the Ashley River with his command of American Volunteers. For this mission, he also had command of the

**While protecting Biggin Bridge, General Isaac Huger put many of his men in camp around the parish church; they were attacked and routed there by Lt. Colonel Banaster Tarleton and Major Patrick Ferguson. The ruins of Biggin Church, surrounded by a cemetery, are on SC Hwy 402 in Monck's Corner near the site of the bridge.**

Royal North Carolina Volunteers. Departing at seven in the evening, they marched 22 miles overnight arriving at Bacon's Bridge in ten hours. With only two hours' rest, they pressed on 15 miles more to Middleton's plantation at Goose Creek, where Tarleton's Legion joined them at one o'clock in the afternoon. Ferguson's weary men rested until well after dark.[25]

Knowing of Huger's presence at the bridge 18 miles away, Tarleton skillfully planned the attack. His mounted infantry and cavalry were still riding the plow horses and swamp ponies they had been able to commandeer at Port Royal and elsewhere. Being so poorly mounted, they could gain an advantage, Tarleton decided, only through a surprise attack in the dark. The mounted troops of Ferguson and Tarleton would advance first, moving swiftly and quietly; Webster's infantry would follow immediately, giving support.

Making little sound as they moved along the road, an advance detachment of Tarleton's dragoons surprised an enslaved man, capturing him before he could escape into the brush. He was carrying a note from Huger to Lincoln. The intercepted message divulged to Tarleton how many and where the Patriots were stationed at Biggin's Bridge. The Legion pressed on. After covering 18 miles in five hours, Ferguson and Tarleton neared the bridge around three o'clock in the stillness and darkness of the night. Apparently, Huger had posted no forward sentries and only one patrol along the road near the bridge.

The British units arrived undetected. When Tarleton gave the signal, he and his dragoons charged through the small party of mounted Continental defenders, over the bridge and into the camp of unsuspecting Patriots. The dragoons, wielding their sabers, slashed at the startled Americans, striking heads, arms, and shoulders with full force. Shouts of fright and cries of agony joined the confusion of whinnying horses and desperate commands yelled out from both sides. The rebels scattered, some attempting to mount their horses. Others, including Lt. Colonel William Washington and General Huger, escaped on foot into the darkness and ran into the surrounding swamp. The attacking dragoons chased down some of the fleeing, capturing many and killing others. With the Continental mounted troops dispersed, the Legion infantry under Major Cochrane charged into the camp with fixed bayonets. They routed the Patriot militia camped around Biggin's Church, killing, wounding, and capturing many of the panicked and unarmed citizen soldiers.[26]

All told, the Patriots lost 14 killed and 19 wounded; Tarleton took 64 prisoners. The real damage extended beyond the loss of men, however. Huger also lost 30 wagons of stores and supplies, each pulled by four horses. Moreover, Tarleton captured the Patriots' superior horses and remounted his own dragoons, thus extending the range and fighting capability of the Legion's mounted infantry and cavalry. Along with their mounts, the fleeing Continentals lost their firearms, sabers, blankets, equipment, and many personal effects.[27] The attack by Tarleton and Ferguson at Monck's Corner was a severe blow to the Patriot strength, forces, and strategy. The road to Charlestown from the backcountry was no longer open to the rebels for reinforcement or for retreat.

**Charlestown Under Siege**

After Lincoln had refused the articles of surrender on April 10 and had declared to Clinton his intent to defend the city, he urged Governor John Rutledge to flee Charlestown. Rutledge did so in the company of some of his council members, crossing the Cooper River on April 13. Leaving in advance of Huger's defeat at Biggin's Bridge, the party of refugees fortunately headed toward North Carolina by a road leading to Lenud's Ferry across the Santee River rather than toward Monck's Corner. Rutledge intended to muster what help he could find outside the Lowcountry — more Continental troops, or perhaps militiamen from the Upcountry.

These principals of South Carolina's government escaped through Christ Church Parrish. That area between the Wando River and the coastal marshes was the only open route through which escape was possible. Indeed, it was just that route and its open status that most concerned Clinton. Capturing Charlestown would be important, he believed, but trapping General Lincoln and his several-thousand-strong Southern Department of the Continental Army in the city would certainly hasten the demise of the rebellion. Clinton was eager to close off the remaining possible escape routes before Lincoln should order his men to evacuate the city by crossing the Cooper

River.

After the governor departed, Lincoln called a council of his officers. Some argued for saving the army by moving the Continentals across the Cooper River immediately. During the week, the garrison gathered boats of all descriptions on the Cooper River for a possible escape. Catching wind of this discussion, the lieutenant governor and some prominent citizens insisted in the strongest terms that Lincoln not abandon the city. One even declared his willingness to open the gates to the British invaders should the Continentals attempt an escape.[28] Perhaps Lincoln had allowed himself to be overly influenced by these civilians — by their reasons and their threats — or maybe it was already too late to escape. Regardless of the reason, he made his choice. Lincoln and his army remained in Charlestown. Their fate was sealed.

**The Cooper River**

From Biggin's Bridge, Ferguson, Tarleton, and Webster began to sweep through the Cooper River area cutting off other routes of reinforcement and taking command of the countryside. Clinton sent his second-in-command, General Lord Charles Cornwallis to oversee the efforts to close off the region east of the city. Clinton did so, in part, to rid himself of a source of disharmony in his command; Clinton and Cornwallis disliked each other and only tolerated working together. Clinton outranked Cornwallis in the army, but within the hierarchy of British aristocracy, Cornwallis held the higher station. On Clinton's orders, Cornwallis took a large detachment of soldiers across the Cooper River on April 24 and joined the men already camped around St. Thomas Church. His command then numbered about 2,300, but even this large corps was not invincible. Allaire captured that night's incident in his journal: "The Rebels sallied out and took eight of the

Light Infantry prisoners, upon which the whole line got under arms; some in their hurry getting out without putting on their coats, were taken by the others for Rebels, and fired on, which unluckily occasioned warm work for a few minutes. Sixty odd of ours got killed and wounded by our own men."[29]

During the following two weeks, under Cornwallis's command, Ferguson's detachment advanced to Lampriere's Point, Mount Pleasant, and Haddrell's Point, capturing a redoubt at the last of these on May 2 with only sixty men. Impressed by this feat, Allaire wrote: "[T]wenty men like the American Volunteers would have defied all Washington's Army." Carrying through on such high self-expectations, Ferguson's corps was present at Fort Moultrie when that Continental garrison surrendered on May 7. Even before the fall of this fort — one previously so essential to the defense of the city — any possible escape across the Cooper River had been lost to Lincoln's Continentals Army trapped in Charlestown.

**Lenuds' Ferry**

Farther away from Charlestown, similarly disheartening defeats of the Patriots played out as well. Colonel William Washington and his surviving cavalry, after their defeat at Biggin's Bridge, had escaped over the Santee River at Murry's Ferry. Washington made his way to the plantation of Thomas Sumter, where he haggled with the retired Continental officer for purchase of a fine English mare for £100. Washington and his men commandeered another 16 horses for remounting their own troops. They then rode off to join with Colonel Anthony White, who had arrived in late April from the north among some hundreds of mounted soldiers, the First Continental Light Dragoons.[30]

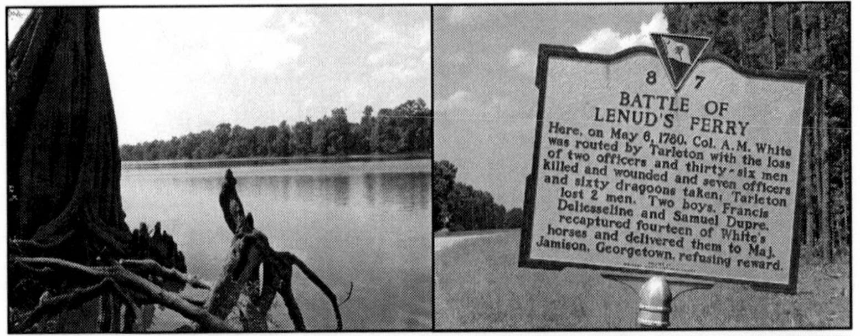


**Lt. Colonel Banastre Tarleton overtook an unsuspecting Colonel Anthony White at Lenud's Ferry over the Santee River, capturing White's superior horses for remounting his troops. A historic marker is on US Hwy 17 two miles NE of Jamestown, Berkeley Co., SC.**

Colonel White, commanding a detachment of 100 dragoons, had some immediate success in capturing a British foraging party of seventeen men south of the Santee River. On May 6, the same day, he took his prisoners to Lenud's Ferry where White rested half his horses, unbridled and unsaddled, while he passed the prisoners over the river, to the infantry of Colonel Abraham Buford's regiment of Virginia Continentals waiting on the opposite bank. Unfortunately for the Patriots, Tarleton was riding toward Lenud's Ferry that same day with 150 dragoons. He learned from a local farmer that White had captured some soldiers of the Legion and was headed to Lenud's. The farmer's story recounted how the Continental dragoons had hacked the Loyalist dragoons in retaliation for the slaughter at Monck's Corner. Tarleton pushed his men on hurriedly toward the ferry in a forced march, arriving around 3:00 p.m. As they had done at Biggin's Bridge, Tarleton's men rode in hard, catching the rebels unprepared. Wielding their sabers furiously, the Legion's dragoons slashed and killed 11 rebels, wounding another 30. When the attack began, the prisoners in the boats jumped their Patriot guards and threw them overboard. Washington and White both swam the river to safety as Tarleton's men fired upon them and others from the riverbank. Other

Patriots attempting to escape drowned in the river and in the waters of the surrounding Hell Hole Swamp. Buford's men on the east bank, separated from White's men by the river, were out of musket range and unable to assist with any firepower. Tarleton captured nearly 70 of the rebel cavalry and some 100 horses: superior, Virginia equine stock he used as before to better mount his cavalry and mounted infantry. Tarleton's men had ridden their own horses so hard, that 20 mounts died of fatigue.[31]

**Buford's Retreat**

After witnessing firsthand Tarleton's battlefield prowess and defeat of Colonel White and knowing the size of Cornwallis's army, Coloenl Buford decided that he could not possibly fight his way into Charlestown. He retreated instead, moving from Lenud's Ferry northwest along the Santee River valley toward Camden. Governor Rutledge accompanied him. Along the way, they arrived at the home of Thomas Sumter and tried to persuade him to join as a leader in the defense of South Carolina. Sumter had previously served under Colonel Andrew Williamson in the 1776 campaign against the Cherokee and later as a colonel of the Sixth South Carolina Continental Regiment. By September 1778, however, Sumter had become frustrated with his military career and his desire to win glory in battle. As a colonel, he had marched his riflemen across many hundreds of miles in four campaigns only to stand by as other units were preferred for engagement and took the credit. He resigned his commission and went home to the High Hills of the Santee. In May 1780, even with the British invading, Governor Rutledge was not able to stir Sumter to join the partisan effort. Thomas Sumter declined.

Rutledge may have failed in his quest to recruit Sumter for any number of reasons, but the governor was no friend of the backcountry types such as Sumter. A member of the Lowcountry elite, Rutledge had referred to the residents of the backcountry as "a pack of beggars." It may be that Sumter's rebuff of the governor's plea was more in response to the solicitor and not the cause.

Leaving Sumter's home, Buford's entourage continued toward Camden and while still in the High Hills of Santee came upon Colonel Richard Caswell and his North Carolina militia who were heading toward Charlestown. Learning the situation from Buford, Caswell also saw the futility of continuing his march; the two armies retreated together continuing north. At Camden, Caswell turned east toward the Pee Dee River; Buford's army of Virginians with Governor Rutledge in tow continued north intending for Salisbury and then Hillsborough. John Rutledge, whose brother Edward had signed the Declaration of Independence on behalf of South Carolina, intended to carry on the state's government in exile.

**The Surrender**

As General Clinton tightened his grip on Charlestown and closed off

**Built in 1771, The Exchange, along the waterfront, was the center of commerce and social entertainments for Charlestown. General Moultrie hid gunpowder in the basement, which the British used to hold suspects temporarily. The Old Exchange and Provost Dungeon, at the east end of Broad Street, offers interpretive tours of the Revolutionary era.**

the surrounding countryside to reinforcements as well as escape, the fate of those trapped inside became unquestionable. On May 8, Clinton again summoned the garrison trapped in Charlestown to surrender. In the formal practice of 18th century warfare, Lincoln responded with proposed conditions. Clinton replied on May 9, accepting some and rejecting others of the proposed articles of capitulation. In light of Clinton's demands, Lincoln decided to fight on, but by May 11 and after receiving petitions from some of the Patriot militia and from some citizens, Lincoln accepted the conditions which Clinton offered. On May 12, the Patriot garrison opened the gates. In a formal ceremony, the British forces marched into Charlestown, struck the American colors, and raised the British standard. Clinton reported capturing 5,600 men, though it is likely that only 4,000 or so of them would have been battle-ready at the time of surrender.[32] Of those surrendered, about 3,500 were soldiers of the Continental Army. Their capture essentially destroyed the Southern Department, eliminating most of the regular troops of South Carolina, North Carolina, and Virginia.[33] Among them was Colonel Nathaniel Gist commanding one of the thirteen Additional Continental Regiments including soldiers from Virginia, Maryland, and Delaware. He remained a prisoner-of-war until January 1, 1781.[34]

In the days immediately following the surrender of Charlestown, Clinton began issuing proclamations for public consumption. One was addressed to the "wicked and desperate Men still endeavoring to support the Flame of Rebellion," warning them against thwarting the efforts of the British forces to reestablish his Majesty's government.[35] He was encouraged by the throngs of locals — many former rebels — who came into Charlestown to join with the British forces.

Clinton also saw the time was right to form a loyal militia. He issued one notable broadside, declaring, "The Time is come, when it is equally the Interest and Duty of every good Man to be in Readiness to join the King's Troops, and assist them in establishing Justice and Liberty, and in restoring and securing their own Property." Their goal, according to Clinton's proclamation, was "driving their Rebel Oppressors and all the Miseries of War far from the Province." To organize these loyalists, Clinton appointed Major Patrick Ferguson as Inspector of Militia for Georgia and the Carolinas. They were to march into the backcountry and to subdue the rebel elements which remained there. Indeed, Cornwallis had declared to Clinton within a week after the surrender that "without some success in the Back Country, our success at Charlestown would but little promote the real interests of Great Britain."[36]

Agreeing with Cornwallis's sentiments about subduing the backcountry and intending to return to New York, Clinton put Cornwallis in command of the British forces. These troops included six regiments of British regulars, three regiments of Hessians, and six provincial regiments of loyalists. To this substantial force of over 6,000 men in arms, Major Ferguson would add what recruits he could muster from the countryside, as Cornwallis marched his army north.[37] To encourage such enlistments, Clinton issued a dramatic proclamation declaring that those who did not pledge their allegiance to the Crown would be considered "Enemies and Rebels." As essential as he might have thought this requirement was to re-establishing control in the province, this bothersome requirement for pledging allegiance to the Crown eventually forced many otherwise neutral residents to take sides; they chose to be against the King. However, confident at the moment in the success of the enterprise he had put in motion, Sir Henry Clinton wrote to Lord Germain as he then sailed for New York in early June: "I may venture to assert that there are few men in South

Carolina who are not either our Prisoners or in Arms with us."[38]

**The Southern Campaign Continues**

During the week or two before Clinton's departure, the British forces marched north on three fronts. To the far west, one column moved up the Savannah River toward Augusta. Lt. Colonel Nisbet Balfour moved north toward Ninety Six. Cornwallis's column moved up the Santee River heading for the Wateree and Catawba rivers; the general had his sights set on victory in North Carolina. Cornwallis only first needed to make his way through South Carolina's backcountry. The Patriot garrisons at Ninety Six and Camden surrendered on learning of the fall of Charlestown. Beaufort and George Town garrisons did the same. Despite their overly exuberant display of soldiering against the Cherokees just four years before, General Andrew Williamson's men elected to take parole and to return home rather than fight the invading British Legion. Immediately after the fall of Charlestown, South Carolina's backcountry was devoid of any army ready to face the advancing British.[39]

**"Bloody Ban"**

On May 18, Cornwallis's column marched from the backcountry east of Charlestown with 2,500 troops toward the Santee River at Lenud's Ferry. After arriving there, he learned of Governor Rutledge's retreat with Colonel Buford's Virginia Continentals toward Camden. Cornwallis wanted to capture the rebel governor.

Realizing that Buford and Rutledge had a ten-day head start, Cornwallis called upon Banastre Tarleton to overtake Buford's entourage if he could. Tarleton commanded 270 men including 130 Legion cavalry, 100 mounted Legion infantry, and 40 British regulars of the 17th Regiment of Horse. Rising to the challenge, Tarleton's men

**Colonel Thomas Sumter left his home in the High Hills of Santee to organize resistance to the advancing British Legion. The graves of Thomas Sumter and his wife, Mary, are among monuments at Genl. Sumter Memorial Park, the home site, in Sumter County, SC.**

departed on May 27 from Nelson's Ferry (near today's St. Stephens about 12 miles upstream from Lenud's Ferry) and rode hard toward Camden, about 60 miles away. They rode through the heat and humidity of late May in South Carolina's interior coastal plains below the fall line. Along the way, their plundering, burning, and ravaging alarmed the Whigs they molested, creating considerable fear and dread among the citizens. Some of the accosted rode off hurriedly to warn others of Tarleton's coming. One such message reached the home of Thomas Sumter. When he heard that Tarleton was torching homes of Patriot citizens, he donned his old Continental uniform and rode away with no particular plans on how he would help oppose the British invasion. The ruthlessness of Banastre Tarleton had accomplished what the coaxing of Governor Rutledge could not: the arousal of Sumter's patriotic passions. Not long after Sumter's departure, some of Tarleton's men, under the command of Captain Charles Campbell, arrived at Sumter's home intending to capture the Whig. Finding that he had fled, they looted food and supplies, manhandled his handicapped wife, Mary, frightened his family and servants, and burned the

Sumter home.

During the night of May 27, Tarleton arrived in Camden where his men rested only a few hours. They departed Camden at two o'clock in the morning on the 28th and at dawn arrived at Rugeley's Mill, about a dozen miles northwest of Camden. (Rugeley's Mill and Cleremont plantation were along a main, high road running north from Camden to Salisbury at the crossing of Grannies Quarter Creek about 10 to12 miles upstream from its confluence with the Wateree River.) Buford and the governor had camped there not long before until Colonel Henry Rugeley, a Tory, warned them of Tarleton's arrival in Camden. Perhaps fearing any retaliation by his Whig neighbors, Rugeley did not want the rebel governor captured at his home. Buford and his men left immediately and pressed on northward. From Camden, Tarleton's troops continued at their arduous pace. His detachment exhausted their horses, riding some to death. Along the way, they commandeered other mounts from local residents. They pressed on, eventually covering just over 100 miles in two-and-a-quarter days.

Learning along the road that Buford's retreating army was only 20 miles ahead, Tarleton sent forward a courier, Captain David Kinlock, with a message demanding Buford's surrender. "Resistance being vain, to prevent effusion of human blood, I make offers which can never be repeated," Tarleton's message read. His continued offer attempted to frighten Buford into surrendering by exaggerating the size of the force that was soon to be upon him. After reading the summons, Buford stopped his army in the Waxhaws, a region just a few miles south of the North Carolina line. He instructed his wagons, artillery, and the governor to continue moving toward Salisbury. He planned to stand and fight. (Buford's protection of the fleeing governor was providential for the new country. Fifteen years later, John Rutledge served as the second Chief Justice of the United States.)

Delaying his reply to the courier until he could get his men into an open field, Buford responded verbally. According to Tarleton, Buford replied: "Sir, I reject your proposals, and shall defend myself to the last extremity."[40] Kinlock departed with the message and rode off to find Tarleton. "By this time," Tarleton later wrote, "many of the British cavalry and mounted infantry were totally worn out and dropped successively into the rear; the horses of the three-pounder likewise unable to proceed."[41]

About 3:00 p.m. on May 29, Tarleton, informed of Buford's refusal of his offer, overtook Buford. In view of the Patriot commander, Tarleton's advance unit destroyed in a brief skirmish Buford's rear guard comprised of five mounted Continentals. Tarleton aligned his men on a rise overlooking the open field in which Buford had arranged his troops. Had Buford encircled his wagons and trained his artillery against Tarleton's exhausted cavalry, Tarleton later suggested that he might not have attacked. As it was, he formed his men into three ranks ready to charge across 300 or 400 yards of open field. Tarleton commanded his left wing rather than the center. When Tarleton heard from across the field Buford order his men to hold their fire until his riders were within ten paces, he instantly realized Buford's error. Knowing the victory would be his, without hesitation Tarleton gave the order and led his dragoons charging across the field. A thunder of hooves rushed toward the Continentals.

Had Buford ordered his men to fire volleys in platoons while there was time to reload and fire again, Buford might have diminished the effect of the cavalry charge. Instead, the Continentals stood at the ready as they watched scores of mounted soldiers ride down upon their force of about 350 Continentals. After the one volley, the saber-wielding British Legion dragoons were in among the Continental ranks slashing and hacking the startled Patriots from the elevated advantage provided by their saddled mounts. Without time to reload, the Patriot troops threw their muskets to the ground and raised their hands. Attempting to surrender, some called for quarter. Accounts differ, but if the Continentals raised a white flag or attempted to present one to the attackers, it was either struck down or not made known to Tarleton. Were the Continentals surrendering or not? Neither side could tell.[42] In the resulting confusion, some Continentals picked up their muskets and attempted to reload. The mounted British Legion continued slashing and sabering the Continental troops. The dragoons granted no quarter, believing that none had been asked.

Buford's one volley had succeeded with one particular effect, dropping the horse from under Colonel Tarleton. With his fall, his Green Horse and the 17th Dragoons believed that Tarleton had been shot. Enraged by that thought, the mounted troops were not only leaderless, but bent on retaliation as well. (Tarleton was, in fact, pinned for a time beneath his fallen horse.) The fighting was vicious and man-to-man. The dragoons slashed one and then another of the doomed Patriots. The wounded Continentals fell to the ground, some instantly dead, but many more were horribly wounded and soon to die. Into the melee marched the dismounted Legion infantry of Major Cochrane with bayonets fixed. These were Americans. They were Loyalists who had decided to fight in support of King George III and Parliament and to maintain their rights as Englishmen. The British Legion stalked the wounded Continentals among the casualties and bayoneted some of the wounded. Later accounts claimed that some even used their bayonets to toss aside those bodies that lay on top of others so they could get at and bayonet the wounded Patriots lying underneath. Others claimed that the mortally wounded begged to be killed to end their pain.

The battlefield experience of John Stokes reveals the horror of the

**Lt. Colonel Banastre Tarleton pursued Colonel Abraham Buford's Virginia Continentals to the Waxhaws, where he charged, with sabers slashing, into the Patriots, who may have been calling for quarter. A mass grave for Patriots killed at the battle is part of the "Buford Massacre 1780" memorial in Lancaster County on SC Hwy 522 south of SC Hwy 9.**

moment. "Early in the sanguinary conflict he [Stokes] was attacked by a dragoon, who aimed deadly blows at his head, all of which, by the dexterous use of his small sword, he easily parried; when another dragoon attacked from the right, and by one stroke cut off [Stoke's] right hand. They both then attacked him, and instinctively attempting to defend his head with his left arm, that was hacked in eight or ten places from the wrist to the shoulder and a finger cut off. His head was laid open almost the whole length of the crown to the eyebrows. A soldier passing asked if he expected quarter. Stokes answered: 'I have not, nor do I mean to ask it; finish me as soon as possible;' whereupon the soldier transfixed him twice with his bayonet." (Stokes survived this battle and was held as a prisoner until 1783. Later he read for the bar and was appointed a U.S. District Judge by President George Washington.)

The failure of Buford's field tactics was immediately obvious, but he, among a few others, escaped the battlefield. Forty years later, the incident would first be tagged a "massacre," but those who were there at the time knew firsthand the true horror of the engagement, regardless of any label. The casualty loses among the Continentals were horrendous: 113 killed and 203 captured including 150 wounded, many horribly disfigured and later to die of the wounds. Members of the community tended the wounded soldiers at the Waxhaw Church. Among the caregivers were Elizabeth Jackson and her son Andrew, then age 13, later to become the seventh president of the United States.

The victorious Tarleton, suffering only five killed and 12 wounded, wrote to Cornwallis, "My Lord, I am extremely fatigued with overtaking the Enemy & beating them — I summoned the Corps — they refused my terms — I have cut 170 Off'rs and men to pieces." Word of the disaster in the Waxhaws spread quickly among the Patriots and with it a new disdain for the invading British force. "Give them Tarleton's Quarter" and "Remember Buford's Quarter" became rallying cries for the Whig rebels across the Carolinas. Tarleton and his dragoons certainly had been feared; but, after May 29th and serving well the purposes of rallying men in the backwoods of the Carolinas to the rebel cause, "Bloody Ban" was now also greatly despised. The wholesale slaughter of Buford's Continentals would not soon be forgotten.

**Ninety Six**

After the embarrassing surrender of the Continentals in Charlestown and after Tarleton's thrashing of Buford's corps on the battlefield in the Waxhaws, Cornwallis imagined little remained to be accomplished to subdue the wayward colony. He had already sent three columns forward. He augmented this distribution of troops by sending other units forward to occupy additional positions across the rebellious colony. They went to Georgetown, Cheraw, Hanging Rock, and Rocky Mount. To support them, he made Camden a depot for supplies. From each of those military positions, the officers were responsible for maintaining the general peace and subduing any partisans they should happen to find. Among the appointments made, Cornwallis sent Lt. Colonel

**Major Patrick Ferguson marched his Loyalist troops to Ninety Six. Ninety Six National Historic Site is on SC Hwy 344 two miles south of the modern town of Ninety Six in eastern Greenwood County, SC.**

George Turnbull and his New York Volunteers to Rocky Mount and Lord Rawdon's Volunteers of Ireland to the Waxhaws.

Under the general command of Lt. Colonel Nisbit Balfour, Major Patrick Ferguson led the American Volunteers as they marched toward Ninety Six. They departed Charlestown on May 26 at three o'clock in the morning. Marching in the cool of the early morning, they passed through Monck's Corner and reached Nelson's Ferry on the Santee River on June 1. Allaire recorded: "By express were informed that Col. Tarleton, Monday, the 29th, fell in with a body of Rebels forty miles above Camden. He summoned them to surrender — received an insolent answer, charged them …"

Following the Santee, Congaree, and Saluda rivers, Balfour's column reached 77 miles from Charlestown by June 3. On the 12th, they reached Congaree Stores, where they laid up a few days. On the 22nd, they forded the Saluda River and marched on six miles to Ninety Six.

Anthony Allaire described the village of Ninety Six as "contain[ing] about twelve dwelling houses, a court-house and a jail." (Construction of the star fort was not begun until December 1780.) The "country town … is situated on an eminence, the land cleared for a mile around it, in a flourishing part of the country, supplied with very good water, enjoys a free, open air, and is esteemed a healthy place."[43] When

Balfour's men arrived, the jail was filled with 40 rebels who had been brought in by the local loyalist militia — the "friends to Government." The loyalists were pleased to turn the tables, it seemed, because some had been hiding in the swamps to avoid persecution by the Patriots when their rebel garrison controlled the post. Indeed, at one court session, 75 loyalists had been condemned and five were executed; the others reprieved. As Allaire noted, from all parts of the countryside loyalist militia were coming to Ninety Six. It was a rallying point for those professing allegiance to the Crown and the King's ministers.

Ninety Six was a cross roads on the South Carolina frontier assuring its importance for commerce and communication. It had a brick jail of two stories and a courthouse, making it prominent in enforcing the law and helping keep order. During the Revolution, the town was a staging area for both Loyalist and Patriot campaigns. It was also the site of the first shooting conflict of the Revolution south of New England. Two thousand Loyalists laid siege to Major Andrew Williamson's 560 Patriot militiamen for three days in November 1775. The Patriots forted within a hastily built stockade around the barn of John Savage. This early conflict confirmed the divided loyalties that characterized the backcountry throughout the war and greeted Major Patrick Ferguson in 1780.

# The Upcountry

### The Rebels Rally

Despite the gathering of Loyalists at Ninety Six and elsewhere, in other parts of the Carolina backcountry, men who believed in Liberty could still be found. During the few days after leaving his home in the High Hills in advance of Tarleton's raid, Thomas Sumter had learned from friends of the fervent desire among many in the Catawba River valley to rally to the Patriot cause. On June 1, he received in Salisbury permission and funds to raise a band of guerilla fighters to harass the British Legion in their advance into the South Carolina Upcountry. William Hill, Edward Lacey, and William Bratton were leaders of the Patriot cause along the Catawba River and in the district reaching west to the Broad River. Hill wrote to Thomas Sumter in Salisbury and asked if he would consent to join them and possibly lead them. Sumter had already departed Salisbury, heading down the Catawba River valley with 200 Catawba Indians and a band of officers who had served under him in the Sixth Continental Regiment.

At a mustering of Patriots at King Hagler's Creek in mid-June, the militiamen and officers under Hill, Lacey, and Bratton agreed on the 15$^{th}$, through backwoods democracy, to follow the command of Colonel Thomas Sumter. They also agreed that he should be a brigadier general. In a letter to Governor John Rutledge, administering South Carolina in absentia from Hillsborough, the militiamen

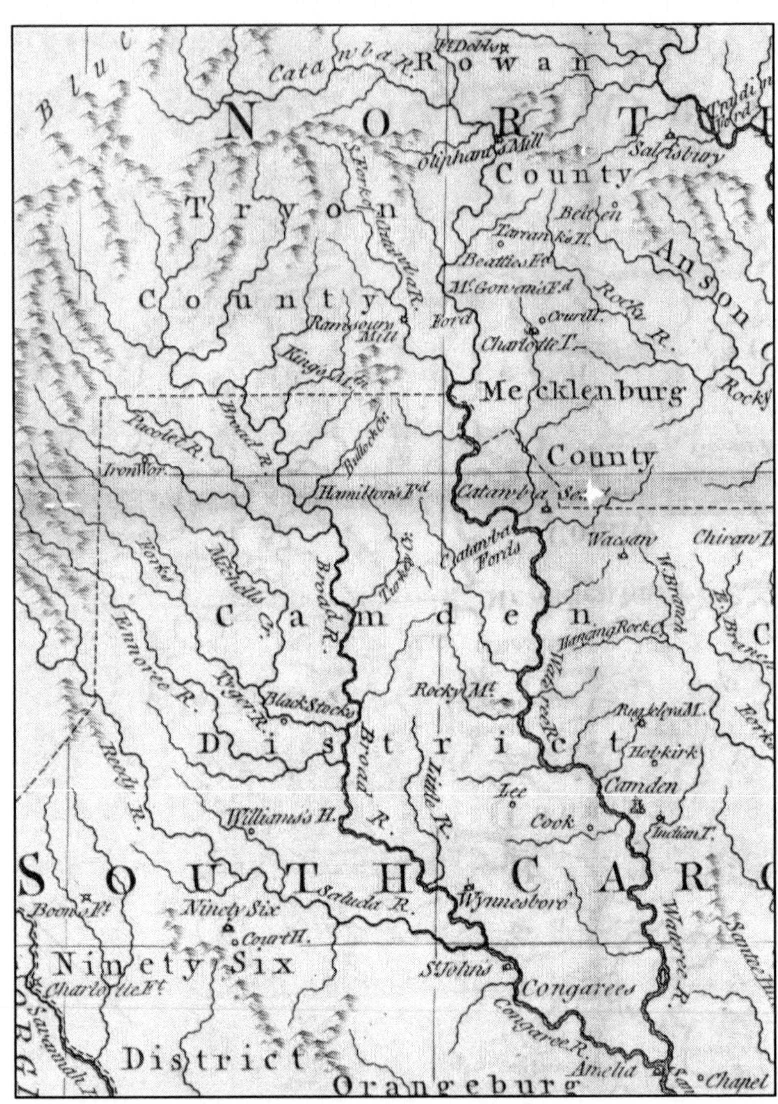


The Upcountry of South Carolina and the lower Piedmont of North Carolina were the scenes of fervent resistance to the advance of the British Legion and the rallying of Tory militia. Detail above is from "A map of the seat of war in the southern part of Virginia, North Carolina, and the northern part of South Carlina," London, 1781. [Reference: http://dc.lib.unc.edu/u?/ncmaps,361]

asked the governor to confirm the appointment. Sumter accepted the role as leader, assuring his new compatriots, "Our interests and fates are and must be identical. With me as with you, it is liberty or death."[1]

William Hill, widely known as Billy, was an Ulster Scot, born in 1741. In 1762, he moved from York, Pennsylvania to the Catawba River valley, where he found iron ore on his property along Allison Creek. Beginning at first with an open-pit mine, he later built an ironworks called the Æra Furnace. From it, he supplied all the cannonballs used by Charlestown during the siege.[2] At that ironworks during the days following the capture of Charlestown, the local community gathered to hear a Tory read a proclamation issued by Sir Henry Clinton. It declared that the Continental Congress had abandoned South Carolina and called for all those who served the rebel cause to take an oath of allegiance to the King. Put off by the arrogance of the British, Billy Hill rose to denounce the claim as a lie. He openly declared, "[We have] all taken an oath to defend & maintain the Independence of the state to the utmost of our power … [W]e could keep in a body, go into North Carolina meet our friends & return with them to recover our State." His spirit was contagious and inspiring. Though Hill was highly vocal in rallying Patriots in the Upcountry, William Bratton and Edward Lacey had also banded together men from the area to fight in defense of Liberty.

South Carolina's Upcountry had a long history of an independent spirit. Since the 1750s, the residents of the region (today's York, Cherokee, and Spartanburg counties) had suffered through Indian wars, government apathy, raids by bands of outlaws, boundary disputes, and the Regulator-Moderator conflicts of the late 1760s. They had learned to take care of their own affairs. When the fighting began in Massachusetts in 1775, the residents took sides, long before

Cornwallis came to their doorsteps. Reflecting their local politics and history, for the most part, the former Regulators sided with the Whig rebels, and the former Moderators (also known as Scovelites) sided with the Loyalists as "friends of the government." The people knew their neighbors and they knew what sides each had taken. The war was a civil conflict in the Carolina backcountry, just as it was in other colonies. Not everyone was a Patriot. Moreover, these backcountry militiamen, on both sides, fought in ways and with weapons unfamiliar to the invading British Legion. With rifle, tomahawk, and scalping knife, they ambushed and skirmished from their hiding places and targeted the officers — tactics considered dishonorable on the battlefields of Europe.[3]

In issuing the proclamation requiring a oath of allegiance, Sir Henry Clinton had perhaps underestimated the extent and fervor of support for the Patriot cause in the Upcountry. Even so, the British and their Loyalist supporters intended to snuff it out.

Being aware of Hill's active and vocal resistance, Colonel George

**Billy Hill's ironworks was a gathering place for Whig supporters in the Upcountry and a supplier of shot to the Continental Army before Captain Huck burned it. The site of the ironworks, now submerged beneath Lake Wylie in York Co., SC, is commemorated by a stone monument and historic marker on SC Hwy 274.**

Turnbull at Rocky Mount sent forward Captain Christian Huck to burn Hill's foundry. Turnbull had written to Cornwallis seeking permission for the expedition, noting that Hill's ironworks was "a Refuge for Runnaways, a Forge for casting Ball and making Rifle Guns &c."[4] Huck was a lawyer from Philadelphia, of German ancestry, and a steadfast supporter of the King. He was particularly unsympathetic toward the Scots-Irish who inhabited the area he was asked to patrol. Relishing his assignment, Huck rode out on June 18. "With a company of horse and about 500 Tories," Hill later wrote, they "destroyed all the property they could not carry away[, b]urned the forge furnace, grist and saw mills together with all other buildings even to the negro huts, & bore away about 90 negroes …"[5] Riding into the Scots-Irish communities along Fishing Creek, Huck took note of the inhabitants' reluctance to take the oath of allegiance. A week earlier, on Sunday, June 11, Huck and his Tory detachment had ridden to Fishing Creek Church where they expected to find the known Whig preaching support for the rebels from the pulpit. To Huck's dismay, the pastor had already taken up arms and joined a local militia group. Angry at missing his chance to take the pastor, Huck burned the Reverend Simpson's home, and one of his men shot a young boy as the lad carried his Bible along the road.

Huck's reckless marauding horrified the residents of the Upcountry community. His actions were regarded as particularly egregious even in light of the bands of Tories (some were actually bandits and outlaws) who rode throughout the Upcountry region wantonly harassing suspected Whigs. These lawless Tories preyed on those who had complied with the proclamation and had taken the oath. Having identified themselves as previously supporting the Revolution, these former rebels attracted the wrath of these vindictive Loyalists. One such victim wrote, "[They] set to Rob us taking all our living, horses, Cows,

Sheep, Clothing, of all sorts, money, pewter, tin, knives, in fine Everything that sooted them Untill we were Stript Naked."[6] Understandable to everyone except the perpetrators of these crimes and the British officers who enabled and tolerated these atrocities, the residents of the Upcountry stiffened their resistance to the British advance. Local Patriot scout James Collins recounted his father's declaration after witnessing the burning of Billy Hill's ironworks: "I have come here determined to take my gun and when I lay it down, I lay down my life with it." Addressing his son, he added with firm resolve, "We must submit and become slaves, or fight."[7]

**The Battle of Ramsour's Mill**

At the Battle of Moore's Creek Bridge in February 1776, the Loyalist sentiment in North Carolina had been beaten back, but not destroyed. After the surrender of Charlestown, Loyalists were newly emboldened. In the North Carolina backcountry counties west of Salisbury and Charlotte, the rival factions — Patriot and Loyalist — were both recruiting ranks of militiamen from among the area residents.

As Cornwallis prepared to march northward from Charlestown, he wanted the Loyalists in North Carolina to prepare to assist him with the invasion of the rebel colony. Cornwallis sent one of his Tory officers, Lt. Colonel John Moore of the Royal North Carolina Regiment, back home to muster volunteers in the area. He returned to his native Tryon County, which the rebel government had then divided into Rutherford and Lincoln counties.[8] In sending Moore, Cornwallis ordered that the colonel take no military action until the British forces arrived. Cornwallis deemed the Loyalist army he asked Moore to raise as absolutely critical to supporting the British Southern campaign and its planned invasion of North Carolina.

After a local meeting on June 10 at his father's home with a small gathering of some 40 Loyalists, Moore sent out word for a muster on June 13 at Ramsour's Mill (also incorrectly reported as Ramseur's and Ramsaur's). With the aid of Major Nicholas Welch, Moore convened about 1,300 men by June 18 at Derick Ramsour's Mill.[9] Welch was a flamboyant fellow who regaled the Loyalist recruits with stories about Clinton's capture of Charlestown and Tarleton's victory at the Waxhaws. He also spread around a few guineas, which helped encourage some men to rally to the King's cause. Many, but not all, were German farmers who had taken an oath of allegiance to King George III during the Regulator Movement of 1771. Others were of English descent. Many were citizen farmers, not fighters. About one-quarter of the men who mustered to the call bore no firearms and were expecting to be provided weapons supplied by the British Legion. The large party camped atop a thinly wooded rise some 300 yards east of the mill site. This was not an army, but an unorganized throng of untrained civilians who came together in support of the British government. Some most certainly wanted to protect their rights as Englishmen. Others came because it seemed most likely that the invading British army would prevail and they wanted to be on the winning side. Others were perhaps interested in gaining a claim on the lands of local Whig rebels should those lands be confiscated by Cornwallis.

At the time of the Loyalist muster, General Griffith Rutherford, commander of the Whig militia for the Salisbury District, was assembling his force of 1,200 men in Mecklenburg County, anticipating the advance of British forces toward Charlotte. Learning of the muster at Ramsour's Mill and being unwilling to reduce his own force at the time, Rutherford sent Colonel Francis Locke to raise Patriot forces within his home Rowan County. He charged Major David Wilson to do the same in the northern part of his home Mecklenburg County. They mustered together between 360 and 400 men, with about 100 of them mounted. The assemblage moved toward Ramsour's Mill uncertain about its next steps. Most certainly they were outnumbered by three or four to one.

Because the Patriot men were all civilians, serving under their elected leaders, no one leader had general command. This was the same difficult situation Captain William Moore had bemoaned four years before in the expedition against the Cherokees. Locke had served under Rutherford then as well. Locke called the Whig leaders into a council of war on the 19th where they discussed their options. They were aware they numbered only about one third of the assembled Loyalists. To some it seemed prudent to avoid direct confrontation until they were reinforced. Others saw it differently and must have leveled an "imputation of cowardice," noted William Graham later, as the cause of such timidity. Immediately after the challenging remarks and a spirited exchange of words, the entire party threw itself headlong and imprudently into planning an imminent attack. Their courage would not be questioned, they declared by their actions. Locke sent an officer as courier ahead hurriedly to inform General Rutherford of their plans.

Rutherford, in the meantime, had seen a favorable change in the British movements in South Carolina's Upcountry. Rutherford then turned his attention and the Patriot militia of 1,200 men toward dealing with the Loyalist force he knew Colonel Moore was assembling. Rutherford sent his own courier to inform Colonel Locke to stand by and to wait for his arrival. The message was too late. The Whig militia under Colonel Locke was already moving.

Before dawn on the 20th, thirty men from the Burke County Militia Battalion joined up with Locke. Their leader, Captain Adam Reep, explained the lay of the land and the placement of the Loyalist militia. "The Tories were encamped on a high ridge, clear of under wood, and covered with large oaks," Major William R. Davie later reported, "their rear was protected by a Mill-pond and their right flank by a strong fence."[10] With this new information, the Patriot force approached the mill on three fronts. Locke's infantry approached along the Tuckasegee Road. Major Joseph McDowell's mounted troops rode along the Sherrill Ford Road. Captain John Hardin's unit approached from the south over a hill and through a ravine.

On the last day of spring, June 21, a heavy fog shrouded the woods. The men could see only so far into the hazy morning. What lay ahead unseen was a mystery and a potential threat. The mounted militia led the advance with two ranks of infantry following. McDowell's Burke County mounted militiamen rode in with Captain Daniel McKisick leading his Lincoln County militia in the charge.[11] Their incursion was first met by a handful of Tory pickets posted some 600 yards away from the encampment. Spotting the Whigs emerging from the fog, the Tories turned and ran toward camp. Describing the battle, Major William A. Graham wrote, "[Major Joseph] McDowell's men had pushed on and reached the enemy about the same time [as Locke's], and both parties, leaving the road, rode up within thirty steps of the enemy and opened fire. The enemy were considerably demoralized at first, but seeing so few (not over one hundred) in the attacking party, rallied and poured such a volley into them that they [McDowell's mounted force] retired through the infantry, some of whom joined them [the mounted in retreat] and never returned."[12]

Initially encouraged by the apparent retreat of the attacking Whigs, the

**The battle at Ramsour's Mill was fought between Patriot and Loyalist units, Americans all. Volunteer living history interpreters reenact the battle at the site of Ramsour's Mill in Lincolnton, NC.**

Tories pushed down the hill, but the Patriots re-formed and pressed back. The Whigs drove the Tories 600 yards toward the hill, laying in such heavy fire that the Tories took cover at the top and beyond the hill where they had camped. Davie wrote, "[T]he enemy drew up behind the trees and baggage, … the enemy's fire was well directed."[13] The Tories recovered and in turn pressed forward, driving the Patriots halfway back down the front slope of the ridge. Few orders were given by officers on either side. The men fought by instinct, taking advantage when and where they could find it, each operating independently.

A haze of gun smoke drifted through the woods across the face of the hill, blending with and then replacing the clearing fog. Throughout the conflict, some of the fighting was hand-to-hand. Neither side had bayonets to force the other into retreat. Some did swing their rifles as clubs at close quarters and used their rifle butts to crush the skull of a foe. By the time the Tories had pushed back a good bit on the Patriot infantry, captains John Hardin and Joseph Sharpe had moved their men of the 1st Rowan Militia into positions on the Tories' right and left flanks. Exploiting this tactical advantage, the Patriots pressed forward with accurate shooting, taking out Loyalist officers, and enfilading the Loyalist ranks with a sweeping fire from across the entire line of Patriot militia. "Captain Hardin," C.L. Hunter wrote, "… under cover of the fence, kept up a galling fire on the right flank of the Tories."[14]

Neither side wore uniforms. Loyalists and Patriots both fought in their hunting shirts and everyday clothing. To distinguish one from the other in battle, the Loyalists wore sprigs of evergreen in their hats. The Patriots placed patches of white paper in theirs. Tragically, the patches of white served as appealing targets to the Loyalist marksmen. Many of Locke's men were shot in the head; nevertheless, the Patriots persevered. When the tide of the battle turned against the Tories, some ripped the evergreen from their hats, tossed it aside, and intermingled with the Patriots moving up the slope. Sensing defeat, other Loyalists farther back in the line turned and ran toward the mill. Patriots shot some of the Loyalists as they retreated. Other Tories unnerved by the Patriot assault scrambled through the trees and made their way to Clark's Creek. In crossing the mill pond, some panicked and drowned.

When the Whigs finally crested the ridge where the Loyalists had encamped, they halted their pursuit. From there they could see a host of Tories across Clark's Creek at Ramsour's Mill. Many of these were the unarmed Loyalists who had fled the camp when the shooting started. Unaware of this fact, the Patriots assumed the fighting would resume anew with this secondary force held in reserve. The Whigs mustered what remained of their force of 400. They counted 84. Another two dozen were rounded up from the rear for a total of 110, both willing and reluctant militiamen.

Two officers rode toward Rutherford to hurry him along.[15] Thinking that his orders to Locke to stand by had been received and being unaware as well of the impending battle, Rutherford had made camp for the night on the 19$^{th}$ at the Dickson plantation.[16] Some of his men had "taken courage" at the nearby Dellinger's Tavern. When the two officers found Rutherford some six miles away and alerted him to the situation, the general immediately sent Major William R. Davie with his 65 mounted militiamen ahead at a gallop. Rutherford followed with his infantry militiamen hurrying at a quickened pace. The two riders had stopped at the Dickson home (near today's Mt. Holly in Gaston County) to tell Captain McKisick's wife, Jane, that her husband had been shot and was lying on the battlefield likely dying. Leaving her two young daughters with the Dicksons, Jane McKisick mounted a horse and rode 16 miles to the battlefield. She searched for her husband, Daniel, among the dead and dying. Finding him alive, she carried him to the Reinhardt cabin. She and the other wives, mothers, and daughters tended to the wounded on both sides for several days. The wounded overflowed the home, the stable, and the smokehouse.[17]

Meanwhile, Colonel Moore played for time. He sent forward under a flag of truce a messenger to propose a cease of hostilities so both sides could tend to their wounded and even bury the dead. At the same time, Moore ordered all but 50 of his Loyalist recruits to scatter and head for their respective homes. They departed immediately, some on foot and some on sad horses. Colonel Locke sent forth Major James Rutherford—a son of the general riding toward them with reinforcements—to hear the messenger. Locke was duly concerned that the Loyalists would discover the weakness of his forces. Refusing the delay, Major Rutherford demanded the Loyalists surrender in ten minutes. The flag bearer returned to Colonel Moore. He and his men immediately fled; some rode with Moore and others headed in their own directions.

Colonel Moore eventually made his way to General Lord Cornwallis with about 30 of his men. His news was not well received. Cornwallis was angry at Moore for disobeying orders not to engage the Patriots before Major Patrick Ferguson arrived with an army of perhaps 2,000 men. The general had Moore arrested and threatened him with court-martial. The Loyalist army, so important to Cornwallis's plans to subdue North Carolina, had been unnecessarily scattered.

The aftermath of the battle was both sobering and somber. Before the battle had started, Christian Reinhardt had taken his wife, two children, and some of their enslaved ("several small negroes") across Clark's Creek to a cane brake along the western bank. In the retreat, the fleeing Tories ran through the cane brake, some exclaiming desperately "We are whipped!" Mrs. Reinhardt made her way back home across the creek to a most disturbing scene. "As the contest raged, and peal after peal of musketry reverberated over the surrounding hills and dales, [the Reinhardt's] dwelling house, smoke-house, and even [the] empty stables were successively filled with the dead, the dying and the wounded."[18] "In a short time, her house was stripped of every disposable blanket and sheet to wrap around the dead, or be employed in

**Neighbors gathering at the Reinhardt cabin cared for the wounded of both sides. A replica cabin, battlefield graves, wayside exhibits, and commemorative monuments interpret the story of the battle at Ramsour's Mill.**

some other useful way. Neighbors and relatives, a few hours before bitter enemies, were now seen freely mingling together and giving every kind attention to the suffering, whether Whig or Tory, within their power."[19]

For several days afterwards, families of the men who had fought there — Patriot and Loyalist — came looking for their loved ones. In some cases, they removed the bodies from the field and buried them at home. Without uniforms, the identities of the dead were not always discernible as to the side for which they had fought. Though some were buried individually, seventy bodies, both Loyalists and Whigs, were buried in a common grave at the site of the battle.

By the time Major Davie and General Rutherford arrived at the scene, the fighting had been over for an hour or two. Rutherford sent Major Davie to overtake and capture escaping Loyalists. Most that he caught were paroled, but a few were sent to the jail in Salisbury to await trials for suspected perpetration of crimes. Rutherford's men remained at the battle site for two days. Rutherford learned that Colonel Bryan (probably Samuel, but perhaps his brother Joseph) was raising a band of Loyalists in the Forks of the Yadkin area. By approaching the region with 600 men, Rutherford caused Bryan to flee the vicinity with his Loyalists. Major Davie would encounter Bryan's Tories soon enough at Hanging Rock, South Carolina, on August 6.

The Battle of Ramsour's Mill had been a battle of neighbors, of friends, and of brothers. These were backcountry citizens engaged in a civil war, fighting for what they believed to be their best destiny—as loyal subjects of the King enjoying the celebrated rights of Englishmen or as rebel heirs to an uncertain future they were free to create. On the face of the slope, 56 bodies lay still. Another 70 lay on the top of the hill and beyond the crest. Each side suffered about one hundred wounded with some of these mortal, ending in later deaths. For the Whigs, suffering 140 casualties out of an initial force of 400 far surpassed the usual carnage inflicted by either side during the American Revolution. Considering that a large part of the Whig force ran away when the shooting began, the percentage of casualties was even higher. The Battle of Ramsour's Mill was indeed a bloody encounter. It was also a costly affair for the Loyalists, hampering for a time their ability to recruit and muster men to their cause. These were men whose presence and activity in support of the King and Cornwallis could well have turned the tide of events yet to unfold not 30 miles away in the same countryside and not four months hence — another confrontation between opposing forces of Americans: the Battle of Kings Mountain.

**Ferguson Responds**

News of the defeat at Ramsour's Mill traveled across the backcountry. It reached Ninety Six on June 23. Lieutenant Allaire recorded receipt of the news and its effects in his journal: "Some friends came in, four were wounded. The militia had embodied at Tuckasegie, on the South Fork of Catawba river — were attacked by a party of Rebels, under command of Gen. Rutherford. The militia were scant of ammunition, which obliged them to retreat. The men were obliged to swim the river at a mill dam. The Rebels fired on them and killed thirty." Allaire added that upon hearing the news, Major Ferguson rode off with forty American Volunteers, "push[ing] with all speed in pursuit of the Rebels." Their prey was about seventy miles away. With optimism in the outcome of the British campaign, Allaire added to punctuate his confidence, "The militia [Tories] are flocking to him from all parts of the country."

The Whig militia's defeat of the Loyalists at Ramsour's Mill may have encouraged the local Patriots, but this skirmish, fought among neighbors in the southern piedmont of North Carolina, did little to forestall the continuing advance of the sizable, invading British Legion. Lord Cornwallis believed confidently that the surrender at Charlestown, the defeat of Col. Buford, and the absence of any organized opposition signaled an end to substantial armed resistance in South Carolina. Noting in particular "the submission of General Andrew Williamson at Ninety Six," he confidently wrote to Sir Henry Clinton on June 30 that several recent victories had "put an end to all resistance in South Carolina."[20]

**Upcountry Stalwarts**

During the Battle of Ramsour's Mill, Sumter and his men had been close enough to hear the shooting well off in the distance, but the fighting was over before they arrived. Sumter applied to authorities for permission to impress into the service of the Patriots items he could gather from the battlefield. With the garnered supplies, he and his men first convened at Hagler's Hill; but, seeking better pasture for their horses, Sumter and his men moved south to Clem's Branch of Sugar Creek (in today's Fort Mill, York Co., South Carolina).[21] There he set up camp and began to train his men. He trained them not with drills and military discipline, but in physical strength with competitions in wrestling, running, swimming, and jumping. He was preparing them for a new type of warfare. More men continued to rally to the cause and to muster at the camp. Some were experienced militiamen and fighters. A few even violated their paroles and thus risked being hanged if captured again by the British. Many more were new to the cause, joining for the first time in 1780. They were young men, many in their twenties. The stories told of Tarleton's brutal slaughter of Buford's men had spurred them to join in resisting what they plainly saw as a British invasion of their Carolina homeland.

One notable Patriot who came forward at this time was Colonel James Williams. He arrived from his Little River plantation and mill in the Ninety Six District. He had served in the campaign against the Cherokees four years earlier, commanding men he had recruited and trained. Williams was passionate about resisting the British incursion, believing that his fighting was "but of necessity," he wrote to his son. He continued, "… I had rather suffer anything than lose my birthright, and that of my children."[22] Williams had served with Billy Hill and Thomas Sumter in the South Carolina General Assembly. Relying on that mutual relationship, Sumter made Williams his commissary officer responsible for gathering and distributing supplies.

After two weeks in camp, Sumter believed he had 500 men well trained and ready for action. On July 4, he moved his camp to Nation's Ford on the Catawba River. From there Colonel James Williams wrote a letter to his wife sharing, perhaps imprudently, many details of gathering Whig and rebel forces. He enumerated 7,700 troops on their way to Camden expected to arrive there "in six or seven days, which may put a different face on

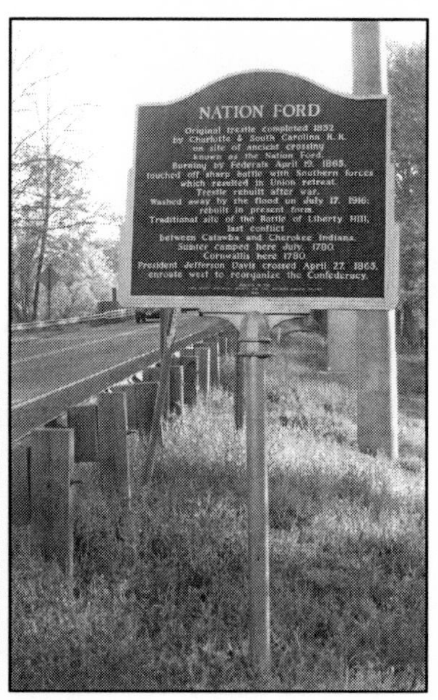


**After training his men along Clem's Branch, building their strength and skills for guerilla warfare, Sumter moved them to Nation Ford. A marker at Nation Ford recounts numerous historic events associated with this crossing of the Catawba River on US Hwy 21 near Ft. Mill, SC.**

matters." With an eye toward protecting his home and family, he also wrote, "I pray God that I may have the happiness of seeing you my love at Mount Pleasant in the course of this month with a force sufficient to repel all the Tories in the upper part of South Carolina."[23]

The Loyalists in the communities just below the North Carolina line took note of Sumter's militia troops-in-training and expressed their concerns to the local British commander. He responded with treachery, authorizing a bribe to entice a Patriot officer to lead Sumter into an ambush. Because Captain Edward Lacey's father was an ardent Tory and perhaps because Lacy himself had served with Major General Edward Braddock at the Battle of the Monongahela in 1755[24], the captain was considered a potential accomplice. As was demonstrated through his later service, no such willingness to betray any Patriot could have been more wrongly surmised.

**Huck's Defeat**

After burning Hill's ironworks on June 18, Captain Christian Huck continued harassing Whigs in the district between the Broad and Catawba rivers, known as the New Acquisition District. He had picked on the wrong population. British officers often spoke of the Irish, meaning the Scots-Irish, of being the settlers most averse to the British government.[25] Huck discovered the truth of that statement for himself. He marched into the New Acquisition District with orders to muster a militia of Loyalists. Going from house to house, his men commanded the male residents to muster. The younger ones had already departed; only the old men remained. But having no choice in the matter, they complied.

At the muster, Huck combined in his harangue both politics and religion, declaring that he would defeat them even "if the Rebels were as thick as trees, and Jesus Christ himself were to command them." These Presbyterian Scots-Irish had plenty of time to talk among themselves about Huck's disturbing blasphemy as they walked back to their homes; Huck's men had confiscated the citizens' horses while they listened to the Legion commander. Hill later wrote: "This ill behaviour of the enemy made an impression on the minds of the most serious men in the little band and raised their courage under the belief that they would be made instruments in the hand of Heaven to punish this enemy for his wickedness and blasphemy …"[26]

On July 11, Captain Huck departed his camp with the intentions of harassing Whigs and rebels in the area, but his plans had been discovered. That morning Joseph Kerr had come into Huck's camp. He was a young man of 19 who had endured a physical handicap since birth. Frequently he used his condition to disarm the suspicions of others, earning him the trust of the people he approached. By this means, he was, in fact, a successful spy for the Whigs. On this occasion, having earned the confidence of the camp, Kerr moved about unchallenged, listening and learning about plans. Though some that day suspected his devious intentions, he protested that he was not a Whig spy. Taking no chances in the matter, however, Huck insisted that Kerr remain with them throughout the day.

Huck departed camp with some one hundred or more men (some accounts say specifically 115 men) including 35 British Legion dragoons, 50 or 60 Tories and the rest New York Volunteers from Rocky Mount. He first descended upon the home of Captain John McClure. Huck was intent on capturing this Whig leader, having heard that some of the gathered Patriots had returned home to check on their crops. In fact, McClure was still away at Sumter's camp, but his son James (some accounts say younger brother) and a son-in-law, Edward

**Huck's men threatened Martha Bratton with a reaping hook on the porch of her home before they rode on to the Williamson plantation. The William Bratton home and the old road bed are preserved and interpreted for visitors at the 775-acre site for Historic Brattonsville, one of the York County Culture and Heritage Museums.**

Martin, were caught there melting the family's pewter plates and utensils and molding the metal into shot for ammunition. As Huck roughed up the family and declared that the two men would hang in the morning, no one noticed that daughter Mary McClure had slipped out of the house. She saddled a horse and rode off to warn her father and brothers.

Huck next rode to the home of William Bratton expecting to capture that rebel leader. He was greeted by Martha Bratton who stood on the porch with her young son and defied the attempts to frighten her with a reaping hook and sword. One of Huck's Tories had stepped onto the porch and threatened to cut off her head if she did not reveal her husband's whereabouts. After previously saying she did not know, her son later wrote that in response to the threat she declared: "I told the simple truth and could not tell if I would; but I now add, that I would not if I could." Other accounts have Martha Bratton defiantly declaring when first asked as to her husband's whereabouts, "in Sumter's army." In either case, her boldness enraged the Tory who might have readily carried out his threat to slash her throat. In an instant, however, he was lying prostrate on the porch having been knocked down by one of the

Legion officers. Continuing to strike the ruffian with the flat of his sword, Captain John Adamson from Camden kicked the Tory trouble-maker off the porch. He apologized for the rough treatment she had received and promised Martha Bratton that she would not be hurt. She and her son stepped back into the house. Despite receiving her own reprieve from harm, Captain Huck did capture three suspected Whigs on the property that day and carried them off, promising to hang them with the others in the morning.

Traveling a short distance from the Bratton home, Huck next arrived at the plantation home of James Williamson. His five sons were serving with Bratton, and it appeared that no one at all lived there at the time. Huck chose to make camp there for the night. He locked his doomed prisoners in a corncrib and took personal shelter in the house. However, he did not with sufficient care post guards and sentinels for his camp.

After Mary McClure arrived at Sumter's camp with word of Huck's marauding, her tale was corroborated by another messenger. Martha Bratton had sent one of the enslaved plantation workers, named Watt, to alert her husband. Watt was soon followed by the arrival of spy Joseph Kerr who had slipped away after dark. The last two arrivals brought word of the location and the layout of Huck's camp. All three carried a message of dire urgency for the lives of the five prisoners to be hanged in the morning.

Several parties of Patriot militia and would-be rescuers departed from Sumter's camp, each riding under the command of its own leader. Communication was not coordinated, and along the way some went off in other directions. Of the some 500 men who started toward the Williamson home, half that number arrived. Those men were under the command of William Bratton, Billy Hill, Edward Lacey, John McClure, and Andrew Neel.

Edward Lacey had to deal with extra burdens as a partisan rebel. His father was a devout Tory, living within a few miles of the Williamson home. His brother, Reuben, was fighting for the Tories. Lacey placed four men to guard his father to prevent him from warning Huck of the pending assault. Despite the four guards, the senior Lacey escaped anyway, and was most likely on his way to inform his Tory son Reuben of the attack. Fortunately, the guards recaptured the runaway only a few hundred yards from the home. Taking no chances with the second confinement, Edward Lacey had his father tied to the bed to prevent his spoiling the eminent Patriot attack.

The Patriot militia arrived at the Bratton home undetected. William Bratton sneaked onto the plantation to scout the placement of guards and to discover where the Tories were bivouacked. All the Tories were in their tents in an area marked off by a split-rail fence. Bratton

**William Bratton's militiamen surprised Captain Huck at dawn and fired from behind a split-rail fence at the startled Tories. Volunteer reenactors come to Historic Brattonsville annually to playout the encounter for hundreds of visitors on a weekend near July 12.**

returned to the other militia leaders to discuss a plan of attack. He would lead one detachment along the road from the direction that led to his house. Lacey would circle around the Williamson plantation and attack along the same road from the other direction. Lacey's men were delayed getting into position, Hill wrote, "with some embarrassments by fences, brush, [and] briars."[27] They were not completely in place when Bratton's men opened fire from their side in the pre-dawn light of July 12.

The element of surprise stunned the Tories. Bratton's men had waited until they were only 75 paces from the tents before they opened fire with buckshot. They dismounted and took positions along the split-rail fence, which provided them some protection but mostly just made them difficult to see. By this time, Lacey's men were in position and likewise began firing from the opposite side into the startled Tories as the defenders scrambled from their tents.

Despite the deadly fire that the Whigs were pouring into the Tory camp, Huck's men rallied enough to form a bayonet charge against the Patriots. Using the fence to steady their rifles and muskets, the Patriots fired into the line with deadly accuracy and turned back three attempted bayonet charges. Amidst the fighting, Captain Huck emerged from the house and mounted his horse. He attempted to rally his men into an effective stand. In short order, Huck was shot from his horse. Some accounts say he was shot in the throat; others say that Thomas Carroll loaded two balls in his rifle and caught Huck behind the ears with both. In either case, when Huck fell, the spirit of the Tories did as well. Some threw down their weapons and surrendered. Others took to the woods and still others ran down the road. The Patriot militiamen pursued some of them for fourteen miles, sometimes taking retribution against those they caught for offenses and crimes the captives

**Tory Captain Christian Huck was killed and his men routed at the battle at Williamson's plantation, thereafter known as Huck's Defeat. The grave stone for the enslaved Watt stands next to a battle monument at Historic Brattonsville in York Co., SC.**

had committed. Some were likely given "Tarleton's quarter," killed in retaliation for the slaughter of Buford's men. Without the discipline of answering to a central commander, many of the militiamen acted rashly and brutally, and they did so with impunity.

Of the 115 or so Tories who rode with Captain Huck, only a reported 24 survived. Some of the victims had been killed outright; the bodies of many others were later found in the woods where the wounded had crawled to escape and then died. Ninety-some Tories had been killed. The Patriots lost only one militiaman. In addition, the spoils of Patriot victory included some one hundred horses, saddles and bridles along with scores of pistols and muskets.

News of the complete victory at Williamson's plantation spread quickly through the Upcountry. It lifted the spirits of Patriots throughout the region. More men began to seek out the partisan bands in which they could fight. Fewer men mustered to the camps of the Loyalists. The battle itself became known more commonly by what it was: Huck's Defeat. That engagement in which Edward Lacey played such a pivotal role was, Hill wrote, "the first check the enemy had received after the fall of Charleston; and was of greater consequence to the American cause than can be well supposed from an affair of [so] small a magnitude—as it had the tendency to inspire the Americans with courage & fortitude & to teach them that the enemy was not invincible."[28] The victory of Huck's Defeat put Cornwallis on notice that he had much more work to do if he intended to subdue the citizens of South Carolina's Upcountry. His letter to Clinton on June 30 had clearly overstated the prospects for a quick victory over the Patriots.

That evening Lieutenant Anthony Allaire was on expedition from Ninety Six in pursuit of a reported band of rebels and camping along Padget Creek. He recorded in his journal: "Wednesday, 12th. … This evening met an express with the disagreeable news of a party of ours consisting of seventeen of the Legion, eighteen York Volunteers, and twenty-five militia being defeated at Colonel Bratton's, at Fishing creek."[29] He added in his next day's entry: "The Rebels, we hear, are collecting in force at the Catawba Nation and Broad river." On the following day, he concluded: "Every hour news from different parts of the country of Rebel parties doing mischief." Only three days earlier, Allaire had penned a more sanguine and confident note: "Monday, 10th. Got in motion at five o'clock in the morning; crossed Saluda in a flat; marched nine miles to a Rebel Col. [James] Williams' plantation, where we halted. Mrs. Williams and the children were at home, and were treated with the utmost civility. Col. Williams is with the Rebels, and is a very violent, persecuting scoundrel."[30]

Cornwallis continued with his strategy to invade and conquer the

**Major William R. Davie attacked and looted a convoy of packhorses delivering supplies to the British outposts. A marker on Flat Rock Road in Lancaster Co. , southwest of Kershaw, commemorates the encounter and escape.**

Upcountry. He marched his British Legion northward, up the Catawba River valley. To supply his advancing army, he sent ammunition and food ahead to outposts. Wagons and packhorses carried these provisions to stations including Hanging Rock and Rocky Mount. These depots made excellent targets for bands of Patriot militia wanting to challenge the British advance and in need of their provisions for war.

### Flat Rock

About a week after Huck's Defeat, Major William R. Davie gathered his North Carolina militia near his home church in the Waxhaws (a few miles north of today's Lancaster, South Carolina). After learning that supplies would be delivered to Hanging Rock on July 20, Davie rallied his men into an all-night march intending to intercept the convoy.

Davie and his mounted militiamen successfully ambushed the Tory guards at Flat Rock on the road from Camden, about four-and-a-half miles south of Hanging Rock. They took from the supplies what they needed and destroyed the rest. The Patriots mounted their prisoners two to a horse and tied each pair together, taking them along to prevent word of the ambush from reaching Cornwallis so quickly. Another band of Tories laid an ambuscade near Beaver Creek along the lane as it passed a plantation. In the predawn hours of the 22nd, Davie's party rode past the cornfield. The hidden Tories fired into the Patriot convoy. The mounted twin-prisoners presented easy targets in the dim light. Mistaking them for Patriots, the Tories shot their own men, killing most, while Davie's men escaped almost unscathed. Davie's detachment left the dead and wounded Tories on the hill and rode away. As they had done on their way to Flat Rock, they successfully passed quietly by the encampment of Tories at Hanging Rock and returned to their camp. Once again, the advancing British convoy was confronted by the craftiness and raw courage of the Patriot militia who would not be so easily subdued.

**Rocky Mount**

With renewed confidence in their ability to oppose both the British invasion and the Tory militia, the leaders of several bands of partisan militia convened at Landsford on the Catawba River. They planned attacks intended to dislodge the British control of the Catawba River valley. At the time, General Thomas Sumter was the leader of the only viable resistance in the area. They knew that General Horatio Gates, the newly appointed commander of the Southern Department of the Continental Army, would soon to be in command of the troops already marching out of North Carolina to confront Cornwallis. Before Gates arrived with his army, Sumter wanted to attempt a campaign of his own. With Billy Hill and Edward Lacey, Sumter planned to capture the installation at Rocky Mount. He asked Major Davie and a party of North Carolina militia to attack Hanging Rock simultaneously with his attack to draw attention there.

Rocky Mount was a fortified camp including three buildings; one was a framed house covered with clapboard. The camp sat along the road from Winnsboro to Camden near where it crossed the Catawba River at a ferry. The site was west of the river and positioned on a ridge above the ferry site, overlooking Rocky Creek. The camp was surrounded by a ditch with abatis (sharpened stakes protruding from the ground) to deter attacks. The immediate area surrounding the camp was generally open although large boulders protruded from the ground. The main building provided loopholes, which afforded the riflemen inside sheltered positions from which to fire on any attackers. Numbering between 150 and 200 men, the New York Volunteers defended the British position there under the command of Lt. Colonel George Turnbull. It was Turnbull who had sent forth Captain Huck to burn Hill's ironworks. No doubt, Hill was pleased for the opportunity to exact some revenge.[31]

On Sunday, July 30, Sumter's men crossed Fishing Creek and then Rocky Creek, attempting to surprise Turnbull and the garrison at Rocky Mount. Their effort was spoiled, however, when they spooked a nearby party of patrolling Tories. The Tories retreated to the fortified camp giving an alarm of the approaching Patriots.

**Thomas Sumter and Billy Hill unsuccessfully attacked the outpost at Rocky Mount. The site of Rocky Mount is marked with a single monument on Catawba Rd. in Fairfield Co. uphill from the Catawba River.**

Sumter's force was three times as large as that of the defenders, so Sumter at first simply demanded Turnbull's surrender. After a time,

Turnbull replied that "duty and inclination induce me to defend this place to the last extremity." Sumter began the attack believing that the clapboard building they saw would be easily riddled with their shot. Colonel Billy Hill recounted later that the defenders had placed small logs inside the house and used dirt to fill the cavity created against the wall. This afforded the occupants greater protection than the clapboard alone had suggested. That explained why Sumter's men fired without effect except when they fired directly at the loopholes themselves.[32]

After eight hours of sporadic gunfire, Sumter succumbed to his growing frustration; he called for a charge and direct assault on the fort. His foolish order resulted in the loss of eight of his men and had no effect at all on the defenders. But Sumter would not quit. After conferring with his militia officers, Sumter asked for two volunteers to approach the fort and to attempt starting a fire by tossing flaming bundles of lightwood onto the roofs of the buildings. After a long pause during which it looked doubtful that anyone would step forward for the hazardous task, Colonel Billy Hill volunteered for the mission; he was joined by Sergeant Jim Johnson. Carrying bundles of the wood, the two men scampered across 100 yards of open ground taking refuge behind large rocks. They were soon chased back by a party of British defenders who emerged from the fortification and charged the men with bayonets. On a second attempt, Hill and his companion reached a position closer to the fort and began lighting and tossing flaming bundles of sticks onto the roofs. When it looked as if the roof of the house would ignite, they retreated across the open field as the Volunteers fired at them from within the fort. Hill later wrote, "… neither of us lost a drop of blood, altho' locks of hair was cut from our heads and our garments riddled with balls." Despite their heroic efforts, just as the fires began to flame, a summer thunderstorm erupt-

**Major William R. Davie moved boldly against the British Legion at Hanging Rock as a diversion while Sumter and Hill attacked Rocky Mount. A marker on US Hwy 521 in Heath Springs, SC commemorates the later battle there.**

ed and doused the fire. Sumter and his men retreated from Rocky Mount "under a great mortification, as ever any number of men endured," Hill wrote. The British Legion retained control of Rocky Mount.[33]

### Davie at Hanging Rock, July 30

Meanwhile, Major Davie, intending only a diversion, was courageously succeeding at Hanging Rock by employing a creative deception. His goal was to keep the British forces there engaged to prevent their reinforcing Rocky Mount. He accomplished much more.

In the early afternoon of July 30,[34] Davie and 80 mounted militiamen approached Hanging Rock. They learned from a local Patriot that three companies of North Carolina Tories (some 60 or 70 mounted infantry of Colonel Morgan Bryan) had just arrived. They were encamped at the farmhouse very near the fortified camp, which garrisoned the British Legion. Taking stock of the situation, Davie devised a plan to get his men into position so they could destroy Bryan's Tory force. Because militiamen on both sides wore not uniforms but their hunting shirts and everyday clothing, he and his men were able to move through the encampment unnoticed. Davie sent 20 of his mounted dragoons to one end of the road beyond the house and another 20 into a field beside the house. He then had the remaining mounted riflemen (20 or 30 or 40; reports vary) ride down the road right by the farmhouse, appearing to be what others were expecting to see: more Loyalist militiamen headed for the encampment at Hanging Rock.

With his men in position along the road, Davie's riflemen dismounted in the road and began firing into the Tories. Davie later wrote, "The astonished Loyalists fled instantly the other way, and were immediately charged by the dragoons at full gallop and driven back in great confusion."[35] Those surprised Tories who ran into the field to escape were attacked by Davie's dragoons, who rode them down and hacked them with sabers. The slaughter was complete as Davie was unwilling to encumber his detachment by taking prisoners. Before the Legion forces could mount a counterattack from within the camp, Davie and his men escaped unscathed by any casualty. They departed the scene having captured sixty horses and a hundred rifles and muskets. It had been two months since Tarleton's slaughter of Colonel Buford's men in the Waxhaws. To the Patriots fighting a desperate, guerilla war, this attack may have felt something like justified retribution.

On August 1 and 2, Lieutenant Allaire added notes to his journal as his detachment camped in the Fair Forest region: "*Tuesday, August 1st.* Lay at Mitchell's creek. Had intelligence that the Rebels had attacked Col. Turnbull at Rocky Mount, on Sunday the 30th; but could not learn the particulars. *Wednesday, 2d.* … Had intelligence that Col. Turnbull beat off the Rebels … commanded by Gen. Sumter. He sent in a flag, demanding the post — Rocky Mount. Col. Turnbull sent word that he might come and take it. Sumter endeavored to do so, but was obliged soon to retreat with considerable loss. Col. Turnbull took two prisoners, who had previously been in his camp, drew ammunition, and then joined the Rebels, and were heard to say when firing, 'take back your ammunition again.' They were both hanged as a reward for their treachery."[36]

### Thicketty Fort

Since Huck's Defeat on July 12, the Whig partisans had skirmished with Legion and Tory groups in several parts of the Upcountry. For the moment, Rocky Mount and Hanging Rock remained in British control, but in other parts of the Upcountry, other Patriot groups were also establishing themselves as forces deserving respect. Partisans patrolling the Spartanburg District west of the Broad River had their own encounters with local Loyalists and the advancing British forces.

In February 1780, as the British were landing on the South Carolina coast, the Council of State for North Carolina had seen the need to prepare for its defense or possibly for sending troops to aid South Carolina. The governor called upon his generals to muster an army of 2,000 militiamen. General Griffith Rutherford, commander of North Carolina's Western Militia District, in turn, issued a call for 200 militiamen to muster from the Overmountain regions.[37] Colonel John Sevier had responded on March 19 in a council of his officers, asking them to raise for this duty 100 men, eight from each Washington County (North Carolina) company. Among the officers listed were Captain Robert Sevier and Lieutenant Landon Carter. Captain Valentine Sevier was away at the time of the council. Isaac Shelby, the colonel of Sullivan County, was in Kentucky at the time of this initial call, surveying land in the Transylvania Purchase to improve his claims.

After the fall of Charlestown in May, General Rutherford rode off with what North Carolina troops he had to join with the remnants of the Southern Army then advancing toward Camden under the command of Baron Johann deKalb. The Overmountain men recruited by Sevier had not yet mustered at the time of Rutherford's departure.

With General Rutherford in the field, Colonel Charles McDowell of Burke County, Rutherford's second in command, issued an immediate call for Colonel John Sevier and Colonel Isaac Shelby to muster men from their regions. Sevier's command responded with 200 mounted men who crossed the mountains and joined McDowell at Cherokee Ford on Broad River. Concerned for the safety of his home settlements in the face of potential attacks by Cherokees, Colonel Sevier remained behind and sent his men forward under the command of Major Charles Robertson. Colonel Sevier's wife, Sarah Hawkins Sevier, had only recently died; he stayed at home as well to attend to the needs of his family.

After McDowell's request for militiamen reached Shelby in Kentucky on June 16th, the colonel immediately returned to his home at Sapling Grove in the South Holston River valley and mustered 200 men from his Sullivan County militia. Shelby's troops arrived at McDowell's camp in mid-July a few days after Sevier's men had arrived. (Some accounts say the 16th, others, the 25th.) Colonel Charles McDowell then commanded a force of 600 men in camp near Cherokee Ford in the Spartan District. Among them were his own Burke County militia and Rutherford County militiamen under Captain Andrew Hampton. With the Overmountain men mustered, McDowell felt ready to harass Loyalist troops that were troubling Patriot residents in the Upcountry.

With the British Legion advancing through South Carolina, the Tories of Tryon County, North Carolina mustered under Colonel Patrick Moore and moved south to join the British. A hundred Loyalists took over a fortification in the Pacolet River basin near Thicketty Creek.

Operating from this small and well-protected stronghold (also known as Fort Anderson), Colonel Moore led men from the garrison on raids throughout the area against suspected Whigs and rebel supporters. He would accost the families of partisan fighters away at the time, loot their homes, plunder their food stocks, steal their cattle and horses, and torch their houses and buildings. In light of this, Colonel McDowell decided to attack the Loyalist fort. The North Carolina partisans were joined by volunteers mustered under Colonel Elijah Clarke of Georgia. Operating independently from McDowell, Colonel Thomas Sumter had sent Clarke's force forward from his Catawba River valley camp on the same mission — take Fort Anderson on Thicketty Creek.

The Loyalist fortification had been built for the protection of settlers during the Cherokee War of the 1760's and later served as a defense against bands of outlaws during the Regulator movement.[38] Thicketty Fort sat on a rise a quarter mile north of Goucher Creek and about two-and-a-half miles above that creek's confluence with Thicketty Creek. The fort's defenses included abatis[39] as well as loopholes high upon its walls. The only entrance was a well-protected, small wicket.

As the ranking officer of the Patriot detachment, Colonel Shelby took command of the expedition against the Loyalists and departed Cherokee Ford at sunset on Saturday, July 29 for a night march. Covering about 20 miles, they arrived at dawn on Sunday. Shelby sent forward Colonel William Cocke under a flag of truce and demanded that Moore surrender, given that he was outnumbered so badly.[40] Knowing that the garrison of Loyalists was well supplied and believing that Major Patrick Ferguson was heading his way with reinforcements well surpassing the number of Patriots Shelby might have brought, Colonel Moore told Cocke that he declined Shelby's offer.

**Colonel Isaac Shelby captured "Thicketty Fort" without firing a shot. The site of the fort is unconfirmed, but as described, it could have been near Goucher School Rd. at Pacolet Highway (SC Hwy 150), shown above as the high ground to the east of Goucher Creek.**

Isaac Shelby decided to intimidate Colonel Moore with a display of force. Shelby had his men move into firing position where they could be seen at the edge of the woods. He then renewed his offer to Moore. On the second offer, Moore waffled in his decision, perhaps having in mind the defeat of North Carolina Loyalists at Ramsour's Mill the previous month. Moore left the fort to meet with Shelby. As he departed, he assured his officers that he still intended to fight just as they had encouraged him to do. When Moore returned, however, he was accompanied by some Patriot officers. They took control of the gate. To the shock and surprise of the Loyalists inside, Shelby's Patriots then marched in and took command of Thicketty Fort without firing a shot. When he had met with Isaac Shelby, Colonel Moore had agreed to surrender the fort on the promise that all his men would be paroled immediately and allowed to go home.

As Shelby's and Clarke's men entered the fort they could see how well defended and prepared the garrison was and how fortunate they were not to have fought a battle. They saw muskets and ball & buckshot enough to defend twice their number of attackers. Shelby paroled the 93 Loyalists, sending them home on their pledge not to take up arms against the Patriot cause. He also captured their generous supplies including 200 firearms. Not knowing how close Major Ferguson was to arriving, Shelby and his men took the supplies and hurried back to the Cherokee Ford where they would wait until the next opportunity to strike out and harass British interests. Later, word of Colonel Moore's surrender of the fort greatly displeased British officers. "Cowardice" was used in describing Moore's actions in so easily relinquishing Thicketty Fort to the partisans.

Three days after learning of Rocky Mount's successful rebuff of Sumter's attack on July 30, Lieutenant Allaire learned of the defeat on the same day at the much nearer Fort Anderson (i.e., Thicketty Fort). He wrote: "Saturday, 5th. Lay in the woods near [Capt.] Bobo's [near Tyger Creek]. Had intelligence that Fort Anderson, in which we had a Sergeant of the American Volunteers, and eighty militia men, was summoned on Sunday the 30th July, and given up in a dastardly manner, without exchanging a single shot."[41]

**Hanging Rock**

On August 5, the day Ferguson's detachment learned of the surrender of Fort Anderson, Major William Davie and Colonel Thomas Sumter reconvened at Landsford after their separate expeditions on July 30 against Rocky Mount and Hanging Rock. Along with colonels Robert Irwin, Billy Hill, and Edward Lacey, they plotted their next steps to impede the British advance and attempts to control the Catawba River valley. Their combined forces in camp numbered about 800 men.[42] They considered again attacking one of the two British outposts along the river. Rocky Mount had fewer troops, they knew, but those defenders were protected by fortified cabins. Indeed, Sumter knew firsthand from his experience just days before the difficulty of attacking there. It was true, they reasoned, that Hanging Rock had more fighting men, but the camp was an open field surrounded by only an earth berm. Moreover, they believed that 300 troops had been sent from Hanging Rock to reinforce Rocky Mount. The colonels agreed that another attack on Hanging Rock offered them the best chance for success. The militiamen, when informed of their mission, "entered into the project with great spirit & cheerfulness." [43]

Leaving Landsford on August 5 with about 600 men, about evenly split between North Carolina and South Carolina militia units,[44] Sumter's men attempted to ford the rain-swollen Catawba River that evening. Men and horses were swept downstream. They emerged on the eastern bank discouraged, with some men having lost their rifles and others their horses. (One account says two hundred men were without rifles or muskets. Hill later wrote that none of the men went into battle with more than five rounds of shot.[45]) Sumter rallied the men's spirits, however, and marched them through the night to arrive near Hanging Rock before dawn having slogged through 16 miles of a muddy and rutted road. The men rested until daylight with their arms at the ready.

Four groups of British Provincials and militia were camped at Hanging Rock in three groups. Together they numbered about 1,400. To the north of the others and separated from them by a ravine and thin woods was a party of North Carolina Loyalists recruited by Morgan Bryan. They were under the command of his son, Colonel Samuel Bryan. Across the ravine were Captain Kenneth McCulloch's and Captain John Rousselet's two companies of infantry from the British Legion. Just south of them was the Prince of Wales American Regiment, commanded by Major John Carden. To his south and on the other side of a local house were artillery, infantry, and cavalry under the command of a Colonel Robinson.

Sumter divided his men into three contingents and ordered each to attack a specific camp. Major Davie and Colonel Richard Winn commanded the reserves. (With Davie on this campaign was 13-year-old Andrew Jackson, to whom Davie gave a pistol and the task to serve as a mounted messenger.) The three groups skulked through the woods guided by three local scouts. Somehow the scouts in error ended up bringing all Sumter's men to the same spot.[46] This error, however, worked in Sumter's favor.

On the morning of August 6, Sumter's men watched from their secluded position as the British and Loyalists soldiers finished their breakfasts and scattered throughout the camp to their duties. Around 6 o'clock, Colonel Irwin's Mecklenburg militiamen began the attack by opening fire at the north end, against Bryan's camp. Hill wrote, "This action commenced under very unfavorable circumstances to the Americans, as they had to march across a water course & climb a steep cliff, being all this time under the enemys *(sic)* fire & could not injure them until they got around the side of their camp."[47] From behind trees and rocks, the Patriot militia delivered a hail of bullets with murderous accuracy. Bryan's men panicked and ran to the center of the camp. Winn's and Davie's men, the reserves, charged into Bryan's camp and scattered the Loyalists. The Patriot militiamen who had lost their rifles in the river picked up weapons, powder, and shot as they moved through Bryan's camp.

The attacking Patriots continued on to McCulloch's Legion camp, but these trained Loyalist soldiers held their ground and formed a line behind a fence and among their brush huts. The Legion and the Royal

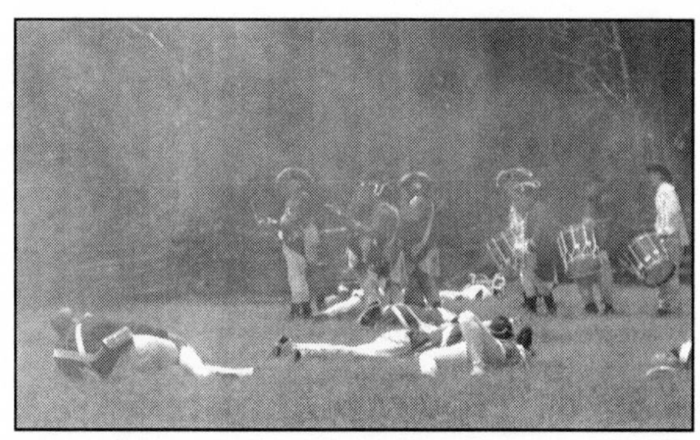

**The British Legion soldiers "fell so fast by their unseen enemy that their officers were obliged to push them forward by their sabers." The attack by Patriot militia at Hanging Rock looked to be a rout.**

North Carolina Regiment prepared for a bayonet charge. Sumter's men rushed on, "fir[ing] on the enemy as they went, with bullets in their mouths and powder in their pockets, … load[ing] as they ran up but by no means … tak[ing] a tree even where trees was."[48] As they rushed on, they shouted the "Indian Hallo."

The Patriots fought hard and pushed the Tories back some only to give up in time the ground they had taken. The men fought hand-to-hand and contested every inch of the field. As dead and dying men lay across the battleground, the Patriots succeeded in killing McCulloch. With the loss of its leader and sixty of its troops, the British Legion fell back in retreat until Rousselet rallied the men into a second charge. With the attention of the Patriots focused on the center, they did not notice that Colonel Thomas Brown's Rangers (the colonel was not present) had "passed a bold and skilful maneuver" through the swampy woods hoping to outflank them. "They poured a Heavy fire onto the Whig militia."[49] The deadly firepower surprised the Patriots. The men under colonels Hill and Lacey and including Davie's riflemen "took instinctively to the trees and brush heaps and returned fire with deadly effect," Davie wrote. Hill described it similarly, adding "these few [his detachment] took to trees and rocks; whilst the British were advancing firing in platoons, and they [Brown's Rangers] fell so fast by their unseen enemy [Patriot militiamen] that their officers were obliged to push them forward by their sabers."[50] Davie added that soon "not a British officer [was] standing, one half of the regiment had fallen, and the others … threw down their arms."[51]

As Colonel Billy Hill rode along his line of militiamen, he was shot below the shoulder blade. As blood spurted from his wound, he was encouraged to leave the field. Defiant, he declared, "If I die, I'll die on Flim Nap [his horse]." He spurred the horse and rode along his line of men rallying them and calling out, "Fight on, my brave boys, I'm mortally wounded."[52]

In the same fight and astride his horse, Thomas Sumter rode along the line urging his men to press on. He knew his men were tiring and running out of ammunition. As he drove them forward, Sumter took a ball to the thigh. The colonel did not let anyone know he was wound-

**As the Patriots were pressing for victory, unexpected British cavalry reinforcements arrived, but Major Davie's mounted militiamen drove them from the field and into the woods.**

BEFORE THEY WERE HEROES AT KING'S MOUNTAIN

ed as he spurred on his men. The Patriots continued to kill score upon score of the enemy, almost completely annihilating the Prince of Wales Regiment.[53] Indeed, with only nine men in his immediate command remaining, Major Carden's courage collapsed and he relinquished general command to Captain Rousselet.

As the Patriots pressed on to what seemed a certain victory, unexpected reinforcements rode into the fray. Forty mounted infantrymen from the British Legion had been riding toward Camden when they heard the sounds of the conflict in the distance. They galloped toward Hanging Rock. When they arrived, they immediately formed a long line and attacked across the front of the conflict. Their efforts turned the tide of the Patriot advance for a moment, but Major Davie's mounted dragoons rode into the fight and drove the Legion's mounted infantry into the woods.

At this point, Captain Rousselet formed his men into an open square, a defensive tactic for the open field. The defenders fixed their bayonets. Sumter's force was unable to make headway against this formation. After three hours of intense fighting, the Patriot militiamen were exhausted. They were also hungry and thirsty, not having eaten in twelve hours. Sumter later wrote, "Men [were] fainting with heat and drought." Many turned their attention to looting the British camp. The militiamen found food and several kegs of Jamaican rum, which they eagerly opened and began sharing among their ranks. More of the Patriots joined in the plundering of the camp. Over the next hour, Sumter's troops ransacked the camp, eating and drinking wildly while the Legion soldiers watched from their defensive position. Not so eager to renew the engagement, the Legion simply looked on as the Patriots pillaged the camp.[54]

In the midst of the drunken frolicking, Sumter received word that Colonel Turnbull was but four miles away with Loyalist reinforcements marching toward them double time. Sumter cautioned his troops, "Boys, it is not good to pursue a victory too far." With commanding authority — but still with some understandable difficulty, Sumter mustered his inebriated men for departure with Major Davie protecting the rear. The Whigs carried their wounded and marshaled their prisoners. Some of the Patriots were wonderfully drunk; they did not look like a victorious army. As the Patriots marched away, the Legion soldiers from a distance gave three cheers for King George III. Urged by Sumter to respond, the retreating Patriot militiamen returned three huzzas for the "Hero of American Liberty," presumed to be George Washington.[55]

Sumter estimated for his report that his men had killed 250 of the enemy (other accounts say 200) and captured 75. His own losses were modest in comparison: 20 killed (others say 12 with perhaps 10 missing) and 40 wounded. Nevertheless, every man lost was important. Among his officers, one of his captains, John McClure, was dead and colonels Winn and Hill had been wounded, as had Sumter.

Miles away in the Fairforest region of the Upcountry, Lieutenant Allaire made note of the news that arrived on August 10: "*Thursday, 10th.* … We marched about seven miles to Culbertson's plantation, on Fair Forest [Creek]. Express arrived from Col. Turnbull at Rocky Mount, with orders to join him. By the express heard that Sumter had attacked Hanging Rock the 6th instant. The North Carolinians were first attacked; they gave way. Brown's corps came up, but were obliged to give way. The Legion Cavalry came in the Rebels' rear, and soon gained the day. Brown's corps suffered much — three officers killed, and three wounded — an hundred men taken prisoners."[56]

# August 1780

**Colonel James Williams**

After the battle at Hanging Rock, Thomas Sumter returned up the Catawba Valley toward his own encampment. He stopped to rest and recover a few days at Major Davie's camp in the Waxhaws. His wound and those of his men were tended. While there, Colonel James Williams approached Sumter with a request to seek volunteers among the men so he could ride west just below the North Carolina border and molest what Tories they could find there. He also hoped in the process, he said, to help drive Major Patrick Ferguson from the area. The Patriots knew that British officer was at the time sweeping north from the Ninety Six District into Fairforest, recruiting Loyalists, and protecting Cornwallis's left flank as he proceeded through South Carolina. Williams had another motive in mind as well. The region through which Ferguson was reportedly advancing was an area well known to Williams. He had property on Little River in the Saluda River Basin not so far from the British outpost at Ninety Six. Williams was concerned for the welfare and safety of his family and property. (James Williams was a cousin to Joseph Williams of the Surry County Militia.)

Sumter granted Williams permission to recruit. Williams took with him some good men including Colonel Thomas Brandon and Major Joseph McJunkin. Williams also took — and without permission —

some of the supplies that Sumter had commandeered from the British and local Tories. Williams made off with horses, wagons, and all manner of provisions, which Sumter had collected for his own use. Williams's act of taking them was considered, if not a theft, at least a breach of trust among fellow officers. Still tending to and favoring his wounded leg, Sumter sent Colonel Edward Lacey, a most trusted officer, along with some men to overtake Williams and to recover the allegedly pilfered supplies.

Lacey soon caught up with Williams at his camp and demanded the return of the goods. Lacey must have thought better of starting a confrontation in William's camp with only his small guard to support him. Instead, Lacey invited Williams to step outside the camp with him, so they could talk privately. Once sufficiently away from the others, Lacey pulled his pistol and pressed it into Williams's chest warning him that if he called for help, he was dead. Lacey then advised Williams to listen carefully as he demanded that the stolen supplies be returned immediately. Williams relented, giving his word to return both men and supplies, but once back in the camp and among his supporters, Williams reneged on the promise. He declared he could not and would not honor a pledge he had made under a threat of death. Instead, he marched away the next morning with the men and the appropriated supplies. He soon made his way to Cherokee Ford on the Broad River where he joined with the partisans there under the command of Colonel Charles McDowell.

Colonel Lacey returned empty-handed to Sumter. Rather than spending time and energy chasing down one of their own, Sumter and his men moved north along the Catawba River to camp at Landsford. From there, they planned to venture out and appropriate more supplies from Tories in the area. As they were preparing to do so, Sumter received word that General Horatio Gates and the Continental Army were advancing toward Camden. Gates had camped only forty miles away on August 7. Sumter changed his plans, deciding to stand by in readiness to support General Gates in his efforts to confront General Lord Cornwallis in South Carolina.

**Lt. Colonel Elijah Clarke**

During the summer after the surrender of Charlestown in May, Lord Cornwallis issued an adamant clarification of Sir Henry Clinton's earlier proclamation that all citizens should take an oath of allegiance to the Crown. Cornwallis added prominently that "every militia man who has borne arms with us and afterward joined the enemy, shall be immediately hanged."[1] In eager compliance, Colonel Thomas Brown, British commander of the garrison at Augusta, Georgia, took five prisoners from the gaol and hanged them.[2]

In the face of this threat and Cornwallis's apparently unstoppable advance, some of the South Carolina Patriot leaders relinquished the fight for independence and accepted paroles.[3] Notable among them were Andrew Williamson and Andrew Pickens. Perhaps Williamson's firsthand knowledge of the defeat at Briar Creek the year before had tempered his appetite for battle. (His reinforcements arrived too late to help General Ashe.) Certainly, a regiment of angry and vengeful 71st Highlanders advancing with the British Legion behind them was a good bit more fearsome than Cherokee villagers trying to escape an invasion by marauders. Or, as was alleged by some, Williamson received benefits from the British for switching his allegiance from the Patriots to the Crown, a claim somewhat ameliorated later by assurances that during that time he actually had spied for the Patriots. For whatever reason, the fact remained that Williamson stopped fighting for the Patriots when they most needed him. The paroled Pickens was beseeched to fight on as well. He replied that he was "bound by conscience and honor" not to break his agreement until the conditions to which he had agreed were infringed.[4] Eventually, Pickens did resume service, declaring that the British had violated the conditions. Nevertheless, during the summer of 1780, resistance to the British advance was left to others in the backcountry. Prominent among those new leaders, in the spirit of Colonel Thomas Sumter, were Colonel Charles McDowell of North Carolina and Lt. Colonel Elijah Clarke of Georgia.

In Georgia, Tory militia Lt. Colonel Thomas Brown and his King's Carolina Rangers controlled the backcountry from their occupation of Fort Grierson. Despite the name, it was really only a fortified home, and Brown heartily sought Cornwallis's support and funding for building a substantial fort suitable for protecting the Georgia backcountry. He was supported by Colonel Nisbet Balfour, then commander at Ninety Six, and by Governor James Wright; but, Cornwallis considered the backcountry of Georgia and the entire province adequately subdued. After his victories in South Carolina, he was looking toward an invasion of North Carolina. Anything remaining to do in Georgia and South Carolina, he believed, was simply a clean-up operation.[5]

Colonel Brown saw matters differently and diligently worked to suppress Whig movements. His Loyalist troops rode through the countryside administering oaths of allegiance to the citizenry. Brown also re-energized the opposition of Creeks and Cherokees to the continuing encroachment of settlers on their lands in Georgia. Regarding the Cherokees, he later wrote to Cornwallis, "They have cheerfully agreed to attack the Rebel Plunderers and Banditti who have taken forcible Possession of their hunting Grounds."[6] His reopening the Indian trade brought more Creeks and Cherokees into Augusta, a situation which further antagonized the backcountry settlers against Brown and his Tory control of their region.

Unlike Williamson who relented to British victories, Colonel Elijah Clarke would not submit his fervor for the Whig cause. He continued to resist the British invasion as best he could through the summer, and he was stern with his men. He told the men who had, in fact, taken the British oath that if they did not muster when he called, he would put them to death.[7] In July, he led 140 mounted Georgians across the Savannah River to harass the Loyalists and Tories in the South Carolina Upcountry. Once out of Georgia, his independent-minded militiamen became ungovernable as some saw no need to follow the laws of their home jurisdiction.[8] Riding with Clarke were men like Captain Patrick "Paddy" Carr, an Irishman with an ill temper toward the Tories, whom he favored hanging sooner rather than later. He claimed to have killed over a hundred of them personally during the war and according to Draper said of himself that "had not God given him a merciful heart, he would have made a good soldier." When Carr was murdered in 1802, assumed done at the hands of Tory descendants, he was eulogized as a "honey of a Patriot," but a man whose name was "mixed with few virtues, and a thousand crimes."[9] Such was the nature of some of the men of Wilkes County who fought for Liberty. In the face of such unruliness, Clarke abandoned his foray and returned to Georgia to await news on which he could act with purpose.[10] After a week or two, Clarke again mustered his men and set out riding along the edge of the southern Blue Ridge Mountains into South Carolina. Without any public funding for provisions, his party foraged off the enemy and the land. In early August, they joined up with North Carolina's Colonel Charles McDowell at Cherokee Ford on the Broad River.

**An Action Severe and Bloody**

From his camp at Cherokee Ford, Colonel Charles McDowell continued to watch for the advance of Major Patrick Ferguson into the Spartan District. Encamped with him, McDowell had militiamen numbering at times several hundred to a thousand. Cornwallis was advancing unimpeded toward North Carolina, and the new Inspector of Militia was protecting the commander's left flank and successfully recruiting Tories to his ranks. Knowing of Ferguson's success, the Patriots expected Ferguson to be advancing into the Upcountry with an estimated 1,500 to 1,800 Loyalist militiamen.

Shortly after Shelby's success at Thicketty Fort, McDowell again detached about 600 men under colonels Isaac Shelby and Elijah Clarke to monitor Ferguson's movements. The men rode twenty-something miles down the Broad River expecting to muster again at the confluence with Brown's Creek.[11] Only a smaller number of the men arrived there before a larger force of Tories — likely a foraging party for Ferguson's troops — forced them to flee. The retreating Patriots rode 30 or 40 miles to the northwest, gathering their full party as they went. The rebel militiamen regrouped in the upper end of the settled area along Fairforest Creek.[12]

After the loss of Anderson (Thicketty) Fort, Major Ferguson was acutely aware of colonels McDowell and Shelby and their bands of partisans. The major hoped to catch Shelby unaware during his patrolling of the Upcountry.

On the afternoon of August 7, Shelby's Overmountain men and Clarke's Georgia militia were scouting the Fairforest area when they stopped to make camp for the night. They chose a spot along Fairforest Creek where the road, which continued to Wofford's Iron

**On August 8, 1780, men under Isaac Shelby and Elijah Clarke skirmished with Ferguson's and Dunlap's troops along a road not far from Cedar Spring. A plaque in Spartanburg Co., SC across from Cedar Spring Baptist Church commemorates the event.**

Works and then to Cherokee Ford, crossed the creek. Cedar Spring lay about one mile to their east. Being near to his home, young Josiah Culbertson was permitted to visit his family that night and then rejoin the men in camp the next morning.

Before dawn on August 8, Patriot scouts returned with information. The wife of a local Patriot reported that Legion troops and Loyalist militia under the command of Major James Dunlap were only a half-mile away. This fact was confirmed immediately when they heard a single shot fired in the distance.[13] The Patriots decamped quickly and rode three or four miles toward Wofford's Iron Works, which sat on Lawson's Fork.[14] They took suitable positions near a peach orchard at Thompson's place.

When Culbertson casually rode back into camp after dawn expecting to find his compatriots, he was surprised to see Dunlap's men there preparing to break camp after a few hours' rest. He rode through the camp slowly taking note of the numbers of men. Dressed in his hunting clothes like so many of the militiamen in camp, he was assumed to be one of their own. When out of sight of the camp, he rode hurriedly in the direction he figured Clarke and Shelby had taken. Finding his corps at the orchard, he informed Shelby and Clarke of what he had seen. A scout rode out to investigate and returned hurriedly with Major Dunlap's Tories following quickly behind him.

Major James Dunlap, who fought with the spirit of his commander, Major Patrick Ferguson, rode in hard with dragoons and mounted militia. From their position along the road, the Whigs opened fire. Dunlap's mounted riflemen recoiled in their first wave of the assault. Dunlap had trouble at first controlling his confused and scattering men, but after rallying them, Dunlap led another charge in which the broadsword-wielding dragoons had some effect. The skilled hunters from the frontier, however, took careful aim and picked off many of the attackers with great accuracy. The fighting became hand-to-hand in places. In the melee, Colonel Clarke was jumped by two large brutes, but he fought successfully with them, knocking one to the ground and causing the other to run away. In the process, however, Clarke received two saber wounds. He was struck on the back of the neck and again on the head. A buckle on a strap had stopped a blade from killing him. The blow to the head, however, destroyed his hat.

**Militia colonels Shelby and Clarke fought a running skirmish with British Major Ferguson along the road to Wofford's Iron Works. A marker on Clifton-Glendale Rd. east of Lawson's Fork in Spartanburg Co., SC, commemorates the ironworks and the fierce fighting.**

"An action severe and bloody ensued for near an hour,"[15] Shelby later wrote, before Dunlap felt compelled to retreat, having lost more than 50 men both killed and taken prisoner. He and his defeated detachment of mounted Tories retreated south along the road for some two miles with Shelby and Clarke pursuing them and continuing to inflict damage for part of that distance. Two miles into his retreat, Dunlap met Ferguson coming up with reinforcements. With Ferguson in command, the reunited Tory force then advanced with renewed spirit. At last, Ferguson was meeting on the field of battle the militiamen of Shelby and Clarke — the backwoods hunters he was coming to despise.

In the face of such overwhelming numbers, Clarke and Shelby staged a fighting retreat moving slowly north along the road. They stopped intermittently to establish fighting positions from which to fend off a rapid Tory advance. This was just the type of Indian-style fighting and running skirmish the frontiersmen from Sullivan and Washington counties preferred. Though Ferguson was determined to recapture the prisoners Shelby had taken, the Patriot militiamen were able to hold the Tories in check long enough to move the fifty prisoners out of reach.

About three miles northeast of Wofford's Iron Works, the Patriot forces crossed the Pacolet River. The men clambered up a steep, rocky hill across the river and waited for Ferguson to arrive. The Patriots stood in plain view to watch what Ferguson would do. As Draper described it, "… when Ferguson and his men came into view, evincing a disinclination to pursue any farther, the patriots, from their vantage-ground, bantered and ridiculed them to their heart's content."[16] Though he had pursued the Patriots for four miles, Ferguson was resigned to abandoning the chase and the captives. The Patriots continued toward Cherokee Ford, Shelby in possession of four dozen Tory prisoners and Clarke conspicuously bare-headed.

Major Patrick Ferguson had experienced his first run-in with North Carolina's Overmountain men on August 8 in the Upcountry of South Carolina, and he was not pleased with the outcome. He had suffered losses of 30 killed and wounded and 50 captured. Shelby and Clarke had lost four killed and 20 wounded. Ferguson, no doubt, puzzled at how this undisciplined rabble could have possibly outfought his trained and well-armed militia. Wisely, however, Shelby did not underestimate Ferguson, later calling him "an officer of great experience and enterprise as a partyzan."[17]

Lieutenant Allaire wrote in his journal that evening about that day's encounter: "*Tuesday, 8th.* … Dunlap and his party rushed into the centre of the Rebel camp, where they lay in ambush, before he was aware of their presence. A skirmish ensued, in which Dunlap got slightly wounded, and had between twenty and thirty killed and wounded . … We pursued them five miles to the Iron Works, but were not able to overtake them, they being all mounted."[18]

### Gates Advances to Camden

As bands of partisan militia resisted the British advance throughout the Upcountry, General Horatio Gates continued to march southward — and foolishly so. Against the wishes of General George Washington, the Continental Congress selected Gates to replace the captured General Benjamin Lincoln as commander of the Southern Department. Little of it remained intact and regiments from other states were reassigned to make up a core of the command. Gates was in Virginia at the time of his appointment and his new command was already marching toward South Carolina. General Baron Jean deKalb

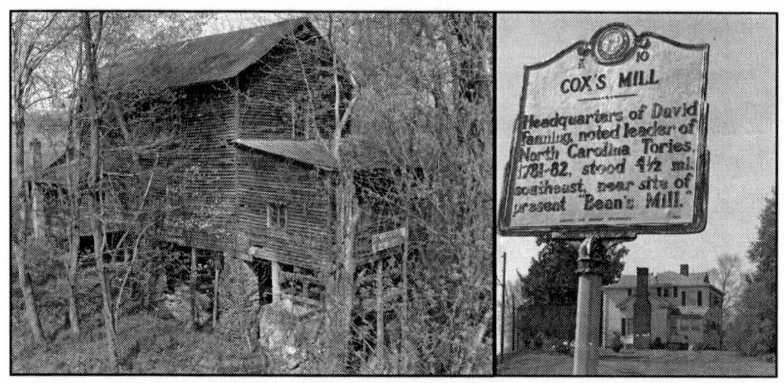


**General Gates took command of the Southern Department of the Continental Army near Buffalo Ford over Deep River near the site of Will Cox's Mill on Mill Creek. A marker in Ramseur, NC points to an old mill (pictured) sitting today near that historic mill site.**

— a man who was not really a baron but had adopted that title — had marched the Continental Army as far as the ford at Deep River. The army camped in the field across from Cox's Mill.[19]

Gates arrived on July 25 and took command. His officers advised him to march to the west in an arc through Salisbury and Charlotte where they might expect to gather more Patriot militia to their ranks and more readily find supplies to feed the army. Perhaps having enjoyed too long and too readily the accolade "hero of Saratoga," Gates ignored his advisors and preferred a more direct route toward Camden. Gates was eager to demonstrate that he was indeed an able and ready field commander. Gates crossed the Deep River, perhaps at Buffalo Ford immediately below Mill Creek. In his eagerness, Gates marched his men at a hard pace through a barren area devoid of food and support. The men grew weary from lack of both food and rest. They lacked flour and resorted to eating green corn when they could find it. They also ate green apples and peaches. So scarce were supplies that the officers used their wig powder to thicken their soup.

Thomas Sumter was pleased to see the Continental Army arriving in South Carolina. He had changed his plans for local action to make his men available to support the general. Learning that Gates was at Rugeley's Mill on August 12, Thomas Sumter suggested to him by express a plan to capture the ferries along the Wateree River. This strategy, he suggested, would confound the British efforts to advance up the Catawba River valley. Gates liked the idea and on August 15 sent along a hundred Maryland Continentals and 200 (or 300) North Carolina militiamen to join Sumter's force. In doing so, Gates imprudently weakened his own strength as he marched toward a confrontation with Cornwallis. Sumter and his men worked down the Catawba and Wateree rivers from Landsford, capturing fords and taking control of ferries. In the process, Sumter discovered that the British had abandoned Hanging Rock and Rocky Mount. The British were, in fact, concentrating their forces at Camden to support Cornwallis. The British general was hurrying from Charles Towne to take field command of the continuing invasion of South Carolina. Cornwallis had left Charlestown on August 10; he arrived in Camden three days later.

Sumter's men had great success raiding along the Catawba River. Riding under Colonel Thomas Taylor, a detachment of Sumter's men captured at one ferry near Camden 30 men and 36 wagons of supplies including corn and rum. Sumter had learned of a British convoy marching his way from Ninety Six. The prize was rich. Fifty light infantrymen required six wagons to carry their baggage and, they drove with them a flock of sheep and 300 head of cattle. Taylor captured both convoys.[20]

Reporting on his success and proving his utility to the general, Sumter sent an express to General Gates on August 15:

> "Have just time to inform you, that early this morning I took possession of all the passways over the Wateree river, from Elkins' ford to Mr. Whitear's ferry, five miles below Camden. The enemy had guards at many different places upon the river, all of which were evacuated last night or this morning, and the guards ordered into Camden …" [21]

Despite his success in capturing these crossings, Sumter soon learned that British troops were crossing the river below his southernmost advance. He broke camp and moved up the Wateree, taking his plunder and booty with him. The much-needed provisions, however, slowed Sumter's retreat considerably.

Cornwallis arrived at Camden on the 13th and spent another two days reviewing the troops and preparing for an advance farther up the Catawba River Valley and into North Carolina. Late on the evening of August 15, Cornwallis's army marched out of Camden headed north. Coincident with Cornwallis's departure, Gates was advancing south having also begun his march at night.

Gates had gauged his numbers poorly believing that he had 7,000

**Advancing up the Wateree River valley, Cornwallis stopped two days in Camden to rest and prepare his troops for advancing into North Carolina. Historic Camden Revolutionary War Site interprets life in the community during the Colonial and Revolutionary Periods.**

troops. One of his officers, incredulous at Gate's overconfidence, revealed by count an army of only about 3,000. Confronted with the facts, Gates dismissively replied, "There are enough for our purpose." To compound his problems, on the night before the final push toward Camden, Gates fed the men by one account "quick baked bread and fresh beef with a dessert of molasses mixed with mush."[22] As the troops marched trough the night, the men broke ranks and dashed into the woods as necessary. The purging of their digestive systems, prompted by the imprudent meal, further weakened the men who were about to face the colonial version of the most formidable army in the world.

The night was dark and quiet. In the hours well before dawn, neither army expected that an encounter was eminent. The advance guards of both armies ran into each other about halfway between Rugeley's Mill and Camden in the wee hours of the morning of August 16. The cavalry units of Patriot Colonel Charles Armand collided with those of Lt. Colonel Banastre Tarleton. They skirmished for a while in the dark with Armand's unit fading in the confrontation until they were steadied by a line of Virginia militia. The two sides then retreated to their respective camps and waited for dawn before attacking.

General Gates arrayed his units for battle, putting his 900 Maryland and Delaware Continentals under DeKalb on the right and the untested 1,200 North Carolina militia and 700 Virginia militia in the center and on his left respectively. The North Carolina units included militia under General Griffith Rutherford and under General Richard Caswell, the former rebel governor of North Carolina and a hero of the Battle of Moore's Creek Bridge. Since that battle, no British forces had entered North Carolina, and Caswell certainly wanted to stall the British advance south of the state boundary. Cornwallis arranged his units in the typical European fashion with his British Regulars on his right. In that alignment, which Gates should have anticipated, the British Regulars would press hard against the opposing and inexperienced militia on Gate's left flank.

### Battle of Camden

At first light on the 16th, the conflict began. It ended as a monumental disaster for the Patriot cause. Unaccustomed to battle in an open field, the untested Patriot volunteers reeled when the British Regulars advanced with bayonets. Col. Otto Williams wrote: "… the impetuosity with which they [British forces] advanced, firing and huzzaing, threw the whole body of the militia into such a panic that they generally threw down their loaded arms and fled in the utmost consternation. The unworthy example of the Virginians was almost instantly followed by the North Carolinians." He added: "Like electricity it [panic] operated instantaneously — like sympathy. It is irresistible where it touches."[23] Two-thirds of Gate's army was militia. The majority, Williams observed, "fled without firing a shot."

**The Continental Army under Horatio Gates and the British Legion under Lord Cornwallis stumbled into one another in the wee hours of August 16, 1780, just north of Camden. The site of the battle is a National Historic Landmark on Flat Rock Road off US 521, nine miles north of Camden.**

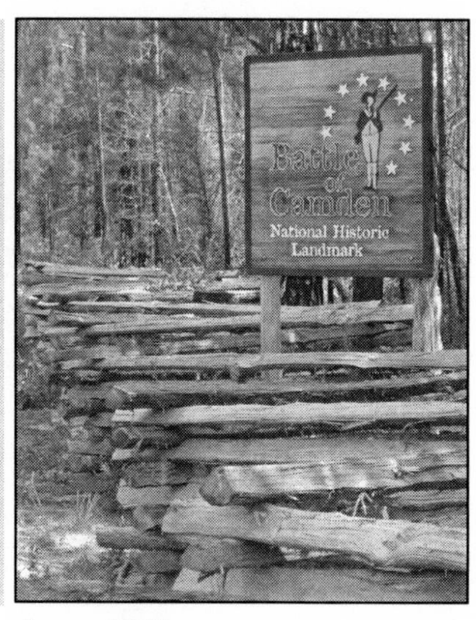

On the Patriot's right, General deKalb and the Continentals were repelling the British attack and making some headway when other British units flanked his position. Joined by one North Carolina unit which held its ground, deKalb's position had a force of 800 Patriots facing 2,000 British Regulars. Williams wrote: "the enemy having collected their corps, and directing their whole force against these two devoted brigades [Maryland and Delaware], a tremendous fire of musketry was, for some time, kept up on both sides, with equal perseverance and obstinancy, until Lord Cornwallis, perceiving there was no cavalry opposed to him, pushed forward his dragoons — and his infantry charging, at the same moment, with fixed bayonets, put an end to the contest."[24] When Banastre Tarlton's cavalry circled around and rode in from the rear, the Patriot resistance collapsed. Many of the men were captured while some escaped into a nearby swamp. Williams wrote; "even the bogs and brush, which in some measure served to screen them from their furious pursuers, separated them from one another."[25]

The refugees scattered, each man making his way toward home as best he could hoping not to be caught. The Virginians knew nothing of the countryside and many started toward home in the direction from which they had come, toward Hillsborough. Brigadier General Edward Stevens commanded the Virginia Militia Brigade. He chased down his retreating volunteers and attempted to rally them. Deciding it was hopeless to band them together for another chance to prove their courage, Stevens released them all from their terms of service. Although Steven's brigade included units from Louisa, Pittsylvania, and Culpeper counties, these retreating militiamen were not of the same caliber as those who had mustered under Andrew Lewis six years earlier to fight at Point Pleasant or fought at Great Bridge in '75. The men of that ilk were elsewhere in 1780, living, hunting, and fighting deeper in the mountain fastness of the Appalachians' secluded and sparsely settled valleys. The frontier had moved west, and with it, the frontiersmen.

Tarleton's cavalry aggressively pursued the fleeing Continentals and militia. Williams described the scene: "[Some of the wagons] had got out of danger from the enemy; but the cries of the women and the wounded in the rear and the consternation of the flying troops, so alarmed some of the wagoners that they cut out their teams, taking each a horse, left the rest for the next that should come. Others were obliged to give up their horses to assist in carrying off the wounded; and the whole road, for many miles, was strewed with signals of distress, confusion, and dismay."

General deKalb suffered eleven wounds and died three days later although he was tended by Cornwallis's personal physician. General Griffith Rutherford, wounded seriously, was captured and held as a prisoner for a year. He was held aboard a ship in Charles Town harbor

**Baron deKalb suffered multiple wounds during the battle. He was tended by Cornwallis's doctor, but succumbed to his injuries in a few days. A monolith marks the site on the battlefield where he fell.**

and later in a dungeon cell of the prison at St. Augustine, Florida. After the debacle, 250 Patriots were dead with another 800 wounded and taken prisoner. The rest had run away. (Other counts of casualties are common. By any assessment, it was a rout of the American Continental Army.) The British casualties were not inconsequential, suffering 68 dead and 256 wounded; but, for the Patriots, the encounter of these two major armies was a catastrophe. Colonel Armand wondered after the battle, "I will not say that we have been betrayed, but if it had been the purpose of the general to sacrifice his army, what could he have done more effectually to have answered that purpose."[26]

General Horatio Gates, "the Hero of Saratoga," turned out to be the coward of Camden. Early in the battle, the North Carolina and Virginia militia broke and ran toward the rear. Crashing into the Maryland Continentals, the deserters even threw those regular troops into disarray. In the face of this collapse of his army, the new commander of the Continental Army's Southern Department abandoned his troops on the field of battle and fled, riding in haste toward Charlotte. He rode in the company of General Richard Caswell, who was also fleeing. The frightened Gates stopped only briefly when he met on the road Major William Davie and his men. He warned them about Tarleton ahead and then galloped away, not stopping until he reached Charlotte that same day, 60 miles away. Incredibly, he covered another 120 miles during the following two days arriving in Hillsborough on August 19. The fearless Major Davie, however, proceeded south for a time and then sent word to Sumter of the complete defeat at Camden. Receiving the disheartening news, Sumter hastened his retreat up the Catawba River as best he could, but his men and his horses were nearing exhaustion, advancing in earnest as they were with their thirty-some wagons of plunder in tow.

Proceeding beyond the battlefield at Camden, Cornwallis stopped his advance at Rugeley's Mill and awaited the return of Banastre Tarleton, whose Green Horse dragoons had pursued the retreating Patriot militiamen for 22 miles, slaughtering many along the way and only stopping when he chased them as far as Hanging Rock. Realizing that Thomas Sumter's men were the only remaining viable fighting force in South Carolina, Cornwallis saw his opportunity to crush completely the partisan resistance. As soon as Tarleton's dragoons returned, Cornwallis sent them in pursuit of Sumter. Tarleton's task was twofold: Destroy Sumter's army of Whig partisans and recover the supplies that had been stolen along the Wateree River.

Lieutenant Allaire and the American Volunteers were aware through a series of expresses that Lord Cornwallis was moving northward and had commanded a major victory. He wrote: "Tuesday, 15th. ...[G]ot intelligence that Gen. Gates lay within three miles of Camden, with an army of seven thousand men. ... Saturday, 19th. Lay at [Rebel Colonel] Winn's plantation. An express arrived from Camden with the agreeable news of Lord Cornwallis' attacking and totally defeating Gates' army on the morning of the 16th; twelve hundred were killed and wounded, left on the field; and one thousand prisoners ..."[27]

In the following weeks, as Cornwallis reveled in his victory over the Patriots, he received at his headquarters a young girl on a mission of mercy. Martha Lenoir, age 12, had learned of the capture of her father, Thomas Lenoir, a brother to William. Knowing that he was wounded and suffering from lack of food and care, she rode 20 miles through desperate countryside to Camden in the company of an elderly, enslaved black man. She carried with her provisions she hoped to give her father. By some good fortune, she gained an audience with the general. After hearing her story of a deceased mother and the children left home alone, Cornwallis rewarded her bravery. "My little miss," he said, as tradition holds, "your father shall not only have this food which you bring, but he shall accompany you home."[28]

**Fishing Creek**

Sumter's retreating expedition pressed northward for two days finally stopping on the 17th when it reached Rocky Mount. Sumter made his camp on the west side of the Catawba River. Tarleton rode hard all day along the east side of the river with 350 men attempting to discover and overtake Sumter. Reaching the ferry at Rocky Mount that night, Tarleton's men spotted the fires of Sumter's camp across the river. They made their own camp in the dark and remained quiet, not wanting to give away their close proximity.

On the 18th, Sumter broke camp from Rocky Mount and continued moving slowly north up the Catawba River, encumbered by the plunder. Sumter's men crossed Fishing Creek at Cow Ford and remained on the west bank of the Catawba River until they reached a camp Sumter had used previously. Perhaps feeling somewhat insulated from any pursuit, Sumter posted only a couple of mounted sentinels to the rear. His men stacked their arms and took camp liberty, which enabled them to bathe in the river below their camp. Sumter, personally exhausted, removed his boots, his officer's garb—his hat with a cock's feather and his blue coat with red trim and gold epaulettes—and lay on the ground in the shade of a captured supply wagon.

Tarlton's men rose early that morning on the east bank and remained quiet. Learning from his scouts that Sumter had struck camp and moved on, Tarleton's men crossed the Catawba River using the ferry; the horses swam the river. Once on the west side, Tarleton pressed

**Encumbered by the booty he had taken from British supply trains, Colonel Thomas Sumter retreated slowly north along the Catawba River to Fishing Creek where he was overtaken and routed by Colonel Tarleton. A historic marker and a stone monument, both on US 21 north of Great Falls, SC, commemorate the Patriot defeat.**

northward to Fishing Creek. There he selected a hundred dragoons and 60 infantrymen. They raced off in pursuit of Sumter, riding two to a horse. Soon enough they came upon the sentinels, who fired at Tarleton's advancing company. While the mounted Patriot sentinels tried to reload, some of Tarleton's dragoons charged them and hacked the men to death with sabers. Tarleton's other men rode hurriedly toward Sumter's camp where they surprised the Patriots, inattentive to their circumstances. The Whig militiamen were bathing, cooking, eating, and sleeping. Some of them had even gotten into some captured kegs of rum and had become too jolly for men at war.

The Green Horse seized their opportunity. Tarleton's dragoons charged into Sumter's camp, separating the men from their stacked firearms. The Patriots who tried to fight their way to the muskets were met by slashing steel. Colonel Lacey rallied some of his men around the wagons where they fought valiantly for a while. Sumter, stirred from his sleep beneath the wagon and lacking his uniform and his boots, jumped onto one of the wagon's horses and cut loose the harness. Riding bareback, he tried to rally his men, but they were panicked beyond help. Some ran into the woods; others tried to swim to safety. Tarleton's men were upon them all.

Seeing Lacey run into the woods, Sumter knew all was lost and he rode after him. Riding with abandon into the woods, Sumter was knocked hard from his horse by a low limb. He lay unconscious in the woods for some time, likely hours, appearing quite dead. When he awoke, he found his horse and made his way in the dark to a local house where he received his first food in 24 hours. He then rode on to Davie's camp where he arrived without his army — and without his boots and coat. Absence of the latter was his good fortune. Had he been wearing the clothing that identified him as a Patriot officer, Sumter most surely would have been killed or captured during the battle.

Three days later, Lieutenant Allaire was delighted to make his journal entry in August:

> "Monday, 21$^{st}$. … About one o'clock a Mr. Duncan came to our camp with the agreeable news that Col. Tarleton, with three companies of the Light Infantry, and the Legion Cavalry, fell in with Sumter about twelve o'clock on Saturday, the nineteenth [actually Friday, 18$^{th}$]. He found them all asleep after the fatigue of two nights' rapid retreat. Their horses were all at pasture. … Col. Tarleton, with his unusual success, gained a complete victory over Gen. Sumter."

Tarleton's defeat of Sumter's army was complete. Tarleton reported capturing 800 horses, killing or wounding 150 men and officers, and taking over 300 Continentals and militiamen as prisoners. As for the supplies, he reported that "two three[-]pounders, two ammunition wagons, one thousand stand of arms, forty-four carriages loaded with baggage, rum, and other stores fell into the possession of the British." Tarleton also recovered one hundred of Brown's men captured at Hanging Rock.

Though many died and were captured, some escaped. Colonel Edward Lacey outran his pursuers through the woods and made good his getaway. Colonels Thomas Taylor and Henry Hampton, while being marched toward Camden as captives, took their opportunity to tumble down a hill into the brush and escaped. By whatever means, some of the men escaped; not all the Whigs were defeated. During the next week or two, partisan Carolinians reconvened with Sumter at Davie's camp in the Waxhaws and recruited many others who had learned of Tarleton's massacres. Within only a week, Sumter had rebuilt his army enough to patrol once again the fords along the Catawba River. Such news was disheartening to Cornwallis. He wrote to Sir Henry Clinton on August 29, "[T]he indefatigable Sumter is again in the field, and is beating up for recruits with the greatest assiduity." By the end of the month, Sumter had at least one thousand men once more under his command, ready to fight for the Patriot cause.[29]

### Musgrove's Mill

After returning to Cherokee Ford, victorious in their encounter with Dunlap and Ferguson at Wofford's Ironworks on August 8, Colonel Isaac Shelby and Colonel Elijah Clarke rested their men for a time. Among their numbers at Cherokee Ford were several notable leaders of patriot militia including Major Joseph McDowell, Captain David Vance, and Captain Valentine Sevier. Carrying along the supplies he had taken from Thomas Sumter, Colonel James Williams and his volunteers from Sumter's camp joined the band of mostly North Carolina and Georgia militiamen at Colonel Charles McDowell's camp.

After a few days, Shelby and Clarke moved their detachment of Patriot militiamen ten miles down the Broad River to Smith's Ford where they camped on the east bank. While there, they learned that 200 Loyalists had arrived at Musgrove's Ford on the Enoree River to guard and protect that crossing. Shelby believed that prize target was particularly vulnerable to attack because Ferguson's main force had already advanced well beyond it. The Patriots expected the Tory troops camped at the adjacent Musgrove's Mill to be overly confident in their security.

The two Patriot officers mustered their men for an immediate expedition against the Loyalists at Musgrove's Mill. Williams was especially eager to join this expedition as it promised to take him even closer to his home on Little River.

Colonel Thomas Brandon, a tall Irishman and part of Williams's company, was familiar with the country and served as a guide, leading the 200 militiamen from Smith's Ford. It was a challenging ride as they planned to cover 40 miles before dawn. For secrecy and to spare their horses the heat of the day, they departed camp about an hour before sundown on August 17. They rode for a time through the woods, and when darkness fell, they entered a road and proceeded at a canter all night, never stopping even once. In their cross-country ride, they made their way up hills and down into valleys, crossing small and larger creeks as they cut across several watersheds and river basins. In succession, they crossed a series of creeks: Gilkey's, Thicketty, Pacolet, and Fairforest. After riding 26 miles, they passed unnoticed only some three or four miles from Ferguson's army which was camped at Fairforest Shoals. Pressing on, they rode another dozen or so miles, crossing the Tyger River. Just before sunrise, they approached Musgrove's Ford.

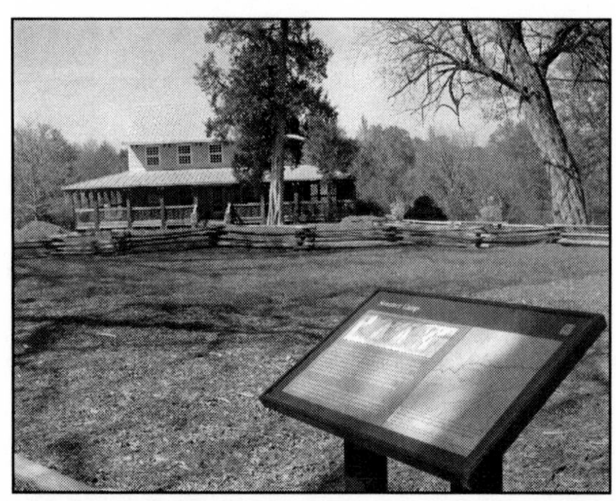

**The British Legion forces camped at Edward Musgrove's Mill to control the Enoree River ford and his mill's capacity for grinding meal. It became a camp for wounded Loyalists as well. A visitor center offers exhibits about the history of the area and the battle.**

Shelby halted the men in an open area, an old Indian field, about a mile north of the ford across the Enoree River. He sent forward a small party of six spies to scout the area. They reached the Enoree River at the mouth of Cedar Shoal Creek and made their way carefully and quietly upstream a mile or so on a small road to Head's Ford, where they crossed the Enoree River. They crept up to the Tory encampment and took note of the numbers of men and the activity. The scouts may have noticed that the camp included more men than they were expecting to find. Returning by the same route to report what they had seen, they were surprised by a Tory patrol that had crossed the Enoree River after the scouts had passed. The two groups skirmished in a sharp fight until the scouts had killed one and wounded two of the Tories. The two other Tories ran for their camp to give the alarm. The Patriot scouts hastened to Shelby and Clarke, two of them slightly wounded, to report on the skirmish and to tell what they had seen.

The Tory camp had heard the shots and when the two Loyalists returned with the news that Whigs were skulking near the ford, the encampment came alive. Colonel Alexander Innes, who had just arrived the night before, was ready to mount his men and ride out to confront whatever size party of Patriots they might find. Colonel Innes, a Scotsman, commanded the South Carolina Royalists, a mounted Tory militia regiment advancing from Ninety Six with another two hundred well-trained men from two provincial regiments. Innes was an experienced military officer. He had served for a time at Long Island on the Holston as the assistant commissary officer and in 1777 had lived among the Cherokee most probably as a protégé of Alexander Cameron, the British Indian agent. He had come not afraid to take decisive action. Colonel Innes made his case to the council of officers at Musgrove's Mill for an immediate attack. Others argued that waiting until a party of about a hundred men returned from their patrol down river would afford them the advantage of a larger force. At the least, they would be able to finish their breakfasts, they argued. However, Innes's sense of urgency in riding immediately to capture the Whigs carried the council. Leaving a hundred men to guard their camp at the home of Edward Musgrove, Innes and the Loyalists mounted up and crossed the Enoree River at the ford. They were bent on chasing down the bothersome Whigs before they could escape. According to Draper, Innes regarded the Patriot militiamen as "a scurvy lot of ragamuffins."[30]

Expecting that the 200 or so Tories they believed to be at the ford might soon come after them, Shelby and Clarke positioned their men on a tree-covered ridge about a half-mile north of Musgrove's Ford and east of Cedar Shoals Creek. While taking their position there, a local friend of the Patriots came to Shelby. Colonel Innes, he told

Shelby, had arrived the night before with 200 provincials and another hundred Tory militia volunteers. With them were Captain Abraham DePeyster and the notorious Tory, Captain David Fanning. These troops were on their way to join with Major Patrick Ferguson for his continuing push through the South Carolina Upcountry and then into North Carolina.

With this disconcerting news, Shelby and Clarke realized they now faced not an even number of Tory militia as they had expected, but potentially a force of 500, including 200 British-trained soldiers. It would be foolish to attack as they had originally planned, the officers reasoned. Likewise, it would be impossible to retreat; they had ridden their horses to exhaustion. The Patriots had no choice but to make a stand where they were. They tied their horses well to the rear and began preparing their defenses along the timbered ridge.

Hurriedly the men built a breastwork of fallen logs and brush. They constructed their rough fortification in a semicircle arcing across some three hundred yards and extending equally on each side of the road, which ascended the hill from the ford. For thirty minutes, the men labored to erect the protection as high as their chests. Shelby's men were on the right and Clarke's on the left. Williams took the position in the middle. Each flank had 20 mounted troops hidden from the view of any approaching enemy. Clarke held forty men behind his lines in reserve.

Patriot Captain Shadrach Inman then volunteered to execute a plan he had suggested as a way to entrap the British forces. He rode to the ford with 25 mounted men and fired upon the Tories across the river to provoke them into attacking. The British troops under Colonel Innes pursued Inman and his men, following them up the road and

**Colonels Shelby, Clarke, and Williams defeated the Loyalists gathered at Musgrove's Mill before escaping to North Carolina. Musgrove Mill State Historic Site on the Enoree River, near Clinton, SC, interprets this Patriot militia victory with a visitor center, battlefield trail, and living history events throughout the year.**

believing they were driving the Patriots into retreat with their bayonet charge. Inman's men executed a fighting retreat as the Patriots had done at Wofford's Ironworks. They fired and fell back, continuing to take new positions behind trees from where they fired again, each time retreating ever closer to their fellow Patriots hidden behind the breastworks.

When Innes's troops were still 200 yards out from the secluded Patriots, they formed a line and advanced another 50 yards. From there the Loyalists fired several volleys with their muskets without much effect, generally shooting over the heads of the Patriots. The Whigs took cover behind trees and behind the breastworks and even sheltered themselves along a fence that paralleled the road. The hidden Patriots held their fire, obeying the orders not to shoot until the enemy was close enough that they could see the whites of their eyes or distinguish the buttons on their coats.

Captain Inman continued his retreating skirmishes. When it appeared to the British that the Patriots were retreating in confusion, Colonel Innes ordered a charge. With the sound of the bugle and the beat of the drum, the provincial guard and Loyalist militia advanced, but in less than military order. The excited Loyalists broke their ranks and rushed forward sensing a victory over the small party of Patriots they had been chasing up the hill. Anticipating victory, they shouted, "Huzza for King George!"[31]

When the Loyalist forces were within 70 yards, the Patriots unleashed a deadly barrage of firepower from behind the breastworks. The unsuspecting Tories were stunned, but they did not retreat. They formed again and continued advancing up the road. The fighting continued in earnest and the provincial guard under Innes began to make some headway against Shelby's men on the right flank. Clarke sent his 40 reserves to join in with Shelby's men and to help stem the advance. As Innes was pressing hard on the right flank and about to sweep over them, William Smith, a rifleman from the Watauga Valley, placed a ball into the Loyalist colonel and knocked him from his horse. "I've killed their commander," he shouted as Innes fell.[32] Some of Innes's men grabbed the colonel and carried him to the rear. Shelby's men, sensing the opportunity, jumped from their covered positions and charged the provincials, fighting furiously as they frightened the enemy with their Indian yells. Clarke's men pressed forward as well on the left flank, yelling and shooting as they attacked the less effective Tory militia aligned against them. Shelby recounted the battle as "one of the hardest ever fought in the United States with small arms. The smoke was so thick as to hide a man at the distance of twenty yards." He added, "The action was bloody & obstinate for upwards for an hour and a half."[33]

The Loyalist troops began to retreat and eventually gave way, falling back completely and descending the road toward the ford as the Patriots pursued them. Draper most effectively described the British retreat:

> "The yells and screeches of the retreating British and Tories as they ran through the woods, and over the hills to the river — loudly intermingled with the shouts of their pursuers, together with the groans of the dying and wounded, were terrific and heart-rending in the extreme. The smoke, as well as the din and confusion, rose high above the exciting scene. The Tories ceased to make any show of defense when half way from the breast-works to the ford. The retreat then became a perfect rout; and now, with reckless speed they hastened to the river, through which they rushed with the wildest fury, hotly pursued by the victorious Americans with sword and rifle, killing, wounding or capturing all who came in their way."[34]

Shelby wrote: "The Tories … broke in great confusion, the slaughter from thence to the Enoree river about half a mile was very great[,] dead men lay thick on the Ground over which our men pursued the enemy."[35]

Amidst this seeming victory, tragedy struck. While Inman was leading the Patriot militiamen in their chase toward the ford, some of the British force stopped and fired, hitting the captain. Inman was struck seven times, receiving a lethal shot in the forehead. In the confusion of this retreat, Tory Colonel Daniel Clary faired better. The bridle of his horse was seized by two strapping Whigs grabbing from opposite sides, as they intended to capture him. With great presence of mind, he shouted, "Damn you, don't you know your own officers!" The startled Patriot militiamen instantly released their hold, and Clary fled the field.[36]

The Tories scrambled desperately across the ford in full retreat, but one fellow had enough spirit left to stop and in a gesture of contempt, bared his buttocks at the Patriots. "Can't you turn that insolent braggart over?" asked Colonel Thomas Brandon of a nearby militiaman. The Patriot took aim and hit his mark exactly, "turning him over"; afterwards two Loyalists carried the wounded man from the opposite hillside.[37]

With changing emotion, about fifty Tories had watched the events of the hour-long encounter from their vantage point on the roof of the Musgrove's house. Their initial cheers as Innes chased the Patriots up the road turned to cries of despair. "We are beaten," they moaned when they saw their comrades retreating toward the ford. Some among these spectators had been paroled previously by the Patriots, and they feared the consequences should they be captured again.

**The field of battle was along a road from the Enoree River ford uphill to the northeast. An interpreted battlefield trail takes visitors across the scene of the intense and decisive battle.**

These anxious Tories grabbed their knap-sacks and scampered off as quickly as they could toward Ninety Six. Those departing so quickly were soon joined in their retreat by a host of dispirited troops. Leaving a sizable number of troops at the mill to tend to and guard the wounded, Captain DePeyster led a party of men toward Ninety Six. Other groups soon followed.[38]

"This action [at Musgrove's Mill]," wrote William Hill later, "was one of the hardest ever fought in the United States with small arms — the smoke was so thick as to hide a man at the distance of 20 yards."[39] The Patriot victory at Musgrove's Mill was a complete rout of the British troops, though many observed that the British-trained troops had fought well and bravely. The Patriots attributed the Loyalists' performance to the discipline and training they had received from Major Ferguson. Regardless of the training, the casualties were heavily one-sided. The provincials and Tories lost 63 killed and 90 wounded. Seventy were taken prisoner. Out of the four or five hundred in the force, this was a devastating loss. The Patriots suffered four killed and nine wounded.

Continuing his journal entry on August 19, Allaire's disposition went from excited confidence to deep concern in a single paragraph. He wrote, "We received orders to pursue Sumter, he having the only remains of what the Rebels can call a corps in these parts at present. … At seven [p.m.] we got in motion. That very moment an express arrived from Col. Innes', who was on his way from Ninety Six to join us, informing us that he had been attacked by a body of Rebels at Musgrove's Mills on Enoree river . … He wished for support as many of the militia had left him. … At eleven at night, we got in motion; marched all night; forded Broad river at sun-rising."[40]

### Flight to Gilbert Town

With their devastating victory over the British force stoking the Patriot militia's confidence, Shelby and Clarke talked of making another grueling ride to Ninety Six, 25 miles south, where they could attack what they had learned was a weakened British garrison. As they were preparing to depart on this campaign, an express arrived with a message from Colonel Charles McDowell. Enclosed was a letter to McDowell from General Richard Caswell advising him of the complete defeat of Gates's Continental Army at Camden on the 16$^{th}$, just two days before. The message warned all the detachments to escape the region before they were cut off. McDowell added that he was moving his men towards Gilbert Town in the Broad River valley of North Carolina. Shelby and Clarke understood immediately their predicament: McDowell was gone and Sumter's men, too; Ferguson was to their north and the troops of Ninety Six were not so far away; Cornwallis was overrunning South Carolina. Holding council from their saddles, the officers decided to take a backwoods route, thus avoiding Ferguson, and to attempt a rendezvous with McDowell in Gilbert Town.

The Patriots had captured 70 Tories and expected to take them along. Each of three riders was assigned a prisoner to carry on his horse in rotation with the others. Each prisoner carried his own musket without its flint. The caravan departed immediately knowing that Ferguson would mount a furious effort to recover the prisoners as soon as he learned of the defeat at Musgrove's Mill. The Patriots rode to the northwest, crossing the headwater streams of the Tyger River and across rough and rocky ground. Though the horses and the men were tired, Colonel Isaac Shelby would not let them rest lest they all be overtaken. The men stripped green corn from the stalks as they rode by and snatched peaches off trees. These pluckings provided their only sustenance during their hard retreat. To rest the horses, the men dismounted and trotted along beside them. They stopped infrequently and then only briefly to water and feed their mounts, slaking their own thirst from the streams flowing out of the mountains toward which they were riding.

Ferguson's men did indeed pursue the retreating Patriots and on the 18th a detachment stopped at a place where only 30 minutes before Shelby and his men had stopped to water their horses. Not knowing how close they had come to overtaking the Patriot militiamen, Ferguson's men halted their chase. Shelby and Clarke rode on, still attempting to outpace the pursuers they believed were behind them. The Patriot militiamen rode all night. On the 19th, they crossed the North Tyger River and later entered North Carolina. By then, Musgrove's Mill was sixty miles behind them and Smith's Ford another forty miles before that. Since leaving the Broad River at sunset on the 16th, they had covered one hundred miles in less than 48 hours, stopping only long enough to fight and win a heroic battle and then escape with 70 prisoners. The grueling pace took its toll on the men. Shelby recounted later, "the excessive fateague … effectually broke every officer on our side that their faces and eyes swelled and became bloated in appearance as scarcely able to see."[41]

Shelby and Clarke joined Charles McDowell in Gilbert Town and after resting some time, considered their prospects for the immediate future. Isaac Shelby was adamant that an army of sufficient size be raised on both sides of the mountains to deal with Ferguson. The officers and men who were consulted on the prospect of following this course agreed whole-heartedly. They knew it could be done. They agreed that Colonel McDowell would send an express to Colonel Benjamin Cleaveland in Wilkes County and Major Joseph Winston in

Surry County apprising them of the need and the plan and asking them to raise volunteers. They agreed as well that McDowell would keep the other colonels apprised of Ferguson's movements as they each retired to their home communities and prepared for the coming invasion by Ferguson and Cornwallis.

Shelby knew that the time of enlistment agreed to by his volunteers and by Sevier's militiamen, then commanded by Major Robertson, had passed. He left the Tory prisoners to the care of Colonel Elijah Clarke and rode off with the Overmountain Men toward the Holston, Watauga, and Nolichucky river valleys. The men from Burke and Rutherford counties, numbering fewer than 200, remained in the Gilbert Town area. Clarke also decided to leave and to head back to Georgia. After Shelby departed, Clarke put the prisoners into the care of Colonel James Williams. Clarke and his men crossed the Savannah River and returned to Wilkes County, Georgia.

Williams conveyed the prisoners successfully to Hillsborough as the colonels had agreed and he delivered his report on the battle to South Carolina's Governor John Rutledge. The governor had been administering his state in exile since April 13, when he slipped out of Charlestown under siege and retreated from his state. Writing years later, Billy Hill charged that Williams had "arrogated the whole honor to himself," implying that he had the major role in carrying out the expedition that ended in a gallant victory at Musgrove's Mill. Thus, did Rutledge praise Williams grandly, Hill claimed, "upon his showing his prisoners to the Governor and deceiving him by taking the whole merit to himself." (Scholars strongly contest Hill's assertions on this point.[42]) Moreover, Hill claimed that the governor bestowed on Williams a "General's Commission."[43] The other officers received no such accolades and approbation for their roles in the victory, Hill said.

(Williams had, in fact, mentioned them all in his report of September 5.) Whether Williams's report was intended or not as a deception, on September 10, the governor of North Carolina, Abner Nash, may have construed the account to the favor of Williams and disregarded the role of his own militia leaders — Shelby, McDowell, Robertson, and others — in praising the victory at Musgrove's Mill. Nash reportedly wrote, "Colonel Williams of South Carolina, two days after this defeat [at Camden], with two hundred men, engaged four hundred of the British cavalry, in a fair open field fight, and completely defeated and routed them …"[44]

Despite the erroneous record of service that was being circulated about the civilian Patriot leaders who were then safely removed from the fields of conflict, Lieutenant Allaire recorded on September 1 his own concerns for the continuing effort to suppress the rebellion two weeks after Gates had seemingly destroyed the organized Patriot army. He wrote: "*Friday, September 1st.* Still remained at Culbertson's. Maj. Ferguson joined us again from Camden with the disagreeable news that we were to be separated from the army, and act on the frontiers with the militia."[45]

# Tory Troubles

**Backcountry Divided**

During the second half of the 18th century, the backcountry of North Carolina and Virginia was filling with people of an independent spirit—Scots Irish, English, Germans, and French Huguenots. They came for affordable and abundant land, for opportunity, and to make new lives of their own choosing as the land would allow. Despite the similarities of their situations, the people on the frontier did not all think alike, and they resented any suggestions that they should.

**William Campbell moved to land along the Middle Fork of the Holston River most likely in 1773. This marker for Aspenvale, his home, is on Seven Mile Ford Rd. in Seven Mile Ford, VA near the hilltop cemetery containing his grave.**

Many parts of the Holston River, New River, and Yadkin River valleys were home to groups who favored the revolution and home as well to groups who abhorred it. Since the beginning of the revolution, these factions, Whig rebels and Loyalists, had been in conflict. Loyalism on the frontiers was not always so much about a love of the British Crown as it was an honest and heartfelt resentment of the gentry class of American colonists, some of whose members were organizing the rebellion. Regardless of the reasons, the divisions by politics were clear, emphatic, and unwavering.

In the backcountry, men on both sides of the revolution claimed to be fighting for justice. A third group professed neutrality, trying to live at peace in communities so divided. Mixed in with all those residents of the backcountry were outlaws and opportunists, who thrived in the chaos. These robbers and horse thieves created a civil disorder that neither the Loyalists nor the Whigs could control. Restoring public order was, in fact, a chief goal of the backcountry Whigs. Only then could they claim governmental authority. Many Loyalists in the area felt the same; they only wanted to restore order to their communities by subduing the rebellious, upstart Whigs.

A year after the Fincastle County Committee of Safety in Virginia had expressed its "unpolished sentiments" regarding liberty through its Fincastle Resolves in 1775, the committee was confronted within the county by a passionate expression of staunch support for the King. An incautious resident along the New River, John Spratt, damned the committee, threatened the life of William Preston, County Lieutenant of Militia[1], and declared that "he could raise one hundred men for the king." The committee took a strong stand against such internal opposition to the Whig rebellion. They captured, tried, and punished such insurrectionist and disaffected citizens during the early years of the war. Nevertheless, in some of the southwestern Virginia counties, half of the citizens were Loyalists.[2]

### Swung to a Limb

Within the first year that William Campbell had returned home from his service in Williamsburg (that is, during 1777), he and his neighbors were continually watchful for strangers and suspicious persons in their counties. The British had agents in the area, it was believed, for the purposes of encouraging the local Tories. One Sunday, the story was later recounted, when Campbell was returning home from church with a party of family and friends, they noticed a stranger walking along the road. The man had a simple bundle slung over his shoulders. When Campbell's group got within about 150 yards of the man, the fellow veered off the road into the woods. Campbell, on horseback, rode into the forest to intercept the man, who then broke into a dead run toward the river. As there was no ford there, Campbell and some of his party dismounted and waded across the river to trap the fellow in an ivy-covered cleft in the bank. Campbell took the man, "dressed very shabbily," it was noted, back to the road where others soon joined them. Campbell interrogated the man, who feigned being a fool and offered flimsy excuses for his behavior. Campbell suspected the man was up to some "vile service," and demanded to search him. After looking through the bundle and all the man's worn-out clothes, Campbell remarked with keen curiosity on the man's wearing a "very good pair of shoes." Using his knife, Campbell removed the soles of the shoes and discovered in each shoe letters "written by the British commander, addressed to the King of the Cherokee Indians." The letters were written on fine paper and each was enclosed in a bladder to protect it from moisture. The letters exhorted the Indians "to send their warriors in every direction and harass the whites as much as possible." The letters recommended their bearer to the Cherokee chiefs as "a man of sense and honesty as one in whose counsels they should place implicit confidence." Confronted with the evidence, the spy confessed that he "had been promised by the British commander a large sum of money to carry these letters to the Indians and to incite them." Campbell conferred briefly with his companions on what course of action to take. Declaring themselves fit dispensers of justice, Campbell and his party passed summary judgment. The fellow was "swung to a limb."[3]

### Uncivil Conflict

After the Virginia legislature demanded that every man at least age 16 take an oath of allegiance, many refused, including nearly one entire militia company in Montgomery County. Disaffected militiamen and others formed bands of opposition to the Whigs. These gangs of Tories roamed through the western counties "stealing horses and robbing … Whig sympathizers." The Patriot militia responded by patrolling the counties, even marching up the New River and dispersing some Tories gathered there.[4] But, the Tories along the New River did not operate in isolation. They communicated with like-minded men from the South Fork of the Holston in Washington County, Virginia and disaffected Loyalists south of and along the Yadkin River in North Carolina.

In March 1779, another British agent was in southwest Virginia encouraging Loyalist support by spreading the rumor that the land where they lived had been sold to the French, so they "might as well" fight on behalf of Great Britain, the agents argued, rather than be ruled by France. (This, no doubt, played on the fears of the frontiersmen aroused earlier by the Quebec Act in 1774.) The agent offered the men money for enlisting with the promise of 450 acres to be quitrentfree for 21 years. The persuaded recruits were drawn into efforts to disarm local Whigs. They even planned a raid on the home of William Preston to capture the supply of armaments there. Indeed, Preston's own neighbors were involved in a "Bloody and Murderous Conspiracy" against him and his family. In response to the insurrection, the local Montgomery County militia, with William Campbell and his mounted militia from Washington County joining in, rounded up the conspirators, capturing fourteen. Nine of the conspirators were released, but two were put in irons awaiting trial. Three others were sent to work in the lead mines although there was no evidence against them at all.[5] The Whigs on the frontier were committed to suppressing any Toryism before it could grow, even if they sometimes, perhaps, overreached the law.

In this uncivil conflict among neighbors, however, over stepping the law and resorting to justice of one's own design was not uncommon. In the summer of 1779, Major Walter Crockett of Montgomery County asked William Campbell for help in suppressing some Tories, who had gathered with the intent to capture the lead mines. Since 1776, the mines had been supplying many tons of lead, so critical to the Continental Army.[6] Crockett and his men seized a group of Tories and "shot one, Hanged one, and whipt several." At another time, Campbell reportedly hanged 12 men from two oaks in the Black Lick Valley. (The notorious, twin "Tory Trees" long stood in what was then Montgomery County, now Mercer Co., West Virginia.[7] )

During the summer and fall of 1779, Colonel Campbell took command of 400 mounted militia and rode into the Yadkin River valley where he set up headquarters in the Moravian towns. Campbell treated the Moravians with respect, more than they received from the nearby Wilkes County Militia.[8] Campbell's men made "excursions from that point [the Moravian towns] after the Tories, some of whom they whipped, others they hanged." Despite being a colonel of the Virginia militia (Washington County), Campbell ranged throughout western North Carolina riding even into the Catawba River valley. Riding under Captain Abraham Trigg, Virginia militiaman Henry Trolinger, on a three-month tour of service, declared that he remained with Campbell's Tory expedition until they reached Quaker Meadows in late October.[9] Campbell and Crockett were so active in suppressing "open insurrection and conspiracy," that in October 1779, Virginia's General Assembly—on a motion by General Thomas Nelson, Jr., a signer of the Declaration of Independence—"indemnified and clearly exonerated" Campbell and Crockett for actions they may have taken not "strictly warranted by law." [10] [11]

**The Boundary Issue**

In the fall of 1779, a matter of jurisdiction initiated a change in the leadership of the Overmountain militia. On September 13, when William Cocke was called upon by a deputy of sheriff Arthur Campbell to pay his taxes, he refused, declaring that he really did not live in Virginia after all. Cocke had served in the Virginia legislature and he and his Carter Valley neighbors along the Holston River had always regarded themselves as Virginians. On this occasion, however, Cocke challenged the right of Virginia to collect taxes. He said "the people were fools if they did pay [the sheriff] public dues," because, he claimed, they all actually lived in North Carolina.[12]

This incident led the two states to commission two sets of surveyors to extend their common boundary (at 36 degrees 30 minutes north) from its previous termination near Steep Rock Creek. Dr. Thomas Walker, the man who "discovered" the Cumberland Gap, represented Virginia. Judge Richard Henderson, the land speculator who had founded Boonesborough in Kentucky, represented North Carolina. Isaac Shelby served as a member of the guards who escorted and protected the surveyors. Although the two parties disagreed after about 40 miles, Virginia continued the line all the way to the Mississippi River. As a consequence of the survey, a third to a half of Washington County, Virginia was revealed to actually lie in North Carolina. The Old North State acted quickly, creating Sullivan County in February 1780. Sapling Grove, the home of Isaac Shelby, was south of the line. He resigned his commission in the Virginia militia, and became the county lieutenant for Sullivan County militia in North Carolina. In this capacity, he received a request from General Griffith Rutherford to provide militiamen for the protection of the state. Isaac Shelby's father, Evan Shelby, also discovered that he lived in North Carolina. When he resigned his commission as colonel of the 70th Regiment of Virginia Militia (Washington County), William Campbell became the new full colonel in April, commissioned by the governor. William Edmiston, Sr. became major.[13]

**We Hung Him, Betty**

Colonel William Campbell's antagonism toward Tories was not reserved to his service at the head of a body of militia. On occasion, he chased down the scoundrels personally. In the spring of 1780, after returning from his Tory hunting excursion with Major Crockett the year before, Campbell was, on one Sunday morning, riding home with this wife, Elizabeth (a sister to Patrick Henry), and a small entourage of friends and family members including his cousin, John Campbell. They noticed a man ahead on the road approaching them on horseback. William Campbell did not know the man, but John Campbell identified him as Francis Hopkins, a notorious Tory bandit. He was a counterfeiter of treasury notes, a criminal who had escaped from jail while awaiting trial. After escaping, he then harassed the Whig citizens of Washington County, stealing their horses and intimidating them in any number of ways. Indeed, Hopkins had posted threats against Colonel Campbell on the gates of Campbell's home, Aspenvale, warning Campbell to desist his persecution of Loyalists. As was his practice and preference, Hopkins was carrying with him that day a rope halter he intended to use in stealing yet another mount from some local Whig.

William Campbell may not have recognized Hopkins, but the latter turned in flight when he saw Campbell approaching. Campbell immediately spurred his horse and took off at a gallop to overtake the fellow. A companion followed behind Campbell. The hunter and the prey rode at full speed along the long stretch of road between the homes of Colonel Greever and Colonel Beattie, Campbell gaining on Hopkins with every stride. "As they reached the branch at the base of the hill a little west of Colonel Beattie's, Colonel Campbell dashed up alongside the fleeing Tory, who, seeing that he would be caught, turned short to the right down the bank and plunged into the river. As he struck the water, Colonel Campbell, who had left his companion in the rear, leaped in beside him, grasped the Tory's holsters and threw them into the stream, and then dragged him from his horse into the water." [14]

Campbell's companion arrived to help drag Hopkins from the stream. The captured Tory was brave, if foolish, and defiantly acknowledged the truth of the charges laid against him, declaring that he would take horses from any Whig wherever he could find them. Campbell would have none of that arrogance from an enemy of the commonwealth. Without benefit of trial, William Campbell used the rope halter to hang the man from a sycamore limb that reached out over the stream.

In his own account of this incident, published in 1881, Lyman C. Draper conflated the stories of Campbell's separate encounters with a spy and with Hopkins as reported by Lewis Preston Summers. Draper added a little drama by having Campbell wrestle with Hopkins in the river, almost being drowned by the stronger man. Although his full account may be somewhat suspect as written, Draper punctuated it with an ending quite telling of Campbell's demeanor: "When Colonel Campbell rejoined his wife, she eagerly inquired, 'What did you do with him, Mr. Campbell?' 'Oh, we hung him, Betty—that's all.'" [15, 16]

**Terror of the Tories**

Across the mountains and to the south of William Campbell's Holston River valley, Benjamin Cleaveland was dealing with the Tories in the Yadkin River valley of North Carolina. After serving as chairman of the Surry County Committee of Safety in 1775 and later, he worked, in the face of a growing population to carve a new county out of Surry and a part of Washington County. Established through his efforts, in part, in 1777, Wilkes County became effective in February 1778. Cleaveland continued to be one of its prominent figures and represented the county in the North Carolina Assembly in 1778 and in the state senate in 1779. Serving as a fellow representative from the western counties in the Halifax session in the fall was Joseph Hardin.[17] As part of the proceedings of the first session, on February 12, Benjamin Cleaveland was appointed a colonel of the newly formed Light Horse militia and Joseph Hardin, a major of the same.[18]

Cleaveland already had a reputation for leadership in the field—and for a ferocious temper. When his militiamen returned on one occasion from ranging through the Yadkin River valley looking for Tories, they had in their possession a great deal of goods and property they had plundered from local residents. Tradition says that Cleaveland was furious at his men for their behavior and he threatened to shoot the ringleaders of such gang activities. He would relent on two conditions, he offered: their returning the stolen property to the rightful owners and their promising to be ever ready to muster at a moment's notice.[19]

Despite such tales likely told years later to clean up the questionable reputation of a favored war hero, Cleaveland was notorious for his pursuit of Tories and his disturbance of neutral communities. Before becoming a captain in November 1776[20], Cleaveland rode as a lieutenant under Captain Jesse Walton, whose rough treatment of residents in the Yadkin Valley was recorded by the Moravians in Salem.

As was Campbell, Cleaveland was also known for quickly dispatching his opponents. On one occasion two of Cleaveland's men, David and John Witherspoon, living with their parents and toward the mountains, were captured by the Tory Captain William Riddle. They were taken as prisoner over the Appalachian Mountains into the Watauga Valley. The two young men were blindfolded and lined up to be shot, when Riddle proposed a remedy to their plight. If they would swear an oath to fight for the King, he said, join his Tory band, and also ride home and return with a prize horse, known as O'Neal's mare, their lives would be spared. The two brothers readily agreed and made careful mental notes about what they had promised. When they reached home, David mounted the O'Neal mare and rode hurriedly to alert Whig militia officer Benjamin Herndon. They quickly raised a party and rode back to the Watauga valley where the Whigs surprised the Tories, killing several, chasing off others, and capturing three: Riddle, Goss, and Reeves. The Witherspoons had indeed kept their promises. They had returned—and with the mare.

When the party of Whigs and three captured Tories reached

Wilkesboro, Benjamin Cleaveland held a quick court martial and sentenced the men to be hanged. Attempting to gain a little favor with the Whig militiamen—or perhaps attempting to effect his escape, Riddle offered to treat the gathering with a round of whiskey. Cleaveland told Riddle it would be a wasted effort as he was to be hanged right after breakfast. That morning, Cleaveland hanged the Tories from a tree at the center of the village, as Riddle's wife, an accomplice to her husband's marauding, looked on. (The Tory Oak stood next to the courthouse in Wilkesboro for more than two centuries, finally succumbing to age and high winds in 1992.)

Benjamin Cleaveland could also be unusually cruel in his persecution of Tories. The story recalled was that Cleaveland rode to the Richmond courthouse, the seat of Surry County affairs, where two horse thieves were in jail. For fear that those scoundrels might yet escape, Cleaveland insisted on hanging them immediately. He took the two out of the jail, stood one on a log with a noose around his neck and the rope slung over a limb. He then kicked the log out of the way. As the victim yet dangled from the rope, Cleaveland turned to the

**Benjamin Cleaveland hanged Tories from a tree on a hill along the Yadkin River. Adjacent to the Wilkes Heritage Museum in Wilkesboro, NC, a wayside exhibit interprets the Tory Oak's history next to a new commemorative planting, replacing the tree which collapsed in 1992.**

Tory accomplice and said, "You have your choice, either to take your place beside him, or cut your own ears off, and leave the country forever." The man took Cleaveland at his word and called for a knife. As Draper recounted the disturbing scene, the man "whetted [the knife] a moment on a brick, then gritting his teeth, he slashed off his own ears, and left with the blood streaming down his cheeks, and was never heard of afterwards." [21]

Such was the character of Colonel Benjamin Cleaveland that gave rise in the fall of 1779 to a perhaps less agreeable piece of business undertaken by the General Assembly. At the Halifax session, the senate sent a resolution for house concurrence on gubernatorial pardons for Colonel Cleaveland, serving as Wilkes's senator, and Captain Benjamin Herndon, serving as a Wilkes representative. The two militia officers and others had killed Lemuel Jones and William Coyle, "two known Traitors, Murderers, Robbers and House [Horse] thieves," the resolu-

**Benjamin Cleaveland was prominent in the governance of Wilkes County, NC, and a notorious Tory hunter. The Wilkes Heritage Museum interprets his life through exhibits including the cabin of his brother Robert. Near the museum is a cement, commemorative statue of Benjamin Cleaveland with its own art history.**

tion read. The militiamen had also beaten James Harvel, who had harbored the two Tories.[22] The two colonels were seeking indemnification and exoneration for those crimes committed in the interest of removing enemies of the state during the Revolution. In that cause, they ranged throughout the Yadkin Valley and up the New River as well. Cleaveland must have made some enemies of his own in the Assembly, as the bill, needing to pass after three readings, failed to pass on the second reading. Introduced a third time on November 9 as the final order of business that day, the resolution was at last approved for sending to the governor with the concurrence of the House. It passed 29 votes, yea, to 24, nay. Notable among the nays was the representative from Surry County, one who—and whose constituents—perhaps knew Benjamin Cleaveland all too well. He was, in fact, known far and wide as the Terror of the Tories.[23]

**The Enemy Was Not Far Before Us**

In early 1780, when word of Sir Henry Clinton's February 8 landing of British troops planning to attack Charlestown reached southwest Virginia, the Loyalists there were greatly emboldened. News of that landing at Tybee Island arrived two weeks later and may have been spread that quickly by British agents. Indeed, soon fifteen agents were working throughout Washington and Montgomery counties rallying Loyalist support. In one neighborhood alone, they raised 75 men as Tory sentiments were strong in the region. When they raised sufficient numbers, the Tories planned to destroy the lead mines and then join with the Cherokee "to burn[,] Destroy and cut their way to the English Army and assist them in reducing the Country." William Preston called out the militia to put down the insurrection. Taking a more conciliatory approach toward the Tories, Preston continued to call on citizens to take the oath of allegiance to the commonwealth. Few took the oath, but, in any case, the Tory effort to execute the planned attack did not succeed. Nevertheless, although lacking such a victory, men with Loyalist leanings were continually encouraged to fight for their King and their rights as Englishmen—as well as, the agents noted, for a recruitment bonus and rent-free land.[24]

The Loyalists were certainly encouraged when Charlestown surrendered on May 12. Arthur Campbell, County Lieutenant for Washington County Militia, alerted his cousin[25] by letter on July 12 indicating Tories, "forty or fifty strong," intended to attack Fort Chiswell. "They may do mischief outside as robbers," Arthur Campbell wrote, "but I hope strength enough will be collected today to chastise them."[26] To that end, William Campbell directed captains William Edmiston, Aaron Lewis, James Dysart, and John Campbell of Royal Oak[27] to muster about a dozen men each and to meet at his home "early next day, equipped to march with me [Campbell] to the lead mines."[28] The Whig militiamen of Montgomery County insisted on mustering their Patriot friends. When they marched out, Campbell's troops numbered 140.

Upon reaching the settlement about 16 miles above the lead mines (meaning upstream on the New River and to the southwest near the North Carolina border), they learned that a party of 40 Tories had captured the son (James) of Captain John Cox. Campbell and his men set out immediately tracking the Tories knowing from reports in the settlement that he and his men were only about two hours behind the captors. "We then followed after them in the best order we could lest they should attempt to surprise us," Campbell later wrote, "until it became so dark that we could no longer follow their track." The men made camp. Campbell wrote, "[We] tied up our horses in the most silent manner we could, conjecturing the enemy was not far before us."[29]

Campbell sent forward a scouting party, "four or five very trusty men, to find if possible where the enemy lay." The men got within twenty yards of the camp when Tory sentries fired upon them. They reported to Campbell that "their encampment was in [a] piece of woods in a large glade and perfectly clear for at least a quarter of [a] mile all around where they lay." (This clearing was known as the Big Glade, also as Round Meadow.)

"As soon as it became so light that we could see a small distance around us," Campbell wrote, "we set out a second time toward the enemy's camp on horseback. We got to the side of the glade just as the sun was rising. The morning was very foggy, which prevented our discovering the flight of the enemy, nor did we know they had fled until Captain Cox's son came to us, who in their hurry they had suffered to escape. Upon going to their camp, we found they had gone off with the greatest precipitation, having left everything behind them excepting their arms. . . . [W]e pursued with all the expedition we could upon the trace; but upon their discovering that we [were] pursuing them, they dispersed and hid themselves among the bushes and weeds. We had not the fortune to find any but one of them, who was immediately shot. The woods were searched upon the way they fled for three of four miles. Some of them ran into the mountains and laurel thickets where it was impossible to pursue them on horseback." [30]

Campbell was actually somewhat relieved that the Tories had escaped. As was William Preston, William Campbell was optimistic about persuading his Loyalist neighbors to support the Revolution. He wrote, "I believe the most of them are now well convinced of their folly, and may yet become very good citizens." Giving up the pursuit and being aware they had not eaten much since the morning of the day before,

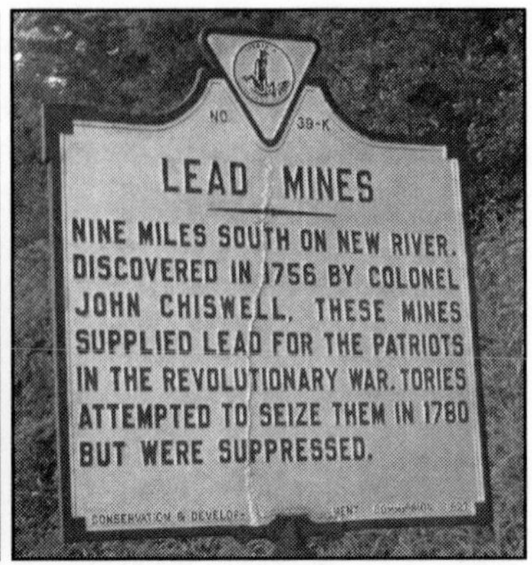

NO. 39-K
LEAD MINES
NINE MILES SOUTH ON NEW RIVER. DISCOVERED IN 1756 BY COLONEL JOHN CHISWELL. THESE MINES SUPPLIED LEAD FOR THE PATRIOTS IN THE REVOLUTIONARY WAR. TORIES ATTEMPTED TO SEIZE THEM IN 1780 BUT WERE SUPPRESSED.


**Tories in then-Montgomery County wanted to capture the lead mines along New River, which provided shot to the Continental Army. A historic marker on US Hwy 52 at I-81 commemorates the history. Attesting to the value of the mineral deposits, a shot tower (used to form lead in a free-fall of 150 feet) from a later era stands at Shot Tower Historical State Park, visible from I-77 at New River.**

Campbell's men, he wrote, "all assembled at the enemy's camp and breakfasted upon the provisions they left behind them."[31]

The men returned to Captain Cox's home that night (by some accounts at the Peach Bottom on New River), and the next morning were met by Colonel Benjamin Cleaveland and 130 of his Wilkes County militiamen. On the day before, he had captured a known Tory, Zachariah Goss, who rode with what the Whigs called "the Plundering Sam Brown gang."[32] Brown and his associate named Coyle were two notorious "murderers, horse thieves, and robbers," Campbell wrote. "Goss was immediately hung," Campbell continued, "I believe with the joint consent of near three hundred men." Reporting in a matter-of-fact manner, he added, "Two other villains were very well whip'd."[33]

William Campbell vehemently disliked troublesome Tories, but as with his optimism for converting the disaffected, he was not without some humanitarian compassion for their families. He ordered Captain Henry Francis to take 60 or 70 men to "collect all the stocks of horses and cattle belonging to the insurgents they possibly could." But knowing those Tory families would suffer, he added "only leaving to each family one horse creature and what milch cattle were necessary for its support."[34]

### Very Equal to Such Duty

William Campbell and his Patriot colleagues in Southwest Virginia faced enemies on three fronts. Campbell was certainly concerned about the British invasion in Charlestown, but any confrontations with that enemy were in the future, though perhaps sooner than he knew. He and his backcountry Virginians faced two more immediate threats: the Tory insurrection, which he was already busily suppressing, and British-fostered Indian attacks against the frontiers.

British efforts to encourage Indian attacks against western settlers spread across the frontier and into the Ohio Valley. Virginia's Governor Thomas Jefferson was concerned about such attacks into Kentucky County from the Shawnee lands across the Ohio River. On May 8, 1780 at Botetourt Court House, militia officers from Washington, Montgomery, Botetourt, Greenbrier, and Rockbridge counties met to plan an expedition across the Ohio River against the Shawnees. William Campbell was the appointed commander, "former experience," Jefferson noted, "having provided him very equal to such duty."[35]

Campbell's expedition to the Ohio River was soon suspended by concerns closer to home. (Colonel George Rogers Clark, however, led a successful expedition of a thousand Kentucky County militiamen across the Ohio River on August 1 and onto the Pickaway Plains to rout the Shawnee on August 8.[36]) Recognizing a rising threat of attacks by Chickamaugas, Jefferson ordered William Campbell instead to command militiamen from Washington and Montgomery counties in a joint expedition with North Carolina militia from the Overmountain region against parties of the renegade Cherokees. Campbell was anxious that the Overmountain militiamen from Washington (North Carolina) and Sullivan counties would not carefully distinguish between friendly (Cherokee) and hostile (Chickamauga) Indians. Fearing that such treatment would prompt a general Indian war, Campbell sought general command of all troops on the expedition so he could better control the behavior of all the troops. Jefferson wrote to North Carolina's Governor Abner Nash[37] on the matter, but this urgent expedition against the Chickamaugas was itself soon delayed by even more urgent threats.

William Preston had hoped Campbell's prior militia raids into the Holston, Yadkin, and New river valleys would have put an end to the Tory uprisings, but the Loyalists were resilient. Through the efforts of a Patriot spy who infiltrated Loyalist planning meetings, Preston learned that the Tories intended to seize the lead mines on July 28. By their plans, they would then join with British troops to march on Charlottesville where they intended to free the British soldiers imprisoned there after their capture at the Battle of Saratoga (1777). By arming those released soldiers, the Loyalist expected to overtake all of Virginia.

Learning of this rising threat of Toryism, Governor Jefferson wrote directly to William Campbell describing the "dangerous insurrection on New River in an attempt to destroy the mines." He changed Campbell's orders and asked him to defend the lead mines a second time "apply[ing] to this object the means and powers put into your hands for the Indian Expedition and to take effectual measures as may secure future safety of that quarter."[38] Foreknowledge of the scheme provided by the spy enabled Colonel William Campbell to lead 500 militiamen from Washington, Montgomery, and Botetourt counties against the brazen Tories. Campbell was joined by Bedford militia under the command of Colonel Charles Lynch.[39] Lynch was the manager of the lead mines on behalf of the commonwealth of Virginia.[40] Campbell and Lynch defeated the Tories and meted out various punishments including 39 lashes, service in the Continental Army for 18 months, imprisonment until trial, parole, and being placed on bond. In the spirit of victors, the Patriot militia plundered the Tories' property and divided it among themselves, such booty being an enticement for many militiamen to serve.

Colonel Lynch soon found himself in late July and early August chasing Tories into Montgomery County where he captured nine and took them to Lead Mines. After extracting confessions from them, he dealt with them in various manners, noting that some "should be made Exampels of." (One writer declares that Lynch "adopted Campbell's method of dealing with Tories and wrong-doers."[41]) Lynch's treatment of Tories was notorious and some suggest that the term "lynch law" comes from "Captain Lynch's law," and is associated with actions such as his. Whether or not he ever hanged anyone without a trial, Colonel Lynch was also exonerated by the Virginia legislature for actions he took in the summer of 1780 to suppress the Tory insurrection, actions that may have been outside the law. [42]

### A Body of 700 Tories and Indians

Although the efforts of colonels William Campbell and Arthur Campbell had diminished the Tory activity in Washington County, threats to the county were not entirely extinguished. The Indian threat rose again. On August 13, 1780, Arthur Campbell wrote to his cousin, William, then chasing Tories in Montgomery County, encouraging him "of the necessity speedily to return with the men from this county." He had just learned by express from Chief Raven at Chota that "a body of 700 Tories and Indians had … set out against the frontiers of this state and Carolina."[43]

Governor Thomas Jefferson had, of course, previously ordered Colonel William Campbell "to take command of the militia ordered to suppress the Tories" and to organize this militia for an expedition against the Chickamaugas.[44] In August, Colonel William Campbell mustered 400 men from Washington County and rode south to prosecute that campaign against those renegade Cherokees. He had expected to join up with militiamen from the Watauga and Nolichucky river valleys, but those men were already engaged east of the mountains. (North Carolina militiamen under Isaac Shelby and Valentine Sevier were serving under Colonel Charles McDowell from his camp at Cherokee Ford in South Carolina.) Nevertheless, Campbell proceeded on his own and was soon reinforced by two Virginia companies from Botetourt County. Overtaking Campbell at the Bend in the Nolichucky River, the reinforcements brought news of Tory uprisings back home in southwest Virginia. Being aware that Cornwallis was indeed marching north from Charlestown, Campbell had reason to be concerned. He called together the officers on the expedition and held a council of war. They decided to proceed no farther. Again, the priorities for protecting their homes had changed. Turning around, they rode back the way they had come. After Campbell and his men rested only a few days back home, he then mustered 300 militiamen for another thrust against the Tories.[45]

### More Than a Hundred Lashes

William Campbell marched his Virginia militiamen into North Carolina to the Moravian town of Bethabara from where he fanned out in search of bands of active Tories in the Yadkin River valley. Colonel Benjamin Cleaveland and his Wilkes County Militiamen joined him. By now, they were generally known among the Whigs as "Cleaveland's Bull Dogs." Among the Tories, they were "Cleaveland's Devils." By any name, for their fighting prowess Cleaveland considered any of his men equal to five regular soldiers.[46]

Campbell's effectiveness in Tory hunting had caught the attention of Patriot General William Smallwood. He wrote to Major General Gates on August 31 from Guilford Courthouse decrying the state of the Continentals and suggesting how best to use such militiamen as rode under Campbell. "The Officers and Soldiers are in a most wretched Situation for want of Cloaths of all kinds, particularly Shoes and Shirts, as also Tents, Camp Kettles, Equipage, &c. If they cannot

**The Gemeinhaus (background) at Bethabara Historical Park in Winston-Salem, NC was built in 1788. Its predecessor, a log structure built atop the stone foundation shown in the foreground, stood witness in Bethabara to the Patriot persecution of Tories in the Yadkin River valley. Bands of both Tories and Patriots came to the Moravian towns for supplies of goods and food during the war.**

immediately be equipped, perhaps it would be eligible to order the Posts at Charlotte and Yadkin to be occupied by Bodies of Militia, Volunteer horse and Riflemen, numbers of which I believe might be got till the Regular Troops could be fitted. Colo. Campbell, with near 300 Volunteer Riflemen from Virginia, well mounted, armed and accoutred, are now in the Moravian Settlement. I would submit to you the Propriety of ordering him to the late Post on the Yadkin." In the same letter, Smallwood also requested instructions on what to do with "twenty British and near thirty Tory Prisoners which I now have under guard, the greatest part taken by Colo. Williams in South Carolina." [47]

Venturing east into Guilford County, Campbell and Cleaveland captured Tory Captain Nathan Read[48] and 17 others. They brought the captives back to Bethabara as prisoners for trial. On September 5, the Moravians recorded, "Another company brought more Tories. Some were tried, and several were whipped, one especially received more than a hundred lashes."[49] On the 8$^{th}$, after his court martial, Read was condemned to be hanged. The Moravians were upset at Colonel Cleaveland's plans to hold the execution on their square and they spoke to Colonel Armstrong. "Then the company was dawn up in two lines," the Moravians recorded, "with this man and the other prisoners between, and so they marched out to the middle bars in the field, where the man was hanged. His name was Rieth [Ried]. As he stood at the foot of the gallows he said that he deserved this sentence, and ought to die quickly."[50] Though Read had been given the chance to serve in the Patriot cause to the end of the war, he declined, "meeting his death heroically," Draper suggested.[51]

On the following day, September 9, Campbell brought the remaining prisoners into the square, which was ringed with Whig militia. He conducted trials for all and whipped four or five on the spot. "In the afternoon all the Virginia troops marched away," the Moravians wrote. "[W]e did not know whither, but we thanked the dear Saviour from our hearts for their departure."[52]

The Moravians had been anxious about the return of Captain Isaac Campbell, whose company had been dispatched a few days before. When he did return and discovered his fellow Virginians had gone, he left his ten prisoners under the guard of other militia at Bethabara and departed. "We were thankful for this also," the Moravians declared.[53]

# Ferguson Enters North Carolina

## To Extinguish the Rebellion

Emboldened by his complete rout of Gates's forces at Camden, Cornwallis wrote to Lt. Colonel John Cruger at Ninety Six recounting his specific orders for punishing the rebels. He wanted all the residents of the Province (South Carolina) who had participated in the revolt to be punished "with the greatest rigor; that they should be imprisoned, and their whole property taken from them or destroyed." Moreover, "every militia man who had borne arms with us, and had afterwards joined the enemy, should be immediately hanged." He concluded his message asking that Cruger "take the most vigorous measures to extinguish the rebellion, in the district in which you command."[1]

On August 29, Cornwallis wrote a report for the Home Government in which he praised the skills of Patrick Ferguson in raising seven battalions as Inspector General of Militia, "consisting of above four thousand men, and entirely composed of persons well-affected to the British Government." The general then denigrated the potential of using such Loyalist militia effectively. "This militia can be of little use for distant military operations," he wrote, "as they will not stir without a horse; and, on that account, your Lordship will see the impossibility of keeping a number of them together without destroying the country." Such a herd of hoof-stock, he conjectured, would rapidly deplete the grain available in any area for feeding anyone — soldiers or civilians.

Despite previous British enthusiasm for a Southern Strategy and their general reliance on rallying "friends of the government" to prosecute the war, among the Loyalist officers, the fighting prowess of these recently recruited militiamen was suspect. In recent skirmishes with Whig militia in the Upcountry, the Loyalist militia had shown signs of timidity and hesitation. The British Legion officers' solution to this problem was apparently to threaten the Loyalist militiamen with severe punishment and loss of property for being delinquent, deserting the battalion, or disobeying a commander's orders. The ultimate punishment, they unanimously devised, was service in the regular army.[2]

Despite such lack of confidence in the Loyalist militia, Cornwallis wrote to Sir Henry Clinton on the same day, explaining his orders for using them nonetheless. He ordered Patrick Ferguson into Tryon County, North Carolina (what the rebels had divided and renamed as Lincoln and Rutherford counties). Ferguson was to command, Cornwallis wrote, "some militia, whom, he says, he can depend upon for doing their duty and fighting well." Cornwallis expressed his serious doubts about the militia, but he, nevertheless, sent Ferguson on a mission far from any reinforcements and without any regular soldiers as part of his command.[3] Ferguson was on his own.

### Plundering What Goods They Desired

Leaving Fair Forest River in the Upcountry on September 2, Ferguson and the various parties of militia beat around the countryside for two or three weeks, visiting upon Whig plantations. On the 2nd, they rode to Wofford's Ironworks, the site of his skirmish with Shelby's and Clarke's men. There, Lt. Anthony Allaire recorded in his diary an incident that brought home another horror of war. "Here was a Rebel militia-man," he wrote, "that got wounded in the right arm at the skirmish at Cedar Spring, the eighth of August. The bone was very much shattered. It was taken off by one Frost, a blacksmith, with a shoemaker's knife and carpenter's saw."[4]

Ferguson's party marched through the Upcountry of South Carolina for a week, crossing into North Carolina over Buck's Creek on the 7th. That night, Ferguson with fifty American Volunteers and 300 militiamen rode out to surprise some Whigs they heard were at Gilbert Town. Again, he was disappointed by the prey's flight in advance of his arrival. Having missed another opportunity to confront the troublesome bands of Whig militia, Ferguson was growing weary of the continuous chase. In August, Shelby and his Overmountain militia had menaced the Loyalists at Fort Anderson, at Cedar Spring, and at Musgrove's Mill; yet, even after the decisive British victory at Camden, Ferguson was unable to overtake them or their like-minded bands of Whig rebels. He wanted to put an end to this cat-and-mouse affair. Ferguson paroled one of the Whig militiamen he had captured at Musgrove's Mill (or at Cedar Spring) and sent him to deliver a stern verbal message to the leaders of the troublesome rebel militia in the Overmountain region of North Carolina. Sam Philips, the parolee, whose wounds had sufficiently healed by then, departed Gilbert Town and headed west toward the mountains, intending for the Watauga, Holston, and Nolichucky river valleys.[5]

During Ferguson's fruitless excursion to Gilbert Town, Allaire had remained at a camp along the Broad River. From there he kept a watch for "some Georgians" reported to be coming their way. Undoubtedly, this was Patriot Col. Elijah Clarke and his men retreating from their siege of Augusta. Ferguson rejoined Allaire's party late on the 10th.

They continued patrols through the Broad River valley.

Majors Patrick Ferguson and James Dunlap had ventured into Tryon and Burke counties, riding at the heads of separate parties, and divided their forces into smaller units as well. The Loyalist bands roamed through the countryside visiting their vengeance upon the homesteads of known Whigs, calling on the families to produce the rebels. The families nearly always declared that the men the Loyalists were seeking were not at home and they did not know where their husbands and fathers were. The Loyalists then plundered from the families what goods they desired. To those residents resigned to defeat, the British Legion administered oaths of allegiance as well. But on occasion, a party of Tories would meet their match at a home where the inhabitants of the community had gathered to protect themselves with what guns and able-bodied men they had, often those too young or too old to serve with the Whig militia. With the women in the house reloading the muskets and rifles as fast as one was discharged, the defenders were on occasion able to drive off a party of marauding Tories, whether actually part of Ferguson's corps or just a band of opportunistic robbers.[6]

## Three Hundred Infamous Villains

On September 12 at two o'clock in the morning, Ferguson left his campaign camp with forty American Volunteers and one hundred militiamen. They marched 14 miles through the mountains to White Oak Springs at the head of Cane Creek, where they expected to surprise a party of rebels.[7] Colonel Charles McDowell and his Whig militiamen had been beating about the backcountry since they left Smith's Ford on the Broad River upon hearing from Richard Caswell[8] about Gates's defeat at Camden. Ferguson learned of McDowell's presence, but McDowell also learned that Ferguson was marching to surprise

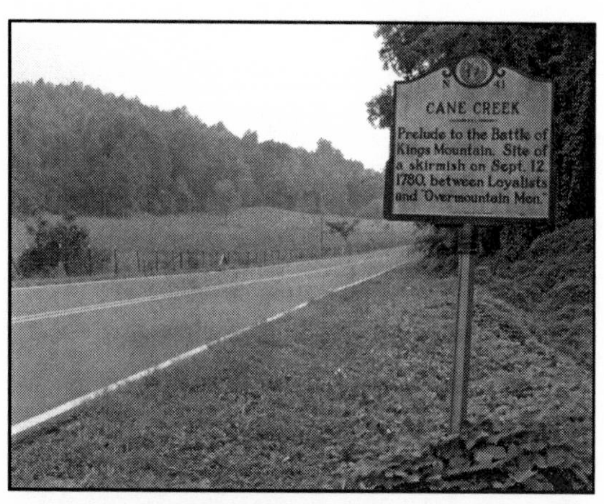


**Colonel Charles McDowell ambushed Ferguson's force on September 12, 1780, near the upper ford on Cane Creek and then retreated to the Overmountain region. A marker stands along US Hwy 64 in Rutherford Co., NC, near the McDowell Co. line.**

him. McDowell's men lay in ambuscade along Cane Creek on a hillside, which commanded the ford at upper Cane Creek.[9] When Ferguson's men were crossing, McDowell's 160 men fired from seclusion; but, the Loyalists rallied, firing back and inflicting casualties among the Whigs. The Patriots could have been routed except for the intrepid spirit of Major Joseph McDowell, the colonel's brother. He was animated along the line, declaring loudly that he would never yield and encouraging his men to fight and die with him if necessary. Firing from cover and moving about through the brush while making good use of their marksman's skills, the Whigs inflicted damage on the Loyalists, including the wounding of Major Dunlap in his leg. The battle was indecisive, and the two parties separated. Ferguson and the Loyalists made their way to Gilbert Town with their wounded. McDowell and his men made their way toward the safety of the distant Appalachian Mountains, crossing during the next week to the Watauga River valley.

Lt. Anthony Allaire recorded a different account of the same encounter, revealing his disdain for the rebels. He bemoaned the Whig's apparent discovery of Ferguson's approach, and then wrote for his September 12 entry: "Mr. McDowell, with three hundred infamous villains like himself, thought it highly necessary to remove their quarters. However, we were lucky enough to take a different route from what they expected, and met them on their way, and to appearance one would have thought they meant sincerely to fight us, as they drew up on an eminence[10] for action. On our approach they fired and gave way. We totally routed them, killed one private, wounded a Capt. White, took seventeen prisoners, twelve horses, all their ammunition, which was only twenty pounds of powder, after which we marched to their encampment, and found it abandoned by those Congress heroes."[11]

**The Most Violent Rebels**

Over the next week and half, Ferguson continued to march around the countryside. On the 13th and 14th, he and his men lay at the plantation of the rebel Colonel John Walker. Allaire remarked, "The poor, deluded people of this Province begin to be sensible of their error, and come in very fast." He also noted some curious experiences, writing, "This creek [Cane] is so amazingly crooked that we were obliged to cross it nineteen times in marching four miles." On the same day he added, of an encounter, "Mrs. Bowman is an exceedingly obliging woman. She had a child about four years old, who had smoked tobacco almost three years."[12]

On the evening of the 15th, Ferguson marched out at 10 o'clock with some American Volunteers and 500 Loyalist militia expecting to surprise McDowell elsewhere. McDowell and his men had departed the day before and were, in fact, headed toward the Overmountain region.

Ferguson continued on to Pleasant Gardens Ford on the Catawba River on September 16. Allaire remarked, "I was surprised to see so beautiful a tract of land in the mountains." He added, "This settlement is composed of the most violent Rebels I ever saw, particularly the young ladies." Ferguson continued ranging up and down the Catawba River camping for a time on the plantation of the rebel Major William Davidson[13], west of Pleasant Gardens. On September 23rd, Ferguson returned to Gilbert Town, having camped the night before once again at the home of rebel Colonel Walker. Allaire noted regarding Gilbert Town, "Took up our ground on a height about half a mile from the town. This town contains one dwelling house, one barn, a blacksmith's shop, and some out-houses."[14] The next day, Allaire reported that "five hundred subjects" had come in, apparently to seek protection, take an oath of allegiance, or otherwise reconcile themselves to the invading British commander, Patrick Ferguson.

Much as Shelby and McDowell had anticipated in August after Shelby's escape from Ferguson following the victory at Musgrove's Mill, the British forces had consumed during the following weeks all the beeves in the Upcountry. They then moved into Burke County, North Carolina to forage for more cattle. During Ferguson's ride along the Catawba River as far west as plantations near the "old fort," he had expected to find more beef steers than he did. Indeed, Colonel McDowell had arranged for the cattle of Patriots to be pastured in remote hollows and meadows far into the foothills of the Blue Ridge Mountains to protect them for use by the Whigs. McDowell had also proposed that some of the most ardent Whigs and upstanding men of the community "take protection" under the British as an additional ruse to guard the beeves. Some refused to compromise their integrity regardless of the benefit to the Patriots. Others, such as Colonel John Carson, some accounts claim, undertook the ruse. When Ferguson and a foraging party returned to the Catawba River valley suspecting that the cattle were being hidden from the Legion, Carson then led Ferguson to a canebrake in which a large herd was feeding. Ferguson's men set about slaughtering about a hundred head. Only when they were well into their work did Carson mention that the cattle likely belonged to three Loyalists who were then in Ferguson's camp. Ferguson admitted later that he had been outsmarted.[15] (Carson's patriotic willingness to participate in the ruse, however, created political friction a generation later and led to the infamous Vance-Carson Duel of 1827, of which Tennessee's Congressman David Crockett was a witness. See *In the Footsteps of Davy Crockett*.)

Ferguson returned to Gilbert Town, convinced — despite occasionally confronting some resistance among the citizens — that he and the British Legion were succeeding in subduing the rebellious Southern colonies. However, all was not well in Cornwallis's continuing advance.

**Tarleton Takes Ill**

After his victory at Camden on August 16, Lord Cornwallis spent three weeks dealing with his prisoners and preparing for his push into North Carolina. He had sent Ferguson ahead with the militia to disturb the countryside. On September 8, Cornwallis began his main advance toward North Carolina. He had not moved far, when Colonel Banastre Tarleton was taken deathly ill the next day with a fever, believed to be yellow fever, though malaria was prevalent among the troops as well. Tarleton lay mostly unconscious — and certainly helpless — for much of the next two weeks, holed up at White's Mill on Upper Fishing Creek.[16] During his illness, his corps of dragoons was unavailable for service as it was needed there to protect the much despised "Bloody Ban." Indeed, Cornwallis delayed his entire campaign awaiting Tarleton's recovery. On September 23, Tarleton

**Marker 46-22: "Site of White's Mill"**
*(About 3.7 miles SW of Rock Hill on SC 72 at intersection of Road 739)*
About 1 ½ miles south of here on Fishing Creek were a house and mill mentioned on a 1766 royal landgrant to Hugh White. British Colonel Banastre Tarleton and his Legion were encamped at White's Mill for several days in September 1780, during which time Tarleton lay "dangerously ill of a fever." Erected by York County Historical Commission — 1983.

[Source: South Carolina Highway Historical Marker Guide, (Columbia: SC Department of Archives and History, 1992), p. 199]

**Tarleton's severe illness with a fever delayed Cornwallis's advance into Charlotte Town for two weeks. A historical marker on Fishing Creek in York County, SC, is missing.**

regained consciousness and was put in a wagon sling for transport. His men carried him toward Charlotte along the Steel Creek road, but the consequences for the British strategy were severe. That two-week delay had enabled the rebel militia ample time to form. They did so among the partisans of North Carolina South Carolina and under the command of Colonel Thomas Sumter.[17]

# The Muster and the March

**With Fire and Sword**

Bad news travels quickly. In the Watauga Valley, reports that caused grave concern among the inhabitants of the Overmountain region for their own safety came in part with the arrival of Colonel Charles McDowell. He and his men were escaping the foothills of the Carolina Piedmont after their confrontation with Major Patrick Ferguson at Cane Creek. The situation was described in a letter from Long Island written by Virginia's Indian Agent Joseph Martin on September 22 to Governor Thomas Jefferson: "We are all on this quarter in great Confusion … On the [18]th Instant Col. McDowell with about three hundred [actually 160] men arrive[d] at Col. Coarters [Carter's] about

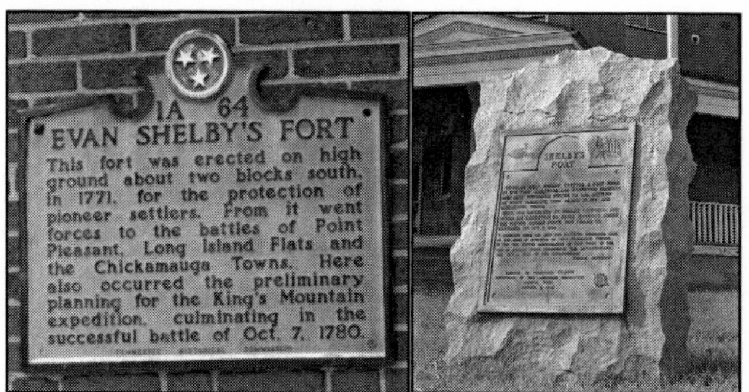


**Isaac Shelby lived at Sapling Grove, the site of his father's fortified home. A marker stands at the site of Shelby's Fort on Anderson Street at 7th Street in Bristol, Tennessee. Another historical marker is mounted on a building wall two blocks north on 7th Street.**

Twenty five miles from [here]."[1] But, another disturbing situation with far more serious consequences for the Overmountain inhabitants had developed about the same time.

Sam Philips, paroled by Ferguson to deliver a message to the rebel leaders in the Overmountain regions of the Holston, Watauga, and Nolichucky river valleys, had arrived in Sullivan County at Sapling Grove, the home of his distant cousin, Isaac Shelby.[2] He imparted to Shelby the direct and succinct message from Ferguson: "If they did not desist from their opposition to the British arms, he would march his army over the mountains, hang their leaders, and lay their country waste with fire and sword."[3] Philips shared in addition what he knew about the location and strength of the Loyalist forces. He may have also shared what he could have learned during his time as a prisoner, that some of the Loyalist troops had lived in the Overmountain region previously and knew their way around that area. One of the former Overmountain Loyalists was especially eager to guide Ferguson into the western waters. Captain Robert Sevier and his rebel light-horsemen had tarred and feathered this fellow for his support of the King. He wanted revenge.[4] By the time Martin wrote his letter to Jefferson, news of Ferguson's insolent threat had circulated among the people. Martin continued, "[We are i]nformed that a body of about fifteen hundred English and Tories was on their way to this place."[5]

Isaac Shelby listened carefully to what Sam Philips shared. He considered Ferguson's threat and the situation in which the Overmountain inhabitants found themselves. After a few days, he saddled up and rode forty miles to confer with his fellow militia leader John Sevier, then living on Limestone Creek where he had a mill.[6] (Although romanticized accounts say Shelby interrupted Sevier's wedding celebration to confer on the matter, Shelby said he caught up with Sevier at a horse race near Jonesborough, a community celebration of great conviviality nonetheless.[7] Although Sevier had recently married Catherine Sherrill, his "Bonnie Kate," — after the death in February of his first wife, Sarah Hawkins Sevier[8] — they were wed in the middle of the previous month, on August 14.[9] Still, the Seviers were indeed newlyweds at the time Shelby conferred with Sevier.)

Shelby related to Sevier the situation and shared with him Ferguson's outrageous threat. He, no doubt, told Sevier of the plans he, Clarke, McDowell, and Williams had made in Gilbert Town after they escaped from pursuit by Ferguson's men after the battle at Musgrove's Mill. They had agreed to enlist the aid of Cleaveland and Winston and to amass their armies when the time was right. Now was that time, Shelby and Sevier decided. All the leaders were to muster their militia, march over the mountains, and destroy Ferguson's army before those marauders could come into their distant homeland.[10]

After Shelby and Sevier conferred on a plan of action, each got busy. Sevier rode to the Watauga River valley to confer with Colonel McDowell and some of his officers, all refugees from their homes in the Piedmont, learning what he could about Ferguson's army and enlisting the aid and support of the men from Burke County. Knowing that some of his men had no horse and lacked adequate equipment for such an expedition, Sevier called upon John Adair for a loan of funds to outfit his men. Adair was the Entry Taker for land sales and had, of course, the only public currency in the region. Hearing Sevier's proposal for the use of the public funds to support the men who would retard the British advance, Adair responded bravely, "Colonel Sevier, I have no authority by law to make that disposition of this money. … But, if the country is overrun by the British, liberty is gone. Let the money go too. Take it." Sevier and

Shelby each pledged themselves for making a proper accounting of the monies to the state.[11]

Meanwhile, Shelby sent his brother, Captain Moses Shelby, into Virginia with a message for William Campbell to join them in their march over the mountains to confront Ferguson.[12] Draper says that William Campbell refused the offer preferring to march south across the plateau to Flour Gap (also Flower Gap, today's Piper Gap on the Blue Ridge Parkway in Carroll County) to prepare to meet Cornwallis's troops whenever they approached and threatened Virginia. He had just spent weeks dispersing and defeating bands of Tories, who had threatened the lead mines. Indeed, Cornwallis's grand plan for subduing the southern, rebellious colonies was to unite with Ferguson in North Carolina and to attack the lead mines with the help of the Tories in southwest Virginia. Their attack would be greatly assisted by the Chickamauga attacking throughout the western settlements even as far north as the New River. Campbell clearly understood the threat to his Virginia in his own countryside. He dared not leave his county exposed. Captain Shelby returned to his brother with Campbell's response.[13]

Colonel Shelby believed, as well, that the Cherokees were preparing for an attack. He knew it would be imprudent to remove all his men for the expedition and thus leave the settlements virtually defenseless. Shelby needed Campbell's men to join in the enterprise, otherwise he would not have enough men to attack Ferguson with a good chance of victory and also defend the home front. Shelby wrote a second letter and sent his brother, Moses, back to see Campbell. He sent a third letter to Arthur Campbell, County Lieutenant for Washington County, by way of John Adair as express. Arthur Campbell had just returned from Richmond where he had learned about the larger plans for opposing Cornwallis. Skillfully, Shelby's letter appealed to emotion, telling the sad story of how the families of McDowell's men had been driven from their homes. Shelby proposed that the Virginia militia escort those families back home to North Carolina. Arthur Campbell was indeed touched, replying that "the tale of McDowell's men was a doleful one, and tended to excite the resentment of the people." He and his brother-in-law, William Campbell, conferred on the matter and heartily agreed at last to join in Shelby's and Sevier's expedition. William Campbell called out half of his militia. He also sent an express up the New River (that is, south) to Wilkes County, North Carolina, calling on his Tory-fighting comrade-in-arms Benjamin Cleaveland to join them.[14] They were to meet at Quaker Meadows.[15]

### "Convinceing Proff of There Friendship"

Had Martin's letter of September 22 arrived quickly enough to Virginia's governor, Jefferson might have changed his earlier orders to William Campbell to muster and pursue the Cherokees. But as events were changing too quickly for decisions to be made effectively from so far away in Richmond, the men on the frontier took matters into their own hands. Governor Jefferson's concerns for the safety of the frontiers were perhaps a little assuaged when he read also in Martin's letter of his success in keeping the Cherokees at bay at least for a while. Martin wrote: "On 2nd instant I left the Cherokee nation where I had a Convinceing proff [proof] of there *(sic)* friendship. Two agents belonging to the Crown of Great Britain came there with about four hundred of the out lying Cherokees [Chickamaugas] in order to take me prisoner & bring me over to there meas[ures?]. All there *(sic)* ... Treats [(or Threats) offered?] ... was nobley *(sic)* Rejected by the old warrior who told them that he would die on the place before he would [give?] up. Ordered them off ameadiatly *(sic)*. [Said t]hat he had nothing to do with them nor goods but still begs for a supply from your

Excellency."[16] Thus did the counsel and intervention of Joseph Martin at a most critical time on the frontier keep the Cherokees from mounting an attack at the very time the militiamen of the Overmountain region were needed across the mountains to confront the threat of a British invasion of their homeland.[17]

### The Muster Begins

On September 22, William Campbell called for his men to muster in a meadow along Wolf Creek, near the Bradley farm.[18] It was just west of Black's Fort, in a community known as Wolf Hills and incorporated since 1778 as Abingdon. Two hundred men gathered there over the succeeding two days, camping along the stream and preparing themselves for yet another ride of great distance into what for many would eventually become unfamiliar territory. They departed on Sunday, the morning of September 24. For the first leg of their journey, the men rode down the familiar Watauga Road, while their commander,

**From the Muster Grounds on Wolf Creek, 200 men marched to Sycamore Shoals to join their leader, Colonel William Campbell. The W. Blair Keller Visitor Center at the Muster Grounds is adjacent to the site at 702 Colonial Road, Abingdon, VA. This site is a trailhead of the Overmountain Victory National Historic Trail.**

Colonel William Campbell, rode separately to the west to meet with Colonel Shelby at Sapling Grove. For some of the men riding south toward Sycamore Shoals, this morning departure from Craig's Meadow, the mustering ground, would be their last glimpse of home.[19]

Campbell's men, riding under Major William Edmiston, second-in-command, soon crossed over the recently surveyed boundary into North Carolina. They passed by the Pemberton Oak on their first day out. It was a noted place for mustering men in previous wars and served in the new Sullivan County to muster Whig militia under Captain John Pemberton. He and his men gathered at Sycamore Shoals under Colonel Shelby. Campbell's Washington County militia-men continued south and camped that first night just north of Womack's fort, one of the fortifications built or strengthened in 1776 in the face of threatened attacks by Dragging Canoe. Captain Jacob Womack (Womach) and his neighbors fortified his home for protection on the north side of the South Holston River, two miles east of Choate's Ford.[20] Womack had the year before (1775) signed the petition along with John Sevier, John Carter, Charles Robertson, James Robertson and others, including David Crockett,[21] asking that North Carolina provide protection for the residents of the Overmountain region.[22] (At the same time, they and others signed a similar petition for protection by Virginia.) Womack and his men mustered at Sycamore Shoals.

On the second day of their ride, Campbell's men crossed the South Fork of the Holston River at Choate's Ford (today's Bluff City, Tennessee) and continued toward the rendezvous. Crossing the shoals of the Watauga River on the afternoon of the 25$^{th}$, they arrived at the fields surrounding Fort Watauga, familiar grounds to many, the site in recent years of both Indian attacks and Indian treaties. There they found friends and comrades-in-arms, fellow militiamen gathering this time for the purpose of protecting their homes in the western waters, not from Cherokees or Chickamaugas, but from the threatened invasion by Ferguson's British Legion and Loyalist troops. Among the gathering militiamen were some of the 160 men under Colonel Charles McDowell and Captain Andrew Hampton, men who had retreated from Cane's Creek. (Some of the men along with McDowell had already returned east of the mountains to prepare for the coming of this corps of militia.) Lt. Colonel John Sevier's men from the Nolichucky River valley numbered 240. Colonel Shelby's men from Sullivan County numbered the same.

With over 800 militiamen mustered, Shelby proceeded with his plans for the march. The mills of Baptists McNabb and Mathew Talbot ground corn into meal. Some of the men reportedly mined lead for shot from the Bumpas Cove region of the Nolichucky River.[23] The militiamen tended to their horses and their equipment, sewing and mending the latter as necessary. Most carried a blanket for sleeping and warmth; none required a tent. They carried a metal cup for drinking from any spring or stream they passed. Some carried a skillet for cooking over a fire. Each had a wallet or a haversack of provisions, usually some parched corn and maple sugar, and perhaps some dried jerked meat. As these were hunters, they expected to procure some game along their ride, sharing their quarry with their fellow militiamen. The plans, however, included driving along with them a herd of beeves to supply them meat.[24]

Among their other preparations, the men cleaned their rifles and marshaled their ammunition. Most men carried a prized Deckard rifle (also Deckhard and Dirkert), a highly accurate, spiral grooved gun from 40 to 48 inches long with a 30-inch barrel. Named for a gunsmith in Lancaster County, Pennsylvania, who built rifles of this design and precision, a weapon of this make and accuracy was cherished by a man of the frontier, whether shooting for food or protection. Accurate at 200 and 300 yards, this rifle, firing shot 70 balls to the pound, had made the "shirtmen" duly feared by those soldiers and opposing militia who were unfortunate enough to face them in battle.

The gathering at Sycamore Shoals was not just men preparing for battle. With them came some of their families — wives, children, parents — to see the men off and to prepare for the life of the community after the men had ridden away. (A painting of the muster at Sycamore Shoals by Lloyd Branson hangs in the Tennessee Museum of History in Nashville.) Ramsey described the scene in his *Annals of Tennessee*: "Scarce a single gunman remained, that day, at his own home. The young, ardent and energetic had generally enrolled themselves for the campaign against Ferguson. The less vigorous and more aged were left with the inferior guns, in the settlements for their protection against the Indians." The old men encouraged the young ones and listened to the colonels for orders on how to defend the stations during their absence. Major Charles Robertson led the militia from Washington County, North Carolina, left to guard the frontier. Colonel Anthony Bledsoe did the same for the Sullivan County home force.[25] The sisters, the mothers, the wives, all said their anxious goodbyes, proud for their men folk. Others brought in produce and supplies, wanting to outfit the expedition from what they could offer — food, clothing, a rifle, a horse — anything that showed their support. Ramsey concluded: "Never did the mountain recess contain within it, a loftier or a more enlarged patriotism — never a cooler or more determined courage."[26]

**Mary Patton manufactured gunpowder for the Overmountain Men. The grave of Mary Patton is in the Patton-Simmons Cemetery on Toll Branch Road in northwest Carter County, Tennessee about two miles south of Milligan College.**

**Mary Patton**

As militiamen converged at Sycamore Shoals, they were provisioned by local planter William Cobb, owner of Rocky Mount. His son, Pharoah, provided many of them additional supplies from his farm at Sycamore Shoals. From the Patton powder mill along nearby Powder Branch, the militiamen received 500 pounds of gunpowder manufactured by Mary McKeehan Patton. Whether Mary Patton donated the powder to the Patriot cause or it was purchased from her by William Cobb is unknown. In either case, at a value of a dollar per pound (when a dollar would buy an acre of land), that quantity was a substantial contribution to the Patriot cause.[27]

Mary Patton probably learned the skill of making black powder as a child in Scotland, perhaps from her father who may have operated an illegal, cottage powder mill in opposition to British laws. She and her husband, John, had operated their mill on Powder Branch since 1777 after moving to the Overmountain region from Carlisle, Pennsylvania, to escape the threatened British invasion there.[28]

Making black powder was a time consuming and dangerous proposition. People died making gunpowder, not from explosions although that was possible, but from falling into the rack of hot, smoldering timbers burned to make an essential ingredient, charcoal. A second ingredient, sulfur, had to be purchased and was probably imported from Italy after being refined by French chemists.[29] America's alliance with France prevented an interruption of the importing of sulfur. It had many uses in the colonial period.

The third essential ingredient, making up about three-quarters of the compound by weight, was created in a rather disagreeable manner. It was made from repeatedly boiling dung. By carefully boiling down animal excrement, Mary created saltpeter. Fortunately for her, she used nitrate-rich bat guano, found in abundance in the nearby Hyder and Gourley caves. (One of the actual kettles used by Mary Patton is on display at the Rocky Mount Living History Museum in Piney Flats, Tennessee.)

**Some of the mustering militiamen gathered at the home of William Cobb who joined them at Sycamore Shoals. The Cobb home is interpreted today at Rocky Mount State Historic Site Museum on US Hwy 19W/11E in Piney Flats, TN.**

**The Overmountain militiamen mustered at Sycamore Shoals in September 1780 to pursue Major Patrick Ferguson. Sycamore Shoals State Historic Area on West Elk Ave. (US Hwy 321) in Elizabethton, Tennessee interprets the history of Fort Watauga and the lives of early pioneers in this area.**

Blending all the ingredients together in the right proportions, removing impurities, and achieving the proper grain size, which regulated burning, were skills essential to the art of powder making that made Mary Patton a valued craftsman in the Overmountain region.[30] Her supply of powder to the men mustering at Sycamore Shoals was a critical part of their preparations for the campaign to pursue Patrick Ferguson.

### More Men

On September 26, as the militiamen at Sycamore Shoals were making their final preparations for departure, they were encouraged much with the unexpected arrival of two hundred additional Virginia militiamen riding under Colonel Arthur Campbell. After his brother-in-law had left Abingdon, Arthur Campbell decided to provide another 200 men to help assure a victory. He had little choice, perhaps, as the men under this command were eager to join in the campaign and solicited him to send them forward rather than have them remain behind to defend Washington County. The scene of their arrival has been masterfully described by an early historian of the event:

> "When nearly ready to begin the march, the sound of

> approaching voices was heard once more. The camp was astir; unexpected visitors were discovered in the distance; nearer they came, and recognition was announced by a wild shout of joy, and Colonel Arthur Campbell led two hundred men into the camp. One thousand and fifty voices now made the welkin ring with their glad acclaim."[31]

Leaving his men at Sycamore Shoals under the command of his cousin, William Campbell, Arthur Campbell rode back to Washington County to muster additional men to protect southwest Virginia from marauding Cherokees and Tories.

**Samuel Doak**

Among those gathered at Sycamore Shoals to see the men off was the Reverend Samuel Doak. This Princeton-educated, Presbyterian minister assembled the men for a blessing before their departure. Tradition says he invoked divine protection for the men and asked that they be guided by God to a victory. He told the Old Testament story from the Book of Judges about Gideon gathering a small number of men to attack the camp of the Midianites, who greatly outnumbered them. With great passion, Doak ended his sermon, giving the men a rallying cry: "The sword of the Lord and of Gideon!" The Scots-Irish Presbyterians and other Christians among those gathered embraced this call to action. They responded, "The sword of the Lord and our Gideons!"[32]

**The Ascent**

The militiamen departed Sycamore Shoals for the gap at Yellow Mountain, the best spot for crossing over the mountains and the route preferred by those occasionally bringing supplies and trade goods over the mountain on packhorses. The route was known as Bright's Trace.

**The militiamen departed Sycamore Shoals for the mountains, marching along Gap Creek, and driving with them, too slowly, a herd of beeves. A marker erected in 1976 by local students stands along Gap Creek Road (TN Hwy 362) in Carter County, TN.**

Most of the men were mounted; some were on foot. Having some difficulty in getting the beeves started on the march, the men made only three miles by midday, stopping along Gap Creek at Mathew Talbot's Mill[33] for a midday meal. Pressing on in the afternoon, they continued up Gap Creek crossing over to Little Doe River and then Doe River, marching upstream to reach the "Resting Place." This was the first flat and open spot that afforded any opportunity for camping for those travelers coming west over the ridge near Roan Mountain, whose peak is 6,300 feet above sea level. The men pastured the cattle and hobbled their horses, letting them graze in the grasses alongside the strong mountain stream. Adjacent to the river was a prominent rock overhang known since, if not before, as Shelving Rock. The men stored their gunpowder underneath the rock ledge to keep it dry during the mist and rain, which began to fall that night.

Knowing that the cattle had slowed the men's progress to this point and anticipating the steep climb over the Yellow Mountain the next day, the officers ordered the men to slaughter some of the beeves and to prepare rations for their trip. They undertook that task in the morning of Wednesday, the 27th, taking up most of the day preparing the meat. They turned around the remaining beeves, sending some of the men to drive them back to Sycamore Shoals. These men may have been part of a group Colonel Campbell also sent back after the march began. They were to provide protection for the Holston River settlements. Among the twelve were James Berry and Thomas McSpadden.[34] The others then pressed on, continuing to follow Bright's Trace in a steep climb and then through the gap between Yellow Mountain and Roan Mountain. The route was well known and well trod. Ensign Robert Campbell wrote at the time, "The ascent over this part of the mountain was not very difficult. There was a road; but not one on which wagons could pass. No provisions were taken, but such as each man could carry in his wallet or saddle-bags."[35]

They covered about four miles in reaching the top at nearly 4,700 feet elevation. Ensign Campbell continued in his diary, "[T]here were about a hundred acres of beautiful table land, in which a spring issued, ran through it, and over into the Watauga." He also reported, "The sides and top of the mountain were covered with snow, shoe-mouth deep."[36] The rain the men had experienced the night before at Shelving Rock at the Resting Place, had taken a different form at the higher elevations of Bright's Trace as the trail passed through the

**At the "Resting Place" on Doe River, the militiamen camped their first night of the march, storing their powder under a rock overhang to keep it dry in a light rain. Shelving Rock is on TN Hwy 143 between US Hwy 19E and Roan Mountain State Park.**

**As the militiamen ascended Yellow Mountain, they could see behind them the valleys of their homesteads. A certified portion of the OVNH Trail in Tennessee climbs from Hampton Creek Cove to Yellow Mountain Gap.**

meadow known as "the Bald of the Yellow."

### Spies

Having reached the bald, the officers gathered their men by company and paraded them, ordering the men to each fire his weapon. At the higher elevations, some men later recalled, the thinner air reduced the report of their rifles, making much less of the expected sound.[37] With the men in ranks and files, each company accounted for its numbers. John Sevier discovered that two of his men were missing: James Crawford and Samuel Chambers. Although these men had mustered with the Whigs, it was known the two fellows had leanings toward the Loyalists. Sevier was concerned that the pair had departed the expedition with the intention of running ahead to warn Patrick Ferguson that this army of a thousand militiamen was crossing the mountains to attack him. The officers agreed it best to alter their route somewhat. As they descended from the bald, they were no longer able to look back and see the hills and the valleys of the Watauga and Holston rivers and the homes in which their loved ones awaited their return and for whose safety they were going off to fight.

### Bright's Trace

The companies of militiamen proceeded east and downhill for about two miles into Elk Hollow, continuing to follow Bright's Trace. At a good spring that fed Roaring Creek, they made their camp for the night of September 27. On the $28^{th}$, the party continued south and east following Roaring Creek to the North Toe River. They followed that course for a mile, where they passed the home of Samuel Bright, the peddler, trader, and guide who followed the same route over the mountains through Yellow Mountain Gap, bringing trade goods from the east side to the Watauga River valley. Bright was a Tory. Taken into court in March 1777 on charges of encouraging the enemies of the state, he took the oath of allegiance to the Patriot cause and received amnesty.[38] The route was really an Indian trail that probably had been used for centuries. As were many such paths, it was most likely a route followed since ancient times by buffalo, elk, and deer in their migrations across the mountains.

The travel was slow coming down the east side of the mountains. Ensign Campbell recounted, "With a very bad road, we were four days in passing the mountains."[39] The men continued down the trace, following the North Toe River until they reached the spring at Davenport's place where they paused at midday on the $28^{th}$. Continuing on, the route was "exceedingly difficult, and not unfrequently dangerous, for horses to pursue," wrote Draper. But he added as well, "The bright, rushing waters tumbling over their rocky beds, and the lofty blue mountains in the distance, present a weird, dreamy,

**At Yellow Mountain Gap, the leaders paraded their militiamen, had them fire their rifles, and discovered that two men, suspected spies, were gone. The OVNH Trail and the Appalachian Trail cross at Yellow Mountain Gap.**

**After crossing through Yellow Mountain Gap, the Overmountain Men proceeded down Yellow Mountain Road along Roaring Creek to the North Toe River. US Hwy 19E in North Carolina follows North Toe River south much of the way toward Spruce Pine.**

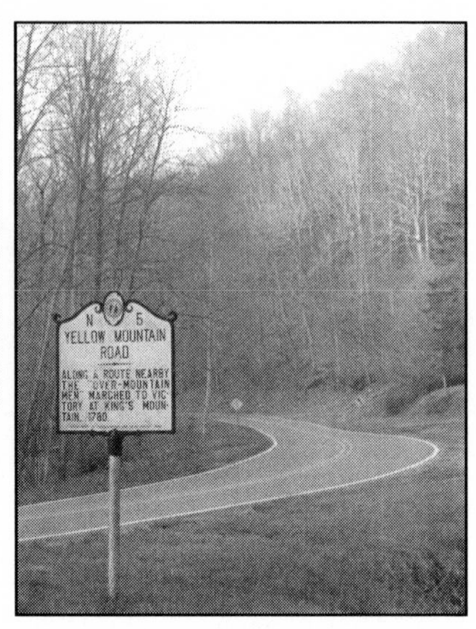


bewildering appearance."[40] Unfortunately for the militiamen, the wilderness terrain could have been hiding hundreds of Ferguson's men lying in ambuscade for them to ride into. The Overmountain Men sent scouts ahead, and they proceeded along the path attentive and alert. They rode on to Cathey's plantation at the mouth of Grassy Creek, where it flowed into the North Toe River. Having covered twenty miles that day, they made camp there for the night of the 28th. They ate a meal of parched corn and what beef remained from their prepared rations. Two days of strenuous riding had given them strong appetites. Ensign Campbell recorded: "On reaching the plane beyond the mountain, they found themselves in a country covered with verdure, and breathed an atmosphere of summer mildness."[41]

**On the third night, the Overmountain Men camped at the mouth of Grassy Creek on the North Toe River. A 1910 DAR marker near the train depot in Spruce Pine, NC commemorates this encampment.**

**The Overmountain Men reached the eastern face of the Blue Ridge Mountains at Gillespie Gap. A marker sits on the grounds of the Museum of North Carolina Minerals, a National Park Service facility on the Blue Ridge Parkway near Spruce Pine, NC.**

## The Choice

On the 29th, the men rode up Grassy Creek some eight or nine miles to its head where they reached the crest of the Blue Ridge Mountains at Gillespie's Gap. Below them, they looked east into the Catawba River valley. The beauty, however, belied the danger. The officers faced a difficult decision. Two routes descended the mountain to the valley below. If they went down one, Ferguson could well have been coming up the other and once behind them would have been unopposed in executing his threat to burn their homes and crops. The other choice was as disagreeable. They could have split their forces and descended by both routes. If one party — half the force — had encountered Ferguson on the way, those men would most surely have been outnumbered and suffered defeat. Dividing one's force in the face of the enemy was a classic military blunder; they faced a decision the militia leaders did not relish making. Isaac Shelby perhaps recalled how six years earlier Chief Cornstalk had attacked the colonial militia at Point Pleasant before the two halves of that expedition united. William Campbell and others then standing at Gillespie Gap would have known of that same dangerous encounter as well. They knew the risks and the consequences. Splitting their forces was, however, the choice they had to make.

Colonel Campbell and his men rode by the southerly route descending six or seven miles to Turkey Cove on the Catawba River. They passed the home of Henry Gillespie, a simple cabin in the wilderness where some of the men camped, questioning Gillespie at length for information about Ferguson. He knew nothing and offered as much, hoping to survive the turmoil of the Revolution by remaining neutral, incurring neither the gratitude nor the wrath of either side. Some of Campbell's men continued on to the home of Colonel William Wofford, fortified, as it was, against Indian attacks. Wofford was a wealthy man and a faithful Patriot, though he may have recently participated in a ruse to protect cattle of Burke County for Patriot use by pretending to take British protection.[42] He had only recently arrived in Burke County where he bought a 900-acre farm and built a grist mill. He had escaped the Upcountry of South Carolina after the fall of Charlestown. It was near his foundry on the Pacolet River, Wofford's ironworks, which Tories had previously destroyed, where Isaac Shelby

**Colonels Shelby and Sevier descended the mountains through McKinney Gap. The gap and the Historic Orchard at Altapass are visible from Blue Ridge Parkway, MP 328. The nonprofit Altapass Foundation owns The Orchard and interprets the OVNH Trail.**

and his mounted Overmountain militiamen had fought a running skirmish with Patrick Ferguson on August 8. On this occasion as the militiamen descended into the Catawba River valley, Wofford had no useful information for the Patriots.

Shelby and Sevier led their men down the face of the Blue Ridge Mountains by a more easterly route descending a similar six or seven miles into North Cove. They slept in the woods along the North Fork of the Catawba River near the mouth of Hunnycut's Creek. There they were joined by Colonel Charles McDowell, who rode up from his home at Quaker Meadows. He had left the Watauga Settlements ahead of his men, attempting to rouse Whig support for the campaign from men on the eastern side of the mountains. He had sent messengers in all directions. He sent James Blair, an express, to find Colonel Cleaveland marching up the Yadkin River and to hurry him along. He also brought word to Shelby and Sevier that Ferguson was believed to be encamped at Gilbert Town. This was news that must have relieved the militia leaders' concerns somewhat, that Ferguson was not closer to the mountains and setting a trap for them. McDowell shared as well news that Cleaveland and Winston were on their way and that militiamen from South Carolina under separate leaders were nearby. McDowell's news was encouraging.

**Along the Catawba**

On September 30, the separated parties of Overmountain militia proceeded toward their rendezvous along the Catawba River. From Turkey Cove, Shelby and Sevier, reunited with McDowell, marched over Silver Mountain and Linville Mountain and then from the ridge descended down Paddy's (Paddie's) Creek to the Catawba River. There they waited for the other party, which had farther to go. Campbell's men marched down the North Fork of the Catawba River, following

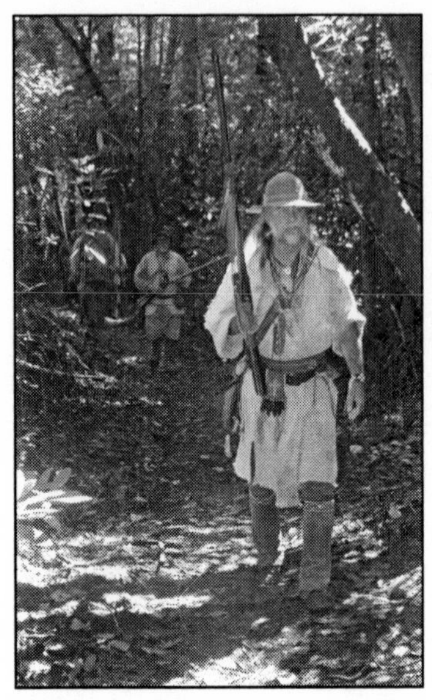

**Shelby's and Sevier's men marched down Paddy's Creek to reunite with Campbell's men along the Catawba River. Members of the Overmountain Victory Trail Association, in period dress, march along the certified, historic segment of the OVNH Trail following Paddy's Creek in Lake James State Park, Burke County, NC.**

a trail along the north side of the river until they met up with Shelby and Sevier. The parties proceeded toward Quaker Meadows crossing over Linville Creek along the way. They arrived at the homes of Charles McDowell and Joseph McDowell that evening.

By then, the two militia groups had covered 31 miles and 23 miles that day, with each having covered 15 miles the day before, after leaving Cathey's plantation. The men were in need of rest. Major Joseph McDowell welcomed them to his home at Quaker Meadows, encouraging the men to use his dry rail fencing as kindling for their cooking fires. Their spirits were lifted further upon the arrival of Colonel Benjamin Cleaveland and Major Joseph Winston in command of 350 men from Wilkes and Surry counties, including "Cleaveland's Bulldogs."

**Cleaveland and Winston**

The Wilkes County Militia and the Surry County Militia had mustered on the Yadkin River at Elkin Creek on September 27. Some of those men, particularly those riding under Colonel Cleaveland, had been harassing and pursuing Tories in and around the Yadkin River valley.

**The Overmountain Men and the Yadkin River valley militia met at Quaker Meadows, the homes of Charles McDowell and Joseph McDowell. Owned by Historic Burke Foundation, the 1812 home of Colonel Charles McDowell stands today off NC Hwy 181 on Saint Marys Church Rd. in Morganton, NC. Nothing remains of the 1780 home.**

Indeed, at the time of the muster, some of Cleaveland's men were already in the saddle, patrolling the headwaters of the New River and suppressing Tories there. Word was sent to them to join in the march to Quaker Meadows.

**Major Joseph Winston mustered his Surry County militia at Elkin Creek and departed on Sept. 27, marching up the Yadkin River. Wayside exhibits overlooking the Mustering Ground (now Elkin City Park on NC Hwy 268) in Elkin, NC mark the trailhead of the eastern leg of the Overmountain Victory National Historic Trail.**

**In Wilkes County, the militiamen under Colonel Benjamin Cleaveland joined with Major Winston's men. Exhibits about the Overmountain Victory National Historic Trail fill one entire room of the Wilkes Heritage Museum in Wilkesboro, NC. The Robert Cleaveland cabin and the site of the Tory Oak are adjacent.**

The Wilkes and Surry militiaman departed the muster grounds at Elkin Creek, riding up the Yadkin River on the north side. They camped that night in the vicinity of the infamous Tory Oak where Cleaveland meted out his own form of justice for Tories. They continued riding southwest some eight miles, crossing over the Yadkin River at the mouth of Warrior's Creek. The contingent of Cleaveland's men riding in the New River valley joined the march along the way. They continued on some dozen or more miles, making a good day's ride along the flat land along the river.

### Fort Defiance

On the night of the 28th, these militiamen camped at the site of Fort Defiance.[43] This was a stockade and fortified home built by then-Lieutenant William Lenoir and others in the summer of 1776 for protection on the frontier from attacks by Cherokees. It was about 24 miles southwest of the Tory Oak and upstream along the Yadkin River. Situated at the tip of a flat ridge, which jutted out above the river bottom, the fort was positioned perfectly as a lookout post, affording a good view of any approaching attackers.[44] That evening when they looked out, they probably saw express James Blair approaching them. He carried a message from Charles McDowell encouraging them to arrive at Quaker Meadows as quickly as possible. He had ridden about 30 miles on this task, and not without incident. Along the route he was shot at and wounded from ambush by some gunman, assumed to be some Tory scout. The Loyalists were apparently aware of the large force of militiamen marching up the Yadkin River. The rascals would try to spoil the effort in any manner they could.[45]

In 1776, a William Gist, then age 16, had helped Lieutenant Lenoir in the construction of the fort. He was likely a member of the families of Christopher Gist and his son, Nathaniel Gist, the Cherokee trader, who had lived along the upper Yadkin River in the 1750s and 1760s. Nathaniel Gist's brother, Richard Gist, was then marching toward

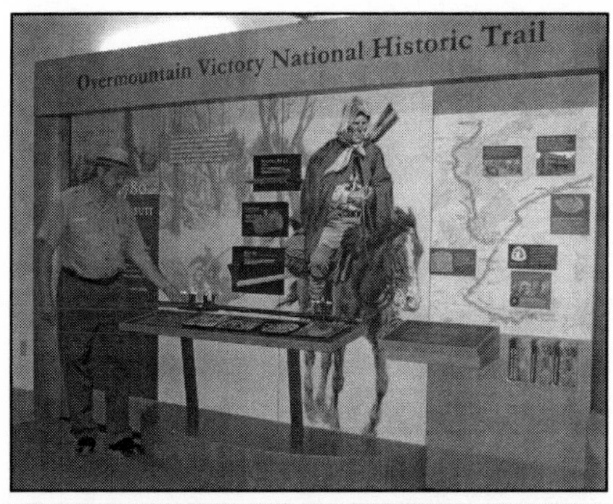


**The Wilkes and Surry militiamen marched up the Yadkin River valley. The US Army Corps of Engineers exhibits a display on the OVNH Trail at its visitor center at W. Kerr Scott Reservoir on NC Hwy 268 southwest of Wilkesboro, NC.**

William Lenoir came early to the Upper Yadkin River valley. His 1795 home sits near the site of his earlier, fortified home of the same name, Fort Defiance. The historic site, open to visitors, is on NC Hwy 268, Caldwell Co., NC.

Quaker Meadows under the command of Captain William Edmiston and Colonel William Campbell. With him was, perhaps a relative, Nathaniel, and, if so, likely named in honor of his uncle. This Nathaniel was marching in another Virginia company under the command of Major William Edmiston and the colonel.[46]

On the 29th, the Wilkes and Surry militiamen continued toward the head of the Yadkin River, crossing over Warrior Mountain and reaching Crider's (Grider's, Krider's)[47] Fort at the settlement known as Tucker's Barn (today's Lenoir).[48] The party of 350 militiamen camped around the fort that night.

On the morning of September 30, the party continued southwest from Crider's intending toward Quaker Meadows and the rendezvous. They crossed John's River and pressed on. At some point in their expedition, Colonel Cleaveland learned of a band of some 100 Tories encamped at Little John's Meeting House. He devised a plan to draw them into an ambuscade and sent William Lenoir ahead with five men of his choosing to get the attention of the Tories and then retreat into Cleaveland's trap. Despite the courage of the effort, Lenoir found the camp empty. He and his men rejoined Cleaveland and continued their march.[49] Cleaveland's and Winston's men came to the home of the McDowells as evening approached. Their arrival was roundly cheered by the Overmountain Men who were already in camp.[50]

### Quaker Meadows

The two parties of Patriot militia converging at Quaker Meadows were heartily encouraged when they saw one another. Old friendships were renewed; many had been comrades-in-arms before. They numbered together some 1,400 armed men with years of experience in traversing rough country and fighting what enemies presented themselves, be they Cherokee, Shawnee, Loyalist Highlanders or Tories. These were backcountry woodsmen, skilled in tracking, hunting, and making do with what they had to accomplish what needed to be done. Writing later about the mustering of Wilkes and Surry men with others at Quaker Meadows, William Lenoir said, "[T]he active Whigs … like patriots at a moment's notice, without any call from the Government, turned out and concentrated in Burke County, without any aid from public stores, of clothing, arms, ammunition, or any article of camp equipage, not having a single tent or baggage wagon amongst them."[51] These men — their determination, their fortitude, their sacrifices — were the true expression of American independence.

On October 1, the united party left Quaker Meadows, heading toward Gilbert Town where they expected to find Patrick Ferguson.

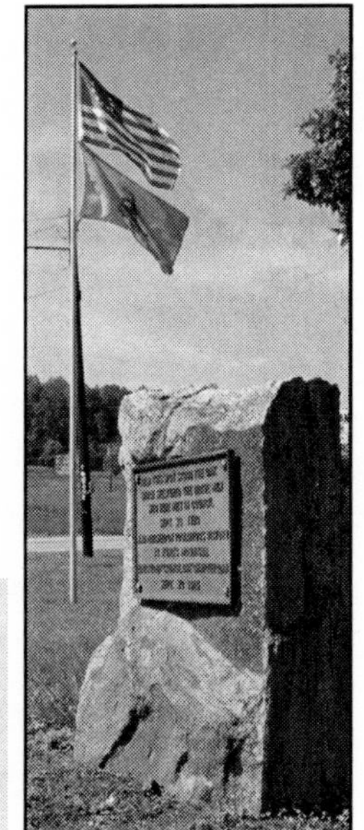

**At Quaker Meadows, the militia leaders met under a spreading oak tree, thereafter called the Council Oak. That tree and the gathering beneath it are commemorated by a monument on NC Hwy 18 in Morganton, NC.**

Compared to their experience in crossing the mountains, they found the roads much preferable. They had indeed been fortunate to get through the mountains without suffering any disagreeable weather. Beginning on that Sunday morning with good weather continuing, they skirted to the west of the South Mountains crossing numerous small streams flowing off those peaks. Within constant view from a great distance was a prominent knob, called Pilot Mountain, set apart from the South Mountains. They set for the gap between the two and made 18 miles before the weather changed and a steady rain set in. They stopped their march early and made camp at Bedford's Hill, just to the south of Pilot Mountain and very near the site along Cane Creek where Major Joseph McDowell and his men had skirmished with Ferguson three weeks before. The rain grew steady and fell through the night.

**Bedford Hill**

On Tuesday, the rain continued at such a pace that the commanders decided to remain in camp. At this point, the Overmountain Men had been in the saddle for six days, the Virginians for eight. For men ready to get on with the business at hand of chastising Ferguson, the unwanted delay made them restless. The tedium of camp life created some tensions among the men, with some coming to blows or nearly so, over one small irritation or another, simply out of frustration.

Knowing that their companies of militia were generally undisciplined to the life of a soldier, the commanding officers convened in the evening of October 2 to discuss their circumstances. Colonel Charles McDowell presided as the senior officer,[52] but that was, in fact, the topic of discussion. McDowell recognized that they needed a general commanding officer, but as they came from different states, no one of them could assume that command. Accordingly, McDowell proposed

**The militiamen camping at Bedford Hill, on a "breakwater" dividing the Catawba and Broad river basins, may have spread across the area drawing water from Magazine Creek and Cane Creek. (As per Albert Dale of Union Mill, NC, local resident and historian.) Looking north from FortuneRoad on Bedford Hill across Magazine Creek toward Pilot Mountain (in photo), one can see the South Mountains to the east and the gap through which the militiamen rode (right center of photo) where today's US Hwy 64 passes.**

they send a messenger to General Gates, then at Hillsborough, asking him to send a commanding officer. The group preferred General William Davidson or General Daniel Morgan. Colonel Shelby, however, was in no mood for such delays. He proposed they select one of their own to command under the advice of the others in council. As they were so close to confronting Ferguson, they needed efficient command and the ability to move quickly. Attentive to the personal politics of the situation, Shelby knew that selecting any officer from North Carolina would be problematic, especially him. They were all colonels; moreover, he was the youngest at 30. He instead proposed that William Campbell take the general command. Campbell was, Shelby offered, the only officer from Virginia, he had brought the most men, and he had come the farthest distance. Although Campbell took Shelby aside and initially protested his nomination, Shelby persuaded him otherwise and he consented to the arrangement, as did the other officers. As Lenoir wrote, "Campbell ... was complimented with the command of the whole detachment."[53] At this point, Colonel Charles McDowell volunteered to ride to Hillsborough to secure a commander from General Gates. The other officers assented to his leaving for their own reasons. Shelby later attributed his own reservations about McDowell to his age; but, he was then only 37. More likely, some had concerns about McDowell's battlefield judgments. In any case, McDowell took the opportunity to leave gracefully and set out on his mission. He retired from camp immediately, passing command of his men to his brother, Major Joseph McDowell.[54]

# The Siege of Augusta

## Militia, Loyalists, and Creeks

After his victories at Wofford's Ironworks and Musgrove's Mill in the company of Isaac Shelby in August 1780, Elijah Clarke decided to deal with the British forces closer to his Wilkes County, Georgia, home. In early September, he devised a scheme to attack the British forces under Lt. Colonel Thomas Brown then occupying Augusta, and he hoped to muster a thousand men for the confrontation. His South Carolina ally in this enterprise, Lt. Colonel James McCall, hoped to unite 500 men from his home region around Ninety Six. The recent defeat of Gates's Continental Army and even the routing of Sumter's militia at Fishing Creek apparently had made many of the potential recruits more cautious about supporting a cause which increasingly looked doomed. McCall only managed to bring 80 militiamen to the rendezvous at Soap Creek about forty miles north of Augusta. Clarke did better in recruiting from those living in Wilkes County, but he also threatened that he would put to death any of his men who did not respond to his call. Even then he only mustered 350 men. Some were interested in potential plunder, but many were stalwart Patriots. Among them was Major William Candler. Born to English parents in Belfast, Ireland, Candler came over to Virginia as a child and then moved with his own family to the Ceded Lands in Wilkes County in 1770, where he served as Deputy Surveyor.[1]

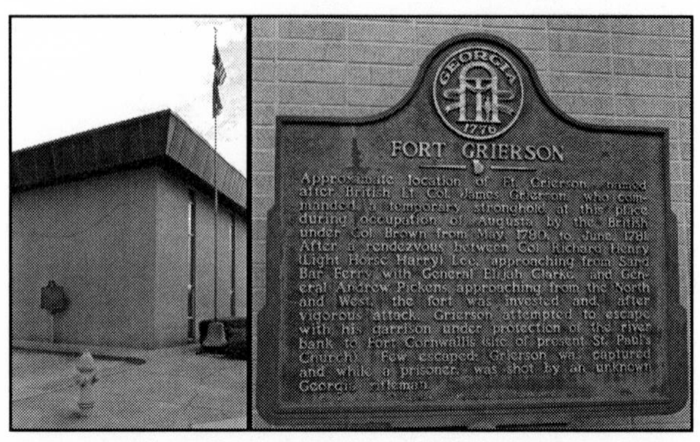


**Colonel Thomas Brown commanded Loyalists troops from Fort Grierson in Augusta. A historical marker stands adjacent to the fire station on Reynolds Street at 11th street.**

Lt. Colonel Brown, in addition to commanding the British garrison at Augusta, was also Superintendent of Indian Affairs for the Eastern Division of the Southern Department. In that capacity, he was treating at the time with 250 Creeks who had come to Augusta to receive their gifts. A larger party of 1,000 Creeks had been on their way to Augusta, led by deputy agent David Taitt. When Taitt fell ill on the journey, most of the entourage stopped to care for him. Only those warriors led by Little Prince of the Tuckabatchees continued on to Augusta. They camped at Indian Springs, about three miles west of Augusta.[2] Brown, at the time, waited inside Fort Grierson with his garrison of 250 rangers, with probably only 150 fit for fighting. The term "fort" overstated the conditions. It was really Grierson's fortified home. The building was small and inadequate for protecting the town, but it was used for storing provisions as was nearby St. Paul's Church. About 70 Patriot prisoners were held at Grierson's fort as well as rifles and muskets captured from these and other Patriots. Also present were 27 wounded Loyalists of the New Jersey Volunteers. These men were recovering from their last encounter with Elijah Clarke at Musgrove's Mill.[3]

**The White House**

Clarke had devised a scheme to attack Augusta on three fronts. They selected September 14 as the day. Major Samuel Taylor attacked the Creek camp west of town. The Creeks fired randomly and without organization at the attacking Patriots while retreating northeast toward MacKay's Trading Post near the Savannah River. At the sound of fighting nearby, Brown led many of his men out of Fort Grierson and marched hurriedly toward the Creek encampment. He met up with his Creek allies near MacKay's. From the east, Clarke was then able to come in behind Brown and take the fort and its small, remaining garrison of 70 Rangers without a fight. He freed the prisoners and then outfitted them with the confiscated arms and ammunition stored there and at St. Paul's Church. Clarke and his men then joined forces with McCall to attack and capture MacKay's Trading Post, known also as the White House. In this place were stored all the presents for the Creeks.

The Patriots first captured the trading post, but Brown regrouped his forces outside the White House on a slight rise to the southwest called Garden Hill. He had 175 of his own provincial rangers and volunteers and two pieces of artillery. The armed Creeks took cover along the river bank only 80 yards from Mackay's. Aided by artillery fire, the Rangers mounted a bayonet charge and chased the Patriots from the trading post. In their retreat, some of Clarke's men circled behind Brown's charge and captured one of the artillery pieces. The Patriots and Loyalists had essentially swapped places; Clarke's men were outside the trading post then occupied by Brown. The Patriots continued to fire their rifles with some effect throughout the rest of the day, and they displaced the Creeks from their position along the river.

That night, Brown's men fortified their position inside McKay's, knocking loopholes in the walls, putting floor boards in the windows, and filling against the walls with earth and wood to protect those in the building against musket fire. Brown ordered the digging of trenches around the post and then placed the Creeks in them to defend his position. Early the next morning, fifty Cherokees arrived at the scene and sneaked into the fort to reinforce Brown's position. Brown armed them from the supplies stored inside. Clarke, however, was not to be outdone. He and his men dug their own circle of trenches and fortifications around those of Brown, specifically cutting off Brown's access to a supply of water. Thus did Elijah Clarke lay siege to the British forces trapped in the trading post.

On the 15$^{th}$, Clarke brought in two artillery pieces from Fort Grierson: six-pounder and four-pounder cannons. He began to fire on the trading post. The Loyalists fired back. Almost immediately the only artillerist among the Patriots was shot and killed. The two groups exchanged sporadic gunfire over the course of the second day. The British suffered casualties. Indeed, Colonel Brown was wounded in both thighs with a single shot. But the siege makers were not unscathed. At night, Cherokee warriors crept quietly to the trenches of Clarke's men and scalped the unwary.[4]

Over the following two days, Brown's men, trapped inside MacKay's, exhausted their rations, subsisting on raw pumpkins and drinking their own urine saved in earthen jars.[5] Dead horses and human corpses lay around the White House, decomposing and filling the air with a nauseating stench. The wounded lying outside the fort called out in anguish for help and for water. Brown's situation was becoming increasingly desperate. Twice on the 17$^{th}$, Clarke summoned Brown to surrender. Brown defied Clarke declaring that he would defend the trading post to the last extremity. Victory would certainly have gone to

**MacKay's Trading Post was the sight of the four-day siege of Colonel Brown's Loyalists by Colonel Elijah Clarke. The chimney for the later Confederate Powder Works on Goodrich Street stands at the approximate site of MacKay's Trading Post. The battlefield between Garden Hill and "the white house" is severed by the 1845 Augusta Canal.**

the Patriots eventually, except Brown knew what Clarke did not: On the first day of the conflict, Brown had sent separate messengers to Ninety Six to alert Colonel John Cruger to the fact of Clarke's attack. On the evening of the 15th, Patrick Houstoun was the first of the messengers to reach Cruger. The colonel departed Ninety Six on a forced march with 350 Loyalist rangers and militia. (Some accounts say 500.)[6] Cruger was 45 miles from Augusta and would need two days to reach Brown with reinforcements.

**Rescue and Retaliation**

On the evening of the 17th, Clarke's spies brought to him the first word of Cruger's march. Clarke's situation had deteriorated since the attack and after the siege began. He was seriously lacking in manpower in the face of Cruger's coming reinforcements. Some of Clarke's men had departed to visit their families and friends in Burke County (Georgia), well south of Augusta. Others of his regiment had decamped the siege, gone back to Fort Grierson, and plundered some of the supplies and stores there and at St. Paul's Church. Clarke's initial force of about 430 men was reduced to about 200.[7]

At 8 o'clock on the morning of the 18th, Colonel Cruger arrived on the east side of the Savannah River.[8] Clarke lifted the siege and departed Augusta by 10 o'clock. He did not have time to take with him his badly wounded troops, numbering 29. They and the dead accounted for his 60 casualties lost in the attack on Augusta. Cruger captured the wounded Patriots holed up at Fort Grierson. If Clarke thought Cruger and Brown would treat them as prisoners-of-war, he was sadly mistaken.

Lt. Colonel Brown did not treat the prisoners with anything other than disdain. Invoking Cornwallis's proclamation to hang all those who had taken the oath and then fought against the Crown, Brown set about executing Clarke's captured men. He hanged 12 of the men from the outside staircase of the White House while he lay on his pallet suffering the pain of his wounds. Among the victims were two Glass brothers, ages 17 and 15. Afterward, Brown delivered up all the bodies to the Indians who had lost 70 of their tribes in the fight. The Creeks and Cherokees scalped the bodies of the executed and mutilated them further before tossing the corpses into the river. The other prisoners were given over to the Indians, too. The Indians encircled them, killing and scalping them, and tossing some of them into fires before they had expired.[9] (Although the horrific accounts of this episode were used to vilify Thomas Brown, some historians believe it more likely that Colonel Cruger carried out the executions as Brown was too weak and in such pain from his wounds.[10])

**Retreat of the Refugees**

The remainder and survivors of Clarke's men rode away from Augusta, crossing over the Little River into Wilkes County. The men rode to their respective homes and said their good-byes to neighbors. The Tories and Indians pursued them immediately and continued to take revenge on all the Patriot settlers in Wilkes County. Brown sent detachments in all directions. His men harassed the citizens, burning homes and crops. They arrested suspects, throwing some in jail and hanging others without trials. Again, Brown declared that those who did not take up arms against the rebels were subject to be hanged. This unexpected demand that residents fight against their neighbors was intolerable to most. More than any other action by the British authorities, some claim, that miscalculation motivated more and stiffer resistance to the British by the backcountry citizens.

Thomas Brown had made it impossible for those who had aligned themselves with Liberty to remain in Wilkes County. Within a few days, Clarke again convened his men, numbering about 300. At the end of September, they provided an escort for their families, some 400 women and children, as they made their way on a 200-mile journey through a wilderness terrain toward the safety of the Overmountain region of North Carolina, the home of the men alongside whom Clarke had fought in August. The refugees lay close to the mountains, following a network of roads that carried them toward the Nolichucky and Watauga River valleys. Clarke's entourage departed with five days' food supply. Most walked and many had no shoes. They walked not knowing from what direction or around what turn they might be attacked by pursuing Tories or attacking Indians. They rested as necessary, in the open without shelter, ready at every moment to move on. When the food ran out, they foraged the woods, subsisting on nuts and arriving on the 11$^{th}$ day of their march in the Overmountain region, starving and in a deplorable condition. They were greeted by the Overmountain settlers with clothing and food and shelter.[11]

Colonel Cruger had pursued the refugees for a time, but found that he was getting too far away from his post at Ninety Six. He sent word to General Lord Cornwallis, who ordered Major Patrick Ferguson to watch in his quarter for Clarke and the escaping Whig rebels. Clarke marched northward, hugging the mountains to keep a good distance from the British forces. Along the way, Clarke learned from Captain Edward Hampton[12] that militia colonels Shelby, Campbell, and Sevier had gathered their forces and were marching over the mountains to confront Patrick Ferguson and to help forestall the advancing British Legion. Elijah Clarke continued leading the homeless Patriots toward safety, but he joined in supporting this Patriot resistance. He dispatched Major William Candler and 30 men, including captains William Johnston and Patrick Carr, along with Candler's oldest son, Henry, to seek out the Patriot campaign. Major Candler and his men rode east in earnest. Ready and eager, these few Georgians were looking to join up with the Overmountain Men.

# Ferguson Retreats

### The Dregs of Mankind

Major Patrick Ferguson returned to Gilbert Town in late September, having ridden throughout the region notifying partisans to submit, issuing pardons, and finding no concerted militia group gathering to challenge his control of the western portion of North Carolina. He had chased Colonel McDowell from the countryside and across the mountains. Lord Cornwallis was advancing into Charlotte as planned, with Lt. Colonel Banastre Tarleton supporting his eastern flank. To Ferguson, the victory of His Majesty's army over the rebellious colonists of the Carolinas may have looked highly promising, if not essentially completed. In late September, probably on the 24th or 25th while in Gilbert Town, Ferguson furloughed some of his militiamen

**Gilbert Town, established in 1779 in Rutherford County, was occupied at different times by both Patriot militia and Ferguson's Loyalist forces. The site of the former Gilbert Town lies two or three miles northeast of Rutherfordton, North Carolina on Rock Rd. about 600 feet northeast of Old Gilbertown Road.**

to visit their families.

Ferguson had learned on September 24 of Colonel John Cruger's rescue of the besieged at Augusta on the 18th, and of the flight of partisan Colonel Elijah Clarke, his men and hundreds of women and children chased from their homes by the Loyalists toward the North Carolina mountains. Ferguson had actually lingered in the vicinity of Gilbert Town longer than he had planned so he might assist in overtaking and capturing Clarke and his Whig militiamen from Georgia. No doubt, Ferguson resented Clarke's escape from their encounter at Wofford's Ironworks on August 8. He may have felt he had a score to settle with Clarke, part and parcel of the umbrage he took with those he regarded as "Back Water men." Indeed, when Ferguson furloughed so many of his Loyalist militiamen from Gilbert Town, he may have expected that some of them might have learned in their travels home something of the whereabouts of Clarke and the refugees. Even though the furlough was given on the condition that the men muster quickly when called, most of Ferguson's militiamen were from South Carolina and thus many miles from his mustering point.[1]

**Gilbert Town was the site of the first courthouse in Rutherford County. That town's history and artifacts from the site of Gilbert Town are on display in the Rutherford County Office Building on N. Main Street (US Hwy 221) in Rutherfordton, NC.**

Hearing nothing in Gilbert Town about Clarke's route in flight from Augusta, Ferguson departed on the 27$^{th}$ to see what he could find out about Clarke. Ferguson marched to the southwest over Mountain Creek, the Broad River at Twitty's Ford, and Green River at McDaniel's Ford, stopping on the 29$^{th}$ at the farm of James Step. There on the 30$^{th}$, Ferguson's sense of assured security as a leader among the victoriously advancing British Legion was profoundly disturbed. Two men, Samuel Chambers and James Crawford, arrived at Step's farm and told Ferguson of an army of a thousand mounted rebel militiamen coming over the mountains and looking for him.[2]

With his militia on furlough, Ferguson immediately recognized his predicament. He sent messengers out to muster his troops and any support he might receive from other Loyalists. He sent a dispatch to General Cornwallis requesting reinforcements and alerting his commander to the circumstances. The dispatch was entrusted to two local Loyalists who knew well the routes through this region: Abram Collins and Peter Quinn. The pair followed a direct route toward Charlotte, but along the way took refreshment at the home of a Whig, Alexander Henry, disguising their purpose. Henry, nonetheless, suspected they were up to no good. His Patriot sons followed the pair along the road so closely that the two messengers became anxious at first and then fearful. Collins and Quinn began to hide by day and travel only at night. By this over-caution, they arrived in Charlotte and delivered the message to Cornwallis a week later, on October 7.[3]

Ferguson also decided upon a deceptive maneuver. He wrote to Colonel Cruger at Ninety Six asking for some number of regiments as reinforcements. (Days later he received a reply from Cruger informing him that only half the number requested were available.) Regardless of what support he expected from Cruger, Ferguson feinted toward Ninety Six in the hopes that any scouts out for the Whigs might report that movement to the leaders of the Overmountain Men and they would make a dash in that direction to overtake him.[4]

On Sunday, October 1, Ferguson continued to the southwest reaching the plantation of Baylis Earle on the North Pacolet River. A detachment "plundered at their pleasure," as Draper described it, killing a beef steer and destroying "four or five hundred dozen sheaves of oats." Such action would have certainly created a tale quickly circulated about Ferguson's presence in that quarter. He then marched back to the Broad River, at Denard's Ford (Dennard's)[5] and made camp. From there he issued an appeal to the Loyalist citizens of the region, sending it out into South Carolina as well:

"Denard's Ford, Broad River, Tryon County, October 1, 1780

> Gentlemen: — Unless you wish to be eat up by an inundation of barbarians … who by their shocking cruelties and irregularities give the best proof of their cowardice and want of discipline; I say, if you wish to be pinioned, robbed, and murdered, and see your wives and daughters, in four days, abused by the dregs of mankind — in short, if you wish or deserve to live, and bear the name of men, grasp your arms in a moment and run to camp.
>
> "The Back Water men have crossed the mountains; McDowell, Hampton, Shelby, and Cleveland are at their head, so that you know what you have to depend upon. If you choose to be pissed upon forever and ever by a set of mongrels, say so at once, and let your women turn their back upon you, and look out for real men to protect them.

Pat. Ferguson, Major 71st Regiment."[6]

**An Object of Some Consequence**

Over the next two days, Ferguson proceeded toward Charlotte, perhaps too cautiously. He marched on October 2 only four miles before making camp to await the return of his furloughed militia as well as reinforcements. He may, as well, have still harbored a desire to hear about Clarke's movements. Getting in motion at four o'clock in the morning of the 3rd, he did cover 20 miles that day, arriving at Tate's plantation in the evening. He spent the next two days in camp awaiting scouting reports about his pursuers. The news he received on the evening of the 5th was not encouraging and he sent off a message to his general:

> "My Lord: — A doubt does not remain with regard to the intelligence I sent your Lordship. They are since joined by Clarke and Sumter — of course are become an object of some consequence. Happily their leaders are obliged to feed their followers with such hopes, and so to flatter them with accounts of our weakness and fear, that, if necessary, I should hope for success against them myself; but numbers compared, that must be doubtful.
>
> "I am on my march towards you, by a road leading from Cherokee Ford, north of King's Mountain.[7] Three or four hundred good soldiers, part dragoons, would finish the business. Something must be done soon. This is their last push in this quarter, etc.
>
> Patrick Ferguson."[8]

Lieutenant Allaire recorded the next day, "Friday, $6^{th}$. Got in motion at four o'clock in the morning, and marched sixteen miles to Little King's Mountain, where we took up our ground."[9] There Ferguson again awaited arrival of his furloughed militiamen and reinforcements, which he hoped were on their way.

**Little King's Mountain**

Ferguson chose for his camp a small eminence at the southwestern end of a 16-mile-long range known as King's Mountain. The dominant feature, a rocky escarpment known as The Pinnacle, was six miles to the northeast of the promontory on which Ferguson camped. He found Little King's Mountain to be 600 yards long and about 250 yards across at the base. Rising some 60 feet in elevation above the surrounding terrain, the top tapered in width from 120 yards at the northern end to some 60 yards at the southern end. The top was shaped not unlike a footprint. Ferguson was pleased with his position high above the surrounding land. Despite an adequate supply of timber that would have allowed for the erecting of breastworks and abatis, Ferguson deigned to fashion either of these defenses, choosing instead simply to circle his supply wagons at the north end of the rise.[10] Years later, accounts by Patriots imputed to Ferguson bold claims of invincibility, perhaps uttered to encourage his militiamen, whose bravery may have been flagging upon word of a thousand "shirtmen" pursuing them. Colonel Hill wrote that Ferguson "defied God Almighty & all the rebels that could be collected to drive him from that camp."[11]

Ferguson needed a victory. He may have thought that the failures of his charges—Moore at Fort Anderson (i.e., Thicketty Fort), Dunlap at Cedar Spring (i.e., Wofford's Ironworks), and Innes at Musgrove's Mill — had sullied his reputation as a capable military leader. The capture of Elijah Clarke in retreat or perhaps the defeat of the pursuing "Back Water men" would certainly have rescued his reputation and substantiated his effectiveness as a military leader. Such success, of course, could have quite possibly led to promotions in the current theater of conflict and any later wars he should have undertaken on behalf of His Majesty. Such rationale along with no desire to be seen as retreating in the face of an approaching enemy may have caused Ferguson to take imprudent risks, lingering in camp as he did on two occasions rather than marching immediately to the protection of General Lord Cornwallis and his British Legion.[12]

On October 6, a cool, fall night atop Little King's Mountain, Ferguson waited as a steady rain began and fell through the night. For Ferguson's troops, the night passed without incident. The major, perhaps, took comfort that evening in the company of Virginia Paul and the red-haired Virginia Sal, two "fine looking young women," supposed to be his mistresses, who served nominally as his cooks.[13]

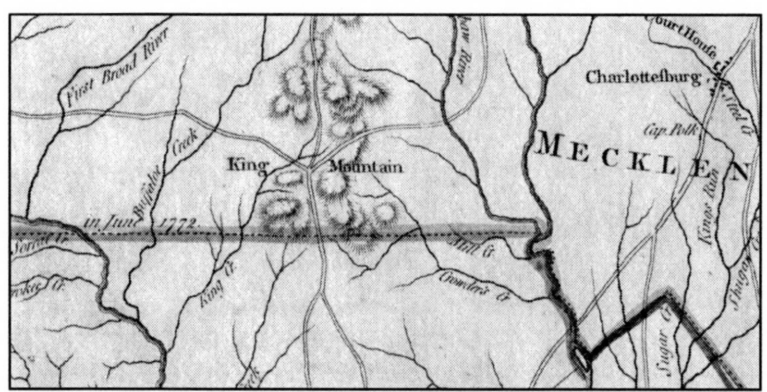


**A British Map from 1775 shows a crossroads called King Mountain toward which Ferguson was heading from Cherokee Ford, seen at the lower left, on his way to Charlotte Town. On October 6, Ferguson camped atop Little King's Mountain along King Creek.**

# The Patriots Pursue Ferguson

### A Question of Command

On October 2, Shelby, Sevier, Cleaveland, Winston, Campbell and McDowell, convened after two rainy days to address the matter of a general commander. As they did so, another colonel, not so far away, was writing a letter to General Horatio Gates with something similar in mind. Colonel James Williams wrote from his camp in Burke County, "seventy miles from Salisbury in the fork of the Catawba" at the Tuckasegee Ford. He advised the general that he had some 450 mounted men in the pursuit of Colonel Ferguson. He continued:

> "This moment another of my express is arrived from Colonels M'Dowell and Shelby: They were on their march, near Burk *(sic)* court house, with one thousand five hundred brave mountain men, and Colonel Cleveland was within ten miles of them with eight hundred men, and was to form a junction with them this day. I expect to join them to-morrow, in pursuit of Colonel Ferguson, and, under the direction of Heaven, I hope to be able to render your honour a good account of him in a few days."[1]

By some accounts, all the men Williams claimed to command were not his.

A month earlier, on September 8, Colonel Williams, a refugee from his home state of South Carolina after his escape from Musgrove's Mill, had received instructions from North Carolina's governor in Hillsborough. Abner Nash authorized Williams to recruit North Carolina militiamen for his command from Caswell County, in particular. Williams recruited there and in the surrounding area with some success. One of his majors also set up camp in Rowan County and recruited mostly refugees from Carolina and Georgia.[2] Dated September 23, the call for recruits was headed, "A call to arms! Beef, bread, and potatoes." Besides promising reliable meals, Williams apparently attracted recruits with the opportunity to plunder Tories, offering, as one Patriot recorded in his memoirs, "as many negroes and horses as they might choose to take."[3] With such men as responded to this call under his command, Williams then reportedly went looking to take control of the militiamen then serving under Colonel Thomas Sumter.

Since losing everything at Fishing Creek, Thomas Sumter had reconstructed his command by recruiting nearly 1,000 men. He continued to be such a nuisance to the advancing British Legion that a price remained on his head. "They … have offered twenty guineas to anyone who will conduct them privately to my camp," he wrote on September 23. Although the British Legion may not have known he was then camped at the Island Ford on the Catawba River, Colonel James Williams did. He paid a visit to the camp apparently while Sumter was away.[4]

According to the accounts written decades later by Colonel William ("Billy") Hill, Colonel Williams allegedly claimed to have been promoted to brigadier general by South Carolina's governor in exile, John Rutledge. Williams rode into Sumter's camp, Hill recalled, "had his commission publically read and required all the officers and men under his immediate command." Williams's claim (if it were actually made[5]) was roundly ignored by Sumter's officers. These were militiamen, not regular army soldiers. They elected their leaders and followed men whom they trusted. Colonel Hill said in his account that the men "refused to have any thing to do with him [Williams] or his commission & if he had not immediately left the camp he would have been stoned out of it."[6] Nevertheless, the challenge by Williams to Sumter's right to command concerned the men. According to Hill, the officers conferred on a plan of action, their "convention" being interrupted by an attack of Legion cavalry. Hill's and Lacey's men marched up the Catawba River and "encamped that night in an uncommon thick wood" where they "were safe from the horse of the enemy."[7]

Continuing their convention, they chose to send a few trusted officers to see Governor Rutledge in Hillsborough. They also decided that Colonel Sumter should go along with the five designees but not appear at Hillsborough until the matter was settled. The entourage arrived in Hillsborough on October 4. Two days later, Governor Rutledge rectified the situation by commissioning Thomas Sumter as brigadier general.[8] Thus, at the time that Shelby, Campbell, Sevier, and Cleaveland were pushing toward a confrontation with Patrick Ferguson, Thomas Sumter was miles away from the pending action. He was absent from the command of his men at a critical time apparently because of his and Williams's personal jealousies and their paralyzing conflict over who was really in charge. Nevertheless, because of his months-long efforts resisting the advance of Lord Cornwallis northward through South Carolina, Thomas Sumter had rallied, mustered, trained, and put into the field a formidable fighting force that stood ready to join in the immediate campaign to confront Patrick Ferguson. Yet, in Sumter's absence, the critical matter still remained: Who would lead them?

**Colonels Hill and Lacey led their detachment of Sumter's militiamen westward from Tuckasegee Ford to Flint Hill. A detail from "A map of the seat of war" (1781) shows the British understanding of the terrain across which Loyalists and Patriots were traveling.**

During his absence in early October, Sumter had given command of his men to his colonels Billy Hill and Edward Lacey. They and their men (a portion of Sumter's corps) departed camp and rode up the Catawba River, crossing at Tuckasegee Ford, where they received information by express from General William Davidson about reports of the movement of a large body of partisans coming from the west (that is, Shelby, Sevier, Campbell and Cleaveland).[9] Hill and Lacey moved out with their 270 South Carolinians, heading west and crossing the Catawba River again at Beattie's Ford. During the day, they were joined by 60 men from Lincoln County, North Carolina, riding under colonels William Graham and Frederick Hambright, both veterans of Rutherford's campaign against the Cherokees four years earlier.[10] That night, Williams again came into camp further pressing the matter of his command, this time "with an air of authority."[11] Hill told him "there was not an officer or man in the whole army that would submit to his command." Williams, fearing he might be rather roughly treated by Hill's and Lacey's men, removed with his recent recruits and camped at some distance from the South Carolinians.

Hill and Lacey, agreeing that they could certainly use the fighting men in Williams's company, proposed an arrangement of command the next day. Williams refused it, reportedly declaring "that by virtue of his commission he would command the whole."[12] Hill told Williams that unless he accepted what was offered, he could not march with the South Carolinians and the Lincoln County militia. Williams relented reluctantly, and the three companies pressed on westward attempting to join up with Shelby, Sevier, Cleaveland, and Campbell. Scouts reported the party of western Patriots as passing through the gap at Cane Creek. Hill, Lacey, Williams and the others marched in that direction reaching Ramsour's Mill and then bearing southwest, crossing the Buffalo River and the First Broad River. They camped on the night of October 3 at the base of Cherry Mountain, then called Flint Hill. That night, Colonel Charles McDowell rode through their camp on his way to Hillsborough. He had no news to share about the imminent plans of the Overmountain Men as he had left the war council in progress.[13]

### The Enemy Is at Hand

While Hill and Lacey dealt with Williams, at Bedford Hill on the morning of October 3, the Overmountain Men and Wilkes/Surry militiamen prepared to renew their march after a day-and-a-half of camp and rain. Before they began, Colonel Cleaveland asked to address the men, "telling them the news," as he called it. He wanted them to know that Ferguson was nearby in Gilbert Town, just 18 miles away, and soon they would have the opportunity to confront the villain. The rough Cleaveland, with his imposing frame — reported to be six-and-a-half-feet tall and variously reported as weighing from 250 to 350 pounds — spoke to inspire the men. "Now, my brave fellows, I have come to tell you the news," he said. "The enemy is at hand, and we must up and at them. Now is the time for every man of you to do his country a priceless service — such as shall lead your children to exult in the fact that their fathers were the conquers of Ferguson. When the pinch comes, I shall be with you. But if any of you shrink from sharing in the battle and the glory, you can now have the opportunity of backing out, and leaving." He offered each man the opportunity to take three steps to the rear if he wanted to leave. Not one man budged and the entire horde of Patriots roundly cheered themselves and their bravery.[14]

"I am heartily glad," said Shelby, then addressing the men, "to see you to a man resolve to meet and fight your country's foes. When we encounter the enemy, don't wait for the word of command. Let each one of you be your own officer, and do the very best you can, taking every care you can of yourselves, and availing yourselves of every advantage that chance may throw in your way. If in the woods, shelter yourselves, and give them Indian play; advance from tree to tree, pressing the enemy and killing and disabling all that you can. Your officers will shrink from no danger."[15]

The men were dismissed with orders to prepare provisions for two meals and to be ready to march in three hours. Benjamin Cleaveland and Joseph McDowell, having secured some liquor of some description, announced to the men that when they were ready to march, they should have a "treat." (Such remedies were used often in the belief they warded off illness brought on by damp and cold. The officers wanted to keep their men healthy as well as amenable to their command.) The men marched out that day, covering only a few miles along

**The Patriot forces descended Cane Creek, passing the log building Brittain Church, erected in 1768. New Brittain Church and cemetery are on US Hwy 64 seven miles north of Rutherfordton, NC.**

Cane Creek, crossing the crooked course of that stream several times. They camped along the stream that night, near Marlin's Knob, taking up the march again on October 4. As they approached Gilbert Town, they learned that Ferguson had already departed. Disappointed that their prey had escaped, the Patriot hunters camped that night near the mouth of Cane Creek, a little north of the town.[16]

On the 5th, the Patriots passed through Gilbert Town and pressed on south following the route they believed Ferguson had taken on his departure. The reports from scouts were consistent with his heading for Ninety Six, one hundred miles away. The Patriots knew that location was heavily garrisoned with Legion regulars and Loyalist militia. They hoped to overtake Ferguson before he could reach that safe haven, if in fact he were actually headed that way. They could not be sure. They crossed the Broad River at Twitty's Ford, where the scouts did not discover evidence of Ferguson's turn to the east.[17] The Patriot militiamen marched on toward the southwest, arriving after two-and-a-half miles at the ford over Green River (today's Alexander's Ford).

They covered, at best, thirteen miles that day.

During the day, Major William Candler and his 30 Georgians joined the Patriots' campaign to overtake Ferguson. These were the militia-men detached by Colonel Elijah Clarke during his escape from Georgia with 400 refugee women and children. Along the Broad River, the Patriots were also joined by 20 men riding under Major William Chronicle from the South Fork of the Catawba River.[18]

The Overmountain Men had left Sycamore Shoals ten days before and had covered some 150 miles since. As Draper described them, "many of the horses had become weak, crippled, and exhausted, and not a few of the trampers foot-sore and weary."[19] The men were tiring, especially the men on foot; and some, who had started the march with such high spirits, were becoming discouraged. Moreover, they were increasingly uncertain in what direction Ferguson was actually headed. William Lenoir later wrote, "[We] received some further but imperfect information of the progress of … Ferguson, who was said to be progressing through the country in various directions, committing great ravages and depredations."[20] Apparently Ferguson's feint and his marauding at the farm of Baylis Earle had worked to circulate stories of his whereabouts.

The leaders considered their circumstances and their options, but they never deterred from their commitment to pursue Ferguson. Lenoir wrote that local Tories were so active in informing Ferguson as to the whereabouts of the Patriots "that men on foot would not be able to overtake him, therefore orders were given for as many as had, or could procure, horses, to go in advance as mounted infantry."[21] Draper wrote, "The whole night was spent in making a selection of the fittest men, horses, and equipments for a forced march, and successful attack on the enemy." They selected from among their ranks about 700 mounted militiamen. About the same number of footmen and riders with weaker horses would follow along. Colonel Campbell put Major Joseph Herndon, from Cleaveland's command, and Captain William Neal (Neill) from his own, in charge of the trailing militiamen. He urged them to follow along as quickly as they could, knowing that they also might be needed in the confrontation they soon hoped to have with Ferguson.[22]

Lenoir's account of his experience in selecting the 700 clearly suggests that many of the men on this campaign made choices as individuals and not as members of some regimented military corps. "I was a Captain of a company of footmen," he wrote, "and left them at Green river, except six of them, who procured horses and went with us. I went as a common soldier, and did not pretend to take command of those who belonged to my company." He fell in behind the command of Major Joseph Winston, along with his companions, Robert Cleaveland and Jesse Franklin. [23]

**All of You That Love Your Country**

On the morning of October 5, a man came into the camp of the South Carolinians at Flint Hill, seeking out the leaders Hill and Lacey. He was "an old gentleman well known to many of us to be a man of veracity," Hill wrote. He had been in Ferguson's camp at Tate's plantation for some time passing himself off as "a great friend of the Royal cause." By that ruse, he had learned the major's plans. Then slipping out of the camp after dark, he had traveled twenty miles through the night to bring this information to Hill and Lacey. He related that Ferguson had sent a message to Cornwallis that he was headed toward Charlotte and would much appreciate his sending mounted troops and soldiers as an escort. As Hill recounted it many decades later, because

"… the Rebels were such Dam—d cowardly rascals that they would ambuscade him."[24] Indeed, Ferguson was marching for Charlotte, not Ninety Six.

As it happened, Hill had observed that morning, while the spy was passing along his information, that colonels James Williams and Thomas Brandon were missing from the line of march. Only at the end of the day did he see them and then apparently upon their first return to camp. Hill confronted the pair, asking where they had been. They evaded giving a straight answer until eventually sharing that they had been to see "the mountain men," which they described as "a set of fine men & well armed." Hill pressed for information about where they were to rendezvous with the Overmountain and backcountry militiamen. Williams replied, "At Lawson's Fork at the old Iron works." Hill knew instantly this was away from Ferguson's route as related by the spy. Hill pressed Williams until Williams admitted that he, as Hill wrote later, "had made a deception to get them to go to Ninety Six." Hill saw that Williams was attempting to steer this army of militiamen into his own neighborhood, to protect his property and perhaps plunder others in the area. By doing so, Hill told Williams, the opportunity to confront Ferguson would be lost as the major would in two days be within the safety of Cornwallis's lines. Williams held his ground, according to Hill, declaring "with a considerable degree of warmth, that the North Carolinians might fight Ferguson or let it alone, & that our business was to fight for our country [meaning South Carolina]."

Hill was outraged at Williams's actions. He went immediately to Lacey and told him what had transpired. They agreed that without the correct information, Shelby, Sevier, Campbell, and Cleaveland would be heading away of the prey they sought. Hill was unable to ride well because of the battle wound he had suffered at Hanging Rock. He gave his horse, a good night traveler, to a local pilot and asked Lacey to carry the message to the Overmountain Men. The pair of messengers departed camp about 8 o'clock in the evening, riding hard through the night toward the Green River ford. "In crossing the spur of the mountain," Hill wrote, "they lost the path, and he [Col. Lacey] was so suspicious that he [the pilot] was taking him to the enemy … that he cocked his gun twice to kill him; but Providence prevented it."[25] After riding a circuitous route through the night, they then found their way some eighteen or twenty miles,[26] finally approaching the camp of the Overmountain Men before day.

Lacey was unknown to the Virginians and backcountry North Carolinians. When he and his pilot approached the ford, the sentinels repulsed their advance. The guards captured Lacey, blindfolded him and took him to the Green River camp for interrogation by Campbell,

**The Patriot militiamen camped along the Green River at today's Alexander's Ford. The old road bed along which the Patriots and Colonel Lacey rode descends the long hill toward the river crossing, passing through the Bradley Nature Preserve in Polk County, NC.**

Shelby, Sevier, Cleaveland and the others. The two intruders were at first taken to be Tory spies. Lacey asked if two men had visited them that day and steered them toward Ninety Six. Were they Williams and Brandon? The leaders acknowledged this was true. Lacey then shared with them the information he and Hill had gained that morning from the spy. Hill wrote, "[Lacey] had the address at last to convince them he was no impostor; he told them where the Royal army was, their force, &c, and urged them, by all means, to come on immediately."[27] The Overmountain leaders were most pleased to learn of Ferguson's true direction of retreat and his plans; but, Hill wrote, "When the officers found themselves thus deceived by Williams, … they expressed the Highest degree of Indignation, as they had come so far with an intention to fight Ferguson & that they were so near being prevented of their intention by this supposed friend."[28]

According to Lacey's 19th century biographer, A.S. Salley, "Campbell had that night in council abandoned the chase and had determined to return over the mountains; but, upon the earnest and continued solicitations of Col. Lacey, they … now resolved to pursue Ferguson as far as King's Mountain."[29] Draper recorded no such dispirited resignation among the leaders of the Overmountain Men, even if some of the militiamen were becoming discouraged. The leaders had already determined to "pursue Ferguson unremittingly, and overtake him, if possible, before he could reach any post, or receive any re-inforcements."[30] Upon the reliable news, which Lacey brought, the band of Overmountain Men and backcountry Patriots then had confidence in the direction their quarry had fled. They agreed with Lacey to rendezvous with the South Carolinians at the Cowpens the next evening, October 6.

After a meal and a few hours' rest, during which his horse was cared for as well, Colonel Lacey returned to his camp in the morning to yet more turmoil, "a likelihood of their being a mutiny in the army," Hill called it. In Lacey's absence, Colonel Williams had made the rounds among the men and officers ordering them to march in the direction of Lawson's Fork. Hill went along behind, he said, "inform[ing] those Officers & men of his [Williams's] wicked designs and request[ing] them to wait Col. Lacey's return."[31] Hill had the presence of mind to parade the men so he could address them all together. He put them to a challenge. "All of you that love your Country & wish to fight for your country, your friends & posterity, & not to plunder your country in a day of distress, you will parade to the right." Those who preferred to follow the intentions of Colonel Williams and to venture into South Carolina with designs to plunder Tory property, as Hill described it, were invited to parade left. Hill was heartily pleased that the vast part of the army paraded to the right.

At mid-morning, Colonel Lacey returned to camp with word of the intended rendezvous. The men immediately prepared to march and got under way toward the Cowpens. The rear guard soon noticed that Colonel Williams and his party were tagging along. So few had joined in his scheme, Hill wrote, that Williams "thought it rather hazardous to March by himself." Williams and his small party were held in such an unfavorable light by the rear guard that "they were throwing stones & otherwise offronting *(sic)* them the whole day."[32]

**The Cowpens**

The South Carolinians arrived at the Cowpens late in the afternoon of October 6 and awaited the arrival of Campbell, Shelby, Sevier, Cleaveland and the others. The sub-divided party of Overmountain Men departed the Green River ford early on October 6. The mounted force pressed onward, following a ridge road south to Sandy Plains

**Riding and marching hard all day October 6, the mounted and foot militia arrived at the Cowpens to join with the South Carolina militia. A segment of the old road into the Cowpens National Battlefield is the route followed by the Patriot militia coming from the Green River ford.**

and then took a better road southeastward to the rendezvous. The footmen followed. That day the Patriots covered 21 miles, getting with each step closer to their prey. They were firmly and resolutely committed to reaching Ferguson before he could retreat to safety.

The separate bands of Patriots convened on the pastures and fields of a well-to-do Tory Englishman named Saunders. He dealt in cattle and had several pens constructed there, hence the name given the well-known location, the Cowpens. The arriving Patriots roused him from his sick bed and treated him pretty roughly, demanding to know when Ferguson had passed by. He denied knowing anything about Ferguson's army and begged the overly eager interrogators to search his house and property if they did not believe him. He even offered them the use of his own supply of pine knots as torches. The Patriot militiamen did search the house, the buildings and the grounds to their satisfaction that Ferguson had not come that way. The men then shot a few of the Tory's beeves[33] and slaughtered them for a hurried meal, intending not to tarry long at this site. Just as quickly, they harvested fifty acres of corn for themselves and for their horses.[34] As the men prepared their meals, roasting strips of beef and ears of corn, "the bright camp fires were everywhere seen lighting up the gloomy surroundings," Draper wrote.[35] These men were, however, on the cusp of completing their mission — pursuing Ferguson and defeating him to prevent his invasion of their homeland. He was at last nearby, but still a long day's ride away. The leaders were concerned that Ferguson was not more than two days out of Charlotte and the safety of Cornwallis. If they wanted to confront Ferguson, they would have to find him and deal with him the next day. They had sent out scouts during the previous days and awaited any news they might bring.

As the men took their short respite from the saddle, they received word from one of their spies, Enoch Gilmer, a man championed for the task by Major William Chronicle of Graham's South Fork Boys. Gilmer had a reputation for creating any credible persona that was called for. "He could cry and laugh in the same breath" and make everyone believe he was sincere in both," Draper wrote. "He was "a shrewd, cunning fellow, and a stranger to fear."[36] Gilmer returned to the camp with some news. He had come across a Tory's home not far from the Cowpens and learned from the unsuspecting man that Ferguson had supposedly been recalled to Cornwallis, who was preparing for a major strike in North Carolina. But, the man provided no specifics that would help the Patriots find the major.

The same evening, another spy returned with more immediately useful information. Joseph Kerr, as part of the South Carolina command and a month shy of his 20th birthday,[37] had left Flint Hill a day or two before, seeking the whereabouts of Patrick Ferguson and his army of British Legion and Tory militiamen. Kerr was championed for the mission by Lt. Colonel James Steen of the South Carolina Refugees as "a faithful and efficient spy" and as one who had proven himself so in mid-July at the skirmish at the Williamsons' home, since known as Huck's Defeat.[38] Kerr found Ferguson's camp at midday on the 6th on the plantation of Peter Quinn, some six or seven miles from Little King's Mountain. Pretending to be a Loyalist looking to take protection under the major, he made his way into the camp. He easily succeeded in this ruse because this area was full of Loyalists, and because Ferguson was eager to gather more militiamen to his ranks. Moreover, Kerr was a generally amiable person, but suffering some disability since birth, his physical condition disarmed the Tories of their caution. He circulated freely among the men at camp, cajoling with them, feigning praise for the Crown, and asking seemingly innocuous questions. He played the part perfectly, showing great interest and delighting in hearing about recent British successes and, most important, Ferguson's immediate plans. Timing his departure carefully, the shrewd spy shrank back from the encampment and faded from their attention. He then made his way back toward the Patriot militiamen, whom he knew were on the move. With good fortune as the sun was setting, he found his fellow South Carolinians and the redirected Overmountain Men gathered at the Cowpens. He shared the news with the commanders, reporting Ferguson's location and that his command numbered no more than fifteen hundred men. The leaders were greatly encouraged that Ferguson was so near and within reach. Their spirits rose.

At the Cowpens, all the militia officers — including, perhaps, the otherwise reportedly shunned Colonel Williams — gathered in a war council. (Writing 50 years later, Kerr pointedly declared "Williams was present at each council that was held."[39] Conversely, Hill declared that "after the attempt to deceive Col. Campbell & the other Officers, he dare not appear before them neither at the council of officers at the

Cowpens nor at the other near the Mountain."[40]) They renewed their faith in Colonel William Campbell as their commander-in-chief, gaining the ascent of the men who had joined since his election on October 2. The number of mounted men arriving from the Green River ford numbered 700. With about 400 North Carolinians and South Carolinians joining from Flint Hill, the combined Patriot force was some 1,100 mounted men, with the uncounted footmen still arriving. From this corps, the leaders selected 910 men — the best marksmen on the sturdiest horses — to ride overnight in pursuit of Ferguson. Among them were, Draper surmises in proportion to their numbers at the Cowpens, 200 under Campbell, 120 each under Shelby and Sevier, 110 under Cleaveland, 90 under McDowell, 60 under Winston, 100 under Lacey, 50 under Graham and Hambright, and 60 under Williams, including the 30 Georgians.[41] These men had been in their saddles all day, covering 21 miles since sunrise. But after only a brief stop at the Cowpens, an hour or so, they remounted their tiring horses and continued their pursuit.

### Enough, If We Can Find Him

At nine o'clock on a cold and dark October 6$^{th}$ night, the Patriot militiamen departed camp for the 12$^{th}$ day of their expedition, a day they wanted to be the last of their long pursuit. The saddle-weary men rode out into a damp night that soon became a drizzling rain and then at times a steady downpour. To keep their powder dry and their rifles ready for firing, some of the "shirtmen" took off their hunting frocks and wrapped them around their rifles. Others used their blankets, if they had them; whatever they had to keep their weapons ready, they used.[42] The roads were muddy and the routes confused in places. Some of the Virginians took a wrong turn. "[T]he path being small & the woods very thick, the troops got scattered & dispersed through the woods thus wondering [wandering] the whole night," Hill wrote. By

**The mounted Patriot militia rode through a cold, rainy night, crossing the Broad River at Cherokee Ford where some of them had encamped earlier under Colonel McDowell. Cherokee Ford is about 1.5 miles south of US Hwy 29 off SC Hwy 239 and off Ford Road.**

daybreak, some of the men were only five miles from where they had started. "This caused them to march uncommonly hard," he continued, "which caused many of the horses to give out as but few of them were shod."[43]

The reunited party of mounted Patriots had intended to cross the Broad River at Tate's plantation, the site of Ferguson's recent camp; but, as they approached it, the leaders thought better of it, supposing that some rear guard of Ferguson's might be lying in ambuscade on the eastern side of the ford. Instead, they rode south some one-and-a-half or two-and-a-half miles to Cherokee Ford, the site of Colonel Charles McDowell's former camp. To see if that ford was guarded as well, they sent forward Enoch Gilmer to scout.

The men reached the river early in the day; the rain continued falling. They had covered 18 miles in their overnight ride. They were still 15 miles shy of King's Mountain, though at the time, they lacked confirmation that Ferguson was there. As they awaited a report from Gilmer, they sat in their saddles continuing to shelter their rifles and their powder. Soon enough they heard a familiar voice from the other side of the river, carrying a tune as best he could, singing verses quite loudly to *Barney O'Linn*, a popular song of the day. That was the signal that all was clear. The men began to ford the river, those with the largest horses crossing first and taking position on the upstream side to stem the flow somewhat so the others could pass through the river. Although the river was rising from the recent rain, all the men made it across, apparently without incident and without a single one taking a ducking.

Once across the river, the men rode on at a quickened pace though they and their horses were showing signs of fatigue. Some of the men had not eaten since Green River, having failed to refresh themselves at the Cowpens. Meanwhile, Gilmer set off at a gallop to scout ahead, hoping to discover Ferguson's encampment.[44]

When the men reached Peter Quinn's place, the site of Ferguson's previous night's camp, they paused for a moment. Some of the men ate what little remained in their wallets. Others grabbed green corn on the stalk as they rode along the road, passing fields not yet ready for harvest. Some they ate immediately. Some they saved for their horses. The rain continued. At this point, the officers convened from their saddles. Some of the mounts were giving out, they noted, having covered to this point over forty miles without pause since Green River, some farther as a result of wandering lost in the rainy woods. Campbell, Sevier, and Cleaveland suggested they stop and let the men and horses rest. Colonel Shelby would have none of it. "I will not stop until night, if I follow Ferguson into Cornwallis' lines," he swore with a measure of indignation and firmness that quickly caused the others to relent. Not another word was uttered. The man who had first received Ferguson's insolent threat, the man who had called for the muster at Sycamore Shoals would not be defeated. He would not fail. The commanders returned to their companies and continued to ride, heading east.

Within a mile, the men came to the home of the aptly named Solomon Beason, a man, who of necessity, wisely declared himself a Whig or a Tory depending on who was asking about his allegiance. He told them Ferguson was but eight miles away. The men's spirits were lifted immensely, having only a mile before considered making a halt. As if on cue with their brightened circumstances, the rain slackened and soon ceased. A gentle breeze welcomed the midday sun.

At Beason's home, the Patriots captured, as well, two Tories, whom they forced to show them the route to King's Mountain. One rode with Shelby; the other with Cleaveland.[45] Five miles farther, they came to another house. The men there would only say that Ferguson was not that far away. As the Patriots began to ride off, "a girl" by Draper's description, followed the men outside and asked simply, "How many are there of you?" "Enough to whip Ferguson if we can find him," came the quick reply. Whether a Patriot or a pragmatist, or perhaps simply impressed by the number of young men or one in particular riding past her home, she responded, "He is on that mountain." She pointed toward Little King's Mountain, still three miles away.[46]

The men rode on and soon spied the horse of Enoch Gilmer tied up at the gate of another cabin. Suspecting the ruse he must have been playing on the inhabitants, Colonel Campbell decided to extract their spy from his situation and discover what he had learned. The men rode at a gallop to the house and stormed inside. Swearing at Gilmer, Campbell shouted, "You damned rascal, we've got you!" Taking the cue, Gilmer shouted back, "A true King's man, by God!" Playing out their respective roles, Campbell snagged a noose around Gilmer's neck declaring he would hang the Tory scoundrel at the gate. Major Chronicle joined in the playmaking, beseeching Campbell to spare the ladies of the house such a scene. They were already in tears. Campbell declared they would hang the wretch from the first tree down the road. The Patriots left and when out of sight, removed the noose from Gilmer's neck. He happily shared his news. When he discovered that the residents of that cabin were Loyalists, he said, he feigned such delight that he gave each of the women a kiss on the cheek. Thus assured of his own allegiances, one of the women said she had taken chickens to Ferguson's camp that day, most likely delivering them to his two cooks, Virginia Sal and Virginia Paul. The encampment the women described to Gilmer was "a ridge between two branches where some deer hunters had a camp the previous autumn."[47] Major Chronicle chimed in. That was his camp, he believed. He knew the area well.

Amidst this exchange, a messenger arrived with news that Colonel William Graham's wife was in some distress and requested him at home immediately. Taking leave for "a woman's affair," Graham rode off, but not without falling under suspicion of some degree of cowardice, though that was dreadfully unfair. Colonel Graham had been in the relief of Charlestown and was at Thicketty Fort and Cedar Spring both with Major Chronicle. He had ridden against the Scots Tories in '76 and that fall rode with Rutherford against the Cherokee town. He was not one to shun a challenge. Major Chronicle took Graham's command of the Lincoln County militia and led his own South Fork Boys to the head of that unit. Lt. Colonel Hambright assented to the major's command as Chronicle knew the terrain. Continuing toward Little King's Mountain, the Patriots captured a couple more Tories,

**The mounted Patriots rode undetected toward Little King's Mountain along the same road Major Ferguson's men had trod the day before. A marker along the entrance road to Kings Mountain National Military Park marks the route both parties traveled.**

who unwillingly corroborated the report they had of Ferguson's position. Still farther on they captured a young lad, John Ponder, carrying a message from Ferguson to Cornwallis. It was another plea for reinforcements and a declaration of his precarious situation. Pressed for additional information, Ponder declared they would know Ferguson when they spotted him. Although Ferguson was the best dressed soldier in the unit, Ponder said the major wore a checked duster covering his uniform.

The leaders designed their plan of attack from the saddle and put it into action as they continued riding toward the ridge. They planned to encircle the mountain and charge up simultaneously. By shooting uphill they would avoid firing into their own men. They divided into two columns with Campbell at the head of one and Colonel Cleaveland at the head of the other. The men were ordered to keep strict silence as they approached the mountain hoping to get as close as possible and perhaps completely encircle the mountain and encampment before Ferguson was alerted their presence. The rain through which they had suffered worked in their favor. They stirred no cloud of dust on their approach. Once on foot, they would have created no rustling of leaves on the ground.

The party of Patriots crossed through the watershed of King's Creek, reaching the east side and the ridge along the headwaters of Long Branch of Clark Fork. They quietly dismounted and tied up their horses, securing to their mounts their blankets, their hunting frocks and everything except what they would need in battle — their rifles, their shot bags and powder horns, their tomahawks, and their hunting knives. The general command went out, "Fresh prime your guns, and every man go into battle firmly resolving to fight till he dies."[48]

The war and the world were about to change.<br>
It was Saturday, October 7,<br>
three o'clock in the afternoon.

# The Battle at King's Mountain

### Kings of King Mountain

Major Patrick Ferguson, in camp atop King's Mountain, was not completely confident in his numbers though he greatly trusted in his position. He had written a message on October 6th to Lord Cornwallis: "I have arrived today at King Mountain and I have taken a post where I do not think I can be forced by a stronger enemy than that against us. … Good soldiers as reserves behind our riflemen and a few real dragoons to second with effect and support the flank of our horse militia upon the enemy's flanks would enable us to act decisively and vigorously …"[1] Ferguson acknowledged to Cornwallis that no help was coming from Colonel Cruger at Ninety Six, but he expected reinforcements of militia under a Colonel Floyd to arrive on the evening of the 7th. Writing to a

**On the evening of October 6, Major Patrick Ferguson set his camp atop Little King's Mountain. The US Monument at Kings Mountain National Military Park stands at the site of Ferguson's camp where the closing events of the battle occurred.**

friend, Major Robert Timpany[2], also on the 6th, Ferguson declared; "Here we are Kings of King Mountain — altho there is indeed another throne or ridge opposite to us where Genl. Sumpter *(sic)* and your humble servant may ... reign [face to face] in day Light ..."[3] Ferguson was keenly aware of General Sumter's army in the region as he had shared in his letter to Cornwallis the day before. He may have supposed that Sumter was at the head of the force reported to be gathering against him. Or, Ferguson may simply have hoped to impress his friend by suggesting that he and his army of militia was appropriate quarry for a rebel general.

Ferguson's fighting force was predominantly militia, as that was his role — recruiting Loyalists throughout the backcountry of South Carolina and North Carolina to fight as "friends of government." He had perhaps one thousand militiamen, whom he had been training continually; but, he relied more heavily on his troops from the British Legion. They numbered perhaps no more than 100 and by some accounts only 70. These were Provincials, or Rangers. He had among them the King's American Volunteers recruited from around New York, the Queen's Rangers, and the New Jersey Volunteers. These men, Americans all, wore uniforms with scarlet coats and green coats and those not mounted were skilled in the bayonet charge, an essential British battlefield tactic.

Ferguson trained the militia in the bayonet charge as well, and he continually drilled his recruits in battlefield maneuvers. Those who carried the British-issued Brown Bess musket could readily affix their bayonets. Some of the militia who had brought their own muskets and rifles had no bayonets. For them, Ferguson had local blacksmiths fashion for each a "plug bayonet," a knife with a handle and shoulder that fit snuggly into the muzzle and served as a makeshift weapon. [4] Still, the bayonet charge was a tactic for experienced soldiers used to fighting in regimental lines and not a maneuver that a citizen militiaman, used to shooting at small game or even an armed opponent from a distance, would take to readily.[5] Nevertheless, having prepared his men, Ferguson believed his militia could fight effectively with perhaps varying degrees of reliability. Ferguson wanted to prove, perhaps, that Loyalist militia properly trained as he had done could rise above the dismissive regard they received among the other Legion commanders, including General Cornwallis. Nevertheless, many of these militiamen had not yet tested themselves in battle.

## The Damned Yelling Boys

The Patriot militiamen, arriving from the west, had dismounted and tied up their horses at some distance from Ferguson's camp. They formed two columns for marching, each two men abreast, and prepared to encircle the mountain. The commanders remained mounted. Campbell led the column to form the right wing with McDowell and Winston in his command. Winston's men, having the farthest to go to get into position at the far end of the eminence to cut off any possible escape, retained their mounts and rode off ahead of the others. They "rode like fox hunters," Lenoir wrote, "as fast as their horses could run, through rough woods, crossing branches and ridges without any person that had any knowledge of the woods to direct or guide them."[6] Shelby and Cleaveland commanded the columns forming the left wing with Williams and Lacey in between them. Sevier was on Shelby's right facing the mountain slope.[7] The left wing also sent a detachment to the far end, commanded by Major Chronicle and Lt. Colonel Hambright. The latter force was to proceed until they met up with Winston coming from the opposite direction. That achieved, the Patriots would completely encircle Ferguson.

Shelby's men had spotted a picket at the southern end of the mountain. The colonel sent out, or he may have led, a small party of experienced fighters with just the right skills. They quietly dispatched the pickets without firing a single shot or otherwise alarming the camp.[8] Indeed, the Patriots were within a quarter mile of Ferguson's camp before they were discovered. The Loyalists began to fire at Shelby's men still reaching their positions. Hearing the gunfire from the opposite side of the mountain, Campbell threw off his coat and yelled out the orders, "Here they are my brave boys; shout like hell, and fight like devils!"[9] The firing began on both sides of the mountain, and, as ordered before they marched, the men all around the mountain erupted in Indian-style war whoops.[10] Ferguson's second-in-command, Captain Abraham DePeyster reportedly remembered his experience at Musgrove's Mill and remarked to Ferguson, "These things are ominous — these are the damned yelling boys!"[11]

### Most Craggy, Rough, and Steep

Campbell had ordered a detachment of Virginians and Wilkes and

**The Centennial Monument, erected at Kings Mountain National Military Park in 1880, stands at the highest point on the promontory and near where William Campbell's Virginians were the first to engage Ferguson's men, who charged them with bayonets. Some of Ferguson's riflemen fired from the rocks nearby.**

Surry militia to sweep across the spur of the mountain on horseback toward the main guard and then return to the lines. According to Joseph Starns, who was with Campbell, "We surprised and took their picket guard without a noise, then a man named Philip Giever … shot a man who came out from the British guard into the woods. This made the enemy's guard retreat to the main body — we advanced toward them before they could form and gave them a fire and before we could load again the British formed and charged on us …"[12] Although the detachment forced the guard to run, the brief exchange was costly as the guard killed two Patriots including Lieutenant Robert Edmiston (the elder),[13] and wounded another. The other Virginians started to climb the slope; "that part of the mountain where Campbell's men were compelled to ascend, was the most craggy, rough, steep, and difficult part of it. His men made the attack under a heavy fire of the enemy."[14] The attack caught Ferguson's attention. He ordered his Rangers to charge down the hill in that sector with fixed bayonets, their first foray. A few Virginians stood their ground and were run through with cold steel. Others turned and fled down the hill, a little farther than the officers thought necessary, as the Rangers stopped at the bottom of the hill, turned and marched back up to the top. Upon retaking their position on the ridge, they discovered that Shelby's men were advancing up the mountain from the opposite side. By this time, Ferguson was ordering his militia to form. The Loyalists then charged down that face of the hill with their bayonets. Shelby's men retreated to the bottom of the hill.

During the charge against Campbell's men, Lieutenant Anthony Allaire, took action which he recalled five month's later: "When our detachment charged, for the first time, it fell to my lot to put a Rebel Captain to death, which I did most effectually with one blow of my sword; the fellow was at least six feet high, but I had rather the advantage, as I was mounted on an elegant horse, and he on foot."[15] Meanwhile, the fleeing Virginians had scampered across the narrow valley to reach a ridge opposite. "For my part, I only retreated about eighty yards," wrote John Craig, "when I was called to by my Lt. Robt. Edmiston [the younger], who told me he was wounded in the arm. We covered ourselves behind a tree, whilst I took his handkerchief and bound up his arm." Colonel Campbell and Major William Edmiston loudly protested their men's hasty departure and coaxed them back to make another charge up the mountain. "Then Edmiston (the younger) remarked to me, 'Come, let us at it again.' We all again attacked and renewed the battle more warmly than ever on both sides."[16] Besides their gallant bravery, they succeeded, in part, because the Loyalists were then on the opposite side of the hill facing down Shelby and chasing his men with a bayonet charge. When Shelby's men reached the bottom of the hill, he rallied them for another charge, saying, "Now, boys, quickly reload your rifles, and let's advance upon them, and give them another hell of a fire!"[17] His brave militiamen again faced the mountain and pressed up the slope a second time as had Campbell's men before.

In these individual acts at the bottom of the hill, these men held victory in the balance. This was the point on which success in the battle turned. Their willingness — and that of their fellow Patriots around the mountain — to face another bayonet charge immediately after just barely escaping from one, was the most essential, elemental, and consequential act of courage displayed that day. They were committed. They were brave. They would not fail.

Ferguson had trained his Loyalist militiamen to charge down the hill with fixed bayonets and to hold their fire until they reached the bottom. After removing the plug bayonets and discharging their muskets,

Loyalist Bayonet Charge
The three bayonet charges by Ferguson's
Loyalists were ineffective because the
terrain was mountainous, and patriot
forces used Indian-style tactics.

**A diorama of the bayonet charge depicts the difficulty the Loyalists encountered in using this tactic on the hill-sides of King's Mountain. The diorama is among the extensive displays in the museum at Kings Mountain National Military Park.**

they turned and marched back up the hill, reloading as they climbed. This was the opportunity that best served the skilled riflemen of the backwoods. As the Rangers and Tories turned, the Patriots picked them off from the bottom of the hill, their rifles being accurate from 200 and 300 yards. It was an effect of fighting in such terrain that shots fired downhill often went high, something every experienced hunter knew. Thus the Loyalists were firing repeatedly high. The buzzing of shot flying through the forest canopy overhead attested to this fact. For the Patriots shooting uphill, their shots were true.[18] Thus had Ferguson given himself another great disadvantage by setting his camp atop Little King's Mountain.

### My Brave Fellows

Colonel Cleaveland's men were not quite in position when the shooting started as they had to cross some boggy terrain. About ten minutes into the battle, they reached their quarter, forced a picket to retreat up the hill toward camp and then followed in steady pursuit. Years later, Cleaveland recounted the sentiments he expressed to his men during the battle, most likely in rougher language and in piecemeal fashion. He professed to have told them, in part: "My brave fellows, we have beaten the Tories and we can beat them again. They are all cowards. … I will show you, by my example how to fight; I can undertake no more. Every man must consider himself an officer, and act from his own judgment. Fire as quick as you can, and stand your ground as long as you can. When you can do no better, get behind trees, or retreat; but I beg you not to run quite off. If we are repulsed, let us make a point of returning and renewing the fight."[19]

All around the mountain the battle was fully engaged after some fifteen minutes. Gunfire flashed on every slope from top to bottom and a haze of sulfurous smoke began to envelop the mountain as nearly two thousand men on both sides fired at each other as quickly as they could reload. The peal of muskets and rifles firing was nearly a continuous din. The visibility of the riflemen through the smoke was likely much less than the range of their weapons. Ferguson had called his men into action by the beat of the drum, but after the fighting began, he gave his orders through tweets on two silver whistles, commands he had practiced time and again with his Tory recruits. The high trills of his whistles carried over the roar of gunpowder explosions.

**Using LED lights, a 3-dimensional model of King's Mountain shows the movements of Loyalist and Patriot troops during the battle. This display, which helps explain the unique aspects of this battle's actions, is part of the exhibits at the Visitor Center at Kings Mountain National Military Park.**

Captain William Edmiston did not shrink from the ferocity of battle — ever. While fighting on the hill, he desired to move to a spot with better advantage. He broke from his protection and dashed forward during a hot part of the battle. When DePeyster's men were charging down the hill, Edmiston fired his rifle and then used it to club the bayoneted musket from the hands of an approaching Tory. Edmiston seized the man around the neck, made him his prisoner, and took him to the foot of the hill. When he returned up the slope to continue fighting, he was shot in the chest. Lying on the hill, he clung to life until the battle was over. After hearing news of the victory, he expired knowing, at least, that he had done his part.

Another brave Virginian shared the same fate. Lieutenant Reece Bowen, a near-40-year-old scout for the Washington County militia, ran up the hill exposing himself to fire without taking cover. Draper recounted that after a fellow militiaman chastised him for not being more careful, he replied indignantly, "Take to a tree — no! Never shall it be said that I sought safety by hiding my person, or dodging from a Briton or Tory who opposed me in the field." No sooner had he declared his courage than he was struck by a ball in the chest. He fell on the slopes of King's Mountain, where he died. Such sentiments and bravado were likely ascribed to him afterwards as testaments to his courage. He was too good a fighter for such foolhardy behavior. He had fought alongside his brother, Captain William Bowen, at Point Pleasant in '74 and gone to the relief of the Kentucky stations in '78.[20] He was a scout and he fought Indian-style with the best. Because his brother, the captain, was ill at the time of the muster in Craig's Meadow, Lieutenant Bowen had taken the command. He was a leader among men, and suddenly sorely missed.

At the north end of the mountain, Major William Chronicle was leading his South Fork Boys up the steep slope. He was well in front of his men with his hat raised in the air and shouting to encourage them, "Face the hill!" Hardly had his men started up from the base, when their major was shot. Lt. Colonel Frederick Hambright, the 53-year-old German, took the command. He was experienced in battle, having gone with Rutherford against the Cherokee towns and riding to the relief of Charlestown.[21] Hambright led the men up the slope where they were confronted by a bayonet charge led by DePeyster. On the slope, Robert Henry, then but 15 years old, took cover behind a log, reloading his rifle, as the bayonet charge stormed down the hill. "When they made the charge," he later wrote, "they first fired their guns [, killing and wounding several of our men.] The Fork boys fired and did considerable execution. I was preparing to fire when one of the British advanc[ed.] I stepped and was in the act of cocking my gun when his bayonet was running along the barrel of my gun, and gave me a thrust through my hand and into my thigh; my antagonist and myself both fell. The Fork boys retreated and loaded their guns. I was then lying under the smoke and it appeared that some of them were not more than a gun's length in front of the bayonets, and the farthest could not have been more than twenty feet in front when they discharged their rifles. The British then retreated in great haste and were pursued by the Fork boys."[22] Finding Henry on the ground, one of his companions pulled the bayonet from his hand and leg to free him, giving Henry's wounded leg a kick to remove the bayonet. Henry said the removal was more painful than the attack. He discovered that he must have pulled the trigger when he was run through. His assailant lay on the ground, blood still draining from his dead body.

**Huzza, Boys!**

The rifle in the hands of the "shirtmen" carried the day. Their accuracy made nearly every shot the ruin of a Tory or a Ranger. William

**Major William Chronicle, leading the South Fork Boys, was killed early in the battle near the bottom of the hill as he encouraged his men to advance. A commemorative marker stands at the spot where he fell.**

Twitty, a stepson to Colonel Graham, had lost a friend fighting by his side and saw the smoke lingering beside a tree, behind which he concluded the assailant was hiding. He trained his aim on the edge of the tree and when the fellow poked his head around, Twitty fired with deadly accuracy, killing, as he later discovered, a neighbor who had chosen to fight for the King.[23] Silas McBee recounted, "During the fight some of the Tories at the west end of the summit were secured among some table or bench rocks. Whenever one popped up his head, a ball from some unerring rifle of the mountaineers pierced through." The bodies of some twenty Tories, shot in the head, were later found among the rocks.[24]

In Cleaveland's quarter the fighting raged on as fierce as anywhere on the mountain. Upon first reaching his position, he had yelled to his Wilkes militia, "Yonder is your enemy, and the enemy of mankind!" As Draper described their assault, "They sought all natural places of protection — trees, logs, rocks, and bushes; when Cleveland would, ever and anon, vociferously urge onward and upward his troops — 'a little nearer to them, my brave men!' And the men of Wilkes and Surry would then dart from their places of concealment, and make a dash for more advanced positions."[25] Their reward for such bravery was a hail of bullets that killed many good men and wounded others, with Lieutenant Samuel Johnson having his hunting frock riddled with seven bullets, one finally striking him in the abdomen. As he lay wounded on the slope, he continued to lead though prostrate, raising his hand in the air and urging on his men, "Huzza, boys!"[26] He was a soldier's soldier. He had been with Rutherford in '76 on the Cherokee expedition. He had ridden against the Scots Tories, too. Just before mustering for the current campaign, he had gone with Cleaveland into the New River valley chasing Tories.[27]

Cleaveland's horse, Roebuck, received two wounds; the officer dismounted near the foot of the hill. Benjamin Sharp recounted, "Although fat and unwieldy, he [Cleaveland] advanced on foot with signal bravery; but was soon re-mounted by one of his officers, who brought him another horse." One of Cleaveland's Bulldogs, Lieutenant Charles Gordon, charged into the midst of a band of Tories, grabbing one by the hair and dragging him down the hill. The partially subdued officer pulled his pistol and fired into Gordon's arm at point blank range, breaking it. Gordon, himself, an officer, pulled his sword and killed the Tory with his good arm.[28] With their arrival and advance, Cleaveland's men had plugged a hole in the Patriot lines, the prospect of which for a time had encouraged the Tories that they might escape in that quarter. "This threw the British and Tories into complete disorder, and Ferguson seeing that all was lost, determined not to survive the disgrace."[29]

The Patriots were moving all around the mountain. When Charles Bowen, a 31-year-old private of Captain William Edmiston's company, heard rumor that his brother Reece Bowen had been killed, he frantically tore around the slope looking for him, desperately hoping to find his brother only wounded. He found first his own captain, shot

**Although the mature forest on the slope in 1780 has been replaced by smaller trees and underbrush, the steepness of the hillside up which Colonel Williams and Colonel Shelby attacked can be seen.**

in the head and dying. Running helter-skelter through the battlefield searching and without regard for his own safety, he ended up near the top of the mountain, no more than twenty paces from the enemy in the quarter where Cleaveland was advancing. The colonel was on foot with rifle in hand. He concluded Bowen's frantic actions to be those of a Tory. Cleaveland called out the sign expecting the countersign. Bowen, so distracted, said nothing, which confirmed for Cleaveland his suspicions. He lowered his rifle on Bowen and pulled the trigger. By great Providence, it misfired. Bowen, still not comprehending what was happening around him, charged the colonel and seized him by the collar. Bowen grabbed his tomahawk from his belt — as his brother William had done at Point Pleasant — ready to slay his attacker, when his arm was grabbed by a man, Buchanan, who knew both Cleaveland and Bowen. Coming to his senses, Bowen shouted the countersign, "Buford." Cleaveland lowered his rifle and hugged the Virginian he had almost dispatched.[30]

**Brothers Against Brothers**

Bowen and Cleaveland did not know one another and they fought for the same side. Others on the mountain that day knew each other well and were enemies. The Logan family of Lincoln County had two sons, William and Joseph fighting for the Patriots and against their brothers, John and Thomas, fighting on behalf of the Crown. Thomas was badly wounded and left on the field of battle. His brother John would be taken prisoner and marched away afterwards.[31] In another instance, a wounded Tory recognized his brother-in-law, a Patriot, and called to him for help. "Look to your friends for help," came the stern rebuke as the Patriot moved on.[32]

One family from Rutherford County lost four sons in the battle. Preston Goforth fought for the Patriots; his three brothers, including John, were among the Tories. Preston and one of his brothers may well have been the pair Colonel Shelby later recalled: "Two brothers, expert riflemen, were seen to present at each other, to fire and fall at the same instant."[33] Another Patriot noticed heavy and accurate fire coming from inside the hollow shell of a chestnut tree, through a hole in it. He fired several shots through the small hole, silencing the firing from within. He later looked inside the shell to discover he had killed his brother, a Tory. The shock and grief overwhelmed the man and "he became almost deranged in consequence."[34]

**And Dashed Onward**

Colonel John Sevier's column, in the left wing by Shelby, advanced up the hill without suffering a direct bayonet attack from the Rangers and Tories, though some in his column supported Campbell's men in their distress. Unhappily, Captain Robert Sevier, the colonel's brother, was severely wounded in the battle. His brother, Joseph, removed the wounded Sevier to the bottom of the hill to quench his thirst at a spring there.[35] Meanwhile, Colonel Sevier rode about the slope rallying his men who had been persuaded by rumor — or by deceptive shouts from the enemy — that Tarleton's dragoons were then at the scene. Tarleton was not there, in fact, but the mention of his name could have made any militiaman's blood run cold for a few moments until he could bolster his courage.

Colonel James Williams took his position in the left wing, his column facing the slope adjacent to Shelby and next to the colonel whose command he had attempted to commandeer, Edward Lacey. Reportedly, Williams had refused earlier to take part in the battle, offended that his superior rank had not been recognized. But when the fighting came, he joined in and acted heroically.[36] "I had seen him … that day," wrote Thomas Young, fighting under colonels Williams and Brandon, "it was in the beginning of the action, as he charged by me at full speed around the mountain. Toward the summit, a ball struck his horse under the jaw, when [the horse] commenced stamping as if he were in a nest of yellow jackets. Colonel Williams threw the reins over the animal's neck — sprang to the ground, and dashed onward."[37] Others on the field of battle also remarked on the courage of the colonel and their respect for him.[38] Indeed, two distinct images of Colonel James Williams emerged from the King's Mountain expedition, leaving each to his own conclusions about the man — hector or hero.

There was no doubt, however, about Williams's commitment to the Patriot cause. He was a cousin with Judge Richard Henderson of Transylvania fame and also with Colonel Joseph Williams of Surry County. James Williams's two sons, Daniel and Joseph, were at King's Mountain with their father.[39] Both these lads, stalwart Patriots and captured at Hayes Station a year later in November 1781, were executed by “Bloody Bill” Cunningham after he reneged on treating them as prisoners-of-war. Daniel was then18, Joseph 14.[40]

**Remember Your Liberty**

Of his own experience, Thomas Young recounted, “I well remember how I behaved. Ben Hollingworth and I took right up the side of the mountain, and fought our way, from tree to tree, up to the summit. I recollect I stood behind one tree, and fired until the bark was nearly all knocked off [from return fire], and my eyes pretty well filled with it. One fellow shaved me pretty close, for his bullet took a piece of my gun-stock. Before I was aware of it, I found myself apparently between my own regiment and the enemy, as I judged from seeing the paper which the Whigs wore in their hats, and the pine twigs the tories wore in theirs, these being the badges of distinction.”[41] “I had no shoes,” he later related, “and of course fought in this battle barefoot; when it was over, my feet were much torn and bleeding all over.”[42]

The other units pressed forward as well. Lt. Colonel Hambright was shot in the leg, the ball passing between his thighbone and his saddle. The severed artery soon filled his boot with blood; yet, he refused attention as it might distract his men from the task at hand — charging toward the summit. He called out instead, “Huzza, my brave boys, fight on a few minutes more, and the battle will be over!”[43]

After more than a half-hour of fighting, Campbell pressed forward, charging up the hill. He was leading his men, so far out in front of them as to be in danger of being shot by them, Draper said. “Boys, remember your liberty!” he shouted. “Come on! Come on! my brave fellows; another gun — another gun will do it! Damn them, we must have them out of this!” A pocket of Tory militia, holed up in a chain of rocks and delivering deadly fire on the Patriots, had worn out the patience of Campbell. He and his shirtmen, joined by Shelby's men, attacked for twenty minutes, finally running the Tories out with their accurate fire as they advanced up the slopes tree to tree and rock to rock. They fired with a precision that startled the enemy. The Tories retreated along the crest of the ridge toward the north end and their camp.[44]

The Patriot militiamen repeatedly charged up the hill and retreated in the face of the bayonet charges. Just as quick as one side retreated, those on the opposite side of the mountain charged up. This continued for three assaults until after an hour during which the slopes of the mountain were engulfed in a cloud of gun smoke, the Patriots pressed near the top from all sides. The men under Campbell, Shelby, and Sevier pressed them hard from the southwest quarter toward the northern end of Little King's Mountain. The Tories began to crowd into the middle of their encampment, the militia declaring to their commanders that they were out of ammunition. As they huddled, they made themselves easier targets, where almost any shot would strike someone with effect. Coming to the crest, Cleaveland, Lacey, and Williams joined in the press, as the men offered up shouts of victory and war whoops.

### What Sweet-Lips Can Do

Ensign Robert Campbell, brother to the commander, reported later, "Ferguson being heavily pressed on all sides, ordered Captain Dupoister [DePeyster] to reinforce some of the extreme posts with a full company of British regulars [Provincial Rangers]. He marched, but to his astonishment when he arrived at the place of destination, he had almost no men, being exposed in that short distance to the constant fire of their [mountaineers'] rifles. He then ordered his cavalry to mount, but to no purpose. As quick as they were mounted they were taken down by some bold marksmen."[45] This small corps of cavalry was 20 men under Lieutenant John Taylor. The loss of this cavalry and his Rangers drove Ferguson to desperation.

Atop the mountain, Captain DePeyster could see their defeat was inevitable. He suggested to Ferguson that they surrender, but the proud major declared he would never surrender to these "damned banditti." Ferguson committed to his own escape through the lines. He wore his checkered duster and was swinging his saber in his left hand. Both were telltale signs that marked him to the Patriots as the British officer who had threatened to march into their Overmountain homeland, hang their leaders and lay their country waste with fire and sword. The latter fact was told to the Patriots by one of Ferguson's cooks, Virginia Paul, as she rode away from the scene of battle on horseback.[46] Her fellow cook and Ferguson's supposed alternate paramour, Virginia Sal, had been struck and killed by some stray shot early in the battle. Why Paul told the Patriots how to identify Ferguson was unknown, but the notion that "Nor Hell a fury, like a women scorn'd"[47] could likely have played into the story. By keeping two mistresses, Ferguson, most certainly, had been living dangerously.

Patrick Ferguson spurred his horse, and with a few other officers following rode toward the northeast quarter of the encircling Patriots, toward Winston's lines. By this time in the battle, men had intermingled in companies scattered around the mountain. Among the men there was John Gilleland, one of Sevier's militiamen and the surveyor of Jonesborough, a man who had come over the mountains to defend the life he was making in the western waters. He drew a bead on Ferguson as the major rode toward him. He pulled the trigger. The flint hit the frissan, but nothing happened. Misfire. He called over to his comrade Robert Young, "There's Ferguson — shoot him!" Taking aim on the checkered duster, the 62-year-old Watauga Valley militiaman, muttered, "I'll try, and see what Sweet-Lips can do," that being the name of his rifle and the pet name for his bride back home. He pulled the trigger. The pan flashed, the barrel erupted, the ball flew. The shot was true and struck Ferguson, knocking him from his horse. His foot caught in the stirrup, some said, and his horse ran wildly around the top of the mountain, dragging the body of the hated Ferguson with it.

The major's body was found to have multiple wounds (Draper reported six to eight. McBee personally counted nine). Indeed, several other militiamen claimed the privilege of having dispatched the arrogant Patrick Ferguson.[48] "On examining the dead body of their great chief," James Collins wrote, "it appeared that almost fifty rifles must have been leveled at him, at the same time; seven rifle balls had passed through his body. Both of this arms were broken, and his hat and clothing were literally shot to pieces."[49] Some of the Tories carried the body in a blanket to a spring at the edge of the hill and propped up the body. Ferguson may have already expired, but if not, he soon did.

**Major Patrick Ferguson was shot from his horse, which precipitated the end of the battle. Several men claimed to have fired their rifles and hit the officer on horseback. A marker on the northeast slope of the battlefield stands to commemorate the spot on the mountain where he was shot.**

**Damned Unfair**

"The action continued an hour and five minutes," wrote Anthony Allaire in his diary, "but their numbers enabled them to surround us. The North Carolina regiment [Loyalist militia] seeing this, and numbers being out of ammunition, gave way, which naturally threw the rest of the militia into confusion. Our poor little detachment [Rangers], which consisted of only seventy men when we marched to the field of action, were all killed and wounded but twenty; and those brave fellows were soon crowded as close as possible by the militia." With Ferguson's death, DePeyster saw that defeat was inevitable. He "saw it impossible to form six men together," continued Allaire, and "thought it necessary to surrender to save the lives of the brave men who were left."[50]

"As soon as Captain Dupoister [DePeyster] observed that Colonel [Major] Ferguson was killed," wrote Ensign Campbell, "he raised a flag and called for quarters. It was soon taken out of his hand by one of the [Patriot] officers on horseback, and raised so high that it could be seen by our line, and the firing immediately ceased. The Loyalists, at the time of their surrender, were driven into a crowd, and being closely surrounded, they could not have made any resistance."[51] "At the close of the action," wrote Benjamin Sharp, "when the British were loudly calling for quarters, but uncertain whether they would be granted, I saw the intrepid Shelby rush his horse within fifteen paces of their lines, and command them to lay down their arms, and they should have quarters. Some would call this an imprudent act; but it showed the daring bravery of the man."[52]

The moment was more confused and perilous than Campbell and Sharp related. Others in the Tory lines had already been waving white flags and continued to do so, fearful of what the closing ranks of these fearsome "shirtmen" might do. Their concerns were warranted, it seemed. "It was some time before a complete cessation of the firing on our part, could be effected," Shelby wrote. "Our men who had been scattered in the battle were continually coming up, and continued to fire, without comprehending, in the heat of the moment, what had happened."[53]

Joseph Sevier, age 18, having heard false reports that his father, Colonel John Sevier, had been killed, continued to fire into the huddle of Tories. With tears streaming down his young cheeks, he declared, "The damned rascals have killed my father, and I'll keep loading and shooting till I kill every son of a bitch of them."[54] The huddled Tories were calling desperately, "Quarters! Quarters!" as some of the Patriots continued to fire into them. Shelby rode in hard, shouting from his saddle, "Damn, you. If you want quarters, throw down your arms!"[55]

Another militiaman, Andrew Evins, age 21 and who had been under the command of Captain William Edmiston before he was killed, also continued to fire into the mass of Loyalists. Colonel Campbell ran up to him and knocked his rifle upward, shouting, "Evins, for God's Sake, don't shoot! It is murder to kill them now, for they have raised the flag."[56] Campbell attempting to regain control, repeated his order, and ran about the area shouting, "Cease firing! — for God's sake, cease firing!"[57] Joseph Sevier did stop firing, but only because his father appeared, of which he was greatly relieved.

As Campbell pleaded with his men to stop shooting, Captain DePeyster, who had raised the white flag, exclaimed in great earnestness to the animated militiaman in shirtsleeves whose name he did not yet know, "It was damned unfair! Damned unfair!" Colonel Campbell, in no mood to be lectured by a Tory officer or to engage in any banter at all with such a foe, sharply ordered DePeyster and the other officers to dismount. Then he called out, "Officers, rank by yourselves; prisoners, take off your hats, and sit down." He then ordered his own men to close up around the prisoners, making first one circle, then two, finally surrounding the prisoners with militiamen four deep. With the defeated Tories sitting in the center and the dead Major Ferguson lying on the ground nearby, Colonel William Campbell called for the men to give themselves three huzzas for Liberty.

### Don't Give Up the Hill

Near the end of the battle, Colonel Williams was shot. (Some say it happened before the surrender; Draper says after.) Thomas Young reported, "I heard a great noise & voices saying, Col. Williams is shot — I ran to him — his son Daniel had raised him up; they ran into a tent and got some water & washed his face so that he could speak. The first words he spoke were, 'For God's sake, boys, don't give up the hill.' We now had the Enemy huddled up on the top of the Mountain; they wheeled to fire a platoon over us, some of our men ran back, but I was too much fatigued to run. They fired, but without effect." Young left Williams in the care of his son and then, as he said, "returned to the field to avenge his fall."[58, 59]

### Fire Upon the Enemy

Tragedy strikes quickly, just as it did at the moment Colonel Campbell had the prisoners encircled and his men cheering for their liberty. Someone fired a shot. It could have come from a Tory foraging party returning to the encampment having heard the gunfire but being unaware of the surrender. If so, they scurried away. It could have come from reinforcements believed to be on their way under Tarleton. Or, it could have come from among the prisoners, perhaps a few conspiring to make an escape with the celebrating Patriots a little distracted. As it was, Campbell let the fear of it get the best of him. He quickly ordered his men to fire upon the enemy. "[W]e killed near a hundred of them after the surrender of the militia," wrote Joseph Hughes, one of Williams's men, "& could hardly be restrained from killing the whole of them." Hughes's number may have been too high, but the execution of more Loyalists was substantial and horrible. He added, "General Williams of So. Carolina was Kill'd after the British raised their flag to surrender by a fire from some Tories." Indeed, by some accounts Colonel James Williams apparently approached the encampment of the subdued Tories after the surrender when a shot was fired from somewhere. If Williams were struck by this single shot after the surrender, the wrath against the Tories displayed especially by Williams's men was understandable. The frenzied shooting continued until Campbell could again restore order and calm. Then the prisoners were ordered to march away from their weapons, lest they attempt an escape, and the Patriots put them under a strong guard elsewhere on the mountain. Meanwhile the Tory officers surrendered their swords to various Patriot leaders.

**Insult and Indignity**

Ferguson's body soon became an object of curiosity. Before the surrender, a Tory had attempted to pick his pockets; but, afterwards, the Patriots gathered around to gaze upon the body of the man they had so despised. Even the wounded wanted to know. Colonel Cleaveland and two other militiamen carried the wounded Lieutenant Samuel Johnson up the hill to see the defeated major. Likewise, the young Robert Henry, with wounds in his hand and thigh, went to see the body of the man he had helped defeat.[60]

The body and personal possessions of Major Ferguson were soon set upon by those who wanted some relic of the major's defeat.[61] Some

**The body of Major Patrick Ferguson was wrapped in a raw cow hide and buried with the body of Virginia Sal, one of his cooks and a supposed mistress. A marker placed in 1930, on the 150th anniversary, stands at Ferguson's traditional Scottish burial cairn. It was placed by US citizens to recognize friendship with British citizens.**

say the corpse was picked clean of mementos, but only Tarleton, who was not there, recounted any hint of the victorious Patriots desecrating the body. "The mountaineers, it is reported, used every insult and indignity, after the action," Tarleton wrote, "towards the dead body of Major Ferguson."[62] Though recorded nowhere else, it is not difficult to imagine that it could have happened, especially given Ferguson's ultimatum of October 1 issued at Dennard's Ford: "If you choose to be pissed upon forever and ever by a set of mongrels …" Still, no evidence or accounts can support any claims of such desecration.

Ferguson's body was wrapped in a raw beef's hide and buried near the spring to which he was carried. Tradition said the body of his cook, Virginia Sal, was buried with him. Recent archaeology confirmed the fact.[63]

## John Broddy

Although these Patriot militiamen were fighting for "Liberty," the freedoms they sought to secure for themselves would not extend to everyone there at King's Mountain on their behalf. Colonel William Campbell was a well-to-do planter as were several of the officers. He had brought along his manservant — an enslaved mulatto — John Broddy. When they arrived at the west end of Little King's Mountain, Campbell had left Broddy to tend to his horse, the black Bald Face, having determined that horse too skittish for the duty in battle. Campbell secured the use of another horse, a bay, from one of his men. During the course of the battle, Broddy became curious and rode forward to get a better view of the action. He was about Campbell's size and from a distance not different in complexion. He was riding the Bald Face and riding in his shirtsleeves, as Campbell was

**The Tennessee State Museum in Nashville exhibits mementos from the Battle of Kings Mountain including items that belonged to Patrick Ferguson and "Sweet-Lips," the rifle fired by Robert Young, who reportedly felled the major during the battle. The bench is made from wood salvaged from the fallen Pemberton Oak.**

attired. Such were the circumstances that led Isaac Shelby, upon spotting Broddy in the rear during the heated part of the battle to mistake him for Campbell and later impugn the bravery and courage of the overall commander of the expedition against Ferguson.[64]

Shelby wrote in 1823, "While I was attempting to rally the men, at the distance of about two hundred yards from where the scene of the action had been, I looked down the mountain, and saw Col. Campbell, sitting on the bald-face black horse, about two hundred yards further off, apparently looking right at me. He was in the same trim — with his coat off — that he had put himself in to fight the battle. I stopped my horse, and raised myself up in my stirrups, to show him that I saw him. He did not move while I looked at him."[65] Shelby may have firmly believed what he thought he had seen, but bolstering his own reputation at the time was politically motivated. The United States found itself again fighting the British in the War of 1812, and Shelby wanted his war record to offset concerns about his age as he again ran for the governorship of Kentucky. He wanted to be seen as the real commander of the Overmountain campaign.[66] Thus, three decades after the battle, Shelby's interpretation of events created a firestorm among veterans of the Battle of Kings Mountain concerning the courage and valor of their chosen commander, Colonel William Campbell.

# Homeward Bound

## The Night After the Battle

As the night passed on King's Mountain, the Patriots were anxious for the dawn. They were eager to get away from the battlefield where they feared Banastre Tarleton and his Light Horse might appear at any moment to attempt a rescue of the prisoners.[1] They also were in need of provisions, having brought none for themselves in their overnight dash to catch Patrick Ferguson and discovering so little among the seventeen wagons they captured of the major's command. The region was sparsely settled; it was a difficult place in which to supply an army. Moreover, what little had been available in the region had already been plundered or foraged by roving bands of Tories, by detachments of the British Legion, and by companies of Whig militiamen, all to the detriment of the civilians.[2]

After securing the prisoners, the Patriots turned their attention to their casualties. "The groans of the wounded and dying on the mountain were truly affecting," wrote John Spelts, "begging piteously for a little water; but, in the hurry, confusion, and exhaustion of the Whigs, these cries, when emanating from the Tories, were little heeded."[3]

The reports after the battle of the number of casualties varied, but later some consensus formed around the losses. The Patriots had suffered 26 killed, and 66 wounded. Ferguson's corps of Loyalists, both

Provincials and militia, suffered 225 killed and 123 wounded; 716 surrendered as prisoners.[4] The entire corps under Ferguson, a good portion of Cornwallis's British Legion had been neutralized in an hour. The British surgeon, Dr. Uzal Johnson, with some assistants tended to the wounded on both sides. He remained behind the following day as well to continue aiding the surviving victims.

One of the wounded, likely tended by Johnson, was William Moore, a militiaman from the Holston River valley. He served under Colonel Campbell and had ridden with him previously against the Tories on New River.[5] Moore's leg was so severely damaged in the battle, it was amputated in the field. His comrades removed him from the battlefield the next day, but they left him at the home of some good soul nearby who was willing to look after him. When his fellow militiamen returned home and told his wife of Moore's plight, she saddled her horse and, beginning her trip in November, as Draper put it, she "rode all the long and dreary journey" to King's Mountain. Such was the hardy nature of the pioneer stock of men and women who dared live on the frontier. She nursed her husband to health well enough to take him home where he recovered and lived another 45 years.[6]

**A Melancholy Sight**

"The victors encamped on the mountain that night," wrote Shelby "and the next morning took up their line of march for the mountains under a bright sun, the first they had seen for many days."[7] The brightening weather mirrored the prospects of the Patriots and filled them with a longing to return home as soon as possible. They had defended their homes by excising the threat from the frontier. Now, they only wanted to see their families again and to put behind them the horrors and discomforts of the past two weeks.

Benjamin Sharp recalled, "The next day [October 8], as soon as we could bury our dead, and provide litters to carry our wounded, we marched off to regain the upper country for fear of being intercepted by a detachment from the army of Lord Cornwallis, for we were partly behind his quarters, between him and the British garrison of Ninety Six. A British surgeon, with some assistants, were left to attend their wounded; but the wounded Tories were unprovided for, and their dead left for their bones to bleach upon the mountain."[8]

The sound of the battle had carried across the Carolina countryside. The enormous roar of musket and rifle fire brought to the battlefield at least two companies of militiamen from Lincoln County under captains John Weir and Robert Shannon, but they arrived after the battle was over. Of more use after the surrender was the arrival of Ellen McDowell and her daughter Jane. Having heard the shooting from their home, they made their way to King's Mountain where they moved around the battlefield tending to different wounded soldiers. They remained there for several days.[9]

After the firing ceased, families and neighbors came to the mountain to look for loved ones. James Collins wrote: "Next morning, which was Sunday, the scene became really distressing; the wives and children of the poor Tories came in, in great numbers. Their husbands, fathers, and brothers, lay dead in heaps, while others lay wounded or dying; a melancholy sight indeed!"[10]

As the Patriots moved out, Colonel Lacey remained behind with 200 men. He gave paroles to the Tories who were unable to march away. Colonel Campbell remained behind as well to finish the job of the burials. They buried the dead Tories in a large, common shallow grave and the men of Ferguson's British Legion in a separate place. Collins continued his description, "We proceeded to bury the dead, but it was badly done; they were thrown into convenient piles, and covered with old logs, the bark of old trees, and rocks; yet not so as to secure them from becoming a prey to the beasts of the forest, or the vultures of the air; and the wolves became so plenty, that it was dangerous for any one to be out at night for several miles around; also the hogs in the neighborhood, gathered into the place, to devour the flesh of men, inasmuch, numbers chose to live on little meat rather than eat their hogs, though they were very fat; half of the dogs in the country were said to be mad, and were put to death. I saw, myself, in passing the place, a few weeks after, all parts of the human frame, lying scattered in every direction."[11]

### The March Homeward

Before leaving, the Patriots rolled the captured wagons over their campfires and burned them. To have taken them along would have encumbered their progress in retreating. Colonel Lacey and others of Sumter's men, no doubt, recalled when Tarleton overtook them on Fishing Creek in August while they were lumbering north with their caravan of captured booty. Those men, wiser for the experience, would not make the same mistake. Their goal was to escape the region as quickly as they could. They understood — or feared — that Tarleton was on his way to attack them and to rescue the prisoners. Indeed, Major Ferguson's failure had been in not retreating as quickly as possible after he learned of the Patriot's pursuit. The Patriots would not share that misstep. They headed west, making their way quickly for the safety of the mountains and remote regions farther north.

Along with the wagons, the Patriots captured a reported 1,500 stand of arms, but some of those weapons were old and used just for training. The Patriots decided to take with them what useable weapons they could and to let the prisoners carry them. The militiamen removed the flints from the locks, so the guns would not fire, and then paraded the prisoners by the pile of arms, telling them to pick up a musket. Some of the healthier men were forced to carry two.

Few spoils of the victory were taken along, save a few souvenirs of a vanquished foe which the Patriots had stripped from the body of Ferguson. The swords of the Legion officers, surrendered as gestures of submission, were also kept by some. One of the colonels rode off the mountain astride Ferguson's horse, the one from whose saddle the despised Scotsman was shot. Draper said, Colonel Cleaveland, whose own horse had been shot from under him, was given, by general consent, "Ferguson's white charger."[12] Colonel Lacey's biographer, A.S. Salley, recounted that Lacey was given the "black English charger" of the defeated major.[13]

The Patriots set off for home following for a while the same route they had taken to King's Mountain, at least as far as the Broad River. They departed the battlefield throughout the late morning and marched their 700-some prisoners under the guard of 800 victors. The wounded Whigs who could not walk were carried away in horse litters — canvas slings fashioned from Tory tents and blankets, and suspended between two poles fastened at each end to the flanks and shoulders of horses walking in tandem. After paroling the hapless victims, the Patriots left the wounded Tories on the battlefield to fend for themselves.

**Resigned to His Fate**

The wound suffered by Colonel James Williams late in the battle and under uncertain circumstances, continued to weaken the colonel over night. He was in a delicate condition when his men put him in a horse litter and removed him from the battlefield. The party carrying Colonel Williams had gone no more than three miles from King's Mountain, when they saw that the colonel was quickly fading. They stopped. He passed away in the early afternoon, no doubt in the presence and care of his two young sons, Daniel and Joseph. The colonel's devoted men were at first determined to convey home his body for burial at his Little River plantation, but they changed their resolve on that matter during the day.

That Sunday, the entourage covered some 16 miles. "About sunset we met the footmen they had left at Green river," wrote Lenoir. He added, as evidence of the deprived conditions in which these victors found themselves, "[they] provided a plenty of rations, & the Whigs who had fought the battle were almost famished."[14] Sharp's account confirmed that some of the men had not eaten since Friday evening at the Cowpens. He continued: "That afternoon we met Capt. Neil coming on with his detachment, and encamped for the night on a large deserted Tory plantation, where was a sweet potato patch sufficiently large to supply the whole army. This was most fortunate for not one in fifty of us had tasted food for the last two days and nights, that is, since we left the Cowpens. Here the next morning, we buried Col. Williams, who had died of his wounds on the march the day before. We still proceeded towards the mountains as fast as our prisoners could bear."[15]

After making camp for the night along the Broad River, the militiamen under Williams's command buried their revered leader with military honors and the firing of volleys.[16] (Years later, his body was reinterred at its present location.) Joseph Kerr, the spy who served under Williams, remembered his passing: "A mortal wound in the groin … terminated his life on the next day after the battle before twelve

**The remains of Colonel James Williams were moved and reinterred in Gaffney, South Carolina. The grave and markers are at 210 N. Limestone Street (SC Hwy 150) at the Cherokee County administration offices.**

o'clock. [I] well remember conversing with him after the battle. He knew he must die and did so cheerfully[,] resigned to this fate."[17]

### Those Villains Divided Our Baggage

The conditions of the retreating Patriots did not improve much in the following days. Thomas Young noted, "After the battle we marched upon the head waters of Cane Creek, in North Carolina, with our prisoners, where we all come very near starving to death. The country was very thinly settled, and provisions could not be had for love or money. I thought green pumpkins, sliced and fried, about the sweetest eating I ever had in my life!"[18] The prisoners were not treated to such bounty. Anthony Allaire, then a prisoner, recorded his sarcasm in his diary during the forced march, "In the evening their liberality extended so far as to send five old shirts to nine of us, as a change of linen — other things in like proportion."[19] He was an officer of the British Legion thusly treated. The ranks of Tory militiamen faired much worse. When food could be found, it was offered to the prisoners uncooked. With the militiamen encircling the prisoners, they flung green pumpkins and raw corn into the huddle of hungry, near-starving men, "like so many farmer's swine," Draper wrote.[20]

On the tenth, the party made its way in a northwest direction toward Gilbert Town, "up main Broad river, crossing First Broad and Sandy run," Draper noted the route, covering some twenty miles. That day six Gage brothers, all prisoners, conspired to escape, wanting to end the dreadful treatment they endured with no food and endless marching. One of them was ill, or pretended to be so, and the others took turns carrying him on their backs. They lagged farther and farther back in the entourage until late in the day. As the march continued into the night and they were crossing a deep creek, they fell down in the water and waited for the rear guard to pass over them in the dark. By such craftiness and courage did they and many others escape along the retreat march. The number of prisoners began to dwindle.[21]

But, not all the reductions in number of prisoners was by escape. Unfortunately, the Patriots dispatched more than a few. Along the march on October 11, Colonel Thomas Brandon, a close friend of the deceased Colonel Williams, discovered that one of the prisoners had ducked into a hollow tree along the road, hoping to escape. The "rough, impulsive Irishman," as Draper described him, dragged the man, burdened with two muskets, out of the hiding place and hacked him to death with his sword. Other such cruelties against the prisoners were so frequent apparently, that Colonel Campbell issued a warning to his men as part of his General Order issued on October 11. If they could not "restrain the disorderly manner of slaughtering and disturbing the prisoners," he would readily use harsh measures and punishments "upon delinquents as [would] put a stop to it."[22] At the hands of revengeful Patriot militiamen moving anxiously through a region deprived of sustenance, the retreat had become something of a death march for the prisoners.

On the 11th, the entourage passed through Gilbert Town, where the prisoners were placed in pens while the Patriots rested. These pens, only days before, had been used by the occupying Tories to hold captured Patriots. The moment of revenge was sweet for some who gloated in their victory and taunted the prisoners. In the afternoon, the guards marched their prisoners on to the home of Colonel John Walker, who lived five miles from Gilbert Town, on the east side of Cane Creek and half a mile above its mouth. They remained in camp there on the 12th, taking liberties with the possessions, if not the personages, of the prisoners. "Those villains divided our baggage," Allaire wrote in his diary with the expectations of a gentleman officer, "although they had promised on their word we should have it all."[23] Exasperated at the militiamen's betrayal of a pledge that he would have all his baggage for tending to the wounded, Dr. Uzal Johnson, wrote, with a hint of his building vindictiveness, "Where honour binds, I find Promise can be broke. … Would not hemp do the business better?"[24]

The day's rest and the slow progress of the march put the Patriots, by Shelby's later reckoning, only forty miles from the battlefield in a week.[25] As it was, Cornwallis had ordered Tarleton, on October 10, to reinforce Ferguson — by then dead three days. Tarleton rode off with light infantry, some British Legion, and a three-pounder cannon with orders to "reinforce Ferguson wherever he could find him, and to draw his corps to the Catawba, if after the junction, advantage could not be obtained over the mountaineers." If he found Ferguson defeated, he was to prevent the "victorious Americans" from entering South Carolina. Tarleton marched to a ford on the Catawba River, where he first learned of Ferguson's fate.[26] Consequently and yet unknown to Campbell, Shelby, and Cleaveland, "Bloody Ban" was not pursuing the

**During the withdrawal, some of the wounded Patriots were left under the care of the community at Brittain Church. Not all of them survived. The headstone of Lieutenant Thomas McCullough, Virginia Rifleman, reads: "Here lies the body of Lieut. Thomas McCullough, belonging to Col. Campbell's regiment Virginia who lost his life in and for the honorable Just and virtious (sic) cause of liberty at the defeating Col. Ferguson's infamous company of bandity. Kings Mountain October 7, 1780"**

retreating Patriots, after all.

## Died Like Romans

On Friday, October 13, the Patriots and their prisoners "moved six miles to Bickerstaff's plantation," Allaire wrote. (It was later known also as Biggerstaff's Old Fields or the Red Chimneys.) This Tory plantation sat along Robertson's (Roberson's) Creek, just west of Flint Hill, and about eight miles northeast of Gilbert Town. The owner, a Loyalist leader at Ramsour's Mill, Captain Aaron Biggerstaff, had been mortally wounded at King's Mountain and left for dead.[27] The militiamen and the prisoners remained at the Biggerstaff's plantation two nights, no doubt unsettling the widow, Martha.[28]

On the 14th, William Campbell issued general orders declaring those militiamen who had left the march without permission to be deserters. He needed all those men to conduct the prisoners to Bethabara. He was plagued more, perhaps, by "the complaints of the inhabitants on account of the plundering parties who issue[d] out from the camp, and indiscriminately rob[bed] both Whig and Tory, leaving our friends, I believe, in a worse situation than the enemy would have done."[29] The undisciplined militiamen, acting independently as was their wont, continued to be a problem for the militia officers.

During the march, the officers and men of the North Carolina and South Carolina Patriot militia had looked over their prisoners. Some recognized a number of the prisoners from previous encounters as troublemakers and scoundrels. They approached Colonel Campbell about the need to deal with these "robbers, house-burners, parole breakers, and assassins," as Draper described them, lest they escape and continue their Tory depredations on Patriot families. Others reminded the colonel that many of their Patriot friends had been hanged at Camden, Ninety Six, and at Augusta quite recently. Disguising their desires for revenge as justice, some of these men believed that retaliation was necessary to quiet the Toryism rampant in the countryside.[30]

Campbell consented to their requests and agreed to convene a court to review the complaints against certain persons. As they were in North Carolina, they sought to convene a civil court under North Carolina law, which they knew required only any two magistrates to summon a jury. As many such men were among their officers, the Patriots proceeded to conduct trials of the prisoners against whom complaints were made. "Ten O'clock in the Morning, their Guard Paraded and formed a circle," wrote Dr. Johnson. "Capt DePeyster and the rest of us Officers were ordered within the ring. They then proceeded to trying the [Loyalist] Militiamen for treason."[31] Conducted more as a court-martial, the trials proceeded as twelve officers heard the charges. Conferring the appearance of some civility to the proceedings, Ensign Campbell wrote, "The court was conducted orderly, and witnesses were called and examined in each case."[32] Johnson took a different view: "We were Spectators of this disagreeable Day's work."[33]

Shelby wrote later, "Under this law, thirty six men were tried, and found guilty of breaking open houses, killing the men, and turning the women and children out of doors, and burning the houses."[34] The evidence presented might have been hurried or prejudiced, but it was nonetheless persuasive. Captain Walter Gilkey was condemned for shooting a lad in front of his house simply for saying his father, the partisan they were hoping to catch, was not at home. The boy had been wounded in the arm, had survived, and was there with the Patriot militiamen, to testify to Gilkey's conduct. John McFall had sought to capture Martin Davenport, a partisan, at home but missed him. He and his men abused the family forcing the wife to fix them a meal and beating a young son for refusing to tend to the feeding of their horses.

Colonel Ambrose Mills was accused, without much evidence, of inciting Cherokee attacks against Patriot families on the South Carolina frontier. If the consequences had not been so dire, the accusation might have been seen as laughably contrived. The Cherokees had killed his first wife, Mourning Stone, and children during the French and Indian War; and, he had ridden against the Cherokees in the 1776 campaign. But, Mills had conspired with David Fanning in 1778 to raise a corps of 500 Loyalists with plans to rally beneath the Royal standard in St. Augustine, Florida. He was betrayed, arrested, and thrown into the gaol in Salisbury. Although he had been released by the Patriots, Mills had fought against the Patriots in recent battles[35] Still, the notion that he, at 58, was a dangerous man — a murderer and assassin — was grossly overstated.[36]

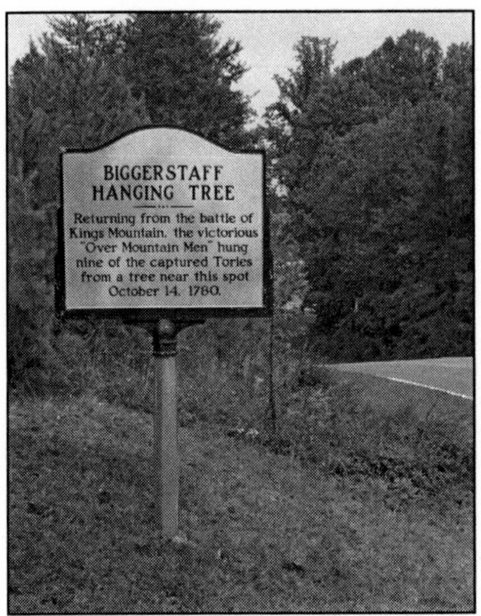


**In camp at Biggerstaff's farm in eastern Rutherford County, the withdrawing Patriot militiamen tried 32 Tory prisoners and hanged nine of them, including Colonel Ambrose Mills. The marker is west of Sunshine on Green Street, about ten miles northeast of Bypass US Hwy 74 in Ruth (adjacent to Rutherfordton), North Carolina.**

The officers considered each charge, but they sometimes differed in their opinion of what conduct deserved the most severe consequences. Major McDowell favored leniency for McFall, but Cleaveland declared in an outburst, "No such man ought to be allowed to live." Other officers, such at Colonel Thomas Brandon, were also adamant about dispatching the guilty. Such was the victims' plight. McFall was one among the guilty, variously reported as numbering between 30 and 40, with 32 being the most-often cited number of condemned.[37]

Others fared better in the hearing of evidence. James Crawford, the Overmountain militiaman who deserted Sevier's company at the Yellow Gap to warn Ferguson, was excused for his traitorous conduct. Colonel Sevier interceded for his old neighbor. Samuel Chambers, who had fled the Patriots with Crawford on their mission as spies, was excused because of his youthfulness, on the notion that Crawford had unduly influenced him. Moreover, the pair reported that Ferguson had not treated them so well. It had been a week after they had first reported to the Scottish major that the pursuing army of one thousand militiamen was after him and no such army had appeared. Ferguson had decided Crawford was guilty of bringing a false report. He condemned Crawford to hang on the evening of October 7.[38] Thus, Crawford, who by rights was a deserter and a traitor, had been spared one fate, undeserved, by the successful attack of the men whom he had betrayed. He was spared another possible hanging, a deserved fate, perhaps, by the same men.

Shelby wrote, "The trial was concluded late at night. The execution of the law was as summary as the trial."[39] The Patriots marched the 32 men out to a sturdy oak and dropped three ropes over a limb. With pine-knot torches casting a low amber light into the darkness, they surrounded the condemned prisoners four deep. Draper wrote, "They were swung off three at a time and left suspended at the place of execution."[40] One of the Georgians, Captain Paddy Carr, a rather stern and unpleasant fellow but a good soldier, pointed to the dangling victims and declared, "Would to God every tree in the wilderness bore such fruit as that!"[41]

Dr. Johnson recorded a more sobering account. "What increased this melancholy scene was the *(sic)* seeing Mrs. Mills take leave of her Husband, and two of Chitwood's Daughters take leave of their Father. The latter were comforted with being told their Father was pardoned. They went to our Fire where we had made a Shed to keep out the Rain. They had scarce set [sat] down when News was brought that their Father was dead." He continued, "Here words can scarce describe the Melancholy Scene, the two Young Ladies swooned away, and continued in fits all Night. Mrs. Mills, with a Young child in her Arms, set [sat] out all Night in the Rain with her Husband's Corps[e], and not even a Blanket to cover her from the inclemency of the Weather."[42]

After nine of the condemned had been hanged, the next three were tied up. One was Isaac Baldwin, a particularly notorious Tory robber and plunderer known well around Burke County. As he was about to be executed, his young brother ran from the crowd in a fit of grief and despair, hugging his brother and crying out pitifully. While everyone present was transfixed by this touching display of affection, the lad managed to cut through the straps confining his brother. In an instant, the prisoner darted through the lines of Patriots surrounding the condemned and escaped into the dark woods. No one pursued him. Three more were tied up and prepared to be hanged, when Colonel Shelby proposed that enough was enough. The other officers agreed and thus the other condemned prisoners were spared execution. Accounts say they were then reprieved by the "commanding officer," but because Campbell was from Virginia, some other officer, perhaps Cleveland or Shelby, may have issued these pardons for convictions produced under North Carolina law.[43]

Lieutenant Anthony Allaire recorded in his journal his own view of those events: "Saturday, 14$^{th}$. Twelve field officers were chosen to try the militia prisoners — particularly those who had the most influence in the country. They condemned thirty — in the evening they began to execute Lieut.-Col. Mills, Capt. Wilson, Capt. Chitwood, and six others, who unfortunately fell a sacrifice to their infamous mock jury. Mills, Wilson, and Chitwood died like Romans — the others were reprieved."[44] Johnson used the same phrase, declaring, "They died like Romans, saying they died for their King and his Laws."[45]

**A Very Disagreeable Road**

After most of the convicted and condemned Tories had been spared the noose at Biggerstaff's on October 14, one of them, in particular, showed his gratitude. He went to Colonel Shelby at 2 o'clock in the morning and declared that a woman had brought the news to some of the prisoners (most likely while at Gilbert Town) that Tarleton was most certainly on his way to recover the captured Loyalist militia and British Legion and that he would arrive the next day. Upon hearing that news, the Patriots decided to press on immediately.[46]

The pace and urgency of the march changed. Allaire recorded on the 15th: "Moved at five o'clock in the morning. Marched all day through the rain — a very disagreeable road. We got to Catawba [River], and forded it at Island Ford, about ten o'clock at night. Our march was thirty-two miles. All the men were worn out with fatigue and fasting — the prisoners having no bread or meat for two days before. We officers were allowed to go to Col. McDowell's [Quaker Meadows], where we lodged comfortably." The prisoners had been on a forced march for eight days with little food. The Patriot militiamen had beaten some and executed others. The prisoners' prospects for survival did not look good to them. Allaire took note of the outcome of this turn in the prisoners' attitude. He wrote on the 15th, "About one hundred prisoners made their escape on this march."[47] Johnson estimated fewer but emphasized the prisoners' desperate condition. He wrote that "thirty-odd of the Prisoners made their escape on the March, tho very much fatigued and all most famished with hunger, having no Meat for three Days."[48]

The plight of the Patriot militiamen was not much different that day. "We set off early next morning," wrote Benjamin Sharp, "and shortly after the rain began to fall in torrents and continued the whole day."

**On the 8th day of marching away from the battlefield, the Patriots and their prisoners arrived at Quaker Meadows where they rested for a day. On a hilltop near the McDowell homes, the Quaker Meadows Cemetery (on Branstrom Drive) contains the graves of many notable persons of the revolutionary era, including the graves of Charles McDowell and Joseph McDowell.**

They quickened their march, wanting to cross the Catawba River before it became impassible. Perhaps such an urgent and demanding pace in such disagreeable weather enabled so many prisoners to slip off into the woods. In any case, the party marched 32 miles, crossing the Catawba River near midnight and discovering the next morning that it had become swollen beyond passage. They felt secure from Tarleton's pursuit, if, in fact, he had been riding after them. They stopped at Quaker Meadows, and Major McDowell rode along the line welcoming the men, telling them this was his plantation, and inviting them to use the rail fencing to build fires. "I suppose everyone felt grateful for this generous offer," wrote Sharp, "for it was rather cold, being the last of October, and every one, from the Commander-in-Chief to the meanest private, was as wet as if he had just been dragged through the Catawba River."[49]

The withdrawing Patriots and prisoners rested for the day. Some of the Overmountain Men took their leave of the expedition from Quaker Meadows, marching west and conveying their wounded with them toward the mountains. The men under Shelby and Sevier, and the footmen under Campbell departed. Colonel Lacey's men also departed for South Carolina. The remainder of the Patriots, some five or six hundred, barely outnumbered the prisoners they escorted. The Wilkes and Surry troops under Cleaveland and Winston along with the mounted troops under Campbell made up the bulk of the guards. Campbell and Shelby accompanied the prisoners, too. Shelby had been burned once before by turning his prisoners over to the control of another. Perhaps that memory of Colonel Williams's misrepresentation figured into Shelby's plans to help escort them to their destination. Or perhaps Shelby had other reasons for continuing on to the Moravian towns. Cleaveland most certainly knew those communities as the home of industrious German settlers — farmers and mechanics — people who could be relied upon to provide for their needs even if the visitors were unexpected.

**Robert Sevier**

Riding back to his Nolichucky River homestead, Captain Robert Sevier was nursing a serious battlefield wound. He had been hit near the kidney by buckshot as he bent over to pick up his ramrod. Dr. Johnson tended to him in the field, attempting to remove the lead ball. He was not able to remove it then, so he dressed the wound and told Sevier to rest for several days when he would then be able to remove the shot. If Sevier traveled before that, the doctor assured him, the kidney would inflame and he would die, most assuredly in no more than nine days.

Sevier was anxious about remaining behind should Tarleton then sweep through the area, so he decided to take his chances and ride for home. Departing the expedition at Quaker Meadows, he headed for the mountains. In the company of his nephew, James Sevier, and nine days after the battle, Robert Sevier ascended Bright's Trace on the eastern slope rising toward the Yellow Mountain Gap. The pair stopped to prepare a meager meal near Davenport Springs, when the captain fell ill. Robert Sevier, a wounded veteran of the battle, died within an hour. James wrapped his uncle's body in a blanket and buried him on a small rise, returning home alone with such sad news for the Sevier family.[50]

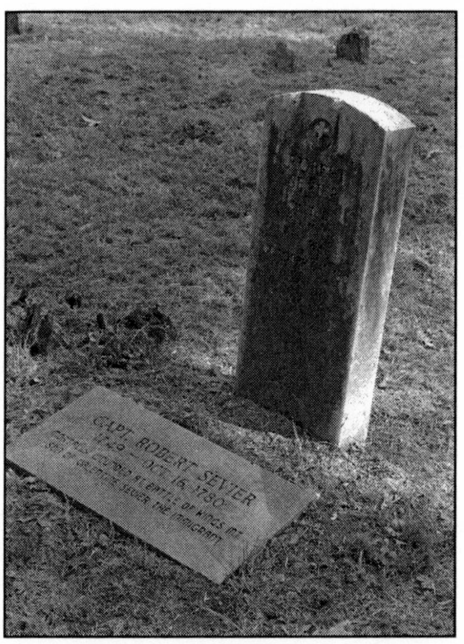


**Captain Robert Sevier died on October 16 during his return trip home after being wounded during the battle at King's Mountain. The marked grave is among others in a cemetery on private land near Davenport Springs about four miles northeast of Spruce Pine, North Carolina; public access is restricted.**

# The Shallow Ford

After the Patriot militia had vented their anger at the Tories by hanging nine of the convicted at Biggerstaff's plantation, they continued their withdrawal from the battlefield, then some 40 to 50 miles behind them. The Patriots were marching their prisoners toward Bethabara, a Moravian community in Surry County[1], still seven days' travel away, down the Yadkin River. There the Patriots expected to find succor and sustenance. As a group, the Moravians were neither Tory nor Patriot. Most had refused, out of conscience, to take the Oath of Allegiance as written and had implored the North Carolina Assembly to alter it in a manner that would enable them to affirm their allegiance without violating their religious convictions. Meanwhile, at a practical level in their daily lives, the Moravians worked diligently in remaining neutral in the conflict between inhabitants of the region. The Patriots, however, often accused them of being Loyalists simply because they tolerated and provisioned men from both sides. To the credit of their industry as a community, the Moravians also worked diligently to keep up with the demands continually imposed upon them by the visitations of various bands of soldiers. The Moravians in both Bethabara and Bethania had been much disturbed during recent weeks. The middle of October brought more of the same as the victors at King's Mountain and their prisoners continued their march toward Bethabara.

## They Were Very Wild

On October 12, the Bethanians wrote: "Before dawn Colonel Gideon Wright and about a hundred men arrived, and inquired whether any Liberty Men were here. They were assured that at the present moment none could be found here. They remained on their horses, and were served there, and those who wished received bread, and then they set off toward Bethabara without doing anything else. It can be considered a direct act of Providence that the last of the Liberty Men set out scarcely an hour earlier, for the town has been full of them since Monday [October 9]. Before midnight another company of more than a hundred passed, also for the king."[2] Meanwhile, in Bethabara, they recorded on the same day, "A company of Whigs had to be fed here. They went on toward the Shallow Ford, and … met a strong company of Tories. The Whigs refused to surrender, and there was a hand-to-hand fight, in which the Tories killed one or two, and took several prisoners. Many of the Tories came here during the night to get bread to eat, but were very mannerly; they were in this neighborhood to see after the Whigs."[3]

The next morning, the record continued, "sixteen horsemen [Whigs] arrived; they were very wild and threatened that this town would be burned to the ground within a few days," because as they were riding toward Bethabara two guns were fired at them. The Moravians assured

**Bethania was visited frequently by Tory and Whig militia. Bethania, established in 1759, is today a community of private homes and is a National Historic Landmark in Forsyth County, NC.**

**Both Loyalist and Whig militia rode into the Moravian towns of Bethania and Bethabara demanding food and information about opposing forces. Historic Bethabara Park hosts interpretive events among the ruins and reconstructions of the 18th century town.**

them "that it was probably the act of spies, whom they had not seen." Nevertheless, the men took away a horse and musket.[4]

The Tories and Whigs were both beating about the Yadkin River valley in the vicinity of the Moravian towns. With so many of the Patriot militiamen — Liberty Men as the Moravians termed them — gone from Surry County with Major Joseph Winston, the Tory faction rose to action. Colonel Gideon Wright and his brother, Colonel Hezekiah Wright, banded their Loyalist men together. On October 3, one party of Tories raided the county seat of Richmond where they killed the sheriff, a Mr. Hedgspeth.[5] Surry's county seat had been built on land owned by Patriots Martin Armstrong and William Sheppard after moving the government from its previous location on land owned by Gideon Wright. The Tories raided and ruined Sheppard's home.[6] The animosity between these factions was as much personal as political. Hezekiah Wright had been severely whipped on September 9 in Bethania by Liberty Men under the command of Captain Isaac

Campbell, although some of the Moravians had tried to stop it. Wright escaped his captors the next day.[7] Indeed, the Liberty Men had perpetrated such injustices against Loyalist and neutral citizens, that they were widely despised — and feared. On October 8, a Sunday, the Tories returned, again attacking Richmond and "tak[ing] back the things of which they had been robbed."[8]

During the following week, on October 11, General Jethro Sumner at Camp Yadkin Ford near Salisbury learned from Colonel Joseph Williams that Colonel Gideon Wright had convened 300 to 400 Loyalists in Surry County and was looking for a way to join up with Cornwallis's army in Charlotte Town. In response, Sumner sent forward, on October 13, Colonel Paisley (Peasley) with a company to disperse Wright's Tories and to prevent their union with Cornwallis.[9] The reputation of the Wrights caused due concern. Major Mark Armstrong had written to Sumner on October 7 from Surry County advising, "… of a truth my present Circumstances are bad. … The County at this time is exposed, for almost every good man that could be collected is now in service … Colo. Wright & his Brother are at the head of these Banditts of Plunderers, whose ignorance is to be dreaded, having not the least principles of Honor or honesty."[10]

Meanwhile, four companies of Virginia Whig militia from Montgomery County under Major Joseph Cloyd were moving south to join with Colonel William Campbell's men in his pursuit of Major Ferguson. Numbering 160 men, they were two weeks late in their departure behind Arthur Campbell's other troops who had joined William Campbell at Sycamore Shoals, but they were no less committed to helping stop the British invasion. Some of these men under captains George Pearis (Parris) and Abraham Trigg moved on foot up the New River from the Lead Mines, "performing a most fatiguing march … nearly to its source, through a most rugged and mountainous country"[11] and crossed into the Yadkin River valley. Others came through the Flour Gap and descended into the Moravian towns from the north. They mustered under captains Isaac Campbell and Henry Francis. An express may have informed captains Pearis and Trigg of the victory at King's Mountain, and that same, or another, express told them of the Tory uprising in Surry County where they could be of service still. The men marched hurriedly east toward the Moravian towns.

Concerned also about the Tory uprisings of early October, Andrew Carr, who lived about 15 miles west of the Yadkin River, rode to Charlotte Town to see General William Lee Davidson, who gave him command of 52 men. Carr and his company returned to Surry County to patrol and confront, if they could, the Tory band of the Wrights. Along the lower Yadkin River valley, the remnants of the Southern Department of the Continental Army remained aware of the Loyalists' movements behind them as they faced toward Cornwallis and his considerable army of the British Legion approaching North Carolina from Camden.

**We Are Whipped**

The local Liberty Men were not waiting around for any reinforcements. They were not likely even aware of the dispatching of Peasley or Carr or the movement of the Virginia militia from Montgomery County. Acting in their own interests, the local Patriots mustered together about 150 men, the remainders of several companies who had sent most of their men in pursuit of Ferguson. They were patrolling their region, expecting to confront any bands of Tories. With great fortune, these Patriot militiamen fell in with the Virginians on the west side of the Shallow Ford probably on the evening of

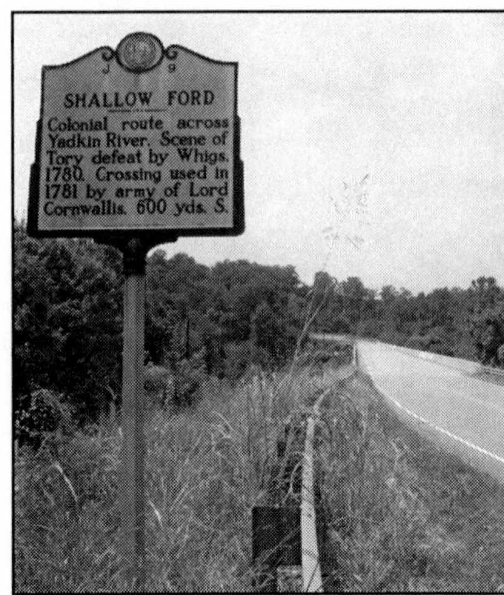


**The Shallow Ford over the Yadkin River was a prominent spot for crossing the river because of its solid rock outcrop. The ford is downstream from the bridge on Shallowford Road on the Forsyth-Yadkin county line.**

October 13, if not before. On the morning of October 14 about nine o'clock, the combined North Carolina and Virginia militia force was riding along the Mulberry Fields Road about a mile west of the Shallow Ford when the united party rounded a bend in the road and saw an approaching band of Tories coming west from the river. Each party was startled and cried out a warning to its men of the approaching enemy. Both sides quickly formed lines for battle, taking to the cover of the trees. Each man fired at will. Both sides were made of men who lived in the backcountry, but among the Virginians were those who knew how to fight Indian-style; and, recalled Henry Trolinger years later, "[we had] some as perfect marksmen as any in the world."[12]

Tory Captain James Bryan fell first; he and his horse receiving five rounds. He was the nephew of Tory Colonel Samuel Bryan through the colonel's brother, Morgan Bryan, Jr. James Bryan's father and uncles William, James, and Joseph Bryan had built Bryan's Station in Virginia's Kentucky County, not far from Fort Boonesborough, named for their brother-in-law, Daniel Boone. These men had found their treatment in the North Carolina community by the Liberty Men particularly troubling and sought to remove themselves from the reach and outrages of punitive partisans such as Benjamin Cleaveland. The young Captain Bryan, like his uncle Samuel, was a staunch Loyalist on the east side of the Cumberland Gap, but he fought differently on the far frontier. He had only recently returned from the Kentucky region where he had served in the summer campaign against the Shawnees alongside Squire Boone, Jr. and under General George Rogers Clark.[13] According to family tradition, when the father and son (Morgan Bryan, Jr. and James) returned together and reached North Carolina, the son rode off to join the Loyalists and the father, a Patriot, rode off to join the men pursuing Patrick Ferguson.[14]

The skirmish developed quickly. Patriot Captain Henry Francis was killed by a Tory ball to the head. He fell near his son, Henry, Jr.; another son, John, fired on the Tory who had killed his father. Despite the loss of one of their captains, the Patriot militiamen kept up a steady fire and soon began to overpower the Tories, who fell back some distance into the woods where they made another stand. In the fight, Captain Isaac Campbell discovered he was not as brave as he had hoped, perhaps. He fled the battle scene, leaving his men to their own devices and fate. Eventually, the precise marksmanship of the skilled frontier Patriots was too much for the Loyalist militiamen. "After several rounds," Trolinger declared, the Tories broke and ran toward the ford where the remainder of their men was still crossing the rock ford across the Yadkin River.[15]

The first of the fleeing Tories to reach the ford called out, "We are whipped, we are whipped." This anxious declaration caused those in the river to turn about and retreat. Those still on the east side of Shallow Ford turned tail as well and rode away in haste. The Tories scattered. In the wake of the Loyalist retreat, one Ball Turner, a black man, though abandoned on the battlefield by his fellow Loyalists, continued to fire on the Patriots from ambush. Watching for the telltale puffs of gunpowder smoke, the Patriots discovered Turner's hiding place and shot him several times.[16]

The gunfire heard from a distance caught the attention of others in the area. Patriot Colonel Joseph Williams — perhaps not yet knowing of his cousin James Williams's death or even of the Patriot victory at King's Mountain — rode with his men toward the sounds of fighting. When he arrived, he stopped a man from crushing the skull of a fallen Tory with the butt of his rifle. Williams ordered the victor instead to bring the victim some water in his hat. While the Patriots were tending to their wounded, they heard the unmistakable sounds of approaching infantry. Fortunately for the militiamen, it was Colonel John Peasley (Paisly), arriving from Salisbury with some 300 men and a few mounted troops. Peasley wrote later to his commander, General Sumner, "Last Saturday [October 14], we were within almost one and a half miles of the Shallow Ford when we heard a foray. Thinking that our light infantry was engaged, we advanced with all possible speed and discovered that the Virginians and some of the Surry Troops had attacked three hundred Tories under Colonel Wright."[17]

The Patriots suffered the loss of Captain Francis and the mortal wounding of Captain Pearis. Three other Patriots were wounded as well. The Tories suffered 15 killed including Captain Bryan and a Captain Burke; a Captain Lakey was mortally wounded and captured as were three other wounded Tories. They buried Captain Francis along the road. The Tories whose bodies were not claimed by family were buried in a common grave. Dr. Bonn, the Moravian physician in Salem, sent his apprentice, Joseph Dixon, to tend to the wounded. Dixon took the victims to Bethania for treatment and care.

## Cold, Wet, and Hungry

After the Battle of Shallow Ford on October 14, the Moravians endured an invasion of demanding soldiers. As the rain began to fall that night and continued on the 15th,[18] they noted in Bethabara, "the arrival of several companies of soldiers, who were so cold and wet that arrangements had to be made to get them under shelter and where they could have fire. At the same time cattle had to be killed and bread baked for them. Toward evening Colonel [John] Paisly [Peasley] arrived with four hundred infantry … in the same condition as the others, cold, wet, and hungry. … Nearly six hundred men were asking for bread and meat from us, and there was also stealing or demanding a tithe of swine, chickens, sheep, ducks, and geese and the spring-house was emptied of all the milk and the small amount of butter. The same thing happened to the apples stored in the old store building."[19] The militia and Continentals effectively plundered Bethabara. "They forced their way into the houses," the Moravian diarist wrote, and "they seized all stores in the town and neighborhood."[20]

"More than two hundred Liberty Men were in Salem," the Moravians at Bethania recorded on October 16, "and more than six hundred in Bethabara, and they behaved badly enough."

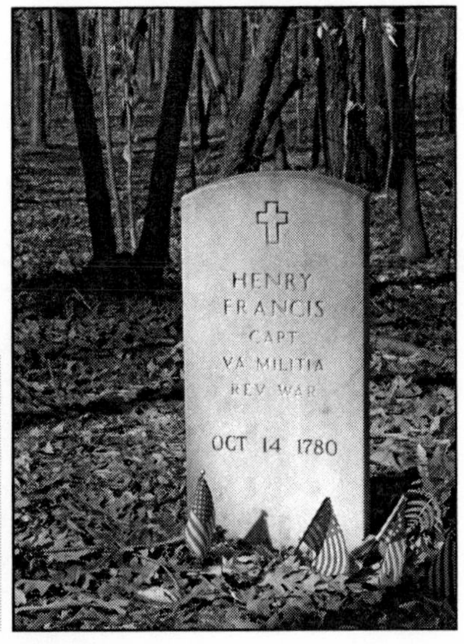


**The Patriot militiamen buried Captain Francis next to the Mulberry Fields Road about one mile west from the Shallow Ford. The old roadbed and the grave are on private property in Yadkin County.**

Their journal read on the 17th: "Everywhere it was said that the woods were full of Liberty Men on horse-back, looking for Tories …"[21] A week made no difference in the circumstances. On the 24th, the Moravians wrote, "From all sides come reports of the bad behaviour of the Liberty Men, especially those from Wilkes County." On the 27th, the Bethanians recorded, "Joseph Holder and his family passed on their way to Schemel's farm. The Liberty soldiers have taken everything from them, and beat him and his wife."[22]

On the 17th and referring to the soldiers, those at Bethabara recorded, "How glad and thankful we were to see them go, in view of the damage they had done to our garden, sheds, and indeed everywhere; and in the evening meeting, we returned our thanks to our dear Lord." The next day the Moravians busied themselves "cleaning in all the houses" and hauling wood "for they had burned more than ten cords at the Gemein Haus …"[23]

The welcome respite for the Moravians was short-lived.

**Victorious Whig militia, riding into Bethabara in need of food and shelter, accepted Moravian hospitality and then took whatever else they needed. Historic Bethabara Park includes a visitor center, foundation ruins of the town, and several buildings near the period.**

# Lord Cornwallis

While the Patriot militia had been in pursuit of Patrick Ferguson during the last week of September and the first week of October, Lord Cornwallis was occupied with this advance toward North Carolina. He marched north along the Catawba River valley from Camden, designing to invade his second rebellious Southern colony at Charlotte Town. As Colonel Banastre Tarleton recalled later, "The appearance of the royal forces, after such brilliant success, would have animated their friends, discouraged their enemies, and continued the confusion and dispersion of the American Army."[1] Instead, the British Legion entered an area devoid of adequate supplies and thin in support by friends of the government; and, many soldiers were sick with malaria. Colonel Tarleton, in fact, was laid up a week and a half with yellow fever.

### A Hornets' Nest

The countryside through which the British Legion had just passed was scarce in forage, "the depredations of both parties having made a desert of the country."[2] Although the town was named for the queen, the wife of King George III, Lord Cornwallis soon learned what was widely shared among his officers, that the people of Mecklenburg and Rowan counties "were more hostile to England than any in America."[3] Riding with the general as he entered North Carolina was another notable gentleman, who also had his hopes set high that he was enter-

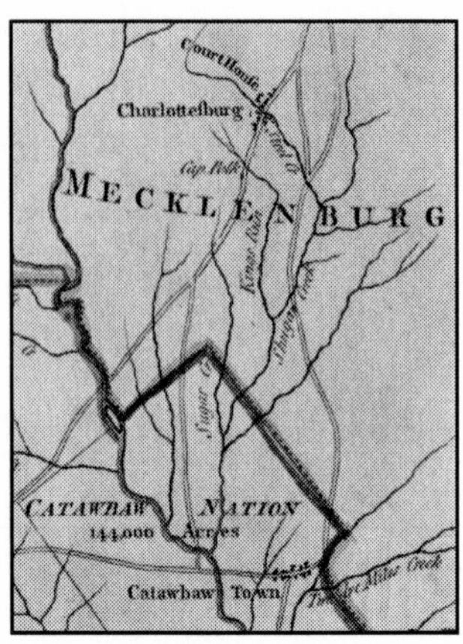


**Lord Cornwallis marched into Charlotte Town from the south. This map is a detail from "An Accurate Map of North and South Carolina With Their Indian Frontiers," Sayer & Bennett, London, 1775.**

ing a region friendly to the British — former royal governor Josiah Martin. Probably not able to resist the gratification that such an act would provide his ego, Martin immediately issued a proclamation declaring that once again North Carolina was under royal control. But, much had changed in the countryside since he escaped from Fort Johnston to the safety of *The Cruizer* in the Cape Fear River in 1775. Simply saying he was back in control did not make it so.

Cornwallis had ordered his advance troops to cross the Catawba River at Blair Ford on September 22. As his entourage of supply wagons rolled toward Charlotte Town, the Legion troops were harassed and ambushed by partisans and Continentals. After the capture of General Griffith Rutherford at the Battle of Camden, Colonel William Lee Davidson was promoted to brigadier general and given command of the militia in the Salisbury District.[4] "On Tuesday last," wrote General Jethro Sumner to Major General Gates, "a Small party of Genl. Davidson's infantry fell in with two of the Enemy's Waggons, with an Escorte, on their way from Cambden *(sic)*, within two Miles of Charlotte, on the Steel-Creek Road; killed two men, took two, & brought off the Waggon Horses, 2 port-mantues, with Officers' Baggage, &c., &c."[5]

Major William R. Davie also harassed the approaching British Legion, skirmishing with them on September 25, taking some prisoners, and afterward retreating with his 150 mounted infantry and dragoons to take a post in Charlotte. Charlotte was but a small village with a courthouse and only a few wooden structures arranged along two intersecting streets. In the surrounding area were several mills where Cornwallis expected to grind meal to feed his army.

On the night of September 25, Lord Cornwallis was encamped seven miles from Charlotte Town. On that same night about 140 miles to the northwest, in the meadows beside Sycamore Shoals, the Overmountain Men, gathered from the hills and vales of the western waters, as they finished their preparations for a campaign in pursuit of Major Patrick Ferguson.

As Shelby, Campbell, and Sevier departed the Overmountain reaches to answer Ferguson's threat to their homes, Major William Davie prepared in Charlotte Town "to give the Lordship some earnest of what he might expect in North Carolina." He placed one dismounted company behind a breast-high stone wall at the courthouse and two other companies behind houses and gardens on both sides of the road. When Cornwallis's Legion marched in, they did so "with a front to fill the street."

Colonel Banastre Tarleton arrived in Charlotte Town as the nominal commander of this dragoons and light infantry. After suffering with yellow fever for two weeks and having only regained consciousness three days before, he was physically weak. He gave command immediately to Major George Hanger.[6] Leading the British light infantry, Hanger charged up the street at a full gallop; Davie's corps held their

**After repelling repeated attacks by British cavalry, the Patriot militia in Charlotte Town retreated along the road to Salisbury. The Battle of Charlotte historic marker is on South Tryon Street, 200 feet from Trade Street.**

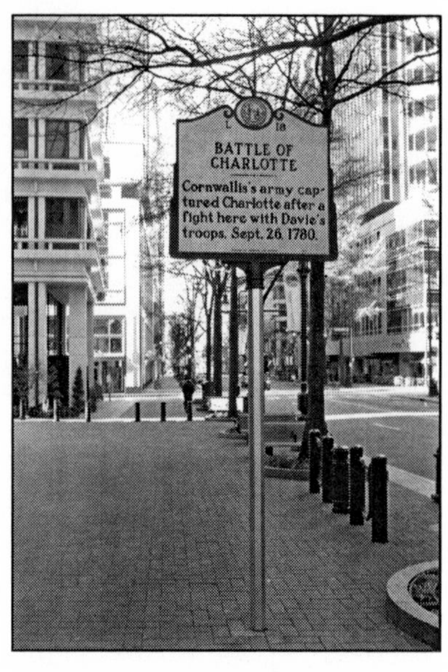


fire until the charge was within 60 yards. They fired "with such effect among the cavalry that they retreated with great precipitation." Davie's men repulsed repeated charges, but eventually gave way and retreated by the Salisbury road. "The enemy followed with great caution & respect for some miles," Davie wrote.[7] As Davie's men retreated north, unknown to either party, a group of militiamen from Surry County departed their camp at the mouth of the Elkin River and began their march up the Yadkin River valley to a rendezvous at Quaker Meadows.

The British general did enter Charlotte on September 28, but over the next two weeks, his men were continually harassed by snipers killing his soldiers from hiding and by partisan raids against the mills and his foraging parties.[8] After this inhospitable greeting, Lord Cornwallis reportedly called the town a "hornets' nest of rebellion."

### Yadkin Ford

In the face of Cornwallis's advance toward Charlotte Town, the Continental generals of the Southern Department had retreated with the remnants of their army so recently routed at Camden. A flurry of messages passed among them as they secured what supplies they could take from Charlotte Town and moved north toward Salisbury, attempting to secure the fords across the Yadkin River to prevent Cornwallis advancing unopposed to Hillsborough. General Sumner wrote on September 29 to General Gates in Hillsborough from his camp on McGoon's Creek, at the Trading Ford, revealing the threat they faced: "The enemy continue in Charlotte, about 2,000," he wrote. "Some enlarge their number to 3,000. On my retreat I endeavored to bring off all the public stores there, and effected it. I have detached Col. [William R.] Davie of the light horse, and Col. Taylor with 200 horse, to Fisher's Mill and in the vicinity, to remain and prevent the enemy's plundering the inhabitants. I every hour expect to hear from them."[9] As he wrote these words, the divided force of Overmountain militia was descending the eastern slope of the Blue Ridge Mountains, camping on the North Fork of the Catawba River at North Cove and Turkey Cove.

Writing the next day on September 30, Gates implored Sumner to defend the Yadkin Ford and not abandon its defense until "forced to do it" by the "near approach of a superior number of the enemy." Gates declared that reinforcements were on their way—General William Smallwood, a Marylander who had stood his ground at Camden and then escaped with his men, and Colonel Daniel Morgan as well as some Virginians gathered near Guilford Courthouse.[10] As Gates penned his encouragement, the Patriot militia of the Yadkin River valley from Surry and Wilkes counties united with the Overmountain Men at Quaker Meadows, their strength in numbers then reaching about 1,400.

On October 4, General Sumner advised Gates that although he could defend that ford, he believed that the Shallow Ford, some thirty-five miles upstream, afforded Cornwallis equally adequate access over the Yadkin River. Indeed, he noted, McKnitt's Road ran directly there

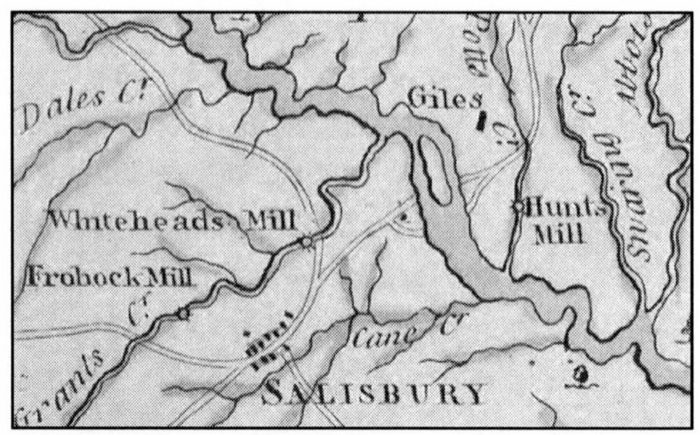


**General Sumner was encamped at the Trading Ford to prevent Cornwallis from crossing the Yadkin River. This detail from the 1770 Collette Map shows the important crossing. The "Trading Ford" historical marker, L-24, is missing from the US Hwy 23/70 bridge over the Yadkin River. The ford was one mile east.**

from Charlotte Town and would afford them access to the Moravian towns once over. The solid rock at Shallow Ford would clearly support Cornwallis's wagons and artillery. Indeed, Sumner noted, Colonel Taylor had recently seen 800 soldiers and two pieces of artillery on that very road.[11] Seventy miles away, Cleveland, Shelby, Campbell, and Sevier discovered their quarry had escaped Gilbert Town.

On October 6, General William Lee Davidson wrote to Gates regarding the situation in Charlotte. "The Enemy is still confined to Charlotte. The small Rifle Companies I have kept hanging upon their lines have been of Service in checking their foraging Parties. They are probably 1,800 Strong, including those Loyalists they have recruited in the Southward. Besides these they have some unformed Tories who follow the Fortunes of the Army, rather a dead Weight than a Benefit."[12] Davidson continued to "annoy" the enemy, but he expressed great concern about the attitude of the citizens. "Almost every Class of Citizens," he wrote, "let their Attention rest directly upon their Property, the Loss of which seems to touch them with more Sensibility than the Loss of their Country's Freedom."[13] That night, ever nearer their goal, the Patriot militia, aroused by a threat to their lives, their families, and their liberty, pressed on. Having been in the saddle for two weeks and for 21 miles already that day, they rode out from the Cowpens at nine o'clock in the evening, on a cold, rainy night to finish the job they had come to do.

On October 7, General Gates related to Sumner his immediate plans for defending North Carolina against Cornwallis's invasion: Daniel Morgan had left that morning to join him (Sumner); Gates would depart for Camp Yadkin Ford "the instant the whole of the troops here [were] in a condition to march," he wrote; General Smallwood would follow in a day or two when he was feeling better; and, the Virginia cavalry would depart on October 9. "I am exceedingly anxious that your provisions should be ample and constant," Gates wrote worriedly, "without that, there is no making a stand with any army in any country."[14] Compared to the needs of the professional army to prepare with adequate supplies and to mobilize when everyone was ready and feeling up to it, the Overmountain Men and the Liberty Men had shown themselves to be the hardiest of rangers. They were willing and able to suffer much hardship and to endure long deprivation for the sake of accomplishing their mission. That day they proved their value to the American cause, defeating Ferguson's forces in battle and removing from Lord Cornwallis's control the left flank of the advancing British Legion.

### An Anxious and Miserable Situation

On October 10, having no word from his left flank on the western frontier, Cornwallis ordered Colonel Tarleton out with his light horse to escort Ferguson back across the Catawba River. Tarleton rode out to a ford (Armor's?) downstream of the forks of the Catawba River, "where he received certain information of the melancholy fate of

Major Ferguson."[15] He sent an express immediately to Charlotte to forward the "mortifying intelligence" to Lord Cornwallis. On hearing the news on October 13, the General was stunned. He had lost one of his best officers and a third of his army. Cornwallis later wrote to Clinton that the defeat at King's Mountain was "without any fault of Major Ferguson's. A numerous and unexpected enemy came from the mountains. As they had good horses, their movements were rapid."[16]

Tarleton recounted later, "Added to the depression and fear [that Ferguson's defeat] communicated to the loyalists upon the borders, and to the southward, the effect of such an important event was sensibly felt by Earl Cornwallis at Charlotte town. The weakness of his army, the extent of poverty of North Carolina, the want of knowledge of this enemy's designs, and the total ruin of his militia, presented a gloomy prospect at the commencement of the [North Carolina] campaign." After Ferguson's defeat by the stealth and fighting skills of the unanticipated Overmountain Men and Patriot militia, Cornwallis "formed a sudden determination to quit Charlotte town, and pass the Catawba river."[17] The general recalled Tarleton from the field and set his army retreating. On the same day, the withdrawing Patriots, guarding their prisoners, marched from Gilbert Town to the plantation of a Tory, Biggerstaff.

### I Shall March After the Enemy

On the evening of October 13, General Sumner wrote to Gates a second time that day. He had learned by express the "agreeable news"[18] that Cornwallis was retreating from Charlotte Town. "I shall … March after the enemy, so as to annoy as much as possible, preventing a general Action," he added. For reasons unexplained, or probably not even yet understood by the Continental Army, Cornwallis had turned around, halting for the moment his pending invasion of North

Carolina.[19]

The British Legion began to move away from Charlotte Town on the evening of October 14 and to march toward the Catawba Ford. Tarleton described the woeful plight of the British Legion: "Owing to the badness of the road, the ignorance of the guides, the darkness of the night, or some other unknown cause, the British rear guard destroyed, or left behind, near twenty wagons, loaded with supplies for the army, a printing press, and other stores belonging to public departments, and the knapsacks of the light infantry and legion." Despite the rising of the Catawba River due to the recent rains, the soldiers were ordered across the river. They crossed successfully, but with difficulty. Seventy-five miles to the northwest, the withdrawing Patriot militia tried 32 of their Tory prisoners and hanged nine of them in retaliation for crimes against their Whig families and friends.

The situation of the retreating British Legion worsened. "The royal forces remained two days in an anxious and miserable situation in the Catawba settlement," wrote Tarleton, "owing to a dangerous fever, which suddenly attacked Earl Cornwallis." Moreover, they lacked supplies and were unable to forage successfully. When the doctors declared that the general could survive the discomforts of transport by a wagon, the army pushed on southward. The Mecklenburg Patriot militia menaced the column until Tarleton's light horse chased them away.

Cornwallis was not the only leader of an army to receive bad news that week. As the British Legion was retreating from Charlotte and Cornwallis was falling ill with a severe fever beside the Catawba River, a letter from Philadelphia arrived on October 16 for Major General Horatio Gates. Sam Huntington, President of the Continental

Congress, informed General Gates that by an Act of Congress on October 5, they had "directed a Court of Enquiry respecting [his] conduct as Commander of the Southern Army."[20] As the fortunes of the Patriots seemed to be turning, Gates's infamous and cowardly flight from the battlefield at Camden and, indeed, from all of South Carolina, had caught up with him. Likewise for Lord Cornwallis, his seemingly unavoidable destiny to subdue North Carolina with relative ease had turned around as quickly as he had with the loss of Patrick Ferguson.

In the middle of October 1780, misery and misfortune were shared in great bounty by two opposing generals. These two leaders shared one more melancholy: Both were despised by the Overmountain militiamen of the western waters and the Liberty Men of the Carolina backcountry. These were men of skill, men of courage, men of commitment. They turned away from no enemy and hesitated not a moment when the call to action was so clear, so immediate, so necessary.

# The Moravian Towns

**Bound for Bethabara**

After resting a day at Quaker Meadows, the withdrawing Patriot militia took leave of one another, each group of men returning to their respective homeland—some of the men physically wounded, some battle scarred in ways that did not show, all eager to see loved ones again. Some would begin telling their accounts of the victory over the man they had despised, Major Patrick Ferguson. Others would put the experience behind them, not talking about it for years. Some chose to get on with living, and to prepare themselves for the next confrontation. They knew all too well that the war was not over.

After these groups of militiamen had departed, the smaller remaining entourage got under way. They departed from Quaker Meadows on Monday, October 16, about two o'clock in the afternoon. Over the next few days, they crossed the Johns River and made their way into the headwaters of the Yadkin River valley. They followed in reverse the route Cleaveland and Winston had taken just three weeks before on their way to join up with the Overmountain Men.

Knowing that the number of guards was much smaller, three Tories tried to escape one evening. Two got away, but a third "was shot through the body." The next day, at "five o'clock in the morning, the Rebels executed the man," Lieutenant Allaire wrote in his journal. The party then marched 18 miles along the Yadkin River to the mouth of Moravian Creek, where they halted. The next morning, Thursday, October 19, they forded the creek, passed the Wilkes County Courthouse, where, no doubt, Colonel Cleaveland pointed out to his weary and wary prisoners the fearsome Tory Oak. He had dispensed his own brand of justice there before and he would have wanted these prisoners to know he would use the tree again when necessary. They continued on, covering sixteen miles that day, and six miles more on Friday, where they halted at the plantation of a Tory named Sale.[1]

On Saturday, October 21, the prisoners received the attentions of local inhabitants of the Yadkin River valley, at least those who were "friends of the government." Allaire wrote, "Several Tory women," probably reasoning that their gender would prevent their being accosted by the Patriots, "brought us butter, milk, honey, and many other necessities of life." That afternoon, the Patriots marched the prisoners another fourteen miles to the plantations of two well-known Tories, both of whom were away in service to General Lord Cornwallis. As was the standing military practice, the Patriots foraged among the civilian supporters of the enemy to feed themselves, and

**Salem was a community of artisans, merchants, and craftspeople such as tailors, cobblers, candlemakers, pewter smiths, bakers, printers, and potters. The Gunsmith Shop at Old Salem Museums and Gardens introduces visitors to the art and craft of making and repairing rifles, muskets, and pistols of the 18th century.**

sometimes their prisoners.

After two weeks of marching north from the battlefield at King's Mountain, proceeding up Cane Creek, crossing the Catawba River, passing Fort Crider[2] and Fort Defiance, and descending the Yadkin River, the Patriots and their prisoners approached the region of the east bend (where the eastward flowing Yadkin River turns south not far from Pilot Mountain). Allaire wrote, "Sunday, 22$^{nd}$. Moved at ten o'clock in the morning. Obtained liberty to go forward with Col. Shelby to Salem, a town inhabited by Moravians. Rode ten miles, and forded Yadkin river at Shallow Ford. Proceeded on fourteen miles farther to Salem. Went to meeting in the evening; highly entertained with the decency of those people, and with their music. Salem contains about twenty houses, and a place of worship. The people of this town are all mechanics; those of the other two Moravian settlements are all farmers, and all stanch [staunch] friends to Government."[3] Dr. Uzal Johnson declared the same in his diary.[4]

Allaire and Johnson may have overstated the Loyalist support of the Moravians. The German-speaking Christians had been diligent in their efforts to be neutral. They sold goods and provisions to both Patriots and Loyalists and feared reprisals from one should they be seen as favoring the other. Still, the Whigs pressed them. In August 1778, the courts had posted a declaration at the tavern in Salem saying that all who did not take the Oath of Allegiance had to leave the country in 60 days, traveling to Europe or the West Indies. The Moravians pressed their point with the North Carolina Assembly to rewrite the Affirmation in a form they would be willing to take. Eventually, with very few exceptions, the Brethren took the Affirmation in support of the Patriot cause before a justice of the peace.[5] Anthony Allaire and Uzal Johnson may have mistaken the Christian generosity of the

**Bethabara and Bethania were communities of farmers. The Visitor Center at Historic Bethabara Park displays a model of Bethabara, siting buildings of the day where the foundation ruins revealed in the park indicate the presence of different homes and buildings.**

Moravians at Salem and the concern for the gentlemen's personal well-being for allegiance to the Loyalist cause.

**Very Kind to All the Prisoners**

The patriotism and patience of the Moravians was again tested soon after the departure of the soldiers following the Battle of Shallow Ford. A larger and more needy group of soldiers and prisoners was about to depend on them. Word arrived in Bethabara of the militia camp across the Yadkin River. The Moravian doctor went to help. The entourage of prisoners and guards then crossed the river and moved into Bethania, coming to Bethabara for supplies of meat and bread. Arriving on October 23rd, the horde of destitute men descended on the town. "This morning the prisoners came [to Bethabara], between five and six hundred men including their guards. They camped on the north side of the big meadow. Bread was in great demand, but little could be done in the bakery" because those in such need pressed in. The Patriots provided a guard. The Patriot officers requested that the

Tory officers be provided a house, so an empty one was made available. "As no cattle came in we had to let them have one of ours. There was much disturbance in the town." Those at Bethabara sent to Salem for some Brothers to help.[6]

Word of the demands on Bethabara arrived in Salem on the day of Allaire's visit. The Moravians there recorded "great concern because a large number of Tories, captured in an action on the Catawba River, and the Whigs who are guarding them, [were] marching toward Bethabara." They recorded the next day sending four of the Brothers to help out in Bethabara "to assist in the work caused by the arrival of a large number of soldiers and prisoner; all of them and their horses [requiring] care … and no notice had been sent in advance. Everything was in confusion."[7] Merchants in Salem sent supplies to Bethabara and went off to Cross Creek to get more salt and to Hillsborough for supplies to sell. "Again all day there were officers riding to and fro; several horses had to be furnished to take them to the Atkin [Yadkin]."

**A horde of hungry Patriot militiamen and Tory prisoners descended upon Bethabara two weeks after the battle at King's Mountain. A thousand men took over the town, including, no doubt, the 1775 tavern whose foundation ruins stand adjacent to the modern community garden at Bethabara Historical Park in Winston-Salem, NC.**

Meanwhile, Allaire "lay at Salem in the evening," he wrote. "Two Continental officers slept at the tavern, on their way to join their army. One Mr. Simons, a Lieutenant of Col. Washington's dragoons, was exceeding polite, pitied our misfortune in falling into the hands of their militia."[8] Allaire wrote the next day, "Moved at ten o'clock in the morning; marched six miles to the old town called Bethabara. Here we joined the company again. This town is about as large as the other; but not so regularly laid out. The inhabitants very kind to all the prisoners."[9]

**No Meal Left for Ourselves**

On the 24th, Colonel William Campbell consented to the request to provide Dr. Johnson and Anthony Allaire a separate room, provided in the Kühnast's house.[10] Allaire recorded in his diary, "This night Dr. Johnson and I were disturbed by a Capt. [Isaac] Campbell, who came into our room, and ordered us up in a most preemptory manner. He wanted our bed. I was obliged to go to Col. Campbell, and wake him to get the ruffian turned out of the room; otherwise he would have murdered us, having his sword drawn, and strutting about with it in a truly cowardly manner."[11]

"Today all our meal had been used," they wrote in Bethabara on October 24. "The officers took our wagons and horses and sent them to Salem with several of the cavalry to bring meal." They had to furnish three more beeves to feed the soldiers. "Many of our neighbors came, bringing apples, bread, and several oxen." On the 25th, they recorded rather factually, "Our circumstances were the same as yesterday. In providing for the people who are here we had no meal left for ourselves, and could not bake." Indeed, the Patriot officers were becoming more demanding and a little testy. After bringing in some cattle to the stable, the Moravians "asked to have a guard set at our stable, so that none should be taken out, for Major Winston had threatened that if one was taken he would set the stable on fire."[12]

On October 26, colonels Campbell and Shelby and other officers rode to Salem and "took breakfast at the Tavern." Afterwards, all of them but Captain Isaac Campbell went "to the camp on the Atkin," assumed to be General Sumner's Camp Yadkin Ford. (Perhaps Captain Campbell feared that word of his cowardice at Shallow Ford had made its way to the Continental officers.) The next day, the Moravians in Salem noted an eclipse of the sun. Those in Bethabara were probably too busy to notice; they were hauling corn, driving cattle, and trying to feed the army and its prisoners which so completely occupied their town. Over the next few days, a routine of sorts set in: The Moravians went out to haul corn and grind meal, and soldiers tried to steal it.

On Sunday, October 29, Colonel Cleaveland asked Captain DePeyster

**Salem Tavern was the town's inn for accomodating visitors with food and lodging. After a fire in 1782 destroyed the tavern, a new one was built atop the same foundation and above the cellar from which visitors including Shelby, Campbell, and Allaire were served.**

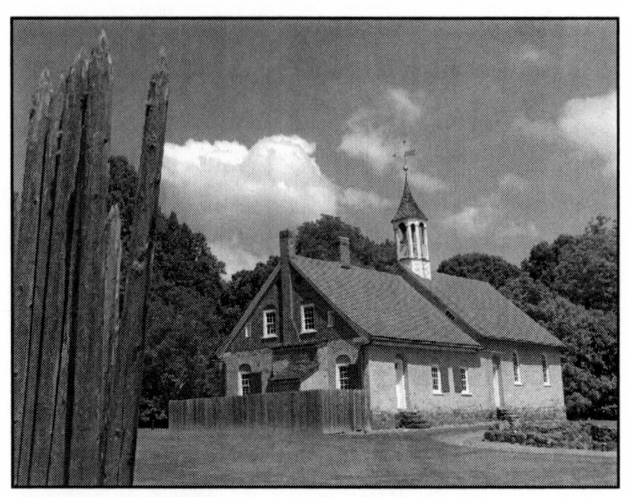

**The Moravians held daily services for the members of the community, most often in German. On occasion, services were offered in English to accommodate visitors. The church building was the center of community life. The Gemeinhaus (above) at Bethabara Historical Park was built in 1788. The replica stockade (foreground left) interprets the period of the Cherokee War, 1759-1761.**

to bring his officers and men to hear a sermon at ten o'clock. The prisoners marched to a hill about a half-mile from the town. The Moravians recorded of the event, "Some of the English officers and soldiers were attentive listeners. In the afternoon there was preaching in the woods between Ranke's and the big meadow. A great crowd of soldiers had gathered, and most our Brethren; it was estimated that about two thousand were present, to whom Mr. Hill [a Baptist minister] preached earnestly on the 63rd chapter of Isaiah [holding a long thanksgiving service for the victory over the Tories]."[13] Allaire recorded his own account: "Here we heard a Presbyterian sermon truly adapted to their principles and the times; or, rather stuffed as full of Republicanism as their camp is of horse thieves."[14]

On the 30th, the town was in a commotion because one of the prisoners was to be hanged for nothing more than insolence toward a guard. "The poor sinner was led to the gallows, and dawn up, but then was pardoned," the Moravians recorded.[15] Colonel Cleaveland stepped in to reprieve the man.[16]

The Patriot militiamen continued to be a problem. Word circulated in Bethabara that the soldiers were planning to rob the houses, but nothing came of it. The Moravians recorded, "It was as disturbed as the other days for there are probably more than a thousand men here and in the camp."[17]

As generous as Colonel Benjamin Cleaveland was one day, he was frequently as peevish the next. Seeing that Dr. Johnson had tended to the wounds of a prisoner whom Cleaveland had cut during the march, the colonel insulted the doctor and beat him. "[G]ot permission from Col. Cleveland to go within the Ring and dress the wounded Prisoners," Dr. Johnson wrote. "When dressing one McCatchum[,] Col Cleveland came to me and said he was a Damnd Villain and deserved the Gallows. I asked him what he was guilty of. He repeated that he was a Damnd Villain as I was and deserved hanging. He then very passionately said he had found out my Villainies and had a great mind to cut me up. No sooner said than done, he struck me over the Head with his Sword, and levild *(sic)* me. He repeated his stroke[,] cut my Hand. I then desird to know my crime. He said I was a damnd traitor to my Country and that he would confine me in the Guard with the other Villains."[18] After that outburst, Colonel Mark Armstrong, commander of the local militia, relieved Cleaveland of his control of the prisoners. Cleaveland and his Bulldogs left Bethabara on November 1. The Moravians wrote, "the town was more quiet this evening."[19]

### The Fruits of That Victory

On November 4, a Continental officer, Major James Reed, arrived with orders for the prisoners.[20] They were to be marched to Lead Mines in Virginia. Indeed, General Horatio Gates had written a letter of thanks and congratulations to "the officers commanding in the late defeat of Maj. Ferguson." The second half of the letter gave the specifics for "the disposal of the prisoners as they may be ready to use in exchange for our valuable citizens in the enemy's hands." He continued, "Send them under proper guards to Fincastle Court House, Virginia."[21] The letter was dated October 12, on which date, the victorious militiamen were on retreat in Gilbert Town and not even yet at Biggerstaff's plantation, dispatching Tories after a trial. It would seem in his letter that Gates was posturing for Congress and others superior to him in the chain of command, especially in asking Governor Thomas Jefferson to forward the news to Congress. Those militiamen among the returning victors from King's Mountain who knew of Gates's scandalous and cowardly flight from the battlefield at Camden in the face of the enemy, would not likely have held his thanks or praise in any high regard. Moreover, Fincastle County, for which Lead Mines had been the county seat, had been dissolved four years earlier with the formation of Washington, Montgomery, and Kentucky counties. Still, at the time, those in the region knew what Gates meant, even if he did not.

News that the prisoners would soon be leaving Bethabara was welcomed by the Moravians. That night "hens, pumpkins, and brandy were stolen."[22] The visitors to the Moravian town, those on both sides of the Revolution, had stayed too long, it seemed.

Some of the prisoners felt the same about having been there too long, and any place called "the lead mines" did not sound too inviting. The

Moravians in Bethabara noted on November 5: "This morning we heard that last night three lower-rank English officers and a Tory captain ran away."[23] Colonel Armstrong, commander of the local militia, sent out some cavalry to catch them. Among the escapees was Anthony Allaire. In his diary, he wrote, "Set off from Bethabara in company with Lieut. Taylor, Lieut. Stevenson, and William Gist, a militia-man, about six o'clock in the evening. We marched fifteen miles to Yadkin river; forded it, found it very disagreeable. We continued on twenty miles farther … [until] daybreak the next morning."[24] On the 9th, twenty more Loyalists escaped from Bethabara, despite the increased guard placed on the prisoners.

Indeed, the whole matter of what to do with the King's Mountain prisoners came to nothing. Colonel William Campbell carried to Governor Jefferson in Richmond, Virginia, the recommendations from Gates, although Gates was dissuaded by Colonel William Preston from sending them to Lead Mines because Montgomery County was rife with Tories. Campbell offered his own suggestions to Jefferson for sending the prisoners north to enlist with General Washington. Jefferson, in turn, referred the matter to Congress. By the time Congress referred it back to Jefferson to act on as he saw fit, it was November 20. The prisoners were essentially all gone. Many had escaped along the march, others from Bethabara. One hundred eighty-eight were taken from that town and bound over for civil trials. Some were paroled and others enlisted in the Patriot militia, some only long enough to defect and to rejoin their Loyalist units. Colonel Henry Lee wrote in January 1781 regarding the prisoners captured at King's Mountain, "The North Carolina government has in a great degree baffled the fruits of that victory. The Tories captured were enlisted into the militia or draft service, and have all rejoined the British; I heard General Greene say, yesterday, that his last return made out sixty in jail, and his intelligence from the enemy declares that two hundred of them were actually in arms against us."[25] In the end, only 130 prisoners from the battle at King's Mountain were marched away from Bethabara, under heavy guard, headed for Hillsborough. Among them was Dr. Uzal Johnson.

Along the way to Hillsborough, the Loyalist prisoners were ill treated by most of the North Carolina inhabitants they encountered. At a tavern near Guilford Courthouse, "the Landlord like most of his Neighbors [was] porofectly *(sic)* disposed to disoblige [us] as much as he could," wrote Johnson. At another tavern, the landlord's "doors were fast and he ... swore vengeance to any that attempted to enter." On the next day in another place, Johnson wrote, "Here again People refused to get us any thing to eat. They all seemed determined to make us fear for the good of our Souls." The soldiers arrived in Hillsborough on November 23, where they were put in the jail. Dr. Johnson and the officers were placed in a house. On the 26th during Johnson's stay, General Nathanael Greene passed through Hillsborough on his way to take command of the Southern Department of the Continental Army. Through aides of Greene,

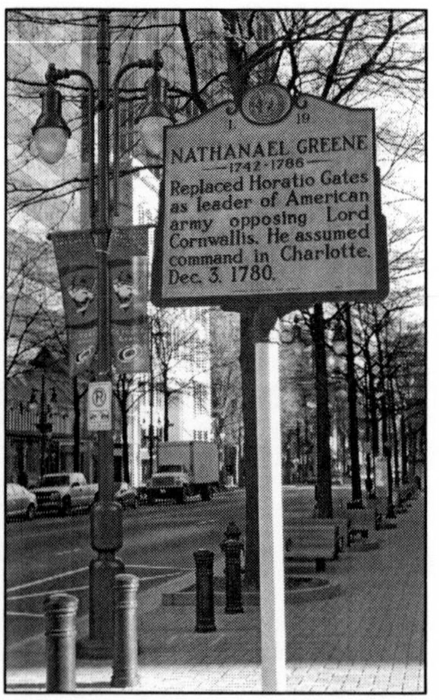


**General Nathanael Greene, George Washington's first choice earlier to command the Southern Department of the Continental Army, took command two months after the victory at King's Mountain had stalled the British advance into North Carolina. A historical marker in Charlotte, NC stands on North Tryon Street at Trade Street.**

Johnson "heard of [their] friends to the Northward."[26]

William Gist, who escaped with Allaire, is a good example of a Tory captured at King's Mountain. He commanded a platoon of mounted men at King's Mountain under Ferguson. He wrote later, "I was made prisoner, tried for my life, handcuffed and marched two hundred miles with little or nothing to Eat and in two months I made my Escape and came to the British line again where I continued till the evacuation of Charles Town where I was obliged to have a wife and five children."[27] Other Americans, as well as the Patriots, it seems, were fighting for their families and their futures.

According to the Moravian accounts at Bethabara, the Patriots enlisted into their ranks the Loyalist prisoners from North Carolina. They also enlisted 140 Tories from South Carolina. When the latter group was released, they spent the night in the town on the square cooking and baking. "The poor men had a pitiful appearance," the Moravians recorded, "most of them having no clothes on their bodies."[28] On November 11, the diarist wrote, "It gave us much pleasure to see the soldiers march away, though we were very sorry for the poor men, who are in great need. They had been in and near Bethabara for nineteen days."[29] Over the next week, the Moravians' record noted, "Every one was busy clearing out and cleaning up inside and outside the houses;" and later, "The farmers finished sowing winter wheat. Several of the English soldiers came from Salem to cut wood for us."[30]

**Return to Charlestown**

Allaire and his companions made their way south with the help of local Tory families. Short phrases from his journal describe the perils he faced: "laying snug in the bushes," "suffered very much from the cold," "passed a Rebel party," and "marched thirty miles." They traveled on Indian paths through the Brushy Mountains and eventually made their way to the Island Ford of the Broad River. Continuing on, they went by the old ironworks at Lawson's Fork and on to Williams's Fort, Saluda and Ninety Six. Setting out from Ninety Six on November 24, Lt. Anthony Allaire reached Charlestown on the 29th. Although he probably referred only to the last leg of the escape in his remarks, his final entry belied the incredible adventure of the last two months as a prisoner of the Patriot militia in North Carolina: "Nothing worth notice on the journey."[31]

# Epilogue

**"The Loss of America"**

The American Revolution did not end, of course, with the victory at King's Mountain. As Thomas Jefferson so eloquently put it later, that victory was but the "joyful annunciation of that turn of the tide of success" inthe American Revolution. The major battles of The Cowpens, Guilford Courthouse, and Yorktown were to follow in 1781 along with a host of other battles and skirmishes throughout the South that kept General Nathanael Greene's Continentals and the Patriot militia of partisan heroes more than occupied. Neither was General Washington idel during the following months. In all quarters, Patriots were pushing for victory. Still, the battle at King's Mountain was a turning point, which Sir Henry Clinton described more somberly in his memoirs. He recalled the battle as "an event that was immediately productive of the worst consequences to

**General Lord Cornwallis's British Legion was trapped on the peninsula at Yorktown by General George Washington with a Patriot force joined by the French Army and French Navy. The Victory Monument at Yorktown, VA commemorates the British surrender on October 19, 1781.**

the King's affairs in South Carolina and unhappily the first link in a chain of evils that followed in regular succession until they at last ended in the loss of America."[1]

The war did end, substantially, on October 19, 1781 when Lord Cornwallis's forces surrendered at Yorktown to the Patriot and French forces under the command of General George Washington. They did so only 12 months and 12 days after the Battle of King's Mountain, although the fighting had persisted without decisive effect for over five years before that battle. Because Lord Cornwallis was too ill—or embarrassed—to present his sword at Yorktown, he left that disagreeable duty to his second-in-command, the Irish General Charles O'Hara. When that officer offered the sword to General Washington, Washington motioned that it be presented to his second-in-command, General Benjamin Lincoln. Lincoln was the Continental officer who had surrendered Charlestown to General Lord Cornwallis only 17 months before, and had been released by the British the following November.

Even though the British forces soon ceased active confrontation with the Continental Army in the East, they continued to pursue dominance over the Ohio River valley, employing their Shawnee and Great Lakes Indian tribe allies against the settlers there. Notably, the last battle of the American Revolution was the Battle of Blue Licks on August 18, 1782, ten months after Yorktown. The confrontation was an ambuscade of the Patriot militia, in today's Kentucky, northeast of Lexington. Daniel Boone's second son, Israel, was killed in the battle, fighting alongside his father. (See *In the Footsteps of Daniel Boone.*)

**Men of Character and Action**

With the end of the war some of the Patriot heroes took on new roles in building the fledgling nation; but, before they did so, most saw additional action in the fighting that continued after the victory at King's Mountain.

Isaac Shelby continued almost immediately additional pursuit of the British near Monck's Corner, South Carolina, responding to a call from General Nathanael Greene to bring 500 Overmountain Men with him. He was joined in that November 1 effort by Colonel John Sevier. Shelby served in the North Carolina legislature that winter before preparing to ride out that spring with 200 Washington County (NC) militiamen against hostile Creeks in the headwaters of the Mobile River. He again served in the North Carolina Assembly before moving to Kentucky County, marrying at Boonesborough in April 1783, and making his new home at his plantation where he lived the next 43 years. He treated with the Cherokees in 1791, helped form the Constitution for Kentucky, and became the new state's first governor in 1792. During the War of 1812, he led the Kentucky troops in a campaign into Canada achieving victory at the Battle of the Thames. Shelby received a sword from the North Carolina legislature for his service at King's Mountain, a gold medal from Congress for his service in 1812, and an appointment as Secretary of War under President Monroe. The last he declined because of his advanced age. He suffered a paralyzing stroke in 1820, but his active mind sustained him until his death in 1826, outliving by 14 days both Thomas Jefferson and John Adams, who died the same day, July 4, 1826, fifty years to the day after the signing of the Declaration of Independence.[2] Isaac Shelby's name honors many towns and counties across the country including Shelby, North Carolina and Shelby County, Tennessee.

John Sevier became the first governor of Tennessee, the 16th state admitted, in 1796. His fame in Tennessee came primarily from events

**The life and spouses of John Sevier are commemorated with monuments on the grounds of City Hall in Knoxville, TN. Southeast of town, the later life of statesman Sevier is interpreted at his Marble Springs plantation home at 1220 John Sevier Hwy (TN Hwy 168).**

that followed the battle at King's Mountain, including his almost immediate confrontation with renegade Cherokees. In November, he joined Shelby in a campaign back to South Carolina to support General Greene. In December 1780, he led 300 men in pursuing hostile Chickamaugas with the help of Colonel Arthur Campbell and Major Joseph Martin.[3] Sevier received additional notoriety when elected as the first (and only) governor of the failed State of Franklin. Serving multiple terms as governor and as US Congressman from Tennessee, John Sevier made his indelible mark on the history of that state.

In the winter and spring of 1781, three months after the battle at King's Mountain, Benjamin Cleaveland began serving three months under General Griffith Rutherford. The general was released by the British in January following his wounding and capture at the Battle of Camden. Together Rutherford and Cleaveland pursued the Tories in southeastern North Carolina. After the war, Cleveland's plantation,

**After losing his claim to his Yadkin River home, "The Round About," Benjamin Cleaveland moved to the Tugaloo River valley in South Carolina where he lived out his days, becoming hugely obese at 450 pounds. A monument on Toccoa Hwy (US Hwy 123) in Old Madison commemorates the life of Patriot Colonel Benjamin Cleveland.**

*The Round About*, was lost to a holder of a better title to the land. He moved to the Tugaloo River valley in South Carolina, then still contested as Cherokee land. He built a new home and plantation where he died on October 15, 1806, sitting at the breakfast table, having achieved, some declare, the enormous weight of 450 pounds.[4] He had received thanks and recognition from a grateful North Carolina legislature in 1781, with the ordering of an "elegant mounted sword." Through a series of oversights, it was finally presented to his family 160 years later in 1941.[5] Cleveland County, North Carolina carries his name.

After returning home from the Moravian towns, William Campbell served at the Battle of Guilford Courthouse in March 1781. After that battle, he contended his riflemen had been abandoned on the field by the movement of Lt. Colonel Henry Lee's cavalry in the face of a charge by Lt. Colonel Banastre Tarleton. As a consequence, Campbell resigned from the Continental Army and returned home to serve again as a colonel of militia.[6] He also then served in the Virginia legislature and was involved in the retreat of legislators (Daniel Boone among them) from Richmond to Charlottesville, to Staunton in the face of a midnight raid by Lt. Colonel Banastre Tarleton, in June 1781. Tarleton intended to capture Governor Thomas Jefferson at

Monticello. As the British advanced into Virginia, Campbell reentered the war as Brigadier General of Militia, serving under Marquis de La Fayette. As Campbell moved his men toward Yorktown that summer, he was taken ill with a pain in his chest and died on August 22, 1781, two months before the British surrendered.[7] His widow, Elizabeth Henry Campbell, later married William Russell, the man who built Fort Patrick Henry, named for her brother. Russell was also the father of Henry Russell, the young man killed along with James Boone, Daniel and Rebecca's first-born child. James was murdered in October 1773 in the Powell River valley as the Boones and Russells first attempted to settle in Kentucky.

Major Joseph Winston also fought at the Battle of Guilford Courthouse, having joined previously with General William Davidson in the pursuit of bands of Tories in North Carolina. After the war, Winston became a noted statesman, serving three terms in the US Congress and five terms in the North Carolina senate. He too was voted a sword by the North Carolina General Assembly in 1781. A first cousin to Patrick Henry, Winston died in April 1815 and was buried at what became Guilford Courthouse National Military Park.[8] After Forsyth County was formed in 1849, the state legislature assigned the name Winston to the new county seat in honor of this Patriot hero.

Indian agent Major Joseph Martin, had held the hostile Cherokees in check during the fall of 1780 just long enough for the Overmountain Men to undertake their pursuit of Patrick Ferguson. But during the winter, Martin joined in confronting the Chickamaugas in the Overhill towns, leading 300 men from Sullivan County along with 300 more under Colonel John Sevier and another 100 under Colonel Arthur Campbell. Through December, the mounted force chastised the hostiles, destroying their principal towns along the Little Tennessee and Hiwassee rivers.[9] Martin continued as Indian agent through the 1780's until he became politically unacceptable because he was seen as too sympathetic to the Cherokees, especially during the Treaty of Hopewell. He retained the support of his long-time friend, Patrick Henry, with whom he harbored hopes for speculating successfully in western lands. When the Southwest Territory was established in 1790, Patrick Henry suggested Joseph Martin for the post of governor, but William Blount was appointed instead. Blount made his residence at Rocky Mount, the home of William Cobb, a mustering point for militiamen on their way to Sycamore Shoals in the fall of 1780.

Before the battle at King's Mountain, William R. Davie interspersed his study of law in Salisbury with command of a troop of Patriot cavalry he had raised and trained. After Davie's heroic stand at the Battle of Charlotte, General Greene asked him to serve as commissary officer, using is knowledge of the countryside and his native intelligence to help supply the army. Davie served with great success in that capacity. After the war, Davie served as a circuit court attorney and for 12 years as a member of the North Carolina Assembly. He earned renown as the "Father of the University" for submitting legislation to create the University of North Carolina.

Thomas Sumter served with distinction amidst controversy, earning over the years his fair share of champions and detractors. He had missed the Battle at King's Mountain because of a dispute over command, but his men soon bested the British at Fish Dam Ford, capturing Major James Wemyss as Sumter barely escaped an attempt to capture him. Later that November, Sumter defeated Lt. Colonel Tarleton at Blackstocks, suffering wounds in the contest sufficient to end his service in the war. Afterward, Sumter served for decades in the state house and in Congress extending his political career to 1810. Living to the age of 98, Sumter was the last living general of the Revolutionary War when he died in 1832. And, of course, Fort Sumter, whose bombardment later began the War Between the States, was named in his honor.

William Lenoir became a noted statesman and servant of the people. He became a major general of militia and served locally as magistrate, county register, clerk of the court, and county surveyor. He served ten years in the state Assembly: three in the house and seven in the senate. Most notably, he served as a Trustee of the University of North Carolina, a man of letters who improved himself continually beyond his woefully limited schooling as a child. He died at Fort Defiance, his home, in 1839 at the age of 88. A county and a city in North Carolina carry his name.

**Three Friends Redux**

People have come to the story of the Patriot heroes of the Battle of Kings Mountain with varied interests in the accounts and from different walks of life. Many who have become enamored of the story have become passionate about sharing the saga with others and assuring that future generations do not forget what happened at that mountain and across the Southeast countryside in the months and years surrounding that event.

Three men, in particular, share a common bond that makes their involvement and activities in commemorating these heroes most interesting:

Harry Smith, from Laurel Bloomery, Tennessee, served as the Safety Marshal during the original commemorative march in 1975 from Sycamore Shoals to Kings Mountain National Military Park, and

**National Park Service Director Gary Everhardt (l), US Senator Jim Broyhill (c), and 1976 Grand Marshal Harry Smith revisted the grounds of Lenoir High School in 2005, The school was built on the site of Crider's Fort, a campsite of the Wilkes and Surry Militia.**

served as the grand marshal in the second march in 1976 during America's Bicentennial celebration.

Gary Everhardt, of Henderson County, North Carolina, served as Director, National Park Service under President Gerald Ford and later as the Superintendent of the Blue Ridge Parkway. He was one of the original signers of the charter forming the Overmountain Victory Trail Association in 1977. His service to the Trail was recognized in 2005.

US Senator James T. Broyhill, most recently a resident of Winston-Salem, served as a longtime US Representative from North Carolina, joining in the 88th Congress after his initial election in 1962. He served in Congress continually for 25 years until his appointment as US Senator. Working closely with a small, dedicated band of interested citizens, he submitted bills to Congress beginning in 1977 to secure the designation of the Overmountain Victory Trail as a National Historic Trail.

As these three men served in time the interests, needs, and development of the Overmountain Victory National Historic Trail from three different perspectives, it is remarkable and certainly worth noting that all three graduated from Lenoir High School in Lenoir, North Carolina. They all knew each other from the community growing up and Harry Smith's school career overlapped with that of the other two. Senator Broyhill graduated in '46, Smith in '47 and Everhardt in '52.[10] Their pioneering work on behalf of the Overmountain Victory National Historic Trail and their childhood friendships make them, perhaps, the modern-day heirs to the mantle, "Three Friends on the Frontier."

As did the Overmountain Men and backcountry militia in 1780, Patriots arise in a time of need in every generation.

The story of America continues.

# Acknowledgments

Many people have played a role in the creation of this book, even if they did not know it.

First and foremost, I express my gratitude to Mary for her support and patience and for tolerance of a project that took time and energy away from the family during four years.

I wish to recognize the prior scholars without whose diligent work, my efforts would have been impossible. Most notable among them is Lyman C. Draper (1815-1891), whose 1881 book, *Kings Mountain and Its Heroes*, remains the basis for all work on the story of the Overmountain Men of 1780. Most appreciated among modern scholars is Bobby Gilmer Moss, with much thanks to a host of others, most of whom I have not met, including all those dedicated investigators such as Steve Rauch, David Paul Reuwer, Patrick O'Kelley, and others who have joined with Charles Baxley in exploring the Southern Campaign of the American Revolution.

Still, I relied principally on a raft of little-known scholars, both contemporary and past as the bibliography attests, whose work during the last two centuries and more has helped fill in the details on a story that grew every larger as I learned more. I thank them for their passionate interest, their diligent research, and for publishing their findings. I thank all the soldiers and their widows who filed pension applications and left us all snippets of their eventful lives. I especially thank two intrepid journal keepers, Lt. Anthony Allaire and Dr. Uzal Johnson, both Loyalists, whose detailed accounts in the summer and fall of 1780 became threads for weaving together a real-time telling of unfolding, monumental events. And I thank the compilers of the "colonial and state records," rich with correspondence of the era, as well as Dr. Adelaide Fries whose life's work included translating the Moravian journals from their German script.

I wish to thank Dr. Greg O'Brien, Professor of History at the University of North Carolina at Greensboro for reading through the chapters addressing American Indian history. I appreciate his guidance, noting, of course, that the responsibility for any errors that may appear in the text is mine alone. I thank as well the small cadre of copy editors and proof readers whose fresh eyes then made obvious what my familiarity had made invisible.

This book is intended to help celebrate and promote the Overmountain Victory National Historic Trail. I recognize the work of OVNHT Superintendent Paul Carson, who since 2003 has helped build broader and stronger appreciation of the Trail in communities spread along its 330 miles across four states. The Trail, of course, has been nurtured since 1975 by patriotic and dedicated citizens and since 1977 by the like-minded members of the Overmountain Victory Trail Association, whose efforts helped the Trail receive Congressional recognition as a National Historic Trail in 1980. I applaud the work of the early OVTA members, many now deceased. I appreciate the dedication of the current president, Alan Bowen, in directing the combined efforts of the ever-growing number of current OVTA members in "Keeping the Story Alive" year after year. The public's interest has not always been so keen. In the leanest years of participation in the annual march from September 25 to October 7, a small, core group, sometimes fewer than a dozen in the 1980s, kept the tradition alive. Most notable among those stalwarts is Mike Dahl, who is appreciated for his dedication to the march over more than 30 years and for skillfully captivating audiences everywhere with his powerful and moving telling of The Story.

I appreciate United States Senator James T. Broyhill and the support he has provided the OVNHT since 1977 when as US Representative Broyhill, he introduced legislation to have Congress designate the National Historic Trail. I thank him for writing the Foreword and for his kind regard toward and encouragement of this book project.

I appreciate the work of Superintendent Erin Broadbent at Kings Mountain National Military Park and all her park rangers, current and past, in telling the story of the events that unfolded there on that hallowed ground on the fateful day, October 7, 1780. The staff's comprehensive knowledge and their skillful programming for visitors provides the anchor for sharing The Story everywhere else.

I am grateful to the Jackson Library at UNC-Greensboro and the award-winning Reynolds Library at Wake Forest University for their superior and superb archives and for research help. I thank also, the librarians of the North Carolina Room at the Winston-Salem Forsyth County Public Library for their help in locating materials both in their collection and by interlibrary loan.

I am grateful to a number of museums who hold and display artifacts and information that tell The Story to the public for letting me photograph some of their exhibits: Tennessee State Museum, Greensboro History Museum, Wilkes Heritage Museum, Hampton History

Museum, and the Corps of Engineers' Visitor Center at W. Kerr Scott Reservoir are among them. I am grateful as well to all the living history artists and reenactors who perform their roles as a way of teaching others about our country's history. I thank them for the use of their images in furthering their teaching efforts. And, I am grateful to all the entities — historic sites and parks — which organize and host reenactment events that enable the public to step back in time and to get a better understanding of life on this southern landscape only a short two-a-half centuries ago. As they all know — and as we all should remember — we are always only one generation away from losing a connection to our heritage. Education about America's story is important work that is worthy of doing.

But aside from my gratitude to all those above, I reserve my strongest and most sincere appreciation for the men and women whose stories we tell. We research it. We read it and write about it. We reenact it and we watch it. But they lived it. The community, the isotation, the challenges, the fear, the pride, the joy, the courage — it all unfolded for them in real time, day by day without an inkling of how it would all turn out. They relied on their own resourcefulness, their confidence in themselves, a strong sense of their independence, and their right to self determination. For those who lived out the story — those on all sides of the issues: Patriots, Loyalists, Cherokees, Shawnees, Mingos, Creeks, enslaved and free blacks, aristocrats, royal ministers, colonists, merchants, farmers, planters, soldiers, militia, men at war, women protecting their homes — I offer a hearty cheer. Huzza! I remain,

Your most humble and obedient servant,

RJ

# Notes

Notes from: **Three Friends on the Frontier**

1 Robert D. Bass, *Gamecock, The Life and Campaigns of General Thomas Sumter*, (Orangeburg, SC: Sandlapper Publishing Co., 2000; originally Holt, Rinehart, and Winston, 1961), p. 6

2 Bass, p. 7

3 Lyman C. Draper, *Kings Mountain and Its Heroes*, (Johnson City: Overmountain Press, 1996, after original 1881), p. 428

4 Other accounts say the militiamen were drunk and themselves unpaid for service. Knowing they could be paid for "Indian scalps" of the French-allied tribes, the Virginians ambushed this party of British-allied Cherokees, killing and scalping them for bounty money.

5 Edward McCrady, *The History of South Carolina under the Royal Government, 1713-1776*, (New York: original 1899, Russell & Russell, 1969), pp. 330-333

6 McCrady, pp. 329-350

7 Today's Tennessee River was called the Cherokee River. Above its confluence with the French Broad, it was known until 1880 as the Holston River.

8 *The Memoirs of Lt. Henry Timberlake*, Duane H. King, ed., (Cherokee, NC: Museum of the Cherokee Indian Press, 2007), p. 9

9 Timberlake, p. 10

10 Timberlake, p. 10

11 Timberlake, p. 11

12 Timberlake,, p. 37

13 The portrait formerly at the College of William and Mary hangs in the National Gallery in Washington, DC.

14 *Emissaries of Peace, Exhibit Catalog*, (Cherokee, NC: Museum of the Cherokee Indian, 2006), p. 45

15 Bass, p. 12-13. *Emissaries of Peace, Exhibit Catalog*, (Cherokee, NC: Museum of the Cherokee Indian, 2006), p. 36

16 Bass says Sumter served as interpreter. (Bass, p. 15); Timberlake mentions only himself in that role (Timberlake, p. 71)

17 Bass, p. 19

18 Bass, p. 22-3

19 Bass, p. 24

20 William Martin, "A Biographical Sketch of Gen Joseph Martin," *Virginia Magazine of History and Biography*, Vol. VIII, No. 4, April 1901, The Virginia Historical Society, Richmond, VA, p. 350

21 Martin, Biography, p. 352

22 Draper, KM, p. 428

23 Probably Angus Rucker, a Culpeper Minuteman later a lieutenant and then captain in the First Virginia State Regiment under Colonel George Gibson. Pension Application S19068. <http://www.southerncampaign.org/pen/s19068.pdf> (March 1, 2010) accessed September 27, 2010

24 Stephen B. Weeks, *General Joseph Martin and the War of the Revolution in the West*, Annual Report of the American Historical Association for the year 1893, Washington, DC, Government Printing Office, 1894, p. 413

25 The number of men with Martin is given as five or six and also as 20-30. Weeks, Martin, p. 414n

26 Weeks, Martin, p. 414

27 Draper, KM, p. 429

28 < http://teresita.com/html/characters.html> (Feb. 28, 2010)

29 <http://chenocetah.wordpress.com> (Feb. 28, 2010)

30 Draper, KM, p. 430
31 Waugh, p. 4

South Carolina Highway Historical Marker, Thomas Sumter's Store
(SC 6, one-half mile below Orangeburg-Berkeley County line)
"About 1765-1767, Thomas Sumter, future hero of the American Revolution, kept a country store near this spot where the stream of colonial traffic to the Up Country divided in the fork where the Nelson' Ferry Road branched off from the Road to the Congarees. Erected by the Cross Community Development Club—1963"

Notes from: **Lord Dunmore's War**

1 The Iroquois name Ohio means "beautiful river."
2 The name Tah-gah-jute is used most often, but perhaps in error, to designate Chief Logan. Other scholars offer Tachnechdorus, Soyechtowa, and Tocaniadorogon. [See Francis Jennings, *American National Biography*, Vol. 13, ed. John A. Garraty and Mark C. Carnes (New York, Oxford University Press, 1999) p. 836-7] He was better known among the whites as Chief John Logan, a name given to him to honor the widely respected Quaker Indian agent James Logan. Chief Logan was the son of a French orphan reared by the Oneida who became in time a chief of the Iroquois. Logan's mother was a Cayuga. Logan lived peacefully around whites all his life and even risked his own life to do so during the uprising in 1763 known as Pontiac's Rebellion.
3 William Hintzen, *The Border Wars of the Upper Ohio Valley (1769-1794),* (Manchester, CT: Precision Shooting, Inc.. 1999), p. 30-1
4 "The Sappington Narrative, Madison County, Feb. 13, 1800" as reported by Hintzen, p.328-30
5 Reuben Gold Thwaites and Louise Phelps Kellogg, *Documentary History of Dunmore's War, 1774.* (Madison: Wisconsin Historical Society, 1905; reprinted Baltimore: Genealogical Publishing Company, 2002) p. 10
6 Robert L. Kerby, "The Other War in 1774: Dunmore's War," *West Virginia History*, (Beckley, WV) Vol. 36, No. 1, p.7
7 Ibid.
8 Thwaites and Kellogg, p. 8; the land was promised in 1754.
9 By tradition, attributed to Washington during his 1770 trip down the Ohio River.
10 George Washington to Presley Neville, June 6, 1794, George Washington Papers, Manuscript Division, Library of Congress.
11 Cresap was born in Maryland and lived there. Dunmore commissioned him a captain to serve in the Virginia militia during Dunmore's War. Cresap later served in the Continental Army raising a company of riflemen from Maryland.
12 William Crawford was promoted to major at the outbreak of Dunmore's War and to lieutenant colonel in 1776. Later he became a full colonel, his rank most often cited.
13 In 1776, Fort Fincastle was renamed Fort Henry to honor Governor Patrick Henry. In time, it became today's Wheeling, West Virginia.
14 Hintzen, p. 37-8
15 Message from Logan reported in Hintzen, p. 33. Logan's mention of "Conestoga" refers to a massacre of Conestoga (Mingo relatives) in 1763 by the Paxton Boys, a group of border ruffians.
16 Thwaites and Kellogg, p. 50-1
17 Shortly after this service, Daniel Boone received a captain's commission in the colonial militia from Colonel Preston. The blank was issued to Preston with Dunmore's signature. That document, which Boone kept for years, helped him when he was interrogated as a prisoner at Fort Detroit in 1778 by Lt. Governor of Quebec, Henry Hamilton.
18 Earl of Dunmore to Earl of Hillsborough, July 2, 1771, as cited by George Morrow, *A Cock and Bull for Kitty*, (Williamsburg, VA: Telford Publications, 2011), p. 16

19 Morrow, *Kitty*, p. 18-9
20 Edmund Randolph, cited by Morrow, *Kitty*, p. 22
21 Morrow, *Kitty*, p. 42
22 Henry Mayer, *A Son of Thunder, Patrick Henry and the American Revolution*, (New York: Grove Press, 1991), p. 199
23 Ibid., p. 198
24 Ibid., p. 198-9
25 Thwaites and Kellogg, Introduction, p. X
26 Kerby, p. 6
27 Stephen B. Weeks, "General Joseph Martin and the War of the Revolution in the West, Washington, DC, Government Printing Office, 1894, p. 415. Culbertson's Bottom (also Crump's Bottom) is in modern Summers County, West Virginia.
28 Kerby, p. 8
29 The Culpeper ranks included men from the families of the Fields, the Greens, and the Slaughters. These were families for whom Daniel Boone had worked around 1760 as a wagoner, driving loads of tobacco to Fredericksburg and crossing the Rapidan River at the community of Germana. For safety during the Cherokee War, Boone had moved his family from the frontier of the Forks of the Yadkin in North Carolina to Culpeper County, Virginia where he lived and worked near Stevensburg. His third and fourth children, daughters Susannah and Jemima, were born there. Men from these families, whom Boone befriended while in Culpeper, joined him later in 1765 for an exploration of the Florida panhandle.
30 Kerby, p. 9
31 Lewis Preston Summer, *History of Southwest Virginia*, (original: Richmond, 1903; reprint:Baltimore, Genealogical Publishing Company, 1966, 1971) p. 156
32 Captain Rees Bowen moved to Maiden Spring in 1772, later to become Washington Co., VA.
33 Draper, KM, p. 403
34 Kerby, p. 9
35 Wm. Fleming to his wife, Sept. 4, 1774, Thwaites and Kellogg, p. 181
36 Thwaites and Kellogg, p. 284
37 The author believes the James McBride listed among the men paid to build canoes at Elk River is his mother's direct ancestor.
38 Thwaites and Kellogg, p. 332, Fleming's Orderly Book.
39 Thwaites and Kellogg, p. 337
40 Thwaites and Kellogg, p. 237
41 George Morrow, *A Cock and Bull for Kitty*, (Williamsburg, VA: Telford Publications, 2011), p. 17;
< http://en.wikipedia.org/wiki/Granville_Leveson-Gower,_1st_Marquess_of_Stafford > (December 21, 2010)
42 Among his many accomplishment, Kenton saved the life of Daniel Boone at Fort Boonesborough in 1777. (See *In the Footsteps of Daniel Boone*, p. 170)
43 Some writers, including Thwaites and Kellogg, have interpreted this to be James Robertson, the Father of Middle Tennessee. Both James Robertson and James Robison appear on the muster roles. Robison was later wounded in the battle. See Thwaites and Kellogg, p. 276.
44 Thwaites and Kellogg, p. 272n
45 Ibid., p. 271
46 Thwaites and Kellogg, p. 341-2
47 Draper Manuscripts, 6C17
48 Thwaites and Kellogg, p. 342
49 Kerby, p. 11
50 Ibid.
51 Draper manuscripts, 6C17
52 Thwaites & Kellogg, p. 275
53 Ibid.
54 Ibid., p. 276

55 Ibid., p. 277
56 Kerby, p.11
57 Fleming to Wm. Boyer, Thwaites and Kellogg, p. 256
58 Some accounts pit 800 warriors against 1,200 militiamen. Others have 1,200 warriors against 800 militiamen. Kerby states 1,000 Shawnee (p. 10). Most accounts suggest the two sides were about evenly matched in numbers with heroes and grievous losses on both sides. That each side suffered about one quarter of its number in casualties is not an improper statement.
59 Kerby, p. 12
60 Michael Cresap was not responsible for the massacre. Either Logan or Gibson was misinformed. However, the accusation stuck and Cresap's reputation suffered from this misattribution for centuries. See Luther Martin, *Letter to Mr. Fennel*, William Cobbett, ed., *Philadelphia Gazette*, March 29, 1797 as reported in "LOGAN'S SPEECH," *The Olden Time, 1846-1847* (February 1, 1847): 49.
61 Ray H. Sandefur, "Logan's Oration—How Authentic?" *Quarterly Journal of Speech* 46 (1960): 291
62 Thwaites and Kellogg, p. xxiii
63 Thwaites and Kellogg, p. 310n
64 Weeks, Martin, p. 418
65 Weeks, Martin. P. 419
66 "Fort Gower Address and Resolutions, November 5, 1774," West Virginia History 153, <www.as.wvu.edu/wvhistory/documents/008.pdf> (June 21, 2010)
67 "Fort Gower Resolutions", *Ohio History Central*, July 1, 2005, <http://www.ohiohistorycentral.org/entry.php?rec=1486> (accessed Dec. 2, 2007)
68 < http://en.wikipedia.org/wiki/Granville_Leveson-Gower,_1st_Marquess_of_Stafford > (December 21, 2010)

**Text for 1932 "George Washington Land" plaque:**
"George Washington acquired 7,276 acres of this land by a grant, dated December 1, 1773, issued to him by John Murray, Earl of Dunmore, last royal governor of Virginia. This tract was surveyed, July 1773, by William Crawford, upon warrants issued to George Washington for 3,953 acres and George Muse 3,323 acres for services in the French and Indian War. It bordered on the Great Kanawha, 12 miles and 227 poles. – Erected by the state of West Virginia 1932."

**Text for "Colonial Army Rendezvous" plaque:**
"Here are Fort Union, built in 1770, a frontier army of 1,100 men assembled in 1774 under command of General Andrew Lewis. On September 12, the army began a march through 160 miles of trackless wilderness to the mouth of the Kanawha River and defeated Cornstalk, gallant Shawnee Chief, and his warriors in the bloody Battle of Point Pleasant on October 10, 1774. The cabin home of Mathew Arbuckle, famous pioneer scout who led the army stood nearby."

Notes from: **Great Bridge and Norfolk**

1 Henry Mayer, *A Son of Thunder, Patrick Henry and the American Republic*, New York, Grove Press (1991), p. 239
2 Mayer, p. 245
3 Mayer, p. 247; Although not expressed explicitly as a tax, each titheable of a county was expected to fund for its defense "half a pound of Gunpowder, a pound of Lead, necessary Flints and Cartridge paper."
4 Mayer, p. 247
5Benjamin Quarles, "Lord Dunmore as Liberator," The William and Mary Quarterly, Third

Series, Vol. 15, No. 4 (Oct. 1958), p. 497; one source says June 5. See W. Hugh Moomaw, "The British Leave Colonial Virginia," *The Virginia Magzine of History and Biography*, Vol. 66, No. 2 (Apr 1958), p. 147

[6] Lyon Gardiner Tyler, *History of Virginia, Vol II, The Federal Period 1763-1861* (Chicago & New York, The American Historical Society, 1924), p. 158

[7] E.M. Sanchez-Saavedra, "All Fine Fellows and Well-Armed, The Culpeper Minute Battalion, 1775-1776," *Virginia Cavalcade*, Vol. 24, No. 1, 1974, p. 5

[8] Mayer, p. 284

[9] "Extract of a letter from Frederick town, in Maryland, dated August 1," *Virginia Gazette* (Pinkney), September 7, 1775, p. 3, transcribed by the author from <http://research.history.org/DigitalLibrary/VirginiaGazette/VGImagePopup.cfm?ID=4812&Res=HI > (accessed March 12, 2010)

[10] Sanchez-Saavedra, p. 6

[11] Sanchez-Saavedra, p 5-6

[12] Draper, KM, p. 382

[13] Sanchez-Saavedra, p. 6

[14] Elizabeth B. Wingo and Elizabeth B. Hanbury, *The Battle of Great Bridge*, (Norfolk: Norfolk County Historical Society, reprinted by Chesapeake Public Schools, 1998) p. 6

[15] Virginia Gazette (Pinkney) September 7, 1775 <http://research.history.org/DigitalLibrary/VirginiaGazette/VGImagePopup.cfm?ID=4812&Res=HI > (accessed Sept 28, 2010)

[16] W. Hugh Moomaw, "The British Leave Colonial Virginia," *The Virginia Magzine of History and Biography*, Vol. 66, No. 2 (Apr 1958), p. 152; John Hunter Holt was editor, not George Holt.

[17] Exhibits at Hampton History Museum, Hampton, VA. (December 4, 2010)

[18] Tyler says Captain John Green led the company of Culpeper Minutemen, p. 156

[19] E.M. Sanchez-Saavedra, "All Fine Fellows and Well-Armed, The Culpeper Minute Battalion, 1775-1776," *Virginia Cavalcade*, Vol. 24, No. 1, 1974, p. 7

[20] Virginia Gazette (Dixon and Hunter) October 28, 1775, page 3, col. 3; <http://research.history.org/DigitalLibrary/VirginiaGazette/VGImagePopup.cfm?ID=4620&Res=HI> (accessed Sept. 28, 2010)

[21] Hampton enjoys another notable claim to primacy. On December 29, 1608, Captain John Smith ate the first Christmas feast in the English-speaking New World at the village of Kecoughtan.

[22] Exhibits at Hampton History Museum, Hampton, VA. (December 4, 2010)

[23] Quarles, p. 497

[24] Quarles, p. 494

[25] "Lord Dunmore's Proclamation." *Black Loyalists: Our history, Our People.* Canada's Digital Collections. <http://www.blackloyalist.com/canadiandigitalcollection/documents/official/dunmore.htm> (accessed May 28, 2010)

[26] Quarles, p. 501

[27] Quarles, p. 502n

[28] Sanchez-Saavedra, p. 7

[29] Quarles, p. 497

[30] Quarles, p. 504

[31] Ibid.

[32] Tyler, pp.159-161

[33] Sanchez-Saavedra, p. 7

[34] Quarles, p. 498

[35] Dunmore to Howe, as reported in Wingo and Hanbury, p. 8

[36] Quarles, p. 502

[37] Ibid.

[38] Quarles, p. 502

[39] Quarles, p. 505

[40] Sanchez-Saavedra, p. 6
[41] Charles W. Carey, "Flora, William," *American National Biography Online*, Feb. 2000, (accessed Oct. 20, 2010); Flora brought his own musket to the fray, a situation suggesting the trust and esteem he enjoyed in the white-dominated community, as even free blacks were forbidden to own guns. He operated a cartage business hauling produce between the wharves and the farms. He also operated a livery stable. He married an enslaved woman, whose freedom he purchased.
[42] Among the captured wounded were two ex-enslaved blacks, James Anderson and Casar. Quarles, p. 503
[43] Woodford referred to him as captain; some references list him as lieutenant.
[44] Quarles, p. 498
[45] Sanchez-Saavedra, p. 11
[46] Benjamin Quarles, "Lord Dunmore as Liberator," *The William and Mary Quarterly*, Third Series, Vol. 15, No. 4 (Oct. 1958), p. 505-6.
[47] Hamilton James Eckenrode, *The Revolution in Virginia*, (New York, Houghton Mifflin Co., 1916), p. 60

Notes from: **All His Majesty's Faithful Subjects**

[1] Adelaide L. Fries, ed. *Records of the Moravians in North Carolina* (Raleigh: Edwards & Broughton Company, 1926), p. 41
[2] William S. Powell, ed. "Tryon's 'Book' on North Carolina," *North Carolina Historical Review*, Vol. XXXIV (August 1957), p. 411
[3] At its founding, Surry (also Surrey) County included today's Stokes, Forsyth, Surry, and Yadkin counties.
[4] Betty Linney Waugh, "The Upper Yadkin Valley in the American Revolution" Benjamin Cleveland, Symbol of Continuity," Doctoral dissertation, University of New Mexico. (Wilkesboro, NC. Wilkes Community College, 1971), p. 53
[5] Waugh, p. 4
[6] Waugh, p. 4
[7] The Third Provincial Congress of North Carolina met at Hillsborough Aug. 20 – Sept 10, 1775. The representatives from all counties and towns established a Council of Safety and divided the province into six military districts for supplying militia.
[8] William L. Saunders, ed., *The Colonial Records of North Carolina* (Raleigh: Josephus Daniels, 1890) Vol. X, 1775-1776, p. 228
[9] Ibid., p. 230
[10] J.G. Hollingsworth, *History of Surry County or Annals of Northwest North Carolina* (original 1935; reprint, Salem, MA: Higginson Book Company, 1997), p. 74
[11] William L. Saunders, ed., *The Colonial Records of North Carolina* (Raleigh: Josephus Daniels, 1890) Vol. X, 1775-1776, p. 188
[12] Hugh F. Rankin, "The Moore's Creek Bridge Campaign, 1776," *The North Carolina Historical Review*, Vol. XXX, No. 1, January 1953, p. 29
[13] built by previous governor William Tryon
[14] David K. Wilson, *The Southern Strategy* (Columbia: University of South Carolina Press, 2005) p. 1
[15] William L. Saunders, ed., *The Colonial Records of North Carolina* (Raleigh: Josephus Daniels, 1890) Vol. X, 1775-1776, p. 46
[16] Wilson, p. 19
[17] Rankin, p. 33
[18] Joseph P. Cullen, "Moore's Creek Bridge," *American History Illustrated.* (January 1970) Vol. 4, No. 9, p. 12
[19] Samuel Cole Williams, "The Founder of Tennessee's First Town: Major Jesse Walton," *The East Tennessee Historical Society's Publications*, Vol. 2, 1930, p. 72
[20] Rankin, p. 32

[21] Rankin, p. 34
[22] Ibid.
[23] Rankin, p. 35
[24] Ibid.
[25] Rankin, p. 34
[26] Rankin, p. 38
[27] Fries, p. 1047
[28] Fries, p. 1048
[29] Ibid.
[30] Fries, pp. 1049-50
[31] Draper, KM, p. 432
[32] Fries, p. 1046
[33] Fries, p. 1048
[34] Fries, p. 1049
[35] Jeffrey J. Crowe, "Liberty Men and Loyalists," *An Uncivil War, the Southern Backcountry During the American Revolution*. eds. Ronald Hoffman, Thad W. Tate, Peter J. Albert (Charlottesville: The University Press of Virginia, 1985), pp. 146-47
[36] Fries, p. 1050
[37] Fries, p. 1048
[38] Fries, pp. 1026-7
[39] Williams, *Walton*, p. 71
[40] Fries, p. 1052
[41] Ibid.
[42] Ibid.
[43] C. Daniel Crews, *Through Fiery Trials, The Revolutionary War and the Moravians* (Winston-Salem, Moravia Archives, 1996), p. 18
[44] Fries, p. 1052
[45] William L. Saunders, ed., *The Colonial Records of North Carolina* (Raleigh: Josephus Daniels, 1890), Vol. X, 1775-1776, p. 452
[46] Rankin, p. 41
[47] Draper, KM, p. 433
[48] Rankin, ,pp. 43-4
[49] Rankin, p. 45
[50] Rankin, p. 44
[51] Rankin, p. 45
[52] Rankin, p. 47
[53] Rankin, p,. 47-8
[54] Rankin, p,. 48-9
[55] Rankin, p. 49
[56] Ibid.
[57] Rankin, p. 50
[58] Vernon O. Stumpf, "Josiah Martin and His Search for Success—the Road to North Carolina," (*North Carolina Historical Review*, January 1976), p. 167
[59] Rankin, p. 53
[60] Rankin, p. 54
[61] North Carolina Provincial Congress, *The journal of the proceedings of the Provincial Congress of North-Carolina, held at Halifax on the 4th day of April, 1776*. (Newbern [N.C.]: Printed by James Davis, printer to the Honourable the House of Assembly, 1776), pp. 3 & 9; Williams and Winston joined the Congress already in session and on the day the vote was taken for the Resolves.
[62] Stumpf, p. 171
[63] Stumpf, pp. 171-2
[64] Williams, *Walton*, p. 72
[65] Ibid.

66 Draper, KM, p. 433
67 Fries, p. 1029
68 Fries, pp. 1063-4

Notes from: **Gwynn's Island to Aspenvale**

1 Henry Mayer, *A Son of Thunder*, (New York: Grove Press, 1991), p. 281
2 Ibid., p. 284
3 Ibid., p. 285
4 Benjamin Quarles, "Lord Dunmore as Liberator," *The William and Mary Quarterly*, Third Series, Vol. 15, No. 4 (Oct. 1958), p. 505. Quarles says "May."
5 Lyon Gardiner Tyler, *History of Virginia, Vol. II, The Federal Period 1763-1861* (Chicago & New York, The American Historical Society, 1924) p. 166
6 Lewis took command in the absence of General Charles Lee, the first Commander of the Continental Forces of the Southern Department, who was then in South Carolina. Lee served as Commander for six months, From March 1 until September. He was captured in camp wearing his night clothes in New Jersey on Dec. 13, 1776 by Banastre Tarleton. He was released in a prisoner exchange.
7 Charles Campbell, *History of the Colony and Ancient Dominion of Virginia*, (Philadelphia: JB Lippincott and Co., 1860; reprint Spartanburg, SC: The Reprint Co., 1965), p. 664
8 *Virginia Gazette*, July 13, 1776, p. 6
9 Campbell, p. 664
10 Campbell, p. 665
11 Hamilton James Eckenrode, PhD, *Revolution in Virginia*, (Boston and New York, Houghton Mifflin Co., 1916), p. 94
12 *Virginia Gazette*, July 13, 1776, p. 6
13 Quarles, p. 504
14 Quarles, p. 505
15 W. Hugh Moomaw, "The British Leave Colonial Virginia," *The Virginia Magazine of History and Biography*, Vol. 66, No. 2 (Apr. 1958), p. 148
16 Quarles, p. 505-6
17 Moomaw, p. 147
18 Quarles, p. 506; Quarles estimates perhaps 800 enslaved reached the British, including about 100 with their masters.
19 Benson J. Lossing, "Virginia in 1775," *Our Country—Household History for All Readers*, Vol. 2, 1877, < *http://www.publicbookshelf.com/public_html/Our_Country_vol_2/virginia1_hg.html*> (accessed Dec. 3, 2007)
20 Mayer, p. 307
21 Thomas Paine, *Common Sense*, Chapter III, (original 1776. New York: Barnes & Noble, reprint 1995), p. 40
22 Ibid. p. 42

Notes from: **Cherokee Resistance**

1 Fries, *Records of the Moravians*, p. 1105
2 Pension Application of Jacob Grider, W3980, Southern Campaign American Revolution Pension Statements, transcribed by Will Graves September 1, 2008, < http://www.southerncampaign.org/pen/w3980.pdf >
3 Judge Avery's Address on the Early History of Burke County, Colonial Records of North Carolina, Vol. X, p.712
4 Rutherford to the Council of Safety, July 14, 1776 in William L. Saunders et al (eds.), The Colonial [and State] Records of North Carolina, 30 vols. (Raleigh 1886-1914), X, 669. Unbeknown to Rutherford, that same day Jemima Boone and the Callaway sisters were kid-

napped at Fort Boonesborough, Fincastle County, Virginia by Shawnee and Cherokee warriors.
[5] Samuel Cole Williams, "Nathaniel Gist, Father of Sequoyah," *The East Tennessee Historical Society's Publications*, Vol. 5, January 1933, p. 47
[6] During the following 20 years, that route was known as Boone's Trace. Eventually the name Wilderness Road was applied to the general route that flowed into Kentucky. (See *In the Footsteps of Daniel Boone*, pp. 100-107)
[7] Also, Chiucanacina. Henry Stuart, *Colonial Records of North Carolina*, X. p. 774. Also, Philip M. Hamer, "The Wataugans and the Cherokee Indians in 1776", *East Tennessee Historical Society's Publications*, III, (January 1931), 110. Pronounced Tsiyu-g□ nsi'nĭ, James Mooney, *Cherokee History, Myths, and Sacred Formulas*, 19th and 7th Annual Reports, Bureau of American Ethnology, 1900 and 1891; reproduced Cherokee, NC: Cherokee Publications, 2006) p. 54
[8] Christina Synder, *Slavery in Indian Country*, (Cambridge, MA: Harvard University Press, 2010), p. 157
[9] The actual boundary was more complicated than a ridge line. For example, in western North Carolina, the treaty boundary ran north from Tryon Mountain to Fort Chiswell, but it was not officially run because of rugged terrain. The ridge line concept served the purpose.
[10] Philip M. Hamer, "John Stuart's Indian Policy During the Early Months of the American Revolution," *Mississippi Valley Historical Review*, Organization of American Historians, Vol. 17. No. 3 (Dec. 1930), pp. 353-4
[11] William L. Saunders, ed., *Colonial Records of North Carolina*, (Raleigh: Josephus Daniels, 1890) Vol. X, p. 392
[12] Philip M. Hamer, "The Wataugans and the Cherokee Indians in 1776," *East Tennessee Historical Society's Publications*, Vol. 3, January 1931, p. 110
[13] Williams says 60 packhorses. It may have been 30 horses with two packs each for balance.
[14] At the time, the Holston River extended to the French Broad tributary. Today that run of river is called the Tennessee River.
[15] Hamer, *Wataugans*, p.115
[16] Samuel Cole Williams, *Tennessee During the Revolutionary War*, (Knoxville, University of Tennessee Press, 1944, 1974), pp. 24-5
[17] Hamer, *Stuart*, pp. 363-4
[18] Cited in Edward J. Cashin, "But Brothers, It Is Our Land We Are Talking About," *An Uncivil War, The Southern Backcountry During the American Revolution,* (Charlottesville: The University Press of Virginia, 1985), p. 242
[19] Colonial Records of thé State of Georgia, 14: 475-76 as quoted by Harvey H. Jackson, "Rise of the Western Members," *An Uncivil War, The Southern Backcountry During the American Revolution,* (Charlottesville: The University Press of Virginia, 1985), p. 280
[20] The backcountry of Georgia in 1774 became Wilkes County in February 1777, "the first county" in Georgia. At the time it included today's Wilkes, Elbert, Lincoln counties and most of Hart, Madison, Oglethorpe, Taliaferro, and Clarke counties.
[21] The Petition of the Inhabitants of the Parish of St. George and St. Paul …, July 13, 1776, cited in Cashin, p. 245
[22] Cashin, p. 245
[23] Cashin, pp. 248-9
[24] Cashin, p. 249
[25] Tonyn to General Henry Clinton, June 8, 1776, as cited in Cashin, p. 250
[26] Drayton to Francis Salvadore, July 24, 1776, as cited in Cashin, pp. 251-2
[27] Brown to Cornwallis, July 16, 1780 … , cited in Cashin, pp. 252-3
[28] Felix Walker was the son of Colonel John Walker who lived along Cane Creek, five miles northeast of Gilbert Town [Draper, *Kings Mountain and Its Heroes*, p. 325]
[29] Felix Walker was one of the thirty axe-men who helped Daniel Boone mark Boone's Trace into Kentucky in the spring of 1775. Walker was severely wounded during an attack by a party of Shawnee, and was nursed back to health by Boone. (See *In the Footsteps of Daniel Boone*, pp. 160-163)
[30] Samuel Cole Williams, *Tennessee During the Revolutionary War*, p. 33
[31] Williams, p. 33n

[32] Williams, p. 34n
[33] Hamer, *Wataugans*, p.111
[34] Colonial Records of North Carolina, Saunders (ed.), Raleigh, 1890, Vol. X, p. 392
[35] Hamer, *Wataugans*, p. 111
[36] Hamer, *Wataugans*, p.115
[37] Williams, p. 26, quoting NC State Records
[38] Williams, p. 27n
[39] Hamer, *Wataugans*, p. 116
[40] Williams, p. 27
[41] J.G.M. Ramsey, *Annals of Tennessee to the End of the Eighteenth Century*, (Charleston: Walker & Jones, 1853; reprinted Johnson City: Overmountain Press, 1967 & 1999),, pp. 106-7
[42] Hamer, *Wataugans*, p. 117
[43] Hamer, *Wataugans*, p. 119
[44] Ramsey, pp. 147-148
[45] Hamer, *Stuart*, p. 365. Ramsey suggests that South Carolina upcountry Loyalist, Col. Moses Kirkland had a hand in the matter. Ramsey, p. 148.
[46] Hamer, *Stuart*, p. 365
[47] Hamer, *Wataugans*, p. 122
[48] Hamer, *Wataugans*, pp.119-20
[49] During the course of the summer, the Wataugans petitioned separately the rebel governments of Virginia and North Carolina for protection. Of interest, David Crockett, grandfather of the later famous Tennessee frontiersman and Congressman signed both petitions with sons William and John ("Davy's" father) each signing one. (See *In the Footstep of Davy Crockett*)
[50] Hamer, *Wataugans*, p.123
[51] John P. Brown, *Old Frontiers: The Story of the Cherokee Indians from Earliest Times to the Date of Their Removal to the West, 1838*, (Kingsport: Southern Publishing, Inc. 1938) p. 142, as reported in Betty Linney Waugh, *The Upper Yadkin Valley in the American Revolution: Benjamin Cleveland, Symbol of Continuity* (Wilkesboro: Wilkes Community College, 1971) p. 37
[52] Hamer, *Stuart*, pp. 365-6, Guy Johnson was the nephew, son-in-law, and successor to William Johnson, the superintendent of Indian affairs for the northern colonies from 1756-1774.
[53] *Colonial Records of North Carolina*, Vol. X, pp. 778-9
[54] Report of Henry Stuart to John Stuart, *Colonial Records of North Carolina*, Vol. X, p. 774
[55] Hamer, *Wataugans*, p. 125
[56] Hamer, *Wataugans*, p. 124
[57] Hamer, *Wataugans*, p. 126
[58] Williams, *Nathaniel Gist*, pp. 49-50
[59] Hamer, *Wataugans*, p. 123
[60] Williams, p. 32
[61] Hamer, *Wataugans*, p. 126
[62] Ramsey, pp. 148-9
[63] Ramsey, p. 150
[64] Letter from Thomas Jones to James Iredell, Halifax, 23rd July 1776, *Colonial Records of North Carolina*, Vol. X, pp. 1032-3
[65] Ramsey, pp. 159-60
[66] Thomas Madison was the son of the Right Rev. James Madison, president (1777-1812) of the College of William and Mary. James organized students into a militia unit in 1777. He was a cousin to James Madison, later President of the United States. Thomas Madison was married to a sister of Patrick Henry.
[67] Captains' report to Col. William Preston, printed in Virginia Gazette. See Williams, p. 39
[68] Ramsey, p. 153
[69] Captains' report to Col. William Preston, printed in Virginia Gazette. See Williams, p. 39
[70] Ramsey, p. 153
[71] Draper, KM, p. 409
[72] Williams, p. 42; Ramsey recounts the Indian throwing a tomahawk and missing while Moore

drew his knife which the Indian grabbed nearly severing this own hand. The battle ended when Moore drew his own tomahawk and cleaved the head of his opponent. p. 155

[73] Ramsey, p. 153

[74] Williams, p. 39; Ramsey, p. 154

[75] Ramsey, p.157

[76] William Tatham, *Knoxville Gazette*, April 6, 1793

[77] Williams, p. 45n; Ramsey, p. 158

[78] Elizabeth Fries Ellet, *Pioneer Women of the West*, (New York: Charles Scribner, 1856) p. 32

[79] Draper, KM, p. 420

[80] Ramsey, p. 158

**Text for marker: "Fort Augusta, Fort Cornwallis, St. Paul's Church"**

... In 1750 there was built the first St. Paul's Church "under the curtain of the fort." In 1763, chiefs of the Cherokees, Creeks, Catawbas, Chickasaws and Choctaws met here with governors of Georgia, North and South Carolina, and Virginia and the King's representative and signed a treaty of peace. Again in 1773, Cherokees and Creeks here ceded two million acres in North Georgia. During the Revolution, the British on this spot erected Fort Cornwallis, which was captured by the Americans by surprise September 14, 1780, but soon abandoned to the British. ...

Notes from: **"A Finel Destruction of the Cherroce Nation"**

[1] Rutherford to Council of Safety, *Colonial Records of North Carolina*, Vol. X, p. 652

[2] Saunders et al. (eds.), *Colonial Records of North Carolina*, XI, 316-17 (as noted in Hamilton, Rev War Diary of William Lenoir, p.252)

[3] *Colonial Records of North Carolina*, Vol. XI, p. 318

[4] Ibid., p. 319

[5] *Colonial Records of North Carolina*, X, p. 727

[6] Adelaide Fries, Stuart Thurman Wright, and J. Edwin Hendricks, *Forsyth, the History of a County on the March*, (Chapel Hill: University of North Carolina Press, 1976 revised ed.) p. 50

[7] J. Edwin Hendricks, "Joseph Winston: North Carolina Jeffersonian," *North Carolina Historical Review*, Vol. XLV, No. 3, July 1968, p. 286. Winston's father, Samuel, was a brother to Sarah, mother of Patrick Henry.

[8] Jeff W. Dennis, "Native Americans and the Southern Revolution, Part II: The 1776 Cherokee War 'Creates' Story of Independence," *Southern Campaigns of the American Revolution*. Vol. 4, No. 3, 2007, p. 22

[9] Ibid., p. 23

[10] Ibid.

[11] Roy S. Dickens, Jr. "The Route of Rutherford's Expedition Against the North Carolina Cherokees," *Southern Indians Studies*, The Archaeological Society of North Carolina and The Research Laboratories of Anthropology, University of North Carolina at Chapel Hill, NC, Vol. XIX, October 1967, p. 4

[12] Despite the plaque on the arrowhead monument in Old Fort, NC, the fort was not built in 1756 and not built to protect the Catawbas. Neither was it built by Hugh Waddell. See Mary M. Greenlee, "Time of Building Old Fort Questioned," *North Carolina Historical and Genealogical Record*, Vol. II, No. 2, April 1933, (Only known copy is in library of Historic Carson House, Marion, NC.)

[13] J.G. De Roulhac Hamilton, ed., "Revolutionary Diary of William Lenoir," *Journal of Southern History*, Vol. 6, No. 2, 1940, p. 251. Lenoir says, "Colonel Joseph McDowell." This regiment was from Rowan County. Burke County was not formed until 1777.

[14] Ibid., p. 252

[15] Despite accounts giving these respective ranks, the North Carolina House made these appointments official on Nov. 25, 1776. See *Colonial Records of North Carolina*, Vol. X, p. 937.

[16] Adelaide Fries, *Records of the Moravians of North Carolina*, Vol. 3, p. 1033

17 Dickens, p. 9

18 Ramsey, *Annals of Tennessee*, p. 164; Harper, p. 9

19 Harper, p. 9. Harper says they rendezvoused at Cathey's Fort.

20 Dickens, p. 9

21 Dickens, p. 5

22 Harper, p. 9

23 Hamilton, p. 254

24 Ibid.

25 Ibid., p. 255

26 where today's US 441/US 23 crosses the Jackson/Macon county line in North Carolina

27 Willie Jones, president NC Council of Safety to Governor Patrick Henry, VA, *Colonial Records of North Carolina*, X, p. 860

28 Letter from Silas McDowell, 1850 as reported in Dickens, pp. 9-10

29 as reported in Dickens, p. 10

30 Hamilton, p. 255

31 See note 35

32 Willie Jones to Patrick Henry, Colonial Records of North Carolina, X, pp.860-1

33 Hamilton, p. 255

34 Hamilton, p. 256

35 Margaret E. Harper, *Fort Defiance and the General*, Hickory NC, Clay Printing Company, 1976, p. 10

36 The historical account of Colonel Williamson's advance into the Cherokee towns is confused. Some accounts place Williamson's ambush by the Cherokees at Wayah Gap; others place "The Black Hole" at "Indian Grave Gap" along the Little Tennessee River a mile north of the mouth of Burningtown Creek. Both encounters are purported to have occurred on September 19. They may be the same or separate encounters. At least one secondary source, in error, conflates these (this?) encounters with the Ring Fight. See *www.ncmarkers.com/Markers.aspx?sp=search&k=Markers&sv=Q-7/*

37 Will Graves, "Arthur Fairies' Journal of Expedition Against the Cherokee Indians from July 18th, to October 11th, 1776," *Southern Campaigns of the American Revolution*, Vol.2, No.10.1, October 2005, pp. 23, Woodward Corporation, online, *www.southerncampaign.org*

38 Dennis, p. 23

39 Graves, *Fairies'*, p. 24

40 Hamilton, p. 257

41 Harper, p. 10

42 Harper, p. 10

43 Hamilton, p. 257

44 Willie Jones, president NC Council of Safety to Governor Patrick Henry, VA, Saunders, ed., *Colonial Records of North Carolina*, X, p. 861

45 The military tactic of "total war" was one the backcountry militiamen had seen used by the British in previous Indian campaigns, most recently by Lt. Col. James Grant during the Cherokee War, 1759-1761. To stop the fighting, they chose to destroy the capacity of the Cherokee to make war. See, Patrick J. O'Kelley, "Rebuttal: The Patriot View of the Cherokee Indian Campaign of 1776," *Southern Campaign of the American Revolution*, Vol. 5, No. 1, p. 56

46 Willie Jones, president NC Council of Safety to Governor Patrick Henry, VA, *Colonial Records of North Carolina*, X, p. 861

47 Virginia Council of Safety to Col. William Christian, August 1, 1776, as reported in Williams, p. 50

48 Letter from Col. William Christian to General Griffith Rutherford, Aug. 18, 1776. Saunders, ed., *Colonial Records of North Carolina*, X, p. 751

49 Williams, *Nathaniel Gist*, p. 49

50 Williams, *Walton*, p. 73

51 Stephen B. Weeks, "General Joseph Martin and the War of The Revolution in the West," *Annual Report of the American Historical Association for the year 1893*, (Washington: Government Printing Office, 1894) p. 424

[52] Draper, KM, p. 410
[53] Weeks, pp. 424-5
[54] Williams, *Nathaniel Gist*, pp. 44-6
[55] Col. William Christian to Gov. Patrick Henry as reported in Williams, p. 56
[56] Ibid., p. 57
[57] a small tribe on the upper Alabama River. The Tawasa of Florida were associated with the Alabama.
[58] *North Carolina Colonial Records*, X, p. 892
[59] Williams, p. 51, n11
[60] Ibid., p. 895
[61] James Mooney, *Cherokee History, Myths and Sacred Formulas*, Cherokee Publications, Cherokee, NC, 1900, reproduced 2006, p. 49; (Stecoee is pronounced Stika-yi)
[62] Judge Avery's Address on the Early History of Burke County, *Colonial Records of North Carolina*, X, p. 713
[63] *North Carolina Colonial Records*, X., p. 896
[64] Ibid.
[65] Ibid.
[66] Ibid., p. 897
[67] Ibid.
[68] Ibid.
[69] Report of Captain Moore to General Rutherford, *Colonial Records of North Carolina*, X., pp.895-8
[70] Wikipedia, Joseph Hardin.
[71] Williams, p. 65; Jesse Walton was the principal proponent and founder in 1779 of Jonesborough, the first town incorporated in North Carolina beyond the Appalachians. It was named for Willie Jones, president of the NC Council of Safety during the Revolution and a noted statesman. Jones promoted the state's westward expansion.
[72] Williams, *Walton*, pp. 73-4
[73] Williams, *Walton*, p. 76
[74] Williams, p. 66
[75] Judge Avery's Address on the Early History of Burke County, *Colonial Records of North Carolina*, X, p. 713
[76] Williams, p. 66, n22
[77] Draper, KM, p. 412
[78] Williams, p. 67
[79] Williams, p. 70
[80] Williams, p. 70
[81] Williams, p. 69
[82] Weeks, p. 426
[83] Williams, p. 71
[84] Williams, p. 71, n35

**Text for marker: Fort Patrick Henry (1 A 41) -** missing 2009
"Erected near here by Lt. Col. William Russell in Sept. 1776 under orders of Col. William Christian, to serve the forces then succesfully campaigning against the hostile Cherokee who had become allies of the British. Capt. Wim. Witcher's Company garrisoned the fort while other troops operated in the lower Indian country."

Notes from: **The Chickamauga Campaign**

[1] Letter of James Robertson to Commissoners Lanier and Winston, Oct. 1777, Samuel Cole Williams, *Tennessee During the Revolutionary War*, (Knoxville: University of Tennessee Press, 1944, third edition, 1974), Appendix E, pp. 271-3
[2] Samuel Cole Williams, *Tennessee During the Revolutionary War*, (Knoxville: University of

Tennessee Press, 1944, third edition, 1974), p. 61n

[3] Williams, pp. 79-80

[4] Williams, p. 82

[5] John Stuart to William Howe, February 14, 1778, as cited in Williams, pp. 82-3

[6] John L. Nichols, "Alexander Cameron, British Agent Among the Cherokee, 1764-1781," *South Carolina Historical Magazine*, Vol. 97, No. 2 (April 1996), p. 111

[7] "Murder of Cornstalk," taken from George W Atkinson, *History of Kanawha County*, (Charleston, West Virginia, 1876), <http://www.rootsweb.ancestry.com/~wvkanawh/Early/murder.html > (accessed November 2010)

[8] William Hintzen, *A Sketchbook of The Border Wars of the Upper Ohio Valley: 1769-1794, Conflicts and Resolutions*, (Manchester, CT: Precision Shooting, Inc. 1999, 2nd edition, 2001), pp. 123-4

[9] Summers, p. 294 says they mustered on April 10.

[10] Draper, KM, p. 412

[11] Summers, p. 295

[12] Nichols, p. 112

[13] Nichols, p. 111

[14] Draper, KM, pp. 412-3

[15] Draper, KM, p. 413

Notes from: **Charlestown**

[1] William Moultrie was promoted to brigadier general on September 16, 1776.

[2] Campbell quoted without citation in "The Capture of Savannah," TheAmericanRevolution.org, < http://www.theamericanrevolution.org/battledetail.aspx?battle=22 > (Dec. 28, 2010)

[3] Patrick O'Kelley, *Nothing by Blood and Slaughter*, Vol. 1, (Barbecue, NC: Booklocker.com, Inc., 2004), p. 216-22

[4] Cited in Cashin, p. 258

[5] Christine R. Swager, *Heroes of Kettle Creek*, (West Conshohocken, PA: Infinity Publishing Co., 2008), pp. 47-54; O'Kelley, Vol. 1, pp. 246-51

[6] O'Kelley, Vol. 1, pp. 253-62

[7] Draper, KM, p. 435

[8] Germain to Alexander Cameron and Thomas Brown, June 25, 1779 as cited by Cashin, p. 259-60

[9] Carl P. Borick, *A Gallant Defense—the Siege of Charleston*, 1780, Columbia: University of South Carolina Press, 2003, p. 23

[10] Borick, p. 17

[11] Borick, p. 26

[12] Borick, p. 40

[13] Borick, p. 57

[14] Draper, KM, p. 485

[15] Draper, KM, p. 484

[16] Draper, KM, pp. 54-5

[17] Buchanan, p. 202

[18] Draper, KM, pp. 62-3, pp. 485-6

[19] Draper, KM, p. 486

[20] Draper, KM, p. 488

[21] Borick, p. 101

[22] Buchanan, pp. 55-6

[23] Buchanan, p. 57

[24] General Clinton Summons Major General Lincoln as reported Ed Southern, ed. *Voices of the American Revolution in the Carolinas*, (Winston-Salem: John F. Blair Publishers, 2009), p. 59

25 Allaire's Diary as reported Lyman C. Draper, *Kings Mountain and Its Heroes*, (1881, reprinted Johnson City: Overmountain Press, 1996.) p. 490
26 Borick, pp. 148-9
27 Draper, KM, p. 490; Buchanan, pp. 61-2; Borick, pp. 148-9
28 Borick, p. 169
29 Draper, KM, p. 492
30 Bass, Gamecock, p. 50
31 Borick, p. 193; O'Kelley, pp. 147-151
32 At the time of the siege, General William Moultrie, the hero of the American resistance to the British attempt on Charlestown in 1776, chose to hide from the invading British a substantial supply of gunpowder. He placed ten thousand pounds of powder in one corner of the cellar below The Exchange and built a false wall to seal it off. His ruse succeeded. Despite the subsequent use of the adjacent space as a prison to hold those Whigs and citizens under suspicion, the British occupiers did not discover the powder. After the war, the hidden ammunition was recovered by the Patriots. Unfortunately, much of it was to damp to use. (Tour guide at The Exchange, Charleston, SC, July 2009)
33 Clinton expected to exchange these prisoners-of-war for the British soldiers surrendered by General Burgoyne at Saratoga in 1777. The Americans were held for months on prison ships, where they succumbed to disease and malnutrition. Of the enlisted men, little more than half survived to be available for exchange.
34 Williams, *Father*, p. 52
35 Borick, p. 233
36 Borick, pp. 235-6
37 Borick, p. 236
38 Borick, p. 239
39 Edgar, p. 53
40 Banastre Tarleton, *A History of the Campaigns of 1780 and 1781 in the Southern Provinces of North America*, (London, T. Caldwell, 1787; reprint, The NY Times & Arno Press, 1968), p. 79
41 Taken from: Southern, p. 69
42 Jim Piecuch, *The Blood Be Upon Your Head, Tarleton and the Myth of Buford's Massacre*. (Luggoff, SC: Southern Campaigns of the American Revolution Press, 2010), pp. 25-6
43 Draper, KM, p. 498-9

Notes from: **The Upcountry**

1 Bass, p. 56
2 Hamilton, p. 367
3 Michael C. Scoggins, *The Day It Rained Militia*, (Charleston: The History Press, 2005), pp. 19-25
4 Lieutenant Colonel Turnbull to Lord Cornwallis, 15 June, 1780, from Scoggins, p. 189
5 A.J. Salley, Jr., ed., *Col. William Hill's Memoirs of The Revolution*, (Columbia, SC: Historical Commission of South Carolina, 1921), p. 8
6 Edgar, p. 71
7 James Collins, *Autobiography of a Revolutionary Soldier*, quoted in Ed Southern, ed., *Voices of the American Revolutioin in the Carolinas*, (Winston-Salem, John F. Blair, Publicher, 2009), p.78
8 Patrick O'Kelly, *Nothing but Blood and Slaughter, The Revolutionary War in the Carolinas*, Vol. Two, 1780. (Barbecue Township, North Carolina: Blue House Tavern Press, 2004) p. 182; The year before, the rebel government had dissolved Tryon County, dividing it into Rutherford and Lincoln counties, named for General Griffith Rutherford, commander of the Militia for the Western District and General Benjamin Lincoln, commander of the Southern Department of the Continental Army. Because Colonel Moore was a fervent Loyalist and a son of the region, he no doubt regarded his home county by the name that honored a prior colonial royal governor, William Tryon. Lincoln County at the time included today's Gaston Co.
9 "The War In Georgia And The Siege Of Savannah, Battle Of Ramsour's Mill," June 20,

1780 by Claude H. Snow, Jr., Piedmont Chapter, Georgia Society SAR http://www.rsar.org/military/garamsou.htm (accessed May 5, 2010)

10 Blackwell P. Robinson, *The Revolutionary War Sketches of William R. Davie*, (Raleigh, NC Division of Archives and History, 1976), p. 7

11 Mary Bolar, "Jane Wilson McKisick: Patriot of the American Revolution," *DAR Magazine*, Feb. 1980, p. 154

12 William A. Graham, *The Battle of Ramsaur's Mill* (1904) <http://carolana.com/NC/Revolution/revolution_battle_of_ramseurs_mill.html> (2008)

13 Robinson, p. 7

14 C.L. Hunter, *Sketches of Western North Carolina*, (Raleigh, 1877) (Baltimore: Regional Publishing Company, 1970), p. 211

15 Major David Wilson and Captain William Alexander (See Bolar)

16 Bolar, p. 154

17 Ibid.

18 Hunter, p. 217

19 Ibid., p. 218

20 Cormwallis to Clinton, June 30, 1780, Clark, ed., *North Carolina State Records*, Vol. XX, p. 251

21 Bass, p. 57

22 Letter from Williams to Son, Daniel Williams, June 12, 1779, Appendix Item #2, Graves, p. 69

23 Mr. Williams to Mrs. Williams, July 4, 1780, Graves, p. 83

24 Hamilton, p. 376a

25 Lt. Col. Banastre Tarleton, *A History of the Campaigns of 1780 and 1781 in the Southern Provinces of North America*, (London: T Caldwell, in the Strand, 1787), reprint (New York: New York Times & Arno Press, 1968), p. 160

26 Salley, *Hill*, p. 9

27 Ibid., p. 10

28 Ibid.

29 Draper, KM, p. 500

30 Draper, KM, p. 500

31 Edgar, p. 102; Bass, p 64

32 Salley, *Hill*, p. 11

33 Ibid., pp.11-2

34 A nearby marker says August 1, in error.

35 Blackwell P. Robinson, ed., *Revolutionary War Sketches of William R. Davie*, (Raleigh: North Carolina Division of Archives and History, 1976), p. 12

36 Allaire's Diary, Draper, p. 502

37 Ramsey p. 211 and Williams, p. 128

38 One account says Fort Anderson was built as late as 1776 by General Andrew Williamson for his campaign against the Cherokee, but that may have been him simply reestablishing the former fort to operation.

39 The fort was surrounded by strategically placed, sharpened, outward-pointing stakes, called abatis.

40 In April 1775, as Daniel Boone had first arrived at the site of Fort Boonesborough amidst vicious attacks by Shawnee, William Cocke had volunteered to ride alone and in great peril through the wilderness to carry a message from rear expedition leader Richard Henderson pleading for Boone to hold his position until he arrived. Cooke's display of bravery contrasts with the incidents at Island Flats in 1776, when reportedly he outpaced his men in retreating to the safety of Eaton's Station.

41 Allaire's Diary, Draper, p. 502

42 Robinson, p. 13

43 Robinson, p. 13

44 O'Kelley, p. 221

45 Salley, *Hill*, p. 12

46 Robinson, p. 14
47 Salley, *Hill*, p. 13
48 Quoted in Patrick O'Kelley, *Nothing by Blood and Slaughter*, Vol 2., (North Carolina: Blue House Tavern Press, 2004), p. 226
49 Robinson, p. 14
50 Salley, *Hill*, p. 13
51 Robinson, p. 14
52 Patrick O'Kelley, *Nothing by Blood and Slaughter*, Vol. 2, (North Carolina: Blue House Tavern Press, 2004), p. 229
53 Salley, *Hill*, p. 13
54 Robinson, p. 15
55 Ibid.
56 Allaire's Diary, Draper, p. 503

Notes from: **August 1780**

1 Hugh McCall, *History of Georgia*, (Atlanta: A.B. Caldwell, 1909), p. 481
2 Hugh McCall, *History of Georgia*, (Savannah: William T. Williams, 1816), Vol. 2, p. 320
3 Edgar, p. 53
4 Hugh McCall, *History of Georgia*, (Savannah: William T. Williams, 1816), Vol. 2, p. 321
5 Steven J. Rauch, "'An Ill Timed and Premature Insurrection,' The First Siege at Augusta , Georgia, September 14-18, 1780," *Southern Campaigns of the American Revolution*, Vol. 2, No. 9. Sept. 2005. p. 3
6 Thomas Brown to Cornwallis, cited by Edward J. Cashin, "But Brothers, It Is Our Land We Are Talking About," Hoffman, Tate, Albert, eds., *An Uncivil War, The Southern Backcountry During the American Revolution,* (Charlottesville, University Press of Virginia, 1985), p. 264
7 Cashin, p. 265
8 Robert Marion Willingham, Jr., *We Have This Heritage—The History of Wilkes County*,(Wilkes Publishing Company, Georgia, 1969), p. 32
9 Draper, KM, p. 341n
10 Willingham, p. 33
11 Now Big Browns Creek and about 10 miles east of Union, SC
12 inside today's city limits of Spartanburg, SC
13 It was later surmised that one of the volunteers riding with Ferguson's detachment may have fired the shot to warn his fellow countrymen of the impending attack and then perhaps pleaded successfully that the discharge was accidental.
14 today's Glendale, SC
15 Letters of Shelby, *Journal of Southern History*., p. 371
16 Draper, KM, p. 94
17 Letters of Shelby, *Journal of Southern History*, p. 370
18 Allaire's Diary, Draper, p. 503
19 Though sometimes referred to as Wilcox's Mill, it was established in 1752 by William (Will) Cox on Mill Creek about four-and-a-half miles southeast of today's Ramseur in Randolph County, NC.
20 Bass, p. 78
21 Bass, p. 79
22 Southern, p. 106
23 Southern, pp. 109-10
24 Southern, pp. 111-2
25 Southern, p. 114
26 Armand, Southern, p. 116
27 Allaire's Diary, Draper, p. 504
28 Margaret H. Harper, *Fort Defiance and the General*, 1976, p. 12
29 Bass, p. 85

[30] Draper, p. 105
[31] Draper, pp. 107-8
[32] Draper, p. 108
[33] Letters of Shelby, *Journal of Southern History*, p. 372
[34] Draper, p. 110
[35] Letters of Shelby, *Journal of Southern History*, p. 372
[36] Draper, p. 109
[37] Draper, pp. 110-11
[38] Draper, pp. 111-12
[39] Salley, *Hill's Memoirs*, p. 26
[40] Allaire's Diary, Draper, pp. 504-5
[41] Letters of Shelby, *Journal of Southern History*, p. 373
[42] William T. Graves, *James Williams: An American Patriot in the Carolina Backcountry*, (iUniverse, 2002), pp. 34-40
[43] Salley, *Hill's Memoirs*, p. 17
[44] This quotation is not in the *State Records of North Carolina* that I can find. This author failed to note at the time the source of this statement. It is provocative, but not substantiated.
[45] Allaire's Diary, Draper, pp. 505-6

Notes from: **Tory Troubles**

[1] In January 1777, William Preston became County Lieutenant for newly formed Montgomery County.
[2] Evans, p. 186-7
[3] Excerpt from manuscript of Captain John Redd as reported by Lewis Preston Summers, *History of Southwest Virginia and Washington County*, (Richmond: 1903, reprinted Baltimore: Genealogical Publishing Company, 1966, 1971), p. 273-4
[4] Evans, p. 188
[5] Evans, p. 191
[6] Agnes Graham Sanders Riley, *Brigadier General William Campbell, 1745-1781*, Historical Society Washington County, Va., Publication Series II, No. 22, May 1985, p. 12
[7] Summers, p. 293
[8] Riley, p. 13
[9] Pension Application of Henry Trolinger, W4087, NARA
[10] Lewis Preston Summers, *History of Southwest Virginia and Washington County*, (Richmond: 1903; reprinted, Baltimore: Regional Publishing Company, 1971), p. 293-4
[11] Evans, p. 194
[12] Summers, p. 299-300
[13] Ibid., pp. 300-02
[14] Charles B. Coale as referenced by Summers, p.276
[15] Draper, KM, p. 385-6
[16] William Campbell was actually at this time a Lieutenant Colonel, but the term "colonel" was appropriately used.
[17] Clark, ed., *North Carolina State Records*, Vol XIII, p. 625
[18] Ibid., p. 734g
[19] Draper, KM, p. 435
[20] Cleaveland was made a captain of Second Battalion of Volunteers for the aid of South Carolina. He then rode under Colonel Armstrong to join with Colonel Rutherford against the Cherokee in fall 1776.
[21] Draper, KM, p. 447
[22] Ibid., p. 888
[23] Ibid., p. 988-9
[24] Evans, p. 195
[25] Arthur Campbell and William Campbell were cousins by blood and brothers-in-law, as well.

Arthur married William's sister, Margaret. Josephine L. Harper, *Guide to the Draper Manuscripts*, (Madison: Wisconsin Historical Society Press, 2004), p. 153

26 Letter from Arthur Campbell at Fort Chiswell to Wm. Campbell, July 12, 1780, *Draper Manuscripts, Kings Mountain Papers*, 8DD3.

27 Distinguished from Captain John Campbell of Rick Valley, also serving in the 70th Regiment of Virginia Militia (Washington Co.)

28 Col. Wm. Campbell against Tories up New River – July 1780, *Draper Manuscripts, Kings Mountain Papers*, 8DD4.

29 Ibid., 8DD4b-4c

30 Ibid., 8DD4c

31 Ibid., 8DD4d

32 See Draper, KM, p. 134-9

33 Col. Wm. Campbell against Tories up New River – July 1780, *Draper Manuscripts, Kings Mountain Papers*,, 8DD4e

34 Ibid. The first name of Captain Francis is provided by Ann Brownlee, "Captain Henry Francis,"
< http://bellsouthpwp.net/w/h/whigkid/shallowford/hfrancis.html > (January 2011)

35 Riley, p. 15

36 "Col George Rogers Clark to Gov. Thomas Jefferson, Louisville, 22 August, 1780, *The Virginia Gazette*, 4 October 1780," as reported in J. Martin West, ed., *Clark's Shawnee Campaign of 1780*, Clark County Historical Society, Springfield, Ohio, 1975, p. 13

37 Abner Nash was elected April 1780, replacing former Governor Richard Caswell with whom Jefferson also had corresponded. Under North Carolina's constitution, Caswell could not succeed himself again as governor. He took command of the North Carolina militia and led them at the Battle of Camden.

38 Thomas Jefferson to William Campbell, Richmond, July 3, 1780, in Boyd, *Jefferson Papers*, III, p.479 (as cited in Riley, p. 15)

39 Evans, p. 199

40 Summers, p. 293

41 Summers, p. 293

42 Evans, p. 202; Others attribute "lynching" to Captain William Lynch of Virginia in the same era.

43 Letter from Arthur Campbell to William Campbell on New River, Aug. 13, 1780, *Draper Manuscripts, Kings Mountain Papers*, 8DD5

44 Summers, p. 304-5

45 Williams, p. 136-7

46 Draper, KM, p. 445

47 Clark, ed., State Records of North Carolina, Vol XIV, p. 581-2

48 Not to be confused with Patriot Captain Nathan Ried, 14th Virginia Regiment

49 Fries, p. 1626

50 Fries, p. 1626

51 Draper, KM, p. 388

52 Fries, p. 1627

53 Ibid.

Notes from: **Ferguson Enters North Carolina**

1 Draper, KM, p. 140

2 Ibid., pp. 143-4

3 Ibid., p. 144

4 Draper, KM, p. 506

5 Draper, KM, p. 167

6 Ibid., pp.144-6

7 Draper, KM., p. 507

[8] After serving as North Carolina's first governor from 1776-1780, Richard Caswell could not succeed himself as governor. In the summer of 1780, he served as commander of the state's militia, leading the men at the Battle of Camden.
[9] Another tradition places the site of the battle three miles north of the Upper Crossing of Cane Creek.. See Draper, KM, p. 198-9. The crossing since became known as Cowan's Ford, not to be confused with the Cowan's Ford on the Catawba River at which General William L. Davidson was killed in February 1781.
[10] Draper, in error, surmised this to be "Bedford's Hill," See footnote, Draper, KM, p. 149. The site of the battle was a mile or two south of Bedford Hill.
[11] Draper, KM, p. 507
[12] Ibid.
[13] Major Davidson was promoted to brigadier general in August 1780.
[14] Draper, KM, pp. 507-8
[15] Ibid., p. 197
[16] This mill site was in today's York County, often confused with White's Mill in today's Chester County built after 1784. See footnotes, Maurice Moore, Sr., *Life of General Edward Lacey*, (originally 1859; Greenville, SC: A Press, Inc., reprint 1981), p. 23
[17] Robert D. Bass, *Gamecock, Life and Campaigns of General Thomas Sumter*, (Orangeburg, SC: Sandlapper Publishing Co., 2000, original 1961), p. 86

Notes from: **The Muster and the March**

[1] "Col. Chs McDowell arrives in Western Waters, Sept. 1780," Joseph Martin, Draper Manuscripts, DD16, p. 12
[2] Draper (p. 169) says Ferguson was in Gilbert Town in "early September" when he paroled Sam Philips. Lt. Allaire's diary puts Ferguson in Gilbert Town on September 7. Ramsey (p. 225) says Philips arrived after McDowell and that Shelby had the message by "late August" (likely in error). McDowell arrived at Watauga on Sept. 18 after fleeing Cane Creek on the 12th. It seems reasonable that Philips reached Shelby between the 18th and 22nd. However, that Shelby could then consider the matter for "a few days," then confer with Sevier and still call a muster for Sept. 25 seems improbable. It may be that Philips reached Shelby before the 18th and that word of the threat, attested by Martin's letter, only reached Watauga when Shelby met with Sevier and reached Long Island later still. In that case, the call to muster for Sept. 25 could have been issued between the 18th and, say, the 22nd. In any case, the Overmountain Men responded quickly.
[3] Draper, KM, p. 169
[4] Ibid., p. 170
[5] Letter from Joseph Martin to Governor Jefferson, Sept. 22, 1780, *Draper Manuscripts*, 16DD12; transcribed by author
[6] Francis Marion Turner, *Life of General John Sevier*, (Johnson City, TN: The Overmountain Press, reprint 1997; original 1910, Neal Publishing Co.), p. vi; Turner places that near today's Telford, TN. Other accounts place Sevier on the banks of the Nolichucky River at this time. In any case, he was living to the southwest of Jonesborough.
[7] Draper, KM, p. 541
[8] Francis Marion Turner, *Life of General John Sevier*, (Johnson City, TN: The Overmountain Press, reprint 1997; original 1910, Neal Publishing Co.), p. vi; others say "between January and late spring." "Biographies of Sevier's Two Wives," JohnSevier.com, <http://www.johnsevier.com/images/Page%20221%20Sevier%20Family%20History.pdf >
[9] August 16 is also reported.
[10] Draper, KM, p. 541
[11] Ramsey, p. 226; Draper, KM, 174
[12] Curiously, Ensign Robert Campbell recorded in his account written decades later that William Campbell and Arthur Campbell "formed a plan to intercept Ferguson and then engaged the commanding officers of Sullivan and Washington Counties," that is, Shelby and

Sevier. (Draper, KM, p. 537)

13 Draper, KM, p. 171

14 Shelby related in an interview 35-40 years later that the Overmountain Men "fell in, accidently, with Col. Cleveland, of North Carolina at Quaker Meadows." This perhaps corroborates the claim that Wm. Campbell, not Shelby, sent a messenger to engage the Surry and Wilkes county militia, despite the plans made at Gilbert Town after Musgrove Mills to keep all informed. (Draper, KM, p. 541)

15 Ibid., p. 173

16 Ibid.

17 Martin's biographer, Stephen Weeks, concluded: "To General Joseph Martin, their leader and representative is due in no small measure the check given the Cherokees in the Revolution. It was largely his diplomatic work that kept them quiet during the British invasion of 1780-81, in spite of the incitement of British agents and the encroachment of whites; this enabled the men of the Watauga Settlement to strike a heavy blow for liberty at King's Mountain which proved to be the beginning of the end." Weeks, p. 408-9

18 Summers, p. 307

19 Ibid.

20 Williams, p. 29, p. 47

21 The grandfather of the later famous Tennessee congressman

22 Pat Alderman, *The Overmountain Men*, (Johnson City: Overmountain Press, 1970), pp. 56-7

23 Alderman, p. 82

24 Draper, KM, pp. 175-6

25 Alderman, p. 82

26 Ramsey, p. 229

27 Robert A. Howard and E. Alvin Gerhardt, Jr., *Mary Patton, Powder Maker of the Revolution*, (Piney Flats, TN: Rocky Mount Historical Association, 1980), p. 2

28 Ibid.

29 Ibid., p. 7

30 The science of gunpowder was understood at the time under the soon-to-be-overthrown phlogiston theory of combustion. During the 1770s and 1780s, Lavoisier in France was at work understanding what became the modern oxygen theory of combustion. That initiated the Chemical Revolution. Mary Patton did not need to understand anything about the science of gunpowder. She used a time-tested process that produced adequate results — it worked!

31 Schenk as quoted by Summers, p. 308

32 Draper, KM, p. 176

33 Draper says the mill was called Clark's Mill at his writing in 1881.

34 McSpadden Pension Application, NARA file S-2813

35 "Diary of Memorandums from a small book kept by Ensign Robert Campbell," Draper, KM, p. 535

36 Ibid.

37 Whether this recollection of "no report" was accurate is unsubstantiated; but some "old soldiers" recalled it that way. See notes, Draper, KM, p. 177

38 Michael Joslin, *Appalachian Bounty*, (Johnson City: Overmountain Press, 2000), pp. 145-151

39 "An Account of the March and the Battle of Kings Mountain By an unknown member of Campbell's regiment," Draper, KM, p. 530

40 Draper, KM, p. 178-9

41 Draper, KM, p. 535-6

42 Draper, KM, p. 181-2

43 This site is "old Fort Defiance," not the later home of William Lenoir currently open to the public for visiting and interpretation.

44 Margaret E. Harper, *Fort Defiance and the General*, (Hickory, NC: Clay Printing Company, 1976), p. 7

45 Draper, KM, p. 180-1

46 Samuel C. Williams, "Nathaniel Gist, Father of Sequoyah," *East Tennessee Historical Society's Publications*, Vol. 5, January 1933, p. 39n

[47] Pension Application of Jacob Grider, W3980, Southern Campaign American Revolution Pension Statements, transcribed by Will Graves September 1, 2008, < http://www.southerncampaign.org/pen/w3980.pdf >
[48] Harper, p. 14
[49] Clarke, ed., North Carolina State Records, Vol. XXII, p. 139
[50] Draper, KM, pp. 185-6; Draper confused the history of this day by including an ambuscade that wounded Lt. Larkin Cleaveland. That incident occurred in 1779 and at Lovelady's Ford on Gunpowder Creek elsewhere in the Catawba River basin. (See *NC State Records*, XXII, p. 138)
[51] William Lenoir as quoted by Harper, p. 14
[52] Draper, KM, p. 186
[53] Harper, p. 15
[54] Draper, KM, pp. 186-90

Notes from: **The Siege of Augusta**

[1] William Candler was the progenitor of a long line of distinguished Georgians, including his grandson, Ignatius Few, the founder of Emory University, and great-grandson Asa Candler, founder of the Coca-Cola Company. Allen D. Candler was governor of Georgia (1898-1902) and a noted chronicler of Georgia history.
[2] Steven J. Rauch, "An Ill-timed and Premature Insurrection, the First Siege at Augusta, Georgia, September 14 – 18, 1780," *Southern Campaigns of the American Revolution*, Vol. 2, No. 9, September 2005, p. 4
[3] Rauch, p. 5
[4] Cruger to Cornwallis, September 19, 1780, BPRO, Cornwallis Papers, 30/11/64, 104-105 as cited by Rauch, pp. 12-13
[5] Charles C. Jones, *History of Georgia*, (Boston: Houghton, Mifflin & Company, 1883), p. 457
[6] McCall, pp. 324-5
[7] Rauch, p. 11
[8] McCall, pp. 325-6
[9] McCall, p. 327. McCall cites letters supporting this account from British officers to friends in Savannah, Charlestown, and London.
[10] Rauch, p. 13
[11] McCall, pp. 332-333
[12] Captain Edward Hampton fought alongside Colonel McDowell's men and a party of volunteers detached from Colonel Clarke during the middle of August in the region of the North Pacolet River. See Draper, pp. 78-83.

Notes from: **Ferguson Retreats**

[1] Draper, KM, pp. 200-01
[2] Ibid., p. 201, p. 509
[3] Ibid., p. 202
[4] Ibid., p. 201, p. 203
[5] Dennard's Ford is a few hundred feet downstream of Pore's (Poor's) Ferry Bridge over Broad River, about one mile below the confluence of the Green River and the Broad River. See "Poor's (Dennard's) Ford: Its Location and Place in History," by Chivous Bradley, Rutherford County (NC) Historian, March 2009. The location of the fords and the correct names for them remains a topic of discussion and research.
[6] Robert M. Dunkerly, *The Battle of Kings Mountain, Eyewitness Accounts*, (Charleston, The History Press, 2007), pp. 135-6; Draper, KM, p. 204; Draper's account changed the original phrase "pissed upon," to "degraded."
[7] "King Mountain" appears to have been a name given to a region of Tryon County, not simply the mountain range or even one specific promontory. The 1775 Sayer and Bennett map of

North Carolina and South Carolina shows a crossroads labeled "King Mountain." This may have been the intersection Ferguson was heading toward from Cherokee Ford to speed his march to Charlotte Town, shown as "Charlottesburg" on this map. The modern City of Kings Mountain cites its beginnings in 1874 and claims the name comes from the battle. (See "An Accurate Map of North and South Carolina With Their Indian Frontiers,"(London. Printed for Robt. Sayer and J. Bennett, Map and Print-Sellers, 1775),
<http://dc.lib.unc.edu/u?/ncmaps,125>
[8] Draper, KM, pp. 207-8
[9] Ibid., p. 510
[10] Ibid., p. 211
[11] Salley, *Hill's Memoirs*, p. 19
[12] Draper, KM, pp. 211-2
[13] Draper, KM, p. 292

Notes from: **The Patriots Pursue Ferguson**

[1] William T. Graves, *James Williams: An American Patriot in the Carolina Backcountry*, (Lincoln, NE, Writers Club Press, an imprint of iUniverse, Inc., 2002), p. 87
[2] Ibid. pp. 36-8
[3] Draper, KM p. 192
[4] Bass, 87
[5] William Hill's account is the only account of this incident. No record exists of Rutledge having made Williams a brigadier general. Both Hill's motives and his mental health at the time of his writing his memoirs have been questioned by historians. Williams may not have been faultless in his pursuit of command, but neither should his reputation be irretrievably sullied by one uncorroborated story. See Graves.
[6] Bass, p. 87
[7] Salley, *Hill's Memoirs*, p. 17
[8] Bass, p. 88
[9] Davidson wrote to Gates on Oct. 6: "A Colo. Ferguson in the British Service has, by a Variety of Mearns, been pernicious to our Interest in the West of both the Carolinas. There has such a force taken the Field against him as will probably rid us of such a troublesome Neighbour." (Clark, ed, *State Records of North Carolina*, Vol. XIV, p. 674)
[10] Draper, KM, p. 476
[11] A.S. Salley, Jr., ed., *Col. William Hill's Memoirs of the Revolution*, Historical Commission of South Carolina, (Columbia: The State Company, 1921), p. 18
[12] Ibid., p. 19
[13] Draper, KM, p. 194
[14] Ibid., p. 195
[15] Ibid., p. 196
[16] Draper places the campsite "near the mouth of Cane Creek, in the neighborhood of Gilbert Town." See p. 213. The official OVNHT map shows the Oct.4$^{th}$ encampment in Gilbert Town.
[17] Twitty's Ford is 2-3 miles north of Alexander's Ford and the likely crossing of Broad River by the pursuing Patriots. Dennard's Ford is downstream of Green River confluence and known today as Pore's Ford. See "Poor's (Dennard's) Ford: Its Location and Place in History," by Chivous Bradley, Rutherford County (NC) Historian, March 2009. The names and locations of Twitty's Ford and Dennard's Ford are confused in the historic record. I believe Draper confused them in his account. I believe Ferguson was at Dennard's Ford when he issued his call to the citizens on Oct. 1. I believe the Patriots were at Twitty's Ford before reaching Alexander's Ford though Draper suggested it was Dennard's Ford.
[18] Draper, KM, p. 214
[19] Draper, KM, p. 216
[20] Draper, KM, p. 551

[21] Draper, KM, p. 552
[22] Draper, KM, pp. 221-2
[23] Draper, KM, p. 554; Jesse Franklin was later governor of North Carolina.
[24] Salley, *Hill's Memoirs*, p. 19
[25] Salley, *Hill's Memoirs*, pp. 20-1
[26] Draper, KM, p. 219; Moore says Lacey rode "sixty miles in one day," likely in error or exaggeration.
[27] Maurice A. Moore, M.D., *Life of General Edward Lacey*, (originally 1859; reprinted Greenville: A Press, Inc., 1981), p. 12
[28] Salley, *Hill's Memoirs*, p. 21
[29] Ibid.
[30] Draper, KM, p. 216
[31] Salley, *Hill's Memoirs*, p. 21
[32] Salley, *Hill's Memoirs*, p. 22
[33] Lenoir says "two beeves." See Draper, KM, p. 552; other accounts say "several."
[34] Statement of Silas McBee, Dunkerly, p. 64
[35] Draper, KM, pp. 223-4
[36] Draper, KM, pp. 225-6
[37] Moss, p. 146
[38] James Steen was a planter of the Upcountry and a veteran of Rocky Mount, Hanging Rock, and Musgrove's Mill. Draper, KM, pp. 469-70
[39] Joseph Kerr Pension Application, 4 Sept 1832, S4469, as reported in Graves, pp. 47-9
[40] Salley, *Hill's Memoirs*, pp. 23-4
[41] Graves, p. 50 gives another breakout of troops by commander: "Campbell (126), McDowell (52), Sevier (57), Clarke (14), Cleveland (117), Shelby (including Winston's command (47), Chronicle (23), with 201 participants not attributed to any particular commander." Graves reports 114 participants under Williams and 61 under Sumter, Hill, Bratton, Liles. Total, 812.
[42] Most of these men probably used a "cow's knee" to protect the lock of their rifles from the rain. This rectangular piece of leather was heavily greased with tallow, placed over the lock along the axis of the barrel and tied underneath. The tallow shed water and caused the leather to cling to the stock thus sealing out the water. (Ref: Conversation with Dave Davis, Curator, Hickory Ridge Living History Museum, Boone, NC, July 2010)
[43] Salley, *Hill's Memoirs*, p. 22
[44] Draper, KM, p. 229
[45] Statement of Silas McBee, Dunkerly, p. 64
[46] Draper, KM, p. 230
[47] Draper, KM, p. 231
[48] Draper, KM, p. 235

Notes from: **The Battle at King's Mountain**

[1] Ferguson's Last Letter to Cornwallis, Robert M. Dunkerly, ed., *The Battle of Kings Mountain, Eyewitness Accounts* (Charleston: The History Press, 2007), pp. 137-8
[2] Major Robert Timpany was Ferguson's second in command of the South Carolina militia, having organized a company of the 4th Battalion, New Jersey Volunteers in1776. After 1778, he served in other capacities. Although a detachment of his company was at King's Mountain, he apparently was not. The 4th Battalion wore coats with green facing. Timpany was a school master and referred to in some letters as "Dr. Timpany." "4th Battalion, New Jersey Volunteers, Major Robert Timpany's Company," *Online Institute for Advanced Loyalist Studies*, < http://www.royalprovincial.com/reenactors/groups/4njv2.shtml > (January 2011)
[3] Ferguson to Robert Timpany, Dunkerly, p. 138
[4] Draper, KM, p. 237
[5] The purpose of the bayonet charge was to "take the field," thus forcing the opposition to run after firing a volley rather than stand and reload. The charge worked because the opposi-

tion was firing muskets inaccurate beyond 60 yards, a distance the charge could close in the time it took to reload. Everything changed in the face of rifles accurate at 200 to 300 yards, but which also required a minute to reload.

6 William Lenoir's Account, Dunkerly, p. 61

7 Early histories of the battle placed Sevier elsewhere, near where some of his men shot Ferguson. Research continues, but NPS interprets his presence next to Shelby. See Robert M. Dunkerly, *Kings Mountain Walking Tour Guide*, (Pittsburgh: Dorrance Publishing Co.,2003), pp. 18-9, 25

8 Benjamin Sharp's Narrative, Draper, KM, pp. 555-6

9 John Craig's Pension Application, Dunkerly, pp. 38-40

10 Statement of James Davison, Dunkerly, p. 41, ". . . Colo Campbell ordered us to dismount, raise the indian halloo and rush up the mountain . . ."

11 Draper, KM, p. 247

12 Joseph Starns's Account, Dunkerly, p. 85

13 Draper, KM, p. 248; on p. 252, Draper cites a second Lt. Robert Edmonson, wounded, both Virginians. Other sources cite a Lt. Robert Edmondson and a private Robert Edmiston. See Alderman, p. 117, p. 121

14 Joseph Philips's Account, Dunkerly, p. 67

15 *Rivington's* Royal Gazette*, New York February 24, 1781*, Dunkerly, p. 129

16 John Craig's Pension Application, Dunkerly, pp. 38-40

17 Draper, KM, p. 252

18 Draper, KM, p. 279

19 Draper, KM, pp. 248-9

20 Bobby Gilmer Moss, *The Patriots at Kings Mountain*, (Blacksburg, SC: Scotia-Hibernia Press, 1990), pp. 23-4

21 Moss, p. 106

22 Robert Henry's Account, Dunkerly, p. 48

23 Draper, KM, p. 259

24 Statement of Silas McBee, Dunkerly, p. 64

25 Draper, KM, p. 260

26 Draper, KM, p. 260

27 Moss, p. 137

28 Draper, KM, p. 261

29 Benjamin Sharp's Narrative, Draper, KM, p. 556

30 Charles Bowen's Pension Application, Dunkerly, p. 18; also, Draper, KM, p. 262

31 Draper, KM, p. 315

32 Draper, KM, p. 266

33 Draper, KM, p. 314

34 Draper, KM, p. 315

35 Draper, KM, p. 266

36 Draper, KM, p. 286

37 Thomas Young's Account, Dunkerly, pp. 91-2

38 Statement of Silas McBee, Dunkerly, p. 64

39 Moss, pp. 268-70

40 Draper, KM, pp. 467-8

41 Thomas Young's Account, Dunkerly, pp. 92-3

42 Major Thomas Young's Narrative, Dunkerly, p. 94

43 Draper, KM, p. 273

44 Draper, KM, p. 278

45 Ensign Robert Campbell's Account, Dunkerly, p. 21

46 John McQueen's Pension Application, Dunkerly, pp. 65-6

47 William Congreve (1670-1729), *The Mourning Bride*, III, viii

48 Draper, KM, p. 275

49 James Collins's Account, Dunkerly, p. 34

50 Diary of Lieutenant Anthony Allaire, Dunkerly, pp. 123-4; also, Draper, KM, p. 510

51 Ensign Robert Campbell's Account, Dunkerly, pp. 21-2
52 Benjamin Sharp's Narrative, Draper, KM. p. 558
53 Ibid.
54 Draper, KM, p. 282
55 Draper, KM, p. 282
56 Statement of Andrew Evins, Dunkerly, p. 120
57 Draper, KM, p. 283
58 Thomas Young's Account, Dunkerly, p. 94
59 Draper disposed of two tired, popular myths in his account. First, it was not true that Williams encountered Ferguson on the battlefield personally before both were killed; and, second, Williams was not shot by one of the South Carolinian Patriots disgruntled by his alleged behavior earlier. More correct to say, Draper did not want to believe it. This second myth came solely from Colonel Hill's accounts, whose veracity had been impugned in some details. Some accounts including Draper's, describe Williams being shot after the white flags were raised, others as "late in the battle." Williams's assailant was unknown. It could have been one of the Tories who were sitting near their rifles just after they had suffered some executions at the hands of angry militiamen. It could have been a returning member of a foraging party known to be out at the time. For certain, the scene was confused with battle and Williams was, in fact, mortally wounded. See Draper, KM, pp. 276-7
60 Draper, KM, pp. 291-2
61 Draper, KM, pp. 307-8
62 Lt. Col. Banastre Tarleton's Account, Dunkerly, p. 145
63 Draper, KM, p. 292; Dunkerly, *Walking Tour*, p. 26
64 Draper, KM, p. 267
65 Colonel Isaac Shelby's Pamphlet to the Public, 1823, Dunkerly, p. 77
66 Agnes Graham Sanders Riley, *Brigadier General William Campbell, 1745-1781*, Publication Series II, No. 22, May, 1985, Historical Society of Washington County, Va., p. 23

Notes from: **Homeward Bound**

1 Statement of John Craig, 1844, Dunkerly, p. 111
2 Draper, KM, p. 307
3 John Spelts's Accounts, Dunkerly, p. 84
4 Robert M. Dunkerly, *Kings Mountain Walking Tour Guide*, (Pittsburgh: Dorrance Publishing Co., 2003), p. 26
5 Statement of William Moore, Dunkerly, pp. 121-2
6 Draper, KM, p. 304-5
7 Colonel Isaac Shelby's Account, 1815, Dunkerly, p. 73
8 Benjamin Sharp's Narrative, Draper, KM, p. 557
9 Draper, KM, p. 306
10 James Collins's Account, Dunkerly, p. 34
11 Ibid., pp. 34-5
12 Draper, KM, p. 308
13 Moore, *Life of General Edward Lacey*, p. 14
14 William Lenoir's Account, Dunkerly, p. 62
15 Benjamin Sharp's Narrative, Draper, KM, p. 557
16 Draper, KM, pp. 323-4
17 Joseph Kerr's Pension Application, Dunkerly, p. 55
18 Thomas Young's Account, Dunkerly, p. 93
19 Allaire's Diary, Draper, KM, p. 510
20 Draper, KM, p. 328
21 Draper, KM, p. 325
22 Draper, KM, p. 326
23 Draper, KM, p. 327; Allaire's Diary, Draper, KM, p. 510

24 Bobby Gilmer Moss, *Uzal Johnson, Loyalist Surgeon*, (Blacksburg, SC: Scotia Hibernia Press, 2000), p. 76

25 Draper, KM, p. 327

26 Lieutenant Colonel Banastre Tarleton's Account, Dunkerly, p. 145

27 Bobby Gilmer Moss, *Uzal Johnson, Loyalist Surgeon*, (Blacksburg, SC: Scotia Hibernia Press, 2000), p. 76n

28 Ibid., p. 78n

29 Campbell's General Orders, Oct. 14, 1780, Draper, KM, pp. 531-2

30 Draper, KM, pp. 330-1

31 Moss, *Johnson,* p. 77

32 Robert Campbell's Account, Draper, KM, p. 540

33 Moss, *Johnson*, p. 77

34 Shelby's Statement, Draper, KM, p. 544

35 Bobby Gilmer Moss, *The Loyalists at Kings Mountain*, (Blacksburg, SC: Scotia-Hibernia Press, 1998), p. 57

36 Draper, KM, pp. 332-3

37 Draper, KM, p. 334

38 Draper, KM, p. 335

39 Shelby's Statement, Draper, KM, p. 544

40 Draper, KM, pp. 339-40

41 Draper, KM, pp. 340-1

42 Moss, *Johnson*, p. 77

43 Draper, KM, p. 343

44 Allaire's Diary, Draper, KM, pp. 510-1

45 Moss, *Johnson*, p. 77

46 Draper, KM, p. 344

47 Allaire's Diary, Draper, KM, p. 511

48 Moss, *Johnson*, p. 78

49 Narrative of Benjamin Sharp, Draper, KM, p. 557

50 Draper, KM, p. 303. Robert Sevier left behind a wife, Kesiah Robertson Sevier and two sons under three years of age. The infant, Valentine, named for his grandfather, had been born in July.
< http://www.johnsevier.com/bio_robertsevier.html > (January 2011)

Notes from: **The Shallow Ford**

1 Surry County at the time included modern Surry, Stokes, Yadkin, and Forsyth counties. Bethabara is in Forsyth County.

2 Fries, *Moravian Records*, p. 1644

3 Fries, *Moravian Records*, p. 1629

4 Fries, p. 1644

5 Clark, *State Records of North Carolina*, XIV, p. 667

6 Ann Brownlee, "The Battle of Shallow Ford," *Early America Review*, Spring 1997, <www.earlyamerica.com/review/spring97/shallowford.html > (August 12, 2010)

7 Fries, *Moravian Records*, pp. 1627, 1643

8 Fries, p. 1643

9 Sumner to Gates, Clark, ed., *State Records of North Carolina*, Vol. XIV, p. 692

10 Armstrong to Sumner, Oct. 7, 1780, Clark, ed., *State Records of North Carolina*, Vol XIV, pp. 675-6

11 Pension Application for Henry Trolinger, W4087, NARA

12 Ibid.

13 David R. Bryan, "Book 5, Morgan Bryan, Jr, the Namesake Son, Third Son of Morgan Bryan, the 'Irish Immigrant,'" *Seven Sons and Two Daughters of Morgan Bryan (1671-1763) – Irish Immigrant and Some of Their Descendants*, Vol II, (Myrtle Beach, SC, privately printed, 2009), pp.

39-40

[14] Conversation with David "Randy" Bryan, Mocksville, NC, August 14, 2010. He confirms that no record of Morgan Bryan, Jr. serving in the Kings Mountain campaign currently has been identified.

[15] Some accounts say the skirmish lasted for 45 minutes; others say four to five hours. Trolinger's account favors the former.

[16] Brownlee, "The Battle of Shallow Ford"

[17] As recorded in G. Galloway Reynolds, *The Shallow Ford*, (Lewisville, NC: privately printed, 1989), p. 9

[18] Fries, pp. 1571, 1629

[19] Fries, *Moravian Records*, p. 1630

[20] Fries, *Moravian Records*, p. 1906

[21] Fries, *Moravian Records*, p. 1644

[22] Fries, *Moravian Records*, p. 1645

[23] Ibid.

Notes from: **Lord Cornwallis**

[1] Lt. Col. Banastre Tarleton, *A History of the Campaigns of 1780 and 1781 in the Southern Provinces of North America*, (London: T. Caldwell, in the Strand, 1787), reprint (New York: New York Times & Arno Press, 1968), p. 155

[2] Ibid., p. 158

[3] "It was evident, and it had been frequently mentioned to the King's officers, that the counties of Mecklenburg and Rohan [Rowan] were more hostile to England than any others in America." Tarleton, p. 160

[4] "Battle of King's Mountain" by General Joseph Graham, in Draper, KM, p. 546.

[5] Sumner to Gates, Clark, ed., *The State Records of North Carolina*, Vol. XIV, p. 692. The date of this particular incident was October 10, but is illustrates the nature of the skirmishing taking place as Cornwallis advanced toward Charlotte Town.

[6] Patrick O'Kelley, "Cornwallis' Attack on Charlotte Town," *Southern Campaigns of the American Revolution*, Vol. 2, No. 10.1, October 2005, p.1

[7] Blackwell P. Robinson, *The Revolutionary War Sketches of William R. Davie*, (Raleigh: NC Division of Archives and History, 1976), p. 24-5

[8] Hugh F. Rankin, *North Carolina in the American Revolution*, (Raleigh: North Carolina Division of Archives and History, 1959), p. 40

[9] Clark, ed., *The State Records of North Carolina*, Vol. XIV, p. 778

[10] Clark, ed., *The State Records of North Carolina*, Vol. XIV, pp. 778-9

[11] Clark, ed., *The State Records of North Carolina*, Vol. XIV, p. 667

[12] Davidson to Gates, Oct. 6, 1780, Clark, ed., *State Records of North Carolina*, Vol. XIV, p. 674

[13] Ibid., p. 675

[14] Clark, ed., *The State Records of North Carolina*, Vol. XIV, p. 783

[15] Tarleton, p. 166

[16] Cornwallis to Clinton, *Observations on Earl Cornwallis's Answer*, by Sir Henry Clinton, (London: J. Debrett, 1783), reprint (Philadelphia: John Campbell, 1866), p. 49

[17] Tarleton, p. 166; October 13, 1780 was a Friday, a most unlucky day for Cornwallis.

[18] Smallwood to Gates, Clark, ed., *The State Records of North Carolina*, Vol. XIV, p. 699

[19] Clark, ed., *The State Records of North Carolina*, Vol. XIV, p. 693

[20] Clark, ed., *The State Records of North Carolina*, Vol. XIV, p. 699

Notes from: **The Moravian Towns**

[1] Allaire's Diary, Draper, KM, p. 511

[2] Also Grider or Krider. Pension Application of Jacob Grider, W3980, Southern Campaign

American Revolution Pension Statements, transcribed by Will Graves September 1, 2008, < http://www.southerncampaign.org/pen/w3980.pdf >
[3]Allaire's Diary, Draper, KM, p. 511. Curiously, Dr. Uzal Johnson's entry is almost identical. See, Moss, *Johnson*, p. 80
[4] Moss, *Johnson*, p. 80
[5] Fries, *Moravian Records*, p. 1281
[6] Ibid., p. 1631
[7] Fries, *Moravian Records*, p. 1573
[8] Allaire's Diary, Draper, KM, p. 512
[9] Allaire's Diary, Draper, KM, p. 512
[10] Fries, p. 1631
[11] Allaire's Diary, Draper, KM, p. 512; Dr. Johnson's account is curiously similar in word choice and phrasing. See Moss, *Johnson*, p. 81
[12] Fries, p. 1631
[13] Fries, p. 1632
[14] Allaire's Diary, Draper, KM, p. 512
[15] Fries, p. 1632
[16] Allaire's Diary, Draper, KM, p. 512
[17] Fries, p. 1632
[18] Moss, *Johnson*, p. 82
[19] Fries, p. 1632
[20] Moss, *Johnson*, p. 83
[21] Gen. Gates' Letter of Thanks for King's Mountain Victory, Draper, KM, pp. 521-2
[22] Fries, p. 1633
[23] Ibid.
[24] Allaire's Diary, Draper, KM, p. 513
[25] Col. Henry Lee to Gen. Wayne, Jan. 7, 1781, as reported in Draper, KM, p. 360
[26] Moss, *Johnson*, pp. 87-90
[27] Dunkerly, pp. 139-40
[28] Fries, p. 1634
[29] Ibid.
[30] Ibid.
[31] Allaire's Diary, Draper, KM, pp. 513-5

Notes from: **Epilogue**

[1] Sir Henry Clinton, *The American Rebellion*, (Yale University Press, 1954), p. 226
[2] Draper, KM, p. 413-16
[3] Draper, KM, p. 390
[4] Draper, KM, p. 451
[5] Stephen O. Addison, *Profile of a Patriot, Colonel Benjamin Cleveland*, (Cleveland, TN: privately printed, 1993), p. 224
[6] Draper, KM, p. 394-5
[7] Draper, KM, p. 395
[8] Draper, KM, p. 554-6
[9] Weeks, p. 429-31
[10] Randell Jones, *A Volunteer Effort,*(Blacksburg, SC: National Park Service - OVNHT ,2005), p. 23

# Bibliography

__________, Emissaries of Peace: Exhibit Catalog, (Cherokee, NC: Museum of the Cherokee Indian, 2006)

__________, "4th Battalion, New Jersey Volunteers, Major Robert Timpany's Company," Online Institute for Advanced Loyalist Studies, < http://www.royalprovincial.com/reenactors/groups/4njv2.shtml> (January 2011)

__________, North Carolina Provincial Congress, The journal of the proceedings of the Provincial Congress of North-Carolina, held at Halifax on the 4th day of April, 1776. (Newbern [N.C.]: Printed by James Davis, printer to the Honourable the House of Assembly, 1776)

__________, "Lord Dunmore's Proclamation," Black Loyalists: Our history, Our People. Canada's Digital Collections. <http://www.blackloyalist.com/canadiandigitalcollection/documents/official/dunmore.htm> (accessed May 28, 2010)

__________, "Fort Gower Address and Resolutions, November 5, 1774," West Virginia History 153, <www.as.wvu.edu/wvhistory/documents/008.pdf> (June 21, 2010)

__________, "Fort Gower Resolutions", Ohio History Central, July 1, 2005, <http://www.ohiohistorycentral.org/entry.php?rec=1486> (accessed Dec. 2, 2007)

Alderman, Pat, The Overmountain Men, (Johnson City: Overmountain Press, 1970)

Atkinson, George W., History of Kanawha County, (Charleston, West Virginia, 1876), <http://www.rootsweb.ancestry.com/~wvkanawh/Early/murder.html > (accessed November 2010)

Bass, Robert D., Gamecock, Life and Campaigns of General Thomas Sumter, (Orangeburg, SC: Sandlapper Publishing Co., 2000, original 1961)

Bolar, Mary, "Jane Wilson McKisick: Patriot of the American Revolution," DAR Magazine, Feb. 1980

Borick, Carl P., A Gallant Defense—the Siege of Charleston, 1780, Columbia: University of South Carolina Press, 2003

Bradley, Chivous, "Poor's (Dennard's) Ford: Its Location and Place in History," March 2009

Brown, John P., Old Frontiers: The Story of the Cherokee Indians from Earliest Times to the Date of Their Removal to the West, 1838, (Kingsport: Southern Publishing, Inc. 1938)

Brownlee, Ann, "The Battle of Shallow Ford," Early America Review, Spring 1997, <www.earlyamerica.com/review/spring97/shallowford.html > (August 12, 2010)

Bryan, David R., "Book 5, Morgan Bryan, Jr, the Namesake Son, Third Son of Morgan Bryan, the 'Irish Immigrant,'" Seven Sons and Two Daughters of Morgan Bryan (1671-1763) – Irish Immigrant and Some of Their Descendants, Vol. II, (Myrtle Beach, SC, privately printed, 2009)

Campbell, Charles, History of the Colony and Ancient Dominion of Virginia, (Philadelphia: JB Lippincott and Co., 1860; reprint Spartanburg, SC: The Reprint Co., 1965)

Cashin, Edward J., "But Brothers, It Is Our Land We Are Talking About," An Uncivil War, The Southern Backcountry During the American Revolution, (Charlottesville: The University Press of Virginia, 1985)

Carey, Charles W., "Flora, William," American National Biography Online, Feb. 2000, (accessed Oct. 20, 2010)

Clinton, Sir Henry, Observations on Earl Cornwallis's Answer, (London: J. Debrett, 1783), reprint (Philadelphia: John Campbell, 1866)

Crowe, Jeffrey J., "Liberty Men and Loyalists," An Uncivil War, the Southern Backcountry During the American Revolution. eds. Ronald Hoffman, Thad W. Tate, Peter J. Albert (Charlottesville: The University Press of Virginia, 1985)

Crews, C. Daniel, Through Fiery Trials, The Revolutionary War and the Moravians (Winston-Salem, Moravia Archives, 1996),

Cullen, Joseph P., "Moore's Creek Bridge," American History Illustrated. (January 1970) Vol. 4, No. 9

Dennis, Jeff W., "Native Americans and the Southern Revolution, Part II: The 1776 Cherokee War 'Creates' Story of Independence," Southern Campaigns of the American Revolution. Vol. 4, No. 3, 2007

Dickens, Jr., Roy S., "The Route of Rutherford's Expedition Against the North Carolina Cherokees," Southern Indians Studies, The Archaeological Society of North Carolina and The Research Laboratories of Anthropology, University of North Carolina at Chapel Hill, NC, Vol. XIX, October 1967

Draper, Lyman C., Draper Manuscripts, Kings Mountain Papers, accessed as microfilm at Reynolds Library, Wake Forest University, Winston-Salem, North Carolina, 2010

Draper, Lyman C., Kings Mountain and Its Heroes, (1881, reprinted Johnson City: Overmountain Press, 1996.)

Dunkerly, Robert M., Battle of Kings Mountain, Eyewitness Accounts, (Charleston, The History Press, 2007)

Dunkerly, Robert M., Kings Mountain Walking Tour Guide, (Pittsburgh: Dorrance Publishing Co., 2003)

Dunkerly, Robert M. and Eric K. Williams, Old Ninety Six—A History and Guide, (Charleston: The History Press, 2006)

Eckenrode, Hamilton James, Revolution in Virginia, (New York, Houghton Mifflin Co., 1916)

Ellet, Elizabeth Fries, Pioneer Women of the West, (New York: Charles Scribner, 1856)

Fries, Adelaide L., ed., Records of the Moravians in North Carolina (Raleigh: Edwards & Broughton Company, 1926)

Fries, Adelaide, Stuart Thurman Wright, and J. Edwin Hendricks, Forsyth, the History of a County on the March, (Chapel Hill: University of North Carolina Press, 1976 revised ed.)

Graham, William A,. The Battle of Ramsaur's Mill (1904) <http://carolana.com/NC/Revolution/revolution_battle_of_ramseurs_mill.html> (2008)

Graves, William T., James Williams: An American Patriot in the Carolina Backcountry, (iUniverse, 2002)

Graves, Will, "Arthur Fairies' Journal of Expedition Against the Cherokee Indians from July 18th, to October 11th, 1776," Southern Campaigns of the American Revolution, Vol.2, No.10.1, October 2005, Woodward Corporation, online, <www.southerncampaign.org>

Hamer, Philip M., "John Stuart's Indian Policy During the Early Months of the American Revolution," Mississippi Valley Historical Review, Organization of American Historians, Vol. 17. No. 3 (Dec. 1930)

Hamer, Philip M., "The Wataugans and the Cherokee Indians in 1776," East Tennessee Historical Society's Publications, Vol. 3, January 1931,

Hamer, Philip M., "The Wataugans and the Cherokee Indians in 1776", East Tennessee Historical Society's Publications, III, (January 1931),

Hendricks, J. Edwin, "Joseph Winston: North Carolina Jeffersonian," North Carolina Historical Review, Vol. XLV, No. 3, July 1968

Hamilton, J.G. De Roulhac, ed., "Revolutionary Diary of William Lenoir," Journal of Southern History, Vol. 6, No. 2, 1940

Harper, Margaret E., Fort Defiance and the General, Hickory NC, Clay Printing Company, 1976

Hintzen, William, A Sketchbook of The Border Wars of the Upper Ohio Valley: 1769-1794, Conflicts and Resolutions, (Manchester, CT: Precision Shooting, Inc. 1999, 2nd edition, 2001)

Hollingsworth, J.G., History of Surry County or Annals of Northwest North Carolina (original 1935; reprint, Salem, MA: Higginson Book Company, 1997)

Howard, Robert A., and E. Alvin Gerhardt, Jr., Mary Patton, Powder Maker of the Revolution, (Piney Flats, TN: Rocky Mount Historical Association, 1980)

Hunter, C.L., Sketches of Western North Carolina, (Raleigh, 1877) (Baltimore: Regional Publishing Company, 1970)

Jackson, Harvey H., "Rise of the Western Members," An Uncivil War, The Southern Backcountry During the American Revolution, (Charlottesville: The University Press of Virginia, 1985),

Jones, Charles C., History of Georgia, (Boston: Houghton, Mifflin & Company, 1883)

Jones, Randell, In the Footsteps of Daniel Boone, (Winston-Salem: John F. Blair, Publisher, 2005)

Jones, Randell, A Volunteer Effort,(Blacksburg, SC: National Park Service - OVNHT, 2005)

Jones, Randell, In the Footsteps of Davy Crockett, (Winston-Salem: John F. Blair, Publisher, 2006)

Joslin, Michael, Appalachian Bounty, (Johnson City: Overmountain Press, 2000)

Kerby, Robert L., "The Other War in 1774: Dunmore's War," West Virginia History, (Beckley, WV) Vol. 36, No. 1

King, Duane H., ed., The Memoirs of Lt. Henry Timberlake, (Cherokee, NC: Museum of the Cherokee Indian, 2007)

Kitchen, Thomas, "A Map of the seat of war in the southern part of Virginia, North Carolina, and the northern part of South Carolina," 1781, (Raleigh: Carolina Digital Library and Archives),<http://dc.lib.unc.edu/u?/ncmaps,361>

Lossing, Benson J., "Virginia in 1775," Our Country—Household History for All Readers, Vol. 2, 1877, <
http://www.publicbookshelf.com/public_html/Our_Country_vol_2/virginia1_hg.html>
(accessed Dec. 3, 2007)

Martin, Luther, Letter to Mr. Fennel, William Cobbett, ed., Philadelphia Gazette, March 29, 1797 as reported in "LOGAN'S SPEECH," The Olden Time, 1846-1847 (February 1, 1847)

Mayer, Henry, A Son of Thunder, Patrick Henry and the American Revolution, (New York: Grove Press, 1991)

McCall, Hugh, History of Georgia, (Atlanta: A.B. Caldwell, 1909),

McCall, Hugh, History of Georgia, (Savannah: William T. Williams, 1816), Vol. 2

Mooney, James, Cherokee History, Myths, and Sacred Formulas, 19th and 7th Annual Reports, Bureau of American Ethnology, 1900 and 1891; reproduced Cherokee, NC: Cherokee Publications, 2006)

Moomaw, W. Hugh, "The British Leave Colonial Virginia," The Virginia Magazine of History and Biography, Vol. 66, No. 2 (Apr 1958)

Moore, Sr., Maurice, Life of General Edward Lacey, (originally 1859; Greenville, SC: A Press, Inc., reprint 1981),

Morrow, George, A Cock and Bull for Kitty, (Williamsburg, VA: Telford Publications, 2011)

Moss, Bobby Gilmer, The Patriots at Kings Mountain, (Blacksburg, SC: Scotia-Hibernia Press, 1990)

Moss, Bobby Gilmer, The Loyalists at Kings Mountain, (Blacksburg, SC: Scotia-Hibernia Press, 1998)

Moss, Bobby Gilmer, Uzal Johnson, Loyalist Surgeon, (Blacksburg, SC: Scotia Hibernia Press, 2000)

Nichols, John L., "Alexander Cameron, British Agent Among the Cherokee, 1764-1781," South Carolina Historical Magazine, Vol. 97, No. 2 (April 1996)

O'Kelley, Patrick, Nothing by Blood and Slaughter, Vol. 1, (Barbecue, NC: Booklocker.com, Inc., 2004)

O'Kelley, Patrick, Nothing by Blood and Slaughter, Vol. 2., (North Carolina: Blue House Tavern Press, 2004)

O'Kelley, Patrick, "Cornwallis' Attack on Charlotte Town," Southern Campaigns of the American Revolution, Vol. 2, No. 10.1, October 2005

Paine, Thomas, Common Sense, Chapter III, (original 1776. New York: Barnes & Noble, reprint 1995)

Piecuch, Jim, The Blood Be Upon Your Head, Tarleton and the Myth of Buford's Massacre. (Luggoff, SC: Southern Campaigns of the American Revolution Press, 2010),

Powell, William S., ed. "Tryon's 'Book' on North Carolina," North Carolina Historical Review, Vol. XXXIV (August 1957)

Quarles, Benjamin, "Lord Dunmore as Liberator," The William and Mary Quarterly, Third Series, Vol. 15, No. 4 (Oct. 1958)

Ramsey, J.G.M., Annals of Tennessee to the End of the Eighteenth Century, (Charleston: Walker & Jones, 1853; reprinted Johnson City: Overmountain Press, 1967 & 1999)

Rankin, Hugh F., "The Moore's Creek Bridge Campaign, 1776," The North Carolina Historical Review, Vol. XXX, No. 1, January 1953

Rankin, Hugh F., North Carolina in the American Revolution, (Raleigh: North Carolina

Division of Archives and History, 1959)

Rauch, Steven J., "An Ill-timed and Premature Insurrection, the First Siege at Augusta, Georgia, September 14 – 18, 1780," Southern Campaigns of the American Revolution, Vol. 2, No. 9, September 2005

Reynolds, G. Galloway, The Shallow Ford, (Lewisville, NC: privately printed, 1989)

Riley, Agnes Graham Sanders, Brigadier General William Campbell, 1745-1781, Historical Society Washington County, Va., Publication Series II, No. 22, May 1985

Robinson, Blackwell P., The Revolutionary War Sketches of William R. Davie, (Raleigh, NC Division of Archives and History, 1976)

Salley, Jr., A.J., ed., Col. William Hill's Memoirs of The Revolution, (Columbia, SC: Historical Commission of South Carolina, 1921)

Sanchez-Saavedra, E.M., "All Fine Fellows and Well-Armed, The Culpeper Minute Battalion, 1775-1776," Virginia Cavalcade, Vol. 24, No. 1, 1974

Sandefur, Ray H., "Logan's Oration—How Authentic?" Quarterly Journal of Speech 46 (1960)

Saunders, William L., ed., The Colonial Records of North Carolina (Raleigh: Josephus Daniels, 1890)

Sayer & Bennett, "An Accurate Map of North and South Carolina With Their Indian Frontiers," (London. Printed for Robt. Sayer and J. Bennett, Map and Print-Sellers, 1775), <http://dc.lib.unc.edu/u?/ncmaps,125>

Scoggins, Michael C., The Day It Rained Militia, (Charleston: The History Press, 2005)

Snow, Jr., Claude H., "The War In Georgia And The Siege Of Savannah, Battle Of Ramsour's Mill," June 20, 1780, Piedmont Chapter, Georgia Society SAR

Southern, Ed, ed. Voices of the American Revolution in the Carolinas, (Winston-Salem: John F. Blair Publishers, 2009)

Stumpf, Vernon O., "Josiah Martin and His Search for Success—the Road to North Carolina," (North Carolina Historical Review, January 1976)

Summer, Lewis Preston, History of Southwest Virginia, (original: Richmond, 1903; reprint: Baltimore, Genealogical Publishing Company, 1966, 1971)

Swager, Christine R., Heroes of Kettle Creek, (West Conshohocken, PA: Infinity Publishing Co., 2008)

Synder, Christina, Slavery in Indian Country, (Cambridge, MA: Harvard University Press, 2010)

Tarleton, Banastre, A History of the Campaigns of 1780 and 1781 in the Southern Provinces of North America, (London, T. Caldwell, 1787; reprint, The NY Times & Arno Press, 1968),

Thwaites, Reuben Gold, and Louise Phelps Kellogg, Documentary History of Dunmore's War, 1774. (Madison: Wisconsin Historical Society, 1905; reprinted Baltimore: Genealogical Publishing Company, 2002)

Turner, Francis Marion, Life of General John Sevier, (Johnson City, TN: The Overmountain Press, reprint 1997; original 1910, Neal Publishing Co.)

Tyler, Lyon Gardiner, History of Virginia, Vol. II, The Federal Period 1763-1861 (Chicago & New York, The American Historical Society, 1924)

Virginia Gazette (Pinkney), September 7, 1775

Washington, George, George Washington Papers, Manuscript Division, Library of Congress

Waugh, Betty Linney, "The Upper Yadkin Valley in the American Revolution" Benjamin Cleveland, Symbol of Continuity," Doctoral dissertation, University of New Mexico. (Wilkesboro, NC. Wilkes Community College, 1971)

Weeks, Stephen B. ,"General Joseph Martin and the War of The Revolution in the West," Annual Report of the American Historical Association for the year 1893, (Washington: Government Printing Office, 1894)

West, ed., J. Martin, Clark's Shawnee Campaign of 1780, Clark County Historical Society, Springfield, Ohio, 1975

Wingo, Elizabeth B., and Elizabeth B. Hanbury, The Battle of Great Bridge, (Norfolk: Norfolk County Historical Society, reprinted by Chesapeake Public Schools, 1998)

Wilson, David K., Southern Strategy (Columbia: University of South Carolina Press, 2005)

Williams, Samuel Cole, "The Founder of Tennessee's First Town: Major Jesse Walton," The East Tennessee Historical Society's Publications, Vol. 2, 1930

Williams, Samuel Cole, "Nathaniel Gist, Father of Sequoyah," The East Tennessee Historical Society's Publications, Vol. 5, January 1933

Williams, Samuel Cole, Tennessee During the Revolutionary War, (Knoxville: University of Tennessee Press, 1944, 1974)

Willingham, Jr., Robert Marion, We Have This Heritage—The History of Wilkes County,(Wilkes Publishing Company, Georgia, 1969)

# Index

CPSIA information can be obtained at www.ICGtesting.com
Printed in the USA
BVOW031135101011

273215BV00001B/1/P